```
PROGRAM name (input, output);        (* header *)


(*Pascal Program Structure *)
(* Declarations *)
LABEL declarations;
CONST declarations;
TYPE definitions;
VAR declarations;
PROCEDURE and FUNCTION declarations;
(*Main Program Statements *)
BEGIN
        Statement;
            •
            •
            •
        Statement
END.
```

A Sample Pascal Program

```
PROGRAM example (input, output);
(* This program reads three integers *)
(* and displays their average.        *)
CONST
    total = 3;
VAR
    grade1, grade2, grade3 : integer;
    average : real;
BEGIN
    (* Prompt for the input values. *)
    writeln ('Please enter the three grades.');
    readln (grade1, grade2, grade3);
    average := (grade1 + grade2 + grade3) / total;
    writeln ('The average grade is ', average:6:2)
END.
```

PROGRAMMING WITH PASCAL

PROGRAMMING WITH PASCAL

John Konvalina
Professor of Mathematics
and Computer Science
University of Nebraska at Omaha

Stanley Wileman
Associate Professor
of Mathematics and Computer Science
University of Nebraska at Omaha

McGRAW-HILL BOOK COMPANY

New York St. Louis San Francisco Auckland
Bogotá Hamburg Johannesburg London
Madrid Mexico Milan Montreal New Delhi
Panama Paris São Paulo
Singapore Sydney Tokyo Toronto

PROGRAMMING WITH PASCAL

1 2 3 4 5 6 7 8 9 0 D O C D O C 8 9 4 3 2 1 0 9 8 7 6

ISBN 0-07-035224-0

This book was set in Times Roman by J.M. Post Graphics, Corp.
The editors were Kaye Pace and Peggy Rehberger;
the designer was Joan E. O'Connor;
the production supervisor was Phil Galea.
The cover illustration was drawn by Anne Green.
The drawings were done by Fine Line Illustrations, Inc.
R. R. Donnelley & Sons Company was printer and binder.

Library of Congress Cataloging-in-Publication Data

Konvalina, John.
    Programming with Pascal.

    Includes index.
    1. PASCAL (Computer program language)   I. Wileman,
Stanley.   II. Title.
QA76.73.P2K66 1987   005.13′3   86-18513
ISBN 0-07-035224-0

ABOUT
THE AUTHORS

John Konvalina is Professor of Mathematics and Computer Science at the University of Nebraska at Omaha. He earned a Ph.D. from the State University of New York at Buffalo. He has written two textbooks and numerous papers in combinatorics and computer science education.

Stanley Wileman is Associate Professor of Mathematics and Computer Science at the University of Nebraska at Omaha. He earned an M.S. degree in Computer Science from the University of Houston under the late Elliott Organick. Professor Wileman has taught computer science courses for over a decade and has coauthored six papers in computer science education. He is an active member of the Association for Computing Machinery.

In memory of our fathers

CONTENTS
IN BRIEF

CONTENTS

PREFACE

Programming with Pascal is designed for a first course in structured computer programming with an emphasis on problem-solving strategies using a top-down approach.
In particular, problem analysis, algorithm design, and implementation using standard
Pascal are stressed throughout. The text is suitable for a variety of introductory computer courses including:

- Introductory computer science courses following the guidelines of CS1 (ACM
  Curriculum '84)
- Introductory computer programming courses using Pascal
- The first half of an advanced placement course in computer science
- Programming language courses using Pascal

In addition, the text includes numerous optional sections on advanced topics such
as loop invariants, analysis of algorithm efficiency, and conformant array parameters.
The advantages of programming in standard Pascal are stressed throughout.

Overview

In the first part of the text (Chapters 1 to 6), the emphasis is on problem solving using
top-down design and stepwise refinement. Chapter 1 is an introduction to computer
science providing an overview of the problem-solving strategies used throughout the
text. Chapters 2 and 3 introduce the Pascal programming language to solve elementary
problems. Chapter 3 also includes an optional section on text file input/output for those
instructors who require the students to use external files early in the semester.

Chapter 4 on top-down design and elementary procedures is fundamental for the remainder of the text. The problem-solving strategy of top-down design together with procedure implementations is carefully developed with the emphasis on the top-down approach. Procedures with parameters are introduced naturally and applied to specific problems. This is actually a soft introduction to parameters. The heavy coverage of parameters is delayed until after the fundamental control structures, selection and looping, have been developed. Chapters 5 and 6 cover selection and looping. Chapter 6 includes an optional section on program correctness and loop invariants. A summary of the fundamental control structures is also included.

The pace of the first six chapters is deliberately slow in order to emphasize the problem-solving strategies used in the rest of the text. After completing Chapter 6, the student should have a firm grasp of the fundamental control structures and should be able to apply them using the top-down approach to problem solving. In the second part of the text the pace is faster since there is a wealth of information to be covered. The emphasis is on data structures but the problem solving strategies with complete Pascal programs are still included in each chapter.

Chapter 7 includes a detailed discussion of procedures and functions, value and variable parameters, and recursion. Chapter 8 covers data types, including enumerated types and an introduction to the set data type. Chapter 9 on arrays includes searching and sorting algorithms and an optional section on analysis of algorithm efficiency. Chapter 10 on character string processing contains an important optional section on conformant array parameters. Included in this section is a complete string manipulation package written in standard Pascal. Chapters 11 and 12 discuss the structured data types records and files. The final chapter is an introduction to data structures, and can be considered as a transition chapter to advanced courses. The appendices include syntax diagrams, reserved words, standard identifiers, order of operators, character set encodings (ASCII and EBCDIC), and miscellaneous Pascal features, such as the GOTO statement and procedures and functions as parameters. A glossary of important keywords follows the appendices.

Each chapter has the following general structure:

- Objectives
- Chapter Overview
- Chapter Contents
- Problem Solving Applications
- Testing and Debugging Techniques
- Pascal Reminders
- Chapter Review
- Pascal Reference
- Preview of the Next Chapter
- Keywords
- Chapter Exercises
- Chapter Problems for Computer Solution

Each chapter begins with a list of objectives and an overview of the contents. Nearly all the chapters contain a section on problem solving with an application and a complete

Pascal program. At the end of each chapter is a Testing and Debugging Techniques

section to aid the student. Included in this section is a list of important Pascal reminders covered in the chapter. Included in each chapter is a chapter review, a summary of the Pascal material covered in the chapter, a preview of the next chapter, a list of keywords, and the exercises.

Exercises

Most sections in each chapter contain exercises the student can do for a self-evaluation of mastery of the material. Answers to all section exercises are found at the end of the text. The chapter exercises are located at the end of each chapter and are divided into three categories: essential, significant, and challenging. Problems for computer solution are also divided into the same categories. These problems include input/output specifications and illustrations of sample executions to make it easier for an instructor to use the problems as assignments without embellishment. Complete solutions to all chapter exercises and problems for computer solution can be found in the instructor's manual. At the end of Chapter 1 a detailed explanation of the graded exercises can be found.

Summary of Features

Programming with Pascal has the following pedagogical features:

- Comprehensive and complete introduction to computer science using Pascal
- Problem solving approach emphasizing top-down design
- Early introduction of procedures and top-down design
- Emphasis on problem analysis and algorithm design
- Numerous sample Pascal programs and applications
- Exercises graded as essential, significant, or challenging
- Graded problems for computer solution with explicit input/output specifications
- Testing and debugging techniques section in each chapter
- Chapter reviews including Pascal reference section that summarizes Pascal syntax, semantics, and usage rules
- Pascal reminders providing checklists for testing and debugging in each chapter
- Chapter keywords listed in each chapter
- Glossary of important keywords

The text also includes the following optional material:

- Early introduction to file input/output
- Program correctness and loop invariants
- Conformant array parameters and a complete collection of string manipulation procedures and functions written in standard Pascal
- Variant records
- Analysis of algorithm efficiency

APEX Supplements

Academic P*ascal* with *Ex*tras (APEX) forms a unique and complete instructional package that has been extensively developed to accompany *Programming with Pascal*. The following figure provides a top-down overview of the APEX supplements:

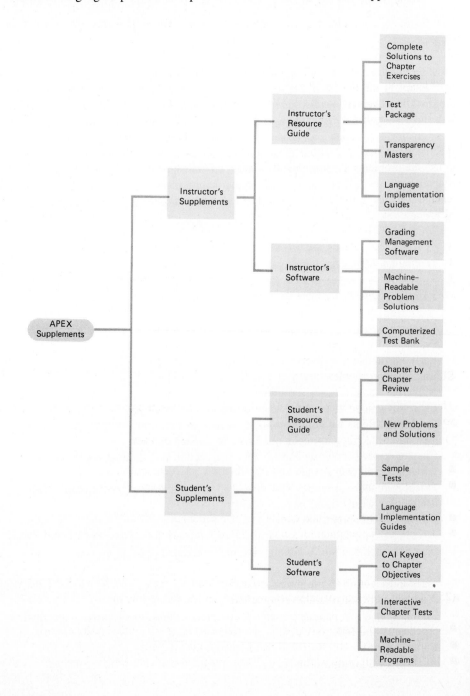

The APEX supplements are divided into two major components: the instructor supplements and the student supplements.

Instructor's Supplements

The instructor's supplements are also divided into two components: the *Instructor's Resource Guide,* and *Instructor's Software.*

The *Instructor's Resource Guide* contains the following items:

- Complete solutions to the chapter exercises and problems for computer solution
- Teaching suggestions
- Test package that includes over one thousand questions
- Transparency masters derived from the text
- Language implementation guides that cover various versions of nonstandard Pascal systems (Turbo, UCSD, Apple, etc.)

The *Instructor's Software* is available for the Apple II family (48 K) and the IBM PC (256 K) and most compatible computer systems and includes the following items:

- Grading management software (in standard Pascal, of course)
- Machine readable solutions for all problems in the text
- Computerized test bank that will generate examinations selected from over one thousand items

Student's Supplements

The student's supplements are divided into two major components: the *Student's Resource Guide* and *Student's Software.*

The *Student's Resource Guide* contains the following items:

- Chapter by chapter review and problem solving techniques
- Numerous new exercises and problems for computer solution with complete solutions
- Sample tests that include questions for each chapter
- Language implementation guides that cover various versions of nonstandard Pascal systems (Turbo, UCSD, Apple, etc.)

The *Student's Software* is available for the Apple II family (48 K) and the IBM PC (256 K) and most compatible systems and includes the following:

- Menu-driven computer-assisted instruction keyed to the chapter objectives
- Chapter quizzes and tests that can be taken interactively
- Complete programs in text available in machine-readable form

APEX is the ultimate computer science instructional system providing a total learning experience that utilizes the current microcomputer technology to improve the educational process.

Acknowledgments

The authors wish to thank the following reviewers for their valuable comments and suggestions: Lionel Deimel, Allegheny College; Kalen Delaney, University of California, Berkeley; Terry Gill, Carnegie-Mellon University; Herman Gollwitzer, Drexel University; Bob Holloway, University of Wisconsin-Madison; Layne Hopkins, Mankato State University; Joseph Lambert, Pennsylvania State University; Patricia Murphy, University of Kentucky; Oskars Rieksts, Kutztown University; Richard Rink, Eastern Kentucky University; Henry Shapiro, University of New Mexico; Jill Smudski, University of Pennsylvania; Mark Stehlik, Carnegie-Mellon University; Ronald Wallace, Blue Mountain Community College; and Jerry Waxman, Queens College.

The authors would also like to thank all the students and colleagues who contributed to this text by reading the manuscript and solving the exercises. Special thanks to Deborah and Rhoda Konvalina, Greg Ostravich, Linda Tuttle, Lori Wernimont, and Peggy Wright.

Finally, a very special thanks are due to Kaye Pace, Shelly Langman, and the staff at McGraw-Hill for their encouragement, support, and commitment to this project.

John Konvalina
Stanley Wileman

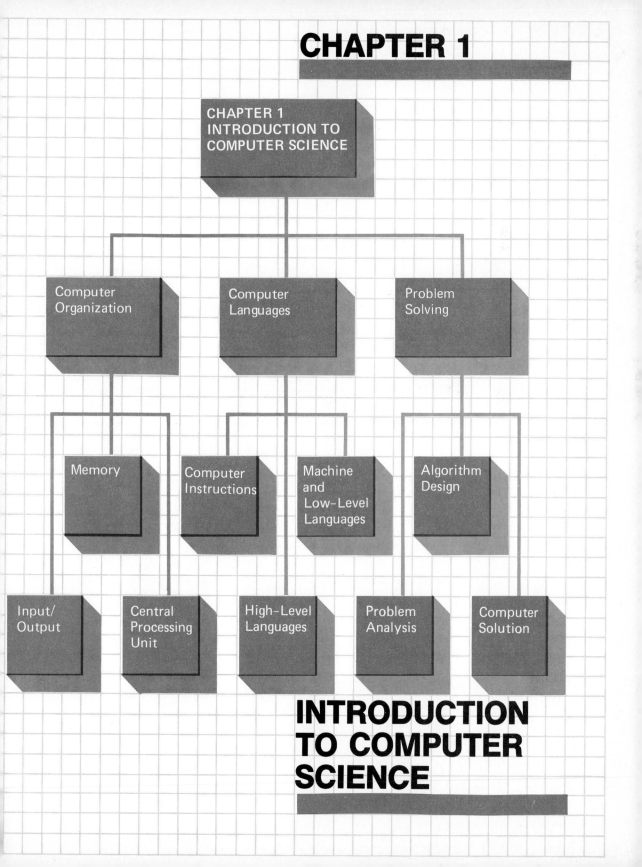

CHAPTER 1

CHAPTER 1
INTRODUCTION TO
COMPUTER SCIENCE

Computer Organization

Computer Languages

Problem Solving

Memory

Computer Instructions

Machine and Low-Level Languages

Algorithm Design

Input/Output

Central Processing Unit

High-Level Languages

Problem Analysis

Computer Solution

INTRODUCTION TO COMPUTER SCIENCE

OBJECTIVES

After completing this chapter you should be able to:

- Describe the major components of a computer: input/output devices, central processor, and memory
- Distinguish between computer languages, such as machine language, assembly language and high-level language
- Describe the major steps in problem solving using a computer: problem analysis, problem solution or algorithm design, and computer solution
- Perform and test the execution of the steps in an algorithm

CHAPTER OVERVIEW

The objectives of a first course in computer science can be summarized as follows: to help you develop and apply computer science principles to problem solving and programming methodology using a programming language. You will not only learn the rules of a computer language, namely Pascal, but develop problem-solving strategies to help you in designing effective computer solutions to a variety of problems. In addition, the course will provide you with a firm foundation for further studies and applications.

Since the computer is the fundamental and underlying tool used in computer science, we begin this chapter with a description of the organization of the computer. Specifically, we will discuss the nature of the major components of a computer: input/output devices, central processor, and memory. Next, we will follow with a discussion of computer instructions and various computer languages and machine language. The details of compiling and executing a high-level language program are also discussed. Finally, the chapter will close with a general discussion of problem solving and program testing which is fundamental to the remainder of the course. In particular, problem analysis, problem solution or algorithm design, and the role of the computer in obtaining the solution are discussed.

SECTION 1.1 COMPUTER ORGANIZATION

A simple way to view a computer is as an information processor. Data and information can be entered into the computer as *input* and then processed to produce *output* (see Figure 1-1).

Figure 1-1   Simple model of a computer.

The physical components of a computer together with the devices that perform the input and output are referred to as *hardware*. A set of computer instructions performed by the computer is called a *computer program*. A significant part of this course deals with problem solving and writing programs to obtain computer solutions to a variety of problems. The set of programs written for a computer is referred to as *software*.

Input/Output

The input/output (I/O) devices allow communication to take place between the user and the computer. Examples of input devices are keyboards, punched cards, and mice (hand-held devices used to move a visual indicator on a display). Examples of output devices are printers, cathode-ray tube (CRT) screens, or video display terminals (VDTs). Terminals include both a keyboard and a CRT and can therefore be used for both input and output. Typical computer installations include other I/O devices such as disk drives and magnetic tape drives for the storage and retrieval of information and data. I/O devices are sometimes referred to as *peripheral devices*, since they are usually external to the computer.

Now let us refine our view of the computer as an information processor and take a closer look at the computer itself (see Figure 1-2).

The computer without the peripherals consists of two major components, the memory unit and the central processing unit (CPU).

Memory Unit

The memory unit consists of thousands of memory cells, each one assigned a unique number known as a *memory address*. We can access each cell by reference to its address, thus allowing for the storage or retrieval of information and data. Also, when computer programs are executed by the computer, they normally reside in the memory unit during the process. The capability of the computer to store a program in the memory unit and then automatically perform, or *execute*, the instructions is one of the major reasons for using computers in problem solving.

The memory unit is frequently referred to as *primary*, or *main*, *memory*. Many computer systems have peripherals, such as disks and tape drives, that can serve as secondary storage devices by providing additional memory. This additional memory, or *secondary storage*, permits the user to permanently store large quantities of information and data on disks and tapes.

Figure 1-2 Refined model of a computer.

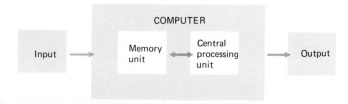

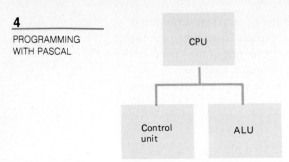

Figure 1-3   Central processing unit (CPU).

Central Processing Unit

The CPU directs and controls the information processing done by the computer. A closer look at the CPU reveals that it consists of two major components: the control unit and the arithmetic-logic unit (ALU) (see Figure 1-3).

The control unit fetches instructions from computer programs residing in memory, interprets the instructions and then directs the execution of the instructions. The computer has the capability of repeating this process millions of times per second with reliability and accuracy. When arithmetic calculations, such as addition, subtraction, multiplication, or division, must be performed, the control unit directs the ALU to perform the tasks. Logical operations, such as comparing two quantities or determining whether a condition is true or false, are also performed by the ALU. This provides the control unit with a decision-making mechanism to alter the flow of a sequence of computer instructions.

Our refined model of the computer as an information processor is shown in Figure 1-4.

This basic knowledge of the organization and structure of the computer is an important aid in the understanding of how the computer executes the instructions of a computer program. These instructions are normally written in some form of computer programming language.

Figure 1-4   Structure of a computer.

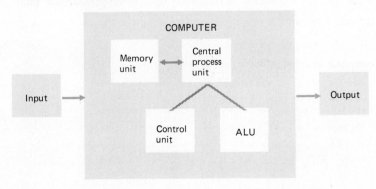

Computer Instructions

Before we discuss computer languages, let us summarize the fundamental types of instructions the computer is capable of executing. More complex instructions in various computer languages can actually be reduced to one of these five fundamental types (see Figure 1-5).

- *Input/output instructions.*   Instructions to transfer information and data between the peripherals and the primary memory
- *Arithmetic-logic instructions.*   Instructions to perform arithmetic operations (addition, subtraction, multiplication, division) or logical operations (results having only two values, true or false) on data stored in the primary memory
- *Selection instructions.*   Instructions that include decision mechanisms to allow selection of alternate courses of action by the computer program
- *Looping instructions.*   Instructions that permit a sequence of instructions to be repeated more than once
- *Procedure instructions.*   Instructions that permit the naming of a group of instructions as a procedure that can then be referenced by a single statement using the procedure name

We will discuss these instructions in more detail in the forthcoming chapters, especially with respect to the Pascal computer language.

Machine Language

If we examined a portion of the memory of a computer, we would find that the content of each memory cell is represented in terms of **bits**, or binary digits (0 and 1). For example, suppose the content of the memory cells is a computer program that starts at memory address 0001 (see Figure 1-6).

Notice the computer instructions and any data in the cells are represented in binary (base 2) code, that is, in sequences of bits. At this level the program is expressed in **machine language**. These machine language instructions depend on the hardware and design of the digital computer. Consequently, different computers may have different

Figure 1-5   Fundamental computer instructions.

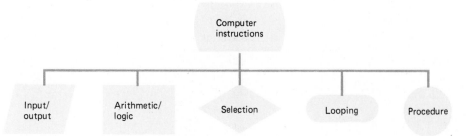

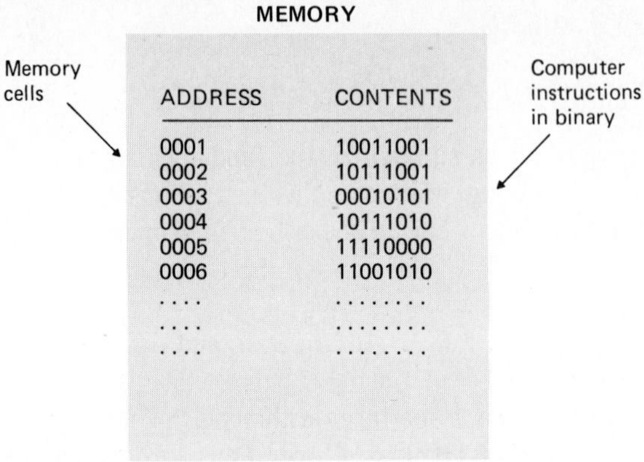

MEMORY

Memory
cells

ADDRESS	CONTENTS
0001	10011001
0002	10111001
0003	00010101
0004	10111010
0005	11110000
0006	11001010
. . . .	. . . .
. . . .	. . . .
. . . .	. . . .

Computer
instructions
in binary

Figure 1-6 Memory cells and computer instructions.

machine codes for each instruction. Programming a computer in machine language can be a tedious and time-consuming process. To improve the situation, computer languages have been created which allow you to write programs using English-like statements. Programs such as assemblers and compilers have been created to translate your programs into the actual machine language.

Low-Level Languages

Since programming in machine language is difficult, *low-level languages* have been developed to simplify the process. These languages are generally machine-dependent; that is, they are dependent on the instruction set of the particular computer. An example of a low-level language is *assembly language*. In assembly language the programmer writes instructions on the machine language level in alphabetic codes known as *mnemonics*. For example, typical mnemonics for the arithmetic operations of addition, subtraction, multiplication, and division could be expressed by the code words ADD, SUB, MPY, and DIV, respectively.

Suppose each operation has a machine code as shown in Figure 1-7. Clearly, it is much easier to remember that the mnemonic ADD means addition than it is to remember that the machine code 1100 also means addition. In fact, the word *mnemonic* is defined as *memory aid*.

Figure 1-7 Machine language code and mnemonic code.

MACHINE LANGUAGE CODE	MNEMONIC CODE
1100	ADD
1101	SUB
1110	MPY
1111	DIV

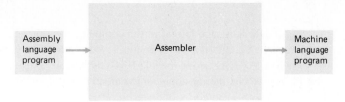

Figure 1-8 Assembler.

After a program has been written in assembly language, it must be translated into the machine language in order to be executed by the computer. Most computer systems have a program called an ***assembler*** that will translate an assembly language program into the corresponding machine language program (see Figure 1-8).

To simplify programming, other computer languages (known as high-level languages) have been developed which are more suitable for general problem solving.

High-Level Languages

Examples of ***high-level languages*** include Ada, BASIC, COBOL, FORTRAN, Lisp, Modula-2, Pascal, and PL/I. In high-level languages the program instructions or statements are written using common names and words to represent the data items to be manipulated and the actions to be carried out. Also, high-level language programs can be written so they are machine independent; that is, the statements in the computer program do not depend on the design or hardware of a particular computer. Consequently, high-level language programs can be translated into machine language and executed by different computers. The program that performs this translation is called a ***compiler***, and programs written in a high-level language are called ***source programs***. The compiler translates the source program into a program called the ***object program***. It is the object program that is used in the execution phase of the program (see Figure 1-9).

An alternate way to execute a program written in a high-level language is to translate it into an object program for a hypothetical computer. Then this object program is *interpreted* using a program (executing on a real computer) that simulates the hypothetical computer.

Figure 1-9 Compiler.

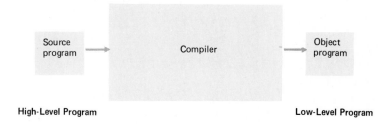

High-Level Program   **Low-Level Program**

Pascal

In this course we will use the high-level language Pascal in the computer solution of problems. The programming language Pascal (named after the seventeenth-century French mathematician Blaise Pascal) was developed in the late 1960s by Niklaus Wirth as a teaching language. Using Pascal we can demonstrate computer science principles and programming concepts together with problem solving in a very organized and highly structured manner.

A Pascal statement when compiled will generally translate into a group of many machine language instructions. Fortunately, we do not have to concern ourselves with the machine language instructions when programming in Pascal. The compiler will perform the translation for us. Here is an example of a Pascal program that computes the area of a triangle. The program obtains the altitude (height) and base of a triangle and then displays the area. (Recall that the area of a triangle is one-half the altitude times the base.)

```
PROGRAM triangle (input, output);
VAR altitude, base, area : real;
BEGIN
        read (altitude, base);
        area := 0.5 * altitude * base;
        write (area)
END.
```

We will study Pascal programming in detail in the next two chapters. However, notice, even if you do not know Pascal, the program statements are understandable and reflect the solution of the problem.

Compiling and Executing

The computer hardware together with the software is called a ***computer system***. The process of compiling and executing a source program in a high-level language, such as Pascal, to obtain results (output) takes place within the computer system. A Pascal program generally acquires input data during the execution of the program. A simple model of this process is represented by Figure 1-10.

In a typical computer system the system software permits the user to process a

Figure 1-10 Computer system.

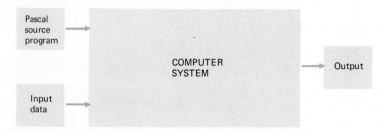

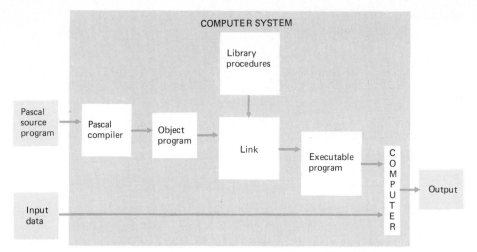

Figure 1-11   Compilation and execution.

Pascal program. The **operating system** is a set of programs that manages this process. For example, to process a Pascal program, we instruct the operating system to *compile* the source program in order to generate the object program. Assuming there are no errors (called **compile-time errors**) in the source program, we instruct the operating system to **link (load)** the object program with any **library procedures** (commonly used software residing in the system library) used or referenced by the Pascal program. The linking process results in an **executable program**. Finally, we instruct the operating system to *execute*, or run, the executable program, using the input data provided. Again, assuming there are no errors during execution (called **runtime errors**), we would obtain the output of the Pascal program. Now our simple model of compiling and executing a Pascal program is represented by Figure 1-11.

The actual instructions or system commands to compile and execute a Pascal program will vary with different operating systems. For example, some systems require only one command to process the Pascal program, whereas others may require separate commands to compile, link, and execute the program. The important point to remember is that once we have the Pascal source program and the input data we can instruct the operating system to compile and execute the program.

SECTION 1.3 PROBLEM SOLVING

When preparing problem solutions for the computer, it is not enough just to know the rules of a programming language. Problem-solving skills are essential to successful programming.

Problem solving using the computer can be broken down into three major steps: problem analysis, problem solution or algorithm design, and the computer solution (see Figure 1-12).

The first step, problem analysis, requires that the problem be defined clearly and

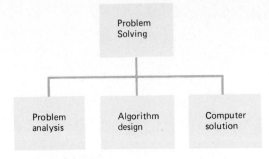

Figure 1-12   Problem solving.

understood so it can be carefully analyzed. It is hardly useful to produce a solution to the wrong problem! Next, the problem solution must be found. This solution can be expressed in terms of an ***algorithm***, or a step-by-step procedure for solving the given problem. Finally, to obtain a computer solution, we must translate the algorithm into a computer language (in our case, Pascal) and then verify or test that the program does indeed solve the given problem. We consider the steps in more detail.

Problem Analysis

A problem specified for computer solution must be clearly stated and understood. The problem must be well defined in order to arrive at a satisfactory solution. Since we are seeking a computer solution, the input and output specifications of the problem must be described in sufficient detail. A well-defined problem and a precise description of the input and output specifications are important requirements for an effective and efficient solution (see Figure 1-13).

Let's return to the problem of computing the area of a triangle:

Write a computer program that computes the area of a triangle.

Figure 1-13   Problem analysis.

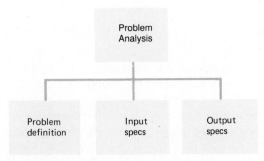

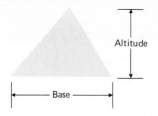

Figure 1-14   Triangle with altitude and base.

This problem is *not* well defined since the input and output specifications have not been described. For example, the following are some questions regarding the input data that have been left unanswered:

- What values will be input?
- How many values will be input?
- What are valid input values?

Also, the following questions regarding the output have been left unanswered:

- What values will be output?
- How many values will be output?
- Should we label the output, and if so, how?
- How many decimal places are required for the output values?

Now consider the following restatement of the same problem:

Problem 1.1

Write a Pascal computer program that inputs the altitude and then the base of a triangle, each of which is a positive decimal number. The program computes the area of the triangle with the given input data. The output includes a copy of the input data and the area with appropriate labels for each. The output values should be printed to two decimal places.

Example input:

10.5   20.5

Example output:

Altitude is 10.50
Base is 20.50
Area is 215.25

At this point we are ready to proceed with the problem solution or algorithm design. A simple problem has been chosen to help illustrate the problem-solving process and to stress the importance of defining precisely even the most basic type of problem. Good problem-solving habits should be developed early in learning how to write computer programs.

Algorithm Design

Complex problems can be effectively solved using the computer when they are broken down into subproblems that are easier to solve than the original. This approach, sometimes called *divide and conquer*, can be applied to the construction of the problem solution and to the writing of the computer program. Consider again the problem of finding the area of a triangle. This problem can be divided into three subproblems: (1) input the data, (2) compute the area, and (3) output the results (see Figure 1-15).

Now we have reduced the solution of the original problem to three simpler subproblems. We proceed to refine each subproblem to obtain a more detailed solution.

subproblem	*refinement*
Input data	Input the altitude and base of the triangle.
Compute area	Area = $\frac{1}{2}$ (altitude) (base).
Output results	Output altitude, base, and area.

We now have sufficient detail to implement a computer solution. This approach of dividing a problem into subproblems, and then dividing the subproblems further until they can be implemented for computer solution, is called ***top-down design***. The process of breaking down the problem at each stage is called ***stepwise refinement***. Although the triangle area problem is a simple case, the power and effectiveness of top-down design will become evident when we attack more complicated problems. At this point, it is highly recommended that the student apply top-down design to all problems for computer solution. The transition to complex problems will then become much easier.

Some of the advantages of top-down design are:

- The problem is easily understood and logically organized into parts called ***modules***. Thus, there is a structure to the solution of the problem.
- Modifications or changes can be easily made to the modules.
- Testing the solution can be easily performed.

Figure 1-15   Top-down design of triangle area problem.

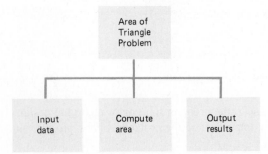

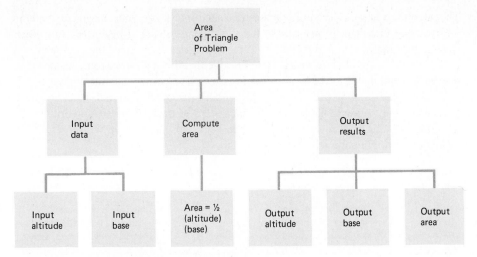

Figure 1-16   Refinement of triangle area problem.

As we study more complicated problems and their solutions, the advantages will become more evident.

Let us return to the triangle area problem and consider our top-down design as represented by Figure 1-16 (known as a ***tree diagram***).

The top-down design is an outline of the solution to the problem. The solution must be translated to a computer language. Observe that in the top-down design we start with a general description of the problem and then refine at each level until the solution is detailed enough for translation to a computer language. This process is also called ***algorithm design***, since we are actually designing the problem solution or algorithm. Before we consider the computer solution of the problem, let us discuss algorithms in more detail.

Algorithms

An ***algorithm*** is a step-by-step procedure to solve a given problem. The instructions should be clear and unambiguous, specific enough to execute, and terminate in a finite number of steps. The execution of an algorithm should be reducible to a clerical or routine task. Thus, an algorithm makes it easier to write the actual computer instructions.

For example, an algorithm to solve the triangle area problem can be expressed as follows:

Triangle Area Algorithm

STEP 1   Input altitude and base.
STEP 2   Compute area $= \frac{1}{2}$ (altitude) (base).
STEP 3   Output altitude, base, and area.

This algorithm is specific enough to be translated into a computer language, such as Pascal. Note that there is an order to the steps. Thus, step 1 is performed first, then step 2, and finally step 3. Once the computer program is written, the computer can execute these instructions in order. Also observe that this algorithm contains the same degree of detail as the lower level of the top-down design tree diagram (Figure 1-16).

To show you a comparison between algorithm instructions and high-level language statements, the following table lists the three steps of the triangle area algorithm and the corresponding Pascal statements. In the next two chapters we will consider the details of writing a complete Pascal program.

step	algorithm	Pascal statement
STEP 1	Input altitude and base.	read (altitude, base);
STEP 2	Compute area = $\frac{1}{2}$ (altitude) (base).	area := 0.5 * altitude * base;
STEP 3	Output altitude, base, and area.	write (altitude, base, area);

Algorithm Execution

The execution of a computer program representing a given algorithm is performed by the computer. However, when there are errors in the program or even the algorithm, it may be necessary for the programmer to execute the algorithm by hand. Here is a simple algorithm sometimes found in puzzle books:

Puzzle Book Algorithm

STEP 1	Think of a number.
STEP 2	Add 3 to the number.
STEP 3	Multiply the result of step 2 by the number 2.
STEP 4	Subtract 4 from the result of step 3.
STEP 5	Divide the result of step 4 by the number 2.
STEP 6	Subtract the original number from step 1 from the result of step 5.
STEP 7	Write out the result of step 6.

Let us execute this algorithm by hand:

step	instruction	result of execution
STEP 1	Think of a number.	5
STEP 2	Add 3.	8
STEP 3	Multiply by 2.	16
STEP 4	Subtract 4.	12
STEP 5	Divide by 2.	6
STEP 6	Subtract original number (5).	1
STEP 7	Write out result.	1 is printed

As an exercise, execute the algorithm by hand with different initial numbers. What is the result? Can you explain why the answer is always 1? (See exercise 1.) Additional exercises in algorithm execution can be found at the end of the chapter. Later in the book we will execute algorithms with instructions from the computer language Pascal.

The preceding algorithm can be simplified significantly when using a high-level language such as Pascal. Instead of thinking of a number, however, we will instruct the computer to obtain a number from the input. The steps can be condensed as follows:

STEP 1 Input number.
STEP 2 Compute result = {[2 (number + 3) − 4]/2} − number.
STEP 3 Output result.

When an algorithm is written in this form, that is, as a mixture of English and computer instructions, the algorithm is said to be written in *pseudocode*. Once we have the pseudocode, it is usually a simple matter to translate to a computer language, such as Pascal. For example, the pseudocode of this algorithm and the corresponding Pascal statements are given below:

step	pseudocode	Pascal statement
STEP 1	Input number.	read (number);
STEP 2	Compute result = {[2 (number + 3) − 4]/2} − number.	result := (2 * (number + 3) − 4) *DIV* 2 − number;
STEP 3	Output result.	write (result);

In the algorithm design phase, after the problem has been analyzed carefully, top-down design is used to divide the problem into subproblems (modules) and to organize our solution. Stepwise refinements help obtain detailed solutions of the subproblems and obtain algorithms written in pseudocode to ease the translation process to a computer language (see Figure 1-17).

Let us apply the algorithm design process to a more difficult problem.

Figure 1-17 Algorithm design.

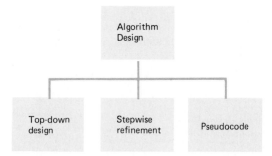

Problem 1.2

The management of Apex Electronics Company would like to determine the median annual salary of its employees in order to provide information for a government study. Write a program which displays the number of employees and their median salary.

The *median* of a set of numbers is the middle number when the numbers are arranged in ascending order (from smallest to largest). For example, the median of the following numbers

85, 53, 98, 86, 42

is determined by first arranging the numbers in ascending order (called *sorting* the numbers)

42, 53, 85, 86, 98

↑

Median

and then selecting the middle number 85. Thus, 85 is the median of the set of numbers. Notice that excluding the median, half of the numbers are above the median and half of the numbers are below the median. In this case there were an odd number of data items (five), so there is exactly one middle number. However, if there are an even number of data items, then there are two middle numbers and the median is defined as the average of the two middle numbers (their sum divided by 2). For example, to find a median for the six data items:

62, 86, 97, 84, 98, 56

we must first sort the numbers into ascending order:

56, 62, 84, 86, 97, 98

↑   ↑

Average = 85

and then take the average of the two middle numbers 84 and 86 to obtain a median of 85. At this point we have a clear definition of the median of a set of numbers, so we can proceed to solve the problem.

If we apply the top-down design process we can divide this problem into three subproblems (see Figure 1-18):

1 Input the data for which the median is desired.
2 Compute the median.
3 Output the result.

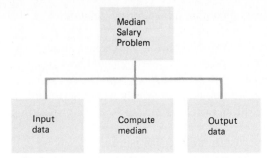

Figure 1-18   Top-down design of median salary problem.

Relatively simple problems were chosen to help illustrate the problem-solving process and show the degree of precision needed even for the most basic type of problem. Next we must refine each subproblem until we can write the pseudocode.

subproblem	refinement
Input the data for which the median is desired.	Input the number of employees and their salaries.
Compute the median.	Sort the salaries into ascending order. Then find the middle salary.
Output the result.	Output number of employees and median salary with labels for each.

The top-down design is shown in Figure 1-19.

At this point it is important to understand that we have avoided the details of solving the subproblems. Using top-down design provides us with an overview of the total

Figure 1-19   Refinement of median salary problem.

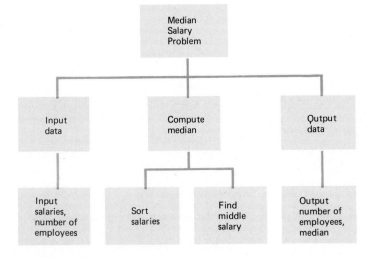

problem and an organized and structured algorithm design for the solution. Now we can proceed to consider the algorithm in more detail.

Looking at the top-down design we find two subproblems that require further analysis: sorting the salaries and finding the middle salary. Sorting algorithms are quite common and available on many computer systems. Thus, we need not concern ourselves with the details of sorting, since we can use a previously written procedure to sort the salaries. Later in this book we will, in fact, learn how to write our own sorting procedures.

To find the middle salary we must consider whether the number of employees is an odd or an even number. If there are N employees, we represent the salaries of the N employees by the symbols $S(1)$, $S(2)$, $S(3)$, $S(4)$, and so on, up to $S(N)$. For example, if there were five employees, N would be 5, the salary of the first employee would be represented by $S(1)$, the salary of the second employee by $S(2)$, and so forth, up to the salary of the fifth employee, $S(5)$. If N is an odd number, then the middle salary is in position $(N + 1)/2$. For example, with N equal to 5, the middle salary is in position $(5 + 1)/2$, or position 3:

$$S(1) \qquad S(2) \qquad S(3) \qquad S(4) \qquad S(5)$$

$$\uparrow$$

Middle salary in position 3

If N is an even number, the two middle salaries are in positions $N/2$ and $(N/2) + 1$:

$$S(1) \qquad S(2) \qquad S(3) \qquad S(4) \qquad S(5) \qquad S(6)$$

$$\uparrow \qquad \uparrow$$

Middle salaries in positions 3 and 4

The median salary is the average of these two salaries:

$$\frac{S(3) + S(4)}{2}$$

Now we have solved the problem of finding the middle salary: If N (the number of employees) is an odd number, then the middle salary is in position $(N + 1)/2$; otherwise, N must be even, and the median salary is the average of the salaries in position $N/2$ and $(N/2) + 1$.

Finally we are ready to write the algorithm in pseudocode:

Median Salary Algorithm

STEP 1   Obtain the number of salaries N from the input data. Obtain the salaries $S(1)$, $S(2)$, . . . , $S(N)$ from the input data.

STEP 2   Sort the salaries $S(1)$, $S(2)$, . . . , $S(N)$ into ascending order.

STEP 3   Compute the median salary.
          If *N* is odd:
              Median is in position $(N + 1)/2$.
          If *N* is even:
              Median is average of salaries in positions $N/2$ and $(N/2) + 1$.
STEP 4   Display the value of *N* and median.

At this point the algorithm can be translated into Pascal. However, a considerable amount of knowledge about the Pascal programming language is required before the program can be written. For example, Pascal has the capability of determining if a number is odd or even. If it did not have this capability, further refinement of the algorithm would be necessary.

An important observation is that in problem solving most of the time should be spent in the problem definition and algorithm design phase. Once a high-level language, such as Pascal, has been learned, the process of translating the algorithm for computer execution becomes routine.

Computer Solution

Once we have designed the algorithm for a problem, we can proceed with the computer solution and implementation phase. The first step is to write, or ***code***, the computer program in a programming language such as Pascal. The next step is to compile and execute the program. This step includes correcting errors, such as compile errors and run-time errors. The third step is to verify or test the correctness of the program (see Figure 1-20).

Pascal Program

After we have designed the algorithm for a given problem, we must write the actual computer instructions in detail. These details will be presented in the next two chapters. Let us assume that we have written a complete Pascal program and would like to

Figure 1-20   Computer solution.

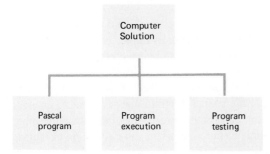

proceed with a computer implementation. The Pascal program must be entered in the system. Two common approaches are known as interactive and batch modes. In an *interactive system* you communicate directly with the operating system, usually through a video terminal. In a *batch processing system* the user submits a program and any input data with all the commands to the operating system to process the program. The user must then wait or return some time later for the output.

An interactive system normally has a program, called the *text editor*, that permits the user to create the Pascal source program and includes editing capabilities to modify the program. The text editor usually creates a *file* to store the source program in the computer system. You can think of a file as a section of storage or memory referenced by a name (created by the user). If your source program needs some corrections, you can use the text editor to recall your source program by specifying the file name.

Program Compilation and Execution

Once the Pascal source program is created it can be compiled and executed. During the compilation process the file containing the source program is read by the compiler and then translated into the actual machine language instructions executed by the computer. The set of machine language instructions is normally stored in a new file. During the compilation process, errors (such as incorrect Pascal usage) are detected by the compiler. These errors are similar to grammatical errors in English and are known as *syntax* errors. When we are informed by the compiler that such an error has been discovered, we determine what correction should be made to the source program, use the text editor to make the correction to the source program, and then recompile. If the program now compiles correctly, then we can proceed with the execution of the resulting object program, which is in machine-readable form.

The last step in processing our program is the execution of the object program. This step will include the processing of any input data provided for the program. Even though a program compiles correctly, this does not mean that the program is error-free. During the execution phase, errors may also occur. For example, if you attempt division by zero, an appropriate message will be displayed. Such errors are usually called *run-time* errors. Obviously, such errors must be corrected. This means the source program must be edited and recompiled, and the object program executed again. Run-time errors, or mistakes in the execution of the program, are frequently called *bugs*, or *semantic* errors. The process of identifying and correcting or removing the bugs is called *debugging*.

It is important to note that the actual commands to compile and execute computer programs vary between different computer systems. For example, your computer may have a Pascal *interpreter* instead of a compiler. When an interpreter is used to process your Pascal program, each statement in the source program is translated and executed before the next statement of the source program is processed. That is, an interpreter translates and executes the statements of the source program one at a time. If an error is located, the process stops and you can correct the error immediately. On the other hand, a compiler will translate the complete source program and only begin execution after all the syntax errors are removed.

Even if the program has no compile errors or run-time errors, the program may not be correct. For example, the output result could be incorrect. The source of this error may be the original algorithm design! This error is sometimes called a *logic error*. If this is the case, we must return to the algorithm design phase and modify our algorithm, change the source program, and compile and execute once more. In order to test the correctness of the program, the program should be executed many times with various inputs. If the results are correct, then our confidence in the algorithm and program is increased. However, this still is not a guarantee that the program is correct, since it may fail on other input data.

Testing a program for correctness is a necessary part of creating a successful computer solution to a given problem. As we proceed in the course, we will present many techniques to aid in program testing. Applying these techniques routinely can reduce the chances of error and increase our confidence in the program's correctness.

SECTION 1.4 TESTING AND DEBUGGING TECHNIQUES

At the end of each chapter you will find a Testing and Debugging Techniques section to provide you with some useful hints in program testing. As you gain experience in writing programs, many of these techniques should be routinely applied in order to arrive at a successful computer solution to a problem. Here is an example of program testing that can be performed during the algorithm design phase of the problem-solving process. Whenever you design an algorithm to solve a given problem, your algorithm should be tested for various inputs by executing the steps by hand. Logic errors and possible omission of steps in the algorithm can be detected early in the problem-solving process. If you avoid early testing of your algorithm, you may find yourself spending many hours on the computer, perhaps buried in the rules of a computer language, searching for an error that may have occurred in the original algorithm design. Flawless execution of a faulty algorithm will not give the correct results.

Let us execute by hand the steps in the Median Salary algorithm presented in Section 1.3. Suppose a small company has five employees. We will test the algorithm for the following five salaries: $75,000, $30,000, $50,000, $40,000, and $60,000. We have chosen a small test case since we are going to execute the algorithm by hand. The larger test cases can be tested during the computer solution phase of the process.

The first step is to obtain the number of employees (N) and the salaries. The next step requires sorting the salaries in ascending order. Finally we must compute the median salary and display the result. Here is a summary of the execution of the algorithm for the test case by hand:

STEP 1 Obtain the number of employees (N) and their salaries.

Result of execution:

$N = 5$

| Salaries: | 75,000 | 30,000 | 50,000 | 40,000 | 60,000 |

STEP 2 Sort the salaries into ascending order.

Result of execution:

Salaries:	30,000	40,000	50,000	60,000	75,000

STEP 3 Compute median.

Result of execution:

Median salary: 50,000

The median salary for this test case was $50,000. Notice that the number of employees is five, which is an odd number. Therefore the median salary occurs in the middle (in this case, the third) position of the list of sorted salaries. As an exercise, execute the Median Salary algorithm by hand for a company that has an even number of employees (see exercise 2).

Another important testing technique is to test for exceptional or special cases. For example, suppose a company had only one employee. Would the Median Salary algorithm still work in this special case? Again, as an exercise, test the Median Salary algorithm for the case of one employee; that is, test the algorithm for $N = 1$ (see exercise 3). What would happen if the input data to the algorithm specified *no* employees?

Testing small cases and exceptional cases by hand is an important algorithm testing technique to help locate logic errors and missing steps in the algorithm before any actual computer language instructions have been written.

SECTION 1.5 CHAPTER REVIEW

The fundamental tool used in computer science is the computer. The major components of a computer are input/output devices, memory, and central processor. The central processor consists of two major components: the control unit and the arithmetic-logic unit (ALU).

There are five fundamental types of computer instructions: input/output instructions, arithmetic-logic instructions, selection instructions, looping instructions, and procedure instructions.

The design of a computer includes computer instructions expressed in binary code at the hardware level. These instructions are collectively known as machine language. Low-level languages, such as assembly language, permit the writing of machine language instructions in symbolic form using mnemonics. Low-level languages are generally machine-dependent. An assembler is a program that will translate an assembly language program into machine language.

High-level languages permit program instructions or computer statements to be expressed in English-like expressions. Compilers and interpreters are programs that translate a high-level language program (source program) into machine language code (object program). Pascal is an example of a high-level language.

The process of compiling and executing a source program in a high-level language involves translating the Pascal source program to the object program, linking the object program with any library procedures if necessary to create an executable program, and then executing (or "running") the executable program to process any input data.

Problem solving using the computer consists of three major steps: problem analysis, problem solution or algorithm design, and computer solution. Problem analysis requires a clear and precise statement of the problem. The problem solution is expressed in terms of a step-by-step procedure known as an algorithm. The algorithm is designed using a top-down design approach, which divides the original problem into simpler subproblems. The subproblems are refined stepwise until they can be implemented for computer solution. The algorithm is usually written in a mixture of English and computer instructions known as pseudocode.

The computer solution is the algorithm written in a high-level language such as Pascal. Then the program is compiled, executed, and tested. During the compilation process, compile-time errors (syntax errors) are detected by the compiler. Run-time errors are detected during the execution process. Errors in algorithm design are called logic errors. The process of correcting errors, or bugs, in a program is called debugging.

Program testing is a necessary part of creating a successful computer solution to a given problem. Testing small cases by hand and larger cases on the computer can reduce the number of bugs in a program and lead to an efficient and effective solution of the problem.

Chapter 2 Preview

If you are overwhelmed by the contents of the first chapter, don't be discouraged! The chapter is basically an overview of the problem-solving process using the computer. Many details have been omitted in order to give you a global view of the computer and its role in problem solving. In the next two chapters we will consider the problem-solving process in more detail using the high-level language Pascal. After you write a few Pascal programs, your understanding of the concepts presented in this chapter should increase significantly.

Keywords for Chapter 1

algorithm
assembler
assembly language
arithmetic-logic unit (ALU)
batch processing
binary
bits
bugs
central processing unit (CPU)
code
compile-time error
compiler

computer program
control unit
debugging
divide and conquer
editor
execute
executable program
file
hardware
high-level language
input device
interactive system

interpreter
library procedures
link
load
logic error
low-level language
machine language
main memory
memory address
memory unit
mnemonics
object program
operating system

output device
peripheral device
primary memory
pseudocode
run-time error
secondary storage
semantic error
software
source program
stepwise refinement
syntax
top-down design

INTRODUCTION TO EXERCISES AND PROBLEMS FOR COMPUTER SOLUTION

Each chapter in the text includes *Exercises*, and all except this chapter include *Problems for Computer Solution*. The Exercises provide a review of the material presented in the chapter but do not require the use of a computer to test your solution. The Problems for Computer Solution, while possibly useful as design problems alone, are really intended as complete statements of problems for which you are to develop solutions (in Pascal). Following these exercises is a synopsis of the form in which Problems for Computer Solution will be presented in later chapters.

Each Exercise and Problem for Computer Solution is classified. You should always attempt those marked *Essential*, since they reinforce fundamental concepts. *Significant* items will normally require more work than *Essential* but are still quite important and are well worth attempting. *Challenging* items are just that; obtaining their solutions may require a significant investment of time. Some of these items may be considered suitable for semester-sized projects.

CHAPTER 1 EXERCISES

The following exercises are not necessarily related to computer problems, but give some practice in hand execution of algorithms. Executing your own algorithms by hand is an excellent way of detecting errors and omissions.

★ ESSENTIAL EXERCISES

1 Execute, by hand, the Puzzle Book algorithm using the number 10. What is the result? Can you determine, mathematically, what the result of the algorithm should be?

2 Execute, by hand, the Median Salary Algorithm for the following set of salaries: $25,000, $20,000, $33,400, $42,500, $31,000, $21,000.

3 Execute, by hand, the Median Salary algorithm for the single salary $21,000. Note whether the answer coincides with the expected answer.

4 What should the median salary be if *no* salaries are provided in the input data? Modify the Median Salary algorithm to handle this case correctly.

5 Devise an algorithm for producing a solution to a problem for computer solution. Develop the algorithm using stepwise refinement, and show all the steps you use at each level and their connection to the steps into which they are refined at the next level.

★★ SIGNIFICANT EXERCISES

6 Assume we have four light bulbs arranged in a circle. The bulbs are labeled with the numbers 1, 2, 3, and 4 in clockwise order. Assume further that we have four switches connected so that each switch controls the light bulb with the corresponding number. Consider the following set of instructions, but do not perform the actions indicated yet.

(1) Turn on the light bulb that is directly across from the single light bulb that is on.

(2) If any odd-numbered light bulb is on, go to step 4.

(3) Turn off the lowest-numbered light bulb, and go to step 5.

(4) Turn off the highest-numbered light bulb.

(5) Turn on the bulb next to the highest numbered bulb that is on, in the clockwise direction.

(6) Turn off any even-numbered bulbs which might be on, and stop.

Perform the instructions four times, each time with only one bulb initially on. That is, turn on bulb 1 and perform the instructions. Then turn on only bulb 2 and perform the instructions. Then repeat for bulb 3 and bulb 4. Based on your experience in executing the instructions, what can you say about the overall result of executing the steps?

7 Assume you have three containers labeled A, B, and C that may contain an arbitrary number of colored marbles. The following set of instructions is designed to be executed starting with step 1. Examine the instructions and then answer the question that follows.

(1) If container C contains any marbles, then move all of them to container A. In any case, continue with step 2.

(2) If container A contains at least one red marble, then move one red marble from container A to container C. In any case, continue with step 3.

(3) If container B contains at least one blue marble, then move one blue marble from container B to container A. In any case, continue with step 4.

(4) If container B or container C contain any blue marbles, then go back to step 2 and continue from there. Otherwise, execution of the instructions has been completed.

Now assume that there are only red and blue marbles in the three containers. What is the overall effect of executing the instructions?

SPECIFICATION OF PROBLEMS
FOR COMPUTER SOLUTION

Each of the following chapters will have problems in this section that adhere to the following format. Each problem is independent of the text in that they do not refer to algorithms or code segments that appear there. Your instructor may, however, suggest modifications to the problems or provide specific data for use in testing your program.

1 *Input data specifications* identify the exact form in which the input data will be provided. If a variable number of input items appear, the limits on the number of such items will be specified. For some problems, multiple sources of input data are required, and the distinction between these sources is explicitly specified.

2 *The problem statement* gives the central goal of the problem to be solved. In those cases where general knowledge is not sufficient for you to produce an algorithm, an introduction to the nature of the problem is given.

3 *Output specifications* give the exact form in which the results should be displayed.

4 *Sample input and output* is provided to give at least one or two simple test cases and to illustrate the required input and output formats.

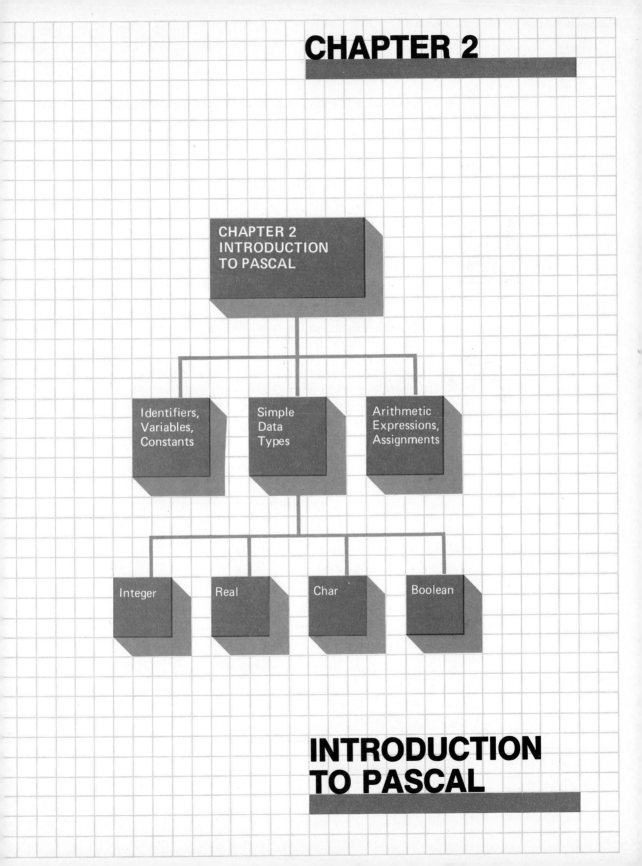

CHAPTER 2

CHAPTER 2
INTRODUCTION
TO PASCAL

Identifiers,
Variables,
Constants

Simple
Data
Types

Arithmetic
Expressions,
Assignments

Integer

Real

Char

Boolean

INTRODUCTION
TO PASCAL

OBJECTIVES

After completing this chapter you should be able to:

- Recognize and create Pascal identifiers, constants, and variables
- Read a syntax diagram
- Declare variables of simple or standard types: integer, real, Boolean, and char
- Recognize and apply the assignment statement
- Construct and evaluate arithmetic expressions using the arithmetic operators (+, −, *, /, DIV, MOD) and the standard (built-in) functions
- Enter, modify, and run a simple existing Pascal program.

CHAPTER OVERVIEW

This chapter contains a detailed discussion of elementary programming concepts using the high-level language Pascal. In the first section we consider the overall structure of a typical Pascal program by examining an example. Next we discuss the details of naming Pascal objects such as the program variables and constants. Pascal contains specific rules for naming objects, and it is necessary for you to know these rules when writing computer programs. Some examples of complete Pascal programs are presented to demonstrate the use of these rules.

Pascal has the capability of storing and manipulating information of various types. In this chapter we consider the four simple data types: integer, real, Boolean, and char. In particular, the integer and real data types are used for numeric data. We discuss the construction and evaluation of arithmetic expressions using the Pascal arithmetic operators addition (+), subtraction (−), multiplication (*), and division (/, DIV, MOD). Also, Pascal includes a number of standard, or built-in, functions. For example, the *sqrt* function computes the square root of a number. We consider some of these functions and give an example of their use.

In the Testing and Debugging Techniques section at the end of the chapter, a discussion of errors arising from arithmetic calculations is presented. Exercises and Problems for Computer Solution are included. After completing this chapter you should be able to enter, modify, and run a simple existing Pascal program. After completing Chapter 3 you should be able to construct and document your own Pascal program.

SECTION 2.1 A PASCAL EXAMPLE

In this course we use the high-level computer language known as Pascal. The language has become widely used for the following reasons:

1 Pascal is a general-purpose language that is applicable to solving a wide range of problems, including both numeric and nonnumeric problems.
2 Pascal is a well-designed introductory programming language ideal for use in teaching the fundamental concepts of computer science.
3 Compilers for Pascal are available on most computer systems.
4 Pascal programs can be written in a highly structured and organized manner, thus making them easy to modify.

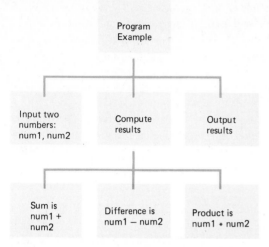

Figure 2-1   Top-down design of program example.

Before going into the details of the language, let us consider the overall structure of a typical Pascal program. For example, suppose we wish to write a simple program to read (or input) two numbers; determine the sum, difference, and product of this pair of numbers; and finally display (print, or output) these results. The top-down design for this program is shown in Figure 2-1, and the corresponding Pascal program is shown below.

```pascal
PROGRAM example (input, output);
(* Program to obtain two numbers from the input and *)
(* display their sum, difference, and product.       *)
VAR
      num1, num2, sum, difference, product : integer;
BEGIN
      (* Obtain the two numbers *)
      write ('Please type two integer values: ');
      readln (num1, num2);
      (* Compute sum, difference, and product *)
      sum := num1 + num2;
      difference := num1 - num2;
      product := num1 * num2;
      (* Display the results *)
      writeln ('The numbers are  ', num1, num2);
      writeln ('The sum is        ', sum);
      writeln ('The difference is ', difference);
      writeln ('The product is  ', product)
END.
```

Let us examine this program line by line. Don't be concerned if you can't understand everything the first time through. We will look at these details and more examples later in the chapter.

Consider the first line of the program:

```
PROGRAM example (input, output);
```

This line is a program heading and is required for all Pascal programs. The name of this program is *example*. The words *input* and *output* indicate that we are using the standard input and output devices defined on the computer system. If you are using an interactive system these devices will likely correspond to your terminal.

The next two lines of the program

```
(* Program to obtain two numbers from the input and *)
(* display their sum, difference, and product.      *)
```

are called ***comments***. Comments are used to include documentation and other information for the programmer and other readers of the source program. That is, comments are used to explain parts of the program to a human reader. Here the comment defines the purpose of program *example*. Comments are always enclosed by the characters (* and *), or the characters { and }, and except for being included in listings of the program, they are ignored by the Pascal compiler.

Following this comment we find:

```
VAR num1, num2, sum, difference, product : integer;
```

This defines (or *declares*) the variables (named ***memory locations***) that will be used in the program. In Pascal, all data items given names by the programmer must be declared before the program statements that use them. In this case the word VAR is followed by the list of names: *num1*, *num2*, *sum*, *difference*, and *product*. These are the names of the variables that will be used in the program statements to follow. The variable list is followed by a colon (:), and the word *integer*. This indicates that the preceding variables will be used to hold only integer values (that is, positive or negative whole numbers).

Following the variable declaration we have the actual program instructions, or ***executable statements***. (The variable declaration is not considered an executable statement since it specifies no actual operations on the data items. The difference between declarations and executable statements in Pascal is similar to the difference between the Declaration of Independence and the American Revolution!)

The executable statements of the program are enclosed by the words BEGIN and END. There are nine statements (or instructions) in program *example*, and they are separated from each other by semicolons. Observe that the last statement before the END does not require a semicolon. Note that BEGIN and END are not statements and are therefore not separated by semicolons. When a single statement is discussed in the text we will omit the semicolon following it, since technically it is not part of the statement. Also note that there are three comments, each enclosed by parentheses and asterisks: (* and *). Let's now look at each of the executable statements in more detail.

```
write ('Please type two integer values: ')
```

This statement instructs the computer to display the message "Please type two integer values: " on the output device. The purpose of this line is to instruct, or prompt, the user to enter the numbers to be processed by the program.

```
readln (num1, num2)
```

Following the prompt we instruct the computer to obtain two numbers (from the input device) and store them in the variables named *num1* and *num2*. If the user had typed 35 and 10, in that order, then the value 35 would be stored in *num1* and the value 10 would be stored in *num2*.

```
sum         := num1 + num2
difference  := num1 − num2
product     := num1 *  num2
```

These statements, known as ***assignment*** statements, perform the addition, subtraction, and multiplication, in that order. (Note that the semicolons have been omitted to emphasize their use as separators; semicolons are *not* used to terminate statements!) In each statement, the variables to the right of the := symbol are added, subtracted, and multiplied. The result of each operation then replaces (stores into, or *assigns* to) the variable to the left of the := symbol, replacing any value it may have had previously. The := symbol, as well as the (* and *) symbols, is formed from two separate characters with no space between them!

Again assume that the value of *num1* is 35 and the value of *num2* is 10. After the computer executes the three assignment statements, the values of sum, difference, and product would be:

Sum	45	(since 35 + 10 = 45)
Difference	25	(since 35 − 10 = 25)
Product	350	(since 35 × 10 = 350)

```
writeln ('The numbers are    ', num1, ' and ', num2)
writeln ('Their sum is       ', sum)
writeln ('Their difference is ', difference)
writeln ('Their product is   ', product)
```

These last four statements instruct the computer to display (on the output device) the results. Each statement displays a single line. When the computer executes the first of these, for example, the message "The numbers are   ," the value of *num1*, the word *and*, and the value of *num2* will be displayed (or output, or printed).

If this program were executed on an interactive computer system we might find the following information on the terminal's screen after execution was complete (the numbers typed by the user are shown here in color):

Please enter two integer values: 35   10
The numbers are   35 and 10
Their sum is   45
Their difference is   25
Their product is   350

Structure of a Pascal Program

A Pascal program consists of two components: a program heading and a program block. The ***program heading*** is a single statement that begins with the word PRO-GRAM. This word is followed by the name assigned to the whole program and a parenthesized list of the names associated with the devices that will be used for input and output. (We will see lists in other places in Pascal; they are just sequences of names or other items separated by commas.) Since the program heading is a statement it must be separated from the remainder of the program by a semicolon.

The ***program block*** is the remainder of the program and consists of two components: the declarations and the executable statements. The ***declarations*** define (or declare) objects that have names (to which we may refer) such as variables and constants. The ***executable statements*** are the instructions that will be carried out by the computer when the program is executed. These statements comprise the *active* part of the program since they, and only they, may cause data manipulation to take place. The entire collection of executable statements is enclosed by the words BEGIN and END. The very end of the program block is marked by a period (which must naturally follow END). Figure 2-2 gives you an overview of the structure of a Pascal program.

In this chapter we consider in detail such fundamental computer science concepts

Figure 2-2   Structure of a Pascal program.

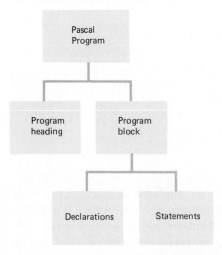

as variables, constants, data types, and assignment statements, as well as how they are related to the Pascal language.

SECTION 2.2 IDENTIFIERS, CONSTANTS, AND VARIABLES

When writing computer programs in any high-level language it is necessary to use names to identify the objects we wish to manipulate. Typically we use names for such things as the entire program, the variables, some constants, and procedures and functions. The word, or sequence of characters, that forms the name of such an object is called an ***identifier***. In the previous Pascal program *example* is an identifier, as is each of the following: *num1*, *num2*, *sum*, *difference*, and *product*.

Identifiers must be constructed so as to conform with specific rules that may vary from language to language. The rules that dictate how individual components may be put together to form a legal program are called ***syntax rules***. The rules for forming legal Pascal identifiers, therefore, are included in the Pascal syntax rules.

Pascal Identifiers

Identifiers used in Pascal programs are comprised of a collection of characters from the letters A through Z and the digits 0 through 9. The only restriction is that the first character of each identifier must be a letter. Many computer systems include devices that include both upper- and lowercase letters, and Pascal permits both these cases to be used. However, an uppercase letter and the corresponding lowercase letter are treated as the same by Pascal.

Here are some legal Pascal identifiers:

```
NUM1                    H2O
num1   (same as NUM1)   SS2468
MaxNum                  MAX
Z2b3004aj19             X
```

Theoretically, identifiers may include any number of characters. However, some Pascal compilers will recognize only the first eight characters in each identifier. If you are using such a compiler, you must be careful to use identifiers which are uniquely defined by their first eight characters, since to do otherwise would result in two or more (apparently different) identifiers being treated as the name of the same object. For example, *interest84* and *interest85* would be treated as the same identifier by such Pascal compilers.

Of course we would like to use identifiers that help us in understanding what a program is doing. We should therefore resist the temptation to use extremely short identifiers (like *A*, *B*, and *C*) or identifiers which are "cute" (*Larry*, *Moe*, and *Curly*), unless they have a direct relationship to the objects they name. Excessively long identifiers may also cause problems, since a misspelling of an identifier will result in two different names when only one was expected.

Here are some identifiers that are illegal:

a + b	(The "+" is not a letter or digit.)
cost of living	(Blanks are not allowed.)
2bornot2b	(It doesn't begin with a letter.)

Some identifiers which would otherwise be permitted as names for programmer-defined objects are reserved for special purpose in Pascal. These identifiers are therefore called **reserved words**. Some of the reserved words used in the program *example* are PROGRAM, VAR, BEGIN, and END. A complete list of these reserved words can be found in Appendix B. Reserved words in this text are written using only uppercase letters. Please note, however, that this is just a matter of typography: When you write the reserved words in your programs, they are formed from the same characters used for other identifiers.

Another group of identifiers used in the program *example* include *integer*, *input*, *output*, *read*, and *writeln*. These are known in Pascal as **standard identifiers**, since they have been predeclared by the compiler. That is, they are automatically associated with certain objects even if your Pascal program does not declare them. If a Pascal program does include a declaration for a standard identifier, the former (automatic) declaration is superceded and the later (programmer-supplied) declaration is the only association which is effective in the program. Such redeclaration of the standard identifiers usually causes confusion and should be avoided. A list of the standard identifiers in Pascal can be found in Appendix C.

Syntax Diagrams

The syntax rules for Pascal can be represented by visual aids known as **syntax diagrams**. The syntax diagram in Figure 2-3 gives the rule for forming identifiers.

To read such a syntax diagram, start at the left side and follow the "path" in the direction indicated by the arrow. We immediately come to the oval labeled "letter," which means that at this point we must select a letter. Continuing from this oval we come to a "branch point" similar to a street intersection. We may choose any of the three alternatives (note that U-turns are *not* permitted!): Continue straight ahead to the exit, follow the path that leads us through the *digit* oval, or follow the path that leads us through the other *letter* oval. If we choose one of the latter alternatives, we must select a digit or another letter for our identifier, after which we find ourselves back at the branch point. We can then choose more letters or digits, or exit.

Syntax diagrams are very useful in verifying the validity of our Pascal programs

Figure 2-3 Syntax diagram for an identifier.

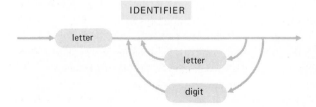

since they give a visual representation of the rules for forming a program. We will have more to say about syntax diagrams in a later section. For now, verify that you understand the syntax diagram for identifiers by showing that the following identifiers are valid:

boxtop   num2   a   c22d46

Constants

Many programs contain certain values that should not change during the execution of the program. Such values are called **constants**. (Note that a variable may also go unchanged during the execution of a program, but this is only because our executable statements did not cause it to change. Executable statements can *never* change the value of a constant.) In Pascal we may use identifiers to provide names for constants that may be referenced in our programs. For example, if we decided to write a program to compute the interest on a savings account which yielded 6 percent, we might include the following declaration:

CONST intrate = 0.06;

The word CONST is reserved and is followed by the identifier naming the constant (*intrate*), an equal sign (= , but not : =), and the value of the constant (0.06). Constant declarations are placed before the variable declarations.

Declarations are separated from other declarations and statements by semicolons, just as statements are separated. Since constant declarations will always be followed by at least one additional declaration or statement, a semicolon will always be required at the end of the constant declaration.

There are two principal reasons for declaring a constant in a Pascal program, both simplify programming. First, identifiers can be chosen by the programmer to reflect the meaning or use of the named object in the program and help make programs easier to understand. Values (like 0.06) could be used in several different contexts in the program, and the use of an identifier for a constant signifies which of these uses are identical. For example, a program might be written to determine the interest on a savings account as well as the income tax to be paid on the interest. Both of these might be 6 percent, and so the constant 0.06 could be used for both. However, giving a name to the interest rate (*intrate*) and a name to the tax rate (*taxrate*) would enable the programmer (or anyone else reading the program) to distinguish between the two uses of the constant.

The second reason for declaring constants is to provide a simple way of altering each occurrence of the constant in the program if necessary. In our income tax example, if the tax rate changed to 5 percent, we would merely have to change the value of the constant in the declaration of the tax rate to 0.05. Then each occurrence of the identifier *taxrate* would represent the modified constant. (Note that this would also require recompilation of the program, since during compilation values are associated with constant identifiers.)

If we wish to declare more than one constant in a program we do not repeat the reserved word CONST, but rather include additional lines of the form *identifier = constant* separated by semicolons:

```
CONST
        intrate  =  0.06;
        taxrate  =  0.05;
```

The syntax diagram for constant declarations is shown in Figure 2-4. Note that in this syntax diagram we have both labeled ovals and labeled rectangles. The characters inside the ovals appear literally (for example, the reserved word CONST must always be included in a constant declaration). The rectangles reference other syntax diagrams. In this case, we must include identifiers and constants in a constant declaration, so we reference their syntax diagrams at the appropriate points. The syntax diagram for constants is shown in Appendix A; for now we can just assume they define values of the type we have been using. Convince yourself that you understand the syntax diagram for constant declarations by verifying that the following is valid:

```
CONST
        size         =  5;
        perfect      =  100.0;
        boilingpoint =  212;
        salestax     =  0.07;
```

The value of a constant is stored in a location in the computer's memory. The identifier used to name the constant refers to that memory location. In this case the identifier is used to name a memory location whose contents are not permitted to change during the execution of the program. If, for example, the constant declaration

```
CONST      pi = 3.14159;
```

is encountered in a Pascal program, a memory location would be reserved and the value 3.14159 would be placed in it. The name *pi* would be associated with the location in such a way that all other references to *pi* in the program would yield the value 3.14159. Figure 2-5 illustrates this concept. You can think of the identifier *pi* as a name tag for the reserved memory location.

Figure 2-4   Syntax diagram for a constant declaration.

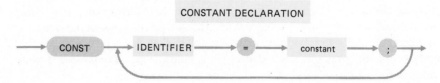

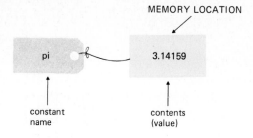

MEMORY LOCATION

pi — 3.14159

constant
name

contents
(value)

Figure 2-5   Storage of a constant.

Variables

Variables are objects in a program that may change value during execution. Fortunately, they do not change value arbitrarily but only in response to the executable statements in the program. Identifiers are used to name variables similar to the way identifiers are used to name constants. As in the case of constants, declaring a variable causes a location in the computer's memory to be reserved and labeled with the corresponding identifier. In the case of variables, however, the content of the memory location (and thus the value of the variable) is permitted to change, and *no definite value is initially placed in the memory location*. This means any use of a variable prior to storing (or assigning) a value to it will yield an undefined (or unexpected) value!

Before further consideration of variables and their declaration, we will examine the manner in which values may be assigned to variables in Pascal. Suppose we have a variable named *time* and we wish it to have the value 60. One way to accomplish this is by using an *assignment statement*, and in this case the assignment statement

time := 60

would achieve the desired result. This is illustrated in Figure 2-6. The assignment statement of this paragraph should be read as "assign the value 60 to the variable named *time*."

It is important to note that assignment statements modify the value of the variable whose name appears to the left of the symbol := with the value from the right. Any

Figure 2-6   Storage of a variable.

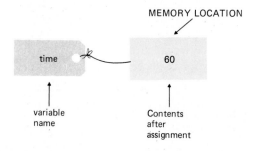

MEMORY LOCATION

time — 60

variable
name

Contents
after
assignment

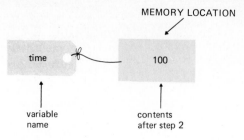

MEMORY LOCATION

variable
name

contents
after step 2

Figure 2-7   Storage of a variable.

value previously stored (or contained) in the named variable is replaced by this new value. For example, consider the following statements:

```
time := 60;
time := 100
```

The first of these assigns the value 60 to the variable *time*. The second assignment statement replaces the current value of *time* (60) with the new value, 100 (see Figure 2-7). There is only one memory location named *time*, and it can only have one value *at a time*.

Variables in Pascal are named by using a valid identifier. The value of the variable can change, but the name does not. A Pascal variable consists of three components: name, type, and value (see Figure 2-8).

To declare a variable, we must specify the name and the data type to be associated with the variable. The name is the identifier which represents the variable. The data type indicates how the value of the variable will be interpreted (real, integer, character). The value of the variable is determined by the statements executed by the computer. Assume, for example, we wish to declare a variable *itemcost*. The variable will represent the cost of a purchased item in dollars and cents. (Actually we will mentally associate dollars and cents with the variable, since literally the variable will only contain a number.) Since we wish to be able to represent decimal fractions with our variable, we choose to use the Pascal data type *real* for *itemcost*. The Pascal declaration for the variable *itemcost* would be[1]

```
VAR itemcost : real;
```

In this declaration we see the reserved word VAR followed by the identifier, a colon, and the name of the data type (in this case, real).

The data type of each variable declared must be specified. In the next section we will consider the so-called simple data types of Pascal: integer, real, Boolean, and char.

---

[1]Once again we must remark about semicolons. Since variable declarations will *always* be followed by other declarations or statements, we include the semicolon in our example. Remember, though, that the semicolon is a separator.

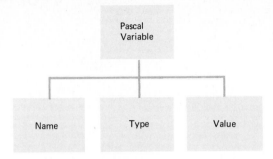

Figure 2-8   Pascal variable.

The concept of **data type** is fundamental to computer science. By specifying a particular data type for a variable we indicate the characteristics of the values that may be stored in the associated variable. (Think of a variable as a container for a value. Then the data type is analogous to the size and shape of the container.)

Pascal is called a *strongly typed* language since each identifier must have an associated type. Thus, the compiler can verify during compilation that only values of appropriate types will be stored into variables. This allows the detection of some problems before the program is ever executed! For example, storing a real number into an integer is not allowed in Pascal, and the compiler would produce an appropriate diagnostic message. An appropriate analogy might be the examination of the size of a container before pouring a gallon of paint into it. If we waited until *execution* and the receiving container was too small—well, perhaps you understand the value of detecting the problem before execution.

The following example shows a variable declaration specifying more than one variable:

```
VAR
    time, speed  : integer;
    distance     : real;
```

Here we have instructed the computer to reserve memory locations for two variables, *time* and *speed*, each of which is of type integer, and an additional memory location for a variable *distance*, which is of type real. Note how we were permitted to specify *time* and *speed* in a list of variables of type integer. In general, we may specify as many variables as we wish in this manner as long as each is to be the same type. The variable *distance* was specified separately, since its type is not the same as that of the other variables.

The third component of a variable, namely its value, is determined during the execution of the program. We have already seen that assignment statements can modify the value associated with a variable. In the statement

```
speed := 55
```

VARIABLE DECLARATION

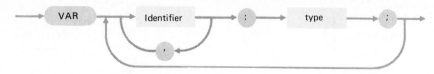

Figure 2-9   Syntax diagram for a variable declaration.

for example, the value 55 is stored into the memory location associated with the variable named *speed*. Remember that Pascal uses the symbol : = to represent assignment of the value on the right (in this case, 55) to the variable named on the left (*speed*). Also, note that a variable must have a value before it can be used in an expression. The value of the variable remains undefined until an executable statement causes a value to be placed in the memory location reserved for the variable.

The syntax diagram for variable declarations is shown in Figure 2-9. Since the data type of a variable must be specified in the declaration, it is explicitly included in the syntax diagram. Again, rectangles are used to refer to other syntax diagrams. Later we will consider the syntax diagram for type in detail, but for now we will use only the simple Pascal types integer, real, Boolean, and char. Using the syntax diagram, you should be able to verify that the following declaration is correct:

```
VAR
      minutes, seconds  :  integer;
      rate              :  real;
      flag              :  Boolean;
      grade, final      :  char;
```

Another Pascal Program

Let us apply some of these concepts to an actual Pascal program called *tax*. This program uses the cost of a purchased item as input data, determines the amount of sales tax at 7 percent, and finally displays the price of the item and the amount of tax. The complete program is shown below.

```
PROGRAM tax (input, output);
(* Program to compute 7% sales tax on purchased items *)
CONST
      taxrate = 0.07;
VAR
      itemcost, salestax : real;
```

```
BEGIN
      (* Obtain cost of item from input data *)
      write ('Please enter cost of item: ');
      readln (itemcost);
      (* Compute sales tax on the item *)
      salestax := taxrate * itemcost;
      (* Display results *)
      writeln ('Item cost is   ', itemcost : 6 : 2);
      writeln ('Sales tax is   ', salestax : 6 : 2)
END.
```

Program Tax

The first line of the program

```
PROGRAM tax (input, output);
```

is the program heading. It contains, as usual, the reserved word PROGRAM followed by an identifier representing the name of the program. In this case we have chosen the identifier *tax* since it gives a clue as to what the program is doing. The program name is followed by the parenthesized list of input/output devices used by the program.

The next line of the program contains only a comment, naturally enclosed by the symbols (* and *). Since comments are ignored by the computer we may safely place them anywhere we wish.

The remainder of the program is the program block containing the declarations and executable statements. The constant and variable declarations are given in exactly that order:

```
CONST
      taxrate = 0.07;
VAR
    itemcost, salestax : real;
```

In the constant declaration the identifier *taxrate* names the constant value 0.07, the decimal fraction representing a 7 percent sales tax rate. The identifiers *itemcost* and *salestax* name the variables that will represent the cost of the purchased item and the sales tax on that item, respectively. Note that each of these variables can store a number with a fractional part.

The executable statements follow these declarations, enclosed by the reserved words BEGIN and END. It is helpful to consider these particular reserved words as always appearing in a pair as they do here, surrounding another group of Pascal statements. In this way, BEGIN and END are very much like parentheses.

The tax program essentially reads the cost of the purchased item, storing the value in variable *itemcost*. Next the assignment statement

```
salestax := taxrate * itemcost
```

multiplies (as represented by the asterisk in Pascal) the *taxrate* by the *itemcost* and assigns this value to the variable *salestax*. The last two statements cause the computer to display the original item cost and the computed sales tax on the output device. The details of these statements will be explained in the next chapter. Finally, the program is terminated with a period, as are all Pascal programs.

Pascal allows any number of spaces (blanks and ends of lines and, on some computer systems, tab characters) between identifiers, constants, reserved words, and operators (like := and *). Some white space must appear between two adjacent identifiers (*otherwisetheywouldcombinetoformonelongidentifier*), but identifiers need not be separated from other symbols. It is usually a good idea, however, to use blanks to separate the various components of the program in order to improve its readability. Consider the program shown below, for example. This program will perform exactly the same computation as the one shown before (program *tax*). Which would you rather read?

```
PROGRAM tax(input,output);(*Program to compute 7% sales tax on
purchased items*)CONST taxrate=0.07;VAR itemcost,
salestax:real;BEGIN(*Obtain cost of item from input data*)
write('Please enter cost of item: ');readln(itemcost);(*Compute sales tax
on the item*)salestax:=taxrate*itemcost;(*Display
results*)writeln('Item cost is ',itemcost:6:2); writeln('Sales tax is ',
salestax:6:2)END.
```

One possible result of running the program is shown below. Those items entered by the user are shown in color.

```
Please enter cost of item: 30.50
Item cost is    30.50
Sales tax is     2.14
```

Note that the cost of the item is entered as 30.50 rather than $30.50 (that is, the dollar sign is omitted). This is because the computer manipulates numbers without considering the units (in this case, dollars) being manipulated. This can easily result in logical errors in program design (such as adding dollars and tax rates), and we will return to this problem later.

Suppose there were many statements in the program using the constant *taxrate*. If this rate should then change to 8 percent, for example, we would only have to change the constant declaration to

```
CONST
        taxrate = 0.08;
```

instead of modifying the many statements using *taxrate*.

EXERCISES FOR SECTION 2.2

1 Determine whether the following identifiers are valid or invalid.

  (a) Average   (b) A1234
  (c) 1234A   (d) Hot Dog
  (e) Program   (f) $XYZ
  (f) A*b   (h) George
  (i) 506-74-3981   (j) 4×2

2 Explain why the following identifiers are invalid.

  (a) 1986   (b) Rate*Time
  (c) End   (d) 1End
  (e) Integer   (f) Var
  (g) Sqrt   (h) $CASH

3 Determine whether the following constant declarations are valid or invalid.

  (a) CONST tax = 0.09;   (b) CONST pi := 3.14;
  (c) CONST ten = 9;   (d) CONST Agrade := 90;

4 Write constant declarations for the following values using meaningful identifiers.

  (a) The number of days in a week
  (b) A person weighing 185 pounds
  (c) A sales tax rate of 8 percent
  (d) A class with 50 students

5 Determine whether the following variable declarations are valid or invalid.

  (a) VAR num1, num2 : real;
  (b) VAR num1; num2 : integer;
  (c) VAR total, sum, count : integer, real;
  (d) VAR studentid, ssnumber : integer;

6 Write variable declarations for variables that can hold the following values using meaningful identifiers.

  (a) Your social security number
  (b) The current year
  (c) The interest rate on a loan
  (d) The average grade on several examinations

7 (a) List five reserved words used in our Pascal programs.
  (b) List five standard identifiers used in our Pascal programs.

SECTION 2.3 THE SIMPLE DATA TYPES: INTEGER, REAL, BOOLEAN, AND CHAR

The computer has the capability of storing and manipulating information (data) of various types. For example, the set of test scores from a computer science or math-

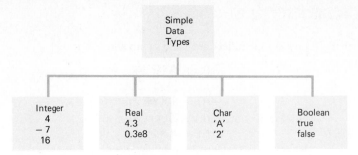

Figure 2-10   Simple data types.

ematics course is an example of numeric data, each score usually being a whole number in the range 0 to 100. The data type for the test scores is known as ***integer***. A different type of numeric data is used for the balance of each checking account at a bank. These balances are normally represented by numbers with fractional parts (the cents being fractions of a dollar). This data type is known as ***real***. Very large numbers like those used in astronomy and very small numbers like those used in atomic physics are also examples of numbers that can be of type real. The computer also has the capability of manipulating nonnumeric data such as the names of the customers at a bank. Programs that process words, like text editors, manipulate such nonnumeric data. The data type used to represent such information is called ***character*** (in Pascal, this type is called ***char***). Finally, we have the data type used to represent only the values true and false, sometimes used for the responses to some examination questions. The data type having only these two values—true and false—is known as ***Boolean*** (usually capitalized, since it is derived from George Boole, a pioneer of mathematical logic). Figure 2-10 summarizes the simple data types.

These four data types—integer, real, char, and Boolean—are the most fundamental and commonly used types, and are therefore known in Pascal as the ***simple***, or ***standard***, data types. The additional data types will be discussed later in the text.

The simple data types describe collections (or sets) of constants with different characteristics and the various operations which may be used to manipulate these constants. For example, the constant 42 is of the integer data type. Some examples of constants of the simple data types are shown in the following table. We consider each data type in detail.

data type	description	examples		
Integer	Positive and negative whole numbers and zero	−30 0	153 96	
Real	Numbers with a decimal point and/or exponent	3.14 1e10	−0.189 6.2e-8	
Char	Characters such as letters, digits, or punctuation, or the blank character	'A' '!' ' '	'a' '%' '{'	'B' ' '' ' ' ''''
Boolean	Logical values	true	false	

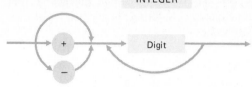

Figure 2-11   Syntax diagram for an integer constant.

The Integer Data Type

The data type *integer* includes positive and negative whole numbers and zero. These numbers *do not* contain fractional parts or decimal points. Examples include 32, − 16, 0, and 8432. If no sign is explicitly included in the number, then it is assumed to be positive. The syntax diagram for integer constants is shown in Figure 2-11.

In Pascal, as in most programming language, commas and blanks are not permitted in integer constants. The following, for example, are not valid integers:

12 5   (blanks not allowed between digits)
1,000,000   (commas not allowed between digits)
5.0   (decimal point not allowed)

Verify that these are not proper integers using the syntax diagram.

A significant difference between numbers represented in a computer and "pure" numbers is due to the computer's finite memory. That is, the number of memory locations in any computer, as well as the size of each memory location, is limited. Each computer therefore has a maximum integer value which can be represented, either as a constant or in a variable. Since different computers may have different maximum values, Pascal has a predeclared standard integer constant called *maxint* whose value is the largest integer which can be represented on the computer in use. We can also write − *maxint* to represent an approximation to the smallest integer which can be stored. (The reason why − *maxint* is only an approximation to the smallest integer will not be covered here.) *Maxint* will vary from computer to computer, but large computers typically have *maxint* equal to 2^{31}-1, or 2,147,483,647, while smaller computers (like personal computers) have *maxint* equal to 2^{15}-1, or 32,767.

Declaring Integer Variables

Suppose we wish to use a variable named *time* to store integer values. Prior to using any variable in Pascal, we must declare it, giving both its identifier and data type.

VAR time : integer;

If we wish to declare more than one variable of the same data type, we may use a list to the left of the colon.

VAR time, rate, distance : integer;

None of these variables are related except for the common data type (integer). (Think of the analogy with three different quart jars; each can store up to one quart, but since each is distinct, they may store different "values.")

The Real Data Type

The *real* data type includes numbers which can be expressed with a decimal point and those numbers which are too large or small to be stored exactly as an integer. If real numbers include a decimal point, they must have at least one digit before and one digit after the decimal point. Also, they may not be written with commas between their digits. Consider the following examples:

invalid form	valid form
.25	0.25
− .007	− 0.007
5.	5.0
1,000.5	1000.5

Very large or very small numbers can be stored in Pascal variables declared as real. These numbers can be represented using a notation similar to scientific notation. The number 357.6 can be represented in scientific notation by moving the decimal point two places to the left and multiplying by 100, or 10^2. The resulting number in scientific notation would then be 3.576×10^2. The number 0.000321 could also be written in this form by moving the decimal point four places to the right and multiplying by 0.0001, or 10^{-4}. The resulting number would be 3.21×10^{-4}.

The following table provides more examples of representing very large or very small numbers in scientific notation. Remember that to put a number into scientific notation, the decimal point is moved until a number between 1 and 10 is obtained. That number is then multiplied by a power of 10. This power (or exponent) of 10 is initially zero, and is increased or decreased by one for each digit past which the decimal point is moved. If the decimal point is moved to the left, the power of 10 increases, and if the decimal point is moved to the right, the power of 10 decreases.

real number	scientific notation
8569.5	8.5695×10^3
100.0	1.0×10^2
0.000035	3.5×10^{-5}
0.0001	1.0×10^{-4}
605.89	6.0589×10^2

In Pascal we can represent real numbers using *floating-point notation*, in which the letter *e* (or alternately *E*) replaces "times 10 to the power" (think exponent.) For example, the real number 3.576×10^2 would be written in our Pascal programs as 3.576e2, or 3.576E2. The number 3.21×10^{-4} would be written as $3.21e-4$, or

3.21E−4. The number before the letter *e* must be an integer or real constant, with or without a sign or decimal point. If a decimal point is included, it must be preceded and followed by a digit, as usual. The number after the letter *e* is a (possibly signed) integer. This number is called the **exponent**. The syntax diagram for constants of the real data type (Figure 2-12) gives the rule more explicitly.

Using this diagram you should be able to verify that the following constants are valid or invalid, as indicated.

VALID REAL CONSTANTS		INVALID REAL CONSTANTS	
floating-point rotation	*scientific notation*	*floating-point decimal*	*reason*
2.6e15	(2.6×10^{15})	1.e2	No digit after decimal point
−3.2e−6	$(−3.2 \times 10^{-6})$	−6.5e3.6	Exponent is not an integer
2e14	(2×10^{14})	.2e3	No digit before decimal point
6.5432e01	(6.5432×10^{1})	3,642.5e−5	Comma is not permitted
−4.6e2	$(−4.6 \times 10^{2})$		
−4.107e32	$(−4.107 \times 10^{32})$		

Declaring Real Variables

Since variables can represent many different values, the question of whether to use an integer or real data type is important. Obviously, if the values include fractional parts, we must choose the real data type. Since integers have limited magnitudes (from −*maxint* to *maxint*), we must also use the real data type to represent those quantities that can exceed this range. The allowable range of values for the real data type will vary between different computer systems.

Since the real data type permits us to store numbers with fractional parts and numbers with much larger ranges than integer, we might ask why we need to use integers at all. The answer lies in the fact that numbers of the real data type are only approximations to exact values. Arithmetic involving real numbers can easily yield apparently incorrect answers; the results are only approximations to the exact values. On the other hand, values of the integer data type are always represented exactly, as long as the results of arithmetic operations do not exceed the allowable range. Examples of some of the problems with the real data type are given in the Testing and Debugging Techniques section at the end of the chapter.

Figure 2-12 Syntax diagram for a real constant.

REAL

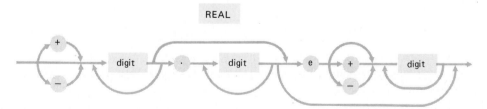

The declaration of the three real variables *tax*, *salary*, and *rate* might be accomplished as shown below:

```
VAR tax, salary, rate : real;
```

The Character (Char) Data Type

Names of persons and objects, words, part numbers, and addresses are just sequences of characters. Each of these characters can be represented by a variable of the character data type, called the **char** data type in Pascal. A character is actually represented internally (in the computer's memory) by a small integer code (typically in the range 0 to 127), but externally (that is, on a keyboard or a printer) the characters are the usual graphics we utilize to represent names and addresses. The graphics we usually find include upper- and lowercase alphabetic characters, decimal digits, and special characters and punctuation marks.

In Pascal constants of the char data type are represented by single quotes, or apostrophes enclosing a single character. As examples of character data type constants consider the following:

```
'A'       'a'       '6'       ' '       '{'       ''''
```

Here the constant 'A' is *not* the same as the constant 'a'. Neither is the char constant '6' the same as the integer constant 6. To represent a blank as data to be manipulated by a program we use ' ', a space inside single quotes. Also, a brace is written '{' to avoid confusing it with a comment. To represent a single quote, or apostrophe, we write '''' (note this is *not* the double quote, "). Such a special form is necessary since single quotes are used to delimit a character constant.

Character variables may store only one character. In Pascal, we can represent constants with more than one character as **character string constants**. The characters appear between the single quotes. Here are a few typical character string constants:

```
'The sales tax is'
'Enter your data, please'
'New York, New York 10020'
```

If we wish to include a single quote in a character string, then we must write two single quotes (*not* a double quote like "). For example, the words *Alice's Restaurant* would be represented by the character string constant 'Alice''s Restaurant'.

Declaring Character Constants and Variables

Single character constants and character string constants may be declared in the CONST section of the program and given names just like integer and real constants. Consider this illustration:

```
CONST
      star     =  '*';
      blank    =  ' ';
      quote    =  '''';
      state    =  'California';
      message  =  'Hello, my name is HAL.';
```

The first three of these constants, *star*, *blank*, and *quote*, are each single character constants, while the last two, *state* and *message*, are character string constants.

The following is a typical variable declaration in Pascal:

```
VAR letter, grade, initial : char;
```

This declaration introduces variables named *letter*, *grade*, and *initial*, each of which can be used to store exactly one character value. To store multiple characters, we must either use multiple variables (with different names) or an array (or list) of characters (to be considered a little later).

The Boolean Data Type

Sometimes information can be represented using only two values, such as yes and no or true and false. For example, a true-false test is an examination in which each question is answered with a true or false response. Surveys often request a yes or no response.

The **Boolean** data type is used to represent the "logical" values true and false. The outcome of many tests in a computer program will be of this type. For example, when we ask if a particular integer value is odd, the answer will be true or false. There are only two Boolean constants, represented in Pascal by *true* and *false*. Here is a valid constant declaration:

```
CONST flag = true;
```

Variable declarations involving the Boolean data type are constructed in a form similar to those for the other simple data types. In the declaration

```
VAR switch : Boolean;
```

the identifier *switch* is used to reference a memory location which can store only the values true and false.

Later we will examine the manipulation of Boolean data in detail, especially with respect to making tests and decisions.

EXERCISES FOR SECTION 2.3

1   Determine which of the following are valid Pascal integer constants.

(a)   189   (b) -2.5 (c)   '33'
(d) -55555 (e)   6,632   (f)   2.5e03
(g) $+199$ (h)   199.   (i)   maxint

2   Determine which of the following are valid Pascal real constants.

(a) -0.01 (b)   .025   (c) -3.6
(d)   69.   (e) $3.6e-06$ (f) $3.e-06$
(g) $+8.3e2$ (h)   1.0E1.   (i)   maxreal

3   Determine which of the following are valid Pascal character constants.

(a)   A   (b)   'A'   (c)   'CAT'
(d)   '8' (e)   '?'   (f)   '??'

4   Write a Pascal real constant representing each of the following values.

(a) 6.21×10^3 (b) 0.15×10^{-2}
(c) 1.66×10^6 (d) 22.4×10^{-8}

5   Write the value of each of the following Pascal real constants without using exponents.

(a)   2.6e03   (b) $-12e-2$
(c)   4.56e10   (d) $-66.5e1$

6   Explain why each of the following is not a valid Pascal real constant.

(a)   10.   (b)   .33   (c) $-2.6e1.5$
(d) $5.25-$ (e) $2.e-03$ (f) $3.14159 \ldots$

7   Determine which of the following are valid Pascal constants.

(a)   'e'   (b)   e   (c)   false
(d)   999   (e)   3.e   (f) $-$maxint
(g) -0.000 (h)   '?'   (i)   !

SECTION 2.4 ASSIGNMENT STATEMENTS AND ARITHMETIC EXPRESSIONS

Assignment

Assignment statements, for example, *num1 := 5*, are used to change the value stored in the memory location of a variable. The symbol : = is used to indicate that assignment is to take place and is called the ***assignment operator***. Note that it is comprised of two separate characters, and must be written in Pascal programs with no spaces separating them.

   The name of the variable whose value is to be modified must be written to the left

ASSIGNMENT

variable → := → expression

Figure 2-13 Syntax diagram for an assignment statement.

of the assignment operator. On the right we place an *expression* which will provide the new value for the variable named on the left. Figure 2-13 shows the syntax diagram for the assignment statement. We will examine expressions in more detail shortly, but before we do so, let us note the important difference between the symbols = and := (the assignment operator). As we have already seen, the equal sign (=) appearing by itself (that is, without the colon preceding it) indicates that the items on either side are *identically* equal, as in the declaration of a constant. The equal sign is also used to test values for equality. On the other hand, the assignment operator changes the value of the variable to its left, working independently of the previous relationship between the values on either side of it. For example, the declaration

CONST speed = 55;

tells the reader and the computer that the identifier *speed* is to be treated exactly like the integer constant 55. The assignment statement

velocity := 55

is an executable statement that directs the computer to change the value the variable *velocity* to the new integer value 55.

The computer performs assignment statements in two basic steps. In the first of these, the value of the expression on the right side of the assignment operator is determined. This step can be quite complicated (as we will see), but the end result is just a value of a specific type. In the second step this value is stored in the memory location for the variable whose name appears to the left of the assignment operator, replacing its previous value.

It is possible to use the same variable name on both the left side of the assignment operator and in the expression on the right side. Since the expression is evaluated first, it is the current value of the variable that is used in the expression's evaluation. Therefore, statements like

velocity := velocity + 1

make perfect sense: determine the current value of the variable *velocity*, add 1 to that value, and then replace the existing value of *velocity* with the result. In short, this statement says "add 1 to velocity." This example emphasizes the fact that the assignment operator does *not* mean equality!

Suppose we have the following variable declarations in a Pascal program:

```
VAR
    num, sum : integer;
    time      : real;
    grade     : char;
    flag      : Boolean;
```

If we wish to assign values to these variables, we must take care to ensure that the values are of the appropriate type. For example, attempting to assign a Boolean value to a character variable does not make sense, and it is therefore not permitted in a Pascal program. Each of the following assignments is correct:

```
grade := 'A'
flag := false
time := 20.15
num := 0
sum := num + 1
sum := sum + 1
```

For comparison, here are a few incorrect assignment statements involving the same variables:

incorrect assignment	reason
grade := B	Single quotes missing in char constant 'B'.
num := 1.0	Here num is integer; 1.0 is real.
num := time	Here num is integer; time is real.
2 := num	Variable must be on left.
sum + num := time	Variable must be on left.

There is one exception to the rule requiring the data type of the variable on the left and the expression on the right side of the assignment operator to be identical. We are permitted to write an assignment statement which directs the computer to store an integer value in a real variable. For example, the statement

```
time := 60
```

is legal, even though *time* was declared (above) as a real variable and 60 is an integer constant. This is because each integer constant has an equivalent real constant. The statement shown above is executed by the computer as if the statement

```
time := 60.0
```

had been written. This conversion from integer to real is automatic, and can be used even if the right side of the assignment operator contains an integer variable. For example, the statement is legal and requires the computer to obtain the value of *num*, convert it to real, and change the current value of *time* to this value. This mixing of data types may also occur in arithmetic expressions, and we will see the consequences in the next section.

Arithmetic Expressions

Consider the following simple arithmetic expression:

5 + 2

The + symbol represents addition and is known as an ***arithmetic operator***. The values 5 and 2 are called ***operands***. The value of the expression 5 + 2 is known as the ***result*** of the expression.

Computations involving real and integer data types use the following *arithmetic operators* (see Figure 2-14):

symbol	meaning	operand types	result type
+	Addition	Integer or real	Integer or real
−	Subtraction	Integer or real	Integer or real
*	Multiplication	Integer or real	Integer or real
/	Division	Real[1]	Real
DIV	Division	Integer	Integer
MOD	Modulus (remainder)	Integer	Integer

[1]Integer operands may be used with the / division operator, but they will be converted from integer to real prior to the division.

Expressions involving variables, unsigned constants,[2] and any of these operators are called ***arithmetic expressions***. The operators are placed between ***operands*** which must

[2]If signed constants were permitted, then an expression like *a* − −*4* would be allowed. Note however, that if *b* is defined (in a CONST declaration) to be a constant whose value is −4, then *a* − *b is* permitted.

Figure 2-14 Pascal arithmetic operators.

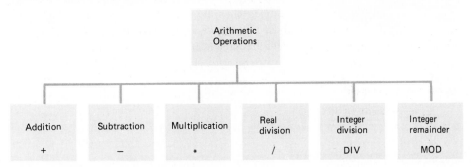

be evaluated before the value resulting from application of the operator can be determined. For example, in the expression

a + b

the value of both variables (operands) must be determined before the addition can take place. In most cases, Pascal expects (and requires) that the types of the variables in an expression be the same. However, the previous exception allowing the use of data of integer type in situations where real data is expected also holds here. To illustrate, suppose we have the following declarations:

```
VAR
    num1, num2 : integer;
    tax, cost    : real;
```

Then the following expressions would be legal, even though they require that the values of the integer variables be converted to real:

```
cost + num1
3.5 * num2
num1 / num2
```

The result of each of these expressions is a real number. Remember that integer values can be converted to real values, but real values cannot be converted to integer.

Here are some more valid arithmetic expressions:

```
2 * num1 + num2        num2 MOD 5 − num1
tax / cost             num1 DIV num2
```

Recall that division by zero is an error detected when the program including the division is executed.

There are two division operators in Pascal: / and DIV. The difference between them is that the real division operator (/) can be used with real or integer operands and has a real result (even with integer operands). The integer division operator (DIV) always yields an integer result; any fractional part is simply discarded. The MOD operator can be used to obtain the remainder of integer division. It, too, requires integer operands and has an integer result. For example, when the integer 15 is divided by the integer 6, the quotient is 2 and the remainder is 3. Figure 2-15 shows the result of the division algorithm to obtain the quotient and the remainder.

Figure 2-15 DIV and MOD operators.

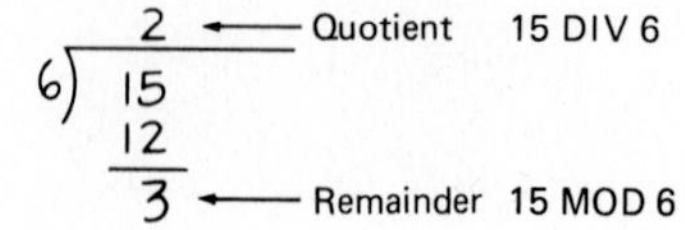

The following examples show the results that would be obtained when the two division operators and the MOD operators are used.

expression	result	expression	result
10.5 / 3.0	3.5	2.0 / 4.0	0.5
1 / 4	0.25	4 / 1	4.0
10 DIV 3	3	10 MOD 3	1
18 DIV 2	9	18 MOD 2	0
20 DIV 20	1	20 / 20	1.0
6 DIV 8	0	6 / 8	0.75

Further illustrations of the MOD operator are necessary to illustrate its properties in detail. MOD always has a positive integer or zero result, and the second operand cannot be negative or zero. In most applications of the MOD operator both operands are positive, and we just get the integer remainder after division. It is only when the first operand is negative that the result is not the remainder. In this case the result of the expression i MOD j is $i - (k * j)$, where k is an integer such that the relation

$$0 \leqslant i - (k * j) < j$$

is true. Here are some examples:

expression	result	reason
−20 MOD 100	80	$80 = -20 - (-1 * 100)$
20 MOD 100	20	normal remainder
−20 MOD −100	error	second operand negative

Unfortunately, some implementations of Pascal do not give the correct result when the first operand is negative; you should verify the proper operation of the Pascal you use before assuming the results of the MOD operator are correct.

Note that the following expressions are all incorrect for the reasons indicated:

expression	reason
25.0 DIV 5	Both operands of DIV must be integer.
15 MOD −5	Second operand of MOD must be positive.
25.0 MOD 5	Both operands of MOD must be integer.
17 DIV 0	Second operand of DIV must be nonzero.
17 / 0	Second operand of / must be nonzero.
21 / −7	Only unsigned constants are permitted.

You may have noticed that there is no operator in standard Pascal to permit exponentiation (that is, raising one number to another power). Pascal does provide the facilities necessary to accomplish exponentiation in the form of built-in, or standard, functions. Built-in functions are considered later in this chapter, and exponentiation is the subject of an exercise at the end of the chapter. Many extended versions of Pascal do include an exponentiation operator.

Assignment Statements and Arithmetic Expressions

As we have already seen, we cannot assign a real value (for example, 6.5) to an integer variable. If we could perform such assignments, the question of what happens to the fractional part of the real value would need to be considered. Two choices are immediately apparent: We could simply ignore the fractional part and use just the integer part of the number (this is called *truncation*), or we could *round* the real value up or down to the closest integer value. Neither of these is actually permitted in Pascal, but some other programming languages do permit such assignments. Truncation and rounding are permitted in Pascal, and we will return to these concepts later.

As mentioned earlier, we can assign integer values (like 12) to real variables, with the conversion of the integer value to its real counterpart (12.0) taking place automatically. The following declarations and assignment statements illustrate both valid and invalid instances of this so-called mixed mode assignment.

```
VAR
      num1, num2, num3 : integer;
      total : real;
      grade : char;
```

assignment statement	remarks
total := num1 + num2 + num3	Integer result converted to real
total := num1 + 3.5	*num1* converted to real
total := num1 DIV num2	Integer result converted to real
total := num1 / num2	*num1* and *num2* converted to real
num1 := total + num2	Invalid, expression is real
num3 := num1 / num2	Invalid, expression is real
num1 := total DIV 2	Invalid, DIV requires integers
grade := '9' + '7'	Invalid, chars cannot be added
grade := num1	Invalid, expression is integer

The following points should be remembered:

- Each expression (or variable or constant) has a type.
- Expressions involving both integer values and real values are evaluated using real arithmetic by first converting the integer operands to real; the result of such expressions is a real value.
- Assignment statements require that the variable to the left of the assignment operator have exactly the same type as the value resulting from the expression to the right of the assignment operator (but integer expressions can be assigned to real variables).

Arithmetic expressions involving more than one operator (such as 2 * 3 + 5) could be evaluated in several different ways, depending on which operator the computer performed first. Since it would be inappropriate to allow such indecision to creep into our Pascal programs, a definite *order of evaluation* is used in the evaluation of Pascal expressions. For example, the expression 2 * 3 + 5 would be evaluated by first performing the multiplication 2 * 3 and then adding 5 to the result:

$$2 * 3 + 5 = 6 + 5 = 11$$

The order in which the various arithmetic operators are applied to their operands is uniquely specified by giving a *hierarchy* for the available operators. This hierarchy is very similar to that used in normal arithmetic and algebra.

In Pascal, the various multiplication and division operators (*, /, DIV, and MOD) are performed before the addition and subtraction operators (+ and −). It is therefore said that the multiplication and division operators have *precedence* over the addition and subtraction operators.

In an expression that involves more than one operator with the same precedence (like 6 DIV 3 * 4), the operators must be performed in order from left to right. Therefore, the preceding expression would yield the integer result 8 (6 DIV 3 equals 2, and 2 * 4 equals 8), not zero (3 * 4 equals 12, and 6 DIV 12 equals 0).

Sometimes the standard order in which operators are applied is not appropriate for a particular situation. Pascal permits parentheses to be used to force certain subexpressions to be evaluated as a unit. As an example, consider the expression 6 DIV (3 * 4). Here, the computer is forced to perform the evaluation of 3 * 4 prior to performing the division.

Naturally, parentheses may be "nested" (grouped inside each other) to indicate order of evaluation even more explicitly. The expression of our previous example might have been written as 6 DIV (3 * (2 + 2)), with exactly the same result as before. Note, however, that the order of evaluation of the *operands* of the operators is not explicitly defined in Pascal; in the expression (3 + 4) DIV (2 + 1) either parenthesized piece could be evaluated first. In this case it really makes little difference to us whether we evaluate 3 + 4 or 2 + 1 first, since both must be done before the division. In other cases, as we shall see later, the order of evaluation may make a difference.

In summary, then, we see that arithmetic expression evaluation is performed using the following algorithm:

Order of Applying Operators

STEP 1 Evaluate any expressions enclosed in parentheses.

STEP 2 Perform the operations indicated by the various multiplication and division operators (*, /, MOD, and DIV). If two or more such operators appear in sequence (as in $a * b / c$), then the operators are performed left to right.

STEP 3 Perform the operations indicated by the addition and subtraction operators (+ and −). If two or more operators appear in sequence (as in $a - b + c$) then the operators are performed left to right.

Some examples of expression evaluation should help illustrate these rules. In these examples we use only integer constants to make the evaluation steps clear. Real constants and integer and real variables may certainly appear as operands of the arithmetic operators. Remember, though, that if one integer and one real operand are used with any operator that permits real operands (specifically, $+$, $-$, $*$, and $/$), the integer operand is automatically converted to real and the result is real.

Example 2.1

```
5 MOD 2  +  14 DIV 3  -  6
1  +  4  -  6      (MOD and DIV before + and -)
5  -  6            (left to right rule)
-1
```

Example 2.2

```
5  +  2  *  (3  +  7)
5  +  2  *  10     (parenthesized part first)
5  +  20           (* before +)
25
```

Example 2.3

```
3  *  (4 MOD (6 DIV 2))  +  5
3 * (4 MOD 3) + 5   (inner parenthesized part)
3 * 1 + 5           (outer parenthesized part)
3 + 5               (* before +)
8
```

You should verify your understanding of arithmetic expression evaluation by working through each of the following expressions.

expression	value
12 DIV 5 * 3	6 (integer)
6 * 5 / 10 * 2 + 10	16.0 (real)
(6 * 5) / (10 * 2) + 10	11.5 (real)
(6 * 5) / (10 * 2 + 10)	1.0 (real)
(6 * 5) / (10 * (2 + 10))	0.25 (real)

Translating Algebraic Expressions to Pascal

Many problems in science and industry require the use of algebraic expressions and formulas, such as the quadratic formula. If we wish to use Pascal to help solve these types of problems, we must translate the algebraic expressions to the form of expressions recognized by Pascal.

The first step in translating any algebraic expression into its Pascal equivalent is to verify that each operation (addition, subtraction, multiplication, and division) is explicitly indicated. For example, the algebraic expression $5x + y$ is quite acceptable for algebraic purposes, since the two terms 5 and x are actually separated by an implied multiplication operator. Pascal, however, does not permit such implied operators, and we are therefore required to rewrite this expression as $5 * x + y$.

The second step in translation from algebraic form to Pascal is concerned with those algebraic operations that require more than one line. These typically include division and exponentiation, as in the expression

$$\frac{a + b^2}{a - b^2}$$

Expressions in Pascal must be written entirely horizontally, so the division and exponentiation in this expression must be indicated as follows:

(a + b * b) / (a − b * b)

Note that this assumes we wish to perform real division and not integer division. A few further examples of algebraic expressions and their Pascal counterparts follow:

algebraic expression	Pascal expression
5 (number + total)	5 * (number + total)
$a^2 + b^2$	a * a + b * b
$\dfrac{x + y}{u + w/a}$	(x + y) / (u + w / a)
$\dfrac{x}{y}(z + w)$	x / y * (z + w)

The expressions shown below are not acceptable in Pascal for the reasons indicated.

incorrect expression	reason
number * + total	An operand must appear between each pair of operators.
x (y + z)	Multiplication must be explicitly indicated.
((a + b) * 4 − 3) / 2)	Parentheses must be balanced.
{[(a + b) − 2] / 4 − 1} + 2	Only parentheses may be used for grouping subexpressions.

Standard (Built-in) Functions

In addition to the various arithmetic operators we have just seen, Pascal provides a number of standard, or built-in, functions. Most of these functions have exact equivalents in algebra. The function *sqrt*, for example, can be used to obtain the square root of any nonnegative number. Other functions are provided to determine the sine of an angle and the absolute value of an arbitrary number. A complete list of the standard functions Pascal provides can be found in Appendix D. In this section we discuss only a few of these. The others will be considered as they are needed.

The standard functions are actually functions that have already been written (based on the appropriate algorithm), compiled, and extensively tested for us. We don't need to actually see the program statements comprising the function in order to use it. Consider the analogy with a telephone: We don't really have to understand exactly how the telephone does it's job or what components it contains in order to use it to make a call.

We must, however, be able to properly request the use of the function. In Pascal we say that a function is *invoked* (or "called") when we request its use. Suppose, for example, that we wish to compute the square root of 100.6 and have the result stored in a real variable named *sqroot*. The following assignment statement will accomplish this for us:

```
sqroot := sqrt (100.6)
```

The expression in this assignment statement consists entirely of a function invocation. Looking at the square root function invocation carefully, we may note the following details:

- The name of the function, *sqrt*, is written first.
- Next follows an expression enclosed in parentheses. This expression is called the *argument* of the function.

The *result* of the function (in this case, 10.03) effectively replaces the function invocation. It is as if we had actually written

```
sqroot := 10.03
```

in place of the original statement. Of course the statement itself really isn't changed; we perform the evaluation of expressions involving such function invocations as if the function's result were written in place of the function invocation. Another example should help clarify this point. Assuming x and y are real variables, the assignment statement

```
x := 2 * sqrt (y)
```

will assign to x a value equal to twice the square root of y. For example, if the variable y contained 169.0, then the sqrt function would yield 13.0 (since 13.0 * 13.0 equals 169.0) and the assignment statement would be treated as if we had written x := 2 * 13.0

which then assigns the value 26.0 to x. If the value of y (the argument) had been other than 169.0, the assignment statement would have stored a different value in x.

The argument of a function can be any valid expression, as long as the type of the argument expression (real, integer, and so forth) matches the type expected by the function. For the square root function the argument may be either real or integer, but the result is always real. If you should use an expression with the wrong type, the Pascal compiler will provide an appropriate complaint and refuse to allow your program to be executed.

Two additional standard functions provided by Pascal are *round* and *trunc*. These functions accept only real arguments, and the result is integer. (They are sometimes known as **transfer** functions, since they transfer, or convert, a value of one type to another.) As you might expect, the **round** function returns the integer closest to its argument. For example:

expression	result
round (5.5)	6
round (−3.5)	−4
round (8.7)	9
round (2.1)	2
round (−3.1)	−3

Notice the difference between rounding positive and negative arguments.

The **trunc** function returns the integer that results after omitting, or truncating, the fractional part of the real number. For example:

expression	result
trunc (5.6)	5
trunc (2.1)	2
trunc (−2.8)	−2

The *sqr* function returns a value equal to the square of its argument with exactly the same type as its argument. *Sqr* (a) therefore is just a shorthand notation for "a * a," where a is the argument of the function. For example:

expression	result
sqr (3)	9 (integer)
sqr (3.0)	9.0 (real)

The last standard function we consider in this section is **abs**, which provides the absolute value (magnitude) of an expression. Like *sqr,* the type of its result is the same as the type of its argument. The examples below illustrate its properties:

expression	result
abs (8)	8 (integer)
abs (−10)	10 (integer)
abs (5.4)	5.4 (real)

Since function invocations appear in expressions, the values they represent must be obtained before any operators can be applied to those values. In the expression

a * sqrt (b) / abs (c)

it should be clear that the multiplication cannot proceed until the value of variable *a* and the square root of variable *b* have been obtained. Once the multiplication has been performed, the division cannot proceed until the absolute value of variable *c* has been computed. But recall our previous note about the order of *operand* evaluation. In the expression

sqrt (a) / sqrt (b)

either square root operation could be performed first. Normally this property (that is, lack of specific order of operand evaluation) will not cause any problems, but we will later revisit this topic when it becomes important.

In summary, we note the following properties of the standard functions:

■ Each standard function implements a tested algorithm for computing useful values.
■ The argument type must match that expected by the function.
■ The type of result obtained from a function is determined by the particular function and, sometimes, by the type of argument.
■ Expressions used as arguments must be evaluated (using the usual rules) before the function invocation occurs.
■ The names of the standard functions are predeclared (they are standard identifiers). If they are explicitly declared, the identifiers then refer to the explicitly declared objects.
■ The order in which expressions are evaluated determines the order in which function invocations are performed.

Here are several additional examples of expressions involving the standard functions.

Example 2.4

```
Evaluate  12 + sqrt (sqr (12) − 4 * 11).
          12 + sqrt (sqr (12) − 44)
          12 + sqrt (144 − 44)
          12 + sqrt (100)
          12 + 10
          22
```

Example 2.5

One solution of the quadratic equation

$$ax^2 + bx + c = 0$$

is given by the algebraic expression

$$x = \frac{-b + \sqrt{b^2 - 4ac}}{2a}.$$

This expression is written in Pascal as

$$(- \text{ b } + \text{ sqrt } (\text{ sqr(b) } - \text{ 4 } * \text{ a } * \text{ c)}) / (2 * \text{ a})$$

Note that all the parentheses in this expression are necessary to correctly represent the algebraic form.

EXERCISES FOR SECTION 2.4

1   Suppose we have the following variable declarations:

```
VAR
      temp, value : integer;
      num,sum :real;
```

Determine which of the following assignment statements are valid.

(a) num := temp + value   (b) value: = num + temp
(c) num := sum   (d) value := temp + 3
(e) value := num + 3   (f) num := num * sum
(g) temp := num * sum

2   Evaluate each of the following expressions.

(a) 6 DIV 2 − 6 MOD 5
(b) 14 MOD 2 * 6 + 3
(c) 3 + 14 MOD (2 * 3)
(d) 5 MOD 8 + 8 MOD 5
(e) 7 MOD2 + 13 DIV 3 − 2
(f) 6 − 2 * (1 + 4) + 5

3   Suppose we have the following variable declarations:

```
VAR
      sales, total, loss : integer;
      score : real;
```

Determine which of the following assignment statements are valid.

(a) score := sales + total + loss
(b) sales := sales + 5.0
(c) score := sales DIV total
(d) score := sales / total
(e) sales := score / total
(f) total := score DIV loss

4 Evaluate each of the following expressions.

(a) sqrt (16)   (e) trunc (−13.8)
(b) round (10.7)   (f) sqr (5)
(c) round (−3.8)   (g) abs (−12)
(d) trunc (10.1)   (h) trunc (8.6) − round (8.6)

5 Assume *acost*, *bcost*, *ccost*, and *dcost* are real variables with the following values:

acost := 4.0;
bcost := 1.0;
ccost := −2.0;
dcost := 5.5;

Evaluate each of the following expressions.

(a) sqrt (acost / bcost − ccost + dcost − 2.5)
(b) trunc (dcost) * abs (ccost * (bcost / acost))

6 Write a Pascal expression for each of the following mathematical expressions.

(a) $\dfrac{x + y}{\dfrac{y}{z} + 3}$ (c) $(x^2 + y^2)^2$

(b) $\dfrac{-b - \sqrt{b^2 - 4ac}}{2a}$ (d) $\dfrac{x + y - z}{2x + y^2 - xyz}$

7 Write an equivalent mathematical expression for each of the following Pascal expressions.

(a) a * b * c / d / e
(b) x + y / z * (a + b)
(c) b * b − 4 * a * c
(d) a − b * c / d + e * f

8 Insert parentheses in each of the following Pascal expressions to indicate the order in which the operators will be applied.

(a) 2 * b − a + b * d / e
(b) f − e * d / c + b * a
(c) a * a − b * c / d + sqrt (e + 2 * f)
(d) d * (a + b) − trunc (e * f / g) + b / (a − b * c)

(e) 6 DIV 2 * 5 MOD 3 − 2 * 3

(f) 2 * 3 MOD (8 DIV 3 + 1) + round (6.5)

9 Determine if each of the following is a valid Pascal assignment statement. Assume *num*, *sum*, and *total* are integer variables, *value* is a real variable, and *chr1* and *chr2* are char variables.

(a) num := num + num

(b) num := num DIV sum / total

(c) sum := num / total

(d) value := total

(e) value := total * num + sum

(f) value := total + chr1

(g) chr2 := chr1

(h) chr2 := chr1 + 1

(i) chr2 := 'chr1'

10 Evaluate each of the following Pascal expressions.

(a) 5 + sqr (3) − 4 + trunc (3.6 − 2.1)

(b) 3 * sqrt (8 MOD 6 * 10 DIV 5)

(c) 6 + 9 * 8 DIV 2 * round (1.362) − 2 * 3

(d) trunc (12 / 5 * sqrt (4 + 4 * 3) / 4)

SECTION 2.5 TESTING AND DEBUGGING TECHNIQUES

When performing arithmetic operations using Pascal, you should be aware of certain errors that can occur. For example, suppose the range of allowable positive real numbers on a particular computer system is 10^{-38} to 10^{38}. If a calculation results in a value exceeding 10^{38}, your computer system will most likely display an error message indicating **overflow** and abruptly terminate the execution of your program. Similarly, an **underflow** will occur if the value calculated is too small (that is, greater than zero but less than 10^{-38} in magnitude). Most systems will not treat underflow in the same way as overflow but instead will return a result of exactly zero.

Another problem arising with computations involving real numbers is the loss of *accuracy*. The number of digits used to represent a real number in the scientific notation form depends on the particular machine. The **precision** of the machine is defined as the maximum number of digits the computer can use to represent a number. Since real values are approximate numbers limited by the precision of the computer, loss of accuracy can result, causing significant errors in our calculations.

Consider the following case. Theoretically, the expression (0.00000234 − 2.0) + 2.0 should yield the value 0.00000234, since −2.0 + 2.0 is exactly zero. However, assume this expression is evaluated on a computer system with a precision of five decimal digits. Since the parentheses indicate that the subtraction should be done first, the computer must first evaluate 0.00000234 − 2.0. (Note that 0.00000234 has only three digits of precision.) Accurate to five decimal places, the result is −2.0000. Now when the addition is performed, the computer yields a result of exactly zero, not

0.00000234! The reason for this loss of accuracy is the combination of very small numbers with relatively larger ones.

Here are several important items to consider when testing and debugging arithmetic calculations:

- Be certain all variables are declared.
- Be certain data types match in input/output statements and assignment statements.
- Do hand testing of calculations with some simple examples.
- Verify the form used for the input data and the *read* and *readln* statements are consistent (see next chapter).
- Review the order in which the arithmetic expressions will be evaluted; if in doubt, use parentheses to guarantee the order of evaluation.

Entering, Modifying, and Running Pascal Programs

Before attempting to write your own Pascal programs, it is usually a good idea to enter or modify an existing Pascal program. This will help you understand the details of editing, compiling, and executing a program on your system. In the chapter exercises you will find problems for computer solution that require you to modify an existing Pascal program, then perform the steps necessary to execute it. In the next chapter we will discuss the details of input, output, and problem solving in Pascal. After completing that chapter, you will be able to write your own complete Pascal programs.

As an aid in testing and debugging your programs, a list of important Pascal reminders follows.

PASCAL REMINDERS

Comments
- Must be delimited by the pairs (* and *) or by braces { and }.

Semicolons
- Separate statements. A semicolon is not necessary before END.
  Example:

```
PROGRAM example (input, output);
VAR a, b, c : integer;
BEGIN
        statement;
        statement;

            .

            .

            .
        statement (* no semicolon*)
END.
```

Pascal programs
- Must end with a period.
- Must have the executable statements enclosed by the reserved words BEGIN and END.
- Should include documentation such as comments and self-documenting variables and constants.

Constants
- Are declared prior to variable declarations.
- Cannot be changed during the execution of the program.

Variables
- Must be declared in Pascal programs using the reserved word VAR.
- Can only be given values of the declared type.
- Must have a value before they may be used in an expression.

Numbers
- Must not contain blanks or commas.
- With a decimal point must have at least one digit before and after the decimal point:

0.05   −2.0

- Of type integer may be freely mixed with numbers of type real in arithmetic expressions, and are converted to equivalent real values in such cases.
- Of type real can be converted to integer using the standard functions *round* and *trunc*.

Characters
- Are enclosed in single quotes:

'A'   'b'   '8'

- Represent single quote as two consecutive quotes:

''''

Assignment statement
- Assigns the value of an expression to a variable.
- Requires "target" variable and expression to have same type (except that integer expressions can be assigned to real variables).
- Examples:

A := 2 * B + 1

count := count + 1

Division
- Of reals uses the operator /
- Of integers use the operator DIV
- Remainder (integer) obtained using the operator MOD

Order of evaluation

- First evalute expressions inside parentheses.
- Next perform multiplication and division, left to right.
- Next perform addition and subtraction, left to right.

SECTION 2.6 CHAPTER REVIEW

In this chapter the details of the Pascal language have been discussed. A Pascal program consists of two components: a program heading and a program block. The program heading is a single statement containing the program name and a list of the file variables which will be connected to external files when the program is executed. The program block consists of the declarations (such as variables and constants) and the executable statements. The overall structure of the Pascal programs in this chapter has the following form:

```
PROGRAM name (input, output);
CONST constant declarations;
VAR variable declarations;
BEGIN
        statement;
        statement;
        . . .
        statement
END.
```

Here is a summary of the Pascal details discussed in this chapter. You should use the summary for future reference.

PASCAL REFERENCE

1   Identifiers, constants, and variables
    1.1   *Identifier:* A word or sequence of characters that forms the name of a program object. An identifier is a sequence of letters and digits that must begin with a letter:

    salestax   H2O

    Reserved word: An identifier reserved for a specific purpose in the Pascal program; such identifiers cannot be redefined:

    BEGIN   END   VAR

Standard Identifier: An identifier predeclared by the compiler that can (but probably should not) be redefined:

input   output   read   integer

1.2   *Constant:* A declared value that does not change during the execution of the program and that is specified by the reserved word CONST:

```
CONST
        taxrate = 0.05;
        pi = 3.14159;
```

1.3   *Variable:* A declared object that has a value which may be changed during execution and that is specified by the reserved word VAR:

```
VAR
        distance, time : real;
        speed : integer;
```

2   Simple data types: Integer, real, Boolean, and char
    2.1   *Integer:* Positive and negative whole numbers including zero:

    -60 45   0   10

    Maxint: The largest integer representable by the particular Pascal compiler in use.

2.2   *Real:* Numbers with decimal points and/or exponents:

    0.5 -2.4 $6.3e-10$

2.3   *Char:* Characters such as letters, digits, and special symbols:

    'A'   'B'   '?'

2.4   *Boolean:* A data type with only two values, true and false.

3   Assignment statement: Assigns the value of the expression on the right side of the assignment operator (: =) to the variable specified on the left side of the operator (the components on each side of the operator must have the same type):

```
time := 60;
grade := 'A';
num := num + 1;
```

4   Arithmetic expressions

4.1   Arithmetic operators:

+	Addition
−	Subtraction
*	Multiplication
/	Division (real quotient)
DIV	Division (integer quotient)
MOD	Division (integer remainder)

4.2   Order of operators:

(1)   Expressions enclosed in parentheses are evaluated first.

(2)   Multiplication and/or division operators (*, /, DIV, MOD) are performed next with evaluation done from left to right when there are two or more such operators.

(3)   Addition and/or subtraction operators are performed last, from left to right when there are two or more such operators.

4.3   Standard (built-in) functions: Predefined functions available to a Pascal program:

sqrt(x)	Square root of x
round(x)	Rounds real argument x to integer
trunc(x)	Truncates real argument x to integer
sqr(x)	Square of argument x
abs(x)	Absolute value of argument x

Other standard functions are listed in Appendix D.

Chapter 3 Preview

In the next chapter we will consider mechanisms used to communicate data between the computer and the "outside world." For example, the results of our computations are frequently displayed on an output device, and data values for our computations are obtained from keyboards or other input devices. In addition to input and output, we will consider problem solving with Pascal.

Keywords for Chapter 2

accuracy	comment
arithmetic operator	constant
argument	data type
assignment statement	declaration
Boolean	delimiter
char	executable statement
character string	floating-point notation

CHAPTER 2 EXERCISES

★ ESSENTIAL EXERCISES

1 Declare variables with meaningful names appropriate for representing the value of each of the following:
   (a) The number of kittens in a litter
   (b) The key in which a particular piece of music is written
   (c) An airline flight number with three digits and one letter
   (d) The value of pi divided by 2
   (e) The ratio of two arbitrary numeric values
   (f) Whether today is Saturday or not

2 Consider the assignment statement $a := b$, where a is a real variable and b is an integer variable. Clearly the value of b must be converted from integer to real before it can be stored in a, but the contents of variable b are not altered. What does this suggest about the ways in which computer memory may be accessed?

3 Determine what your Pascal compiler produces for each of the following expressions. Which results conform to the result obtained in standard Pascal?

   (a) 5 MOD 2   (b) 5 MOD −2
   (c) −5 MOD 2   (d) −5 MOD −2

4 Assume a three-digit number has the form abc. For example, if the number was 730, then a represents 7, b represents 3, and c represents 0. Write Pascal expressions that yield the "numbers" cba and $accb$.

5 Determine which of the following statements are legal. Assume that all variables are appropriately declared so no type mismatches occur.

   (a) v := a(*integer*)DIV b
   (b) v := aDIVb
   (c) v:=a DIV b
   (d) v (*sometimes*) := (*about*) a DIV b
   (e) s := '(*Message*)'
   (f) s := (*Message*)'Number Two'

6   Insert parentheses in the following expressions to make their meaning clearer. Do not change the value of the expressions. Indicate the type of each expression.

(a)   4 + 6 MOD b DIV c

(b)   j DIV k / 17.04e-5 / 2.0

(c)   1 + 2 DIV 3 * 4 + 5 DIV 6

(d)   2 / sqrt (17.03 - a DIV 21 * j MOD k) * 1.0001

★★ SIGNIFICANT EXERCISES

7   Some Pascal compilers (or computer systems) cause variables to be initialized when their storage is allocated. Determine if this is the case for your Pascal by running the following program several times. If you are using a microcomputer, turn the computer off between runs.

```
PROGRAM verify (output);
VAR
      i : integer;
      r : real;
BEGIN
      writeln (i, r)
END.
```

8   Can you think of data types other than integer, real, char, and Boolean which might be useful in a programming language? Could you fabricate values of these data types from combinations of existing Pascal standard data types?

9   Experiment to determine what happens as a result of each of the following assignment statements:

```
toobig := maxint + 1;
toosmall := -maxint - 1;
```

What do these results suggest about the representation of integers?

10   Devise a scheme to obtain the exponent (power of 10) of an arbitrary real number. For example, the exponent of $3.56E-10$ is -10, and the exponent of $4.526E+7$ is 7. (Hint: Consider the use of the *ln* function to determine the logarithm of the number to the base 10.)

11   The standard function *ord* will yield an integer indicating the relative position of any ordinal constant (integer, char, or Boolean) within the set of other constants of the same type. Determine the ordinal value of each of the following constants. (The *ord* function is considered in detail in Chapter 8.)

(a)   true   (b)   'A'   (c)   ';'   (d)   0   (e)   −1   (f)   maxint

(g)   false   (h)   'a'   (i)   ' '   (j)   '"'   (k)   1   (l)   −maxint

12 Mathematically, $\ln a^b = b \cdot \ln a$, and $e^{\ln x} = x$. Use these properties and the standard Pascal functions *ln* and *exp* to write a Pascal expression giving the value of a^b. For which values of a and b will this expression fail?

13 Suppose you decided to test a program with a certain portion of it deleted. Rather than delete that portion of the source program, you consider just making it into a comment by enclosing it in (* and *). In this way, the deleted portion can be restored by just removing the comment delimiters.
   (a) Why might you think this would work?
   (b) Why will it not work?

14 Do the expressions

   sqr (sqrt (2.0))   and   sqrt (sqr (2.0))

   yield the same value? Are you certain? Is the value of

   sqr (sqrt (2.0)) − sqrt (sqr (2.0))

   always zero? Why?

★★★ CHALLENGING EXERCISES

15 Determine the smallest positive real number which can be stored in a real variable. What happens when this number is divided by 2?

CHAPTER 2 PROBLEMS FOR COMPUTER SOLUTION

To gain some experience with entering, compiling, and executing Pascal programs, enter and execute each of the following programs. Some additional changes are suggested for each problem.

★ ESSENTIAL PROBLEMS

Enter each of the following programs. Try to anticipate what the output will be. Then execute them, and compare your output expectations with what is actually displayed.

```
1  PROGRAM sample1 (output);
   CONST
           pi = 3.1415926535;
           r1 = 2.0;
           r2 = 5.0;
   VAR
           area : real;
```

```
              BEGIN
                    area := pi * r1 * r1;
                    writeln (r1, area); (* Display value of r1 and area *)
                    area := pi * sqr (r2);
                    writeln (r2, area)   (* Display value of r2 and area *)
              END.
```

2   ```
    PROGRAM sample2 (input, output);
    VAR
          num : real;
          a, b : integer;
    BEGIN
          readln (num);   (* Get a value for num *)
          a := round (num);
          b := trunc (num + 0.5);
          writeln (num, a, b)   (* Display num, a, and b *)
    END.
    ```

When the program expects input, enter a real number. Run the program several times using both positive and negative numbers with fractional parts greater than, less than, and exactly equal to 0.5.

## ★★ SIGNIFICANT PROBLEMS

3   The following program computes the arithmetic mean of four real numbers provided as the single line of input data. Modify it to compute the geometric mean of the data instead. The geometric mean of $N$ data values, $V1, V2, \ldots, VN$ is defined as

$$(V1 * V2 * \ldots * VN)^{1/N}.$$

```
PROGRAM average (input, output);
VAR
      v1, v2, v3, v4 : real;
      avg : real;
BEGIN
      readln (v1, v2, v3, v4);      (* Obtain data values *)
      avg := (v1 + v2 + v3 + v4) / 4.0;
      writeln ('Average = ', avg)      (* Display average *)
END.
```

4   The following program converts a real temperature obtained from the input data from Fahrenheit to Celsius. Modify the program so it converts the temperature from Celsius to Fahrenheit.

```
PROGRAM convert (input, output);
CONST
```
```

```
        factor1 = 32.0;
        factor2 = 0.5555555555;     (* 5 / 9 *)
VAR
        fahrenheit,
        celsius : real
BEGIN
        readln (fahrenheit);
        celsius := factor2 * (fahrenheit - factor1);
        writeln (fahrenheit, celsius)
END.
```

★★★ CHALLENGING PROBLEMS

5   The following program, which you may not completely understand at this point,
    determines the length of the shortest and longest lines in the input data, as well
    as the average length of the input lines. Try creating data which produces the
    output:

```
Shortest line has 1 characters
Longest line has 10 characters
Average line has 5.00 characters
```

Then try creating data which has at least one line, that produces the output

```
Shortest line has 0 characters
Longest line has 0 characters
Average line has 0.00 characters
```

```
PROGRAM linelength (input, output);
VAR
        shortest : integer;     (* length of shortest line *)
        longest : integer;      (* length of longest line *)
        total : integer;        (* total number of characters *)
        number : integer;       (* total number of lines *)
        average : real;         (* average characters per line *)
        length : integer;       (* length of current line *)
        ch : char;              (* current input character *)
BEGIN
        shortest := maxint;
        longest := 0;
        number := 0;
        total := 0;
        WHILE NOT eof(input) DO
        BEGIN
            length := 0;
            WHILE NOT eoln(input) DO
```

```
            BEGIN
                    read (ch);
                    length := length + 1
            END;
            readln;
            IF length > longest
            THEN longest := length;
            IF length < shortest
            THEN shortest := length;
            total := total + length;
            number := number + 1
        END;
        IF number = 0
        THEN BEGIN
                    shortest := 0;
                    average := 0
                END
        ELSE average := total / number;
        writeln ('Shortest line has ', shortest:1, ' characters');
        writeln ('Longest line has ', longest:1, ' characters');
        writeln ('Average line has ', average:4:2, ' characters')
END.
```

Sample Input:

Column One
↓
Certainly only basic operations limit.
Short
Unusual characters
Keep studying

Sample Output:

Shortest line has 5 characters
Longest line has 38 characters
Average line has 18.50 characters

CHAPTER 3
PASCAL INPUT AND
OUTPUT AND
PROBLEM SOLVING

Input and
Output

Problem
Solving
with
Pascal

Text File
Input and
Output
(Optional)

PASCAL INPUT
AND OUTPUT
AND PROBLEM
SOLVING

OBJECTIVES

After completing this chapter you should be able to:

- Recognize and apply Pascal input/output statements such as *read* and *write*
- Construct and document a simple Pascal program
- Solve, test, and debug a simple Pascal program
- Optionally, recognize and apply text file input and output

CHAPTER OVERVIEW

In this chapter we discuss the task of getting data in and out of the computer. Without the capability to input and output data, our ability to perform computations rapidly and accurately is worthless; it must be possible to communicate with the "outside world." We examine some of the facilities provided by Pascal for input and output (I/O). Additionally we will present a detailed discussion of problem solving using Pascal.

In the first section we consider the problem of obtaining numeric and nonnumeric data from an input device (usually a keyboard) for use by a Pascal program. We also consider the output problem, that is, displaying different types of data on a printer or display terminal. In particular, the details of controlling the appearance of the output, or formatting, are presented. An optional section discusses input and output to files stored on magnetic disks and tapes.

The chapter also includes a discussion of applications of Pascal to problem solving. We present two problems and their complete solutions using the strategies discussed in Chapter 1. These include problem analysis, problem solution using top-down design, and the computer solution. The complete Pascal program for the solution of each problem is included. The Testing and Debugging Techniques section focuses on common input and output errors. After completing this chapter, you should be able to construct and document a simple Pascal program.

SECTION 3.1 INPUT AND OUTPUT

In this section we consider the details of reading and writing data in Pascal. A program may operate on the data that has been supplied by an input device. The results are sent to an output device. Our discussion will include the manipulation of both numeric and nonnumeric data.

Numeric Input

We have already seen that the assignment statement is one method used to change the value of a variable. Another way to supply a value for a variable is to provide it as input data. Pascal provides two statements—*read* and *readln*—to transfer data from an input device into the computer's memory.[1] Consider the following statement:

---

[1] Technically speaking, *read* and *readln* are not statements but are rather *procedures*. For the most part, this difference is relatively unimportant to us, and we will continue to refer to *read* and *readln* as statements.

read (hours, min, sec)

The *read* statement is followed by the variable identifiers, separated by commas and enclosed in parentheses. Assume the variables *hours*, *min*, and *sec* have been declared as integers. The *read* statement instructs the computer to obtain three integers from the input source and store the values, in order, into the memory locations of the listed variables. For example, if the input source is a terminal keyboard and the user types the integer constants

3   25   30

then the computer will assign the value 3 to the variable *hours*, the value 25 to the variable *min*, and the value 30 to the variable *sec*. Note that the values are separated by spaces. An end of line or tab character also is acceptable as a separator.

When executed, the *read* statement causes the values to be stored in the same order as specified. For example, suppose *tax* is declared as a real variable and *num* is declared as an integer variable. Then the read statement

read (tax, num)

would cause the computer to expect a real constant, at least one blank (or end of line or tab character) and an integer constant. For example, if the data

0.05   7

was typed, then the value 0.05 would be stored in *tax* and the value 7 would be stored in *num*. We note that this *read* statement could also have been written as two separate *read* statements:

read (tax);   read (num)

The other input statement, *readln*, is similar to the *read* statement. To completely understand the difference between the two we need a little more background about the organization of the data on an input device.

Frequently we will work with data organized into **lines**. Each line typically consists of an arbitrary number of characters (like digits, decimal points, plus and minus signs, and so forth). Each line can be thought of as having an "invisible" character marking the end of the line, corresponding closely to the return key which you press at the end of each input line. Naturally, this character is called the ***end-of-line character*** (written here as ⟨*eoln*⟩). Most of the time, these end-of-line characters, as well as blanks and tab characters, are treated as separators between real and integer constants in the input but otherwise ignored.

The *readln* statement gives us a little more control over the processing of input data formatted into lines. Specifically, the *readln* statement performs exactly the same functions as the *read* statement, with one exception. When a value has been obtained and stored for each variable in the input list, then the *readln* statement causes the computer to ignore anything that remains unused on the last line processed, including the end-of-line character. This means that the next *read* or *readln* statement will process the data at the beginning of the *next* complete line of input.

As an example suppose the input data is arranged as follows:

```
5      13      17⟨eoln⟩
2       9⟨eoln⟩
```

Assume *num1*, *num2*, and *num3* are declared as integer variables. Then the sequence of input statements

```
readln (num1);
readln (num2, num3)
```

would result in the value 5 being stored in *num1*. Since we executed a *readln* statement, the remainder of the line is skipped. The next *readln* statement begins processing the data on the second line of the input. So the value 2 is stored in *num2*, and the value 9 is stored in *num3*.

The following table contains four examples which indicate the values stored in *num1*, *num2*, and *num3* after the execution of *read* and *readln* statements. In each case we assume the use of the the data shown above. Study these examples carefully, and try to explain the differences between the *read* and *readln* statements.

ASSIGNED VALUES

Example	num1	num2	num3
1 readln (num1, num2); readln (num3)	5	13	2
2 read (num1, num2); readln (num3)	5	13	17
3 readln; readln (num1, num2)	2	9	?

4 readln (num1);
    read (num2);
    readln (num3)
	5	2	9

As another example, consider the following sequence of input statements (assume that all variables mentioned have been declared as integers):

```
read (x, y);
readln (z);
readln (s, t);
read (w)
```

Suppose the following integer constants appear in the input, arranged in lines as shown:

```
5     6     9     3⟨eoln⟩
1     4     7     2⟨eoln⟩
8⟨eoln⟩
```

The first statement

read (x, y)

would cause the value 5 to be assigned to x and the value 6 to be assigned to y. Notice that there are data values left on the first line.

The second statement

readln (z)

will cause the value 9 (the next integer constant that has not yet been processed) to be assigned to z and *then skip the remainder of the line*. This includes the blanks before the 3, the 3 itself, and the end-of-line character.

The third statement

readln (s, t)

will cause the value 1 to be assigned to s and the value 4 to be assigned to t. Since this is a *readln* statement, the remainder of this line is also ignored, including the end-of-line character.

The last statement

read (w)

will cause the value 8 to be assigned to w. Note in this case that the end-of-line character on the third line has not been skipped.

Using *readln* to skip data is not necessarily an error. Typically, *readln* is used when we must begin processing some data at the beginning of a line, so we skip everything, including the end-of-line character, remaining in the preceding line. The characters skipped are usually only blanks and the end-of-line character, but as we have seen, it can be data that could otherwise be processed. It is the joint responsibility of the person preparing the input data and the person preparing the program to ensure that the input data and the *read* and *readln* statements are synchronized to prevent the loss of useful data.

In summary, here are several important points to remember when preparing *read* and *readln* statements for numeric input:

■ The data type of the value that appears in the input must match the data type of the corresponding variable in the *read* or *readln* statement. (If it doesn't, an appropriate error message will be issued.)
■ Each numeric data item in the input must be separated from other data items by at least one blank, tab, or end-of-line character. (More than one, or a combination of these, may be used to separate data values.)

■ The *readln* statement causes the unused part of the last line processed to be ignored, including the end-of-line character.

■ If there are not enough data items on the current input line to match the number of variables specified in the *read* or *readln* statement, then the end-of-line character is skipped and the input continues with data from the next line.

■ If the end of the input data is encountered before a value has been obtained for each variable in a *read* or *readln* statement, an error will occur.

Character Input

Character data is processed by *read* and *readln* in a manner similar to numeric data. The difference is that blanks, tabs, and end-of-line characters are never skipped when a character variable is to be read. Instead, the very next character in the input data is read and assigned to the character variable specified in the *read* (or *readln*) statement's variable list. Usually, blanks, tabs and end-of-line characters are all treated as blanks, but in some systems the tabs and end-of-line characters are treated differently. Refer to the documentation for the particular Pascal you are using for details on the treatment of these characters.

Consider the following example in which the variables are all of type char. The *read* statement

```
read (char1, char2, char3, char4)
```

will read four characters. If we represent the (usually invisible) end-of-line character with ⟨eoln⟩, then the input line

```
12D  ⟨eoln⟩
```

would assign '1' to *char1*, the character '2' to *char2*, 'D' to *char3*, and the blank (' ') to *char4*. The end-of-line character would not be read! The next *read* or *readln* statement would first have to deal with the end of line. Note that, unlike character constants, the actual input data does not require and should normally not include the single quotes around each character of input data.

On the other hand, suppose we used the following *readln* statement:

```
readln (char1, char2, char3, char4)
```

Now exactly the same characters will be assigned to the variables, but the end of line would be skipped.

Finally, consider the following statement:

```
read (char1, char2, char3, char4, char5)
```

If we use the same input data, the same characters are assigned to *char1* through *char4*. When we are ready to read a value for the variable *char5*, the input "mechanism" is positioned at the end-of-line character. Then the end-of-line character would be read, leaving the input mechanism at the first character of the next line, and variable *char5* would be assigned a blank character. (Some nonstandard Pascal versions might produce a different character, or characters, when the end of line is read.)

Mixed Input: Character and Numeric

Care must be taken when reading both numeric and char variables from the same line. As might be expected, the variable list of the *read* and *readln* statements may contain a combination of integer, real, and character variables.[2] Recall that when a numeric variable is read, any leading blanks, tabs, and end-of-line characters are skipped and a numeric constant is read. Reading continues as long as the next character is a legal part of the numeric constant. The value of the constant just read is then assigned to the corresponding numeric variable. The first character not used in the numeric constant is left for the next input operation.

For example, suppose the statement

```
read (num1, char1, num2)
```

is to be processed, where *num1* and *num2* are of type integer and *char1* is of type char. If we provided the input data

```
172.0534
```

for the *read* statement to process, then variable *num1* would be assigned the value 172 (since a period may not appear in an integer constant), *char1* would be assigned the character value '.', and *num2* would be assigned the value 534. Notice that if the same input data was processed with the statement

```
read (real1)
```

where *real1* is of type real, then *real1* would be assigned 172.0534.

Output

Now we consider the various ways of displaying data as output in Pascal. Two output statements—*write* and *writeln*—are provided, which, like *read* and *readln*, include a list of items to be output, enclosed in parentheses and separated by commas.[3] The output list may contain expressions (which include variables) of integer, real, char, Boolean, or string (of character) types.

---

[2] Pascal permits variables of other types to be read, but only integer, real, and char types (but not Boolean) are required to be processed in a predefined manner. You should refer to the documentation for your particular Pascal compiler to determine if variables of other data types may be read and if so, how they should appear in the input.

[3] Once again we have taken the liberty of treating *write* and *writeln* as statements. Like *read* and *readln*, they are really procedures.

Consider the following Pascal program segment, with *test* declared integer and *grade* declared char:

```
test := 95;
grade := 'A';
write ('Letter grade ', grade, ', Numerical score ', test)
```

The output produced by the *write* statement might look something like this:

```
Letter grade A, Numerical score      95
```

Each item (variable, expression, or constant) that is displayed appears in its own *field*, or group of consecutive columns. We assume here (and throughout this section) that integers will always be displayed in a field of 10 columns, with leading zeroes replaced by blanks. This may, in fact, vary among Pascal implementations, since the default for the number of columns used when displaying various types of data (called the *fieldwidth*) is implementation-dependent. Data of type char is always displayed with a default (or assumed) fieldwidth of one. Methods for explicitly specifying the field-width will be discussed later in this section.

Consider the following assignment statements (*r* and *s* are integer and *t* is char):

```
r := 4;
s := 5;
t := 'B'
```

The following *write* statements would then produce the output shown.

write statement	output
write (r)	_ _ _ _ _ _ _ _ _ 4
write (r, s)	_ _ _ _ _ _ _ _ _ 4 _ _ _ _ _ _ _ _ _ 5
write ('Total is', r+s)	T o t a l _ i s _ _ _ _ _ _ _ _ _ _ 9
write (t)	B
write ('R= ', r)	R = _ _ _ _ _ _ _ _ _ 4

Note that the integer values are printed in a field of columns equal to the fieldwidth and that the values are *right-justified*. That is, any unused spaces to the left are filled with blanks. Thus, in the first *write* statement, there are nine blanks before the 4. Further note that we may write expressions (such as $r + s$) in the output list, as illustrated in the third *write* statement.

When a real expression appears in the output list, a decimal representation of the expression's value, rounded to a predefined number of digits, is displayed. The decimal representation used will be the same used for real constants. For example, if *tax* is a real variable with value 0.05 (in scientific notation, 5.0×10^{-2}) and the default fieldwidth for real expressions is 20 columns, then the statement write (tax)

would result in the output

5 . 0 0 0 0 0 0 0 0 0 0 0 0 e – 0 2

Note that trailing zeroes are used to fill the unused spaces in the field.
    Consider the following short Pascal program that illustrates the *write* statement:

```
PROGRAM writeon (input, output);
(* Program to display numerical grade and letter grade *)
VAR
        number : integer;
        grade : char;
BEGIN
        number := 90;
        grade := 'A';
        write ('Score is ', number);
        write (', grade is ', grade)
END.
is
```

The output would look something like the following:

S c o r e _ i s _ _ _ _ _ _ _ _ _ _ _ _ _ 9 0 , _ g r a d e _ i s _ A

    The *writeln* statement is similar to the *write* statement with the same output list,
except that after all values have been written, an end-of-line character is also written.
Since the end of line has the effect of beginning a new line, the following statements

```
writeln ('one');
writeln ('two')
```

would result in two lines of output, with the next *write* or *writeln* statement beginning
its output on the third line:

one
two

Note that if we had used *write* statements instead of *writeln* statements, the output
would be significantly different:

onetwo

would have been produced, and the next *write* or *writeln* statement would continue
placing output on the same line.
    Writeln can be used without an output list to cause a single end-of-line character to

be written to the output. In this case, the parentheses used to enclose the output list are omitted. For example, the statements

```
writeln('one');
writeln;
writeln('two');
```

would produce three lines of output, with the second line entirely blank:

one

      (This line is blank.)

two

Here is another short Pascal program illustrating the *writeln* statement:

```
PROGRAM right (input, output);
VAR
    number : integer;
    realnum : real;
BEGIN
    number := 12;
    realnum := 12.3456;
    writeln ('The value is ', number);
    writeln ('Real value is ', realnum)
END.
```

The expected output should appear something like this:

```
The  value  is          12
Real  value  is    1.23456000000000e+01
```

Note that a lengthy sequence of *write* statements with no intervening *writeln* may produce extremely long lines. Many Pascal compilers have a maximum line length which may not be exceeded. Further, many output devices have inherent limitations on line lengths. Many CRT terminals, for example, display a maximum of 80 characters per line, while most printers cannot display more than 132 characters per line. If this length is exceeded, the result is almost certainly unacceptable. The organization of each program's output should be carefully considered, and the correct combination of *write* and *writeln* statements should be used.

As we have seen in the preceding examples, character strings can be displayed. The strings are enclosed inside single quotes, and just those characters in the string are displayed. The default fieldwidth for such strings is equal to the number of characters in the string. Note that blanks in a string are counted in determining the default fieldwidth.

Boolean expressions may also be included in the output list of a *write* or *writeln* statement. The value of the expression, true or false, is treated as a string, and this string is then displayed. (Whether upper- or lowercase letters are displayed depends on the particular Pascal compiler.) Note that the default fieldwidth is then either four or five characters, respectively. The following statements illustrate the output of Boolean values.

statement	output
write (true)	T R U E
write (false)	F A L S E

Formatted Output

If we use *write* and *writeln* statements in the manner just described (that is, we use the default fieldwidths selected by the designer of the particular Pascal implementation), we have no control over how many columns are used for numeric expressions. Additionally, we are "stuck" with the default fieldwidths specified by Pascal for char, string, and Boolean data types. While these default fieldwidths may be adequate for some applications, we will frequently need to control the placement of values on output lines more carefully.

Pascal allows the programmer to explicitly specify fieldwidths for each output expression. These explicit widths override the default fieldwidths that would normally be used. To see how such fieldwidths are specified, consider the following program segment. All variables used are declared integer.

```
num1 := 4;
num2 := -12;
write (num1:5, num2:7, 'Junk':6)
```

These statements would produce the following output:

```
    4    -12    Junk
```

Each of the expressions in the output list has been followed by a colon and an integer expression (in this example, an integer constant) specifying the fieldwidth we wish to use for the display of the expression's value. As with default fieldwidths, the values are right-justified in the field, with leading blanks being used to fill the field to the specified width. This technique (filling a field with leading blanks) is used for all data types when the explicit fieldwidth specified is larger than necessary. If the explicit fieldwidth is "just right," then no leading blanks appear.

Explicit Fieldwidths for Integer Expressions

But what happens if the fieldwidth we specify is too small for the correct display of an integer expression's value? Consider the case where a fieldwidth of 2 is specified for the value −12. Remember the negative sign must be displayed too.

writeln (− 12:2)

We might assume that part of the number is omitted, but this could lead to serious problems with interpretation of the output. For example, one might assume that leading characters in the value are omitted, in which case the value − 12 would be displayed exactly like the display for 12! This could certainly mislead someone trying to use the output.

Instead of dropping characters from the display for integer values when the fieldwidth is too small, Pascal automatically "widens" the field so the value can be correctly displayed. In our last example, the fieldwidth of 2 would be ignored and the value − 12 would instead be printed in a field of three columns. Such widening of fields also takes place for real values; we will discuss fields for real values in more detail later.

Explicit Fieldwidths for Char and String Expressions

In output lists, we may treat an expression of type char exactly like a string of one character. Also recall that a Boolean value in an output list is treated like the appropriate string 'TRUE' or 'FALSE'.

The explicit fieldwidth specified for a string is never modified by Pascal. If the fieldwidth is more than adequate, then leading blanks are added to fill the field. Fields that are too small to display all characters of the string result in display of only the leftmost fieldwidth characters of the string; the rightmost characters will be truncated. The following examples illustrate these points:

statement	output	observations
write ('Message')	M e s s a g e	Default width is string length.
write ('Message':9)	_ _ M e s s a g e	Leading blanks.
write ('Message':4)	M e s s	Only 4 characters written.

It is frequently useful to include the char constant ' ' in an output list with a fieldwidth greater than one to force alignment of the following field with a specific column. Consider, for example, the following statement:

write (' ':15, 'Message')

Assuming a new line is being written, we would observe

_ _ _ _ _ _ _ _ _ _ _ _ _ _ M e s s a g e

being displayed.

Real expressions may also include an explicit fieldwidth. In fact, there are two forms that may be used for formatted output of real values:

- A real expression may be followed by a colon and a fieldwidth (as for integers and characters):

```
write (realnum : 10)
```

- A real expression may be followed by a colon and a fieldwidth and another colon and an (integer) expression specifying the total number of fraction digits which are to appear after the decimal point:

```
write (realnum : 10 : 5)
```

In the first form, the value of the real expression is written in the familiar exponential form (scientific notation). The display actually includes:

- The sign character (a minus sign if negative, a blank space if positive)
- The first significant digit of the expression's value
- The decimal point
- Some number of digits after the decimal point (this depends, of course, on the actual fieldwidth specified)
- The letter e or E (lower- or uppercase depends on your version of Pascal)
- The sign of the exponent ("+" or "−")
- The exponent (usually two or three decimal digits)

Note that the exact output resulting from the use of a single fieldwidth for real expressions depends to some extent on the particular Pascal compiler you are using. The following program was compiled using a popular computer system and produced the output shown below.

program	output
PROGRAM realdemo (input, output);	
BEGIN	
writeln (12345.67 : 8);	␣ 1 . 2 e + 0 4
writeln (12345.67 : 9);	␣ 1 . 2 3 e + 0 4
writeln (12345.67 : 10)	␣ 1 . 2 3 5 e + 0 4
END.	

Note that the output always has an exponent, and the fractional part is *rounded* by adding 5 to the first fractional digit not displayed. The actual number of columns used (essentially, the minimum fieldwidth) is at least six more than the number of digits in the exponent. Note also that no additional leading blanks (that is, other than the one used in place of the + sign if the number is positive) are produced using this format. The extra columns are filled with digits after the decimal point. On the system used above, for example, the minimum number of columns that will be used is six, since the exponent always requires two decimal digits.

The second form for formatted real output produces a *fixed-point* representation; that is, no exponent is displayed, and the number appears in its decimal format. The expression after the first colon, as usual, determines the minimum fieldwidth used for output. The expression after the second colon determines the number of digits printed after the decimal point. Here is a program similar to the preceding example, with the corresponding output:

program	output
PROGRAM realdemo2 (output);	
BEGIN	
writeln (12345.67 : 9 : 2);	`_ 1 2 3 4 5 . 6 7`
writeln (12345.67 : 10 : 3);	`_ _ 1 2 3 4 5 . 6 7 0`
writeln (12345.67 : 11 : 2)	`_ _ _ _ 1 2 3 4 5 . 6 7`

In fixed-point representation leading blanks are used to make the field as wide as specified. (Note the third *writeln* statement.) In addition, one column before the first digit will always be used for the sign (a minus sign if negative, a blank space if positive). Try to explain why we obtained the indicated output from the second *writeln* statement.

EXERCISES FOR SECTION 3.1

1 Suppose we have the following sequence of input statements (assume each variable has been declared integer):

```
read (x, y, z);
readln (a);
readln (b, c);
read (d)
```

Find the values of the variables (a, b, c, d, x, y, and z) if the following input data was used:

```
8    7    2    1    3
1    4    4    6    2
3    7
```

2   Given the following variable declarations

    VAR
        a, b, c : integer;
        x, y, z : real;

and the following input data

    3   2.3   −6.5
    1   5   2.1

then find the errors, if any, in each of the following read statements.

(a)   read (x, y, z)
(b)   read (a, b, x)
(c)   read (a, x, y);
      read (b, z, c)
(d)   readln (a, x);
      read (b, c, y, z)

3   What will be displayed (on the output device) when the following Pascal statements
    are executed?

    writeln ('Value1 is', 3);
    writeln ('value2 is', 5);
    writeln ('Sum is', 3 + 5)

4   What will be displayed when the following Pascal statements are executed?

    writeln (86, 39);
    writeln ('a = ');
    writeln (32.5);
    writeln ('a = ', 86, 'b = ', 32.5)

5   What will be displayed when the following Pascal program is executed?

    PROGRAM guess (input, output);
    VAR
        a, b, c : integer;
        x, y, z : real;
    BEGIN
        a := 0;
        b := 2;
        c := 1;
        x := 5.2;
        y := 3.6;
        z := 4.1;

```
        write ('Values are');
        write (a, b, c);
        writeln (x, y, z);
        writeln ('Sum is', x + y + z);
        writeln ('Product is', a * b * c)
    END.
```

6 Determine the *exact* output of the following Pascal program.

```
    PROGRAM outa (input, output);
    VAR
            a : char;
            b : integer;
    BEGIN
            a := 'x';
            b := -12;
            writeln (a:2, b:5)
    END.
```

7 Suppose a, b, c, and d are integer variables. Find the values in a, b, c, and d after execution of the following statements with the data shown.

statement		data		
readln (a, b);	2	15	6	4
readln (c);	1	-3	7	9
read (d)	8	12	-1	5

8 Suppose m and t are integer variables with values 4 and -18, respectively. Determine the *exact* output of the following statement:

```
write ('Value':8, m:2, t:4)
```

9 Suppose a, b, and c are integer variables. A user types the following sequence of characters at the terminal (where ⊘ represents a space):

```
1 ⊘ 2
3 ⊘ 4
```

Which statement or group of statements will not result in the values $a = 1$, $b = 2$, and $c = 3$?

(a) ```
    read (a);
    readln (b);
    read (c)
    ```
(b) ```readln (a, b, c)```
(c) ```read (a, b, c)```
(d) ```read (a);```
    ```

```
        read (b);
        readln;
        read (c)
(e)  readln (a);
     readln (b);
     readln (c)
```

10   Which of the following statements will cause the word *FIRST* to be written in columns 1 to 5, the value of the integer variable *next* to be written so as to end in column 20, and the word *LAST* to be written in columns 77 to 80?

    (a)   write ('FIRST', next:15, 'LAST':60)
    (b)   write ('FIRST':5, next:20, 'LAST':80)
    (c)   write (FIRST:5, 'NEXT':15, LAST:60)
    (d)   write ('FIRST', 'NEXT':20, 'LAST':80)
    (e)   write ('FIRST':5, next:5, 'LAST':56)

11   Suppose x, y, and z are integer variables. Given the following program segment

```
readln (x);
readln (y);
readln (z)
```

what will be stored in x, y, and z if a user types in the following lines when the program segment is executed?

```
1 2 ⌀ 3 4 ⌀ 5 6
7 . 0 ⌀ 9 ⌀ 1 . 0
⌀ ⌀ ⌀ ⌀ ⌀ ⌀
⌀ 1 1 ⌀ 2 2
```

(Assume ⌀ represents a typed space.)

12   What will be the *exact* output produced when the following program is executed?

```
PROGRAM test (input, output);
CONST hi = 'HELLO';
VAR r, s : real;
BEGIN
        r := 6.1;
        s := 7.2;
        writeln (hi : 6);
        write ('R = ');
        write (r : 5 : 2);
        writeln;
        write ('S = ');
        write (s : 3 : 1)
END.
```

SECTION 3.2 PROBLEM SOLVING WITH PASCAL

In this section we apply the problem-solving process outlined in Chapter 1 to problems having simple solutions. This permits us to find computer solutions using the Pascal language features presented to this point. In later chapters we will give more complex problems and their solutions.

Consider the following problem.

Problem 3.1

Determine the total and average (rounded to the nearest integer) of four integer examination scores.

After carefully reading and analyzing the problem statement, we find a simple solution. The problem is divided into four distinct subproblems (see Figure 3-1):

SUBPROBLEM 1: Obtain the examination scores from the input.
SUBPROBLEM 2: Compute the total of the examination scores.
SUBPROBLEM 3: Compute the rounded average.
SUBPROBLEM 4: Display the results.

Note that the input and output of data was not explicitly included in the problem statement. We will frequently encounter problems which are written in such a way that we can infer the presence of values for the *givens* (in this case, the four examination scores), and we will need to understand which of these givens represent constants and which represent variable data values. Likewise, a person using paper and pencil to solve a problem will immediately see the result of the calculations, since they appear on the paper. The results obtained by computer solution will need to be explicitly transferred from variables and expressions in the computer's memory to the output device.

We must now refine each subproblem to a form that permits immediate translation to Pascal. One possible refinement is:

Figure 3-1 Top-down design of average program.

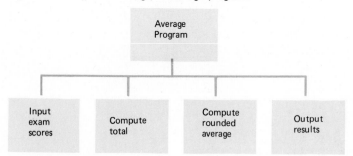

SUBPROBLEM 1: Input *exam1*, *exam2*, *exam3*, and *exam4*.
SUBPROBLEM 2: Total = *exam1* + *exam2* + *exam3* + *exam4*.
SUBPROBLEM 3: Average = *round* (total / 4).
SUBPROBLEM 4: Output *exam1*, *exam2*, *exam3*, *exam4*, *total*, *average*.

This is definitely not Pascal, but the statements are sufficiently close to Pascal to permit their immediate translation. In refining the earlier statements we have introduced more detail: The input data items now have names (*exam1*, *exam2*, *exam3*, and *exam4*), and the algebraic notions of sum and average have been introduced. We still have some generality in our refinement of step 3: We assume the existence of a function *round* to accomplish the rounding of a real value to the nearest integer value. Prior to translation to some languages, we would need to refine our concept of rounding further, but Pascal includes just such a function.

Now we are ready to translate this refined form of the solution to the Pascal source program. While we have given names to the variables we will use, we must still choose a name for the program. As usual, we will choose a name that has some **mnemonic**, or memory aid value, like *examsavg*. This certainly gives an uninformed reader of our program some idea what it is about. The first line in our program will therefore be:

```
PROGRAM examsavg (input, output);
```

While the current refinement of our solution makes no statements about the type of data with which we are dealing, it might have been a good idea to include a summary statement describing the type and use of each data item. Such a summary might look like this:

variable	type	use
exam1,exam2, exam3,exam4	Integer	The four exam scores as provided in the input
total	Integer	Sum of the 4 exam scores
average	Integer	Rounded average of exam scores

If we prepare such a variable summary for each of our problem refinements, we are well prepared to produce the variable declarations of our Pascal program. Note how similar the Pascal declarations and the variable summary appear:

```
VAR
      exam1, exam2,            (* The four exam scores as *)
      exam3, exam4 : integer;  (* provided in the input *)
      total : integer;         (* sum of 4 exam scores *)
      average : integer;       (* rounded avg of exam scores *)
```

Finally, we translate each of the four subproblem refinements to their Pascal equivalents, remembering to enclose the whole group of statements by the words BEGIN and END. The first step is to obtain the four examination scores. We might choose to prompt the user to type the appropriate values by writing a brief message, and we do that in our translation of step 1:

```
write ('Please type the examination scores: ');
readln (exam1, exam2, exam3, exam4);
```

Next we compute the total of these scores:

```
total := exam1 + exam2 + exam3 + exam4;
```

Then we compute the average by using the Pascal built-in function *round*. This function will yield the integer value closest to the value of the real expression provided to it. The real division operation (/) is used to provide the real value for round:

```
average := round (total / 4);
```

Finally we will display the results. In our refinement of step 4 we have chosen to display not only the total and average of the examination scores but also the examination scores themselves. Displaying input data values is sometimes called **echo printing**, or simply an **echo check**, and allows the user of a program to verify that the data provided to the program was indeed that which was intended. Small interactive programs such as the one we are currently considering may usually be written without echo checks, since the data is echoed by the computer as it is typed. We include the echo check here only to illustrate its implementation.

Each of the various output values is written with an identifying message. Imagine the hapless user who gets six integers and has no idea of which is which!

```
writeln ('The examination scores are:');
writeln ('     ', exam1, exam2, exam3, exam4);
writeln ('The examination scores total is ', total);
writeln ('The rounded average score is ', average)
```

The complete program is shown below. We have additionally included comments enclosed by (* and *) to improve the readability of the program. Semicolons are used to separate the various statements (but note that none is used following the last statement). One possible display resulting from the execution of this program is also shown.

```
PROGRAM examsavg (input, output);
VAR
      exam1, exam2,              (* The four exam scores *)
      exam3, exam4 : integer;    (* as provided in the input *)
      total : integer;           (* sum of 4 exam scores *)
      average : integer;         (* rounded avg of exam scores *)
```

```
BEGIN
        (* Obtain the four examination scores from the input *)
            write ('Please type the examination scores: ');
            readln (exam1, exam2, exam3, exam4);
        (* Compute the total and rounded average *)
            total := exam1 + exam2 + exam3 + exam4;
            average := round (total / 4);
        (* Display the results *)
            writeln ('The examination scores are:');
            writeln ('      ', exam1, exam2, exam3, exam4);
            writeln ('The examination scores total is ', total);
            writeln ('The rounded average score is ', average)
END.
```

Program examsavg

Please type the examination scores: 100 96 83 75
The examination scores are:
   100 96 83 75
The examination scores total is   354
The rounded average score is   89

Program examsavg: Sample Execution

Now let us consider another problem for computer solution. This time we will utilize formatted output to enhance the readability of the output.

Problem 3.2

Roland Tool and Die Company is in the process of converting from the English system to the metric system of measurement. Write a Pascal program that will perform the following task. Given a length expressed in feet and inches, determine the metric equivalent, rounded to two decimal places, in both meters and centimeters.

Using top-down design this problem can be divided into three major subproblems:

SUBPROBLEM 1: From the input data, obtain the length in feet and inches.
SUBPROBLEM 2: Convert the length to its metric equivalents, first in centimeters and then in meters.
SUBPROBLEM 3: Display the results of the conversion.

The conversion subproblem can be further subdivided into three subproblems (see Figure 3-2):

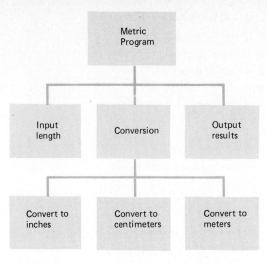

Figure 3-2   Top-down design of metric program.

SUBPROBLEM 2.1: Convert feet and inches to inches.
SUBPROBLEM 2.2: Convert inches to centimeters.
SUBPROBLEM 2.3: Convert inches to meters.

Algorithmically, we have the following sequence of steps:

STEP 1: Input length.
STEP 2: Convert length to inches only.
STEP 3: Convert length in inches to centimeters.
STEP 4: Convert length in inches to meters.
STEP 5: Display results.

We now refine each of these steps to produce a form of the algorithm which is closer to that required by Pascal.

STEP 1: Input length in feet and inches (variables *lenft* and *lenin*).
STEP 2: Convert length in feet and inches to length in inches only (variable *inonly*):

inonly = lenft * 12 + lenin

(since 1 foot = 12 inches).
STEP 3: Convert length in inches to length in centimeters (variable *lencm*):

lencm = inonly * 2.54

(since 1 inch is exactly 2.54 centimeters).

lenm = inonly * 0.0254

(since there are 2.54 centimeters in 1 inch and 100 centimeters in one meter).
STEP 5: Output length in feet and inches, rounded meters, and rounded centimeters.

Here is the summary of the variables we are using:

variable	type	use
lenft	Integer	Length (in feet) from input
lenin	Integer	Length (in inches) from input
inonly	Integer	Length (in inches only)
lenm	Real	Length (in meters)
lencm	Real	Length (in centimeters)

You might be wondering why we converted directly from inches to meters in step 4, instead of converting the length in centimeters (*lencm*) directly to meters. There are actually two reasons for this apparently obscure decision. First, note that the refined subproblem states that we will convert from length in inches to length in meters. Technically, we would not be implementing this step correctly if we used the result of step 3 (length in centimeters) to determine the length in meters. You are certain to assume this is a small detail, and it is. If we do not adhere closely to the small details of our subproblem refinements, we cannot expect the overall, more complex problem solution to have the precise behavior we have designed into it during the top-down design. After all, top-down design only works because a complex problem's solution is comprised of a large number of small problem solutions.

The second reason we did not use our previous result (the length in centimeters) when converting to meters is rather more difficult to explain at this point in our study of computer science. Let us just observe that when we perform numerical computations, it is better to work with the original data than with data resulting from intermediate steps, if we can. (Consider the following frivolous analogies: When searching for buried treasure, it's probably better to use the pirate's original treasure map than one which has been redrawn from the original! When something is told to one person, who tells it to a second person, who in turn tells it to a third person, and so on, the final person may be told something that is considerably different from what the first person was told.)

We now have sufficient detail to write a complete Pascal program called *metric*. It is shown below. The display resulting from one execution of the program is also shown. Note that we have used the rounding property of formatted real output to solve the rounding requirement of the problem statement.

```pascal
PROGRAM metric (input, output);
    (* A program to determine the metric equivalents (meters *)
    (* and centimeters), accurate to two decimal places, of   *)
    (* a length given in feet and inches.                     *)
VAR
        lenft : integer;    (*length (in feet) from input*)
        lenin : integer;    (*length (in inches) from input*)
        inonly : integer;   (*length (in inches only)*)
        lenm : real;        (*length (in meters)*)
        lencm : real;       (*length (in centimeters)*)
BEGIN
        (* Obtain the length in feet and inches *)
        writeln ('Please enter the length in feet and inches.');
        write ('Feet:     ');
        readln (lenft);
        write ('Inches     ');
        readln (lenin);
        (* Convert the length (feet and inches) to inches only *)
        inonly := lenft * 12 + lenin;
        (* Convert length (inches) to centimeters *)
        lencm := inonly * 2.54;
        (* Convert length (inches) to meters *)
        lenm := inonly * 0.0254;
        (* Display input data and metric equivalents *)
        writeln ('The input length was ',
            lenft : 1, ' feet and ',
            lenin : 1, ' inches.');
        writeln ('The equivalent length in centimeters is ',
            lencm : 8 : 2);
        writeln ('The equivalent length in meters is ',
            lenm : 8 : 2)
END.
```

Program metric

Please enter the length in feet and inches.
Feet: 3
Inches: 6
The input length was 3 feet and 6 inches.
The equivalent length in centimeters is   106.68
The equivalent length in meters is   1.07

Program metric: Sample Execution

SECTION 3.3 INTRODUCTION TO TEXT FILE INPUT AND OUTPUT
[OPTIONAL]

101

PASCAL INPUT AND
OUTPUT AND
PROBLEM SOLVING

In a program header such as

```
PROGRAM triangle (input, output);
```

the identifiers *input* and *output* are called ***file variables*** and are used when we wish to perform input or output on external files. Normally *input* and *output* correspond to your terminal in an interactive computer system. *Input* and *output* are known as standard files in Pascal. It is sometimes necessary for us to read data from other external files (located on disk or magnetic tape) or perhaps to save our output in an external file. Pascal provides a mechanism to handle such external text file input and output.

Any external text files you might use in your program must have corresponding file variables. These must be listed, by name, in the program header and must also be declared of type text in the declaration part of the program. When we do this, we are indicating that the file is organized in lines, each of which contains zero or more characters and an end-of-line (⟨eoln⟩) character. The standard files *input* and *output* are automatically declared of type text when they are listed in the program header. Suppose we wish to use two external text files, one for input and one for output. We might choose the file variables named *infile* and *outfile* for input and output, respectively. The following declaration for a program named *process* will allow us to use the external text files:

```
PROGRAM process (infile, outfile);
VAR
     infile, outfile : text;
```

Next we need to be able to read and write these files in a way similar to that used for the standard files *input* and *output*. The *read*, *readln*, *write*, and *writeln* statements provided by Pascal automatically use the files *input* and *output* unless we specify a different file name in the statement. For example, to read data into an integer variable *number* from the external text file associated with the file variable *infile*, we would use the statement

```
read (infile, number)
```

This statement instructs the computer to read an integer value from the external text file associated with file variable *infile* and to store the resulting value in variable *number*. Since *infile* is declared text, we are reading a string of characters that represent the value of the integer. This reading is done using *exactly* the same process that is used when we enter data from the terminal, using the standard input file.

An important step in file input and output is the *opening* of the file. If an external file is to be read, it must be opened, or connected to the associated file variable, before reading can commence. In Pascal, the ***reset*** statement will accomplish this opening operation. For our current problem, the appropriate statement would be

```
reset (infile)
```

When the *reset* statement is executed, the computer system will locate the appropriate external file (if it cannot be located, a run-time error will occur) and arrange things so that any *read* or *readln* statements referring to file variable *infile* will process the corresponding external file, starting at its beginning.

In a similar manner, the **rewrite** statement

```
rewrite (outfile)
```

will connect the file variable *outfile* with a new external file. (If the external file already exists, its previous contents are deleted; otherwise, a new external file is created. Inability to create this file will cause a run-time error.) This new file is initially empty. *Rewrite* must be used prior to executing any *write* or *writeln* statements that refer to *outfile*. After the *rewrite* we may execute the statement

```
write (outfile, number)
```

to put into *outfile* exactly the same characters that would have been written to the terminal if we had executed the statement

```
write (number)
```

The exact external file that is associated with a file variable when a *reset* or *rewrite* is executed varies depending on the computer system you are using. In many systems, the **file name** of the external file is the same as the name of the file variable, but facilities may be available to permit the connection of a file variable with an arbitrary external file. Some Pascal compilers also have slightly different forms for *reset* and *rewrite* (or other facilities) that allow you to specify the name of the external file that is to be connected with the file variable. You should refer to the documentation of your Pascal for details on these deviations from standard Pascal.

Now suppose we wish to write a Pascal program named *copy* that will read three real values from an external text file and copy them to a different external text file. We will assume the file variables *indata* and *outdata* are used. Here is one way to accomplish the task.

```
PROGRAM copy (indata, outdata);
(* Program to copy three real numbers from file variable *)
(* indata to file variable outdata. *)
VAR
        num1, num2, num3 : real;            (* real data *)
        indata, outdata : text;             (* file variables *)
BEGIN
        reset (indata);                     (* "open" indata *)
        rewrite (outdata);                  (* "open" outdata *)
        read (indata, num1, num2, num3);    (* get 3 numbers *)
        write (outdata, num1, num2, num3)   (* put 3 numbers *)
END.
```

We will return to file variables in Chapter 12 but here are a few important points about text file input and output to remember for now:

- More than one input or output file can be specified in the program header.
- *Input* and *output* are automatically declared to be file variables of type text if they appear in the program header and are automatically opened for reading and writing, respectively.
- All other file variables appearing in the program heading must be declared to be of type text in the variable declaration part of the program.
- Input from, or output to, external text files is done with *read*, *readln*, *write*, and *writeln* statements that specify a file variable as the first name in the parameter list.
- Prior to executing the first *read* or *readln* statement using a file variable other than *input*, that file variable must be opened using the *reset* statement.
- Prior to executing the first *write* or *writeln* statement using a file variable other than *output*, that file variable must be opened using the *rewrite* statement.

SECTION 3.4 TESTING AND DEBUGGING TECHNIQUES

In this section we will consider some common errors encountered when performing input and output.

Input Errors

A common input error is to enter a value whose data type does not match that of the variable being read. For example, if the variable *number* is declared as an integer, then the *read* statement

```
read (number)
```

requires the next item in the input to be an integer constant. If you enter a character other than a sign (+ or −) or a digit (0 to 9), then an input error will be reported. In a later chapter we will discuss techniques for validating input data so such errors can be detected and corrective action can be taken. Checking for input errors is an important part of testing and debugging.

Another common input error is the failure to obtain sufficient data to satisfy the *read* or *readln* statement being executed. For example, if *num1*, *num2*, *num3*, and *num4* are integer variables, then the statement

```
read (num1, num2, num3, num4)
```

requires four integer constants in the input data. If only three values are provided, then an error will occur. If there are other values in the input (intended for other *read* or *readln* statements), then the first of these will be read (incorrectly) for *num4*, possibly causing an erroneous result to be computed. If the end of file follows the value for *num3*, then an error will be immediately reported.

The order of the input data is important. For example, suppose *grade* is a char variable, *test* an integer variable, and *average* a real variable. The statement

```
readln (grade, test, average)
```

will expect the input data to look something like this:

```
A  95  82.6
```

When the *read* statement is executed, *grade* will become *A*, *test* 95, and *average* 82.6. Recall that blanks are used to separate real and integer values. Suppose the order of the variables is changed, as in the *readln* statement

```
readln (average, grade, test)
```

If we then enter the data values

```
82.6  A  95
```

then *average* will become 82.6. Now a character value is expected, and the "input pointer" is positioned to the blank separating the value 82.6 and the character *A*. It is this character (' ') that will be assigned to the variable *grade*. Following this the input pointer is positioned to the letter *A*. The *readln* statement will attempt to obtain an integer value for *test* starting with the character *A*, and will naturally fail. Remember that *only* blanks, tabs, and end-of-line characters are skipped prior to reading integer and real values, and *no* characters are skipped, not even end-of-line characters, prior to reading a character value.

The final potential input error we will present concerns the use of single quotes, or apostrophes, around char data. In an expression involving character constants, like that in the assignment statement

```
grade := 'A'
```

quotes must be used around the character to create a valid character constant. These quotes must not be used when the same character appears in the input data. For example, the statement

```
read (grade)
```

will take the next input character as the value of *grade*. If the input data contains

```
'A'
```

then the quote character will be assigned to *grade*, not the letter *A*.

Output Errors

A common output error is to forget the quote marks surrounding any text to be displayed. For example, the statement

writeln (The number is, number)

is erroneous since the quotes are missing around

The number is

When using formatted output the fieldwidths must be integer values. The statement

writeln (3.5 + 3.6 : 3.0)

is erroneous since the fieldwidth is not an integer. The statement should be

writeln (3.5 + 3.6 : 3)

There are many types of output errors that can occur from syntax errors such as those just illustrated. To help locate those output errors that result from improper formatting of the output data, you should experiment with the various forms of output on your system. Include *write* statements, such as echo printing, to validate your input data if you are having input and/or output errors. If you are doing arithmetic calculations, include *write* statements to display any intermediate results. These debug *write* statements can be safely removed when your program has been tested and debugged.

As an aid in testing and debugging your program, a list of important Pascal reminders for input and output follows.

PASCAL REMINDERS

Input
- Of integer or real values must be separated by blanks (or tabs or end-of-line characters)
- Of variables of mixed data types must be done with care since the order is important
- Using *readln* will cause the next *read* or *readln* statement to begin processing the next line of input

Output
- Of integer values can be formatted by suffixing a colon and an integer fieldwidth:

  write (inumber : 5)

- Of real values can be formatted by suffixing a colon, an integer fieldwidth, another colon, and an integer specifying the number of decimal places after the decimal point:

```
write (rnumber : 10 : 3)
```

■ Will automatically expand a fieldwidth if too small to represent a value correctly; for example,

```
write (inumber : 0)
```

will always use a field of a least one column

SECTION 3.5 CHAPTER REVIEW

In this chapter the details of Pascal input and output have been discussed. An optional section on text file input and output was also included. Two problems were completely solved using the top-down design approach to problem solving. Complete Pascal programs were written for both problems. Common input and output errors were presented in the Testing and Debugging Techniques section.

Here is a summary of the Pascal input and output details discussed in this chapter.

PASCAL REFERENCE

1 Input/output
   1.1 Input: *Read* and *readln* followed by a parenthesized list of variable identifiers can be used to obtain data from an input device:

```
read (num1, num2);
readln (principal, interest, tax);
```

Readln will cause any data remaining on the input line to be skipped after reading values for the variables specified in the list.
   1.2 *Output:* *Write* and *writeln* followed by a parenthesized list of identifiers, text (delimited by quotes), or expressions can be used to display data values on an output device:

```
write (sum, product);
write ('The value is ', value);
writeln ('Double the input value is ', 2 * value);
```

Writeln will cause the display produced by the next *write* or *writeln* statement to start on the next line.

Formatted output: In the *write* or *writeln* statements, a data item (identifier, quoted text, or expression) followed by a colon and an integer (and an additional optional colon and integer for real values) changes the default fieldwidth:

```
writeln (number : 5);
write ('Average is' : 15, mean : 6 : 2);
```

For real values, the integer following the second colon indicates the number of fractional digits that are to be displayed.

Chapter 4 Preview

After completing this chapter, you should be able to write complete Pascal programs to solve some basic problems. To solve more difficult problems, we will apply the top-down design approach to divide the problem into subproblems and continue to refine the subproblems until a computer solution is possible. To implement this approach using Pascal, we will introduce program segments known as procedures that will implement the solution to each subproblem. Procedures are actually subprograms that are contained within our Pascal main program. Each procedure should be a self-contained, independent subprogram that solves one of the subproblems. As we shall see in the next chapter, using top-down design and writing procedures will provide an organized and structured solution to our problem.

Keywords for Chapter 3

echo print	read
file	readln
file name	reset
file variable	rewrite
formatted	write
input	writeln

CHAPTER 3 EXERCISES

★ ESSENTIAL EXERCISES

1 How are tab characters treated on input by your system? To find out, execute the following program and enter a tab character, a period, and a carriage return as input data.

```
PROGRAM tab (input, output);
VAR c1, c2, c3 : char;
BEGIN
      read (c1, c2, c3);
      writeln (ord(c1), ord(c2), ord(c3))
END.
```

2 What will the following program produce as output when the input line

1.2.3.4

is typed?

```
PROGRAM funnyi (input, output);
VAR
       c : char;
       r : real;
       i : integer;
BEGIN
        readln (r, c, i);
        writeln (r, c, i)
END.
```

3 What is displayed by the following statements (assume *r* is a real variable)?

```
r := 91.2;
writeln (r : 3 : 0)
```

★★ SIGNIFICANT EXERCISES

4 The *read* and *readln* statements carefully shield us from the true identity of the end-of-line character. Can you determine how individual lines are separated on your computer system?

5 Does your Pascal permit Boolean variables in *read* statements? If so, what must be entered to provide the data values true and false?

★★★ CHALLENGING EXERCISES

6 Determine the length of the longest line that can be displayed on your system. Note that this is *not* the width of your terminal. (Some systems may not have a maximum line length.)

CHAPTER 3 PROBLEMS FOR COMPUTER SOLUTION

★ ESSENTIAL PROBLEMS

1 Two times are given in the input data as integers in the form *hhmm*, where *hh* represents the hours (less than 24) and *mm* represents the minutes (less than 60). Determine the sum of these two times, and display as *d hhmm*, where *d* is days (either 0 or 1).

Example input:

1345   2153

Example output:

1 1138

2 The relative error in a measurement *m* is given as the ratio of the absolute difference between the measurement and the true value *v* to the true value. Assume the input data is a single line that includes two real numbers representing the measurement

m and the true value *v*. Compute the relative error in the measurement, and display it along with the measurement and the true value. Be certain to include descriptive labels for the values you display.

Example input:

```
51.0      51.3
```

Example output:

```
Measurement = 5.1000000000e+01
True Value = 5.1300000000e+01
Relative Error = 5.8479532161e-03
```

3   A computer cannot be used to generate real random numbers since an algorithm must be used to generate the numbers, and hence the actual numbers can be predicted. Computers can, however, generate pseudorandom numbers (numbers that look random, statistically). An old technique that does not give good results is called the ***middle-square*** method. It works like this. Given one number *a*, we generate the next number in the sequence by extracting the middle digits of a^2. For example, if *a* is 53, then a^2 is 2809, and the next pseudorandom number would be 80. If we continue, we see that 80^2 is 6400, so the next pseudorandom number is 40. Continuing this process we obtain 60, 60, 60, ... Write a Pascal program which reads a two-digit integer and determines the next pseudorandom number which would be generated using the middle-square method. Assume the single input line contains the two-digit integer. Display the original two-digit integer, the square of this integer, and the next number, all with appropriate labels.

Example input:

```
53
```

Example output:

```
Input Number = 53
Square of Input = 2809
Next Pseudorandom Number = 80
```

4   Write a Pascal program which reads two integers representing the weight of an object in pounds and ounces. Then display the input weight and its equivalent in kilograms in a form similar to that shown below. Note that 16 ounces equals 1 pound and 2.2046 pounds equals 1 kilogram.

Input:

```
5 3   (representing 5 pounds and 3 ounces)
```

Output:

```
A weight of 5 pounds and 3 ounces is 2.353 kilograms.
```

5 A solenoid is a coil of closely wound wire with a given length and radius. An electrical characteristic of a solenoid is its inductance, which is determined by its length, the area of the cross section, and the number of turns per unit length. The exact formula is

$$L = mu \cdot \text{length} \cdot n^2 \cdot A$$

where L = the inductance in henries
       mu = the permeability constant $4 \cdot \pi \cdot 10^{-7}$
   $length$ = the length of the solenoid in meters
         n = the number of turns of wire per unit length
         A = the area of a cross section in square meters

Write a program which obtains n, the length (in inches), and the radius of the solenoid (in inches) from the input and displays the inductance (in microhenries). Note that 1 inch is 2.54 centimeters, or 0.0254 meters, and there are 10^6 microhenries per henry. Display all results accurate to one fractional digit. (Hint: Do not forget to convert from inches and turns per inch to meters and turns per meter.)

Example input:

100.0 5.0 1.0

Example output:

Solenoid dimensions:
    Radius: 1.0 inches
    Length: 5.0 inches
    Turns/inch: 100.0

Electrical characteristics:
    Inductance: 5013.8 microhenries

6 The Pascal function *exp(x)* computes a value equal to the sum of the infinite series

$$1 + x/1! + x^2/2! + x^3/3! + \cdots$$

where $1! = 1$, $2! = 2 * 1$, $3! = 3 * 2 * 1$, and so forth. Assume the input data contains a single real value for x between 0.0 and 1.0. Determine the sum of the first five terms of the infinite series, and the value of *exp(x)* using the standard function. Display these values and the input value of x using appropriate labels.

Example input:

0.5

Example output:

```
Input Value = 5.0000000000e-01
Series Sum  = 1.6484375000e+00
Exp(x)      = 1.6487212707e+00
```

★★ SIGNIFICANT PROBLEMS

7   Using the result of exercise 12 of Chapter 2, write a program to determine the square root of a positive number a by computing $a^{0.5}$. The input will consist of a single line containing the real number a. Display a, $a^{0.5}$, and $sqrt(a)$ with appropriate labels.

Example input:

12.7

Example output:

```
Input value           = 1.2700000000e+00
Computed Square Root  = 3.5637059362e+00
Pascal's Square Root  = 3.5637059362e+00
```

8   The single input data line contains a real number r and an integer p. Note that p indicates the position of the digit at which r is to be rounded, as follows:

$$r = x\,x\,x \bullet x \quad x \quad x$$
$$\quad\quad \uparrow\uparrow\uparrow \quad \uparrow \quad \uparrow \quad \uparrow$$
$$p = 2\,1\,0 \quad -1 \quad -2 \quad -3$$

For example, if $r = 35.89$ and $p = -1$, then the rounded value should be 35.9. Write a Pascal program which performs this rounding operation. (Hint: Consider multiplication by a power of 10, rounding using the standard function *round*, and division by a power of 10.) Display the input values, r and p, and the rounded value. Use appropriate labels for these values.

Example input:

35.89   −1

Example output:

```
Input Value       = 3.58900000000000e+01
Rounding Position = -1
Rounded Value     = 3.59000000000000e+01
```

9   Write a program which has as its only input a five-digit octal (base 8) number. Display the original octal number and the equivalent base 10 number. For example, the three-digit octal number 415 is equal to the decimal value $4 * 8^2 + 1 * 8^1 + 5 * 8^0$, or 269. (Hint: Recall that Pascal will treat the input value as a decimal number.)

Example input:

217

Example output:

Octal 217 = Decimal 143

10 Given a date expressed as five integers—*M* (month), *D* (day), *C* (century), *Y* (year), and *L* (leap-year indicator)—we can determine the corresponding day of the week as an integer in the range 0 to 6. This calculation can be done using the following formula:

$$W = [D + (2.6 * M - 0.2) + Y + (Y / 4) + (C / 4) \\ - 2 * C - (1 + L) * (M / 11)] \bmod 7$$

where W = the weekday (0 = Sunday, 1 = Monday, and so forth)
   M = the month number *beginning with March* = 1,
   C = the century (the first two digits of current years)
   Y = the year within the century (the last two digits)
   D = the day of the month
   L = 1 for a leap year and 0 for a non-leap year

Expressions in parentheses (M / 11), for example, represent the value of the expression truncated to an integer. Consider January 1, 1985, as an example. We have M = 11 (since March = 1), D = 1, C = 19, Y = 85, and L = 0. Therefore,

$$W = [1 + (2.6 * 11 - 0.2) + 85 + (85 / 4) + (19 / 4) \\ - 2 * 19 - (1 + 0) * (11 / 11)] \bmod 7 \\ = (1 + 28 + 85 + 21 + 4 - 38 - 1 * 1) \bmod 7 \\ = 100 \bmod 7 \\ = 2.$$

Since W = 2, we know that January 1, 1985, fell on Tuesday. The input data will consist of the current month number (*with January* = *1*), the day of the month, the year (not the separated *century* and year as required by the formula) and the leap year indicator (0 or 1). Determine the weekday on which the input date occurred. The output should contain the input data values and the integer representing the weekday, all appropriately labeled.

Example Input:

3   12   1985   (representing March 12, 1985)

Example Output:

Month   = 3
Day   = 12
Year   = 1985
Weekday = 2

★★★ CHALLENGING PROBLEM

11 Given a real loan amount P, a real interest rate R, and an integer number of years
in which we wish to pay off the loan N, determine the amount A which must be
repaid every year. The following expression can be used to determine A:

$$A = [P * (1 + R / 100)^N * R / 100 / [(1 + R / 100)^N - 1].$$

The input data will contain P, R, and N. Determine A, and print P, R, N, and A
with appropriate labels in appropriate formats. Assume R is specified as a percentage including a single fractional digit.

Example Input:

40000 10.0 30   ($40,000 at 10% interest for 30 years)

Example output:

Loan Amount   = $40000.00
Interest Rate = 10.0 percent
Loan Period   = 30 years
Annual Payment = $4243.17

CHAPTER 4

CHAPTER 4
TOP-DOWN DESIGN
AND ELEMENTARY
PROCEDURES

Procedures
and
Top-Down
Design

Problem
Solving
with
Simple
Procedures

Procedures
with
Parameters

Problem
Solving
and
Procedures
with
Parameters

Top-Down
Design and
Testing

TOP-DOWN DESIGN AND ELEMENTARY PROCEDURES

OBJECTIVES

After completing this chapter, you should be able to:

- Apply top-down design to solve a given problem
- Write a computer program in terms of procedures
- Write a procedure with parameters
- Distinguish between formal and actual parameters
- Distinguish between input (value) and output (variable) parameters
- Distinguish between local and global variables
- Apply top-down testing and debugging techniques to procedures

CHAPTER OVERVIEW

In this chapter we discuss applications of the top-down design approach to problem solving. In particular, the process of dividing a problem into subproblems and then refining each subproblem until a computer solution is possible is discussed. The computer solution of each subproblem is in terms of subprograms known as *procedures*.

In the first section we discuss the placement, invocation, and execution of simple procedures, that is, procedures without parameters. Next, we follow with a detailed solution of a problem using only simple procedures. The emphasis is on problem solving using top-down design, algorithm development, and computer solution in terms of procedures. Passing information to and from procedures is presented in Section 3. In particular, formal and actual parameters together with input (value) and output (variable) parameters are discussed. Several examples are included to illustrate the application of procedures with parameters. Local and global variables are also introduced.

The chapter closes with a detailed solution of a more advanced problem using procedures with parameters. Also, a discussion of testing procedures is included.

SECTION 4.1 INTRODUCTION TO PROCEDURES AND TOP-DOWN DESIGN

One approach to solving a complex problem is to divide it into subproblems and then solve the simpler subproblems. These subproblems can in turn be divided repeatedly into smaller problems until these smaller problems are easily solved. This technique of dividing the main problem into subproblems is sometimes called *divide and conquer*. During this process each subproblem is solved. This approach of designing a solution for a main problem by obtaining the solution for its subproblems is known as *top-down design*. It is called top-down design since we start "at the top" with a general problem and design specific solutions to its subproblems. In order to obtain an effective solution for the main problem, it is desirable that the subproblems be independent of each other. Then each subproblem can be solved and tested by itself. This approach is quite useful and provides an effective method of managing the solution of the complex main problem.

Top-down design solutions of complex problems can be easily implemented for computer solution by using structured high-level languages such as Pascal. The main problem is solved by the corresponding *main program* (also called the ***driver***) of the Pascal program. Solutions to the subproblems are provided by subprograms, known as *procedures*, or *functions*, in Pascal. A procedure performs or executes the computer instructions required to solve a given subproblem. Writing a computer program in terms of procedures provides a manageable computer solution to a given problem. The correspondence between the top-down design of a problem and the computer solution in terms of the main program and its procedures is considered in more detail in this chapter (see Figure 4-1).

Consider again the problem of computing the area of a given triangle. This problem can be divided into three subproblems:

SUBPROBLEM 1: Input altitude and base.
SUBPROBLEM 2: Compute area.
SUBPROBLEM 3: Output results.

The algorithm written in pseudocode would then be as follows:

STEP 1 Input the data (altitude and base).
STEP 2 Compute the area (area = 0.5 * altitude * base).
STEP 3 Output results (altitude, base, area).

Next let us write a Pascal procedure to solve each subproblem.

1   The following Pascal procedure will obtain the input data:

```
PROCEDURE getinput;
(* Obtain the altitude and base of the triangle *)
BEGIN
        write ('Enter altitude of triangle: ');
        readln (altitude);
        write ('Enter base of triangle: ');
        readln (base)
END;
```

Figure 4-1   Top-down design and procedures.

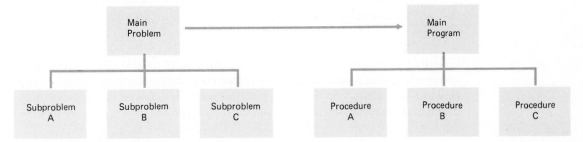

Observe that a procedure must begin with the reserved word PROCEDURE followed by an identifier. This identifier names the procedure (our current procedure is named *getinput*). Also note that a procedure will always have a semicolon following its END, since something must always follow a procedure. As usual, no semicolon is required before the END.

Other than the two points just noted, the structure of a procedure is very similar to that of an entire Pascal program. In fact, we will later see that procedures may include constant and variable declarations, as well as information concerning data to be input and output by the procedure. This allows procedures also to be written as self-contained, independent program modules.

2 The following procedure will compute the area of the triangle, given the altitude and base:

```
PROCEDURE computearea;
(* Compute area of triangle from base and altitude *)
BEGIN
        area := 0.5 * altitude * base
END;
```

3 Finally, the following procedure will display the results:

```
PROCEDURE printresults;
(* Display results of triangle area computation *)
BEGIN
        writeln ('The altitude of the triangle is ', altitude:6:2);
        writeln ('The base of the triangle is ', base:6:2);
        writeln ('The area of the triangle is ', area:6:2)
END;
```

We now have computer solutions to the three subproblems. Next we examine the structure of a main program that will incorporate these procedures. As shown below, the main program contains just three statements:

```
(* The main program begins here *)
BEGIN
        getinput;          (* invoke proc. to obtain input *)
        computearea;       (* invoke proc. to compute area *)
        printresults       (* invoke proc. to show results *)
END.
```

Notice that the statements we have used in the main program consist only of the names of the procedures. In Pascal, a statement consisting of a procedure name is executed by "calling," or "invoking," the procedure, resulting in the execution of the statements in the procedure itself. After executing the procedure, the program continues at the next statement (the line after the procedure invocation). Thus, in the main program, the statement

getinput;

directs the computer to invoke the procedure *getinput* that solves subproblem 1. After executing the *getinput* procedure, the computer will execute the next instruction,

computearea;

which, of course, causes procedure *computearea* to determine the area of the triangle. After completing the computation, the last statement,

printresults

invokes procedure *printresults* performing the task of displaying the appropriate results.

Our final step is to write the complete program. The only components missing are the program heading and the declarations. In addition to the declaration of all variables, Pascal requires the declaration of all procedures. These declarations are placed before the main program and after the variable declarations. The complete Pascal program, called *triangle*, is shown below.

```
PROGRAM triangle (input, output);
(* Program to compute area of a triangle given the base *)
(* and altitude.                                         *)
VAR
        altitude, base : real;    (* input data *)
        area : real;              (* computed area *)
PROCEDURE getinput;
(* Obtain the altitude and base of the triangle *)
BEGIN
        write ('Enter altitude of triangle: ');
        readln (altitude);
        write ('Enter base of triangle: ');
        readln (base)
END;
PROCEDURE computearea;
(* Compute area of triangle from base and altitude *)
BEGIN
        area := 0.5 * altitude * base
END;

PROCEDURE printresults;
(* Display results of triangle area computation *)
```

```
BEGIN
        writeln ('The altitude of the triangle is ', altitude:6:2);
        writeln ('The base of the triangle is ', base:6:2);
        writeln ('The area of the triangle is ', area:6:2)
END;

(* The main program begins here *)
BEGIN
        getinput;          (* invoke proc. to obtain input *)
        computearea;       (* invoke proc. to compute area *)
        printresults       (* invoke proc. to show results *)
END.
```

Program triangle

Let us execute this program by hand for the values altitude = 4.0 and base = 5.0. The first statement, *getinput*, will obtain the values altitude = 4.0 and base = 5.0. The next statement, *computearea*, will compute the area of the triangle:

```
area = 0.5 * 4.0 * 5.0 = 10.0
```

The last statement, *printresults*, will display the results:

```
The altitude of the triangle is 5.00
The base of the triangle is 4.00
The area of the triangle is 10.00
```

We have presented a simple example in order to emphasize the correspondence between the top-down design of the problem and the actual computer solution in terms of procedures. In many cases nothing is gained by writing a sequence of Pascal statements as a procedure. After some experience with problem solving using top-down design, it will become clearer which subproblems should be written as procedures. The effectiveness of this approach will become evident when we solve some of the complicated problems presented in the remainder of this chapter.

Procedure Structure

As we have observed, a Pascal procedure has a structure that imitates a Pascal program. It has a header, then declarations of identifiers used exclusively within that procedure (known as **local** identifiers), and finally the executable statements that are to be performed when the procedure is invoked.

The procedure header is the mechanism used to give a name to the procedure, just like the program header is used to give a name to the entire program. In the next section we will see that the procedure header is also used to identify those values that can be communicated between the procedure and its invocation. Consider the following example of a procedure header:

PROCEDURE getinput;

The reserved word PROCEDURE is followed by the identifier (*getinput*) we have chosen to name the procedure. Note that the semicolon following the identifier is actually separating the procedure header from the statements that must follow (not shown above).

We should use only unique identifiers when naming our procedures. The reason is obvious: If two (different) procedures were both named *getinput*, which one would be used when *getinput* is invoked? With only one procedure named *getinput*, the selection is unambiguous, but with more than one, the computer would be forced to decide for itself (and computers cannot think yet).

Following the procedure header, there may be declarations (for example, constant declarations and variable declarations) of those identifiers that will be used exclusively in the procedure being defined, called its local variables. For now, we will omit these declarations and use those variables declared in the main program, commonly called *global* variables. We will, however, return to the topic of local identifiers in the next section when we discuss how to make procedures self-contained and independent modules.

The third component of a procedure, the executable statements, follows the declarations or, in the absence of declarations, the procedure header. These statements are preceded by the reserved word BEGIN and followed by the reserved word END, just like those of the main program. Again, a fine point to remember is that the END of the main program is followed by a period to indicate that there is no more program, while the END of a procedure is always followed by a semicolon, since there *must* be more program code following the procedure.

Here is a summary of the major rules for writing simple procedures:

Simple Procedure Summary

Declaration

1 The header: PROCEDURE identifier;
2 The declarations: (Not used in simple procedures)
3 The executable   BEGIN
   statements   statement;
                              .
                              .
                              .
                           statement
                    END;

Placement

Simple procedure declarations appear just before the BEGIN that starts the main program and after all constant and variable declarations.

Invocation

A simple procedure is invoked by writing its name as an executable statement, followed by a semicolon (if necessary) to separate it from the next statement. When a procedure is invoked (1) the location of the statement after the procedure invocation is "remembered" by the computer, (2) the executable statements in the procedure are executed, and (3) execution returns to the "calling" program at the remembered location.

Procedure Invocation and Execution

Since procedures are similar to programs, it is normally a routine matter to change a program to a procedure. For example, the program *tax* from Section 2.2 is shown below rewritten to use a procedure called *onetax*.

```
PROGRAM tax (input, output);
(* Program to compute 7% sales tax on purchased items *)
CONST
        taxrate = 0.07;
VAR
        itemcost, salestax : real;
PROCEDURE onetax;
BEGIN
        (* Obtain cost of item from input data *)
        write ('Please enter cost of item: ');
        readln (itemcost);
        (* Compute sales tax on the item *)
        salestax := taxrate * itemcost;
        (* Display results *)
        writeln ('Item cost is      ', itemcost : 6 : 2);
        writeln ('Sales tax is      ', salestax : 6 : 2)
END;

BEGIN (* the main program *)
        onetax(* invoke the procedure *)
END.
```

Program tax with procedure onetax

The main program consists of only one statement:

```
BEGIN
        onetax  (* invoke the procedure *)
END.
```

This statement is used to invoke the procedure *onetax*. It is probably apparent that there is no immediate benefit from writing *onetax* as a procedure and invoking it in this way. If we were to require the calculation of the tax on a variety of items, then *onetax* could be invoked several times, each time with only one statement. This is clearly more efficient than writing the entire group of statements contained in the *onetax* procedure several times! For example, suppose we wanted to calculate the tax on three items. The main program would be:

```
BEGIN
        onetax;      (* first invocation *)
        onetax;      (* second invocation *)
        onetax       (* third invocation *)
END.
```

It is very useful and instructive to follow the sequence of steps actually performed by this group of statements. As an aid, imagine a pointer (a "finger") which indicates the next statement to be executed by the computer. If our main program contained only the three statements shown above, the pointer would be positioned to the first of the three when the program starts. We will show this as follows:

```
→onetax;
  onetax;
  onetax
```

When this statement (a procedure invocation) is executed, two important things happen, *in the order given below*.

1   The position of the statement after the procedure invocation is noted and saved for later reference. (We'll show this position with a pointer like this: $\Rightarrow$).
2   The finger pointer (the one that points to the next statement to be executed) is moved to the first executable statement in the named procedure. (There is more to procedure invocation when parameters are included, but we will address this later.)

Now let's follow the action in the procedure invocation and execution.

Step 1.

The program begins execution.

main program	procedure

→ onetax;
  onetax;
  onetax
	PROCEDURE onetax;
	BEGIN
	    writeln('Input cost of item');
	    read(itemcost);

main program	procedure
	(* Compute sales tax on item *)
	salestax := taxrate * itemcost;
	(* Output sales tax *)
	writeln('Item cost is ', itemcost);
	writeln('Sales tax is ', salestax)
	END;

Step 2.

The procedure onetax is invoked. Note the position of the return pointer ($\Rightarrow$) and the next statement pointer ($\rightarrow$).

main program	procedure
onetax;	PROCEDURE onetax;
$\Rightarrow$ onetax;	BEGIN
onetax	$\rightarrow$ writeln('Input cost of item');
	read(itemcost);
	(* Compute sales tax on item *)
	salestax := taxrate * itemcost;
	(* Output sales tax *)
	writeln('Item cost is ', itemcost);
	writeln('Sales tax is ', salestax)
	END;

Step 3.

The statement "writeln ('Input cost of item')" is executed.

main program	procedure
onetax;	PROCEDURE onetax;
$\Rightarrow$ onetax;	BEGIN
onetax	writeln('Input cost of item');
	$\rightarrow$ read(itemcost);
	(* Compute sales tax on item *)
	salestax := taxrate * itemcost;
	(* Output sales tax *)
	writeln('Item cost is ', itemcost);
	writeln('Sales tax is ', salestax)
	END;

Steps 4 through 7.

The other statements in *onetax* are executed. (Note that the comments are ignored during execution.)

main program	*procedure*
onetax;	PROCEDURE onetax;
⇒ onetax;	BEGIN
onetax	writeln('Input cost of item');
	read(itemcost);
	(* Compute sales tax on item *)
	salestax := taxrate * itemcost;
	(* Output sales tax *)
	writeln('Item cost is ', itemcost);
	writeln('Sales tax is ', salestax)
	→END;

Step 8.

The procedure terminates and execution returns to the caller. Note that the return pointer becomes the next statement pointer and, further, that no pointers remain in the procedure.

main program	*procedure*
onetax;	PROCEDURE onetax;
→ onetax;	BEGIN
onetax	writeln('Input cost of item');
	read(itemcost);
	(* Compute sales tax on item *)
	salestax := taxrate * itemcost;
	(* Output sales tax *)
	writeln('Item cost is ', itemcost);
	writeln('Sales tax is ', salestax)
	END;

For each of the two remaining procedure invocations, steps 2 through 8 are repeated, exactly as before (except for the position of the return pointer). Naturally, the potential exists for processing different data values each time. It is in this capability to perform the same actions on different collections of data that we find the real power of the procedure.

Let's test this program by hand execution with some actual numbers. Suppose the three items cost $100, $200, and $300, respectively. These numbers will be the input data for our problem. After the first invocation of the procedure *onetax*, the following lines would be displayed:

```
Item cost is   100.00
Sales tax is     7.00
```

After the second invocation the following is displayed:

```
Item cost is   200.00
Sales tax is    14.00
```

Finally, after the last invocation the following is displayed:

```
Item cost is   300.00
Sales tax is    21.00
```

When to Use a Procedure

Procedures are not necessary in all programs. In fact, many useful programs of hundreds of lines may never use a procedure. So when should we use a procedure? What criteria should be applied in making the decision?

One of the most obvious reasons for writing a sequence of statements as a procedure is that the sequence is used several times in different places in the program. Certainly the program is still correct if those statements are written at each point in the program where they are needed. There are several problems with this approach, however.

First, and most obviously, the program is larger than it needs to be. This makes reading, writing, entering, and maintaining (making changes and correcting errors in) the program more difficult. Further, larger source programs require more of the computer's memory (a very important consideration for users of small computers).

Second, the nature of the computation performed by the program is obscured. We come to expect that a particular computation should be done in the same way everywhere it is needed in our programs. If this is not done, then we become suspicious and wonder, "Why is this code repeated; is there some devious little difference between this and its previous appearance?"

So much for repeated code motivating the use of procedures. Is there another reason for installing procedures in our programs? Yes! And it has nothing to do with repeated code. Grouping statements, such as is done when a procedure is written, suggests that those statements have some singular purpose. A simple example of this is shown below:

```
BEGIN          (* the main program *)
      getinput;
      processdata;
      putresults
END.
```

Each of the lines between BEGIN and END is just a procedure invocation. The procedure names were chosen to be suggestive of the functions performed by the procedures: reading some input, doing some processing of that input, and then printing some results. We have no clues as to the particular processing the program performs, but we do know a great deal about its structure. We know that the statements in procedure *getinput* will handle any details associated with the reading of the input data, that procedure *processdata* will contain those statements forming the heart of the computation, and that procedure *putresults* will manage the display of our results. This section of code is obviously very readable, even without a single comment!

Note that each procedure in the same program could conceivably be written by different programmers. As long as the problem has been carefully subdivided and interaction between the individual solutions has been minimized, each procedure can be totally independent of the others. This ability to allow separate programmers to develop procedures for the same program is very important when a large program (including tens or even hundreds of procedures) is being written.

It may seem that we dwell unnecessarily on program readability. However, it is appropriate to observe at this point that the greatest portion of time spent attending to programs is not that expended on their invention, but rather on their maintenance! That is, more programmer time is consumed in the tasks associated with program correction and modification than is spent in the original creation of the program. Hopefully, the benefits of proper program decomposition into procedures will improve this situation.

Placement of Procedures and Strong Typing

As you learned in Chapter 2, all identifiers used in a Pascal program must be declared (in a header, a CONST declaration or a VAR declaration) before they may be used. This rule also applies to procedures. In order to *declare* a procedure, the entire procedure (the header, local declarations, and executable statements) must be written ahead of the executable statements of the program that uses it. Specifically, the procedures are placed just before the reserved word BEGIN that marks the start of the executable statements of the main program. (We will later see that procedures can also appear *within* other procedures.)

This placement of procedures *before* the statements that use them will probably look a little strange at first. After all, the executable statements in the procedure are not actually performed until some later statement invokes them. So why must we put the procedures first?

To understand the answer to this question we must first understand something of the *strong typing* rules used by Pascal. Pascal restricts the use of identifiers to those contexts where the identifier makes obvious good sense. For example, it is meaningless to attempt to add 4 to the procedure *onetax* shown previously. In a similar fashion, it would not make sense to add 3 to a Boolean variable. The Pascal compiler will detect all attempts to perform such meaningless operations *while it is translating your program*. In some other programming languages, these errors are not detected until later (during the execution of the program) when they may have caused serious problems.

So why does this strong typing require that procedures be declared before they are invoked? Answer: The Pascal compiler must know *before* invocation that an identifier refers to a procedure so it can perform the appropriate type checking!

SECTION 4.2 PROBLEM SOLVING USING SIMPLE PROCEDURES

In this section we present the detailed solution of a problem using simple procedures.

Problem 4.1

Given a 24-hour clock and a time represented as an integer in the form hhmm, *where* hh *represents the hours (00 to 23) and* mm *represents the minutes (00 to 59), determine the time after 5 hours and 23 minutes have elapsed. The result should be expressed in the same form as the input. For example, given the input 1230 (representing 12:30 P.M.), the output should be 1753 (representing 5:53 P.M.).*

This problem can be divided into three subproblems:

SUBPROBLEM 1: Input the time.
SUBPROBLEM 2: Compute the new time.
SUBPROBLEM 3: Display the new time.

Subproblems 1 and 3 can be solved by simple input/output statements. Subproblem 2 requires further analysis. Suppose the input time is 1230 (an integer). In this case, to compute the time 5 hours and 23 minutes later, we could just add 0523 directly to 1230 yielding the proper result, 1753. But our program must work correctly for arbitrary input times. Consider an input time of 2359 (1 minute before midnight). It is obvious that the result should be 0522 (representing 5:22 A.M.), but adding 2359 and 0523 directly yields 2882. This is clearly incorrect.

The difficulty is due to the way the input is presented. We are provided with a single integer in a single "unit" which represents two integers in two different units (hours and minutes). The output must be in the same form, so we can easily see that subproblem 2 can be subdivided into three subproblems:

SUBPROBLEM 2.1: (*Split*) Separate input time into hours and minutes.
SUBPROBLEM 2.2: (*Add*) Add 5 to the hours and 23 to the minutes.
SUBPROBLEM 2.3: (*Join*) Convert hours and minutes to an integer for output.

The overall top-down design of this problem is shown in Figure 4-2.

To solve subproblem 2.1, we must determine how to split an integer such as 1230 into two separate integers, 12 and 30. Integer division and modulus operations, rep-

Figure 4-2 Top-down design of time conversion problem.

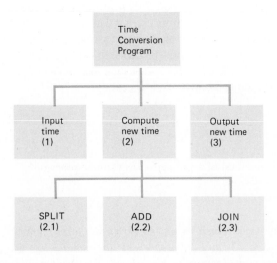

resented in Pascal by the operators DIV and MOD, can be used to achieve such a separation. This technique, which we will examine now, can be used for many other similar problems.

Observe that integer division by 100 effectively removes the rightmost two decimal digits from the number being divided. For example, 1230 DIV 100 equals 12; the 30 has been "removed." Note also that a number MOD 100 effectively yields the rightmost two digits. Thus, 1230 MOD 100 equals 30; the high-order digits have been removed.

Once we have determined the hour and minute components of the input data, we can solve subproblem 2.2 by adding 5 to the hours and 23 to the minutes. But we're not ready to move on to subproblem 2.3 yet since this addition can result in a minutes value greater than 59 or an hours value greater than 23. Therefore, these values may require adjustment before conversion to a single integer. Once again we may use the division operation (the Pascal DIV operator) to determine the number of full hours in our new minutes value and the modulus operation (the Pascal MOD operator) to extract the excess minutes from the new value. Next, subproblem 2.3 converts the hours and minutes back to an integer to be displayed by multiplying the hours by 100 and then adding the minutes.

Consider the hours and minutes resulting from an input value of 2159. After adding minutes, the new minutes value will be 59 plus 23, or 82. This represents 1 hour and 22 minutes, and can be computed in Pascal as 82 DIV 60 (1 hour) and 82 MOD 60 (22 minutes). After adding 5 to the original hours, the hours we extract from the minutes value must be added to the new hours. Then this value must be converted to a number in the range 0 to 23, again using the MOD operator. Using the 2159 input value, we obtain an hours value of 21. Adding 5 hours yields 26, and after adding the 1 hour excess extracted from the minutes value, we have 27 hours. This is converted to 3 hours using the expression 27 MOD 24. The following table summarizes these results.

SUBPROBLEM 2.1

input	hours	minutes
2159	2159 DIV 100 = 21	2159 MOD 100 = 59

SUBPROBLEM 2.2

Combine minutes:	59 + 23 = 82	
Adjust minutes:	82 DIV 60 = 1 hour	
	82 MOD 60 = 22 minutes	

SUBPROBLEM 2.3

Combine hours:	21 + 5 = 26	
Increment hours:	26 + 1 = 27 (if minutes >= 60)	
Adjust hours:	27 MOD 24 = 3 (if hours >= 24)	

We now have sufficient detail to write the algorithm in pseudocode. The result is shown below:

Pseudocode for Problem 4.1

STEP 1 Input time: Get an input value representing the time on the 24-hour clock.
STEP 2 Compute new time.
  STEP 2.1 Separate input time into hours and minutes.
  STEP 2.2 Add 5 hours and 23 minutes.
  STEP 2.3 Convert hours and minutes to an integer appropriate for output.
STEP 3 Display the value resulting from step 2.3

The complete Pascal solution to the problem using procedures and sample output is shown below. Notice the two procedures *split* and *join* were used to convert from the integer representation of a 24-hour time to the equivalent hours and minutes and to convert back to an integer. Also note that nothing would be gained by writing the input and output statements as procedures. *Split* and *join* are useful, however, and are important examples of how various tasks necessary in problem solving can be *encapsulated*. In fact, these procedures could be used in many other problems dealing with times represented on a 24-hour clock. The exercises, for example, include the general problem of adding two arbitrary times to give a result. Having the *split* and *join* procedures already written and tested goes a long way toward producing the solution.

```
PROGRAM timeconv (input, output);
CONST
        hour = 60;      (* minutes per hour *)
        day = 24;       (* hours per day *)
VAR
        itime,          (* the input time *)
        otime;          (* the output time *)
        mins,           (* separate minutes *)
        hrs : integer;  (* separate hours *)


PROCEDURE split;
(* Procedure to separate an integer time in the format *)
(* "hhmm" in variable "itime" into separate hours and     *)
(* minutes in variables "hrs" and "mins".                 *)
BEGIN
        hrs := itime DIV 100;   (*removes minutes *)
        mins := itime MOD 100   (* removes hours *)
END;


PROCEDURE join;
(* Procedure to store into variable "otime" the integer     *)
(* value in the form "hhmm" corresponding to "hrs" hours *)
(* and "mins" minutes. Excess hours in "mins" are added  *)
(* to "hrs", and excess days in "hrs" are removed.        *)
```

```
BEGIN
        hrs := hrs + mins DIV hour;      (* add excess hours *)
        mins := mins MOD hour;          (* remove excess hours *)
        hrs := hrs MOD day;             (* remove excess days *)
        otime := hrs * 100 + mins       (* compute new otime *)
END;

BEGIN  (* the main program *)
        (* Prompt the user for the input data *)
        write ('Enter a time in the form "hhmm": ');
        readln (itime);

        (* Separate itime into hrs and mins *)
        split;

        (* Add 5 hours and 23 minutes *)
        hrs := hrs + 5;
        mins := mins + 23;

        (* Adjust the time, and create new output time *)
        join;

        (* Display the resulting time *)
        writeln ('The time 5:23 later is ', otime)
END.
```

Program timeconv

```
Enter a time in the form "hhmm": 1230
The time 5:23 later is      1753

Enter a time in the form "hhmm": 2150
The time 5:23 later is       313
```

Program timeconv: Sample Executions

EXERCISES FOR SECTION 4.2

1   Determine the output obtained when the following program is executed.

```
PROGRAM velocity (input, output);
VAR  distance, speed, time : integer;
```

```
                        PROCEDURE outspeed;
                        BEGIN
                                speed := distance DIV time;
                                writeln ('Speed is ', speed, 'mph.');
                        END;
(* Main program begins here *)
            BEGIN
                        distance := 100;
                        time := 2;
                        outspeed;
                        distance := 400;
                        time := 10;
                        outspeed
            END.
```

2 Determine the output obtained when the following program is executed.

```
            PROGRAM exercise (input, output);
            VAR  a, b, c : integer;
                        PROCEDURE achange;
                        BEGIN
                            a := a + 1
                        END;
                        PROCEDURE bchange;
                        BEGIN
                            b := b + 2
                        END;
                        PROCEDURE cchange;
                        BEGIN
                            c := c - 1
                        END;
(* Main program begins here *)
            BEGIN
                        a := 1;
                        b := 2;
                        c := 3;
                        achange;
                        bchange;
                        cchange;
                        writeln (a, b, c);
                        achange;
                        achange;
                        writeln (a, b, c)
            END.
```

3 Write a Pascal procedure called *trisum* that computes the sum of the three variables *num1*, *num2*, and *num3* (assume the variables are declared as integer in the main program), and stores the sum in the variable *total*.

4 Write a Pascal procedure called *mean* that divides the value in the integer variable *total* by 3 (using integer division) and stores the result in the integer variable *average*.

5 Write a complete Pascal program called *compute* that obtains three integer values for variables *num1*, *num2*, and *num3*, then invokes the procedures *trisum* and *mean* from problems 3 and 4, and finally displays the average value with an appropriate message. Declare all the variables in the main program.

6 Write a procedure called *circle* that computes the area of a circle given the radius declared as real in the main program.

7 An integer variable *nickels* represents a number of nickels. Describe the purpose of the following procedure (assume the variables *nickels* and *value* are declared in the main program).

```
PROCEDURE worth;
BEGIN
    value := 0.05 * nickels
END;
```

8 The integer variables *nickels*, *dimes*, and *quarters* represent the number of nickels, dimes, and quarters, respectively, in the drawer of a cash register. Write a procedure called *money* to determine the equivalent number of dollars in the cash register, storing the result in the real variable *dollars*. Assume all variables are declared in the main program.

SECTION 4.3 PROCEDURES WITH PARAMETERS

Procedures are most effective when they are self-contained and independent program modules. The reason for this is that when a problem is very complicated, the programs written to solve the problem will most likely be just as complex. In order to manage an effective solution of the problem, we apply a top-down design and divide the problem into subproblems. If the corresponding procedures which solve the subproblems are self-contained modules, we can solve and test each procedure *independently* of any of the other procedures. This generally breaks a difficult problem into more manageable parts. The divide and conquer approach is commonly used by managers of large programming projects.

The simple procedures used previously are not self-contained since they operate on specific variables declared in the main program. In order to make procedures self-contained programs, many high-level languages allow information to be *passed* to and from procedures by objects known as ***parameters***. Parameters enable procedures to manipulate different sets of values, and so the same procedure can be used several times in the same program. Before we discuss parameters with Pascal procedures, we'll first consider how a procedure is similar to a program.

A computer program, just like a digital computer, can be considered as an information processor with input and output data. Similarly, if a procedure is considered as a self-contained program, then it is also an information processor with input and output (parameters). See Figure 4-3.

Information and data can be provided as input to the procedure, and during execution the procedure will produce output.

Let us return to our triangle area problem. Suppose we wish to write a self-contained, independent Pascal procedure to find the area of a triangle. What information is needed by this procedure? Certainly, knowing the altitude and base would be sufficient input. The output is the area of the triangle. In a Pascal procedure this information (known as the *parameters*) can be included in the procedure header. Thus, for the triangle area problem we have the following parameters:

Input parameters: Altitude and base

Output parameter: Area

The actual Pascal procedure (*triangle*) including parameters is shown below:

```
PROCEDURE triangle (altitude, base : real; VAR area: real);
(* A procedure to compute the area of a triangle, given *)
(* the base and altitude.                                *)
BEGIN
      area := 0.5 * altitude * base
END;
```

Procedure triangle

In Pascal, the parameters listed in the program header are called **_formal parameters_**. They serve as placeholders for the actual values supplied when the procedure is invoked.

Figure 4-3   Program and procedure similarities.

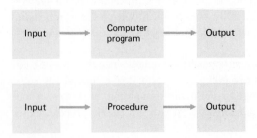

In the procedure *triangle*, what is the value of the altitude? Since altitude is a formal parameter, it has no value until the procedure is invoked by the calling program that will pass the actual value of the altitude.

Let us consider the procedure header in more detail. After the procedure name we have listed the input parameters (called *value parameters* in Pascal) *altitude* and *base*, followed by a colon and the data type of the parameters. Pascal requires the data types of all parameters to be specified in the parameter list. The input parameter list ends with a semicolon. Following this is the output parameter list (called *variable parameters* in Pascal). This list begins with the reserved word VAR followed by the output parameters, including their data type. Figure 4-4 illustrates this.

Let us summarize our discussion of the parameter list for this procedure. The input (value) parameters *altitude* and *base* are of type real, and the output (variable, or VAR in Pascal) parameter *area* is also of type real. We will consider value and variable parameters in more detail in Chapter 7. At this point it is important to remember the following facts in order to write self-contained and independent procedures:

- Any input information or data needed by a procedure should appear in the formal parameter list as input (value) parameters (that is, without the reserved word VAR).
- Any results determined by the procedure that are required by the calling program should appear in the formal parameter list as output (variable) parameters and must be preceded by the reserved word VAR.

Once more it is important to realize that the parameters listed in the program header are formal parameters. In fact, changing the names of the parameters will not change the effects of the procedure. For example, consider the following version of procedure *triangle*:

```
PROCEDURE triangle (height, tribase : real; VAR triarea: real);
(* A procedure to compute the area of a triangle, given *)
(* the base and height.*)
BEGIN
        triarea := 0.5 * height * tribase
END;
```

Procedure triangle, revised

Figure 4-4   Procedure header with formal parameters.

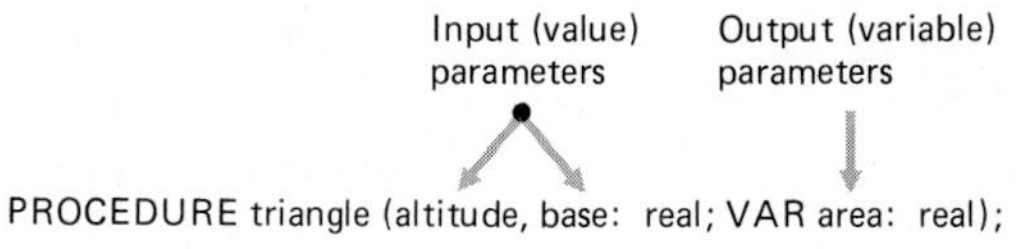

```
PROCEDURE triangle (altitude, base:  real; VAR area:  real);
```

This version of the procedure is effectively the same as the previous one. The input parameters *altitude* and *base* have been renamed *height* and *tribase*, and the output parameter *area* has been renamed *triarea*. The identifiers used to name the formal parameters are only placeholders for the actual values, and so do not depend on the identifiers used in other procedures and the main program.

Later (in Chapter 7) we will see that VAR parameters can be used for both input and output. We will avoid using VAR parameters in this way until they are discussed further.

Procedure Invocation with Parameters

There is one other important aspect of procedure parameters, specifically, how the actual values for the formal parameters are supplied and retrieved. Let us begin by returning once again to our triangle area problem. We would certainly use a procedure to perform the area calculation if we were interested in obtaining the area of several different triangles. For example, suppose we wish to compute the area of a triangle with an altitude of 3.0 units and a base of 4.0 units and store the area in a variable named *triarea*. The following procedure invocation in the main program would perform the task:

```
triangle (3.0, 4.0, triarea)
```

The parenthesized list following the procedure name is called the ***actual parameter list***. The order of the actual parameters in the procedure invocation must be the same as the order of the formal parameters in the procedure header.

The procedure invocation statement is executed in several steps. For each of the input (value) formal parameters a copy of the actual parameter's value is stored in a new location in memory and given the name of the corresponding formal parameter. Instead of creating a new memory location for the output (variable) parameters, the original memory location for each is given an additional name (an alias), as specified by the corresponding formal output (variable) parameters. This difference is important, as we will soon see.

Then the location of the statement following the procedure invocation is "remembered," and the first executable statement of the procedure being invoked is executed. These last steps are, as you recall, exactly the same as for the simple procedures (without parameters) we covered earlier.

Let us apply these steps to the invocation of the first triangle area procedure. First, the values 3.0 and 4.0 are stored in new memory locations named *altitude* and *base*, respectively. Then an additional name, *area*, is associated with the memory location for the variable named *triarea*. This new name is an alias for *triarea* known *only* in *procedure* triangle. The correspondence between actual and formal parameters is shown in Figure 4-5. Notice the actual parameters, 3 and 4, are passed to the procedure and stored in the memory locations for the formal input (or value) parameters, *altitude* and *base*. The formal output (variable) parameter *area* and the actual parameter *triarea* refer to the same memory location containing the result that is passed back to the main program. Figure 4-6 illustrates these concepts.

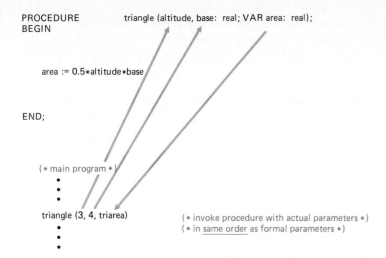

```
PROCEDURE        triangle (altitude, base: real; VAR area: real);
BEGIN


        area := 0.5*altitude*base



END;



( * main program * )
    •
    •
    •
triangle (3, 4, triarea)        ( * invoke procedure with actual parameters * )
    •                           ( * in same order as formal parameters * )
    •
    •
```

Figure 4-5   Invoking a procedure and passing actual parameters.

Pascal verifies (during compilation) that the types of the actual parameters and the corresponding formal parameters match. If the type of at least one actual parameter does not match the type of the corresponding formal parameter, the compiler will issue an appropriate error message, and no executable program will be produced.

An actual parameter that corresponds to an input (value) parameter may be a constant or an expression, since a copy of its value is created when the procedure is invoked. For example, the following program segment could be used to compute the area of

Figure 4-6   Names and locations of parameters.

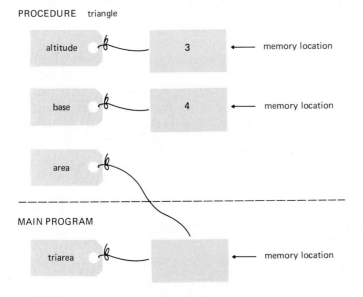

PROCEDURE   triangle

altitude ——— 3 ◄——— memory location

base ——— 4 ◄——— memory location

area

MAIN PROGRAM

triarea ◄——— memory location

the same triangle as in our previous example (the variables *base*, *height*, and *triarea* must be declared as real variables in the main program):

```
height := 3.0;
base := 4.0;
triangle (height, base, triarea);   (*invoke procedure*)
```

Or we could read the values for *height* and *base* prior to invoking the procedure:

```
read (height, base);
triangle (height, base, triarea);   (*invoke procedure*)
```

The most important points to remember about actual parameters are:

■ Those actual parameters corresponding to the input (value) parameters of the procedure header must have a value before the procedure is invoked.
■ Those actual parameters corresponding to the output (variable) parameters of the procedure header must be specified as variables.

In the above example, *height* and *base* must have values before the procedure is invoked since they act as input to the procedure. Further, it is mandatory that a real variable be supplied as the third actual parameter to *triangle*; a real constant or expression will not be allowed for a real formal parameter that is declared an output (variable) parameter since neither have named memory locations associated with them.

Now let us write a complete Pascal program that will invoke the self-contained procedure *triangle* twice with different actual input (value) parameters. In the main program we will declare variables *height*, *base*, *triarea* for the triangle area problem. Actually, we could use the same variable names as those used in the procedure *triangle*. This would make no difference since the variables listed in the procedure header are just formal parameters that act as placeholders.

The program *compute* (shown below) will calculate the area of two different triangles and output the results. Notice there is a procedure *printdata* to display the results, which avoids repeating the same sequence of statements after each procedure invocation. Also observe that the procedure *printdata* has no output (variable) parameters in the formal parameter list since none are required for this procedure. In general, a procedure declaration may contain no parameters (such as a simple procedure), or only input (value) parameters, or only output (variable) parameters, or finally both input (value) and output (variable) parameters. We will consider examples of all these cases in the remainder of this chapter.

```
PROGRAM compute (input, output);
(* Compute the area of two different triangles using a *)
(* procedure with parameters                           *)
VAR
        height,       (* height of a triangle *)
```

```
        base,              (* base of a triangle *)
        triarea : real;    (* area of a triangle *)
PROCEDURE triangle (altitude, base : real, VAR area : real);
(* Compute area of triangle from altitude and base *)
BEGIN
        area := 0.5 * altitude * base
END;


PROCEDURE printdata (altitude, base, area : real);
(* Display altitude, base, and area of a triangle *)
BEGIN
        writeln ('The altitude of the triangle is ', altitude : 5 : 2);
        writeln ('The base of the triangle is ', base : 5 : 2);
        writeln ('The area of the triangle is ', area : 7 : 2)
END;


BEGIN  (* the main program *)
        (* Find area of the first triangle *)
        height := 3;
        base := 4;
        triangle (height, base, triarea);
        printdata (height, base, triarea);
        (* Find area of the second triangle *)
        height := 10;
        base := 6;
        triangle (height, base, triarea);
        printdata (height, base, triarea)
END.
```

Program compute

```
The altitude of the triangle is 3.00
The base of the triangle is 4.00
The area of the triangle is 6.00
The altitude of the triangle is 10.00
The base of the triangle is 6.00
The area of the triangle is 30.00
```

Output of program compute

Local and Global Variables

Recall that in a simple procedure (no parameters) the variables or constants referenced by the procedure are declared in the main program. These variables are called *global variables* since any procedure in the main program can reference them. However, to make the procedures independent of the main program, we have to pass the variables as parameters. Since a procedure can be a self-contained program, variables, constants, and even other procedures can be declared within the procedure. Such declarations are local to the procedure. **Local variables** are declared in a procedure and are known only within that procedure. For example, consider the following procedure *timeout* that has one input (value) parameter (*time*) and prints the time from a 24-hour clock in terms of hours and minutes with a colon between. Thus, if the actual value parameter is the integer 1230, the formatted output would be

The time is 12:30

```
PROCEDURE timeout (time : integer);
(* Display time in the form "hhmm" on the output as *)
(* hours and minutes separated by a colon.          *)
CONST  colon = ':';         (* local constant    *)
VAR hours, mins : integer;  (* local variables   *)
BEGIN
        hours := time DIV 100;
        mins := time MOD 100;
        writeln ('The time is ', hours : 2, colon, mins : 2)
END;
```

Procedure timeout

In this procedure the variables *hours* and *mins* are local variables known only within the procedure. Also, *colon* is a local constant. Later in Chapter 7 we will find that the input (value) parameter *time* can also be considered as a local variable.

This procedure is completely self-contained and independent of any other procedure and of the main program, since any value can be used for the actual parameter. The only requirement is that the formal and actual parameters match. In fact, we can declare this procedure (and any such self-contained procedure) *as is* in any main program as long as the procedure name *timeout* was not declared previously for some other purpose.

What if the main program has declared variables with the same names as *hours* and *mins*? In Pascal it makes no difference if the names are identical. Although they have the same identifiers, in the procedure the local variables are used, whereas in the main program the global variables are used. In the procedure the local variables have *precedence* over the global variables, and in the main program they are unknown. The obvious advantage of this is that procedures previously written can be declared in any program with a minimal amount of effort and (hopefully) no modifications. We will consider local and global variables in more detail in Chapter 7.

1   Identify the input (value) and output (variable) parameters of the following procedure header:

PROCEDURE check (x, y, z : integer; VAR a, b, c : integer);

2   What is the difference between a formal parameter and an actual parameter?

3   Consider the following procedure header:

PROCEDURE start (time, space : real; VAR day : real; sign : char);

Suppose the following procedure invocation is in the main program:

start (3.5, 6.0, hour, 'Z')

Identify the formal parameters and the actual parameters. After the procedure is invoked, what are the values of the formal parameters specified in the procedure header?

4   Consider the following procedure header:

PROCEDURE test (x, y : integer; VAR z : real);

Find the error in the following procedure invocation, assuming *time* is a real variable:

test (1, 2.0, time)

5   Consider the following procedure header:

PROCEDURE test (x, y : real; VAR z : real);

Find the error in the following procedure invocation:

test (2.0, 3.0, 4.0)

6   Consider the following procedure header:

PROCEDURE right (VAR z : real; x : char);

Find an error in the following procedure invocation, assuming *zero* is a real variable):

right (zero, Z);

Exercises 7 through 12 refer to the following program:

```
PROGRAM scope (input, output);
VAR tum, num, temp : integer;
PROCEDURE prog (a, b : integer; VAR c : integer);
VAR clock : integer;
BEGIN
        clock := a * b;
        clock := clock + 1;
        c := clock + a;
        writeln (a, b, c, clock)
END;
(* Main program *)
BEGIN
        tum := 1;
        num := 2;
        prog (tum, num, temp);
        writeln (temp);
        tum := 0;
        num := 1;
        prog (num, tum, temp);
        writeln (temp)
END.
```

7 Identify the global variables of the main program.

8 Identify the local variable declared in the procedure *prog*.

9 Identify the formal parameters of the procedure *prog*. Determine the input (value) parameters and the output (variable) parameters.

10 Determine the actual value parameters when the procedure is first invoked.

11 Determine the actual value parameters when the procedure is invoked the second time.

12 Determine the output of the program. How many lines of output are produced?

SECTION 4.4 PROBLEM SOLVING USING PROCEDURES WITH PARAMETERS

In this section we apply procedures with parameters to problem solving. In particular we include a detailed discussion of the three major components of problem solving: procedure analysis, problem solution, and computer solution. Consider the following problem.

Problem 4.2

The input contains the coordinates in the plane (Cartesian coordinates) of the three vertices of a triangle as real numbers. Determine and display the area of the triangle represented by this data.

Problem Analysis

Figure 4-7 shows one possible set of three input points, each consisting of an x and y value, with the appropriate edges drawn between the points to form a triangle. The three sides are labeled with the letters a, b, and c. The vertices of the triangle are represented by the capital letters A, B, and C. We are provided with input data having the x and y coordinates of each vertex: $A = (x_1, y_1)$, $B = (x_2, y_2)$, and $C = (x_3, y_3)$. Given the coordinates of the vertices, we can compute the length of the three sides by using the formula (from the Pythagorean theorem of analytic geometry) for the distance between two points. For example, the distance between the points represented by (x_1, y_1) and (x_2, y_2) is given by the formula

$$\text{Distance} = \sqrt{(x_1 - x_2)^2 + (y_1 - y_2)^2}.$$

Now, given that we can compute the length of the three sides, we have to compute the area of the triangle. Fortunately, there is a formula from geometry (Heron's formula) that says, given the lengths of the three sides of a triangle, a, b, and c, the area is computed by

$$\text{Area} = \sqrt{s\,(s - a)\,(s - b)\,(s - c)},$$

where s is one-half the perimeter of the triangle. That is,

$$s = (a + b + c) / 2.$$

Figure 4-7   Triangle specified by vertices in the plane.

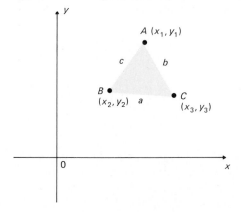

Let us work through a specific example. Suppose the x and y coordinates of the vertices are the following:

$$A = (0,0) \qquad B = (0,3) \qquad C = (4,0)$$

The lengths of the three sides of the triangle formed by the vertices A, B, and C are

$$a = 3 \qquad b = 4 \qquad c = 5.$$

The value s (one-half the perimeter) in this case is

$$s = (3 + 4 + 5) / 2 = 6.$$

Then the area is

$$\begin{aligned} \text{Area} &= \sqrt{6\,(6 - 3)\,(6 - 4)\,(6 - 5)} \\ &= \sqrt{36} \\ &= 6. \end{aligned}$$

Now we have analyzed the problem sufficiently to allow us to begin our top-down design (see Figure 4-8).

Top-Down Design

This problem can be divided into four subproblems:

SUBPROBLEM 1: Obtain the coordinates of the vertices.
SUBPROBLEM 2: Compute the lengths of the three sides.
SUBPROBLEM 3: Compute the area of the triangle.
SUBPROBLEM 4: Display the area of the triangle.

Since we must obtain three sets of coordinates, we will write a procedure called *vertex* to input a single set of coordinates. Also, we must compute the length of the

Figure 4-8 Top-down design of triangle area problem.

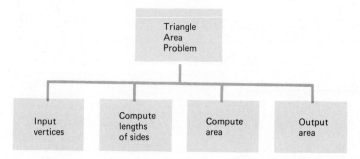

three sides, so a procedure called *length* to compute the distance between any two points would be appropriate. Finally, a procedure called *findarea* to compute the area of a triangle using Heron's formula will be written in case we are required to perform this computation again.

Algorithm

Next, we must refine each subproblem and write the algorithm. The pseudocode for the algorithm would be as follows:

Pseudocode for Problem 4.2

STEP 1. Obtain the coordinates of the three vertices from the input by calling the input procedure (*vertex*) three times with different actual parameters.
STEP 2. Compute the length of each side of the triangle by calling the appropriate procedure (*length*) three times, each time with the appropriate parameters.
STEP 3. Compute the area of the triangle using Heron's formula.
STEP 4. Display the area of the triangle.

Computer Solution

Now we can begin writing a procedure to solve each subproblem. The procedure to obtain a vertex from the input data, called *vertex*, will have two output (variable) parameters. Let us call these parameters x and y to represent the x and y coordinates of the point to be returned to the calling program. The procedure itself is relatively simple:

```
PROCEDURE vertex (VAR x, y : real);
(* Procedure to input x and y coordinates of a point *)
BEGIN
        write ('Please enter x coordinate of point: ');
        readln (x);
        write ('Please enter y coordinate of point: ');
        readln (y);
        writeln ('The coordinates are: ', x, y)
END;
```

Procedure vertex

Next a procedure to determine the distance between two given points, say (x_1, y_1) and (x_2, y_2), must be written. In this case the coordinates are input (value) parameters. The distance, represented by formal parameter *distance*, is an output (variable) parameter, since this result must be returned to the main program. Note the additional use of local variables and the built-in square root function (*sqrt*) in the procedure. The *sqrt* function does not have to be declared since it is predeclared in Pascal.

```
PROCEDURE length (x1, y1, x2, y2 : real; VAR distance : real);
    (* Determine distance between the points (x1,y1) and *)
    (* (x2,y2), placing the result in "distance".         *)
    VAR
        xchange,            (* change in x, squared *)
        ychange : real;     (* change in y, squared *)
    BEGIN
    (* compute terms in square root expression *)
        xchange := sqr (x1 − x2);
        ychange := sqr (y1 − y2);
    (* compute "distance" using distance formula *)
        distance := sqrt (xchange + ychange)
    END;
```

Procedure length

Finally, we must write a procedure called *findarea* to determine the area of the triangle using Heron's formula. Again, local variables are used to store the perimeter of the triangle. The input (value) parameters are the lengths of the three sides *a, b,* and *c,* and the output (variable) parameter is the area of the triangle.

```
PROCEDURE findarea (a, b, c : real; VAR area : real);
(* Determine area of triangle with sides a, b, c, *)
(* placing the result in "area". *)
VAR
        s,          (* half-perimeter of triangle *)
        perimeter : real;   (* perimeter of triangle *)
BEGIN
(* Compute perimeter and half-perimeter of triangle *)
        perimeter := a + b + c;
        s := perimeter / 2;
(* Compute area of triangle using Heron's formula *)
        area := sqrt (s * (s − a) * (s − b) * (s − c) )
END;
```

Procedure findarea

Figure 4-7 shows the relation between the variables used in the program and their physical interpretation. Now, let's complete the program by combining the procedures with the main program. The program *Heron* is shown below. The display that would result from one possible execution follows the program.

```
PROGRAM Heron (input, output);
(* Determine the area of a triangle given the coordinates *)
(* of the vertices. Heron's formula is utilized for the     *)
(* area calculation.                                        *)
VAR
    x1, y1,          (* coordinates of first vertex *)
    x2, y2,          (* coordinates of second vertex *)
    x3, y3,          (* coordinates of third vertex *)
    sidea,                   (* length of side a *)
    sideb,                   (* length of side b *)
    sidec,                   (* length of side c *)
    area : real;             (* area of triangle *)

PROCEDURE vertex (VAR x, y : real);
(* Procedure to input x and y coordinates of a point *)
BEGIN
    write ('Please enter x coordinate of point: ');
    readln (x);
    write ('Please enter y coordinate of point: ');
    readln (y);
    writeln ('The coordinates are: ', x, y)
END;

PROCEDURE length (x1, y1, x2, y2 : real, VAR distance : real);
(* Determine distance between the points (x1,y1) and *)
(* (x2,y2), placing the result in "distance".        *)
VAR
    xchange,         (* change in x, squared *)
    ychange : real;      (* change in y, squared *)
BEGIN
    (* Compute terms in square root expression *)
    xchange := sqr (x1 − x2);
    ychange := sqr (y1 − y2);
    (* Compute "distance" using distance formula *)
    ldistance := sqrt (xchange + ychange)
END;

PROCEDURE findarea (a, b, c : real; VAR area : real);
(* Determine area of triangle with sides a, b, c, *)
```

```
                    (* placing the result in "area".                    *)
                    VAR
                        s,           (* half perimeter of triangle *)
                        perimeter(* perimeter of triangle *)
                    BEGIN
                        (* Compute perimeter and half-perimeter of triangle *)
                        perimeter := a + b + c;
                        s := perimeter / 2;
                        (* Compute area of triangle using Heron's formula *)
                        area := sqrt (s * (s − a) * (s − b) * (s − c) )
                    END;

                    (* Main program for problem 4.2 *)
                    BEGIN
                        (* Input the coordinates of the three vertices *)
                        vertex (x1, y1);
                        vertex (x2, y2);
                        vertex (x3, y3);
                        (* Determine the length of the sides, saving the *)
                        (* results in sidea, sideb, and sidec.           *)
                        length (x1, y1, x2, y2, sidea);
                        length (x1, y1, x3, y3, sideb);
                        length (x2, y2, x3, y3, sidec);
                        (* Determine the area of the triangle *)
                        findarea (sidea, sideb, sidec, area);
                        (* Display the computed area *)
                        writeln ('The area of the triangle is ', area:7:2)
                    END.
```

Program Heron

Please enter x coordinate of point: 0
Please enter y coordinate of point: 0
Please enter x coordinate of point: 0
Please enter y coordinate of point: 3
Please enter x coordinate of point: 4
Please enter y coordinate of point: 0
The area of the triangle is   6.00

Program Heron: Sample Execution

1   Determine the exact output of the following program.

```
PROGRAM main (input, output);
VAR a, b, c : integer;
PROCEDURE sub (x : integer);
VAR a, b : integer;
BEGIN
        a := 1;
        b := 2;
        x := a + b;
        writeln (a, b, x)
END;
BEGIN (* Main program *)
        a := 3;
        b := 5;
        c := 4;
        sub (c);
        writeln (a, b, c)
END.
```

2   Write a procedure called *cube* which has an input (value) parameter called *length* and an output (variable) parameter called *volume*. The procedure should compute the volume of the cube having an edge of the specified length. All variables are real.

3   Write a procedure called *magnitude* which has two input (value) parameters *x1* and *x2* and an output (variable) parameter *distance*. The procedure should compute the absolute distance between the points *x1* and *x2*. All variables are real.

4   Write a procedure called *digit* which has an input (value) parameter called *number* and an output (variable) parameter called *lowest*. The procedure should extract the units digit from the value of *number* and return it in *lowest*. For example, if *number* is 234, the value stored in *lowest* would be 4, the units digit. If *number* is 1200, the value stored in *lowest* would be 0. (Hint: Use the MOD operator.)

Consider the following problem. A rectangular floor measuring 12 feet by 15 feet is partially covered by circular rugs. The radius of one rug is 1 foot; the radius of the other is 2 feet. Exercises 5, 6, and 7 are concerned with finding the area of the uncovered part of the floor.

5   Write a procedure with two formal parameters that determines the area of a circle. The first formal parameter is the radius, and the second is the corresponding area. Assume both are real.

6   Write a procedure with three formal parameters that computes the area of a rectangle with a given length and width.

7   Write a complete Pascal program that includes the procedures developed in exercises 5 and 6. The program should include procedure invocations to determine the area of each circle and a procedure invocation to determine the area of the rectangular floor. Then the main program should determine the uncovered area of the floor and display that result.

SECTION 4.5 TOP-DOWN DESIGN AND TESTING

The most difficult part of top-down design is often making the decisions concerning the division of work. At the beginning of a design it is not always possible to see problems which may arise during the solution of a lower-level problem. These difficulties are invariably due to two reasons: the inappropriate division of the work involved in the problem solution or inappropriate choice of data structures (how data is stored and processed). This latter problem will be taken up in more detail in a later chapter. The former problem, inappropriate work division, can frequently be attributed to an incomplete understanding of the problem at hand.

Regardless of the source of the difficulty, errors in design should not be considered minor problems to be corrected and forgotten or "black marks" to be hidden from view. If there are problems, each design difficulty should be analyzed carefully to identify the source of the problem. If this approach is used, the designer will benefit by being less likely to make the same mistakes when similar problems are encountered in other design tasks.

Next, by means of example, we will give the first levels of subdivision in a moderately large problem. By doing this, we hope to convince you that large problems really can be readily decomposed into simpler parts. The solution includes some examples of how decisions are made in Pascal programs. The first decision-making constructs will be developed in detail in Chapter 5.

Spelling Checking

A program frequently used by organizations that do a great deal of text processing is a spelling checker. This program attempts to identify each of the misspelled words in a piece of text and display the line number in which the misspelled word appears. The program typically has a list of correctly spelled words (a dictionary) available for reference.

Our first version of the solution is as follows:

STEP 1 Read the text.
STEP 2 Find all misspelled words, and print them with their line numbers.

A little analysis is appropriate before proceeding too quickly to the next step. We need to determine the maximum size of the input text. If we cannot determine a maximum size or if the maximum size is larger than the available data storage in our computer system, it will not be possible to complete step 1. To avoid these problems, a better approach might be to read only a portion of the text, process it, and then repeat until all the text has been processed. Our revised first version might then be:

STEP 1 Read a suitably sized portion of the text.
STEP 2 Find all misspelled words in the portion just read, and print them with their line numbers.
STEP 3 If more text remains to be processed, return to step 1.

We are now in a position to refine any of the three steps in our revised first version. To refine step 1, we should decide what "a suitably sized portion" is to be. Many different choices make sense, but in this development we will assume the portion to be read is a single line. This will help us keep a record of the line number on which misspelled words appear as well. Here, then, is the refinement of step 1 (remember that we are processing one line at a time):

STEP 1.1 Set the number of words to zero.
STEP 1.2 If we are at the end of the line, then skip it (recall *readln's* treatment of the end of line) and proceed to step 1.4.
STEP 1.3 Read the next word, increment the number of words read, and return to step 1.2.
STEP 1.4 Increment the line number. (We will start with line number set to zero.)

Step 2 is the essence of the spelling checker. We assume that the dictionary can be searched for a particular word, resulting in either an indication that the word was found or that it was not found. This portion of the program will not be shown here. An advantage of the top-down development procedure is that we can assume a particular task can be done and we can develop the rest of the program even if the procedure that accomplishes that task has not been completed. Here, then, is our refinement of step 2.

STEP 2.1 Repeat steps 2.2 through 2.4 for each of the words found in step 1.
STEP 2.2 Search the dictionary for the current word.
STEP 2.3 If the word was found (it was spelled correctly), then no action is necessary.
STEP 2.4 If the word was not found (it was misspelled), print the line number and the word.

Step 3 is rather straightforward and will not be refined further in this discussion.

Let us execute this "program" in its current form. (You should continually do this with your own programs to convince yourself that the program is working as you expected. There are few reasons for a Pascal program to fail if you have checked it thoroughly during development!)

Assume our input has several lines of text as follows:

Every formula which the Analytical Engine can be
required to compute consists of certain algebraical
operations to be performed upon given letters, and of
certain other modifications depending on the numerical
value assigned to those letters.[1]

Although we haven't explicitly stated it, we now realize that our program must take into account punctuation, hyphenated words, and various forms like plurals. We need not concern ourselves with this right now, but later refinements need to address such concerns.

Step 1 will process the first line of text:

Every formula which the Analytical Engine can be

and produce the following list of words (which have been written in lowercase letters for conformity):

every
formula
which
the
analytical
engine
can
be

After the word *be* has been read from the input line, we discover that no more words are present, and we then turn to step 2 to process these eight words, with the line number equal to 1.

Step 2 will first attempt to find the word *every* in the dictionary. Since this is spelled correctly, and is probably in most dictionaries, no output will occur. The word *formula* is checked with similar results. The other words on the line are checked, one after another, until step 2 reaches the word *analytical*. While this word is spelled correctly, assume it is not in the dictionary. Since our assumption was that all correctly spelled words were in the dictionary, we will assume that *analytical* is misspelled. (Most sophisticated spelling checkers will permit the use of supplementary dictionaries and modification of existing dictionaries.) Therefore, step 2.4 will display a message something like, "Line 1, analytical."

Once all the words on line 1 have been processed, step 3 determines if more lines are present. Since there are, we return to step 1 to process the next line. Eventually step 3 will find no more input, and the program will terminate.

[1]Charles Babbage and His Calculating Engines, Philip and Emily Morrison, editors, Dover Publications, New York, 1961.

At the outset we must realize that testing a program does not guarantee it will *never* fail. Testing can only be used to show the presence of errors, not their absence.

Still it would be foolish to assume a program works correctly without doing some testing since careful testing often catches most errors. There are two important parts to testing which we consider here: the selection of test data and the top-down and bottom-up testing of a program.

Test data selection should be made with the intended application of the program in mind. In many cases test data is best collected from those people who will be using the program when it is complete. This has two benefits. First, the test data is very realistic, as it is a sampling of real data. Second, it will locate possible failings in the documentation of what the program expects as input data.

For example, suppose we have a program that requires a three digit number in columns 1 through 3 of an input line. A user may believe the first three columns may have any number, with leading, trailing, or embedded blanks, and prepare test data using that assumption. Since the program will likely fail unless the data is properly prepared, a problem has been located early and can be corrected before the program is put into production.

Incidentally, most good production programs will perform exhaustive checking of the input data to assure compliance with expectations. It is not unusual to find that more than half the code in a program is concerned with data validation.

In addition to testing typical data, it is important to test exceptional cases to ensure that incorrect values will not cause the program to fail.

Incremental testing of a program can proceed in two directions, sometimes simultaneously. *Top-down* testing is done by exercising the procedures at the top of the development tree, while *bottom-up* testing exercises the low-level procedures before they are joined with others.

Since top-down testing is often done before all the procedures have been written, it is necessary to fake the program into believing it is complete. After all, considering the spelling checker program, we assumed the existence of a correct procedure to obtain the next word from the input and of a procedure to determine if a word could be found in a dictionary. To perform this sleight of hand, we use very simple procedures known as *stubs*. A stub is just a procedure that behaves exactly like the "real thing," except it yields results that are not necessarily correct but which are predetermined. Stubs also allow us to determine that the formal and actual parameters are in agreement.

Let us consider the use of stubs in top-down testing of the spelling checker. Rather than produce a procedure which gets the next word from an input line (taking care of punctuation, hyphenation, and so forth) we might produce a stub which just returns one of a collection of predefined words, some spelled correctly and others spelled incorrectly. (Note that it is imperative for us to know what the stub will do so we can interpret the output.)

We might also write a stub for the dictionary search. Instead of processing an entire dictionary (which typically requires sophisticated search techniques), we might just search a brief list of those correctly spelled words which the *get-a-word* stub could produce.

Using these two stubs and the remainder of our program, we can get everything working together correctly. Next, we could write the *real* procedure to get the words from the input and keep our stub for the dictionary search. If this fails, we know the problem is in the input procedure and not in any of the other coding which was already tested. Finally, we replace the dictionary search stub with the real procedure.

Bottom-up testing proceeds in the other direction. That is, the individual solutions to the smallest subproblems are tested first and then combined to produce the larger solution to the entire problem. This form of testing requires that small main programs be written to test each small subproblem solution. In addition, these small subproblem solutions will have to be tested by a main program to ensure that they will function well together.

While some programmers may choose to use top-down testing or bottom-up testing exclusively, most of the time a combination of the approaches is used. Whichever you choose, be certain to select test data carefully, since only by doing so can you hope to obtain a solution that is close to perfect!

SECTION 4.6 TESTING AND DEBUGGING TECHNIQUES

If you have written a procedure with parameters that is a self-contained program, then you should test your procedure with various inputs. The approach is similar to the testing of programs discussed in the previous chapter. However, since we must pass the actual parameters, we can simulate or imitate the execution of the main program by providing some actual parameters to the procedure as test cases.

One common approach to testing is to insert *read* and *write* statements to aid in debugging. These *read* and *write* statements can be safely removed after the procedure has been debugged.

Let us consider a specific example. Here is a procedure that computes the average of three integers:

```
PROCEDURE mean (num1, num2, num3 : integer;
        VAR average : real);
VAR total : integer;
BEGIN
  total := num1 + num2 + num3;
  average := total / 3
END;
```

To test this procedure, we can write a program that reads the three numbers and passes these values to the procedure. We can insert a *write* statement either in the procedure or in the main program to verify the performance of the procedure. The following is a sample test program that includes a *write* statement in the procedure for debugging. This statement will be removed after the procedure has been debugged.

```
PROGRAM test (input, output);
(* Program to test a procedure *)
VAR
      value1, value2, value3 : integer;
      avg : real;
PROCEDURE mean (num1, num2, num3 : integer; VAR average : real);
VAR total : integer;
BEGIN
  total := num1 + num2 + num3;
  average := total / 3;
            (* DEBUG WRITE STATEMENT *)
          writeln ('Average for test case is ', average:7:2)
END;
(* Main program *)
BEGIN
      write ('Enter three numbers to test: ');
      readln (value1, value2, value3);
      (* call procedure *)
      mean (value1, value2, value3, avg)
END.
```

Program test

Notice that the debug *write* statement could have been inserted in the main program after the procedure invocation. In this case the actual (output) parameter in the main program is called *avg*. So the write statement would be as follows:

```
writeln ('Average for test case is ', avg:7:2)
```

When the problems become complex and the programs more difficult to manage, the employment of debug *write* statements will become increasingly useful in the testing and debugging phase.

The following list gives some points to keep in mind when testing and debugging procedures.

PASCAL REMINDERS

- Procedures must be declared and are placed after the constant and variable declarations but before the main program's executable statements.
- A procedure is invoked by writing the procedure's name followed by the parenthesized actual parameter list (if needed).

- The executable statements of a procedure are enclosed by the reserved words BEGIN and END.
- A procedure must end with a semicolon.
- The actual parameters must match the type and the order specified for the corresponding formal parameters.
- Actual parameters corresponding to input (value) parameters must have a value before the procedure is invoked.
- Actual parameters corresponding to output (variable) parameters must be specified as variables.
- Input (value) parameters do not permit the values of the actual parameters in the main program to be changed, while output (variable) parameters do permit the values of their corresponding actual parameters to be changed.
- Variables declared in the main program are global and can be referenced by any procedure in which they are not redeclared.
- Variables declared in a procedure are local. They are known only within that procedure and have precedence over variables with the same identifiers in the main program.

SECTION 4.7 CHAPTER REVIEW

Using top-down design, we can divide a complex problem into subproblems. Each subproblem is successively refined until a computer solution is possible. Computer solutions to the subproblems can be expressed in terms of subprograms known as procedures. A Pascal procedure has a structure that imitates that of a Pascal program:

```
PROCEDURE name (parameter list);
CONST declarations;
VAR declarations;
BEGIN
    statement;
    statement;

    . . .

    statement
END;
```

Procedures written as self-contained and independent program modules can provide an effective computer solution to a complex problem. Consequently, procedures can be debugged and tested independently. Changes to a procedure can be made more efficiently when the procedure is written as a self-contained subprogram.

Information is passed to and from a procedure by objects known as parameters. The formal parameters are specified in the procedure header's parameter list. The formal parameters can be input (value) parameters or output (variable) parameters. The actual parameters are specified in the procedure invocation statement.

The following is a detailed summary of Pascal procedures that can be used for future reference.

1 Procedures
   1.1 *Procedure header:* Includes the name of the procedure and an optional parenthesized parameter list.
   1.2 Procedures are placed after the constant and variable declarations of the main program and before the executable statements of the main program.
   1.3 Procedures are invoked by writing the name of the procedure followed by the parenthesized actual parameter list that matches the order and scope of the formal parameter list.
2 Parameters
   2.1 *Formal parameters:* Specified in the parameter list of the procedure header.
   2.2 *Input (value) parameters:* Provide input values to the procedure.
   2.3 *Output (variable) parameters:* Must begin with the reserved word VAR in the parameter list and provide a method of communicating results of procedure back to the corresponding variables in the procedure invocation.

Example:

```
PROCEDURE name (a, b, c: real; VAR x, y: real);
```

Thus, *a*, *b*, and *c* are input (value) parameters, and *x* and *y* are output (variable) parameters.
3 Variables
   3.1 *Global variables:* Declared in the main program and referenced by a procedure in which they are not redeclared.
   3.2 *Local variables:* Declared in a procedure and known only inside that procedure.
4 Example of procedure structure within a Pascal program:

```
PROGRAM example (input, output);
CONST declarations;  (* global *)
VAR declarations;    (* global *)
PROCEDURE name (formal parameter list);
CONST declarations;  (* local *)
VAR declarations;    (* local *)
BEGIN
        statement;
        statement;
        . . .
        statement
        END;
(* Main program *)
BEGIN
        statement;
        name (actual parameter list);       (* procedure invocation *)
```

. . .
    statement
END.

Keywords for Chapter 4

actual parameter	local variable
bottom-up testing	main program
driver	output (variable) parameter
formal parameter	parameter
global variable	procedure
input (value) parameter	stub
invocation	top-down testing

Chapter 5 Preview

Can the computer make decisions? In the next chapter we consider an important program construct used in making decisions and selecting alternate courses of action. In particular, we discuss the IF-THEN-ELSE and CASE statements in Pascal. These statements will permit us to solve more complicated problems that involve choosing different actions depending on the state of some condition.

CHAPTER 4 EXERCISES

⭐ ESSENTIAL EXERCISES

1 We have discussed two types of parameters that may be used with Pascal procedures: input (value) and output (variable) parameters. Is there also an *update* parameter that can be used to provide input to a procedure and through which a value may be returned?

2 Given two arbitrary 24-hour times, each represented by an integer in the form *hhmm*, write a procedure *tsum* which yields (as an output parameter) the sum of these times as an integer in the form *dhhmm* where *d* represents the number of days.

3 Suppose the value of integer variables *a* and *b* represent a rational number *a/b*. Write a procedure *ratadd* that will determine the sum of two such rational numbers. That is, find integers *e* and *f* such that

$$\frac{e}{f} = \frac{a}{b} + \frac{c}{d},$$

where *a, b, c, d, e,* and *f* are integers. The fraction *e/f* need not be reduced to its simplest form.

4 Write a procedure *conv3* which will convert three characters, each of which contains a decimal digit, to the equivalent integer. For example, if the input parameters were '1', '2', and '3', then the resulting integer would be 123.

5 Pascal does not include standard functions for cotangent, secant, or cosecant. Why should this omission cause no problems?

★★ SIGNIFICANT EXERCISES

6 Standard Pascal provides a facility for using precompiled, *external* procedures. One such procedure frequently found in many systems provides the current time of day. If this is the case in your system, write a Pascal program that, when executed, will display the current time.

7 Could you use a time-of-day procedure, such as that mentioned in exercise 6, to determine the total execution time of a program? What would happen if such a time-measuring program was executed several times in a multiple-user computer system?

8 Can you find a way to determine the value in a local variable as soon as the procedure in which it is declared is executed for the *second* time?

9 The solution of a system of simultaneous linear equations with two unknowns can be easily solved using Cramer's rule. Assume the system of equations is

$$ax + by = c \qquad \text{and} \qquad dx + ey = f.$$

Then Cramer's rule states that if there is a solution,

$$x = \frac{ce - fb}{ae - db} \qquad \text{and} \qquad y = \frac{af - dc}{ae - db}.$$

Write a Pascal procedure with input parameters *a, b, c, d, e,* and *f* that determines the solution to the corresponding simultaneous equations, yielding the results in the output parameters *x* and *y*.

★★★ CHALLENGING EXERCISES

10 Write a Pascal procedure *MAX* with two integer value parameters *A* and *B* and an integer variable parameter *C*. Using only the Pascal language features presented in Chapters 2 and 3, procedure *MAX* is to return in parameter *C* the larger of the positive, nonzero integer parameters *A* and *B*. (Hint: Consider the use of the *trunc* and *round* functions.)

CHAPTER 4 PROBLEMS FOR COMPUTER SOLUTION

★ ESSENTIAL PROBLEMS

1 Write a Pascal procedure to determine the area of a four-sided figure given the coordinates of the vertices of the figure. Utilize the triangle area procedure developed in the chapter.

2   A leap year is any which is divisible by 4, except those years which are divisible by 100, which are leap years only if also divisible by 400. For example, 1984, 2000, 2008, and 2400 are leap years, but 1700, 1961, and 2317 are not. Write a Pascal procedure *leaptest* which has a year as its input parameter and as its output parameter a Boolean value which is true if the input parameter is a leap year.

3   Write a procedure to compute the value of the polynomial

$$ax^3 + bx^2 + cx + d,$$

where a, b, c, and d are integer input parameters and x is a real input parameter. The value of the polynomial is the output parameter. Then write a main program which utilizes the output to find the value of

$$f[g(x)] \qquad \text{and} \qquad g[f(x)]$$

where $f(x) = ax^3 + bx^2 + cx + d$, and $g(x) = jx^3 + kx^2 + lx + m$, where a, b, c, d, j, k, l, m, and x are obtained from the input data.

★★ SIGNIFICANT PROBLEMS

4   Given a circular path of radius R for a sports car, what is the maximum speed possible? The coefficient of *adhesion* (friction) between the road surface and the wheels of the car is about 0.8 under good conditions, and the force required to move the car sideways is given by the product of the weight of the car and the coefficient of friction. The centripetal force acting on the car is equal to $m \cdot v^2/r$, where m is the mass of the car and v is its velocity. Write a procedure and a complete Pascal program to determine the maximum speed possible, given a coefficient of adhesion of 0.8 and the car's weight and the curve's radius as input data. The weight of the car is the product of its mass and the acceleration of gravity (about 32.174 feet per second squared at the earth's surface).

5   Given an integer n, write a Pascal program that uses a procedure to draw a square box whose sides are composed of asterisks, centered on the output device. Assume a maximum value of 20 for n. For example, if the input was 5 and the output device has a width of 65 columns, the output would look like this:

```
                         *****
                         *   *
                         *   *
                         *   *
                         *****
```

Notice that the box will not really look like a square, since the number of lines per inch and the number of characters per inch are not the same on most output devices. For example, many printers display 10 characters per inch but only 6 or 8 lines per inch. As a slightly more complicated problem, consider the perspective problem in your solution.

6 The input contains five real numbers representing angles measured in radians. Build a table of values of the trigonometric functions sine, cosine, tangent, cotangent, secant, and cosecant at the given angle, accurate to two fractional digits. The results should be printed in the form shown in the example.

Example input:

```
0.40    0.23    0.90    0.50    0.71
```

Example output:

Angle	0.40	0.23	0.90	0.50	0.71
Sine	0.39	0.23	0.78	0.48	0.65
Cosine	0.92	0.97	0.62	0.88	0.76
Tangent	0.42	0.23	1.26	0.55	0.86
Cotangent	2.37	4.27	0.79	1.83	1.16
Secant	1.09	1.03	1.61	1.14	1.32
Cosecant	2.57	4.39	1.28	2.09	1.53

CHAPTER 5

CHAPTER 5
SELECTION

Boolean
Expressions

IF
Statements

CASE
Statement

Problem
Solving
with Selection

SELECTION

OBJECTIVES

After completing this chapter you should be able to:

- Evaluate Boolean expressions that include Boolean and relational operators
- Recognize and apply the IF-THEN and the IF-THEN-ELSE statements to decision problems
- Recognize and apply nested IF statements
- Recognize and apply the CASE statement
- Solve, test, and debug problems involving selection

CHAPTER OVERVIEW

Many problems require alternate courses of action to be taken depending on the state of some condition. For example, converting a student's numeric grade in a course (ranging from 0 to 100) to a letter grade (such as A, B, C, D, or F) is such a problem. We might decide that a numeric grade of 95 should be converted to a letter grade of A and a numeric grade of 85 to a letter grade of B, and so on. The programming presented so far does not include a mechanism to compare values and choose alternate courses of action. In this chapter we discuss and apply decision making, or selection, and introduce the Pascal language features that enable us to use these features in our programs.

The Pascal programs presented up to this point have a common structure that is reflected in the order of the execution of the statements. More specifically, the statements in the programs are executed sequentially, starting with the first statement of the main program and then continuing with the next statements in order until the last statement is executed (see Figure 5-1).

Structured high-level languages, such as Pascal, contain statements that can alter the flow of a sequence of instructions. Technically, these statements are known as *control structures*. Actually, the procedure statement used in the previous chapter is an example of a control structure. When the procedure is invoked, control is automatically transferred from the main program to the procedure and then back to the main program. In this chapter we will consider a fundamental control structure known as *selection*. Using selection, statements can be executed conditionally. That is, if a certain condition is true, then one sequence of statements will be executed; but if the condition is false, then a different sequence of statements will be executed. For example, suppose a variable named *num* is declared as an integer and contains some value. We wish to determine whether *num* contains an even or an odd number and then print this fact. Figure 5-2 represents the flow of control of this decision process, or selection.

Thus, the condition to be tested (indicated by the diamond in Figure 5-2) is whether *num* contains an even number. If the content of num is an even number, then the condition is true and control transfers to the statement that displays the message "Number is even." If *num* contains an odd number, then the condition is false and control transfers to the statement that displays the message "Number is odd."

The actual Pascal statement (known as an IF-THEN-ELSE statement) corresponding to this control structure is shown below:

```
IF num MOD 2 = 0
THEN writeln ('Number is even.')
ELSE writeln ('Number is odd.')
```

Figure 5-1   Sequential execution.

Recall that MOD produces the remainder after integer division. In this case the remainder is either 0 or 1, which indicates that the number is either even or odd, respectively. In this chapter we consider conditional structures and decision making using Pascal selection statements IF-THEN-ELSE, IF-THEN, and CASE in more detail. Another fundamental control structure known as *looping* will be considered in the next chapter. Looping permits the repeated execution of a sequence of statements while some condition is true.

Figure 5-2   Example of selection control structure.

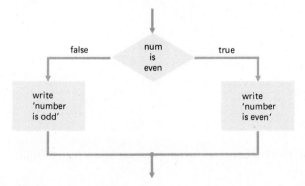

SECTION 5.1 BOOLEAN EXPRESSIONS

Notice, in the previous example, the condition "num MOD 2 = 0" was tested to determine the next statement to execute. The condition "num MOD 2 = 0" is an expression that is either true or false, depending on whether *num* contains an even or odd number. An expression that is either true or false is called a ***Boolean expression*** (named after the nineteenth-century British mathematician George Boole). In this section we study Boolean expressions in detail. The importance of these expressions will become evident in the next section when we consider the IF-THEN-ELSE statement.

Boolean Variables

A Boolean expression in Pascal can be a Boolean variable. Boolean variables can be assigned only the values true or false. Consider the following declaration of a Boolean variable named *switch*.

VAR switch : Boolean;

The following statement assigns the value true to the Boolean variable *switch*:

switch := true

The following statement assigns the value false to *switch*:

switch := false

It is important to note that in standard Pascal the values of a Boolean variable *cannot* be obtained from input data using the *read* statement. (Recall, however, that they may be displayed using *write* and *writeln* statements.)

Relational Operators

Boolean expressions in Pascal can contain the following *relational* operators:

Pascal	English
=	Equal to
<>	Not equal to
<=	Less than or equal to
>=	Greater than or equal to
>	Greater than
<	Less than

Suppose *num1* and *num2* are both declared as integer, then the following are valid Boolean expressions in Pascal:

```
num1 > num2
num1 = num2
num1 <> num2
num2 <= num1
```

Depending on the values of *num1* and *num2*, each of these Boolean expressions is either true or false. For example, if *num1* contains the integer 3 and *num2* contains the integer 5, then the Boolean expression "num1 > num2" is false, since "3 > 5" is false. The table shown below includes more examples with the truth value of Boolean expressions for specific values of *num1* and *num2*.

num1	*num2*	*Boolean expression*	*truth value*
2	5	num1 < num2	true
0	1	num1 > num2	false
3	2	num1 > num2	true
8	7	num1 <> num2	true
7	7	num1 <= num2	true
7	7	num1 <> num2	false

The relational operators are also applicable to other data types. The use of real variables yields similar results. Next consider an example in which grade is declared char in Pascal. Then the expression "grade > 'A' " is a valid Boolean expression. In this case, the relational operator > refers to the ordering of the characters on the computer system, known as the ***lexicographic ordering***, or ***collating sequence***. If the character stored in variable *grade* appears after the character 'A' in the ordering for the particular computer system, then the Boolean expression is true; otherwise, it is false.

The ordering of characters may vary between implementations of Pascal on different computer systems, but standard Pascal requires that certain relations must hold in all cases. These requirements are:

- The character values representing the digits 0 to 9 must be in the expected order, with no intervening characters. That is, '0' < '1', '1' < '2', . . . , '8' < '9'. Notice although the relations are the same as for integers and reals, these are characters, not numbers.
- The uppercase letters *A* to *Z* must appear in the expected order ('A' before 'B', 'B' before 'C', and so forth), but there may be intervening characters. (For example, large IBM computer systems may have some characters between the uppercase alphabetic characters.)
- If the lowercase characters are available, they must obey the same ordering rule required for the uppercase alphabetic characters (so 'a' < 'b', 'b' < 'c', and so forth). Note that this rule does *not* require the lowercase letters to come before the uppercase letters. Hence, we may not assume, in general, that 'a' < 'A'.

Note that these rules mean that 'A' > '2' could be true or false, depending on the particular lexicographical ordering in use on the computer system. Many computer systems use the ASCII (American Standard Code for Information Interchange) character set, which defines the ordering shown in Appendix F. The EBCDIC (Extended Binary-Coded Decimal Interchange Code) is frequently used with large IBM systems and is also shown in Appendix F.

When using the relational operators, the values being compared must be of the same data type with the exception that integers may be compared to reals. For example, each of the following Boolean expressions is *invalid*, since the data types of the values being compared are different.

$$5 > \text{false} \qquad \text{'B'} = 5.0 \qquad \text{'0'} >= 0$$

Expressions of the data type real can lead to problems when they are used with relational operators. For example, the Boolean expression "(1.0 / 3.0) * 3.0 = 1.0" appears to be true. But since the result of evaluating (1.0 / 3.0) * 3.0 will probably be 0.99999 . . . (due to the limited precision of real arithmetic on computers), the Boolean expression will likely be false.

Therefore, sometimes we will have to exclude the real data type from our discussion. The other simple data types—integer, char, and Boolean—are called **ordinal data types**. These data types are called ordinal because the values are ordered and can be specified by a list. For example, the integers are ordered and can be listed from $-maxint$ to *maxint*. As we have seen, the characters are also ordered and can be listed. The Boolean values true and false are ordered since false $<$ true in Pascal.

Boolean Operators

Boolean expressions can be combined to form more complex expressions by using the three Boolean (or logical) operators AND, OR, and NOT. For example, suppose we wish to test whether the integer *num* is between 1 and 10; that is, if "1 $<$ num $<$ 10." This is not a legal Pascal statement. However, the two Boolean expressions "(1 $<$ num)" and "(num $<$ 10)" can be combined using the Boolean operator AND to form the Boolean expression

$$(1 < \text{num}) \text{ AND } (\text{num} < 10)$$

This expression is true if both "(1 $<$ num)" and "(num $<$ 10)" are true. In general, if P and Q represent Boolean expressions, then the Boolean expression "P AND Q" is true only when both P and Q are true. Otherwise, the expression "P AND Q" is false. We can summarize the truth value of the expression "P AND Q" with the following *truth table* showing the result of "P AND Q" for all possible truth values of P and Q.

P	Q	$P \text{ AND } Q$
false	false	false
false	true	false
true	false	false
true	true	true

For example, if P is false and Q is true, then using the second line of the table, we find that "P AND Q" is false. Suppose a Pascal program contains the following declaration:

```
VAR flag, switch, test : Boolean;
```

Then the Pascal program segment

```
flag := 5 > 10;
switch := 'A' < 'B';
test := flag AND switch
```

will result in the equivalent assignments

```
flag := false
switch := true
test := false
```

when the program is executed.

The expression "P OR Q," where P and Q are Boolean expressions, is true when either P is true, *or* Q is true, *or* both P and Q are true. The truth table shown below summarizes the use of the OR operator.

P	Q	$P\ OR\ Q$
false	false	false
false	true	true
true	false	true
true	true	true

Using the table we can see that the Boolean expression

```
(5 > 10) OR ('A' < 'B')
```

is true, since "('A' < 'B')" is true.

The addition, subtraction, multiplication, and division operators are called **binary** operators, since they are applied to two operands. Likewise, the Boolean operators AND and OR are also known as binary operators, since they, too, are applied to two operands.

Operators that apply to single operands are called **unary** operators. For example, if j is an integer variable, then the expression $-j$ involves the use of the unary operator $-$. The Boolean operator NOT is also a unary operator which reverses the truth sense of its operand. For example, the Boolean expression "NOT (5 > 10)" is true, since "(5 > 10)" is false. The following truth table summarizes the effect of the NOT operator.

P	NOT P
false	true
true	false

The following table further illustrates the properties of NOT, AND, and OR. Here, *num* is an integer variable whose value is 3, and *flag* is a Boolean variable whose value is true.

Boolean expression	truth value
(1 > 0) AND (2 = 2)	true
NOT flag	false
(0 < 1) OR (0 > 1)	true
(5 <= 6) AND (2 > 3)	false
NOT (2 <> 2)	true
(num = 1) OR (5 >= 4)	true
NOT (num <= 3)	false

Order of Operators

Recall that the operators in arithmetic expressions are applied in a specific order when more than one operator is present in the expression. Similarly, Boolean operators and relational operators have an order of precedence. For example, the following Boolean expression (assuming p, q, and r are Boolean variables)

NOT p OR q AND r

is evaluated in steps, as shown below:

NOT p	(NOT has the highest precedence)
q AND r	(AND has the next highest precedence)
NOT p OR q AND r	(OR has the lowest precedence)

Therefore, in expressions involving more than one of the three Boolean operators, the order of precedence is NOT first, AND next, and OR last. As with arithmetic expressions, parentheses may be used to force an expression to be evaluated in any desired order. For example,

NOT (p OR q AND r)

would be evaluated by performing the AND operation first, then the OR operation, and finally the NOT operation.

The table below contains further examples. The order of evaluation is shown using parentheses.

Boolean expression	order of evaluation
NOT p OR q	(NOT p) OR q
p OR q AND r	p OR (q AND r)
NOT p AND q OR NOT r	((NOT p) AND q) OR (NOT r)

A frequent problem area in Pascal involves Boolean expressions with both relational operators ($>$, $<$, and so forth) and Boolean operators (NOT, AND, and OR). The relational operators have a precedence *lower* than the Boolean operators, so an expression like

NOT 4 $>$ 5

is erroneous, since the NOT operator would be applied first to the integer operand 4. The use of parentheses is required in this case to obtain the desired result

NOT (4 $>$ 5)

which will yield the value true. As another example, consider the expression

1 $<$ num AND num $<$ 10

with *num* declared to be an integer variable. Since the AND operation has higher precedence than the relational operator $<$, the expression "num AND num" would need to be evaluated first. Naturally, this will result in an error, since the AND operator requires Boolean operands. The proper form for this expression is

(1 $<$ num) AND (num $<$ 10)

The order of precedence for all operators can be found in Appendix E. When in doubt about the order in which the operators in an expression will be evaluated, use parentheses to force the order of evaluation you intend. In addition to indicating the order in which expressions should be evaluated, parentheses can improve the readability of the program.

EXERCISES FOR SECTION 5.1

1 Determine whether each of the following Boolean expressions is true or false.

(a) 2 $<$ 4   (b) $-2 < 0$ (c) 0 $>$ 1
(d) '5' $<$ '6'   (e) 'Z' $<$ 'A'   (f) true $<$ false

2 Determine whether each of the following Boolean expressions is true or false.

(a)   ('b' $<$ 'd') AND (0 $<$ 1)
(b)   ('c' $>=$ 'f') OR ('C' $<=$ 'C')

(c) $(5 < 1)$ OR $(0 > -1)$

(d) NOT $(2 = 2)$ AND (maxint $<$ maxint)

3 Determine the value of each of the following Boolean expressions. Assume $p =$ true, $q =$ false, and $r =$ true.

(a) NOT p OR q AND r

(b) NOT p AND p

(c) q AND p OR NOT r

(d) NOT $(p$ AND q AND r$)$

(e) NOT $(p$ AND NOT q AND r$)$

4 Determine the value of each of the following Boolean expressions. Assume $p =$ true, $q =$ true, and $r =$ false.

(a) $(p$ AND q$)$ AND $(3 < 5)$

(b) NOT $(p$ AND r$)$ OR $(p$ OR q$)$

(c) $('0' < '2')$ AND $(p$ AND r$)$

(d) NOT $(p$ AND r$)$ OR NOT $(p$ AND q$)$

5 Determine the order in which the operators are performed for each Boolean expression by inserting parentheses. Assume *flag*, *switch*, and *test* are Boolean variables.

(a) NOT flag OR NOT switch

(b) flag OR test AND NOT switch

(c) NOT $($flag AND switch OR test$)$

(d) test OR switch AND flag

6 Convert the following to valid Boolean expressions by inserting parentheses. Assume *num* is an integer variable.

(a) NOT 1 $<$ num

(b) 2 $>$ num OR num < -2

(c) NOT 0 $<$ num OR num > 10

(d) 1 $>$ num AND num > 0

SECTION 5.2 SELECTION USING THE IF STATEMENT

Now that we know the fundamentals of Boolean expressions, we are ready to continue with the selection control structures used in Pascal. The first control structure we consider is the IF-THEN-ELSE statement. This statement has the following structure:

IF Boolean-expression
THEN statement-1
ELSE statement-2

The statement begins with the reserved word IF followed by a Boolean expression. This is followed by the reserved word THEN and a Pascal statement (or a group of statements). Finally, the reserved word ELSE is written, again followed by a Pascal statement (or group of statements). Observe that there is *no* semicolon immediately preceding the ELSE.

The IF-THEN-ELSE statement is executed as follows. The Boolean expression is evaluated, yielding a true or false value. If the expression is true, then statement-1 is executed and statement-2 is ignored. If the expression is false, then statement-1 is ignored and statement-2 is executed.

Consider the earlier example of determining whether the content of the integer variable *num* is an even or odd number. The IF-THEN-ELSE statement

```
IF num MOD 2 = 0
THEN writeln ('Number is even.')
ELSE writeln ('Number is odd.')
```

causes the Boolean expression "num MOD 2 = 0" to be evaluated. If the number is even, then the Boolean expression is true, and the statement "writeln ('Number is even.')" will be executed and the statement following the ELSE is ignored. If the number is odd, then the Boolean expression is false, and the statement writeln "('Number is odd.')" will be executed, ignoring the statement following the THEN.

The syntax diagram for the IF-THEN-ELSE statement is shown in Figure 5-3. This diagram also specifies the syntax for the IF-THEN statement, considered later in this section.

Note carefully that the IF-THEN-ELSE statement is a *single* Pascal statement, and must be separated from any statement that follows it by a semicolon.

Problem 5.1

Given two integer variables num1 *and* num2, *determine the larger value and display it.*

The following IF-THEN-ELSE statement will solve this problem:

```
IF num1 > num2
THEN writeln ('The larger number is ', num1)
ELSE writeln ('The larger number is ', num2)
```

Suppose, however, we wish additionally to store the larger value in the integer variable *max*. We would have to write two statements in both the THEN part and the ELSE part of the statement. Pascal requires that if more than one statement is placed in the THEN or ELSE part of an IF-THEN-ELSE statement, they must be grouped together with BEGIN and END. The reserved word BEGIN is placed before the first

Figure 5-3 Syntax diagram for an IF statement.

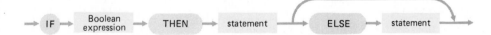

statement of the group, and the reserved word END is placed after the last statement of the group. The solution to the modified problem then looks like this:

```
IF num1 > num2
THEN BEGIN
            writeln ('The larger number is ', num1);
            max := num1
      END
ELSE BEGIN
            writeln ('The larger number is ', num2);
            max := num2
      END
```

As usual, the individual statements grouped together by the BEGIN and END symbols are separated by semicolons, but no semicolon is used before the ELSE.

Let us consider the general structure of an IF-THEN-ELSE statement included with another statement before and another statement after, as well as several statements in the THEN and ELSE parts. This would appear something like this:

```
statement;     (* before the IF statement *)
IF Boolean-expression
THEN BEGIN
            statement;
            statement;

                  .
                  .
                  .

            statement
      END
ELSE BEGIN
            statement;
            statement;

                  .
                  .
                  .

            statement
      END;
statement     (* following the IF statement *)
```

Here is another, more specific example. *Count* is an integer variable and *letter* is a character variable. The program segment might be used as part of a loop (without the statement "count := 0") to determine the number of characters occurring before 'Z' in the lexicographic ordering.

```
count := 0;     (* initialize count to zero *)
read (letter);     (* read a character *)
```

```
IF letter < 'Z'
THEN BEGIN
            writeln (letter, ' occurs before Z.');
            count := count + 1
      END
ELSE BEGIN
            writeln (letter, ' does not occur before Z.');
            writeln ('This character will not be counted.')
      END
```

Note that when a statement follows an IF-THEN-ELSE, there must be a semicolon separating the IF-THEN-ELSE and that following statement.

Figure 5-4 illustrates the control structure of the IF-THEN-ELSE statement. In this figure, statement-1 and statement-2 can be a group of Pascal statements, suitably enclosed by the reserved words BEGIN and END.

The IF-THEN Statement

Suppose we wish to execute a sequence of statements only if a certain condition is true, and otherwise do nothing (but continue with the next statement). For example, a program that maintains the balance in your checking account may include a selection statement that displays a warning if the account is overdrawn. Otherwise, the program continues with the next statement. Suppose an overdrawn account is represented by a negative balance. The following IF-THEN statement (without the ELSE) would display the warning:

Figure 5-4   IF-THEN-ELSE control structure.

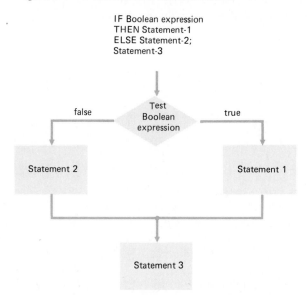

```
IF Boolean expression
THEN Statement-1
ELSE Statement-2;
Statement-3
```

```
IF balance < 0
THEN writeln ('Your account is overdrawn.')
```

This is a situation where an IF-THEN-ELSE statement could be used, except the ELSE part is not required—there should be no statement in the ELSE part of the IF-THEN-ELSE statement. Because this situation occurs with frequency in our problem solutions, Pascal provides that we may not only omit the statement following the ELSE but also the reserved word itself.

For example, suppose we want to display a warning if a test score (represented by the integer variable *testscore*) is outside the range 0 to 100. The following IF-THEN statement will accomplish this task.

```
IF (testscore < 0) OR (testscore > 100)
THEN writeln ('Invalid test score.')
```

In this case the error message is printed only if the test score is less than 0 or greater than 100. If the test score is valid (that is, in the range 0 to 100), no action is specified by the IF-THEN statement and execution continues with the statement following the IF-THEN. The general structure of the IF-THEN statement with a statement preceding and following it is

```
statement;      (* before the IF-THEN *)
IF Boolean-expression
THEN statement;
statement       (* after the IF-THEN *)
```

Figure 5-5 shows the control structure of the IF-THEN statement. As noted previously, the IF-THEN statement is a variant of the IF-THEN-ELSE statement. In fact, the IF-THEN statement is entirely equivalent to the following statement:

Figure 5-5   IF-THEN control structure.

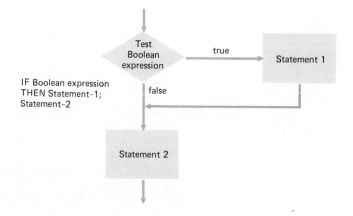

The "statement" following the ELSE is really a Pascal statement! It is called the **empty statement** and is included specifically for use in such situations. While in most cases the use of the empty statement is optional, as we will see, some situations require its use.

Some problems can be solved by using many IF-THEN statements in sequence. Consider, for example, the following problem.

Problem 5.2

Determine if the integer variable number *is evenly divisible by 2, 3, or 5, and display an appropriate message.*

This problem is conveniently solved by using three separate IF-THEN statements, each using a Boolean expression involving the MOD operator to test for divisibility. Here is the solution:

```
IF number MOD 2 = 0
THEN writeln ('The number is evenly divisible by 2.');
IF number MOD 3 = 0
THEN writeln ('The number is evenly divisible by 3.');
IF number MOD 5 = 0
THEN writeln ('The number is evenly divisible by 5.')
```

If the value of *number* is 4, then only the first message will be displayed. However, if the value of *number* is 30, then all three messages will appear in the output.

Nested IF Statements

IF statements can occur inside (be **nested** within) other IF statements. For example, suppose we wish to determine which of two given integers, *num1* and *num2*, is larger. Since it is possible for the numbers to be equal, we should test for this condition and display a message indicating that fact. The following Pascal segment solves this problem:

```
IF num1 >= num2
THEN IF num1 = num2
        THEN writeln ('Both numbers are equal to ', num1)
        ELSE writeln ('The larger number is ', num1)
ELSE writeln ('The larger number is ', num2)
```

This example uses a nested IF statement. Nested IF statements can become increasingly complex and difficult to read. We have indented the nested IF statement to make it easier to read and comprehend. *Remember that how we indent when writing the Pascal statements does not affect the manner in which the statements are executed by the computer.* For example, suppose we nest an IF-THEN-ELSE within an IF-THEN statement and do not indent. We might write such a statement on a single line, as shown below:

```
IF a > b THEN IF a > c THEN max := a ELSE max := 0
```

Here we have two IF statements and one ELSE. Which IF statement contains the ELSE? This is often known as the **dangling ELSE** problem in Pascal. To answer the question, we note the rule that an ELSE is always matched with the nearest preceding THEN that does not already have an ELSE matched with it. So, the above statement, written with appropriate indentation, becomes

```
IF a > b
THEN IF a > c
        THEN max := a
        ELSE max := 0
```

As we can now see, we actually have an IF-THEN-ELSE statement nested within an IF-THEN statement. Of course, the indentation has nothing to do with the way the statement is actually executed. In Pascal, the ELSE will always be matched with the nearest preceding THEN that has no ELSE. To emphasize this fact, consider the following "rewrite" of the statement:

```
IF a > b
THEN IF a > c
        THEN max := a
ELSE max := 0
```

This deceptively looks as if the ELSE belongs to the outer IF statement. That is, the statement "max := 0" looks as if it will be executed only if the Boolean expression $a > b$ is false. However, this is incorrect, since the ELSE is associated with the nearest THEN. But note how the misleading indentation suggests a different (and incorrect) interpretation. The best solution to avoiding confusion is simple: Use indentation to suggest the *proper* order of evaluation of the statements in a Pascal program.

But this suggests an additional question: How do we write the statement if we really want an IF-THEN-ELSE with an IF-THEN inside? This can be accomplished by enclosing the IF-THEN statement with a BEGIN-END pair. This effectively *shields* the IF-THEN statement from the matching process used to associate the ELSE with the nearest THEN. This solution is coded as follows:

```
IF a > b
THEN BEGIN
        IF a > c
        THEN max := a
```

```
ELSE max := 0
```

Now consider the following problem in which we use a nested IF-THEN-ELSE statement to find the largest of three numbers.

Problem 5.3

Given three integer variables num1, num2, *and* num3, *find the largest of these three numbers and store it in an integer variable named* max.

To solve this problem requires that two IF-THEN-ELSE statements be nested within another IF-THEN-ELSE statement. Since each statement has its own ELSE, no special attention is required to force the proper association of the ELSE components. We will still use good indentation practices, however. Here is the solution:

```
IF num1 > num2
THEN  IF num1 > num3
         THEN max := num1
         ELSE max := num3
ELSE  IF num2 > num3
         THEN max := num2
         ELSE max := num3
```

It will be very instructive to study this solution carefully, executing it several times with different values for *num1, num2,* and *num3*. For example, as an exercise, test this solution for the values *num1* = 8, *num2* = 10, and *num3* = 5. What would happen when all three numbers are equal?

In the next problem we illustrate one solution to the problem of converting a numeric grade to the corresponding letter grade.

Problem 5.4

Obtain an integer test score from the input, and verify that it is within the range 0 to 100. If it is, then display the corresponding letter score using the grading scale 90 to 100 = A, 80 to 89 = B, 70 to 79 = C, 60 to 69 = D, and 0 to 59 = F. If the test score is outside the allowed range, then display an appropriate error message.

The solution to this problem involves several nested IF statements, each processing one of the various ranges in which the test score may lie. Again, it is a good exercise to hand test the solution using various input values.

```
read (testscore);
IF (testscore < 0) OR (testscore > 100)
```

```
        THEN writeln ('Invalid test score: ', testscore)
        ELSE IF testscore >= 90
                THEN writeln ('Grade is A')
                ELSE IF testscore >= 80
                        THEN writeln ('Grade is B')
                        ELSE IF testscore >= 70
                                THEN writeln ('Grade is C')
                                ELSE IF testscore >= 60
                                        THEN writeln ('Grade is D')
                                        ELSE writeln ('Grade is F')
```

EXERCISES FOR SECTION 5.2

1 Consider the following statement:

```
IF (grade >= 90) OR (grade < 60)
THEN write ('Extreme')
ELSE write ('Median')
```

(a) What is displayed if *grade* equals 90?
(b) What is displayed if *grade* equals 0?
(c) What is displayed if *grade* equals 70?

2 Consider the following nested IF statement:

```
IF a > b
THEN IF a > c
        THEN write ('A is largest')
```

Write a single IF statement that is equivalent to this one but is not nested.

3 Consider the following program segment:

```
x := 7;
y := 8;
IF x > y
THEN x := x + 1
ELSE y := y + 1
```

Find the value of each variable after execution.

4 Consider the following program segment:

```
a := 5;
b := 4;
```

```
IF a > b THEN
c := 999;
d := 999;
```

After this segment is executed, which of the following is true?

(a) Both c and d are undefined.
(b) Variable $c = 999$ and d is undefined.
(c) Variable $d = 999$ and c is undefined.
(d) Both $c = 999$ and $d = 999$.

5   Consider the following program segment:

```
x := 10;
y := 11;
z := 12;
IF (x > y) OR (z > y)
THEN IF x > z
        THEN IF y > z
                THEN writeln ('Finished.')
                ELSE writeln ('Not finished.')
ELSE writeln ('Never gets to here.')
```

Determine which of the messages, if any, are displayed when the segment is executed.

6   Consider the following program segment, with x, y, and z declared as integer variables:

```
x := 1;
y := 2;
z := 3;
IF x > y
THEN IF y > z
        THEN IF x > z
                THEN writeln (x)
                ELSE writeln (y)
        ELSE writeln (z)
```

Determine what is displayed when the segment is executed.

7   What is displayed when the following segment of code is executed?

```
a := 0;
b := -1;
IF a > 0
THEN writeln ('A')
```

```
ELSE IF b < 0
    THEN writeln ('B')
    ELSE writeln ('C')
```

SECTION 5.3 SELECTION USING THE CASE STATEMENT

Suppose you are solving a problem that requires a selection from many alternatives. This selection could be performed using many nested IF statements, but Pascal provides a more appropriate mechanism: the CASE statement.

The CASE statement in Pascal is a control structure that permits the selection of a course of action from a list of many choices. The IF-THEN-ELSE statement permits selection from two alternatives, but CASE permits more than two. For example, consider the problem of converting the letter grade A, B, C, D, or F to the numeric grade point equivalents 4.0, 3.0, 2.0, 1.0, or 0.0, respectively. Suppose the variable *lettergrade* is declared char and *points* is declared real. The following Pascal IF statement converts the letter grade to a numeric grade point equivalent.

```
IF lettergrade = 'A'
THEN points := 4.0
ELSE IF lettergrade = 'B'
        THEN points := 3.0
        ELSE IF lettergrade = 'C'
                THEN points := 2.0
                ELSE IF lettergrade = 'D'
                        THEN points := 1.0
                        ELSE points := 0.0
```

Although this code is correct, it can be written more succinctly using the CASE statement. Here is what the equivalent statement would be:

```
CASE lettergrade OF
    'A' : points := 4.0;
    'B' : points := 3.0;
    'C' : points := 2.0;
    'D' : points := 1.0;
    'F' : points := 0.0
END
```

The reserved word CASE is followed by an expression known as the **selector**. The selector can only have a value which is of one of the ordinal data types (that is, it cannot be real). The value of the selector determines the statement to be executed. Following the reserved word OF is a list of statements, each of which is labeled with a constant of the same data type as that of the selector expression. The CASE statement then ends with the reserved word END.

The previous CASE statement is executed as follows. First, the value of *lettergrade* is determined and compared to the list of constants used to label the statements in the body of the CASE statement. When a match is found, the corresponding statement is executed.

The statement following each constant label can be a single Pascal statement or any group of Pascal statements enclosed in a BEGIN-END pair. Also, note the CASE statement itself does *not* require a BEGIN to match the END of the CASE.

Observe that the constant labels are separated from the statements themselves by colons. The syntax diagram for the CASE statement is shown in Figure 5-6. The actual control flow of the CASE statement is shown in Figure 5-7.

Observe that an IF-THEN-ELSE statement is just a special instance of the CASE statement. Since the Boolean data type is ordinal, we may paraphrase the general IF-THEN-ELSE statement

```
IF Boolean-expression
THEN statement-1
ELSE statement-2
```

as the following CASE statement:

```
CASE Boolean-expression OF
      true : statement-1;
      false : statement-2
END
```

What happens if the value of the ordinal expression (selector) does not match one of the constant labels? The outcome is unpredictable. That is, in some Pascal systems an error will occur when the program is executed, while on other systems all the statements in the body of the CASE statement may be ignored without any indication that such was the case. Note that some Pascal implementations provide a nonstandard *otherwise* label for a statement to be executed if none of the other constant labels match the selector. Consider the following Pascal code that determines whether an integer variable named *number* is between 1 and 10 (inclusive) and then, using a CASE statement, displays whether the number is even or odd:

Figure 5-6 Syntax diagram for the CASE statement.

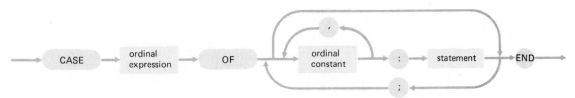

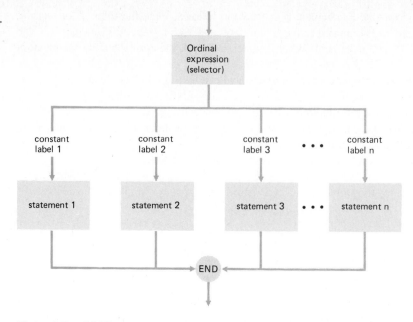

Figure 5-7 CASE control structure.

```
IF (number >= 1) AND (number <= 10)
THEN CASE number OF
      2, 4, 6, 8, 10 : writeln ('The number is even.');
      1, 3, 5, 7, 9 : writeln ('The number is odd.')
      END
```

Note that if the selector (*number*) is 2, 4, 6, 8, or 10, then the statement identifying the number as even is executed; if the number is 1, 3, 5, 7, or 9, then the other *writeln* statement is carried out. If the number is not in the range 1 to 10, the CASE statement is never even executed. This CASE statement illustrates how several constants can be combined with commas to label the same statement.

The following points concerning the CASE statement are important:

> ■ If two or more constants refer to the same statement, then the constants must be separated by commas.
> ■ A constant label cannot appear twice or correspond to two or more different statements.
> ■ The order of the constant labels is arbitrary.
> ■ All values that may result from evaluation of the selector must be specified in the constant label list. If no action is required for a certain value of the selector, then that value should appear as the constant label of an empty statement.

```
CASE lettergrade OF
      'A', 'B' : writeln ('Great grade!');
      'C' : writeln ('Quite satisfactory.');
      'D' : writeln ('Too much MTV!');
      'E' : ;     (* no such grade *)
      'F' : writeln ('Sorry, try again later.')
END
```

If the *lettergrade* has the value 'E', then the empty statement is executed and the computer does nothing but continue to the statement following the CASE. In effect, the CASE statement is skipped.

The next problem is concerned with determining the number of days in a given month of the year. The CASE statement is ideal for this type of problem.

Problem 5.5

The input data contains an integer which is supposed to be in the range 1 to 12. Read this integer and verify that it is in the proper range, and if not, print an appropriate message. Otherwise, use the integer as the number of a month (for example, 1 = January, 2 = February, and so forth). Display the number of days in the corresponding month. If the input value is 2 (February), prompt the user to enter an indication of whether the current year is a leap year or not.

The following program represents a Pascal implementation of the solution to this problem. Note that in the CASE statement the constant label 2 corresponds to a statement that contains more than one statement, and a BEGIN-END pair is required to *bracket* the statements. Actually, this group of statements could be written as a procedure, and then a single statement (namely, that which invokes the procedure) would suffice, eliminating the need for the BEGIN-END.

```
PROGRAM days (input, output);
(* Program to determine number of days in a given month. *)
(* Month must be in the range 1 to 12, inclusive.         *)
VAR
      month : integer;    (* month number          *)
      leap : char;        ('Y' or 'y' if leap year *)

BEGIN
      write ('Please enter month number (1 to 12): ');
      readln (month);
      (* Validate the month number *)
      IF (month < 1) OR (month > 12)
```

```
THEN writeln ('Sorry, the month number is invalid.')
ELSE CASE month OF
          1, 3, 5, 7, 8, 10, 12 : writeln ('31 days');
          4, 6, 9, 11 : writeln ('30 days');
          2 : BEGIN
                      write ('Is this leap year (Y or N)? ');
                      readln (leap);
                      IF (leap = 'Y') OR (leap = 'y')
                      THEN writeln ('29 days')
                      ELSE writeln ('28 days')
              END
      END
END.
```

Observe that in this program we allow the user to answer yes to the leap year question by entering an upper- or lowercase *y*. Further, note the series of ENDs required and the use of indentation to suggest the matching of each END to the corresponding BEGIN or CASE. The table that follows illustrates the output that would be obtained if various data were supplied to the program.

input data	output
1	31 days
2 Y	29 days
2 N	28 days
4	30 days
13	Sorry, the month number is invalid.

EXERCISES FOR SECTION 5.3

1 Find the value displayed after execution of the following CASE statement:

```
letter := 'E';
CASE letter OF
      'A': writeln ('Value is 1.');
      'E': writeln ('Value is 5.');
      'I': writeln ('Value is 9.');
      'O': writeln ('Value is 15.');
      'U': writeln ('Value is 21.')
END
```

2 Write a CASE statement equivalent to the following IF statement:

```
IF k = 0
THEN r := r + 1
ELSE IF k = 1
        THEN s := s + 1
        ELSE IF (k = 2) OR (k = 3) OR (k = 4)
                THEN t := t + 2
```

3 Consider the following code:

```
CASE i OF
        1:    a := a + 1;
        2:    b := b + 1;
      3, 4:   c := c + 1
```

Which of the following statements is true concerning the code?
(a) The CASE statement will compile without error.
(b) The CASE statement must terminate with an END.
(c) The CASE statement must have a BEGIN-END pair.
(d) The symbol i can be a real variable.

4 Write a CASE statement equivalent to the following IF statement.

```
IF (grade = 'D') OR (grade = 'F')
THEN writeln ('Poor job.')
ELSE IF (grade = 'C') OR (grade = 'B')
        THEN writeln ('Good job.')
        ELSE IF grade = 'A'
                THEN writeln ('Outstanding job.')
```

SECTION 5.4 PROBLEM SOLVING WITH SELECTION

Consider the following calendar problem for computer solution, which is based on some of the earlier problems we have been discussing: Given the month, day, and year written numerically, display the name of the month, the day of the month, the year, and the day of the year. For example, if the input data is "3 15 1987," then the output should be "March 15, 1987 Day 74." If the input data represents a leap year, such as "3 15 1988," then the corresponding output would be "March 15, 1988 Day 75."

Using top-down design, we can divide this problem into the following subproblems:

SUBPROBLEM 1: Obtain the month, day of the month, and the year from the input data.
SUBPROBLEM 2: Display the name of the month.

SUBPROBLEM 3: Compute the day of the year.
SUBPROBLEM 4: Display the day, year, and day of the year.

Figure 5-8 gives a graphic representation of this design.

The only subproblem requiring some additional analysis is the computation of the day of the year. One way to determine the day of the year is to compute the total number of days in the months prior to the given month and then add the given day of the month. However, if the year is a leap year and the month comes after February, then an extra day must be added to the total. The number of days in each month for a non-leap year is given in the following table:

month	Jan	Feb	Mar	Apr	May	Jun	Jul	Aug	Sep	Oct	Nov	Dec
Days	31	28	31	30	31	30	31	31	30	31	30	31

The pseudocode for our algorithm should then be:

STEP 1 Obtain month, day, and year from input data.
STEP 2 Display the name of the month.
STEP 3 Compute the day of the year: day of year = (total days of prior months) + day of month. If leap year and month > 2, then add 1 to day of the year.
STEP 4 Display day, year, and day of year.

We can now proceed to write the Pascal program. We use the CASE statement to display the name of the month since there is a direct relation between the month number and the month name. A CASE statement is also used to determine the day of the year. A procedure *leaptest* determines whether the year is a leap year or not. In the Pascal

Figure 5-8 Top-down design of calendar problem.

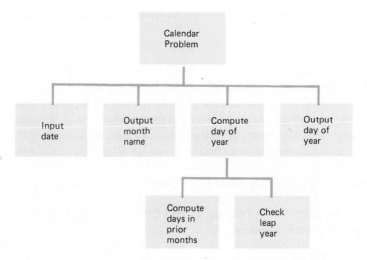

program that follows, the actual statements required for the procedure *leaptest* have been purposely omitted. Their specification is an instructive exercise for the student.

```
PROGRAM calendar (input, output);
(* Convert numerical representation of month, day and *)
(* year to month name, day, year, and day of year. *)
VAR
      month, day, year, dayofyear : integer;
      leap : Boolean;
PROCEDURE leaptest (year : integer; VAR leap : Boolean);
(* Procedure to determine if "year" is a leap year. *)
(* If so, the variable "leap" will be assigned true, *)
(* and false otherwise.*)
BEGIN
        (* The completion of this procedure is the *)
        (* subject of exercise 4.*)
END
(* The main program follows ... *)
BEGIN
(* Obtain the month, day, and year from the input data *)
readln (month, day, year);
(* Validate the month number and output month name *)
IF (month < 1) OR (month > 12)
THEN write ('INCORRECT')
ELSE BEGIN
              CASE month OF
                1 : write ('January ');
                2 : write ('February ');
                3 : write ('March ');
                4 : write ('April ');
                5 : write ('May ');
                6 : write ('June ');
                7 : write ('July ');
                8 : write ('August ');
                9 : write ('September ');
               10 : write ('October ');
               11 : write ('November ');
               12 : write ('December ')
              END;
              (* Compute day of year *)
              CASE month OF
                1 : dayofyear := day;
                2 : dayofyear := 31 + day;
                3 : dayofyear := 31 + 28 + day;
```

```
      4 : dayofyear := 31 + 28 + 31 + day;
      5 : dayofyear := 31 + 28 + 31 + 30 +
          day;
      6 : dayofyear := 31 + 28 + 31 + 30 +
          31 + day;
      7 : dayofyear := 31 + 28 + 31 + 30 +
          31 + 30 + day;
      8 : dayofyear := 31 + 28 + 31 + 30 +
          31 + 30 + 31 + day;
      9 : dayofyear := 31 + 28 + 31 + 30 +
          31 + 30 + 31 + 31 + day;
     10 : dayofyear := 31 + 28 + 31 + 30 +
          31 + 30 + 31 + 31 + 30 + day;
     11 : dayofyear := 31 + 28 + 31 + 30 +
          31 + 30 + 31 + 31 + 30 + 31 +
          day;
     12 : dayofyear := 31 + 28 + 31 + 30 +
          31 + 30 + 31 + 31 + 30 + 31 +
          30 + day
  END;
  (* Check for leap year *)
  leaptest (year, leap);
  IF leap AND (month > 2)
  THEN dayofyear := dayofyear + 1;
  (* Display the day, year, and day of year *)
  write (day:1, ',', year:1, ' Day ', dayofyear:1)
  END
END.
```

Program calendar

- -

```
3    5    1990
```

March 15, 1990 Day 74

- -

Program calendar: Sample Execution

Note that in program *calendar* the main program is essentially an IF-THEN-ELSE statement. In fact, most of the program is contained in the ELSE part of the statement. Observe further that it must be enclosed by the BEGIN-END pair, since there is more than one statement. Actually, the CASE statements corresponding to the same constant label can be combined into one CASE statement with the two statements enclosed by a BEGIN-END pair. Finally, the computation of the day of the year in

the sums in each statement could be computed before writing the program. Then, for
instance, the statement with label 3 would be

3 : dayofyear := 59 + day;

and the statement with label 4 would be

4 : dayofyear := 90 + day;

and so forth. Another method of computing the day of the year uses looping, which
will be considered in the next chapter. Still another method for performing this computation uses recursion, a topic which will be developed in Chapter 7.

SECTION 5.5 TESTING AND DEBUGGING TECHNIQUES

Boolean Expressions

The misuse of Boolean expressions in Pascal program can be the source of many
errors. For example, the Boolean expression

NOT (P AND Q)

is *not* the same as the Boolean expression

NOT P AND NOT Q.

For example, suppose P is the Boolean expression "num $= 0$" and Q is the Boolean
expression "sum $= 1$". To say not both P and Q are true is logically the same as
saying either not P is true *or* not Q is true. That is, either *num* $\neq 0$ or *sum* $\neq 1$. So,
the relations

NOT (P AND Q)   and   NOT ((num = 0) AND (sum = 1))

are logically the same as

(NOT P) OR (NOT Q)   and   (num <> 0) OR (sum <> 1).

Similarly,

NOT (P OR Q)   and   NOT ((num = 0) OR (sum = 1))

are logically the same as

(NOT P) AND (NOT Q)   and   (num 0) AND (sum 1).

These logical relations are known as ***DeMorgan's Laws.***

Parentheses

Parentheses should be used in Boolean expressions containing Boolean operators and relational or arithmetic operators. For example, suppose we wish to test whether the value in a character variable *letter* is between 'A' and 'Z'. We would write the following Boolean expression:

(letter $>=$ 'A') AND (letter $<=$ 'Z')

Parentheses are required in this expression, since their omission would result in the AND operator being applied to the operands 'A' and *letter,* neither of which is Boolean.

Even if parentheses are not required in an expression, it is sometimes wise to include them, since the readability of expressions is frequently enhanced by the inclusion of parentheses. If you are uncertain about the order in which evaluation of operators is performed, you can enforce a particular order by using parentheses. For example, assume variables *number, character,* and *logical* are all declared to be of type Boolean. Then the expression

NOT number OR character AND logical

is easier to read and understand when written as

(NOT number) OR (character AND logical).

Validation

Some errors can be traced to invalid input data values. To avoid these errors, we should include in our programs a test for such invalid data after the values have been entered. For example, the program segment shown below is expecting a positive number named *deposit,* indicating the number of dollars deposited into a checking account. An IF statement is used to validate the input.

```
read (deposit);
IF deposit <= 0
THEN writeln ('Invalid data.')
```

When using a CASE statement, it is always prudent to validate the range of the value used as the selector. In standard Pascal, if the value of the selector does not match one of the constant labels, the result is undefined. For example, suppose a character variables named *code* ranges over the letters 'A', 'B', 'C', 'D', 'E', 'V',

'W', 'X', 'Y', and 'Z'. Then the following IF statement will validate the value of the selector, resulting in execution of the CASE statement or the *writeln* statement which displays a diagnostic:

```
IF ((code >= 'A') AND (code <= 'E') OR
      (code >= 'V') AND (code <= 'Z'))
THEN  CASE code OF
        'A','B','C','D','E': writeln ('Early code letter.');
        'V','W','X','Y','Z': writeln ('Late code letter.')
      END
ELSE writeln ('Invalid code letter: ', code)
```

The following list includes some important reminders to aid you in testing and debugging your Pascal programs when selection is involved.

PASCAL REMINDERS

- Boolean expressions when evaluated yield only the values true or false.
- The AND operator yields a true value only when both operands are true; otherwise, the value is false.
- The OR operator yields a true value when either operand is true or when both operands are true; a false result is obtained only when both operands are false.
- The NOT operator reverses the truth value of the operand.
- The logical operators NOT, AND, and OR are evaluated in that order, and before any relational or arithmetic operators in the same expression unless parentheses are used to force a different order of evaluation. A clever way to remember the order of evaluation of these operators is to note that their names do not appear in alphabetical order:

  <u>N</u>ot   <u>A</u>lphabetical   <u>O</u>rder

  <u>N</u>OT   <u>A</u>ND   <u>O</u>R

- In some cases, parentheses must be used to avoid a syntax error:

  ```
  (num > 0) AND (num < 10)
  ```

- In an IF-THEN-ELSE statement, a semicolon must *not* appear immediately before the ELSE:

  ```
  IF a > 0
  THEN b := b + 1;     (* ERROR! *)
  ELSE a := a + 1
  ```

- A semicolon immediately following THEN or ELSE implies the empty statement occurs before the semicolon:

  ```
  IF a > b
  THEN ;     (* empty statement *)
  ```

```
IF b < 0
THEN b := b + 1
ELSE ;      (* empty statement *)
```

- A BEGIN-END pair is required when more than one statement is to be included in the THEN or ELSE part of an IF statement.
- In a CASE statement the selector value must be of an ordinal type (not real).
- The selector must evaluate to one of the values specified by the constant labels.
- In a nested IF statement, the ELSE is matched with the nearest unmatched THEN preceding the ELSE. Indenting can improve the readability of nested statements.

```
IF num = 0
THEN IF sum = 0
        THEN count := count + 1
        ELSE total := total + 1
ELSE num := 2 * num
```

SECTION 5.6 CHAPTER REVIEW

In this chapter we have discussed decision making, or selection, using the Pascal language. Statements that can alter the flow of a sequence of instructions are known as control structures. The control structures IF-THEN and IF-THEN-ELSE use Boolean expressions to determine the flow of control. The IF-THEN statement selects an additional instruction (or group of instructions enclosed in a BEGIN-END pair) to perform if the Boolean expression is true. The IF-THEN-ELSE statement selects one of a pair of instructions (or group of instructions) based on the true or false value of the Boolean expression. IF statements of both types can be nested, so that an IF statement can include other IF statements.

The CASE statement is a general control structure in Pascal that permits the selection of one of potentially many alternative instructions based on the value of an expression which yields an ordinal value.

The following reference summarizes the selection features present in the Pascal language.

PASCAL REFERENCE

1 Boolean expressions
  1.1 Boolean variables can be assigned only the values true and false:
       switch := false
  1.2 Relational operators

$$= \qquad <> \qquad <= \qquad >= \qquad < \qquad >$$

1.3   Boolean operators:

```
AND       OR       NOT
```

1.3 Boolean operators:

```
AND       OR       NOT
```

1.4 Typical expressions (*flag* and *switch* are declared Boolean; *num* is declared integer):

```
flag AND switch
NOT switch OR flag
(num > 0) OR switch
(num >= 1) AND (num <= 10)
```

1.5 Order of operator evaluation in absence of parentheses:

```
NOT
AND       /       DIV       MOD       *
OR        +       −
=         <>      <=        >=        <       >
```

2   IF-THEN-ELSE statement

2.1 General form:

```
IF Boolean expression
THEN statement-1
ELSE statement-2
```

Specific example:

```
IF num > 0
THEN writeln ('Number is positive.')
ELSE writeln ('Number is negative or zero.')
```

2.2 IF-THEN statement:

```
IF Boolean expression
THEN statement
```

Specific example:

```
IF (grade >= 90) AND (grade <= 100)
THEN writeln ('Your grade is A.')
```

2.3 The empty statement:

```
IF Boolean expression
THEN statement
ELSE ;      (* empty statement before semicolon *)
```

SELECTION

IF Boolean expression
THEN ;   (* empty statement before semicolon *)

2.4   Nested IF statement (IF statement inside an IF):

```
IF grade1 < grade2
THENIF grade1 < grade3
     THEN small := grade1
     ELSE
ELSEIF grade2 < grade3
     THEN small := grade2
     ELSE small := grade3
```

3   CASE statement
General form:

```
CASE  ordinal expression OF
      constant-label-1:   statement 1;
      constant-label-2:   statement 2;
      . . .
      constant-label-n:   statement n
END
```

Specific example:

```
CASE  lettergrade OF
      'A': writeln ('Excellent.');
      'B': writeln ('Very good.');
      'C': writeln ('Good.');
      'D': writeln ('Fair.');
      'F': writeln ('Poor.')
END
```

Chapter 6 Preview

So far we have discussed three control structures: sequence, procedure, and selection. Sequence was discussed in Chapter 2 and consists of statement execution in the order written, one after another. In Chapter 4 procedures were introduced. They alter the flow of the program to execute a named group of statements as a unit by referencing the procedure name and possibly an actual argument list as a statement. In this chapter decision making using selection (Boolean expressions and IF statements and ordinal expressions and CASE statements) was discussed.

In the next chapter we will introduce looping, another control structure of great importance in preparing solutions to problems. Looping permits the controlled repetition of a sequence of statements. We will see several forms of looping control structures.

As you will discover, these four control structures (sequence, procedure, selection, and looping) are sufficient to write structured programs in Pascal to solve almost any problem you will encounter.

Keywords for Chapter 5

AND operator
binary operator
Boolean expression
Boolean operator
Boolean variable
CASE statement
collating sequence
control structure
empty statement
IF-THEN statement

IF-THEN-ELSE statement
lexicographic ordering
nested IF statements
NOT operator
OR operator
ordinal data types
relational operators
selection
selector
unary operator

CHAPTER 5 EXERCISES

★ ESSENTIAL EXERCISES

1   What happens in your system when the following segment of code is executed?

```
val := 3;
CASE  val OF
        1:  writeln ('one');
        2:  writeln ('two')
END;
writeln ('After case')
```

If you can enable and disable diagnostic checking, try the execution of the segment both ways.

2   Nonstandard implementations of Pascal frequently include an OTHERWISE or ELSE component of CASE statements to provide a statement which is executed only if the selector value does not match any of the constant labels. Determine if your Pascal compiler has such a feature, and use it to handle the problem of exercise 1.

3   Indicate the steps involved in evaluation of the expression

$$(a < b) < (c < d)$$

where a, b, c, and d are all the same type. Evaluate the expression for a, b, c, and d equal 1, 2, 3, and 4, respectively, and 4, 3, 2, and 1.

4   Determine the approximate number of decimal digits which may be stored in a real variable on your system. Do so by determining the first of the following which yields the value true. Try to explain the reason this method works.

$$1.01 = 1.0$$
$$1.001 = 1.0$$
$$1.0001 = 1.0$$
$$1.00001 = 1.0$$
and so forth

5   Students are told that their grade for the class is determined by taking the average of the four highest grades from among the five grades earned in the class. Write a procedure *classavg* with five input parameters (the earned grades) and one output parameter (the average grade) that performs this calculation. As a more difficult variation, do the same problem, but assume the grade is based on the average of the four highest scores out of six earned grades.

★★ SIGNIFICANT EXERCISES

6   Write a procedure *comma* which displays an integer value of seven digits or less with commas in the usual positions. For example, the integer 1279621 would be displayed as 1,279,621.

7   Beginning with the first character, the input data is to contain a valid Pascal char constant. Write a program which will determine if this input data is valid. (Recall that the usual form is a single quote, the character, and another single quote. Don't forget the case '''', however.)

★★★ CHALLENGING EXERCISE

8   The value of *n*! (read as *n* factorial) can be defined *recursively* as follows:

n	*n*!
0	1
> 0	$(n - 1)! \cdot n$

Write a Pascal procedure which determines the value of *n*! given an input parameter *n*. If $n < 0$, then display an appropriate error message and return the value -1.

CHAPTER 5 PROBLEMS FOR COMPUTER SOLUTION

★ ESSENTIAL PROBLEMS

1   The cost for mailing a first-class letter is $0.22 for letters weighing less than 1 ounce and $0.22 plus $0.17 per additional ounce or fraction thereof for letters weighing more than 1 ounce. Given a letter's weight as a real number of ounces, display the cost of mailing the letter in the form shown in the example.

Example input:

1.01

Example output:

Weight   Cost
1.01   0.39

2 Read a positive integer n (with no more than four digits) and a positive integer d (with exactly one digit). If d appears in the decimal representation of n, then print the number n with a circumflex (^) below each occurrence of d. Otherwise, print the message "d does not appear in n."

Example input:

100   0

Example output:

100
 ^ ^

Example input:

152   3

Example output:

3 does not appear in 152.

3 Determine the roots of the quadratic equation

$$ax^2 + bx + c = 0$$

where a, b, and c are given as real numbers with values less than 100 in the input data. Display the values of a, b, and c and the roots in one of the following forms:

$$a = xx.x \qquad b = xx.x \qquad c = xx.x$$

   Two unequal real roots: $xxx.xxx$ and $xxx.xxx$
or Two equal real roots: $xxx.xxx$
or Two unequal imaginary roots: $xxx.xxx \pm xxx.xxx\ i$
The number of digits used for printing the roots of the equation may vary.

Example input:

2.0   3.0   1.0

Example output:

a = 2.0   b = 3.0   c = 1.0
Two unequal real roots: − 1.000 and −0.500

4   The input data contains an integer. When this integer is written as a four-digit number, with leading zeroes if necessary, the leftmost two digits represent an hour value in the range 00 to 23 and the rightmost two digits represent a minute value in the range 00 to 59. Write this integer in the form *hh:mm*. Arrange to have all four digits appear, even if they are zeroes.

Example input:

402

Example output:

04:02

★★ SIGNIFICANT PROBLEMS

5   Given an input value that represents a dollar amount less than $1000, display the amount and its equivalent as words:

Input:

357.98

Output:

Three hundred fifty seven dollars and ninety eight cents

6   Convert a four-digit positive hexadecimal number to its base 10 equivalent. A hexadecimal digit is one of the digits 0 to 9 or A (10), B (11), C (12), D (13), E (14), or F (15). The decimal equivalent of a hexadecimal number of the form *abcd* is $a \cdot 16^3 + b \cdot 16^2 + c \cdot 16 + d$.

7   The input data for this problem is a discount rate table for bulk purchases of a particular product (as input data in the format shown in the example below), a specified tax rate on the purchase, a discount rate for paying cash, the number of units of the product desired, and the unit cost. Determine the total cost. The first character in the input will be *C* if payment is in cash and *X* if the purchase is to be charged. The result will be the discount amounts, rounded to the nearest cent, and the final price of the purchase. If appropriate, the bulk purchase discount is applied first, and then the cash discount. Display your results in the format shown below. There will be between 1 and 5 lines in the discount table.

Example input:	(Comments; not part of input)
C	(paid cash)
0.05	(5% discount for cash)
712	(number of units purchased)
12.04	(each unit costs $12.04)
5	(number of lines in the table)
10 0.00	(1 to 10, no discount)
25 0.02	(11 to 25, 2 percent)
100 0.04	(26 to 100, 4 percent)
500 0.07	(101 to 500, 7 percent)
0.11	(over 500, 11 percent)

Example output:

```
Cash purchase of 712 units at 12.04 each.
Net price: 8572.48.
Bulk discount (11 percent): 942.97.
Cash discount (5 percent): 381.48.
Please pay: 7248.06.
```

8 Given a real number representing a dollar amount less than $9,999.99, display the amount with a dollar sign and a comma, if appropriate. Do not include blanks between the dollar sign and the first digit.

Example input:

```
25.04      4012.04
```

Example output:

```
$25.04      $4,012.04
```

9 Produce a truth table for an arbitrary Boolean expression with three variables. That is, given the Boolean expression (but not as input), produce a table that shows the value of the expression for all possible combinations of the variables.
   Example: Suppose the Boolean expression was

```
a AND (NOT b OR c)
```

The output should then be similar to the following:

```
a  b  c  expression
F  F  F      F
F  F  T      F
F  T  F      F
F  T  T      F
```

```
T  F  F     T
T  F  T     T
T  T  F     F
T  T  T     T
```

★★★ CHALLENGING PROBLEMS

10 Given a collection of three decimal digits in the range 0 to 8, determine the number of unique decimal numbers that can be formed, with replacement, assuming sixes can be inverted to form nines. A more difficult problem is to display the integers as well.

Example input:

0   3   6

Example output:

19 unique integers

(Specifically 0, 3, 6, 30, 36, 39, 60, 63, 90, 93, 306, 309, 360, 390, 603, 630, 903, and 930.)

11 Scuba divers must perform decompression stops if they dive for periods of time exceeding certain limits. The table below shows decompression stops for dives to 70, 80, and 90 feet and the required decompression times.

DECOMPRESSION STOPS
(TIMES IN MINUTES)

depth	time at bottom (in min)	at 30 ft	at 20 ft	at 10 ft
70 ft	100		...	33
	110		2	41
	120		4	47
	130		6	52
80 ft	100		11	46
	110		13	53
	120		17	56
	130		19	63
90 ft	100		21	54
	110		24	61
	120		32	68
	130	5	36	74

The input data contains the depth (in feet) and duration (in minutes) of the dive. Determine the proper decompression times and display these. Assume the input will match one of the entries in the table. Include the following message in your output: "WARNING: DO NOT DIVE WITHOUT PROPER INSTRUCTION!"

Example input:

80   120

Example output:

For a dive to 80 feet for 120 minutes, the following
decompression stops are required:
  17 minutes at 20 feet
  56 minutes at 10 feet
WARNING: DO NOT DIVE WITHOUT PROPER INSTRUCTION!

CHAPTER 6

CHAPTER 6
LOOPING

WHILE
Statement

Other Loop
Structures

Problem
Solving
with Looping

Program
Correctness
and Loop
Invariants

REPEAT
Statement

FOR
Statement

LOOPING

OBJECTIVES

After completing this chapter you should be able to:

- Recognize and apply the WHILE statement to problems using looping
- Recognize and apply the REPEAT-UNTIL statement to problems using looping
- Recognize and apply the FOR statement to problems using looping
- Apply the problem-solving approach to problems using looping
- Test and debug a Pascal program using looping
- Optionally, demonstrate the correctness of a loop

CHAPTER OVERVIEW

As you have seen, the computer has the capability of executing a sequence of instructions accurately and repeatedly. In this chapter we concentrate on how you can control the repeated execution of a sequence of statements through a programming technique known as *looping*. In particular, we will study looping control structures that permit the repeated execution of a sequence of statements while some condition is true. We will continue to use Boolean expressions to represent these conditions. One form of a looping control structure is shown in Figure 6-1.

In this case if the Boolean expression is true, then a sequence of statements (known as the *body* of the loop) is executed. After execution, the Boolean expression is tested again. As long as the Boolean expression is true, the body of the loop will be executed repeatedly. When the Boolean expression is false, control transfers to the next statement following the loop. It is important to realize that the Boolean expression will be evaluated and tested after each execution of the body of the loop. The sequence of events in this loop is therefore "test, execute, test, execute, . . . , test". For example, consider the following problem:

> *From the input data obtain a list of an unknown number of letter grades (A, B, C, D, or F) terminated by the letter S, and determine how many of these grades are A.*

The flow of control for this problem is shown in Figure 6-2. The variable *acounter* will count the number of letter grades equal to A. Initially, the value of *acounter* must be set to zero, since no A's have yet been encountered. Then the first letter grade is read.

Figure 6-1   Looping control structure.

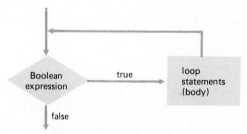

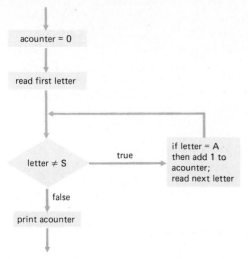

Figure 6-2   Flow of control for sample problem.

Next, the loop begins. "While" the letter grade just read is not equal to S, do the following: If the letter grade is A, add one to *acounter*; then read the next letter. Control transfers to the beginning of the loop, and the loop will be executed while the letter grade is not equal to S. If and when a letter grade of S is read, the body of the loop will be skipped and control will transfer to the print statement following the loop.

There are several looping constructs available in Pascal. A solution of this problem using the Pascal WHILE statement is shown below (assume *acounter* is declared integer and *letter* is declared char):

```
acounter := 0;
read (letter);
WHILE letter <> 'S' DO
BEGIN
      IF letter = 'A'
      THEN acounter := acounter + 1;
      read (letter)
END;
writeln ('The number of A grades is ', acounter:1)
```

Note that a fieldwidth of 1 has been used in the *writeln* statement for displaying the value of *acounter*. Recall (from Chapter 3) that this does *not* imply we will have less than 10 A's, but that we want to use the minimum number of columns possible for the display of the value; if the value of *acounter* is greater than 9, Pascal will automatically increase the number of columns used for the display. By doing this, the output produced by the program will not have an implementation-dependent number of blanks between the word *is* and the number of A grades. Attention to such small details is necessary to produce solutions that are not only correct but are also tailored to use by humans. Programs that exhibit such niceness are sometimes called *user-friendly*.

We consider looping control structures in this chapter. In particular, the Pascal looping statements WHILE, REPEAT-UNTIL, and FOR will be discussed in detail with applications to problem solving. An optional section on program correctness and loop invariants is also included in this chapter.

SECTION 6.1 THE WHILE STATEMENT

The WHILE statement illustrated in the previous example is the first looping construct we will discuss. The WHILE statement in Pascal is an example of a looping control structure that has the following general form:

```
WHILE Boolean-expression DO
    statement-1;
statement-2
```

The reserved word WHILE is followed by a Boolean expression and then by the reserved word DO. While the Boolean expression is true, statement-1 (or a group of statements enclosed by a BEGIN-END pair) will be executed. The WHILE statement will be repeatedly executed until the Boolean expression is evaluated and found to be false, at which time control transfers to the next statement after the WHILE statement (statement-2). The syntax diagram and flow of control of the WHILE statement are shown in Figure 6-3.

Consider the following sequence of Pascal statements (where *num* and *counter* are declared integer):

Figure 6-3   The WHILE statement.

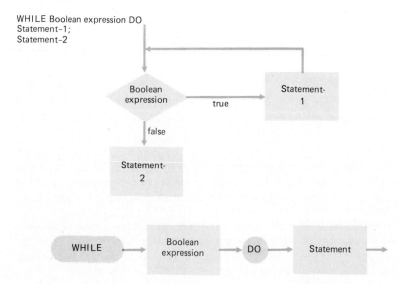

```
counter := 0;
read (num);
WHILE num > 0 DO
BEGIN
        count := count + 1;
        read (num)
END;
writeln ('Number of positive integers =', counter:1)
```

This sequence of Pascal statements when executed will perform the following: *counter* is initially set to zero, an integer (*num*) is read, the WHILE loop is executed repeatedly as long as *num* is positive. This Pascal segment of code will count the number of positive integers entered as input. When a zero or negative number is entered, the body of the loop is skipped and the *writeln* statement will be executed. Observe that the body of the loop contains two statements, and these must therefore be enclosed by a BEGIN-END pair. Suppose the input is the following sequence of integers: 12, 25, 10, and −9. Given this input, the program segment will be executed as described by the following pseudocode.

	pseudocode	explanation
STEP 1	counter := 0	Initialize counter to 0
STEP 2	read (num)	Read first number
STEP 3	WHILE (num > 0) DO	Test if num > 0. If so, continue with step 4. If not, continue with step 7
STEP 4	add 1 to counter	Increment counter
STEP 5	read (num)	Read the next number
STEP 6	return to step 3	To evaluate and test the Boolean expression
STEP 7	write (counter)	Display result

Notice that step 3 through step 6 will be executed as long as the input number is positive. When the −9 is read (after three passes through the loop), the evaluation of the Boolean expression "num > 0" yields false and control transfers to the *writeln* statement. The value of counter at that point will be 3. The following table shows the values that will be assigned to variables counter and num during the execution of this program segment.

step	1	2	3	4	5	6	3	4	5	6	3	4	5	6	3	7
Counter	0	0	0	1	1	1	1	2	2	2	2	3	3	3	3	3
Num		12	12	12	25	25	25	25	10	10	10	10	−9	−9	−9	−9

As we have seen, hand-testing the algorithm with actual values can be of valuable assistance in testing and debugging our programs.

It is important to note that the *read* statement inside the body of the loop is critical. Without the *read* statement, the program would be in an **infinite** (or endless) **loop**. That is, the program would never be able to exit from the loop. Thus, without the *read* statement, the following WHILE statement would be in an infinite loop (assuming *num* > 0):

```
WHILE num > 0 DO
BEGIN
      count := count + 1
END
```

In this loop the value of the Boolean expression never changes. Consequently, the loop will be executed indefinitely.

Suppose we know before writing the program that 20 integers are to be read, and we would like to count and display the number of positive integers. In this case the WHILE statement needs to keep track of the number of times the loop body has been executed. We can use a variable known as a **loop control variable** for this purpose. The following Pascal segment would perform this task (assume i, *count*, and *num* are declared integer):

```
count := 0;              (* Initialize count. *)
i := 1;                  (* Initialize loop control var. *)
WHILE i <= 20 DO         (* Continue until i > 20. *)
BEGIN
      read (num);        (* Obtain the next input item. *)
      IF num > 0
      THEN count := count + 1;
      i := i + 1          (* Increment loop control var. *)
END;
writeln ('The number of positive integers is ', count:1)
```

Observe that the loop control variable i must be initialized to a value (in this case, 1) because the computer cannot determine the value of $i <= 20$ without knowing the value of i. Inside the loop body the loop control variable must be changed in order to avoid an infinite loop. In this case when $i = 21$, the loop will not be executed since the Boolean expression "$i <= 20$" becomes false, but *count* will be less than or equal to 20. Control then skips to the *writeln* statement.

Example 6.1

Consider the following Pascal statements. What will be displayed, and how many times is the body of the loop executed?

```
j := 0;
WHILE j < 5 DO
BEGIN
        write (j);
        j := j + 1
END
```

The output is the value of the loop control variable j at the beginning of each execution of the loop body: 0, 1, 2, 3, and 4. The loop is executed five times.

What would happen if we changed the order of the two instructions in the body of the loop? That is, what is the output of the following Pascal statements?

```
j := 0;
WHILE j < 5 DO
BEGIN
        j := j + 1;
        write (j)
END
```

The output would then be 1, 2, 3, 4, and 5. The loop body is still executed five times. Observe that when $j = 4$, the Boolean expression is true and the body of the loop is executed. Then $j = 5$, and the write statement is executed. The Boolean expression is then evaluated again. This time the expression's value is false and the WHILE statement has completed execution.

Sentinels and Looping

A *sentinel* is a special value used to indicate the end of a list of data items. For example, suppose we have a list of student grades (each grade in the range 0 to 100). Also, there is an unknown number of grades, but the list is terminated by the number -999 (the sentinel). Figure 6-4 illustrates such a list. We can use a WHILE statement to control the loop body that obtains the grades from the input data. The Boolean expression in the WHILE statement will be used to test for the end of the list by detecting the sentinel.

Problem 6.1

One or more student scores in the range 0 to 100 appear in the input data followed by the sentinel value -999. Determine and display the total of all the grades excluding, of course, the sentinel.

The solution to this problem appears below. The variables *grade* and *total* are assumed to be declared as integers.

GRADES

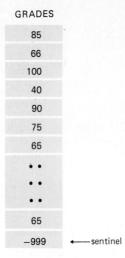

←—— sentinel

Figure 6-4 List of grades with a sentinel.

```
total := 0;
read (grade);
WHILE grade <> -999 DO
BEGIN
        total := total + grade;
        read (grade)
END;
write ('The total of all grades is ', total:1)
```

Observe that *total* is initialized to zero before the WHILE statement. Inside the loop body the partial totals of the grades are computed by the statement

```
total := total + grade
```

When the loop terminates, the contents of the variable *total* will be the sum of all the grades. As an exercise the student should verify the execution of this Pascal segment for the input data

```
85      100      90      50      -999
```

Problem 6.2

This problem is the same as problem 6.1 with the exception that the average of the grades is also to be displayed.

To compute the average grade, we must divide the total of the grades by the number of grades. Thus, inside the loop body we must update a counter that will maintain an indication of the number of grades obtained from the input. This counter must be initialized to zero before the WHILE loop. Assume the variable *counter* has been declared integer and a variable *average* has been declared real. The following segment of Pascal code will compute and display both the total of the grades and their average.

```
total := 0;                    (* initialize total grade *)
counter := 0;                  (* count number of grades *)
read (grade);                  (* obtain the first grade *)
WHILE grade <> -999 DO         (* test for sentinel *)
BEGIN
        counter := counter + 1;   (* increment counter *)
        total := total + grade;    (* add new grade *)
        read (grade)               (* obtain next grade *)
END;
writeln ('The total of the grades is ', total:1);
(* Compute the average grade *)
average := total / counter;
writeln ('The average grade is ', average : 6 : 2)
```

Loop Control Using Boolean Variables

It is possible to have compound Boolean expressions in Pascal WHILE statements using the Boolean operators AND, OR, and NOT. Boolean variables (sometimes called *flags*) can be used to control the execution of a WHILE statement. Consider the following problem, where more than one condition is tested for loop control.

Problem 6.3

The input data contains a single positive integer. Determine if this integer has any proper divisors, and print an appropriate indication of your findings. A positive integer has a proper divisor if it is divisible by any positive integer other than itself and 1. For example, 6 has proper divisors of 2 and 3, while 7 has no proper divisors.

Let us use the variable *num* to store the positive integer read from the input data. Then to solve this problem we will use a "brute force" approach and divide *num* by all the integers between 1 and *num*, not including 1 and *num*. That is, we will divide *num* by the integers 2, 3, 4, . . . , *num* − 1. If any of these numbers divides *num* evenly, then *num* must have a proper divisor and we want to terminate the loop used to "cycle" through all the potential integer divisors.

To do this we use a variable named *flag*, which we declare as Boolean. This variable is initialized to false and indicates whether or not *num* has a proper divisor. If, during execution of the loop, we determine that *num* does have a proper divisor, we will set *flag* to true. If *flag* is true when we evaluate the Boolean condition controlling the loop, then we know a proper divisor has been found, and the loop's execution need not continue.

What happens if we try all integers between 1 and *num* and a proper divisor is not found? The variable *flag* is still false, but we need to terminate the loop. We need to test for this condition too. Therefore the Boolean expression we use in our WHILE statement will consist of two pieces: "NOT flag" and "divisor < num." The following Pascal segment illustrates the solution.

```
read (num);
flag := false;       (* assume no proper divisor yet *)
divisor := 2;        (* start division test with 2 *)
WHILE NOT flag AND (divisor < num) DO
BEGIN
        flag := num MOD divisor = 0;
        divisor := divisor + 1
END;
write ('The number ', num:1, ' ');
IF flag
THEN writeln ('has a proper divisor.')
ELSE writeln ('does not have a proper divisor.')
```

The assignment statement

```
flag := num MOD divisor = 0
```

may appear somewhat strange to you at first glance. However, recall that the expression

```
num MOD divisor = 0
```

is a Boolean expression and will be evaluated as true or false; the resulting value is then assigned to the Boolean variable *flag*. An alternate way to perform this assignment uses an IF statement:

```
IF num MOD divisor = 0
THEN flag := true
ELSE flag := false
```

You should convince yourself that this method is equivalent to the single assignment statement. Since they both work, you can use them interchangeably.

Observe that as soon as a proper divisor is found (*flag* will be set to true), the WHILE loop will be terminated, since the Boolean expression will be false ("NOT flag" will be false). Also, if *num* has no proper divisor, the loop will terminate when the divisor (which is incremented by one each time through the loop) equals the value of *num*. The IF-THEN-ELSE statement will display the appropriate conclusion depending on the value of *flag*. Note that the major purpose of the Boolean variable *flag* is to terminate the execution of the WHILE loop when a proper divisor has been found. Without this Boolean variable, the loop would be repeatedly executed until the divisor equals *num*. This is very inefficient, especially if *num* has a small proper divisor. For example, if *num* is a large even number, say 1200, then with the *flag* variable, the body of the WHILE loop is executed just once since "1200 MOD 2 = 0." However, without the *flag* variable available to terminate the WHILE loop, the body will be executed 1198 times!

Some important points to consider when using the WHILE statement are as follows:

- You should initialize any loop control variables before the loop.
- The Boolean expression in the WHILE statement is evaluated before the loop is entered.
- The loop control variable must be modified inside the loop to prevent an infinite loop.

Nested WHILE Statements

Recall that a statement inside the body of a WHILE loop can be any Pascal statement or group of statements. Specifically, this can include another WHILE statement. A nested WHILE statement is a WHILE statement within another WHILE statement.

Let us consider an example. Suppose we are given the population of each of the 25 largest cities in 10 different states, and we want to identify and display the population of the largest city in each state.

This problem can be divided easily into two subproblems as follows:

SUBPROBLEM 1: Repeat subproblem 2 for each of the 10 states.
SUBPROBLEM 2: Find and display the largest population in one state.

If we can obtain the solution to subproblem 2, we can solve the entire problem. Since there are exactly 25 populations for each state, the solution to subproblem 2 involves reading the 25 populations and identifying and displaying the largest. The Pascal coding for this is simply written using a WHILE loop. We assume that *pop*, *largest*, and *i* are all declared to be integer variables.

```
largest := 0;          (* the "default" largest pop *)
i := 1;                (* initialize the city counter *)
WHILE i <= 25 DO  (* more populations to test? *)
BEGIN
      read (pop);      (* get population of next city *)
      IF pop > largest  (* new largest population? *)
      THEN largest := pop;      (* yes, so save it *)
      i := i + 1      (* increase the city counter *)
END;                    (* of the loop for one state *)
writeln ('The largest population is', largest:1)
```

Note that *largest* is initialized to zero, and then each time a new population is greater, *largest* is set to this value. Subproblem 1 requires the repetition of subproblem 2 exactly 10 times. We can accomplish this by including the solution to subproblem 2 in the body of a WHILE loop which is designed to execute 10 times. To create such a loop, we must use another integer loop control variable, say *j*. Note that we cannot use *i* to control this loop because its value would be changed by the code for subproblem 2. The solution to the entire problem then looks like this:

```
j := 1;                              (* initialize state counter *)
WHILE j <= 10 DO                        (* more states? *)
BEGIN
      largest := 0;                  (* the "default" largest pop *)
      i := 1;                           (* count the cities *)
      WHILE i <= 25 DO               (* more populations? *)
      BEGIN
            read (pop);              (* get population of next city *)
            IF pop > largest         (* new largest population? *)
            THEN largest := pop;         (* yes, so save it*)
            i := i + 1               (* increase the city counter *)
      END;                               (* of the cities loop *)
      writeln ('The largest population is', largest:1);
      j := j + 1                     (* increase state counter *)
END                                     (* of the states loop *)
```

Notice that each time the inner WHILE loop completes execution, the outer WHILE loop resets *largest* to 0 and *i* to 1.

EXERCISES FOR SECTION 6.1

1 Assume that the following code is part of a correct Pascal program.

```
x := 10;
WHILE x > 0 DO x := x − 3;
writeln (x)
```

Determine the exact output after execution of this code.

2 What values are displayed when the following program segment is executed?

```
sum := 0;
i := 3;
WHILE i <= 7 DO
BEGIN
      sum := sum + i;
      i := i + 2
END;
writeln (i, sum)
```

3   Given the input values

    10   5   2   −5

and the code segment

```
sum := 0;
positive := true;
WHILE positive DO
BEGIN
        read (x);
        IF x < 0
        THEN positive := false
        ELSE sum := sum + x
END;
writeln (sum)
```

what will be displayed when the code is executed?

4   Given the input values

    10   20   0   30

and the code segment

```
sum := 0;
i := 0;
read (x);
WHILE x > 0 DO
BEGIN
        i := i + 1;
        sum := sum + x;
        read (x)
END;
writeln (sum, i, x)
```

what will be displayed when the code is executed?

5   What values are displayed when the following program segment is executed?

```
outctr := 1;
WHILE outctr <= 3 DO
BEGIN
        inctr := 5;
        WHILE inctr > outctr DO
                inctr := inctr − 1;
```

```
                              outctr := outctr + 1
       END;
       writeln (outctr, inctr)
```

6 What are the contents of *sum* and *value* after the following program segment has been executed. Assume the following input data: 5, 6, 7, −3, −4, 0, 5, 8, and 9.

```
n := 8;
sum := 0;
i := 1;
flag := false;
WHILE (i <= n) AND NOT flag DO
BEGIN
        read (value);
        IF value > 0
        THEN sum := sum + value
        ELSE IF value = 0
                THEN flag := true;
        i := i + 1
END;
writeln ('End of test ', sum, value)
```

SECTION 6.2 OTHER LOOPING STRUCTURES

There may be situations in which you want a loop to be executed at least once *before* testing whether to repeat execution of the loop. In the WHILE statement, if the value of the Boolean expression is initially false, the body of the loop will not be executed. For example, consider the following Pascal segment (assume *num* and *counter* are declared as integer variables):

```
count := 0;
read (num);
WHILE num > 0 DO
BEGIN
        count := count + 1;
        read (num)
END
```

If the first number to be read is negative or zero, the body of the WHILE loop will not be executed. The WHILE statement tests the value of the Boolean expression first to determine whether to execute the body of the loop. In some cases it may be necessary to execute the body of the loop first and then perform the test. This looping control structure is available in Pascal by means of the REPEAT-UNTIL statement. In these loops the loop body is executed first, and then the Boolean expression is evaluated.

The REPEAT-UNTIL statement has the following general form:

REPEAT
    statement;
    statement;

    .
    .
    .

    statement
UNTIL Boolean-expression

   The reserved word REPEAT is followed by a Pascal statement which forms the body of the loop. The statement is executed repeatedly until the value of the Boolean expression is true. Thus, the REPEAT-UNTIL loop is executed while the value of the Boolean expression is *false*, just the opposite of the WHILE statement. As usual, a group of statements can be used for the loop body, but a BEGIN-END pair is *not* necessary after the word REPEAT if more than one statement is specified. The words REPEAT and UNTIL effectively perform the *bracketing* function. Figure 6-5 shows the syntax diagram and flow of control of the REPEAT-UNTIL statement.

   Consider the following Pascal segment (assume *num* and *counter* are declared as integer variables):

Figure 6-5   REPEAT-UNTIL statement.

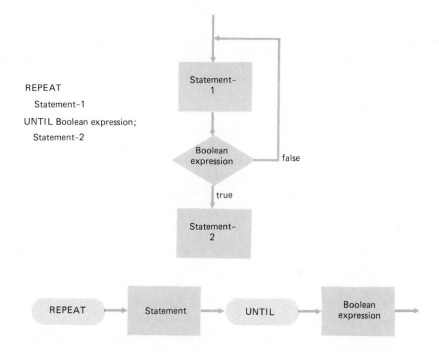

```
count := 1;
REPEAT
    read (num);
    count := count + 1
UNTIL count > 20;
writeln ('Twenty numbers read.')
```

In this Pascal sequence the body of the REPEAT loop is executed until *count* exceeds 20. This will happen after 20 executions of the loop body. Then the *writeln* statement will be executed. Note that no BEGIN-END pair is necessary.

In the following example, we are to search for the first digit in a sequence of characters appearing in the input data.

Example 6.2

The input data contains a sequence of characters. Determine the first decimal digit contained in this input data, and display it in an appropriate message.

In this problem we must read at least one character before any testing can take place, and if the test fails (that is, the character we read is not a decimal digit), then we must read again. This requirement to perform some action repeatedly until reaching a condition that is true is ideally implemented in Pascal using the REPEAT-UNTIL statement. Let us assume a character variable *ch* has been declared. Then the solution takes advantage of the ordering of characters:

```
REPEAT
    read (ch)
UNTIL (ch >= '0') AND (ch <= '9');
writeln ('The first decimal digit is ', ch)
```

Recall that Standard Pascal requires the decimal digits to be ordered so that '0' is less than '1', '1' is less than '2', and so forth. It further requires that no other characters be found between any two decimal digits. So if *ch* is greater than or equal to '0' and less than or equal to '9', we have verified that it is a decimal digit.

Let us consider the same problem but attempt to use a WHILE loop instead of a REPEAT-UNTIL loop. As noted earlier, we *must* read a character before the test for a decimal digit can be performed, so our solution would look like this:

```
read (ch);
WHILE (ch < '0') OR (ch > '9') DO
    read (ch);
writeln ('The first decimal digit is ', ch)
```

Comparing the two loop control structures above, we see that the opposite of the Boolean expression "(ch < '0') OR (ch > '9')" is the expression "(ch >= '0') AND (ch <= '9')." In general, if *P* and *Q* are Boolean expressions, then "NOT (P AND

Q)" is logically the same as "NOT P OR NOT Q." Also "NOT (P OR Q)" is logically the same as "NOT P AND NOT Q." These two properties are known as ***DeMorgan's Law***.

As another example, the following Pascal segment uses a REPEAT-UNTIL statement to print the numbers 1 to 100:

```
num := 1;
REPEAT
    writeln (num);
    num := num + 1
UNTIL num = 101
```

The final example shows how a REPEAT-UNTIL loop can be used in data validation. In this case the program is expecting a month number in the range 1 to 12. If the value obtained from the input is incorrect, an appropriate message is displayed for the user and an additional value is obtained.

```
write ('Please enter the month number: ');
REPEAT
    readln (month);
    IF (month < 1) OR (month > 12)
    THEN write ('Please enter a value between 1 and 12: ')
UNTIL (month >= 1) AND (month <= 12)
```

This loop-checking technique is very useful when you are using an interactive computer system, since it allows immediate correction of an input error.

The FOR Statement

Sometimes we know in advance exactly how many times we want to execute the statements in a loop. In this case, the FOR statement can be used. The FOR statement in Pascal is a loop control structure that will execute a loop body a specified number of times and automatically keep track of the number of "passes" through the loop body. The following FOR statement, for example, will read n integers and determine their sum (assume that n, i, num, and *total* have been declared as integer variables).

```
total := 0;
FOR i := 1 TO n DO
BEGIN
    read (num);
    total := total + num
END
```

Using a WHILE statement, we must initialize the loop control variable (in this case, i) and increment it each time through the loop body. We could then write the above example using a WHILE statement as:

```
total := 0;
i := 1;                    (* initialize loop control var *)
WHILE i <= 20 DO
BEGIN
        read (num);
        total := total + num;
        i := i + 1    (* increment loop control var *)
END
```

The FOR statement in this example initializes the loop control variable to 1 and increments it each time the end of the loop body is reached. This continues until the loop control variable reaches 20. Then the loop body is executed one last time, and execution continues with the first statement following the loop.

Note that the value of the FOR loop control variable (also frequently called a ***counter***) is undefined when the loop terminates. (This is not the case with WHILE loops; the value of the control variable *is* known when the loop terminates.) Any variable which has an ordinal type may be used as a loop control variable. The general form of the FOR statement is

```
FOR counter := initial value TO final value DO statement
```

The statement must begin with the reserved word FOR and is followed by what looks like an assignment statement giving the initial value to the counter variable. This is followed by the reserved word TO and the final value of the counter. Finally, the reserved word DO appears, followed by the statement (or group of statements enclosed by a BEGIN-END pair) that forms the loop body. The counter variable, the initial value, and the final value must all have the same ordinal type. The steps in executing a FOR statement are as follows (refer to Figure 6-6):

STEP 1 The counter variable is assigned the initial value.

STEP 2 If the counter variable is less than or equal to the final value, then the loop body is executed, the counter variable's value is replaced by its successor, and step 2 is repeated. (For integer variables, the successor is just the next sequential integer. Successors of other ordinal types are considered further in Chapter 8.)

STEP 3 After the FOR loop has completed, the value of the counter variable is made "undefined." That is, the value of the counter variable cannot be assumed to have any specific value after the loop has completed execution.

Example 6.3

The FOR statement

```
FOR i := 0 TO 5 DO write (i)
```

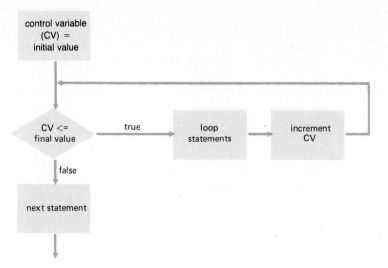

Figure 6-6 FOR control structure.

will display the value of the control variable during each execution of the loop body. Since the loop body is executed six times, the output will contain 0, 1, 2, 3, 4, and 5.

Example 6.4

The FOR statement

FOR letter := 'A' TO 'E' DO write (letter)

will also display the value of the control variable (letter, assumed to be declared as a char variable) during each execution of the loop body. This time the loop will execute five times, and the output will contain ABCDE. The successor of a char value is the character that immediately follows it in the lexicographic ordering (or collating sequence) for the particular computer system in use.

The counter variable in a FOR loop also can be decremented. The reserved word DOWNTO is used in place of TO when writing the FOR statement. For example, consider the statement

FOR i := 10 DOWNTO 0 DO write (i)

This will display the values 10, 9, 8, 7, 6, 5, 4, 3, 2, 1, and 0, in that order. The steps in executing a FOR loop using DOWNTO are similar to those previously presented:

STEP 1   The counter variable is assigned the initial value.
STEP 2   If the counter variable is greater than or equal to the final value, then the loop body is executed, the counter variable's value is replaced by its predecessor, and step 2 is repeated.
STEP 3   The value of the counter variable is made "undefined" after completion of the loop.

Example 6.5

Character-valued control variables can be decremented too. Consider the following FOR loop:

```
FOR letter := 'e' DOWNTO 'a' DO write (letter)
```

This will display the letters edcba.

Note that for the body of the FOR-TO-DO loop to be executed at all, it is necessary for the initial value to be less than or equal to the final value. Likewise, for the body of the FOR-DOWNTO-DO loop to be executed, it is necessary for the initial value to be greater than or equal to the final value. It is not an error to specify a FOR loop whose body is never executed; in many cases the initial value or the final value is specified by an expression whose value is not known until the program is executed.

Example 6.6

Consider the following FOR loop:

```
read (num);
FOR i := 10 TO num DO write (i)
```

If *num* is less than 10, the FOR loop body will not be executed.

It is important to note that any FOR statement can be replaced by an equivalent set of assignment statements and a WHILE statement. But *not* every WHILE statement can be replaced by an equivalent FOR statement, since FOR statements must specify both initial and final values for the loop control variable. The following important points about FOR statements and their loop bodies should be remembered:

■   The loop control variable of a FOR loop may be of any ordinal type (that is, not real), and the initial and final values must be of the same type.
■   The loop control variable must be declared as a local variable within the procedure containing the loop:

right	*wrong*
`PROGRAM a (input,output);`	`PROGRAM x (input,output);`
`VAR i : integer;`	`VAR i : integer;`
`PROCEDURE b;`	`PROCEDURE y;`
`VAR j : integer;`	`BEGIN`
`BEGIN`	`    FOR i := . . .`
`    FOR j := . . .`	`END;`
`END;`	`. . .`
`. . .`	`END.`
`END.`	

■ The loop control variable may not be changed within the loop. In addition, it may not be a formal variable parameter to a procedure containing the FOR loop, or passed as an actual variable parameter to any procedure invoked within the FOR loop body. The following code segment is therefore incorrect (assume that *proc* is a procedure that has a variable parameter):

```
PROCEDURE wrong (VAR i : integer);
BEGIN
     FOR i := 1 TO 10 DO proc (i)
END
```

■ The initial value and final value of a FOR loop may be modified within the body of the FOR loop without changing the number of times the loop is executed. This is because the initial value and final value are determined and saved in "secret" variables prior to the first execution of the loop body. For example, the following loop will print the integers 1 to 10, even though the final value is modified within the loop body (assume all variables are integers):

```
final := 10;
FOR i := 1 TO final DO
BEGIN
     final := 999;
     write (i)
END
```

■ After the execution of a FOR statement, the value of the loop control variable is totally undefined. The control variable must be assigned another value before attempting to use it in an expression.

■ If the initial value and final value are the same, then the loop is executed exactly once. For example, the following FOR statement will display only the number 1.

```
FOR i := 1 TO 1 DO write (i)
```

■ The initial and final values of a FOR loop are arbitrary expressions that may include variables, constants, and operators. For example, the following FOR loop will have its body executed exactly six times (assume that all variables are integers):

```
low := 0;
high := 3;
FOR index := low + 1 TO 2 * high DO
BEGIN
        read (num);
        write (num)
END
```

■ In this case the value of the variable *index* will vary from 1 to 6.
FOR statements may be nested, as may WHILE and REPEAT statements. Thus the following FOR statements (with all variables declared as integers) will produce six lines of output containing 1 1, 1 2, 1 3, 2 1, 2 2, and 2 3. Note that the control variables of nested FOR loops may not be the same.

```
FOR  i := 1 TO 2 DO
        FOR j := 1 TO 3 DO writeln (i, j)
```

Next, we consider a problem where the FOR statement can be used effectively.

Example 6.7

Determine and display the value of 1 + 2 + 3 + · · · + num, where num is an integer greater than zero.

We will need an integer loop counter (*i*) and a variable in which to store the partial sums (*sum*). Then the solution is as follows:

```
sum := 0;
FOR i := 1 TO num DO sum := sum + i;
writeln ('The sum is ', sum:1)
```

Note that no BEGIN-END pair is required with the FOR loop since there is only one statement in the loop body.

Problem 6.4

The input data contains the month number and day of the month in a non-leap year. Determine and display the corresponding day of the year (in the range 1 to 365) using a loop.

Recall that this problem was solved in Section 5.4 using a CASE statement to select the sum of the days in months preceding the month of interest. The solution can be simplified by using a FOR loop to compute this sum. If we assume that *month*, *day*, *index*, and *dayofyear* are all integers, then the following Pascal coding will solve the problem.

```
read (month, day);     (* get month number and day *)
dayofyear := 0;        (* initialize sum *)
FOR index := 1 TO month − 1 DO
     CASE  index OF
               1,3,5,7,8,10 : dayofyear := dayofyear + 31;
               2 :            dayofyear := dayofyear + 28;
               4,6,9,11 :     dayofyear := dayofyear + 30
     END;
dayofyear := dayofyear + day
```

Note that the FOR loop and CASE statement body are used to determine the sum of the number of days in each month prior to the month of interest (*month*). This is the reason for using "month − 1" as the final value in the FOR loop. Clearly *index* will assume each value between 1 and "month − 1," in turn. If *month* is specified as 1, then the FOR loop body is not executed at all. Since *month* can be no larger than 12, the CASE statement must provide for each of the values 1 through 11. The last statement increases *dayofyear* by the day number of the month of interest.

Indefinite or Definite Control Structures?

In this chapter we have presented three Pascal control structures: WHILE, REPEAT-UNTIL, and FOR. The FOR statement implements what is commonly called a ***definite control structure***, since the number of executions of the loop body is determined exactly by the initial and final values specified for the loop control variable. When designing the solution to a problem, keep in mind the limitations of the FOR loop:

- The number of times the loop body is to be executed must be determined before execution of the loop is started.
- No "early" termination of a FOR loop is possible.

For example, if we wish to determine the average income for a group of exactly 50 people, then a FOR statement is appropriate, since exactly 50 executions of the loop body (which obtains one income from the input and adds it to the partial sum) must be performed.

If, however, there are an unkown number of persons in the group, then an *indefinite control structure*, such as that implemented by the WHILE and REPEAT-UNTIL statements, must be used. The indefinite control structures may be used when the loop exhibits the following characteristics:

■ The number of times the loop body is to be executed is not necessarily known prior to execution of the loop.
■ More than one condition may be used to terminate execution of the loop.

Recall that the REPEAT-UNTIL loop will always execute the loop body at least once.

Note that the FOR statement should not be used when more than one condition may be used to terminate the loop. Consider the following problem.

Problem 6.5

It is known that at most one checking account balance in a list of exactly 1000 such balances is negative. Find and display the negative balance and its position in the list, if it exists.

The following FOR loop will solve this problem, but it is clearly inefficient since all 1000 balances must be processed regardless of the position or presence of the negative balance; *balance* is declared real and *index* is declared integer.

```
FOR index := 1 TO 1000 DO
BEGIN
        read (balance);
        IF balance < 0
        THEN writeln ('Balance ', index:1, ' is ', balance:6:2)
END
```

In problems such as this we would like to terminate execution of the loop once the desired condition has been met (here it was discovery of the negative balance or testing of all 1000 balances). Many high-level programming languages, including Pascal, provide a statement called an *unconditional transfer statement* that causes execution to continue at a reasonably arbitrary point in the program. In Pascal, unconditional transfer is provided by the GOTO statement. In the negative balance problem a GOTO statement could have been used to cause the loop to terminate and execution to continue elsewhere. (More details on the GOTO statement are found in Appendix G.) This approach is *definitely not* recommended, however, and most programmers consider almost any use of the GOTO statement an extremely bad practice.

When more than one condition is used to determine when a loop is to terminate, a WHILE or REPEAT-UNTIL statement should be used. The solution of the negative balance problem can be written using a REPEAT-UNTIL statement as follows:

```
index := 0;              (* initialize position in list *)
REPEAT
    read (balance);          (* obtain a balance *)
    index := index + 1       (* update the index *)
UNTIL (balance < 0) OR (index = 1000);
IF balance < 0
THEN writeln ('Balance ', index:1, ' is ', balance:6:2)
```

Observe that when a negative balance is read, the loop will terminate ("balance < 0" is true) and control will transfer to the *writeln* statement. Also note that a WHILE statement could have been used instead of the REPEAT-UNTIL statement.

Given that Pascal provides two indefinite control structures (WHILE and REPEAT-UNTIL), which one should be used for a particular problem? In general, it makes little difference which of these is chosen since the two are very similar. However, consider the situation suggested by the following illustration.

Daily sales data from a certain company is to be processed each day to provide timely inventory information. A loop is to be written that will process the record of each sale. Should a WHILE loop or a REPEAT-UNTIL loop be used, or is it unimportant which one we choose? A problem will occur if there are no sales on a particular day and a REPEAT-UNTIL statement is used to implement the loop, since at least one execution of the loop body is required. The WHILE statement should clearly be used since its Boolean condition may be used to verify that data exists before continuing.

EXERCISES FOR SECTION 6.2

1   Determine the number of times the REPEAT-UNTIL loop body will be executed in the following segment.

```
a := 6;
b := 5;
REPEAT
    a := a + 1
UNTIL a > b
```

2   Consider the following program segment:

```
i := 0;
REPEAT
    writeln ('Primitive.')
UNTIL i = 0
```

Determine the exact output when the segment is executed.

3   What is the value displayed when the following segment of code is executed? Assume *a* and *b* are integer variables.

```
FOR b := 1 TO 3 DO
BEGIN
        IF b <= 1 THEN a := b - 1;
        IF b <= 2
        THEN a := a - 1
        ELSE a := a + 1
END;
writeln (a)
```

4 Consider the following three segments of code, each of which is embedded in a correct Pascal program.

```
I.   FOR  i := 1 TO 3 DO
          FOR j := i + 1 TO 3 DO
              write (i, j)
```

```
II.  i := 1;
     j := 1;
     WHILE (i <= 3) AND (j <= 2) DO
     BEGIN
           write (i, j + 1);
           i := i + 1;
           j := j + 1
     END
```

```
III.  FOR  i := 1 TO 2 DO
           write (i, i + 1)
```

Determine which of the following statements is correct.
(a) All three segments produce the same output.
(b) Segments I and II produce the same output.
(c) Segments II and III produce the same output.
(d) Segments I and III produce the same output.
(e) No segment produces output identical to any of the others.

5 Assume that the following code has been embedded in a correct program.

```
lo := 1;
FOR k := lo TO 3 DO
BEGIN
        lo := lo + 2;
        write (k, lo)
END
```

Determine the display resulting from execution of this code.

6 Determine the display resulting from execution of the following code.

```
hi := 4;
FOR  k := hi DOWNTO 3 DO
        writeln (k, hi)
```

SECTION 6.3 PROBLEM SOLVING USING LOOPING

In this section we apply looping to a specific problem. Consider the following word processing problem for computer solution (see Figure 6-7).

A student has completed a term paper for a particular course. Determine the following statistical information about the paper that is required by the instructor:

- *The number of sentences in the paper*
- *The number of words used in the paper*
- *The average number of words in each sentence*
- *The number of words having 10 letters or more*

To simplify the problem, assume that a period is used to mark the end of each sentence. Thus, the last word of each sentence will be followed by a period. Further assume that a dollar sign is used as a sentinel to mark the end of the paper.

This problem can be divided into three subproblems, as follows:

SUBPROBLEM 1: Read the characters in the text.
SUBPROBLEM 2: Count the number of words, sentences, and words of 10 or more letters.
SUBPROBLEM 3: Display the results.

The most difficult subproblem to solve is the first, reading the data. Since there are an unknown number of characters terminated by a sentinel ("$"), we can use a WHILE

Figure 6-7   Top-down design of word processing problem.

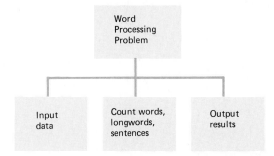

statement to search for the end of the paper. Another WHILE statement can be used to search for the end of a sentence. Inside this WHILE statement we will read and count the words used in a given sentence.

The following algorithm written in pseudocode outlines this solution in more detail.

Word Processing Algorithm

Initialize counters.
Read a character.
While not end of paper ("$"):
   While not end of sentence ("."):
      Read a word.
      Increase count of words.
      If length of word is greater than 10 letters then increase count of longwords.
   Increase count of sentences.
   Read a character.
Display number of sentences.
Display number of words and longwords.
Compute and display average words per sentence.

The only step requiring further analysis is "Read a word." Since words are separated by special characters (such as blanks, commas, and semicolons) we can ignore all characters until an upper- or lowercase letter is read. The refinement of "Read a word" is then the following:

Read a word:
   Skip nonletters.
   Read letters.
   Count letters.

We may now proceed to write our first version of the Pascal program called *wordstat*.

```
PROGRAM wordstat (input, output);
(* Determine number of words, sentences, long words *)
(* (more than 10 letters), and average words per     *)
(* sentence in the input data. The input ends with   *)
(* a dollar sign ("$").                               *)
CONST sentinel = '$';
VAR
      length : integer;    (* length of current word *)
      words : integer;     (* total words read       *)
      longwords : integer; (* no. of longwords        *)
```

```
        sentences : integer;   (* no. of sentences    *)
        average : real;        (* words / sentence     *)
        ch : char;      (* input character             *)


(*---------------------------------------------------------------------------------*)
BEGIN
        (* Initialize all counters *)
        words := 0;
        longwords := 0;
        sentences := 0;
        (* Main loop *)
        read (ch);
        WHILE ch <> sentinel DO   (* not end of paper *)
        BEGIN
                WHILE ch <> '.' DO   (* not end of sentence *)
                BEGIN
                (* Ignore nonletters *)
                        WHILE NOT ((ch >= 'A') AND (ch <= 'Z'))
                            AND NOT ((ch >= 'a') AND (ch <= 'z'))
                        DO read (ch);
                        length := 0;    (* starting new word *)
                        (* read the new word *)
                        WHILE (ch >= 'A') AND (ch <= 'Z') OR
                                (ch >= 'a') AND (ch <= 'z') DO
                        BEGIN
                                length := length + 1;
                                read (ch)
                        END;
                        words := words + 1;
                        IF length > 10
                        THEN longwords := longwords + 1
                END; (* of WHILE ch <> '.' *)
                sentences := sentences + 1;
                read (ch)
        END; (* of main loop *)
        (* Display results *)
        writeln ('Number of sentences:    ', sentences:8);
        writeln ('Number of words:    ', words:8);
        writeln ('Number of long words:    ', longwords:8);
        average := words / sentences;
        writeln ('Avg. words per sentence:', average:8:2)
END.
```

Program Wordstat

I think, therefore I am. I think Descartes said that.
According to Artificial Intelligence magazine, computers can think.
Therefore, they are. $

Number of sentences: 4
Number of words: 21
Number of long words: 1
Avg. words per sentence: 5.25

Program Wordstat: Sample Execution

The above program can be modified to handle other problems related to punctuation and English grammar (question marks, apostrophes, and so forth) as well as checking for misspelled words (see the example in Chapter 4). It can also be used to verify that specifications have been met for a term paper, magazine article, or even a book! Character data handling will be studied in more detail in a later chapter.

SECTION 6.4 PROGRAM CORRECTNESS AND LOOP INVARIANTS [OPTIONAL]

After you have written a program to solve a given problem, how do you know with absolute certainty that the program does solve the problem? You can run numerous test cases of input data and verify that the program's output is correct for those cases. But the program may still fail for other untested input data. If the program is large, it would be very impractical (if not impossible) to verify that the program is correct for all possible inputs.

Techniques for establishing program correctness have been developed by computer scientists in an area of theoretical research known as ***program verification***. In this section we consider some of these techniques, especially those related to proving the correctness of loops. The proofs of correctness can often be complicated and lengthy. However, there are many cases where the cost of proving a program correct is small compared to the cost resulting from running an incorrect program. Think of the potential danger of running a faulty program that controls a nuclear power plant.

Preconditions and Postconditions

The method for program verification presented here is based on a series of observations about the variables of a program before, during, and after the execution of a program segment. These observations, called ***assertions***, are statements about the program variables that are expected to be true. These program assertions are used to describe the state of the program at each step of the execution. In addition, these assertions describe program variables and their relationships during various stages of the execution of the program. Assertions are usually expressed by Boolean expressions. The following are examples of assertions enclosed by comment brackets { and }.

```
{ num is positive }
{ x + y > z }
{ divisor <> 0 }
{ num > 0 and index < num }
{ Counter is the sum of all integers from 1 to 100 }
```

Establishing the correctness of a program (or program segment) is accomplished by precisely specifying the task to be performed. One way to do this is by stating the **precondition** and **postcondition**. The precondition is an assertion that describes the state of the program variables before execution begins. If there is nothing known or assumed about the program variables, the precondition is the Boolean constant true. The postcondition is an assertion that describes the state of the program variables after execution ends. If the precondition and postcondition correctly specify the task to be performed by a program segment, then the question of program correctness can be considered.

The following simple example shows a program segment that is correct (assume *num1* and *num2* are integer variables):

```
{ true }
num1 := 4;
num2 := 5
{ num1 = 4 and num2 = 5 }
```

Observe that no assumptions have been made before the program segment begins execution, so the precondition is true. The postcondition describes the state of the variables *num1* and *num2* after execution of the program segment.

The divide and conquer approach to problem solving can also be applied to proving the correctness of a program. We can construct a correctness proof of a program by successively dividing it into a series of correctness proofs for smaller program segments. If we can prove the correctness of these smaller program segments, then we can combine them to obtain a correctness proof for the whole program. Let's consider the following example, in which a, b, c, and d are integer variables.

```
a := b DIV d;
c := a + b
```

The precondition of the first statement is the assertion that assures the divisor d is not zero:

```
{ d <> 0 }
```

The postcondition of the first statement is the assertion

$\{\, a = b \text{ DIV } d \,\}$

This postcondition will act as the precondition for the second statement before execution. After execution of the second statement, the postcondition for this program segment is

$\{\, a = b \text{ DIV } d \text{ and } c = a + b \,\}$

This is equivalent to the assertion

$\{\, c = b \text{ DIV } d + b \,\}$

So, if the two program parts

$$\{\, d <> 0 \,\} \qquad\qquad\qquad \{\, a = b \text{ DIV } d \,\}$$
$$a := b \text{ DIV } d \qquad \text{and} \qquad c := a + b$$
$$\{\, a = b \text{ DIV } d \,\} \qquad\qquad\qquad \{\, c = b \text{ DIV } d + b \,\}$$

are both correct, then the program

$\{\, d <> 0 \,\}$
$a := b \text{ DIV } d;$
$c := a + b$
$\{\, c = b \text{ DIV } d + b \,\}$

is correct. Notice by the assumptions above, the intermediate assertion "$\{\, a = b \text{ DIV } d \,\}$" can be safely removed.

Loop Invariants

The examples presented so far were kept simple in order to illustrate the ideas of precondition and postcondition. Verifying the correctness of loops is more difficult since we must verify not only that the loop is doing what it is supposed to do but also that it will eventually terminate.

A *loop invariant* is an assertion that is true before a loop is entered and that continues to be true after each iteration of the loop. So a loop invariant remains unchanged after each pass through the loop. A *loop variant* is an assertion that changes with each pass through the loop. It is used to ensure the eventual termination of the loop by reaching or passing a value called a ***threshold***. The loop invariant relates the precondition of the loop to the postcondition. As you will see, if the invariant and variant assertions are appropriately determined, they can be used to prove the correctness of the loop.

Consider the following program segment that computes *product (number * count)* for two integers, *number* and *count* (where *number* is nonnegative), by repeated addition. That is, *product* is initialized to zero and then *count* is repeatedly added to *product*. The precondition and postcondition of the program segment are also included.

```
{ number >= 0 }
index := 0;
product := 0;
WHILE index < number DO
BEGIN
        product := product + count;
        index := index + 1
END
{ product = number * count }
```

In order to prove that this loop is correct with respect to the precondition and postcondition, we must determine an invariant assertion and a corresponding variant assertion. Determining the loop invariant is often a difficult step since there is always more than one invariant for a loop. For example, the assertion "{ index >= 0 }" is true before the loop and after each pass through the loop, so it is a loop invariant. But this invariant is not very useful in proving the correctness of the loop. The loop invariant should assert more information about the action of the loop. Since *index* and *number* are both nonnegative and related by the WHILE condition "(index < number)", we conclude that the following assertion is a useful loop invariant:

{ index <= number }

Notice that for any nonnegative value of *number*, this loop invariant will be true before the loop and after each iteration of the loop.

If the loop is correct, the value of *product* should also be correct. We must therefore find a loop invariant related to computation of *product* inside the loop. The assertion

{ product = index * count }

will be true before the loop is entered and after each pass through the loop, and is therefore another useful loop invariant. Now the final loop invariant can be written as

{ index <= number, and product = index * count }

It gives us confidence that our loop will correctly perform the task of computing *product* by repeated addition.

We must now provide some proof that the loop will eventually terminate by determining the loop variant. Since "(index <= number)" and *index* increases each time through the loop, the loop will terminate when *index* reaches the threshold, in this case, the value of *number*. So the variant assertion is

{ index < number and index increases }

and assures us that the loop will eventually terminate.

The program segment with precondition and postcondition for each statement is shown below.

```
{ number >= 0 }
index := 0;
{ number >= 0, and index = 0 }
product := 0;
{ number >= 0, index = 0, and product = 0 }
{ index <= number, and product = index * count }
WHILE index < number DO
{ index < number, and product = index * count }
BEGIN
        product := product + count;
        { index < number, and product = (index + 1) * count }
        index := index + 1
        { index <= number, and product = index * count }
END
{ product = number * count }
```

At this point we can conclude that the program segment is correct with respect to the precondition "{ number >= 0 }" and the postcondition "{ product = number * count }." The technique of demonstrating program correctness described in this section can be summarized as follows:

- Describe precisely the precondition and postcondition of the program (or program segment) in order to specify the task to be performed.
- Divide the program (or program segment) into successively smaller segments, describing the precondition and postcondition for each segment.
- Establish the correctness of each of the smaller program segments with respect to its precondition and postcondition.
- Finally, conclude the program (or program segment) is correct with respect to the original precondition and postcondition.

Program verification requires quite a bit of work even for an elementary program. More complicated programs can often be proved correct by using sophisticated techniques from logic and mathematics. Also, computer programs have been developed to aid in the process of verifying the correctness of a program. However, program verification as a discipline is in its infancy, and most programs are not formally verified for correctness. So why bother trying to prove the correctness of a program? In some cases, such as loop verification, proving program correctness can be beneficial. For example, it allows us to document the loop very carefully by including program assertions and gives us confidence that the loop will perform correctly as claimed. Another important reason is that an understanding of program verification techniques can be very effective when applied to solving, testing, debugging, and documenting your program. In other words, it can make you a better programmer! Finally, testing can never show the absence of errors, only their presence.

At this point we look back at the last six chapters and summarize the fundamental control structures used in programming languages like Pascal. So far we have discussed the following four control structures: (1) sequential execution, (2) procedure definition and invocation, (3) selection, and (4) looping. We now have all the control structures necessary to write structured computer programs. Much of the remainder of this course is concerned with applying these control structures, all of which are available in Pascal, to the solution of a variety of problems, especially problems involving different forms of data representation and structure. Note that the control structures are a fundamental part of most structured high-level programming languages, but may be represented by the language using different syntactic rules (see Figure 6-8).

Summarizing the fundamental control structures we have the following.

1   *Sequential execution* is the execution of a sequence of statements, one after the other. In Figure 6-9, for example, statement-1 would be executed, then statement-2, and so forth until the last statement is executed.

2   *Procedure* declaration and invocation permits the naming of a group of statements which may then be used by writing a single statement (the invocation). Actual parameters in the main program specify values in the procedure which are associated with formal parameters (*placeholders*), allowing one procedure to be used with different values each time it is invoked. Figure 6-10 illustrates a procedure with an example in Pascal.

3   *Selection* permits alternate courses of action to be chosen depending on the value of an expression. The IF-THEN-ELSE, the IF-THEN, and the CASE statements provide selection capabilities in Pascal. Figure 6-11 illustrates the IF-THEN control structure.

4   *Looping* control structures provide the means for specifying controlled repetition of one or more statements. The repetition can be controlled by a Boolean expression (whose value indicates when to continue the repetition of a WHILE or REPEAT-UNTIL loop body) or by a range of ordinal values (in a FOR statement). Pascal provides two indefinite looping control structures (the WHILE and REPEAT loops) and one definite looping control structure (the FOR loop). Figure 6-12 illustrates the Pascal WHILE control structure.

Figure 6-8   Fundamental control structures.

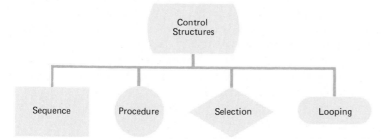

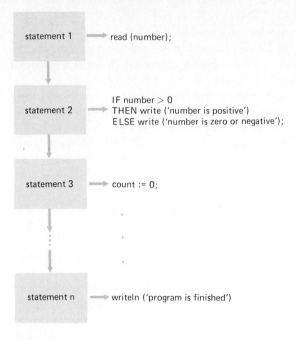

Figure 6-9 Sequential control structure and Pascal example.

Figure 6-10 Procedure control structure and Pascal example.

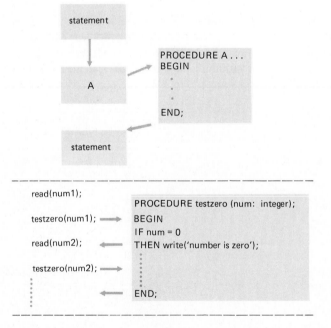

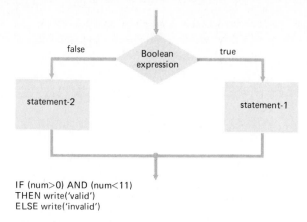

IF (num>0) AND (num<11)
THEN write('valid')
ELSE write('invalid')

Figure 6-11   Selection control structure and Pascal example.

SECTION 6.6 TESTING AND DEBUGGING TECHNIQUES

Infinite Loops

How can you determine if your program is in an infinite loop? If your progam is running and does not terminate, it may be in an infinite loop. What are the sources of error? The following list gives a number of points you might check:

- Be sure the control variable was initialized before the beginning of each WHILE loop.
- Be sure the loop control variable is modified inside the body of the loop.
- Check that the Boolean expression is not always true. For example, the statement

  WHILE (1 + 1 = 2) DO

  will always result in an infinite loop.
- Check that an empty statement does not immediately occur after the DO. For example, assume *num* is initially greater than 10. Then the statement

  WHILE (num > 10) DO ;

Figure 6-12   Looping control structure and Pascal example.

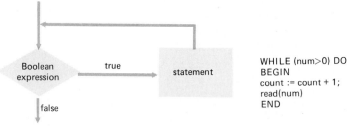

```
WHILE (num>0) DO
BEGIN
count := count + 1;
read(num)
END
```

is an infinite loop, since the loop control variable *num* never changes. If you put a semicolon immediately after the DO by mistake, the Pascal compiler will not report a syntax error. The empty statement is assumed to be the statement you wish to execute repeatedly.

■ In a REPEAT-UNTIL statement be sure the Boolean expression is not always false. Consider the following example:

```
REPEAT
     statement
UNTIL (num > 1) AND (num < 0)
```

Here "(num > 1) AND (num < 0)" is never true; so the REPEAT statement will be an infinite loop.

Loop Errors

A common error in coding loops is the off-by-one error. Consider the following example, which is supposed to print the odd numbers from 1 to 11.

```
num := 1;
REPEAT
     writeln (num);
     num := num + 2
UNTIL (num = 11)
```

The actual output will be the odd numbers 1, 3, 5, 7, and 9. The odd number 11 is not displayed since the Boolean expression is true when *num* = 11, and the loop terminates. We can correct the program by changing the Boolean expression to *num* = 13. What would happen if we change the condition to *num* = 12? Checking a few iterations of the loop by hand will show that you are in an infinite loop!

When writing loops, you should check that the loop is entered under the appropriate conditions. Be sure that the loop control variable is initialized before the loop and that the loop will eventually terminate. Verify the execution of the loop by checking a few values by hand. Be sure to check the initial and final values. These are called the *boundary conditions*. Many loop errors are traced to either an initial value not being correct or a final value never being reached.

The following is an example of a loop that is entered incorrectly. The program segment should read an unknown number of nonnegative numbers, keep the total of these values, and terminate when a negative value is read, without adding the negative value to the total. Assume *number* and *total* are integer variables.

```
total := 0;
WHILE number >= 0 DO
BEGIN
          read (number);
```

```
        total := total + number
END
```

The loop is entered incorrectly since the value of the variable *number* is undefined. Suppose we initialize the variable *number* so the loop will be entered. Then will the following code solve the problem?

```
total := 0;
number := 1;
WHILE number >= 0 DO
BEGIN
        read (number);
        total := total + number
END
```

Let's test the proposed solution by hand to see if it is correct! Suppose the input data was a single positive number and a sentinel:

```
100          -999
```

The previous loop will not, work correctly. The value of total should be 100 after the loop terminates. However, the actual value, as you can verify, is $-999 + 100$, or -899.

The problem can be solved correctly using a technique known as **priming**. The value of *number* can be initialized before entering the loop by reading in the first value. This value is processed inside the loop. The last statement in the loop will read the next value of to be processed, either as a data value or a sentinel. The following code segment correctly implements a solution to the problem. You should verify its correctness for the values 100 and -999, as well as additional test data values. For example, why would the single data value -999 be a useful test case?

```
total := 0;
read (number);                    (* initialize number *)
WHILE number >= 0 DO              (* no sentinel yet *)
BEGIN
        total := total + number;    (* add a non-sentinel *)
        read (number)   (* obtain next data value or sentinel *)
END
```

Once again the importance of testing your solutions using small collections of data has been illustrated. Virtually all the difficulties with solutions to programming problems can be explained if careful hand execution of small program segments is done *before utilizing the coding in a larger program segment*. This technique cannot be recommended too highly!

A list of important reminders appropriate when using the looping constructs of Pascal follows.

PASCAL REMINDERS

- Hand testing of code can identify virtually *all* the problems present in problem solutions.
- The Boolean expression in the WHILE statement must be true for the loop to be executed.
- The Boolean expression in the REPEAT-UNTIL statement must be false for the loop to repeat.
- The REPEAT-UNTIL loop is always executed at least once.
- In a WHILE or REPEAT-UNTIL statement, a counter variable keeps track of the number of times the loop body has been executed.
- Boolean variables known as *flags* can be used to control the execution of a WHILE or REPEAT-UNTIL statement.
- If more than one statement appears in the body of a WHILE or FOR statement, then a BEGIN-END pair must enclose the statements.
- The value of the counter variable in a FOR loop is made "undefined" after the completion of the loop.

SECTION 6.7 CHAPTER REVIEW

In this chapter we discussed looping and related loop control structures in Pascal. In particular, the three loop control structures WHILE, REPEAT-UNTIL, and FOR were discussed. The WHILE statement is a loop that is executed as long as the specified Boolean expression is true. When the expression becomes false, the loop body is skipped and the statement following the loop is executed. Sentinels and flags can also be used to control the loop.

The REPEAT-UNTIL statement is a looping control structure that is executed at least once, and then a Boolean expression is tested. If the Boolean expression is false, the loop is repeated. When the expression is true, the loop terminates and execution continues with the statement following the REPEAT-UNTIL statement. A FOR statement can be used when the number of times the loop is to be executed is known prior to entering the loop (as the value of an expression or a constant). The FOR statement is called a definite control structure.

In this chapter we compared the three loop control structures and discussed the conditions that were favorable for their use. Problem solving using looping was also presented with a detailed example involving word processing. A summary of the fundamental control structures was also presented. The following summary of the Pascal looping constructs described in this chapter can be used for future reference.

PASCAL REFERENCE

1 WHILE statement: While the condition is true execute the loop body.

```
WHILE Boolean-expression DO
    statement
```

Example:

```
WHILE (number > 0) DO
BEGIN
        count := count + 1;
        read (number)
END
```

2 REPEAT-UNTIL statement: Repeat loop body until condition is true.

```
REPEAT
        statement;
        statement;

        . . .
        statement
UNTIL Boolean-expression
```

Example:

```
REPEAT
        read (number);
        count := count + 1
UNTIL (number > 100)
```

3 FOR statement: Execute loop from initial value to final value.

```
FOR count := initial-value TO final-value DO statement;
FOR count := initial-value DOWNTO final-value DO statement;
```

Example:

```
FOR i := 1 TO 10 DO
BEGIN
        read (number);
        sum := sum + number
END
```

4 Fundamental control structures
   4.1   Sequential execution
   4.2   Procedure
   4.3   Selection
   4.4   Looping

Chapter 7 Preview

Thus far we have presented the fundamental control structures in Pascal. Next, we will consider procedures, functions, and parameters. In particular, we will consider nesting procedures, standard Pascal functions, user-defined functions, and recursive functions.

Keywords for Chapter 6

assertion	looping
definite control structure	postcondition
flag	precondition
FOR statement	program verification
GOTO statement	REPEAT-UNTIL statement
indefinite control structure	sentinel
infinite loop	threshold
loop control variable	WHILE statement
loop invariant	unconditional transfer
loop variant	

CHAPTER 6 EXERCISES

★ ESSENTIAL EXERCISES

1 Write a program to display the multiplication table from 1 times 1 to 9 times 9. It should begin something like this:

```
      1  2  3
   1  1  2  3
   2  2  4  6
```

2 Rewrite the code

```
REPEAT
    body
UNTIL Boolean-expression
```

using a single WHILE loop.

3 The buttons on a push-button telephone are arranged in the following pattern:

1	2	3
4	5	6
7	8	9
*	0	#

The input data will contain seven integers, each in the range 0 to 9, representing a telephone number (not including * or #). Write a Pascal program that will display the row and column numbers of the buttons to be pressed in order to dial the number.

Example input:

```
5 6 7 8 0 1 3
```

Example output:

```
2    2
2    3
3    1
3    2
4    2
1    1
1    3
```

4   Assume the input data contains lines, each of which contains a letter in the first column followed by a real value representing a dollar amount. The last line contains only the letter *X* in column 1. The first line contains the letter *P* and the previous balance in a checking account. Each other line contains the letter *D* and a deposit amount or the letter *W* and the amount of a withdrawal. Determine the *exact* balance in the account after the transactions have been processed.

Example input:

```
P  1200.35
D  64.12
W  390.00
W  289.67
D  13.02
W  51.07
X
```

Example output:

The final balance is 546.75.

★★ SIGNIFICANT EXERCISES

5   Consider the function

$$f(x,y,z) = x^2 + 2xy - 3yz + xz$$

where *x*, *y*, and *z* are integer values. Find the largest value of the function for values of *x*, *y*, and *z* in the range −3 to 3. Display the corresponding values of *x*, *y*, *z*, and $f(x,y,z)$.

6 Suppose Pascal allowed real variables to be used as control variables in FOR loops in the form

```
FOR r := start TO finish BY increment
```

where *r, start, finish,* and *increment* are all of type real. What problems can you see in such a loop? In particular, how would the approximate nature of the real data type affect the property that FOR loops always execute the loop body a definite number of times?

7 The input data for this problem consists of the amount of a periodic savings account deposit (as a real number) and the number of periods for which deposits are made. Determine the amount of compound interest for each of the following interest rates: 8, 8.5, 9, 9.5, and 10 percent.

★★★ CHALLENGING EXERCISES

8 There are a large number of problems found in game and puzzle books similar to the following problem. The diagram given below shows the positions of the decimal digits in a multiplication problem. Also, A, B, and C represent three unique decimal digits, and each * represents some decimal digit. Devise a suitable search scheme to find the values of A, B, and C.

```
            A    B    C
            B    A    C
    ------------------------
        *    *    *    *
        *    *    A
    *   *    *    B
    ------------------------
    *   *    *    *    *    *
```

CHAPTER 6 PROBLEMS FOR COMPUTER SOLUTION

★ ESSENTIAL PROBLEMS

1 The input data contains one or more positive real numbers terminated by a negative number (the sentinel). Determine the standard deviation of this data (excluding the sentinel). The standard deviation of a collection of numbers $x_1, x_2, \ldots, x_n$ is defined as the square root of the expression $(s/n) - a^2$, where a is the average of the x values—(that is, $(x_1 + x_2 + \cdots + x_n)/n$)—and s is the sum of the squares of the x values—that is, $x_1^2 + x_2^2 + \cdots + x_n^2$). Display your result as shown in the example, using two digits on either side of the decimal point.

Example input:

```
25.0    23.0    22.0    2 1.0    17.0
 9.0     6.0     5.0    - 1.0
```

Example output:

The standard deviation is 7.60

2 Given a input data line containing 20 decimal digits with *no spaces,* read them into five integers of four digits each.

3 Given a piece of text terminated by a sentinel $, determine the number of double consonants and double vowels. For example, the text "This is foolish" has two double consonants (*Th* and *sh*) and one double vowel (*oo*).

4 Determine and display the largest and smallest numbers in a set of input integers terminated by the number -9999.

5 Display all the prime numbers between *A* and *B*, where *A* and *B* are positive integers obtained from the input data. A prime number is any positive integer greater than 1 that is divisible only by itself and 1. A simple way to determine if a given number *N* is a prime number is to attempt division of *N* by 2 and by each odd integer greater than 1 and less than the square root of *N*. If any of these numbers divides *N*, then it is not a prime number.

6 Each line of the input contains a person's name and address with each "line" of the address separated by a vertical stroke (|), and terminated by a dollar sign. The last line contains only a dollar sign. Display the data as if printing was being done on mailing labels. Each label is assumed to have five lines. For example, the input data was

John Smith|32 Tenth Avenue North|Bellvue, Wa. 60123$
Bryan Meeks|1201 E. 89th #21|Nowhere, Ontario$
$

then the output would be

John Smith
32 Tenth Avenue North
Bellvue, Wa. 60123

Bryan Meeks
1201 E. 89th #21
Nowhere, Ontario

7 Use an infinite series to determine the value of e^x. Use the formula

$$e^x = 1 + x + \frac{x^2}{2!} + \frac{x^3}{3!} + \cdots + \frac{x^n}{n!}$$

Assume the input data contains a positive value *x* and a positive value *eps*. Compute and add terms to the sum as long as the absolute value of each term is greater than *eps*.

8 A list of input integers is supposed to be in ascending order. The last integer in the list is 999. Read the list, and if it is correct, then display the message "CORRECT." Otherwise, print the two numbers preceding the erroneous value (if there are two; otherwise print only the one) and the erroneous value. For example, if the input data was

5 7 12 31 95 89 112 999

then the output would be

31 95 89.

If the input was

5 7 12 31 95 98 112 999

the output would be

CORRECT.

Finally, if the input was

53 45 59 999

the output would be

53 45.

★★ SIGNIFICANT PROBLEMS

9 Computers can easily perform encryption of messages. Given an integer *n* on the first line of input data, "rotate" a message terminated by $ on the second line by *n* characters, and display the result. The message will contain only blanks and uppercase alphabetic characters. Rotation of an alphabetic character by *n* characters can be illustrated as follows. First write the alphabet in each of two lines. Then shift all the characters in the second line left by *n* characters, with those "falling off" the left end being placed on the right end. For example, if *n* is 3, we obtain the following figure:

A B C D E F G H I J K L M N O P Q R S T U V W X Y Z
D E F G H I J K L M N O P Q R S T U V W X Y Z A B C

The message "SEND THE CAVALRY$" would then be encrypted to produce the message "VHQG WKH FDYDOUB."

10 Repeat problem 9, but this time do the inverse transformation. That is, given an encrypted message, "unrotate" it to produce clear text.

11 Determine the value of pi (3.14159 . . .) by estimating the area of a quadrant of a circle. The area of the quadrant can be determined by counting the number of "darts" that land inside the quadrant of a circle drawn inside a square with an edge equal to the radius of the circle. The position of the dart is determined by generating two random numbers in the range 0.0 to the circle's radius and using these random numbers as the coordinates of the position hit by the dart. Most computer systems include an external function to compute such random numbers. (See Chapter 7.)

★★★ CHALLENGING PROBLEMS

12 Print all the twin primes between A and B. Twin primes are pairs of prime numbers that differ by exactly 2. For example, 3 and 5 are twin primes, as are 11 and 13, and 17 and 19.

13 Assume the largest number of decimal digits that can be stored in an integer variable is 4. Therefore, the largest integer value that can be stored is 9999. The input data consists of 10 twenty-digit integers that are to be added to produce a result having a maximum of 22 digits. Compute and print the result. (Hint: Note that the maximum result of adding 2 four-digit numbers is 19,998, which can be treated as a sum of 9998 and a carry of 1.)

14 The input data contains a list of names, each enclosed in single quotes and no longer than 20 characters, and a score for each person named. The sentinel $ will be used to mark the end of the input. Display each name in columns 1 to 20 of an output line and the corresponding score (in the range 0 to 100) in columns 23 to 25 of the same line. Finally, display the word *AVERAGE* in columns 1 to 7 and the average score (rounded to the nearest integer) in columns 23 to 25 on the last line.

Example input:

```
'FRANK G.'  73    'MARY B.'   100    'PAUL K.'  86
'SUSAN F.'  91    'BARRY M.'  100    $
```

Example output:

```
FRANK G.            73
MARY B.            100
PAUL K.             86
SUSAN F.            91
BARRY M.           100
AVERAGE             90
```

15 A group of documents are characterized as having one or more of seven attributes. Each document is specified by a single line having the presence or absence of the attributes specified by an *X* or a blank in the first seven odd-numbered columns (1, 3, 5, 7, 9, 11, and 13) and the name of the document, terminated by a period, starting in column 15. The first line of input will have an attribute "mask" in the first 13 columns followed by an integer representing the number of attributes that must coincide with a document if that document is to be retrieved. The last line of the input will have $ in column 1. Produce a list of the documents that match the request in a form similar to that shown in the example.

Example input:

```
x x x x x x x 4
x    x       x Pascal for Everyone.
x x x x x x x Introduction to CS with Pascal.
x x       x   x Pascal made Difficult.
x    x       x x Men, Machines, and Pascal.
$
```

Example output:

```
Introduction to CS with Pascal.
Pascal Made Difficult.
Men, Machines, and Pascal.
```

16 A sensor is placed in a roadway to measure traffic volume on a one-lane street. Each time a set of wheels passes over the sensor, a line containing the time (as a real number of seconds) is output. The maximum vehicle length expected is 60 feet, and the maximum expected vehicle speed is 80 miles per hour (we do assume people exceed the speed limit). However, these values should be able to be changed easily (that is, use constants for them!). All signals occurring within the period of time allowed for the passage of one vehicle will count as one vehicle. Determine the number of vehicles that passed during the measurement period, as well as the average number of vehicles per minute. As an added (more difficult) problem, determine the maximum and minimum vehicle speeds (assuming that all vehicles have at least two axles).

17 Perform the functions of a simple calculator. The input will be a sequence of decimal digits and the operators +, −, *, and /, all terminated with an equal sign. Ignore embedded blanks. The operators are applied in the order they appear in the input, and produce integer results.

Example input:

```
4 + 3 / 2 * 8 − 4 =
```

Example output:

```
20
```

18 Repeat the calculator problem (problem 17), except that in addition to decimal digits and operators, there may also be *S n* following a decimal digit or *R n* in place of a decimal digit, where *n* is 0, 1, 2, or 3. These represent storing the result of a calculation into a "register" or recalling a previous result. Recalling a result which has not been stored should result in an error.

Example input:

```
4 + 3 S 0 / 2 + R 0 =
4 + 3 S 0 / 2 + R 1 =
```

Example output:

```
10
ERROR
```

19 Given an integer *n* (as input data), print lines 1 to *n* of Pascal's triangle. Line *i* of Pascal's triangle contains the coefficients of the polynomial expansion of $(x + 1)^{i-1}$. For example, for an input value of 5 the output would be as follows:

```
            1
        1       1
    1       2       1
  1     3       3       1
1     4     6     4       1
```

20 Print a table of all integral temperatures from *A* to *B* degrees Celsius including the integral Fahrenheit temperatures. The Fahrenheit temperature corresponding to *C* degrees Celsius is given by the expression

```
32 + 9 * C / 5
```

For example, if $A = 0$ and $B = 5$, the output should look like this:

```
Celsius         Fahrenheit
   0                32
                    33
   1
                    34
                    35
   2
                    36
                    37
   3
                    38
                    39
   4
                    40
   5                41
```

21 A sequence of 10 integer values, each less than 60, is given as input data. Produce a horizontal bar graph similar to that shown in the example for this data.

Example input:

5 12 17 35 52 42 12 28 31 8

Example output:

```
       ******
    5  ******
       ******
       *
       *************
   12  *************
       *************
       *
       ******************
   17  ******************
       ******************
       *
       ************************************
   35  ************************************
       ************************************
       *
       *********************************************************
   52  *********************************************************
       *********************************************************
       *
       **********************************************
   42  **********************************************
       **********************************************
       *
       *************
   12  *************
       *************
       *
       *****************************
   28  *****************************
       *****************************
       *
       ********************************
   31  ********************************
       ********************************
       *
       *********
    8  *********
       *********
```

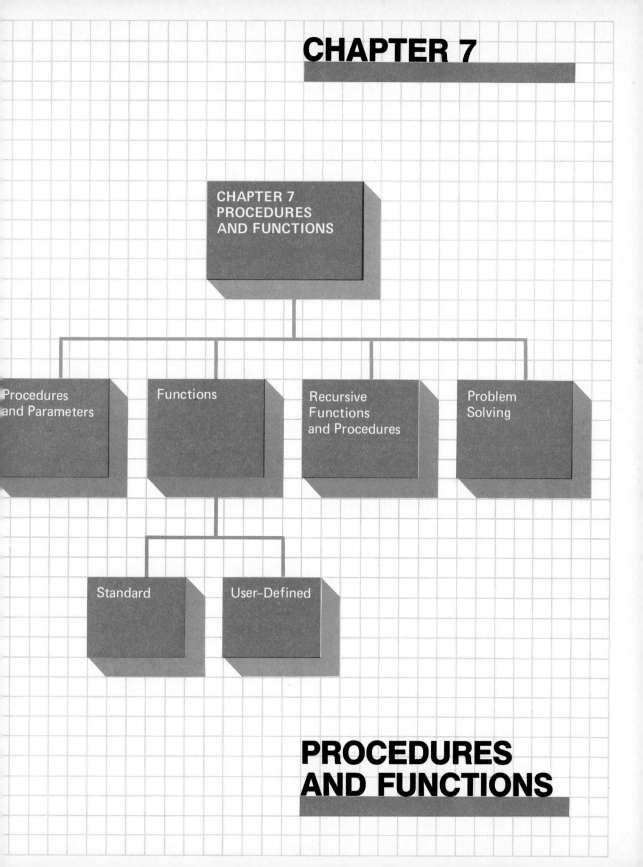

CHAPTER 7

CHAPTER 7
PROCEDURES
AND FUNCTIONS

Procedures
and Parameters

Functions

Recursive
Functions
and Procedures

Problem
Solving

Standard

User–Defined

PROCEDURES
AND FUNCTIONS

OBJECTIVES

After completing this chapter, you should be able to:

- Recognize and apply value and variable parameters in procedures and functions
- Distinguish between formal and actual parameters
- Write nested procedures
- Determine the scope of procedures, functions, and local and global identifiers
- Recognize and apply the Boolean standard functions: *odd*, *eoln*, and *eof*
- Write user-defined functions, including recursive functions
- Recognize and apply random number generating functions
- Solve, test, and debug problems using procedures and functions

CHAPTER OVERVIEW

This chapter contains a wealth of information on procedures and functions and their applications. We start by reviewing procedure parameters. In particular, we discuss value and variable parameters and distinguish between formal and actual parameters. Next a discussion of nested procedures (that is, procedures inside other procedures) is presented. We include some examples and pay particular attention to the local declarations that each procedure may have. In particular, we examine the scope of the local identifiers. In other words, we examine the portion of the program where the identifier is known. Local and global identifiers are discussed in relation to nested procedures.

In Section 7.2 we discuss functions, both standard and user-defined functions. The standard functions we consider are the Boolean functions: *odd* (test integer for odd), *eoln* (test for end of line), and *eof* (test for end of file). After this a discussion of user-defined functions is presented. Applications of functions are also included. In Pascal a function can call itself. Such a function is called **recursive**. We will present a carefully developed example to provide you with some insight into the nature of recursive functions. Several more examples are also included.

At the end of the chapter we apply procedures and functions to a problem dealing with a game-playing program for multiplying numbers. In Section 7.4 we discuss random number generators and the employment of such a function to this problem. Finally, we close the chapter with a discussion of side effects, changing the order of procedure and function declarations, and portability.

SECTION 7.1 PROCEDURES AND PARAMETERS REVISITED

In this section we examine parameters and procedures in more detail and apply the result later to functions. Let us review what we know so far with an example. Suppose you are required to write a Pascal procedure that computes the area and circumference of a circle with a radius of r (see Figure 7-1). Recall the following two formulas for circles, where pi is a constant approximately equal to 3.14159:

$A = \text{pi} \cdot r^2$ (area = pi *times* radius squared)
$C = 2 \cdot \text{pi} \cdot r$ (circumference = 2 *times* pi *times* radius)

 Area (shaded region) = pi $* r^2$ 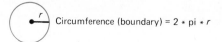 Circumference (boundary) = 2 $*$ pi $* r$

Figure 7-1   Area and circumference of circle.

Remember a procedure is a subprogram that can have input (value) and output (variable) parameters. What are the input (value) parameters? That is, what information must be sent as input to the procedure? In this case, the radius r is the only input (value) parameter. The constant pi (approximately 3.14159) can be declared inside the procedure. The output of this procedure will be the area and circumference of the circle. Thus, area and circumference will be the output (variable) parameters of the procedure. The following procedure called *circle* will perform the required tasks:

```
PROCEDURE circle (radius : real; VAR area, circum : real);
(* Procedure to determine area and circumference of *)
(* a circle, given its radius.                       *)
CONST
        pi = 3.14159;
BEGIN
        area := pi * sqr(radius);
        circum := 2 * pi * radius
END;
```

Note that we have used the standard (built-in) Pascal function *sqr* to square the radius when computing the area. Recall the reserved word VAR does not appear with the input (value) parameter *radius*.

Value and Variable Parameters

The procedure header contains the name of the procedure and an optional list of variable names with data types. The variable names in the procedure header are called *formal parameters*, since the actual values are not known until the procedure is called or invoked. The syntax diagrams for parameter lists and procedure headers are shown in Figure 7-2.

Notice that each formal parameter must include a data type in the header and that some parameters begin with the reserved word VAR. Some information, such as the *radius* in the *circle* procedure, is provided to a procedure as input and is not to be changed in the calling program. The formal parameter corresponding to input to a procedure is called an input (value) parameter. In Pascal it is simply called a *value parameter* and we will now use this terminology. In the program header the list of value parameters does *not* include the reserved word VAR.

The formal parameters corresponding to the output of the procedure, such as the area and circumference of the circle, are known as output (variable) parameters. In Pascal they are simply called *variable parameters*. When we list these parameters,

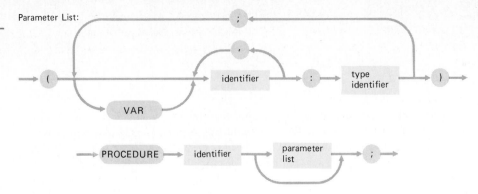

Figure 7-2 Syntax diagram for parameter list and procedure.

the reserved word VAR must be used. This will guarantee that the actual parameters in the calling program will change. For example, if we invoke the procedure *circle* using the following statement that includes the actual parameters

circle (5, area, circumference)

then the contents of the variable parameters *area* and *circumference* would be changed by the procedure. Notice the value parameter 5 will not change. When a procedure is invoked, the order and data type of the actual parameters must match the order and data type of the formal parameters (see Figure 7-3).

Figure 7-3 Procedure invocation.

```
PROCEDURE  circle    (radius : real;  VAR  area, circum : real);

CONST

     pi = 3.14159;

BEGIN

area := pi * sqr(radius);

circum := 2 * pi * radius

END;

( * main program * )

BEGIN
.
.
.
( * procedure invocation * )

circle  ( 5, area, circumference)
.
.
.
END.
```

The actual parameter for a value parameter can be a variable, constant, or an expression. When the procedure is invoked, the value parameter is determined and then passed to the procedure. For example, the following procedure invocation passes an arithmetic expression as the actual value parameter:

```
circle (2 * 3 - 1, area, circumference)
```

When the procedure is invoked, the formal value parameter *radius* will contain the computed value of 5. On the other hand, the actual parameter for a variable parameter must be a variable. Thus, the procedure invocation

```
circle (5, 2, 1)
```

is *not* valid since the second and third parameters are output or variable parameters and 2 and 1 are not variables.

We have considered parameters as either input to or output from a procedure. However, some parameters can serve as both input and output. In Pascal these parameters are also called variable parameters and must include the reserved word VAR in the formal parameter list of the procedure header. Let us look at an example in which variable parameters serve as both input and output. Consider the problem of writing a procedure called *switch* that switches, or interchanges, the contents of two memory locations called *memory1* and *memory2*. If you study this problem carefully, you will note that we cannot exchange the contents of the locations directly in the following fashion:

```
memory1 := memory2;
memory2 := memory1
```

This sequence of statements will not work since the first assignment statement will destroy the contents of *memory1*. We need to save the contents of *memory1* temporarily before making the exchange. The following procedure will solve this problem. Note the use of a local variable to store the contents of *memory1* temporarily. In this procedure *memory1* and *memory2* serve as both input and output, since the contents of each location will change.

```
PROCEDURE switch (VAR memory1, memory2 : integer);
(* Switches contents of memory1 and memory2 *)
VAR
        temp : integer;              (* temporary location *)
BEGIN
        temp := memory1;              (* save memory1 *)
        memory1 := memory2;       (* switch memory2 *)
        memory2 := temp              (* switch memory1 *)
END;
```

When writing procedures, how do you decide whether to use value or variable parameters? In general, if the procedure is sending information back to the calling program, then use variable parameters. On the other hand, if information is being passed to the procedure as input only, then use value parameters. There are some exceptions to this rule that we will consider in later chapters. But why not only use variable parameters? Basically, the reason is that when you use a value parameter, a copy of the value is made and the copy is used by the procedure. This will guarantee that the procedure cannot change the original value parameter. However, value parameters can be costly. As you will see later, we may want to pass as input to a procedure a collection of many values (such as a table of names or a file of characters). Even though these values may serve only as input, we should usually declare them as variable parameters. Otherwise, the computer will waste time and memory locations copying the collection of values. But care must be taken that these values are not inadvertently changed in the procedure.

Here is a summary of some important points regarding value and variable parameters:

- The formal parameters are listed in the procedure header.
- The actual parameters are passed by the procedure invocation statement.
- Formal and actual parameters must match in order and data type.
- Variable parameters must include the reserved word VAR in the formal parameter list of a procedure header.
- The actual parameter for a variable parameter must be a variable.
- The actual parameter for a value parameter can be a variable, constant, or an expression.

Nested Procedures

When procedures are written within procedures they are said to be ***nested***. Let us look at an example.

Problem 7.1

Suppose we would like to write a procedure called search *that reads a character string containing a name followed by a salary represented by an integer with a dollar sign. The purpose of this procedure is to display the salary if it is above a limit; otherwise set the salary equal to zero. A typical input string looks like this:*

JOHN SMITH $50000

Our procedure *search* will contain two procedures called *dollar* and *wage*. Procedure *dollar* will read characters until a dollar sign is found, while procedure *wage* will read the integer *salary* following the dollar sign and determine whether it is over the limit.

Procedure *search* will display a message if the salary is above the limit or return a value of zero to the main program if the salary is not above the limit.

Let us write procedure *dollar* to read and ignore characters until just after the first occurrence of a dollar sign.

```
PROCEDURE dollar;
(* Reads until $ is found *)
VAR
        inchar : char;
BEGIN
        REPEAT
            read (inchar)
        UNTIL (inchar = '$')
END;
```

Notice a char variable *inchar* was declared inside the procedure to store the incoming character. This variable is a *local variable* known only to the procedure *dollar*. This procedure has no formal parameters because we know in advance that the last character read will be a dollar sign.

Now let us write the procedure *wage* to read the salary (an integer) following the dollar sign. Since we want to pass the salary to the procedure *search*, we must declare it as a variable parameter. Also a Boolean variable is included to indicate whether the salary is over the limit (a value parameter).

```
PROCEDURE wage (limit : integer; VAR salary : integer;
                    VAR flag : Boolean);
(* Reads salary and determines if over the limit *)
BEGIN
        read (salary);
        flag := salary > limit
END;
```

Observe that in the procedure header the reserved word VAR occurs twice. If the last VAR (prior to *flag*) was omitted, then *flag* would be a value parameter and the assignment statement

```
flag := salary > limit
```

would not change the actual parameter. Note, however, that *flag* would be changed locally in this case.

Now we can write the main procedure *search* that has a value parameter called *limit* and a variable parameter called *pay*.

```
PROCEDURE search (limit : integer; VAR pay : integer);
(* Procedure to find if salary is above limit *)
VAR test : Boolean;

        PROCEDURE dollar;
        (* Reads until $ is found *)
        VAR
                inchar : char;
        BEGIN
                REPEAT
                    read (inchar)
                UNTIL inchar = '$'
        END;


        PROCEDURE wage (limit : integer; VAR salary : integer;
                        VAR flag : Boolean);
        (* Reads salary and determines if over limit *)
        BEGIN
                read (salary);
                flag := salary > limit
        END;

(* Procedure search begins here *)
BEGIN
        dollar;                         (* search for $ *)
        wage (limit, pay, test);        (* read salary *)
        IF test
        THEN writeln ('Salary exceeds limit: ', pay)
        ELSE pay := 0
END;
```

Scope Rules

When we have nested procedures we must concern ourselves with local and global variables and their scope. The *scope* of an identifier is that portion of the program where the identifier is known. To see this, look closely at the previous example of procedure *search*. The scope of the local variable *inchar* in procedure *dollar* is only the procedure *dollar*. The variable *inchar* is not known to the main program or to procedure *wage*. On the other hand, the variable *test* in procedure *search* is a global variable known to procedures *dollar* and *wage*. Since any procedure can have CONST or VAR declarations, the identifiers are known as local constants or local variables to the procedure. Each identifier is known to all segments of the procedure, including nested procedures that do not have an identifier with the same name. For example, consider the following nested procedure structure (observe each procedure block).

```
PROCEDURE outer (x : integer; VAR y : integer);
CONST
        t = 60;
VAR
        a, b, c : integer;

    PROCEDURE inner1 (x, y : integer);
    VAR
            a, z : integer;
    BEGIN
            .
            .
            .
    END; (* inner1 *)


    PROCEDURE inner2 (VAR a : integer);
    VAR
            v, w : integer;

        PROCEDURE innermost (VAR x, y : integer);
        VAR
                a : integer;
        BEGIN
                .
                .
                .
        END; (* innermost *)

    BEGIN
            .
            .
            .
    END; (* inner2 *)

BEGIN
        .
        .
        .
END; (* outer *)
```

We have put boxes around the procedures to help you see the scope of the identifiers. First the constant $t = 60$ and the variables a, b, and c declared in procedure *outer* are local identifiers to the procedure *outer*. However, the scope of these identifiers includes all of procedure *outer* (main box). Since procedures *inner1*, *inner2*, and *innermost* are included in the main box containing procedure *outer*, they are within the scope of these identifiers. Actually, these identifiers are global to the procedures *inner1*, *inner2*, and *innermost*. In other words, the constant $t = 60$ and the variables a, b, and c in the VAR declaration of procedure *outer* are known to the procedures *inner1*, *inner2*, and *innermost*. Also, the formal parameters x and y of procedure *outer* are actually local variables to the procedure *outer* and have the same scope rules as the constant and variable declarations of procedure *outer*. Thus they, too, are global variables to the procedures *inner1*, *inner2*, and *innermost*.

Now let us consider the procedure *inner1*. The scope of the variables in the declaration is the box containing the procedure *inner1*. Notice that the variable name a occurs both in the main procedure (*outer*) and the procedure *inner1*. They do not refer to the same variable. Any reference to the name a in procedure *inner1* will be to the local variable a in procedure *inner1*. *Local variables having the same name as global variables take precedence over the global variables.* To reference the global variable, you must pass it as a parameter. The parameters of procedure *inner1* (x and y) are also local variables of procedure *inner1*.

Finally, let's consider procedure *inner2*. The local variables v and w of this procedure are known only within the box containing procedure *inner2*. So to the procedure *innermost* contained within procedure *inner2*, the variables v and w are actually global variables. Also, the variables a, b, and c declared in the main procedure *outer* are global variables to the procedure *innermost*. Procedure *inner2* has a local variable a (the variable formal parameter) that is also global to procedure *innermost*. However, procedure *innermost* has a local variable with the same name a. Again, in this case, any reference to the variable a inside procedure *innermost* will be to the local declared variable a inside the procedure *innermost*.

What about procedure invocations? Procedure names have scope just like variable names. Procedure *inner2* can call procedure *inner1* since it (procedure *inner2*) comes after procedure *inner1*. Procedure *inner1* cannot call procedure *inner2*. Also, procedure *innermost* can call procedure *inner1*. Note that procedure *innermost* cannot be called by any procedure outside the box containing procedure *inner2*, since it is unknown outside of procedure *inner2*.

Let us summarize our findings on the scope rules of global and local identifiers.

procedure	known identifiers	other known variables or constants	procedures within scope
outer	t, a, b, c, x, y	None	inner1, inner2
inner1	a, z, x, y	t, b, c (in *outer*)	None
inner2	v, w, a	t, b, c, x, y (in *outer*)	innermost
innermost	a, x, y	t, b, c (in *outer*) v, w, (in *inner2*)	None

Remember that even though you can reference a global variable from a procedure within the scope of the variable, *it is usually not a sound idea*. Preferably, the variable should be passed as a parameter. Global variables should not be changed by a direct assignment statement in the procedure (this is an example of a **side effect**). Your procedures should be self-contained independent modules. Side effects can often lead to serious problems, as demonstrated in the Testing and Debugging Techniques section.

EXERCISES FOR SECTION 7.1

For exercises 1 to 4 answer according to the block diagram shown below.

```
PROGRAM main (input, output);
VAR a, b : integer;

    PROCEDURE a1 (VAR x : real);
    VAR c : char;

        PROCEDURE a2 (y : char);
        VAR d : integer;
        BEGIN
        . . .
        END;

    BEGIN
    . . .
    END;

    PROCEDURE b1;
    VAR e : integer;
    BEGIN
    . . .
    END;

BEGIN
. . .
END.
```

1 Within the scope of procedure *a2*, which of the following variables could be referenced?
   (a)   *d* and *y* only.
   (b)   *d*, *y*, and *c* only.
   (c)   *a*, *b*, *c*, *d*, *x*, and *y* only.
   (d)   none of the above.

2 Within the scope of procedure *al*, which of the following variables could be referenced?
   (a)   *d*, *y*, and *c* only.
   (b)   *d*, *y*, *c*, *a*, and *b* only.
   (c)   *d*, *y*, *a*, *b*, *c*, and *x* only.
   (d)   none of the above.

3 Within the scope of procedure *bl*, which of the following variables could be referenced?
   (a)   *e* only.
   (b)   *e*, *a*, and *b* only.
   (c)   *e*, *a*, *b*, and *c* only.
   (d)   none of the above.

4 The main program could call the following procedures:
   (a)   *al* and *bl* only.
   (b)   *al*, *a2*, and *bl* only.
   (c)   *a2* and *bl* only.
   (d)   none of the above.

5 Determine the output of the following program if the input contains the single integer 4.

```
PROGRAM main (input, output);
VAR x : integer;
PROCEDURE a (VAR y : integer);
BEGIN
        y := y * 2
END;
PROCEDURE b (x : integer);
BEGIN
        x := x + 5
END;
BEGIN
        readln (x);
        b (x);
        writeln (x);
        a (x);
        writeln (x)
END.
```

Study the following Pascal program and then answer questions 6 through 9.

```pascal
PROGRAM scope (input, output);
VAR
        num, clock, temp : integer;
PROCEDURE pascal (num : integer; VAR sum : integer);
VAR
        clock : integer;
BEGIN
        temp := 2 * num + sum;
        clock := temp * sum;
        num := num + 1;
        sum := sum * num;
        writeln (temp, clock, num, sum)
END;
BEGIN
        num := 1;
        clock := 0;
        temp := 0;
        pascal (num, temp);
        writeln (num, clock, temp);
        temp := temp + 1;
        pascal (temp, num);
        writeln (num, clock, temp)
END.
```

6   Determine the output of program *scope*.

7   Which of the following statements is true about program *scope*?
(a)   The scope of the variable *temp* does not include the procedure.
(b)   The main program cannot reference the local variable *clock* of the procedure.
(c)   The procedure could be placed after the main program.
(d)   The local variable *clock* is illegal since it is declared in the main program.
(e)   The variable parameter *sum* must precede the value parameter *num*.

8   Which of the following statements is *false* about program *scope*?
(a)   The procedure can reference the global variable *temp*.
(b)   The procedure name *pascal* is not a valid identifier.
(c)   The local variable named *clock* is a valid identifier.
(d)   The scope of the local variable *clock* is the procedure.
(e)   The *writeln* in the main program will not display the contents of the local variable *clock* in the procedure.

9   Which of the following statements is *false* about program *scope*?
(a)   The value parameter *num* in the procedure declaration is a formal parameter.

(b) The parameter *num* in the procedure call statement is the actual parameter.
(c) The formal parameter *num* is a local variable.
(d) The global variable *num* is identical to the formal parameter *num*.
(e) The scope of the global variable *num* does not include the procedure.

10 Determine the output of the following program.

```
PROGRAM telltale (input, output);
VAR
        a, b, c, d : integer;
PROCEDURE pal (y : integer; VAR z : integer);
VAR
        c : integer;
BEGIN
        b := y * z;
        c := b + z;
        y := y + 1;
        z := z * (z + 1);
        writeln (b, c, y, z)
END;
BEGIN
        a := 2;
        c := 3;
        d := 5;
        pal (c, d);
        writeln (a, b, c, d);
        b := 4;
        pal (b, a);
        writeln (a, b, c, d)
END.
```

SECTION 7.2 FUNCTIONS

Functions are subprograms that compute a single value. For example, the standard function *sqrt* computes the square root of a nonnegative number. In this section we discuss functions in Pascal, both the standard (or built-in) and user-defined functions.

Standard Functions

The standard functions are predefined functions available in standard Pascal (see Appendix D). We have already seen the following arithmetic functions: *sqrt*, *sqr*, *abs*, *round*, and *trunc* (see Chapter 2). The remaining arithmetic functions are the trigonometric functions **sin**, **cos**, and **arctan** and the exponential and natural log functions **exp** and **ln**. We will return to these functions later in this section.

The standard functions also include the four ordinal functions **pred**, **succ**, **ord**, and **chr**. These will be discussed further in the next chapter.

The remaining standard functions are those that yield Boolean results. Specifically, these functions are:

odd	Determines if its argument is an *odd* integer
eoln	Determines if the next input character is an *end of line*
eof	Determines if the next input character is an *end of file*

Functions that return Boolean results are sometimes called **predicates**. We consider each of these functions in detail in this section.

The *Odd* Function

The function **odd** will return a value of true if the integer argument is an odd number and returns a value of false if the argument is an even integer. For example, the following Pascal segment expects the user to enter an integer and then appropriately displays the word *ODD* or *EVEN*. We assume that *number* has been declared an integer variable.

```
read (number);
IF odd (number)
THEN writeln ('ODD')
ELSE writeln ('EVEN')
```

An alternate way to determine if a number is odd (which is necessary in programming languages that do not have a function similar to *odd*) is to use the MOD operator to determine if the remainder after division by 2 is nonzero:

```
read (number);
IF number MOD 2 <> 0
THEN writeln ('ODD')
ELSE writeln ('EVEN')
```

The *odd* function is preferable since it improves the readability of your work. Note that you may also use the *odd* function to determine if a number is even:

```
IF NOT odd(number)
THEN . . .
```

The *Eoln* and *Eof* Functions

The data you enter when your program is executing and the data you enter into a file by use of a text editor must be terminated in such a way that a program reading the data can determine when it has reached the end. When data is stored on a disk or tape, a special sentinel (added by the computer system when the file is originally created) marks the end of the data. When data is entered from the keyboard, however, you must usually manually enter the sentinel by pressing a special key or group of keys (typically the CONTROL and z keys or the CONTROL and D keys pressed simultaneously). When a Pascal program is used to create an output file, this sentinel is automatically appended. When a Pascal program encounters such a sentinel in the input data, no variables are modified, but instead, note is made of the fact that the end of file has been encountered. This sentinel is called the ***end-of-file***, and the standard function that detects that it has been encountered is called *eof*. We will represent the end of file in this text as <eof>.

Text files are not just an arbitrarily long sequence of characters terminated by the end of file. They are subdivided into lines, each of which is typically displayed as a single row of characters on your terminal when you enter it. There is no predefined minimum or maximum number of characters that must appear in a single line of text. (That is, standard Pascal defines no explicit limit, but most systems will have limits on the maximum length.) Therefore, each line has appended a special sentinel known as the ***end-of-line*** character, represented in this text by <eoln>. The *eoln* function permits the Pascal programmer to determine when the very next input character is the end of line. You can think of the <eoln> character as being generated when you press the RETURN or ENTER key on your terminal (if you are using an interactive system).

Both the *eof* and *eoln* functions require a single argument, specifically the name of the file (the file variable) that is being tested for the specified condition. Standard Pascal will permit you to omit the argument (and the parentheses) entirely if you wish to test the standard file *input*. Therefore, these two statements are usually equivalent:

```
IF eoln(input) THEN . . .
IF eoln THEN . . .
```

The lines below are the representation of a text file with the ends of line and end of file explicitly represented. Note that each line contains a person's name and an annual salary. We will refer to this file in our discussion of the *eoln* and *eof* functions.

```
John Dunston            $40000<eoln>
Sandra Floyd            $45000<eoln>
Anna Maria Escadillo    $43713<eoln>
Ethel Arnold            $51529<eoln>
<eof>
```

The functions *eoln* and *eof* return true when the next character in the file is the <eoln> or <eof>. Similarly, when the next character in the file is *not* the <eoln>

or <eof>, then the functions return false. Let us see how the *eoln* function can be used to read and display the first line of our data file.

When the *eoln* function is invoked, the next character in the file (that is, the one just after the last character actually read) is examined without actually reading it. Note that to use the *eoln* function, you do *not* read a character and then check to see if it is the end-of-line character, but rather ask if the next character in the input is the end of line.

Here, then, is the Pascal code to read and display the first line of our file. Assume that *inchar* is declared as a char variable.

```
WHILE NOT eoln DO          (* while not at end of line *)
BEGIN
        read (inchar);     (* get the next character *)
        write (inchar)                   (* display it *)
END;
writeln;            (* "display" an end of line character *)
readln         (* and skip past the end of line in the input *)
```

There is an important point that we must make about this example. The WHILE loop itself does not illustrate any new concepts except the use of the *eoln* function. However, note that when this loop terminates, the end-of-line character has not been read. The following points should be noted about <eoln> processing:

- The *eoln* function tests for the presence of the <eoln> character, but does not read it.
- The *write* statement can never write an <eoln>character.

In the previous code, therefore, we must have the final two statements to write the <eoln> (the *writeln*) and to read the <eoln> (the *readln*).

The reason we cannot simply read the <eoln> into *inchar* and then write *inchar* to produce an end of line on the output is that the <eoln> is transformed into a blank (' ') when it is read. This guarantees that our program will work correctly on all standard Pascal systems regardless of the potentially different techniques used to internally represent the <eoln> character. If we should read and then write the <eoln> character we would only find an additional blank in the output, but *no new line!* This fact makes it easy for us to ignore the <eoln> characters when we are not interested in the line structure of the input file. The *only* way to detect an end-of-line character is the *eoln* function!

Now let us try to read and display the entire file. We will use our solution for a single line from above and add a test for the end of file using the *eof* function. When the *eof* function is invoked, the next character in the input file is tested to see if it is the end-of-file character; it is never actually read. Any attempt to read the end-of-file character will result in a (usually fatal) diagnostic message and unceremonious termination of your program. Here is the solution to our problem:

```
WHILE NOT eof DO              (* while not at end of file *)
BEGIN
        WHILE NOT eoln DO      (* while not at end of line *)
        BEGIN
                read (inchar);      (* get the next character *)
                write (inchar)                (* display it *)
        END;
        writeln;          (* "display" an end of line character *)
        readln    (* and skip past the end of line in the input *)
END
```

The main loop of this program segment says, in effect, that as long as we are not at the end of file, process another line. The inner loop is exactly the same as in our previous problem. Since we were assuming the standard input file in these problems, we were permitted to omit the parameters to the functions. If we were processing a different file, however, we would be required to indicate explicitly the name of the file variable.

Once again we must note that the end of file must *not* be read. It is for this reason that we used a WHILE loop instead of a REPEAT-UNTIL loop. It is impossible to predict the next character in an input file. (It is possible to *anticipate* the next character in an input file, but we must be prepared for all eventualities.)

While it is unusual, we should note that files can sometimes be created without an end-of-line character preceding the end of file. This complicates the processing of an input file, but does not make it impossible.

The use of the *eoln* and *eof* functions as described above is very common when processing characters from an input file. We will return to the topic of text processing in a later chapter.

User-Defined Functions

User-defined functions in Pascal are similar to procedures except that the purpose of a function is to return only one value to the point from which it was called. For example, suppose we wish to write a function called *fourth* that returns the fourth power of a number that is of type real. That is, if the number is called *num*, then we want to compute

$$num^4 = num \cdot num \cdot num \cdot num$$
For example,

$1.0^4 = 1.0$
$2.0^4 = 16.0$
$3.5^4 = 150.0625$

The following Pascal function will perform this calculation for us:

```
FUNCTION fourth (number : real) : real;
(* Compute the fourth power of the argument *)
BEGIN
        fourth := sqr(sqr(number))
END;
```

Notice the function header looks similar to a procedure header. The reserved word FUNCTION is followed by the function identifier and the parameter list. This is followed by a colon and the type identifier that specifies the type of value that the function result will have. In the case of *fourth*, the result will be a real value. The syntax diagram for a Pascal function is shown in Figure 7-4.

The mechanism Pascal functions use to specify the value to be returned is to *assign the value to the name of the function*. In the function *fourth* the assignment statement

```
fourth := sqr(sqr(number))
```

assigns the fourth power of *number* to the function name, thus specifying that this value is to be returned as the value of the function when it terminates. Several assignments may be made to the function name, but only the last value assigned will be returned. Note also that *if the computation requires more than one value to be returned, then a procedure should be used instead of a function*. Since a function returns just a single result, and to emphasize the similarity between mathematical functions and user-defined Pascal functions, variable parameters are not usually used with functions.

It is important not to consider the function name the same as a variable. Using the function name in an expression (for example, on the right-hand side of an assignment statement) will not yield the value that was last assigned to the function name, but rather will specify that the function is to be invoked and yield a value as a result of this invocation.

Let us consider some more examples. Suppose we need a function called *parity* with two integer value parameters *num1* and *num2*, such that *parity* returns true if *num1* and *num2* are both even or both odd, and false otherwise (that is, one is even and the other is odd). The Pascal coding that follows is one solution to the problem:

```
FUNCTION parity (num1, num2 : integer) : Boolean;
(* Returns true if num1 and num2 are both even *)
(* or both odd, and false otherwise.           *)
BEGIN
```

Figure 7-4 Syntax diagram for function.

```
      parity := (odd (num1) AND odd (num2)) OR
               (NOT odd (num1) AND NOT odd (num2))
END;
```

Note the use of the *odd* function. Again, observe that the data type of the result must follow the parameter list and a colon. The function does contain an assignment statement with the name of the function on the left side of the assignment. The resulting value is always assigned to the function name.

The next example function will compute the tangent of an angle. Standard Pascal does not include a tangent function (although some implementations may offer it as an extension), so we will use the relation

$$\tan x = \frac{\sin x}{\cos x}$$

in the function. The code itself is quite straightforward:

```
FUNCTION tan (x : real) : real;
BEGIN
      tan := sin (x) / cos (x)
END;
```

Realistically, we should validate the function arguments. For example, some values of x will cause "tan (x)" to produce a run-time error (for example, when cos (x) = 0).

Finally, consider a function to compute the value of a^b. That is, we want a function to compute a raised to the b power. We use the property that

$$a^b = e^{b \ln a}$$

(where $\ln a$ is the natural logarithm of a) to accomplish the task of the function. Here is the Pascal code, using the standard functions *exp* and *ln*:

```
FUNCTION power (a, b : real) : real;
BEGIN
      power := exp (b * ln (a) )
END;
```

Function Invocation

As with procedures, a function invocation requires that the order and data type of the actual parameters match exactly with the order and data type of the formal parameters. To do otherwise will be detected by the compiler and reported to the user as an error.

Function invocation is not the same as procedure invocation. The reason for this difference is that a function returns a value to the point of invocation, though not through the parameters themselves, as would be the case for a procedure. As a result, user-defined functions are invoked by writing their name and parameter list in an expression, just like the standard functions. For example, to determine the value of 2 to the third power and store this value in variable x, we would write

```
x := power (2.0, 3.0)
```

and to compute and display the tangent of 17.3, we would write

```
writeln ('Tangent of 17.3 = ', tan(17.3))
```

noting that a *write* or *writeln* statement may display the value of an expression.

Function invocations are treated just like any other value of the type returned by the function. We can even combine functions. For example, to compute the tangent of x raised to the third power and then assign half this value to y, we would write

```
y := power (tan (x), 3.0) / 2.0
```

Next we will solve an applied problem utilizing a user-defined function.

Problem 7.2

Write a Pascal program using a function that reads a list of N test scores (non-negative integers) and finds the highest score. If the highest score is above 90, then display a message indicating this fact. The value of N will be supplied as the first data value.

A complete Pascal program called *greatest* appears below. This program uses a function called *high*. The number of values N will be read in the main program and passed as a parameter to the function. In the function *high*, the N scores are read and used but are not provided to the calling program. This is acceptable since the scores are not needed outside the function.

```
PROGRAM greatest (input, output);
(* Determine the largest of N scores read from the input *)
(* and display a message if it is greater than 90.        *)
VAR
        number : integer;
FUNCTION high (N : integer) : integer;
(* Read and return the largest of N integers. *)
VAR
        index : integer;
        score : integer;
        max : integer;
BEGIN
        max := 0;   (* initialize the highest score *)
        FOR index := 1 TO N DO
```

```
          BEGIN
              write ('Enter a score: ');
              readln (score);
              IF score > max
              THEN max := score        (* new highest score *)
          END;
          high := max        (* return highest score *)
      END
(* Main Program *)
BEGIN
          write ('Enter the number of test scores: ');
          readln (number);
          IF high (number) > 90    (* function invocation *)
          THEN writeln ('Highest score greater than 90.')
END.
```

Recall that the function name must appear on the left side of at least one assignment statement inside the function itself to communicate the result of the function to the point of invocation. The function name usually should not appear on the right side of an assignment statement, as previously noted. For example, suppose we would like to write a function that computes the tenth power of an integer. That is, if x is an integer argument, then the result we want is x^{10}. Suppose we call this function *power10*. The following Pascal function will *not* solve this problem, since the function name appears on the right side of the assignment statement.

```
FUNCTION power10 (x : integer) : integer;
(* A function that will NOT work! *)
VAR
      i : integer;
BEGIN
          power10 := 1;       (* initialize the result *)
          FOR i := 1 TO 10 DO
              power10 := power10 * x
END;
```

We can modify this function by adding a temporary variable to store the partial result and then include a statement to assign the final result to the name of the function. Here is the modified, correct solution:

```
FUNCTION power10 (x : integer) : integer;
(* Return x to the tenth power *)
VAR
      i, temp : integer;
BEGIN
          temp := 1;       (* initialize the result *)
          FOR i := 1 TO 10 DO
```

```
            temp := temp * x;
        power10 := temp
END;
```

When the function name appears in an expression, the function is invoked. This is true even for expressions within the function. Functions that invoke themselves are called *recursive* functions. In the next section we will consider some examples.

EXERCISES FOR SECTION 7.2

1 Determine the result of each function invocation
   (a) odd (2)   (b) odd (0)
   (c) odd (-3)   (d) odd (5 − 1)
   (e) odd (2 * trunc (3.6))

2 Consider the following program and the input data. Determine what will be displayed when the program is executed.

```
PROGRAM quiz (input, output);
VAR
        num : integer;
BEGIN
        read (num);
        WHILE NOT eoln DO
        BEGIN
                writeln (num);
                read (num)
        END
END.
```

Input data:

```
2    4    5<eoln>
6<eoln>
<eof>
```

3 Consider the following program and input data. Determine what is displayed when the program is executed.

```
PROGRAM test (input, output);
VAR
        num1, num2, count : integer;
BEGIN
        count := 0;
        WHILE NOT eof DO
```

```
                    BEGIN
                        readln (num1, num2);
                        count := count + 1
                    END;
                    writeln ('The count is ', count:1)
            END.
```

Input data:

```
2      4      5<eoln>
6      7<eoln>
5      10     6<eoln>
<eof>
```

4 Which of the following functions would correctly return the integer portion of x, where x is defined as a real variable?

```
(a)  FUNCTION test (VAR x : real);
     BEGIN
             x := trunc(x)
     END;
(b)  FUNCTION test (x) : integer;
     BEGIN
             test := trunc(x)
     END;
(c)  FUNCTION test (x : real) : integer;
     BEGIN
             test := trunc(x)
     END;
(d)  FUNCTION test (x : real) : integer;
     BEGIN
             x := trunc(x)
     END;
(e)  FUNCTION test (x : real) : integer;
     BEGIN
             trunc(x)
     END;
```

5 Consider the following program segment:

```
PROCEDURE exchange (VAR x, y : integer);
VAR temp : integer;
BEGIN
        temp := x;
        x := y;
        y := temp
END;
```

```
FUNCTION mult (x : integer) : integer;
BEGIN
        mult := x * x
END;
```

Which of the following is a correct invocation of the above procedure and/or function if *x*, *y*, and *z* are integer variables?
(a)   exchange (mult (x), x);
(b)   exchange (3, 4);
(c)   mult (10);
(d)   y := mult (10);
(e)   z := exchange (x, y);

6   Determine what is displayed when the following program is executed.

```
PROGRAM final (input, output);
VAR
        apples, bananas, oranges : integer;
PROCEDURE grade (a, b : integer; VAR c : integer);
VAR
        apples : integer;
FUNCTION what (d : integer) : integer;
BEGIN
        what := d * 2
END;
BEGIN
        b := what (a);
        apples := 16;
        c := what (a)
END;
BEGIN
        apples := 2;
        bananas := 3;
        oranges := 6;
        grade (apples, bananas, oranges);
        writeln (apples, bananas, oranges)
END.
```

7   Write a Pascal function called *lastdig* that expects a single positive integer parameter. *Lastdig* returns the last digit of its parameter. For example, "lastdig (2456)" must return 6.

8   Write a Pascal program that reads an unknown number of grades (between 0 and 100, inclusively) and displays the total number of grades and the minimum grade. Assume there is one grade per line and the end of file terminates the data.

SECTION 7.3 RECURSIVE PROCEDURES AND FUNCTIONS

A function or procedure that calls, or invokes, itself is called *recursive*. You may think that recursive functions are curiosities and not very useful. However, recursive functions (and also recursive procedures) can be quite powerful in problem solving, especially in applications of advanced computer science. In this section we consider some elementary examples and applications to give you some insight into the elegance and simplicity of recursive functions.

Recursive functions are quite suitable to use when a problem can be defined in terms of itself (recursively). For example, consider the following problem definition:

> *A financial institution pays 12 percent annual interest at the beginning of every year on the money left there during the previous year. We wish to determine how much an initial investment of $1000 would be worth if it and the interest were left for* n *years.*

This problem can be rewritten recursively by making the following observations. Let a_n be the amount of money accumulated at the beginning of year n. Thus

$$a_0 = 1000 \qquad \text{(the initial investment)}$$
$$a_1 = 1000 + 0.12 * 1000 \qquad \text{(amount at the end of the first year)}$$
$$a_2 = a_1 + 0.12 * a_1 \qquad \text{(amount at the end of the second year)}.$$

In general, we see that

$$a_i = a_{i-1} + 0.12 * a_{i-1}$$

is the amount invested at the end of the year i. If we simplify this expression by adding the terms we have

$$a_i = 1.12 * a_{i-1}$$

and our problem statement yields the recursive definition shown below:

$$a_0 = 1000$$
$$a_i = 1.12 * a_{i-1}$$

Now the problem is how to compute a_n, given a value for n. For example, if $n = 3$, how much money will have accumulated by the end of the third year? Substituting into the recursive definition, we know

$$a_3 = 1.12 * a_2$$

but we also know that

$a_2 = 1.12 * a_1$

and that

$a_1 = 1.12 * a_0$

.We know the value of a_0, however, and can therefore compute a_1, a_2, and a_3:

$a_1 = 1.12 * 1000 = 1120$
$a_2 = 1.12 * 1120 = 1254.40$
$a_3 = 1.12 * 1254.40 = 1404.93$

Pascal will do all these calculations for us if we simply transform the recursive problem statement into a recursive Pascal function. Remember the recursive definition of the problem:

$a_0 = 1000,$ and $a_i = 1.12 * a_{i-1}$

If we want to compute the value of a_n for an arbitrary value of n (possibly zero), we would write the following pseudocode:

If $n = 0$
Then $a_n = 1000$
Else $a_n = 1.12 * a_{n-1}$

This can be translated directly into a Pascal function! We merely add the usual parameter definition (for n) and replace the name a_n by a Pascal variable. Here, then, is the complete Pascal function to determine the value of the investment after n years:

```
FUNCTION amount (n : integer) : real;
(* Recursive function to compute amount in an *)
(* account at 12 percent interest with initial  *)
(* investment of $1000.00.                      *)
BEGIN
      IF n = 0
      THEN amount := 1000.0
      ELSE amount := 1.12 * amount (n-1)
END;
```

Two important observations should be made at this point. Notice the function name on the right side with the actual parameter. This will cause the function *amount* to call itself. Also, observe how our Pascal solution mirrors the recursive definition of the problem. This close correspondence of the Pascal recursive function and the problem statement makes it easy to use Pascal for implementing solutions to recursive problems. Actually, the investment problem we have just examined can be written more concisely without recursion (see problem 3 at the end of the chapter). However, the recursive solution is more suitable since it reflects the problem solution more naturally.

How does the computer actually compute the result in the recursive function *amount?* Look at our previous hand computation for $n = 3$. That illustration should give you some idea of the technique used by the computer! When it encounters a recursive function call, it must temporarily delay the computation to evaluate the recursive function call. Whatever information is needed to continue the computation after the recursive call is saved by the computer. When the result of the recursive call is obtained, the computation of the function will resume. This process is repeated even if there are many levels of recursive calls. Imagine the number of levels necessary in determining the amount in the account after 50 years! The computer will accurately maintain the entire collection of temporary results until the final result is obtained.

When a procedure or function is invoked, whether recursively or not, the values of the caller's local variables and constants are saved on a **stack**. Stacks are discussed in Chapter 13, but for now you can just think of a stack as being similar to the mechanism sometimes used to dispense plates in a cafeteria. The top plate is currently available, and when it is removed, all the others are "popped up." When a plate is added to the top, all the plates previously present are "pushed down." So it is with function and procedure invocations. When a procedure is invoked, the caller's local values are saved on a stack, and when it terminates (that is, returns control to the point where the procedure was invoked), the local values are restored from the stack. Note that this mechanism is used for all procedures and functions, recursive or not.

Let us consider a different problem which can be solved using recursive functions.

Problem 7.3

Write a recursive function to determine the sum of the integers 1, 2, 3, . . . , n. That is, recursively compute $1 + 2 + 3 + \cdots + n$.

First, let us define the problem recursively. If we call the sum of the first n integers S_n, then we have

$$S_0 = 0, \qquad \text{and} \qquad S_i = i + S_{i-1}$$

We can verify this by hand checking for a particular value, say 5:

$$
\begin{aligned}
S_5 &= 5 + S_4 \\
&= 5 + 4 + S_3 \\
&= 5 + 4 + 3 + S_2 \\
&= 5 + 4 + 3 + 2 + S_1 \\
&= 5 + 4 + 3 + 2 + 1 + S_0 \\
&= 5 + 4 + 3 + 2 + 1 + 0 \\
&= 15
\end{aligned}
$$

Our Pascal solution again mirrors the recursive definition of the problem:

```
FUNCTION sum (n : integer) : integer;
(* Recursive function to compute sum *)
(* of the integers 1, 2, 3, ..., n *)
BEGIN
        IF n = 0
        THEN sum := 0
        ELSE sum := n + sum(n-1)
END;
```

Our next problem solution will illustrate the use of nested functions with a recursive function. This problem has already been solved twice, the first time using selection (Section 5.4) and the second time by looping (Section 6.2).

Problem 7.4

The input data contains the month number and day of the month in a non-leap year. Determine the corresponding day of the year (in the range 1 to 365) using Pascal functions.

We must compute the total number of days in the months prior to the input month and add to this the day of the month. The main function *dayofyear* will contain a single statement to accomplish this. To compute the total number of days in the months prior to the input month, we will invoke a recursive function *daysinmonth*. This function will, in turn, invoke another function *monthlydays* that returns the number of days in any given month. The recursive definition to compute *daysinmonth* is the following (where m_n denotes the total number of days in the months prior to month n):

$m_1 = 0$ (no days prior to January)

$m_n = m_{n-1} +$ days in month number $(n-1)$

Now we are ready to write our functions. The following Pascal function will solve the problem using a recursive function.

```
FUNCTION dayofyear (month, day : integer) : integer;
(* Function to compute day of year given month and day *)
(* Month must be in the range 1 to 12.              *)
    FUNCTION monthlydays (number : integer) : integer;
    (* Return number of days in specified month *)
    BEGIN
            CASE number OF
                1,3,5,7,8,10,12 : monthlydays := 31;
                2               : monthlydays := 28;
                4,6,9,11        : monthlydays := 30
            END
```

```
END;
FUNCTION daysinmonth (month : integer) : integer;
(* Recursive function to return total number of *)
(* days in those months prior to argument month *)
BEGIN
        IF month = 1
        THEN daysinmonth := 0
        ELSE daysinmonth := daysinmonth (month − 1)
                            + monthlydays (month − 1)
END
(* Main Function *)
BEGIN
    dayofyear := daysinmonth (month) + day
END;
```

Recursion and Iteration

The examples presented in this section can be written without using recursion. For example, the function *amount* can be written nonrecursively, or *iteratively*, as follows:

```
FUNCTION amount (n : integer) : real;
(* Nonrecursive or iterative function to compute *)
(* amount in an account at 12 percent annual*)
(* interest with an initial investment of $1000.00 *)
VAR
        temp : real;
        index : integer;
BEGIN
        temp := 1000.00;
        FOR index := 1 TO n DO
            temp := temp * 1.12;
        amount := temp
END;
```

This method of computing is called **iteration** and is nonrecursive. If a programming language such as Pascal supports recursion and iteration, which of the two methods should be used to solve a given problem? Remember that in a recursive solution the computer must keep track of each recursive call, and this can require a large amount of time and storage. As a result, a recursive solution to a problem is often less efficient than an iterative solution. In general, use a recursive solution only if the solution cannot be easily translated to the equivalent iterative solution or if the efficiency of the recursive solution is satisfactory.

all have answers in back

1 Determine what is displayed when the the following program is executed.

```
PROGRAM recursive1 (input, output);
FUNCTION unknown (num : integer) : integer;
BEGIN
        IF num = 0
        THEN unknown := 5
        ELSE unknown := unknown (num − 1) + 1
END;
BEGIN
        writeln (unknown (10))
END.
```

2 Determine what is displayed when the the following program is executed:

```
PROGRAM recursive2 (input, output);
FUNCTION what (num : integer) : integer;
BEGIN
        IF num = 1
        THEN what := 10
        ELSE what := what (num − 1) + 10
END;
BEGIN
        writeln (what (5))
END.
```

3 The function $f(n) = n!$ computes the product of the integers $1, 2, 3, \ldots, n$. That is,

$$n! = 1 \cdot 2 \cdot 3 \cdots n$$

For example, $3! = 1 \cdot 2 \cdot 3 = 6$.
(a) Define $n!$ recursively.
(b) Write a recursive Pascal function to compute $f(n) = n!$

4 The function $power\ (x, n) = x^n$, where $n > 0$, computes $x \cdot x \cdot x \cdots x$ (n factors of x), for a real number x. For example, $power\ (4.0, 3) = 64.0$.
(a) Write a nonrecursive Pascal function to compute $power\ (x, n)$.
(b) Define x^n recursively.
(c) Write a recursive Pascal function with two parameters x and n to compute x^n.

5 The Fibonacci sequence is defined recursively as follows:

$$f_1 = 1$$
$$f_2 = 1$$
$$f_n = f_{n-1} + f_{n-2}$$

The first ten terms of the sequence are as follows:

1, 1, 2, 3, 5, 8, 13, 21, 34, 55

Write a recursive Pascal function to compute the nth Fibonacci number f_n.

SECTION 7.4 PROBLEM SOLVING USING PROCEDURES AND FUNCTIONS

In this section we apply some of the techniques in this chapter to a specific problem, namely the creation of a simple game for teaching multiplication.

Multiplication Game Problem

An elementary school teacher would like to write a game-playing program that will drill the children in the class on the multiplication table shown below.

×	0	1	2	3	4	5	6	7	8	9
0	0	0	0	0	0	0	0	0	0	0
1	0	1	2	3	4	5	6	7	8	9
2	0	2	4	6	8	10	12	14	16	18
3	0	3	6	9	12	15	18	21	24	27
4	0	4	8	12	16	20	24	28	32	36
5	0	5	10	15	20	25	30	35	40	45
6	0	6	12	18	24	30	36	42	48	54
7	0	7	14	21	28	35	42	49	56	63
8	0	8	16	24	32	40	48	56	64	72
9	0	9	18	27	36	45	54	63	72	81

The central part of this problem is to generate pairs of integers repeatedly, each of which is within the range 0 to 9. These numbers will then be displayed for the child to read and multiply. If the child correctly answers 10 problems in a row, then he or she "wins" the game. Otherwise the child does not win. In either case the child is given the option to play again.

This problem can be subdivided into three subproblems (see Figure 7-5):

SUBPROBLEM 1: Randomly generate multiplication problems.
SUBPROBLEM 2: Display problem, obtain child's answer, and test correctness.
SUBPROBLEM 3: Display results and process the continuation option.

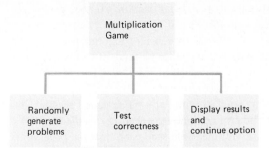

Figure 7-5   Top-down design of multiplication game.

We will use the following procedures to solve the problems:

1 Procedure *problem* randomly generates a multiplication problem (no value parameters, two VAR parameters each receiving a random integer in the range 0 to 9).
2 Procedure *test* validates the child's answer and updates the score appropriately
   (value parameters are the two random integers from procedure *problem* and the
   child's answer; the VAR parameters are the updated score and a right/wrong
   indication).
3 Procedure *display* displays the results and gives the child the option of playing
   another game (value parameter is the score; VAR parameter is the continuation
   indication).

   The algorithm uses two loops, the outer loop to continue playing games and the
inner loop to continue generating problems. We can write our algorithm as follows:

Multiplication Game Algorithm
While more games are to be played
   While correct answer and number correct < 10:
      Generate a multiplication problem.
      Validate answer.
      Update the score.
   Indicate game won/lost status, and give another game option.

   After studying the algorithm, we find the most difficult part to be randomly generating
the multiplication problems. Let us briefly digress to consider this problem in some
detail.

Random Number Generators

Programs or functions to generate random numbers are very common on computer
systems and are often available in the system library. Many Pascal systems have
predefined random number generating functions. Since the emphasis in this book is

on portability and standard Pascal, we have included a random number generating function that should be suitable for use on most Pascal systems.

Random number generators normally produce a sequence of real numbers (usually between 0 and 1) that for all practical purposes appear to be random. Actually, since the numbers are generated by a program, they are not truly random. In fact, the generated numbers are often called *pseudorandom numbers*.

Most random number generators start with an initial real value called a *seed*. The remainder of the random numbers are determined once the seed is specified.

A random number generator can start with the same seed each time the program is executed. This is beneficial when debugging your program, since the random numbers can be regenerated. However, we can change the seed each time we run the program either by entering a different seed as input or using a nonstandard function (such as the time of day from the system).

Here is a random number generating function written in standard Pascal that will operate on most computer systems, including microcomputers. You should not be overly concerned at this point if you do not understand its operation. There are many excellent sources that discuss pseudorandom number generating functions in detail (for example, see Knuth, *The Art of Computer Programming* (Vol. 2): *Seminumerical Algorithms*).

```
FUNCTION random (VAR seed : real) : real;
(* Seed is any positive real number less than m, *)
(* a constant whose value is shown below.        *)
CONST
        a = 93.0;
        m = 8192.0;
        c = 1.0;
BEGIN
        (* Note modification of seed is the side effect! *)
        seed := a * seed + c;
        seed := round (((seed / m) - trunc (seed / m)) * m);
        random := seed / m
END;
```

To use this function, we must initialize the seed in our main program and invoke the function. Note that seed is used both in the main program and the function and, therefore, must be a variable parameter. Here is a sample program to generate 10 random numbers using this random number generator starting with a seed of 0.7823.

```
PROGRAM testrand (output);
(* Program to test the random number generator *)
VAR
        index : integer;
        seed : real;
```

```
FUNCTION random (VAR seed : real) : real;
(* Seed is any positive real number less than m, *)
(* a constant whose value is shown below.*)
CONST
        a = 93.0;
        m = 8192.0;
        c = 1.0;
BEGIN
        (* Note modification of seed is the side effect! *)
        seed := a * seed + c;
        seed := round (((seed / m) − trunc (seed / m)) * m);
        random := seed / m
END;
(* Main Program *)
BEGIN
        seed := 0.7823;
        FOR index := 1 TO 10 DO
                writeln ('A random number is ', random(seed))
END.
```

The output from running this program on a particular computer system is shown below. When you run this on your system you may obtain different results.

```
A random number is 9.03320E-03
A random number is 8.40210E-01
A random number is 1.39648E-01
A random number is 9.87427E-01
A random number is 8.30811E-01
A random number is 2.65503E-01
A random number is 6.91895E-01
A random number is 3.46313E-01
A random number is 2.07275E-01
A random number is 2.76733E-01
```

We can see that the pseudorandom numbers generated by this program are real numbers greater than or equal to 0 and less than 1. In our program we need to generate integers from 0 to 9. To transform the real numbers into integers, we can multiply by 10 and then discard the fractional part. Multiplication by 10 results in a real number greater than or equal to 0 and less than 10. That is, the number is of the form $x.yyyyy$, where x is 0, 1, 2, . . . , 9 and $yyyyy$ is an arbitrary fractional part. Therefore, the expression we use to generate a random single-digit integer is trunc (10 * random (seed))

If we apply this to the 10 random numbers generated previously, we obtain the following 10 integers:

0 8 1 9 8 2 6 3 2 2

Now let us return to the computer solution of the multiplication game problem.

Complete Solution of the Multiplication Game Problem

The complete Pascal program to solve this problem is shown below, with the display resulting from a sample execution. Observe the use of Boolean variables to terminate execution of the loops. Also, if your system has a random number generator, then you may replace function *random* below with a function declaration of your system's random number generator.

```
PROGRAM game (input, output);
(* The Multiplication Game *)
VAR
        number1, number2,        (* numbers to multiply *)
        score,                   (* number of correct answers *)
        answer : integer;             (* the child's answer *)
        right,    (* does answer = number1 * number2? *)
        moregames : Boolean;            (* play again? *)
        seed : real;             (* for random number *)
FUNCTION random (VAR seed : real) : real;
(* Seed is any positive real number less than m, *)
(* a constant whose value is shown below. *)
CONST
        a = 93.0;
        m = 8192.0;
        c = 1.0;
BEGIN
        (* Note modification of seed is the side effect! *)
        seed := a * seed + c;
        seed := round (((seed / m) − trunc (seed / m)) * m);
        random := seed / m
END;
PROCEDURE problem (VAR num1, num2: integer; VAR seed: real);
(* Generate the next multiplication problem for the child *)
BEGIN
        num1 := trunc (10 * random (seed));
```

```pascal
            num2 := trunc (10 * random (seed))
END;
PROCEDURE  test (num1, num2, answer : integer;
                 VAR correct : Boolean;
                 VAR score : integer);
(* Validate the child's answer and update the score *)
VAR
       product : integer;             *                       (* num1     num2 *)
BEGIN
        product := num1 * num2;         (* generate correct answer *)
        IF answer = product             (* was the answer correct? *)
        THEN BEGIN
                score := score + 1;   (* yes, update score *)
                correct := true;
                writeln ('Correct')                 (* and tell the child *)
                END
        ELSE  BEGIN
                correct := false;                     (* nope *)
                write ('Sorry, that''s wrong.');         (* tell *)
                write (' The correct answer is ');
                writeln (product:1, '.')
                END
END;
PROCEDURE display (score : integer; VAR moregames : Boolean);
(* Display game results, and determine new game status *)
VAR
        ch : char;       (* Answer to new game question *)
BEGIN
        IF score = 10
        THEN writeln ('Your score is a perfect 10, a winner!')
        ELSE writeln ('Your score is ', score:1, '. Please try again!');
        ch := ' ';
        WHILE (ch <> 'Y') AND (ch <> 'y') AND (ch <> 'N')
            AND (ch <> 'n') DO
        BEGIN
            write ('Play again (answer Y or N)? ');
            readln (ch)
        END;
        moregames := (ch = 'Y') OR (ch = 'y')
END;


(* The Main Program for the Multiplication Game *)
BEGIN
        seed := 0.7823;      (* initialize variables *)
        moregames := true;
```

```
          WHILE moregames DO
          BEGIN
                writeln ('Starting a new game.');
                score := 0;
                right := true;
                WHILE (score < 10) AND right DO
                BEGIN
                    problem (number1, number2, seed);
                    write ('What is ', number1:1, ' times ', number2:1, '?');
                    readln (answer);
                    test (number1, number2, answer, right, score)
                END;
                display (score, moregames)
          END
END.
```

Program game

```
Starting a new game.
What is 0 times 8? 0
Correct
What is 1 times 9? 9
Correct
What is 8 times 2? 16
Correct
What is 6 times 3? 36
Sorry, that's wrong. The correct answer is 18.
Your score is 3. Please try again!
Play again (answer Y or N)? Y
Starting a new game.
What is 2 times 2? 4
Correct
What is 7 times 4? 28
Correct
What is 5 times 7? 37
Sorry, that's wrong. The correct answer is 35.
Your score is 2. Please try again!
Play again (answer Y or N)? K
Play again (answer Y or N)? N
```

Program game: Sample Execution

In this section we discuss some of the problems that can arise when using procedures and functions.

Side Effects

A function should perform some task using the input parameters and return a *single* value. However, since a function is similar to a procedure, it can do all the same things as a procedure. For example, a function can have variable parameters in addition to the value parameters in the formal parameter list. A function can also modify the contents of a global variable and perform input/output statements. These operations when used with functions are known as *side effects*. In most cases side effects should be avoided (an exception was the random number generating function in Section 7.4). Side effects can cause program bugs that may be difficult to isolate. All information passed to or from a procedure or to a function should be done through the parameter list and not through global variables. This will make the procedure or function a self-contained independent module, which can be tested and debugged on its own. We do not have to be worried about other parts of the program affecting our procedure or function in some subtle way.

Forward Declaration

Recall that a procedure cannot be invoked unless the procedure declaration appears before the statement that invokes it. However, sometimes it may be necessary to call a procedure that has not been declared before the invoking statement. For example, we may have procedures *one* and *two*, each of which calls the other:

```
PROCEDURE one (a : integer; VAR b : real);
declarations . . .
BEGIN
        statements . . .
        two ( actual parameters );
        statements . . .
END;
PROCEDURE two (x : integer; VAR y : integer);
declarations . . .
BEGIN
        statements . . .
        one ( actual parameters );
        statements . . .
END;
```

As written above, procedure *two* is correct, since it references procedure *one* which has been defined. But procedure *one* is erroneous, since it references procedure *two* which has not been defined. Reversing the order of the declarations does not solve the problem; in that case procedure *two* will inherit the error.

Pascal permits us to change the usual order of declarations by using the ***forward declaration***. Essentially, the word *forward* is added to the complete procedure header. This forward declaration is placed before the calling procedure, and the actual declaration of the called procedure (the local declarations and statements) does not contain the parameter list. Procedures *one* and *two* could be written by placing the forward declaration of procedure *one* before procedure *two* as follows:

```
PROCEDURE one (a : integer; VAR b : real); forward;
(* The body of procedure one is omitted here *)

PROCEDURE two (x : integer; VAR y : integer);
declarations . . .
BEGIN
        statements . . .
        one (actual parameters);
        statements . . .
END;

(* parameter list omitted, but given as a comment for clarity *)
PROCEDURE one (* a : integer; VAR b : real *);
declarations . . .
BEGIN
        statements . . .
        two (actual parameters);
        statements . . .
END;
```

Observe that the word *forward* is followed by a semicolon. While not reserved in standard Pascal, the use of the identifier *forward* for other purposes should be avoided. Also, note the parameter list of the called procedure *one* is omitted in the actual procedure declaration since it is already contained in the forward declaration. However, it is good programming practice, as shown above, to include the parameter list as a comment in the declaration of the called program.

The forward declaration can also be applied to functions. Here is an example of such a declaration:

```
FUNCTION filter (a : char) : char; forward;
```

Portability

In this text we have emphasized the use of standard Pascal. The main reason for this emphasis is that programs written in standard Pascal can be moved from one computer system to another with a minimal amount of change. Programs that exhibit this characteristic are called ***portable***. A portable program that has been developed, tested, and debugged on one computer system will require very little additional testing and de-bugging when moved to another computer system.

One problem which adherence to the Pascal standard does not completely solve is that of character set differences. Many computer systems use the ASCII character set, but large IBM systems use the EBCDIC character set, and other manufacturers have defined still additional character sets. The principal problem is that the relative position of a character may differ between various character sets. This may give different results for character comparisons on different machines. For example, the value of 'A' < '0' is true when evaluated on large IBM computers, but on many other systems (including IBM and Apple personal computers) this expression is false. There is no universally acceptable solution to this problem. Many solutions are based on translation from one character set to another.

If you do use the extensions provided in a particular Pascal system, either because they simplify the solution of a problem or improve its efficiency, at least clearly identify with comments those portions of your program where nonstandard features have been used. Then when the program is moved to a different computer, you can easily identify those statements which will probably require modification.

Here is a list of some important Pascal reminders related to procedures and functions.

PASCAL REMINDERS

- A procedure or function should be declared physically before it is invoked (unless a forward declaration is used).
- The formal and actual parameters must match in order and data type.
- An actual parameter corresponding to a formal VAR parameter must be a variable.
- A value parameter can be a variable, constant, or an expression.
- Value parameters serve as input to a procedure or function.
- The reserved word VAR must precede the variable parameter for each data type in the formal parameter list:

  procedure ex (VAR n : real; VAR ch1, ch2 : char);

- Global variables should not be referenced directly from inside a procedure or function.
- Variables and constants used only by a procedure or function should be local variables.
- A local identifier having the same name as a global identifier has precedence inside the procedure or function.
- Local identifiers cannot be referenced from outside their scope.
- The *eoln* Boolean function returns a value of true if the next character to be read is the end-of-line character (<eoln>).
- The *eof* Boolean function returns a value of true if the next character is the end-of-file (<eof>).
- The data type of the function result must be included in the function header:

  FUNCTION power (base, exponent : real) : real;

- The function name must appear on the left side of at least one assignment statement in the function.

- The function name should not appear in an expression within the function unless it is being invoked as a recursive function.
- Function invocations are invalid when written like procedure invocations; they must appear as components of expressions.

```
power (2.0, 3.0)      (* invalid *)
x := power (3.0, 3.0)  (* valid *)
```

- Functions are used when only one value is to be returned; procedures are used otherwise.

SECTION 7.6 CHAPTER REVIEW

In this chapter we have discussed procedures and functions. The input parameters of procedures and functions are known as *value parameters*. If a variable is used for output only or for both input and output, then define it as a variable (VAR) parameter in the parameter list. Procedures as well as functions can be nested. Scope rules apply to the main program, procedures, functions, and local and global identifiers. The scope of an identifier is that portion of the program where the identifier is known. Consider the following nested procedures:

```
PROCEDURE outer;
VAR a : integer;

    PROCEDURE inner;
    VAR b : integer;

        PROCEDURE deep;
        VAR a : integer;    . . .


    . . .

. . .
```

Procedures *inner* and *outer* can reference the global variables declared in their larger, containing procedures. Local variables declared in contained procedures cannot be referenced from outside the procedure and have precedence over the same variable name used in their larger, containing procedures. The same scope rules apply to procedure names.

Two types of functions were discussed in this chapter: standard and user-defined. The standard functions are predefined functions available in all Pascal implementations. In this chapter we discussed the Boolean standard functions: *odd*, *eoln*, and *eof*. The *odd* function will test whether an integer is even or odd. The *eoln* and *eof* functions test whether or not the next character in a text file is the end-of-line character (<eoln>) or the end-of-file character (<eof>).

User-defined functions are written by the programmer and are very similar to procedures with one major exception: Functions return exactly one value to the point of invocation. Many examples of functions were presented. A discussion of recursive functions, or functions that can invoke themselves, was presented in Section 7.3. Recursive functions are quite natural to use when the problem solution has a recursive definition.

An application of procedures and functions to a multiplication game problem was presented in this chapter. A discussion of generating random numbers was also included. The chapter closed with a discussion of side effects and the forward declarations that permit us to change the order of the declarations.

The following is a summary of the Pascal discussed in this chapter, and can be used for future reference.

PASCAL REFERENCE

1 Parameters
   1.1   Value: Input parameter to functions or procedures.
   1.2   Variable: Output parameters, or both input and output parameters.
Example:

```
PROCEDURE (num1 : integer; VAR score : integer);
                ↑                          ↑

          value parameter      variable parameter
```

2 Nested procedures: Procedures written within other procedures.
Example:

```
PROCEDURE main (parameters);
declarations

    PROCEDURE inside (parameters);
    declarations

        PROCEDURE innermost (parameters);
        declarations
        BEGIN
            statements
        END (* innermost *)
```

```
    BEGIN
        statements
    END (* inside *)
```

```
BEGIN
    statements
END; (* main *)
```

The scope of identifiers is in the block indicated except nested blocks where identifiers are redeclared.

3 Functions.
   3.1 Standard functions: Predefined in standard Pascal.
        Boolean functions:
            odd: Tests for odd integers
            eoln: Tests for the <eoln>
            eof: Tests for the <eof>
   3.2 User-defined functions: Written by the programmer (similar to procedures).
        Example:

```
FUNCTION cotangent (angle : real) : real;
BEGIN
    cotangent := cos(angle) / sin(angle)
END;
```

        Function name must appear at least once on the left side of an assignment statement. Data type of result must be specified in the function header.
   3.3 Recursive functions: Functions that either directly or indirectly invoke themselves.

        Example:

```
FUNCTION total (n : integer) : integer;
BEGIN
        IF n = 1
        THEN total := 1
        ELSE total := n + total(n – 1)
END;
```

4 Forward declarations: Permit a function or procedure name to appear, and thus be capable of invocation, prior to definition.
   Example:

```
PROCEDURE last (number: integer); forward;
```

In the next chapter we will consider data types in more detail. In particular, we will discuss an attractive feature of Pascal, the user-defined data types. These data types (known as enumerated types) are defined by the user and can improve the design and readability of our programs. Also, we will look at restricted data types, called **subrange data types**, and some of their applications. The type declarations discussed in the next chapter will be quite useful later in the course when we study more complicated data structures.

Keywords for Chapter 7

actual parameter	PROCEDURE
eof function	pseudorandom number
eoln function	random number
formal parameter	recursive function
forward	scope
FUNCTION	seed
global identifier	side effect
local identifier	standard function
odd function	user-defined function
parameter	value parameter
portability	variable parameter

CHAPTER 7 EXERCISES

※ ESSENTIAL EXERCISES

1 How would you arrange to count the number of times a particular procedure or function was invoked in a Pascal program? How easy is it to do this as an after-thought, that is, after the program was written?

2 Consider the following PROCEDURE statements, where *t1* and *t2* are unique type identifiers.

(1) PROCEDURE p (VAR f1 : t1; f2 : t2);

(2) PROCEDURE p (VAR f1 : t1; VAR f2 : t2);

(3) PROCEDURE p (f1 : t1; f2 : t2);

For each of the following invocations of procedure *p*, determine which of the procedure statements above could be used. Assume *v1* and *v2* are variables of type *t1* and *t2*, respectively, and *e1* and *e2* are expressions of type *t1* and *t2*, respectively.

(a) p (v1, v2);   (c) p (e1, e2);
(b) p (v1, e2);   (d) p (e1, v2);

3 In the program skeleton shown below (intentionally without the usual indentation), draw boxes to indicate the scope of the identifiers.

```
PROGRAM boxes (input, output);
PROCEDURE A;
PROCEDURE B;
END;
PROCEDURE C;
PROCEDURE D;
END;
END;
END;
PROCEDURE E;
FUNCTION F;
END;
END;
END.
```

4 In the program skeleton shown below, abbreviated CONST and VAR definitions and declarations are shown. At each of the three comments marking the location of statements for the procedures and the program, indicate each identifier that is accessible, what it represents (CONST or VAR), and where it was declared (program x, procedure y or z).

```
PROGRAM x;
CONST
        a, b, c;
VAR
      d, e, f;
PROCEDURE y;
CONST
VAR
      b, e;
PROCEDURE z;
CONST
VAR
      f, g;
BEGIN
      (* statements for procedure z *)
END;
BEGIN
      (* statements for procedure y *)
END;
BEGIN
      (* statements for program x *)

END.
```

5   For each of the problems below, indicate whether the solution would most appropriately be expressed as a procedure or function.

(a)   Given a prime number, determine the next larger prime number.

(b)   Given a positive, nonzero integer N, determine the number of unique factors of N and the two (or fewer) largest unique factors.

(c)   Given a character in the ASCII character set, determine its ordinal position in the EBCDIC character set.

(d)   Given a number of years N and a desired amount A, determine the annual interest rate necessary to obtain A in N years if interest is compounded annually and the annual interest rate necessary to obtain A in N years if interest is compounded monthly.

★★ SIGNIFICANT EXERCISES

6   Some languages allow external compilation of procedures and functions. That is, procedures and functions can be compiled independently and then linked together to form an executable program. Why is this not desirable for standard Pascal?

7   Suggest a procedure for determining the number of positions in an output line required to represent a signed integer correctly. For example, $+403$ requires a minimum of three positions, but -403 requires four. Note that 0 requires one position in the output, not 0 positions.

★★★ CHALLENGING EXERCISES

8   Ackermann's function is defined as follows, where m, n and the result are all integer values:

$$
\begin{aligned}
A\,(m,n) &= n + 1 &&\text{if } m = 0 \\
         &= A\,(m - 1, 1) &&\text{if } m \text{ is nonzero and } n = 0 \\
         &= A\,(m - 1, A\,(m, n - 1)) &&\text{if both } m \text{ and } n \text{ are nonzero}
\end{aligned}
$$

Write the Pascal function that computes the value of Ackermann's function, given the parameters m and n. (You may choose to utilize this function in a test program, but be warned that arguments larger than about 2 or 3 for m and n will result in extremely large execution times!)

CHAPTER 7 PROBLEMS FOR COMPUTER SOLUTION

★ ESSENTIAL PROBLEMS

1   Write a Boolean function called *multiple* which has two integer arguments m and n. *Multiple* should yield true if m is an integer multiple of n or n is an integer multiple of m. Write a program to test this function that reads a pair of integers from each input line, invokes *multiple*, and then displays the integers and the result from *multiple*.

Example input:

```
 4    7
 4    8
16    8
```

Example output:

```
 4    7    False
 4    8    True
16    8    True
```

2 Write a procedure with three variable real parameters *a*, *b*, and *c*. The effect of the procedure should be to "rotate" the values in the parameters to the right, such that after execution, the value originally in *a* is in *b*, that originally in *b* is in *c*, and that originally in *c* is in *a*. Test your procedure with a program that reads three real numbers from each line of the input, then displays the rotated real numbers.

Example input:

```
 4.7     1.003      7.5
-12.5          6.5e-4     2.005e+5
```

Example output:

```
7.5000e+00       4.7000e+00       1.0030e+00
2.0050e+05      -1.2500e+01       6.5000e-04
```

3 Write a function *invest* which has three parameters. The first parameter, a real value, specifies the annual interest rate paid at the beginning of each year on investments left in a financial institution during the previous year. The second parameter, also a real value, specifies the initial investment, in dollars. Assuming that interest is reinvested at the beginning of each year, the function is to return the value of the investment after the number of years specified by the third parameter, an integer value. Use iteration to determine the value of the investment. You should also write a main program to test function *invest*. The program should read lines containing interest rates, initial investments, and investment periods, then invoke function *interest* to perform the calculation, and display the results.

Example input:

```
0.12      1000.0    5
0.125     1000.0    5
```

Example output:

```
Interest Rate = 0.120
Investment = $1000.00
Period = 5 years
Yield = $1762.34
```

Interest Rate = 0.125
Investment = $1000.00
Period = 5 years
Yield = $1802.03

★★ SIGNIFICANT PROBLEMS

4   Write a function which obtains an octal number from the input data and returns
its value as an integer. The octal number is presented in the same manner as an
integer. That is, you must skip leading blanks, tabs, and end-of-line characters,
then read octal digits (possibly preceded by a plus or minus sign) and accumulate
the number's value. An octal number may include only the digits 0 through 7.
The value of such a number is determined by evaluating

$$d_i * 8^i + d_{i-1} * 8^{i-1} + \cdots + d_1 * 8^1 + d_0 * 8^0$$

where the digits of the octal number, left to right, are d_i, d_{i-1}, . . . , d_1, d_0. Also
write a main program which tests your function. The input data should have exactly
one octal number per line, and the output should be the decimal equivalent of the
number.

Example input:

```
      -701
 +42
     377
```

Example output:

```
-449
 34
255
```

5   Write a procedure which has as its single-value parameter an integer value. The
procedure should display the value of the integer in the minimum space required
using only write statements with a character parameter. This can be done by treating
the printing as a recursive problem. Assume the integer to be displayed is called
N. Then the following steps will solve the problem:

(1)   If N is negative, then display ' − ' and set N to −N.
(2)   If N is greater than or equal to 10, then recursively invoke this procedure
      with an actual argument of N DIV 10.
(3)   Display N MOD 10.

Write a main program to test the procedure. It should read integer values from the
input until an end of file is encountered and display the integer values (using the
procedure) separated by a comma and a single space. You may assume that this
output will fit on a single line.

Example input

4   −0031   1000   315   −00099   0099

Example output:

4, −31, 1000, 315, −99, 99

★★★ CHALLENGING PROBLEMS

6 Write a function to yield the smallest prime factor of its positive integer argument. A prime number N is divisible evenly only by N and 1. Write a main program that uses this function to display all the prime factors of the integers that appear in the input; display the results for each input value on a single output line, preceded by the integer itself and an equal sign, and separate the prime factors by asterisks.

Example input:

39   42   1517

Example output:

39 = 3 * 13
42 = 2 * 3 * 7
1517 = 37 * 41

CHAPTER 8

CHAPTER 8
DATA TYPES

User–Defined or Enumerated Types

Subrange Data Types

Standard Ordinal Functions

Problem Solving

Sets

ord

chr

pred

succ

DATA TYPES

OBJECTIVES

After completing this chapter, you should be able to:

- Declare and apply user-defined (enumerated) data types
- Declare and apply subrange data types
- Recognize and apply the standard ordinal functions: *ord, chr, pred,* and *succ*
- Recognize and apply the set data type
- Solve, test, and debug problems using enumerated data types

CHAPTER OVERVIEW

One of the attractive features of Pascal is the flexibility permitted in the definition of new data types more suited to the problem being solved. In this chapter we will discuss such user-defined, or **enumerated types**. For example, suppose we would like to define a new data type called *color* whose value can be any one of the following constants:

red, white, blue, black.

In Pascal we can define this data type by the following TYPE definition:

TYPE color = (red, white, blue, black);

Following this statement we can declare variables whose values can range over the data type *color*. As you will see in this chapter, enumerated data types can be manipulated according to the same rules as the standard data types.

Given an ordinal data type, such as integer, char, or Boolean (but not real) or an enumerated type, Pascal permits us to restrict the range of values of the data type. These restricted data types are known as **subrange data types**. They provide an automatic check for values being outside of the specified range.

Included in this chapter is a discussion of the standard ordinal functions: *ord, chr, pred,* and *succ.* These functions are extremely valuable when using ordinal data types. An application to character manipulation is also presented.

At the end of the chapter an application of enumerated types to a specific problem is presented. Also, an introduction to the set data type is included. The Testing and Debugging Techniques section considers the problem of type compatibility when using enumerated types.

SECTION 8.1 USER-DEFINED OR ENUMERATED DATA TYPES

Pascal permits you to define and declare your own data types. This feature can be quite useful when translating an algorithm into the actual Pascal code. In this section we consider these user-defined or enumerated data types.

Recall that a simple data type, such as integer, char, and Boolean (but not real) is called **ordinal** since the values (or constants) defining the data type are precisely ordered. For example, the Boolean constants are ordered as follows:

false < true

Also, character constants have an ordering that includes the following:

'A' < 'B' < 'C' < 'D' < 'E' < ... < 'Z'

The user-defined or enumerated types will also be ordinal types, as we shall see.

Enumerated Data Types

A user-defined or ***enumerated data type*** is an ordered list of constants named by the user. For example, suppose we wish to define a data type called *vowel* consisting of the following ordered constants:

A, E, I, O, U

In this case the ordering is as follows:

A < E < I < O < U

Note that these constants (*A, E, I, O,* and *U*) are *not* the same as the character constants 'A', 'E', 'I', 'O', and 'U'. In Pascal we can declare this ordinal data type using a ***TYPE definition:***

TYPE vowel = (A, E, I, O, U);

Another example illustrating the usefulness of a user-defined data type is the following TYPE definition for the days of the week:

TYPE day = (Sunday, Monday, Tuesday, Wednesday,
                Thursday, Friday, Saturday);

The syntax diagram for enumerated data types is shown in Figure 8-1.

At this point it is important for you to understand that the TYPE definition merely defines the ordinal data type. To actually use the data type, we must declare variables of the given type. In Pascal the variable declarations follow the TYPE definitions in the declaration part of the program. Consider the following declarations:

Figure 8-1 Syntax diagram for enumerated type.

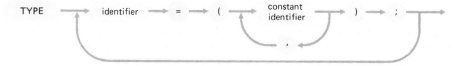

```
TYPE   vowel  =  (A, E, I, O, U);
       day    =  (Sunday, Monday, Tuesday, Wednesday, Thursday,
                  Friday, Saturday);
VAR    letter :  vowel;
       birthday,
       holiday :  day;
```

In this example, the variable *letter* is of type *vowel* and the variables *birthday* and *holiday* are of type *day*. There is an alternate form of declaring these variables that permits the TYPE definition to be included in the variable declaration. The following declaration is equivalent to the one above:

```
VAR letter : (A, E, I, O, U);
    birthday,
    holiday: (Sunday, Monday, Tuesday, Wednesday, Thursday, Friday,
             Saturday);
```

The variables can be assigned any constant value specified in the TYPE definition. For example, the following are valid assignment statements:

```
letter := E;
birthday := Sunday;
holiday := Saturday;
letter := A;
birthday := holiday;
```

The following are *invalid* assignment statements:

```
letter := 'A';              (* 'A' is of data type char *)
letter := Monday;           (* cannot mix data types *)
letter := B;              (* B is a variable, not a constant *)
birthday := day;            (* day names the data type *)
holiday := mon;               (* not a valid constant *)
```

Observe from the previous examples that we cannot mix different user-defined data types. However, since the data types are ordinal, we can compare values. For example, the following IF statement is valid:

```
IF letter = U
THEN writeln ('Vowel is U.')
ELSE writeln ('Vowel is not U.')
```

Another example of comparing values using the ordering is the following:

```
IF (Sunday < holiday) AND (holiday < Saturday)
THEN writeln ('Holiday falls on a weekday.')
ELSE writeln ('Holiday falls on a weekend.')
```

Enumerated data types can be manipulated just like the simple data types with one major exception. In standard Pascal we *cannot* read or display the constants of enumerated data types directly. From the previous example, the variable *letter* is declared of type *vowel*. To display the contents of *letter*, we can use a CASE statement with the ordinal value of *letter*, as the selector. Thus, the following statement would display the value of *letter*:

```
CASE letter OF
        A : writeln ('Vowel is A.');
        E : writeln ('Vowel is E.');
        I : writeln ('Vowel is I.');
        O : writeln ('Vowel is O.');
        U : writeln ('Vowel is U.')
END
```

Problem 8.1

Write a Pascal program using enumerated data types to display the number of days in each month (of a non-leap year) from January to December, in order.

The following Pascal program will display the desired results. Observe the use of the FOR and CASE statements. An advantage in using an enumerated type is the improvement in the readability of the program.

```
PROGRAM daysinmonth (input, output);
(* program to display number of days in each month *)
(* of a non-leap year *)
TYPE montype = (Jan, Feb, Mar, Apr, May, Jun,
                    Jul, Aug, Sep, Oct, Nov, Dec);
VAR month : montype;
BEGIN
        FOR month := Jan TO Dec DO
            CASE month OF
                    Jan,Mar,May,Jul,
                    Aug,Oct,Dec         : writeln ('31 days.');
                    Apr,Jun,Sep,Nov     : writeln ('30 days.');
                    Feb                 : writeln ('28 days.')
            END
END.
```

TYPE Definitions

In a Pascal program the TYPE definitions are placed between the CONST and VAR declarations. Thus, the structure of a Pascal program now takes on the following form:

```
PROGRAM name (input, output);
CONST declarations;
```

```
TYPE definitions;
VAR declarations;
PROCEDURE or FUNCTION declarations;
BEGIN
        statement;
        statement;
        .
        .
        .
        statement
END.
```

TYPE definitions can also appear within a procedure or function as local definitions. Here is a list of some important rules regarding TYPE definitions:

■ Constants used in an enumerated type must be distinct from those used in any other data type. For example, the following TYPE definition is *not* valid since the constants belong to the char data type:

```
TYPE grade = ('A','B','C','D','F');
```

However, the following would be a valid TYPE definition as long as the constants are not previously defined:

```
TYPE grade = (A, B, C, D, F);
```

■ The same constant cannot appear in two or more different TYPE definitions. For example, the following is not valid since the constant *Friday* is used in both definitions:

```
TYPE
    weekday = (Monday, Tuesday, Wednesday,
                Thursday, Friday);
    weekend = (Friday, Saturday, Sunday);
```

■ The TYPE definition merely defines an enumerated data type. A variable declaration will actually reserve the necessary memory locations to store a value of the specified type. The type name should never appear in the executable part of the program. Think of what happens with the standard data types. We never use the names of the standard data types (integer, real, char, and Boolean) in the executable part of our programs. To do so would result in a different meaning of the name and some confusion, no doubt.

■ TYPE definitions can be included as part of the VAR declarations. For example, the following definition

```
TYPE status = (single, married, divorced);
VAR marital : status;
```

can actually be written as a single VAR declaration:

VAR marital : (single, married, divorced);

However, this form of the TYPE definition cannot be used in the header of a procedure or function. That is, TYPE definitions are not allowed in the formal parameter list of a procedure or function. For example, the following procedure header is *not* valid:

PROCEDURE search
(VAR marital : (single, married, divorced));

To permit value and variable parameters to assume values from an enumerated type, we must define the enumerated type globally (to the procedures referencing the enumerated type) using a TYPE definition. Thus, the following is an acceptable way of declaring a formal parameter as an enumerated data type:

TYPE status = (single, married, divorced);
VAR declarations;
PROCEDURE search (VAR marital : status);
.
.
.

In this case the enumerated data type *status* is globally defined and known in all procedures and functions within the scope of the definition. The scope rules for TYPE definitions are the same as those for constants, variables, procedures, and functions.

EXERCISES FOR SECTION 8.1

1 Define an enumerated type for the following definitions:
   (a) States in the United States whose names begin with the letter *A*.
   (b) Your relatives.
   (c) Soft drink types.
   (d) Ice cream flavors.

2 Determine which of the following statements are valid given the following declaration:

TYPE color = (red, white, blue, purple);
VAR coloring : color;

   (a) read (red);
        writeln (red);
   (b) read (coloring);
        write (coloring);

(c) coloring := white;
     writeln (coloring);
(d) coloring := white;
     CASE coloring OF
          red : writeln ('red');
          white : writeln ('white');
          blue : writeln ('blue');
          purple : writeln ('purple')
     END;
(e) coloring := blue;
     CASE coloring OF
          red : writeln (red);
          white : writeln (white);
          blue : writeln (blue);
          purple : writeln (purple)
     END;
(f) IF coloring = blue
     THEN writeln ('blue')
     ELSE writeln ('not blue')

3 Determine whether each of the following TYPE definitions is valid or invalid:
   (a) TYPE letter = ('X', 'Y', 'Z');
   (b) TYPE language = (Pascal, Fortran, Basic);
   (c) TYPE subjects = (math, history, computers, biology);
             major = (math, computers);
   (d) TYPE status = (resident, citizen, alien);
             nationality = (American, European, African, Asian,
                            other);
   (e) TYPE code = (1, 2, 3, 4, 5);
   (f) TYPE code = (c1, c2, c3, c4, c5);

4 Determine whether the following are valid or invalid declarations.
   (a) TYPE status = (single, married, engaged, divorced);
        VAR type : status;
   (b) TYPE city = (NewYork, LosAngeles, Chicago, Houston);
        VAR city : type;
   (c) VAR city : (NewYork, London, Paris, Rome);
   (d) PROCEDURE find (VAR city : (NewYork, London, Rome));
   (e) TYPE jobtype = (whitecollar, bluecollar, colorless);
        PROCEDURE search (VAR job : jobtype);

5 Consider the following program.

```
PROGRAM good (input, output);
TYPE
        subject = (math, history, compsci, geography, physics);
VAR
        a, b : subject;
```

```
BEGIN
      a := math;
      b := compsci;
      IF a > b
      THEN write ('superb')
      ELSE write ('excellent')
END.
```

Which of the following statements is true?
(a) In the IF statement, *a* and *b* cannot be compared since they are not numbers.
(b) The program will display "superb."
(c) The program will display "excellent."
(d) The IF statement will cause a run-time error.
(e) None of the statements is true.

6 Determine the output of the following program:

```
PROGRAM test (input, output);
TYPE
      city = (Boston, NewYork, Miami, Chicago);
VAR
      city1, city2 : city;
PROCEDURE display (citya, cityb : city);
BEGIN
      IF ((citya >= Boston) AND (citya <= Chicago)) AND
         ((cityb >= Boston) AND (cityb <= Chicago))
      THEN  IF citya > cityb
              THEN CASE citya OF
                      Boston: writeln ('Travel to Boston');
                      NewYork: writeln ('Travel to NewYork');
                      Miami: writeln ('Travel to Miami');
                      Chicago: writeln ('Travel to Chicago')
                   END
              ELSE writeln ('Travel not recommended.')
      ELSE writeln ('Error on input.')
END;
(* Main Program *)
BEGIN
      city1 := Chicago;
      city2 := NewYork;
      display (city1, city2);
      city1 := Boston;
      city2 := Miami;
      display (city1, city2)
END.
```

7 Write a Pascal procedure using enumerated types that will display the name of the month given the abbreviated month name as a parameter. For example, if the month name Mar is passed to the procedure, the word *March* will be displayed. Be certain to globally define the enumerated type.

SECTION 8.2 SUBRANGE DATA TYPES

Suppose we are writing a Pascal program that calculates student exam scores, each of which can range from 0 to 100. We can use a variable declaration with a restriction on the range of the integers to the numbers 0 to 100 as follows:

VAR examscore : 0..100;

The variable *examscore* is followed by a colon and the range of values starting with the first or smallest value (0) and the last, or largest, value (100). The first and last values are separated by *two* periods. In Pascal ordinal data types that are restricted to a specific range are called **subrange data types**.

The advantages of using subrange data types are the following:

1 The range of values is explicitly stated, thus improving the design and readability of the program.
2 If the value assigned to a variable declared with a subrange data type is not within the range specified, the computer will provide an appropriate diagnostic message.

Subrange types can be derived from any standard or user-defined ordinal type except real. The following declarations use subrange types derived from the standard data types:

```
VAR  scale: 1..10;        (* range includes 1,2,3,4,5,6,7,8,9,10     *)
     uppercase: 'A'..'Z';  (* range  includes  'A','B',...,'Z'        *)
     internal: -3..3;      (* range includes -3,-2,-1,0,1,2,3         *)
```

Assume we have the following enumerated data type definition:

TYPE day = (Sun,Mon,Tue,Wed,Thu,Fri,Sat);

Then the following is a valid subrange data type declaration:

VAR weekday : Mon..Fri; (* range includes Mon,Tue,Wed,Thu,Fri *)

An attempt to assign a value outside of the valid range to *weekday* will result in a run-time error.

Here are some more valid declarations involving subranges of the standard data types:

```
        grade: 'A'..'F';            (* range includes
                                      'A','B','C','D','E', and 'F' *)
        positive: 1..maxint;        (* range includes all positive
                                      integers up to maxint *)
        temperature: −50..100;      (* range includes all integers
                                      from −50 to 100 *)
        shift: Wed..Sat;            (* range includes Wed, Thu,
                                      Fri, and Sat *)
```

A few rules regarding the use of the subrange data type should be noted:

■ The lower and upper values in the subrange type declaration must be of the same data type. This is called the *host* data type. The lower value must be less than or equal to the upper value. The following examples, therefore, are *not* valid:

```
VAR lowercase: 'z'..'a';        (* wrong order *)
    digits: 0..'9';          (* not same data type *)
```

■ Subrange values include all constant values between and including the lower and upper values. For example, a subrange of the first five even integers is not possible.
■ Different subranges of the same type may be mixed in expressions and assignment statements. However, an error will result if a value is outside the specified range. For example, consider the following declarations:

```
VAR test: 0..100;
    total: integer;
    scale: 1..10;
```

The following assignment statements are valid, but the range checking will still be in effect during their execution:

```
scale := total DIV test;
total := scale * test;
```

In the Testing and Debugging Techniques section we will look at type compatibility in more detail.
■ To use subrange type declarations with formal parameters in a function or procedure header, we must globally define the subrange type using a TYPE definition. Consider the following example:

```
TYPE score = 0..100;
VAR declarations;
PROCEDURE test (exam : score);
```

In this case the value parameter *exam* can assume values from the subrange datatype score (range 0 to 100). The following is an *invalid* procedure header:

```pascal
PROCEDURE test (exam : 0..100);
```

■ Subrange types can be defined in terms of previously declared constants. For example, the following Pascal segment uses the constant declarations in the TYPE definition:

```pascal
PROGRAM example (input, output);
CONST low = 0;
        high = 100;
TYPE score = low..high;
VAR test : score;
```

The next problem is an example of using subrange data types.

Problem 8.2

A pair of dice is tossed 500 times. The outcome of each toss is entered as input to a program. Write a Pascal program that counts and displays the number of outcomes having a total value of 7. Note the range of values for each outcome is 2 through 12.

The following Pascal program implements the solution to this problem. Observe the use of the subrange data types.

```pascal
PROGRAM seven (input, output);
(* Count and display the number of sevens *)
(* resulting from tosses of a pair of dice. *)
CONST
        low = 2;                (* lowest possible toss *)
        high = 12;              (* highest possible toss *)
        max = 500;              (* number of tosses *)
TYPE
        value = low..high;      (* permitted input values *)
VAR
        index : 1..max;         (* counts tosses *)
        toss : value;           (* value of current toss *)
        counter : 0..max;       (* counts tosses of 7 *)

BEGIN
        counter := 0;
        FOR index := 1 TO max DO
```

```
      BEGIN
            read (toss);
            IF toss = 7
            THEN counter := counter + 1
      END;
      writeln ('Number of tosses is ', max:1);
      writeln ('Number of sevens is ', counter:1)
END.
```

EXERCISES FOR SECTION 8.2

1   Define a subrange type for each of the following definitions:
    (a)   The nonnegative integers.
    (b)   The integers greater than 100.
    (c)   The characters in the first half of the alphabet.
    (d)   The characters in the second half of the alphabet.

2   Find the range of values for the variable *time* in the following declaration:

```
CONST
        min = 99;
        max = 1000;
TYPE
        duration = min..max;
VAR
        time : duration;
```

3   Consider the following declarations:

```
TYPE
        daytype = (Monday, Tuesday, Wednesday, Thursday,
                        Friday, Saturday, Sunday);
VAR
        day : daytype;
        workday : Monday..Friday;
        weekend : Saturday..Sunday;
```

    (a)   Will assigning the value *Tuesday* to *weekend* result in a run-time error?
    (b)   Will assigning the value *Friday* to *workday* result in a run-time error?

4   Determine the range of values of each variable.

```
TYPE
        month = (Jan, Feb, Mar, Apr, May, Jun);
```

VAR
      letter : 'A'..'Z';
      negative : $-$maxint.. $-$1;
      somedigits : '0'..'3';
      temp : $-$32..32;
      spring : Mar..Jun;
      halfyear : Jan..Jun;

5   Assume the following are declared in a correct Pascal program:

VAR
      low : 1..5;
      mid : 1..10;
      high : 6..20;
      big : '1'..'10';

If the value of *high* is 7, which assignment will *not* generate either a compile or run-time error? Each assignment is independent of the others.
(a) low := high;
(b) high := 3 * high;
(c) big := high;
(d) mid := high;
(e) mid := high $-$ 7;

6   Which one of the following is a valid subrange declaration?
(a) TYPE label1 = '0'..9;
(b) TYPE label2 := $-$3..6;
(c) TYPE label3 = $-$1..$-$3;
(d) TYPE label4 = 0.0..9;
(e) TYPE label5 = 1..1;

7   Write a Pascal program with subrange declarations to determine whether a sequence of five digits entered as input is a numeric palindrome. A ***numeric palindrome*** is a sequence of digits that reads the same backwards and forwards. For example, the five-digit numbers 12321, 11211, 54345, and 22222 are numeric palindromes. Read each digit as a character, and display a message indicating whether the sequence is a palindrome.

SECTION 8.3 STANDARD ORDINAL FUNCTIONS: *PRED, SUCC, CHR,* AND *ORD*

When we are using ordinal data types, including enumerated types, it is often necessary to perform some manipulation of the data. To aid in this process, Pascal provides the following four standard (predefined) ordinal functions: *pred, succ, chr,* and *ord*. Here is a brief summary of the four functions, giving the required data type of the argument each expects and a description of the result each computes.

standard ordinal function	description	argument type	result type
pred(x)	Predecessor of x	Any ordinal type	Same type
succ(x)	Successor of x	Any ordinal type	Same type
chr(x)	Character whose code is x	Integer	Char
ord(x)	Position of x in its data type	Any ordinal type	Integer

Let's take a closer look at each function.

Pred and *Succ*

The function ***pred(x)*** yields the predecessor of the argument x in its ordinal data type. This is just that constant immediately preceding x in the data type that contains x. In an ordinal data type, each constant other than the first has an immediate predecessor. For example,

```
pred('C')    equals    'B'
pred('8')    equals    '7'
pred(3)      equals    2
```

Suppose we define the following enumerated data type:

TYPE days = (Sun, Mon, Tue, Wed, Thu, Fri, Sat);

The following examples illustrate the effect of applying the pred function to the constants of the enumerated data type:

```
pred(Sat)    equals    Fri
pred(Wed)    equals    Tue
pred(Mon)    equals    Sun
```

Note that the value of "pred(Sun)" is undefined, since the constant *Sun* has no immediate predecessor. For the same reason, "pred(-maxint)" is undefined.

The function ***succ(x)*** yields the successor of the argument x in its ordinal data type. This is just that constant immediately following x in the data type that contains x. Each constant in an ordinal data type other than the last has an immediate successor. For example,

```
succ('a')    equals    'b'
succ(0)      equals    1
succ(-3)     equals    -2
```

succ(false)	equals	true
succ('X')	equals	'Y'
succ(Sun)	equals	Mon

Note that "succ(Sat)" is undefined for the enumerated type defined previously. Similarly, "succ(maxint)" is undefined, since the integer *maxint* has no immediate successor in Pascal.

The argument and result of both functions, *pred* and *succ*, can be any ordinal data type, including enumerated types. The following table gives further illustrations of the *pred* and *succ* functions.

example	result
pred(10)	9
pred('1')	'0'
pred(true)	false
pred(false)	undefined
succ(pred(' '))	' '
pred(succ(2))	2
succ(succ(8))	10

Ord and Chr

The constants of an ordinal data type are ordered by their position in the data type. The function **ord(x)** yields the ordinal position of the argument x in its data type. That is, *ord(x)* yields an integer indicating the position of x in the ordering of constants of the same data type as x. Consider the following enumerated TYPE definition:

ordinal pos. = 0   1   2   3   4   5   6   7   8   9   10   11

           ↓   ↓   ↓   ↓   ↓   ↓   ↓   ↓   ↓   ↓   ↓   ↓

TYPE month = (Jan, Feb, Mar, Apr, May, Jun, Jul, Aug, Sep, Oct, Nov, Dec);

Note the ordinal position of the first constant in this, and each, enumerated data type is zero, *not* one. Thus, we have the following results:

ord(Feb)	equals	1
ord(Dec)	equals	11
ord(Jun)	equals	5
ord(Jan)	equals	0

In any enumerated type the ordinal position of the first constant in the type is zero. This includes the Boolean data type, so that "ord(false)" is zero. The ordinal position of any integer equals the integer itself. Thus, "ord(8)" equals 8, and "ord(-6)" equals -6. The *ord* function can be applied to a value of any ordinal data type and always yields an integer result. In particular, the *ord* function can be used to convert values of the char data type to integer values. Recall that characters are represented internally in the computer by integer values. The actual values used for this representation depend on the particular computer system and character set being used. For example, many computer systems, such as many of those manufactured by Digital Equipment Corporation, and most personal computers use the ASCII coding scheme. Others, such as the large computers manufactured by IBM, use the EBCDIC coding scheme. Appendix F gives the actual codes used for these schemes.

If a computer system uses the ASCII coding scheme, we would obtain the results shown below from the ord function:

```
ord('A')    equals    65
ord('B')    equals    66
ord('C')    equals    67
ord('O')    equals    48
ord('1')    equals    49
```

The function *chr(x)* is the inverse of the *ord* function applied to char arguments. That is, if *x* is an integer that represents an ordinal position in the character set, then *chr(x)* is the character at that position. You should compare the following examples with those shown above. Again, we assume the ASCII coding scheme is in use.

```
chr(65)        equals    'A'
chr(66)        equals    'B'
chr(67)        equals    'C'
chr(48)        equals    'O'
chr(49)        equals    '1'
chr(ord('A'))  equals    'A'
```

Now let us consider a program that displays the ordinal positions and the corresponding characters for a given character set with N (a positive integer) characters.

Problem 8.3

A particular computer has N characters in its character set. Write a Pascal program to display the ordinal positions and the characters at those positions. Assume that N cannot be greater than 512.

The following program will assume the actual number of characters in the character set, *N*, will be provided as input data (variable *num* will contain its value). The actual characters and their ordinal positions are displayed. Note the upper boundary of 512 for each subrange type.

```
PROGRAM display (input, output);
(* Display the characters with ordinal values *)
(* in the range 1 to N. N is provided as input *)
VAR
```

```
      num : 1..512;     (* number of characters *)
      index : 0..511;     (* ordinal position *)
BEGIN
      write ('Enter the number of characters in the set: ');
      readln (num);
      FOR index := 0 TO num-1 DO
          writeln ('Ordinal position: ', index:1, ' ':5,
              'Character: ', chr(index):1)
END.
```

Note that the ASCII character set (and each character set used with Pascal) has the digits ordered contiguously. That is, the digits occur in an ascending sequence with no other characters between them. The following table shows the order of the digits and their ordinal positions in the ASCII character set.

digit	'0'	'1'	'2'	'3'	'4'	'5'	'6'	'7'	'8'	'9'
ordinal	48	49	50	51	52	53	54	55	56	57

Sometimes it may be necessary to convert the character representation of a decimal digit to its integer equivalent. For example, consider the conversion of the character '5' to its integer equivalent 5. The integer value of '5' is equal to its distance from '0' in all character sets used with Pascal, so we can see, for example, that

```
ord('5') − ord('0') = 53 − 48 = 5
ord('6') − ord('0') = 54 − 48 = 6
ord('0') − ord('0') = 48 − 48 = 0
```

Thus, we see that to convert any arbitrary character variable containing a decimal digit (we call it *digit*) to its integer equivalent, the expression

```
ord(digit) − ord('0')
```

will do the task. Since the digits are contiguous in all character sets used with Pascal, this result will work in any program. Although the value of "ord('0')" may vary (depending on the particular computer system in use), the Pascal compiler for that computer system will cause the correct value to be produced. All we need to do is subtract that value from "ord(digit)" to yield the integer equivalent.

We can also reverse the process shown above when we wish to obtain a character equivalent to the value of an integer variable containing a value in the range 0 to 9. Notice the result of the following expressions:

```
chr (0 + ord('0')) = '0'
chr (1 + ord('0')) = '1'
```

chr (9 + ord('0')) = '9'

So the expression

chr (val + ord('0'))

can be used to convert from an integer value *val* in the range 0 to 9 to its equivalent character value.

Let's apply the ordinal functions to a problem that reads a nonnegative integer from a character string and converts it to the actual numeric value.

Problem 8.4

Write a Pascal procedure that reads a sequence of characters, ignoring them until the first decimal digit is found. Then the procedure should convert the decimal digit and any digits immediately following it (up to the first nondigit) to the integer equivalent. This integer value is to be assigned to the single variable integer parameter.

The following procedure called *convert* implements a solution to this problem. Note that as each new digit is encountered, we multiply our previous result by 10 and add the value of the new digit. This approach is a direct consequence of the property that a decimal number, say the three digit number $d_1d_2d_3$, is equal to $(d_1 * 10 + d_2) * 10 + d_3$. For example, $471 = (4 * 10 + 7) * 10 + 1$.

```
PROCEDURE convert (VAR num : integer);
(* Skip leading nondigits and convert a sequence of    *)
(* decimal digit characters to integer equivalent, num *)
(* Stop after first nondigit following the number.      *)
VAR inchar : char;                    (* input character *)
BEGIN
      num := 0;
      REPEAT                     (* look for first digit *)
         read (inchar)
      UNTIL (inchar >= '0') AND (inchar <= '9');
      REPEAT                   (* convert to integer *)
         num := num * 10 + ord(inchar) - ord('0');
         read (inchar);    (* obtain next character *)
      UNTIL (inchar < '0') OR (inchar > '9')
END;
```

This procedure is quite useful in programs that manipulate character strings, as we shall see in a later chapter. As an exercise, test the procedure for the following input string:

Blaise Pascal was born in the year 1623.

EXERCISES FOR SECTION 8.3

1 Determine the result of each expression.
   (a) pred (8)   (b) succ (1)
   (c) succ (−3)   (d) pred ('8')
   (e) succ (true)   (f) pred (−maxint)

2 Determine the result of each expression.
   (a) pred (pred (0))   (b) pred (succ (100))
   (c) succ (pred ('0'))   (d) succ (succ ('2'))
   (e) pred (pred (pred (9)))   (f) succ (pred (succ ('A')))

3 Consider the following definition:

   TYPE
        weird = (googol,noodle,broodle,coodle,zoodle,boodle);

   Determine the value of each expression.
   (a) ord (googol)   (b) ord (zoodle)
   (c) succ (broodle)   (d) succ (boodle)
   (e) pred (googol)   (f) ord (succ (zoodle))

4 Find the value of each expression.
   (a) ord ('7') − ord ('0')
   (b) ord ('1') − ord ('1')
   (c) chr (3 + ord ('0'))
   (d) chr (0 + ord ('0'))

5 Verify procedure *convert* in this section for the following input strings:
   (a) The year 2001 is near.
   (b) $37.00 is the amount.

6 Consider the following declaration:

   TYPE
        vowel = (a, e, i, o, u);
   VAR
        letter : vowel;
        inchar : char;

   Will the following Pascal code execute without an error?

```
letter := a;
WHILE letter <= u DO
BEGIN
        read (inchar);
        writeln ('Input character is ', inchar);
        letter := succ (letter)
END
```

7 Using the declaration of problem 6, will the following code execute without an error?

```
letter := u;
REPEAT
        read (inchar);
        writeln ('Input character is ', inchar);
        letter := pred (letter)
UNTIL letter = a
```

8 Rewrite procedure *convert* in this section using WHILE loops instead of REPEAT-UNTIL loops.

SECTION 8.4 PROBLEM SOLVING USING ENUMERATED TYPES

In this section we solve the following problem using an enumerated data type, which makes the Pascal program more readable.

An English professor needs a text classification program that classifies each character in a sentence as either an uppercase vowel, an uppercase consonant, or a special character and reports the total number of characters in the sentence and the percentage of each character found. The professor assumes that the sentence in which the characters appear is terminated with a period and that the only special characters (other than the period) that may be included are blanks, commas, colons, and semicolons.

This problem can be subdivided into three subproblems as follows (see Figure 8-2):

Figure 8-2 Top-down design of classification problem.

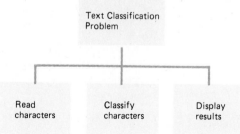

SUBPROBLEM 1: Read each character, and update the total number of characters read.

SUBPROBLEM 2: Classify each character, and update the appropriate class counter.

SUBPROBLEM 3: Display the total number of characters, and compute and display the percentages.

A detailed algorithm can be expressed as follows:

Text Classification Algorithm

Initialize all counters to zero.
Read a character.
While the character is not a period:
    Update the total character counter.
    Classify the character.
    Update the appropriate counter.
    Read another character.
Display total and percentages.

The actual Pascal program is shown below. Note the use of the enumerated data type "class = (vowel, consonant, special)."

```
PROGRAM textclass (input, output);
(* Program to classify each character in a sentence *)
(* as a vowel, consonant, or special character, and  *)
(* and display total characters and percentages.      *)
TYPE
        class = (vowel, consonant, special);
VAR
        inchar : char;                      (* the input character *)
        total,                          (* total number of characters *)
        vcount,                              (* number of vowels *)
        ccount,                           (* number of consonants *)
        scount : 0..maxint;  (* number of special characters *)
        category : class;                   (* the character type *)
BEGIN
        total := 0;                     (* initialize total count *)
        vcount := 0;                    (* initialize vowel count *)
        ccount := 0;               (* initialize consonant count *)
        scount := 0;                  (* initialize special count *)
        read (inchar);
        WHILE inchar < > '.' DO
        BEGIN
```

```
         (* Increase total character counter *)
         total := total + 1;
         (* determine character class *)
         IF (inchar = 'A') OR (inchar = 'E') OR
            (inchar = 'I') OR (inchar = 'O') OR
            (inchar = 'U')
         THEN category := vowel
         ELSE IF (inchar = ' ') OR (inchar = ',') OR
                 (inchar = ':') OR (inchar = ';')
              THEN category := special
              ELSE category := consonant;
         (* increase appropriate category counter *)
         CASE category OF
              vowel : vcount := vcount + 1;
              consonant : ccount := ccount + 1;
              special : scount := scount + 1
         END (* case *)
         read (inchar)     (* get the next character *)
   END; (* while *)
   (* display results *)
   writeln ('There were ', total:1, ' total characters.');
   writeln (vcount / total * 100 : 6 : 2,
            ' percent were vowels.');
   writeln (ccount / total * 100 : 6 : 2,
            ' percent were consonants.');
   writeln (scount / total * 100 : 6 : 2,
            ' percent were special characters.')
END.
```

Program Textclass

Input: TO BE OR NOT TO BE.
Output: There were 18 total characters.
        33.33 percent were vowels.
        38.89 percent were consonants.
        27.78 percent were special characters.

Program Textclass: Sample Execution

In the next section we will discuss the set data type, which will enable us to write an elegant solution to this problem.

SECTION 8.5 INTRODUCTION TO THE SET DATA TYPE

Consider the following problem: A character is to be read and classified as either a decimal digit, like '0' or '8', or as some other type of character. One way to solve this problem is to use an IF statement which determines whether or not the character to be classified is in the range of decimal digits (recall that Pascal requires that the characters corresponding to the decimal digits appear as a single contiguous sequence). This statement might be written as follows, assuming the character to be classified is in variable *inchar*.

```
IF (inchar >= '0') AND (inchar <= '9')
THEN writeln ('The character is a digit.')
ELSE writeln ('The character is not a digit.')
```

An alternative approach we may use in Pascal solutions is to construct a value of a data type called **set**. A set is a collection of objects of the same ordinal data type. For example,

```
['0'..'9']
```

represents the set containing the character representation of each decimal digit. This set may then be used to determine if the character (*inchar*) is one of the characters in the set. The solution to the previous problem could then be written as follows:

```
IF inchar IN ['0'..'9']
THEN writeln ('The character is a digit.')
ELSE writeln ('The character is not a digit.')
```

The expression

```
['0'..'9']
```

is called a **set constructor**, because it produces a value of the data type set, just like 'X' produces a value of the data type char. As we shall see, set constructors build sets containing a variable number of members depending on the ordinal values included in the constructor.

The expression

```
inchar IN ['0'..'9']
```

is true if the value in *inchar* is in the set of digits "['0'..'9']" and false otherwise. In this case the set of digits is specified using a pair of character values separated by "..". This means that the pair of characters, and each character between them, is in the set. The reserved word IN is a relational operator whose result is true if the value to its left is in the set that appears to its right.

A set constructor is a (possibly empty) list of ordinal expressions, or ordinal expression pairs separated by "..", enclosed in square brackets [and]. All the ordinal expressions appearing between the square brackets must be of the same type. If more than one expression or expression pair are placed between the brackets, then they must be separated from each other by commas. The set constructor

['0', '1', '2', '3', '4', '5', '6', '7', '8', '9']

could have been written instead of "['0'..'9']."

Some more examples of set constructors are shown below. Note that the order in which the individual elements of the list are written is unimportant, but when the elements are constants, they are usually written in ascending order to improve the readability of the program. Further note that a pair of ordinal expressions separated by ".." must be written so that the second expression in the pair is no smaller than the first.

In these examples, assume that the following assignment statements have been executed:

```
i := 5;
j := 10;
c1 := 'A';
c2 := 'D';
```

set constructor	members of set
['A', 'E', 'I', 'O', 'U']	'A', 'E', 'I', 'O', 'U'
[c1..c2]	'A', 'B', 'C', 'D'
[succ(c1)..pred(c2)]	'B', 'C'
['a'..'c','A'..'B']	'a', 'b', 'c', 'A', 'B'
[5..10]	5, 6, 7, 8, 9, 10
[i..j]	5, 6, 7, 8, 9, 10
[i, j]	5, 10
[i..i+3, j]	5, 6, 7, 8, 10
[i+1..j]	6, 7, 8, 9, 10
['0', '1', '5'..'7']	'0', '1', '5', '6', '7'
[ ]	None; this is the *empty set*.

Building on these examples, we can verify that the following expressions yield the Boolean value indicated.

Boolean expression	Boolean value
'A' IN ['A'..'Z']	true
'A' IN [c1..c2]	true
c1 IN [succ(c1)..c2]	false
3 IN [0..10]	true
(j DIV 2) IN [i..j]	true

A frequent use of Boolean expressions using the IN relational operator is to verify that the CASE selector matches one of the values in the constant label list. As an example, consider the following segment of code. Here the value of grade should be that of a letter grade ('A', 'B', 'C', 'D' or 'F'):

```
IF grade IN ['A'..'D', 'F']
THEN  CASE grade OF
              'A','B' : writeln ('Very good.');
              'C'     : writeln ('Good.');
              'D'     : writeln ('Poor.');
              'F'     : writeln ('Try again later.')
       END;
```

We may also verify that a value is *not* in the specified set by negating the outcome of the test. In this case we must use parentheses to guarantee that the IN operator is performed before the NOT operator. For example, here is the correct way to test for an invalid grade:

```
IF NOT (grade IN ['A'..'D', 'F'])      (*correct*)
THEN writeln ('Letter grade is not valid.')
```

Now compare the correct solution with one that is *wrong*:

```
IF grade NOT IN ['A' 'D', 'F']      (*correct*)
THEN writeln ('Letter grade is not valid.')
```

As an application of sets, consider the following problem.

Problem 8.5

Write a procedure named letter *that finds the first occurrence of an upper- or lowercase vowel in the input. This character should be stored in the char variable parameter* inchar.

The Pascal coding shown below effectively solves this problem by repeatedly reading characters from the input until one meets the requirements.

```
PROCEDURE letter (VAR inchar: char);
(* Read until an upper- or lowercase vowel is located *)
(* in the input, returning the vowel found in inchar. *)
BEGIN
      REPEAT
            read (inchar)
      UNTIL inchar IN ['a', 'e', 'i', 'o', 'u', 'A', 'E', 'I', 'O', 'U']
END;
```

In the following problem solution we rewrite the text classification program using sets. Note that the final case statement is unchanged.

Problem 8.6

Rewrite program textclass from section 8.4 using sets.

```
PROGRAM textclass (* revised *) (input, output);
(* Program to classify each character in a sentence *)
(* as a vowel, consonant, or special character, and  *)
(* and display total characters and percentages.     *)
TYPE
        class = (vowel, consonant, special);
VAR
        inchar : char;               (* the input character *)
        total,              (* total number of characters *)
        vcount,                     (* number of vowels *)
        ccount,                 (* number of consonants *)
        scount : 0..maxint;         (* number of special
                                                 characters *)
        category : class;        (* the character type *)
BEGIN
        total := 0;              (* initialize total count *)
        vcount := 0;             (* initialize vowel count *)
        ccount := 0;          (* initialize consonant count *)
        scount := 0;            (* initialize special count *)
        read (inchar);
        WHILE inchar <> '.' DO
        BEGIN
                (* increase total character counter *)
                total := total + 1;
                (* determine character class using sets *)
                IF inchar IN ['A', 'E', 'I', 'O', 'U']
                THEN category := vowel
                ELSE IF inchar IN [' ', ',', ':', ';']
                    THEN category := special
                    ELSE category := consonant;
                (* increase appropriate category counter *)
                CASE category OF
                    vowel : vcount := vcount + 1;
                    consonant : ccount := ccount + 1;
                    special : scount := scount + 1
                END; (* case *)
                read (inchar)      (* get the next character *)
        END; (* while *)
```

(* display results *)

```
writeln ('There were ', total:1, ' total characters.');
writeln (vcount / total * 100 : 6 : 2, ' percent were vowels.');
writeln (ccount / total * 100 : 6 : 2, ' percent were consonants.');
writeln (scount / total * 100 : 6 : 2,
              ' percent were special characters.')
END.
```

Sets can be combined to form new sets using several operators. Also we can define set types corresponding to any ordinal type, including enumerated types. We will consider these types in a later chapter.

EXERCISES FOR SECTION 8.5

1 Determine the members of each set.
   (a) [0, 1, 2, 3]
   (b) [0..10, 13, 15]
   (c) ['A'..'J', 'L'..'Z']
   (d) ['a'..'m', 'A'..'M']
   (e) ['0'..'5', '9']

2 Determine which of the following are valid set constructors.
   (a) [0, 1, '9']
   (b) ['A'..'F', 'G']
   (c) [0..100)
   (d) ['0'..'9', 'A'..'Z']
   (e) [0..9, A..Z]

3 Determine the truth value of each Boolean expression.
   (a) 'A' IN ['B'..'S']
   (b) 0 IN [-3..5]
   (c) 7 IN [1..4, 6..8]
   (d) ' ' IN [ ]

4 Determine the truth value of each Boolean expression, assuming *num* = 3 and *inchar* = 'B'.
   (a) 10 IN [3..3*num]
   (b) 5 IN [num+2..10]
   (c) 'A' IN [inchar..'T']
   (d) 'B' IN ['A'..succ(inchar)]

5 Determine the truth value of each Boolean expression. Assume *num* = 100 and *grade* = 'D'.

(a) NOT (num IN [1..200])
(b) NOT (grade IN ['A'..'F'])
(c) NOT (grade IN ['F'..'Z'])
(d) (num IN [99..199]) AND NOT (grade IN ['A'..'C'])

6   Determine the output of the following program assuming the input data is R2D2.

```
PROGRAM guess (input, output);
VAR
        achar : char;
PROCEDURE inspect (VAR inchar : char);
BEGIN
        REPEAT
            read (inchar)
        UNTIL inchar IN ['0'..'9']
END;
(* Main Program *)
BEGIN
        inspect (achar);
        writeln (achar);
        inspect (achar);
        writeln (achar)
END.
```

7   Write a Pascal program using sets that reads a sequence of 80 characters and displays the number of nondigit characters read.

SECTION 8.6 TESTING AND DEBUGGING TECHNIQUES

In this section we consider problems that can arise from the failure to use identical or compatible data types. Also, an input validation problem is discussed.

Type Compatibility

Consider the following declarations:

```
TYPE
        testscore = 0..100;
        letter = 'A'..'F';
VAR
        quiz : 0..100;
        midterm,
        final : testscore;
        total : char;
        grade : letter;
```

Notice that *final* and *midterm* are of the same type, namely *testscore*. In this case we say the two variables have **identical types**. Now consider the variables *final* and *quiz*. It appears that both variables have the same subrange data type, 0..100. However, Pascal does *not* consider these two as having identical types since they were explicitly defined twice. Instead, these variables are said to have **compatible types**. Two types *T1* and *T2* are said to be compatible if one of the following conditions is true:

1 *T1* and *T2* are the same type.
2 *T1* is a subrange of *T2*, or *T2* is a subrange of *T1*.
3 Both T1 and T2 are subranges of the same host type.

(There are a few other rules concerning compatibility of other data types that we will discuss later.) For example, the variables *total* and *grade* have compatible types since the type of the variable *grade* is a subrange of the type of the variable *total*.

A type can have additional names associated with it by writing a TYPE declaration of the form

```
TYPE t1 = t2;
```

In this case, type *t1* is identical to type *t2*, since the definition of type *t1* is the same as that of type *t2*. For example, as a result of the declaration

```
TYPE
      a = integer;
      b = −maxint..maxint;
```

type *a* is identical to the type *integer*, but type *b* is only compatible with the type *integer*.

It is important to note that two variables can be said to have identical types if they are declared using identical type names or if their names appear in the same list in a variable declaration. For example, in the following code variables *hightemp* and *lowtemp* have identical types, but *avgtemp* is only type compatible with them:

```
TYPE
      temp = −50..150;
VAR
      lowtemp : temp;
      hightemp : temp;
      avgtemp : −50..150;
```

All three variables in the following code may be said to have identical types, but no other variable can have a type identical to theirs, since it would need to have been declared in the same list.

```
VAR
     ltemp,
     htemp,
     mtemp : -50..150;
```

The distinction between identical and compatible types is important when specifying a variable parameter in a procedure or function heading. The type of the actual argument (appearing in the invocation) must have a type that is *identical* to that of the formal variable parameter. For example, in the procedure header

```
PROCEDURE tempindex (VAR atemp : temp);
```

the variable parameter *atemp* has a type identical to that of the variables *lowtemp* and *hightemp* from the preceding declaration, and therefore either of the following procedure invocations are valid:

```
tempindex (lowtemp);
tempindex (hightemp);
```

Procedure invocations using any of the other variables (*avgtemp*, *ltemp*, *htemp*, *mtemp*) are incorrect, since the types of these variables are not identical to the type of the variable parameter *atemp*.

More flexibility is allowed with value parameters. When a value parameter is used with a procedure or function, then any value with a compatible type may be used as the actual parameter, as long as the value of the actual parameter is one of the values allowed by the type of the formal parameter. For example, consider the following program segment.

```
TYPE
     upper = 1500..5000;
     middle = 500..2500;
     lower = 0..1499;
VAR
     boost0 : integer;
     boost1 : middle;
     boost2 : lower;
PROCEDURE range (boost: upper);
. . .
END;
BEGIN     (* Main Program, or other procedure *)
     boost0 := 4900;
     range (boost0);     (* allowed *)
     boost1 := 1700;
     range (boost1);     (* allowed *)
     boost2 := 750;
     range (boost2);     (* NOT allowed *)
```

```
         boost1 := 750;
         range (boost1);     (* NOT allowed *)
END
```

In each of the procedure invocations the value of the actual parameter is in the set of values allowed by the type of the formal parameter. Note that the types *lower* and *upper* are compatible, since they are both subranges of the same type, but the value of a variable of type *lower* could *never* be passed as an actual argument to a procedure which expects a parameter of type *upper*.

The last disallowed procedure invocation in the example involved two types that are not **assignment compatible**. Given two types *T1* and *T2*, then a value of type T1 can be assigned to a variable of type *T2* if one of the following conditions is true:

1   *T1* and *T2* are the same type.
2   *T1* is integer, or subrange of integer, and *T2* is real.
3   *T1* and *T2* and compatible ordinal types (including integer, Boolean, char, enumerated types, and subranges of them), and the value of type *T1* is in the set of values allowed by type *T2*.

For example, consider the following declarations.

```
TYPE
      scale = 1..10;
VAR
      number : 1..10;
      value : integer;
      final : scale;
```

The types of the three variables are not identical, but they are compatible. In the assignment statement

```
value := number + final;
```

the expression "number + final" is assignment compatible with the type for the variable *value* since both types are compatible. In the assignment statement

```
number := final + value;
```

if the value of *value* is 15, then the assignment is not permitted, since the value yielded by the expression is outside the range of values permitted by the subrange type *1..10*.

Input Validation

Suppose a character is to be read and a digit ('0' to '9') is expected. What is a good way to validate that the input character is proper? We will consider three methods: (1) brute force, (2) looping, and (3) sets. Assume *inchar* is declared to be a char variable, and *okay* is a Boolean variable to be assigned the value true if the input data is satisfactory.

Method 1: Brute Force

```
read (inchar);
okay := (inchar = '0') OR (inchar = '1') OR (inchar = '2') OR
        (inchar = '3') OR (inchar = '4') OR (inchar = '5') OR
        (inchar = '6') OR (inchar = '7') OR (inchar = '8') OR
        (inchar = '9');
```

While this method works, you are right if you believe there is a better way!

Method 2: Looping

Assume *digit* is a char variable.

```
okay := false;
read (inchar);
FOR digit := '0' TO '9' DO
    IF digit = inchar
    THEN okay := true
```

This is better, but it can still be improved. Try to determine why the statement

```
okay := digit = inchar
```

could not be used in place of the IF statement.

Method 3: Sets

```
read (inchar);
okay := inchar IN ['0'..'9']
```

Ah, that is more like it! Validating the input using sets is the better of the three methods since it is concise, readable, and efficient.

Here are some Pascal reminders to aid you when testing and debugging.

PASCAL REMINDERS

Type Definitions
Are placed between the CONST and VAR declarations.
Are not allowed in the formal parameter list of a procedure or function.

Enumerated Constants

Cannot be read or displayed directly.

Must be unique identifiers distinct from those used for any other purpose.

Have ordinal values determined by the order in which they appear in the TYPE definition; the lowest ordinal value is always zero.

Subrange Types

Require that the lower value be less than or equal to the upper value.

Ord

Yields the position of its argument in the constants of the same data type as the argument.

Chr

Yields the character in the position specified by the integer argument.

Pred and Succ

Yield the element in a data type whose ordinal value is one larger (*pred*) or one smaller (*succ*) than the argument's ordinal value.

Yield undefined values when *pred* is used on the smallest element or *succ* is used on the largest element in a given data type.

Set Constructors

Must be enclosed in square brackets.

Must use ordinal constants or variables of the same type.

May include multiple elements, element subranges separated by commas, or no elements (the empty set).

The IN Operator

Yields true if the value to its left appears in the set to its right, and false otherwise.

May not be immediately preceded by the NOT operator (instead, enclose the IN expression in parentheses and place the NOT before it).

Identical Types

Are required for a variable formal parameter and the corresponding actual parameter.

Compatible Types

Are required for a value formal parameter and the corresponding actual parameter. In addition, the value of the actual parameter must be in the range allowed by the formal parameter's type.

SECTION 8.7 CHAPTER REVIEW

In this chapter we discussed various data types and their applications in Pascal programs. In particular, user-defined, or enumerated, types were presented as a mechanism to assist us in producing readable and easily maintainable programs. Pascal permits us to give names to our own ordinal data types by using a TYPE definition. Enumerated types are not without their disadvantages, though. Variables of such types cannot be read or written directly; they are designed strictly for internal use.

Subrange data types permit us to restrict the range of values that a variable may represent. An automatic range check (which must be explicitly enabled in some Pascal systems) is included every time a new value is stored into variables of subrange data types. These features improve program readability and design.

The four standard ordinal functions *pred*, *succ*, *ord*, and *chr* were discussed in this chapter. They can be quite useful when manipulating data with ordinal types. The *ord* function yields the position of its argument in the list of constants associated with the underlying data type, while the *chr* function returns the character value at the position specified by its argument. These two functions provide a general mechanism for dealing with the char data type, allowing us to convert between external and internal (or coded) representations.

This chapter also presented a specific problem (text classification) and a Pascal solution using enumerated data types. The solution was later revised to use the set data type. Set constructors and the IN operator were presented to allow simple testing for membership of an ordinal value in an arbitrary collection of ordinal values. In the Testing and Debugging Techniques section the concept of identical and compatible types was introduced, as well as the concept of assignment compatibility. The importance of these concepts was illustrated with examples of parameter passing to procedures and functions.

The following summary of the Pascal concepts described in this chapter can be used for future reference.

PASCAL REFERENCE

1 Enumerated type: User-defined ordinal data type.
   Example:

```
TYPE  color = (red, blue, green);
      texture = (soft, smooth, hard, rough);
```

2 Placement of TYPE definitions:

```
PROGRAM name (input, output);
CONST declarations;
TYPE definitions;   (* between CONST and VAR *)
VAR declarations;
  . . .
```

3 Subrange data type: Restricted range of values.
   Examples:

```
TYPE
      class  = (freshman, sophomore, junior,
                  senior, graduate);
      upperclass = junior..senior;
```

```
VAR
    score : 0..100;
    lettergrade : 'A'..'F';
    positivenum : 1..maxint;
```

4 Standard ordinal functions:
   4.1 *Pred(x)*: Predecessor of argument *x*.
   4.2 *Succ(x)*: Successor of argument *x*.
   4.3 *Ord(x)*: Position of argument *x* in ordinal data type.
   4.4 *Chr(x)*: Char value whose ordinal position in data type char is given by argument *x*.

5 Set: A collection of ordinal values (elements). Set values can be created using set constructors.
   Examples:

```
['A', 'B', 'C', 'X', 'Y', 'Z']
['B'..'R']
[low..mid,high]
[Monday..Friday]
```

The IN operator yields true if the value to its left appears in the set to its right.
Examples:

```
'a' IN ['a', 'e', 'i', 'o', 'u']        (* true *)
3 IN [4..10,25]                         (* false *)
NOT (low + 4 IN [low..low + 50] )       (* false *)
NOT (2 IN [-5..0])                      (* true *)
```

6 Type compatibility: Identical and compatible types.

   Example:

```
TYPE
    avg = integer;
    score = 0..100;
VAR
    test : 0..100;
    quiz1, quiz2 : score;
    final : integer;
    aver : avg;
```

Variables with
   6.1 Identical types: *quiz1* and *quiz2*; *final* and *aver*
   6.2 Compatible types: *test*, *quiz1*, *quiz2*, *final*, *aver*

In the next chapter we will discuss the first of the structured data types, the array. An array is a collection of many elements each having the same data type but referenced using a single identifier. Its use is essential when a problem requires that we keep numerous related data values in memory simultaneously. Many applications of the array data type will be presented.

Keywords for Chapter 8

assignment compatible

chr function

compatible types

enumerated type

host data type

identical types

IN operator

ord function

pred function

set constructor

set data type

standard ordinal functions

subrange data type

succ function

TYPE definition

user-defined type

CHAPTER 8 EXERCISES

★ ESSENTIAL EXERCISES

1 In memory, values of an enumerated type are stored as integers representing the ordinal value of the particular constant of the enumerated type. For example, if we have the declaration

VAR stuff : (thing1, thing2, thing3);

and the assignment

stuff := thing3

then the value actually stored in the memory cell for *stuff* is 2. How does this explain Pascal's inability to display the value (for example, *thing3*) of a value with an enumerated type?

2 How is a set different from a collection of variables of the same type? For example, consider the set constructed by

['A', 'D', 'Y']

and the variables

VAR
       ch1, ch2, ch3 : char;

initialized as follows:

```
ch1 := 'A';
ch2 := 'D';
ch3 := 'Y';
```

★★ SIGNIFICANT EXERCISES

3 Some Pascal systems have unfortunate limits on the size of a set.
   (a) If you could not reference the documentation for your compiler, how would you determine what the maximum set size was?
   (b) Give a particular set size limitation that would be unfortunate.

4 Why do you think Pascal does not allow the definition of a type in a procedure header? That is, why does Pascal not allow constructions like the following?

```
PROCEDURE schmata (VAR rag : 0..9);
```

5 Is there any technique you can use in Pascal to specify the desired number of significant digits in real numbers? Some Pascal systems permit more than one type of real number representation. Determine if this is the case on your system and, if so, the number of significant digits permitted in each type.

CHAPTER 8 PROBLEMS FOR COMPUTER SOLUTION

★ ESSENTIAL PROBLEMS

1 The input data contains three integers. Using a set constructor, write a program to determine if the first integer is in the range specified by the second and third integers. You may assume that the second integer is less than or equal to the third.

Example input:

```
5        12     70
31      -10     50
0         0      0
```

Example output:

```
5 is not in the range 12..70
31 is in the range -10..50
0 is in the range 0..0
```

2 The input data contains the name of a day of the week D and a positive or negative integer N separated by at least one blank on each line. Determine the day of the week that occurs N days after day D. Use an enumerated type for the days of the week to represent D.

Tuesday   4
   Saturday   3
Wednesday -31

Example output:

4 days after Tuesday is Saturday.
3 days after Saturday is Tuesday.
31 days before Wednesday is Sunday.

3   The first line of the input data contains a positive integer K. Each remaining line contains text terminated, as usual, by the end-of-line character. Encode the text and display the resulting encoded message by replacing each character of the text by the *printable* character in your character set that appears K characters later. For example, in the ASCII character set the alphabetic characters are contiguous, so the message "HELLO" would be encoded with K equal 3 as "KHOOR." Special characters must be included in the encoding scheme.

Example input:

3
HELLO
Hello

Example output (assuming the ASCII character set):

KHOOR
Khoor

4   Consider the encoding scheme developed in problem 3. Produce a program that expects K as the single integer on the first input line, followed by lines of encoded text. Decode the messages and display the resulting clear text.

Example input:

3
KHOOR
Sdvfdo

Example output (assuming the ASCII character set):

HELLO
Pascal

★★ SIGNIFICANT PROBLEM

5 Write a program that uses an integer subrange type to simulate a limitation on the number of fractional digits in arithmetic operations on real numbers. (Hint: Multiplication of a real number by 10^n to yield an integer, which is then divided using real arithmetic by 10^n, will leave only n fractional digits.) Use this new "type" with various limits to determine the sum of $1/2 + 1/3 + 1/4 + \cdots + 1/z$, where z is the largest value that has a nonzero reciprocal in the new "type."

CHAPTER 9

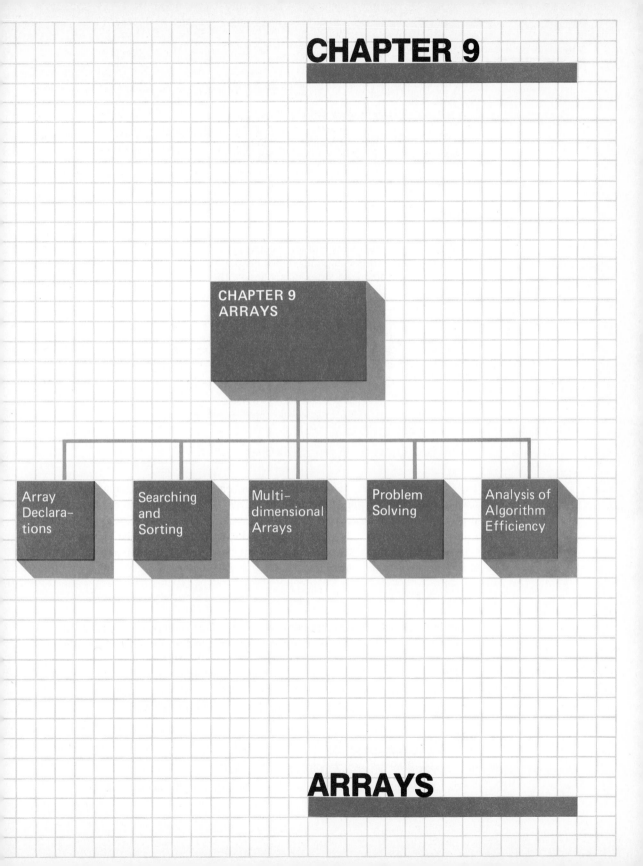

CHAPTER 9
ARRAYS

Array Declara-tions

Searching and Sorting

Multi-dimensional Arrays

Problem Solving

Analysis of Algorithm Efficiency

ARRAYS

OBJECTIVES

After completing this chapter, you should be able to:

- Define and declare array data types
- Recognize and apply a linear search and a binary search
- Recognize and apply a sorting algorithm
- Solve, test, and debug problems using arrays
- Optionally, analyze the efficiency of some algorithms

CHAPTER OVERVIEW

In this chapter we discuss one of the most applicable data types in computer science, namely arrays. An *array* is a group of elements or components, each having the same type and referenced by an index or subscript. The whole group of elements is given a single name.

In the first section we present the details of defining and declaring arrays. One of the most common uses of arrays is in searching and sorting. We present two search techniques, linear and binary searching. Also, a sorting algorithm is included and applied to a problem. Multidimensional arrays are discussed in Section 9.3. Two problems using arrays are solved in Section 9.4. The Testing and Debugging Techniques section includes some common errors arising from using arrays, especially subscript errors. The chapter also includes an optional section on analyzing the efficiency of algorithms.

SECTION 9.1 ARRAY DECLARATIONS

The data types integer, real, char, Boolean, enumerated, and subrange are called *simple data types*. Using the simple data types, we can build more complex data structures known as *structured data types*. Pascal includes the following built-in data structures: arrays, records, files, and sets. In the remainder of the course we will consider these in more detail. These data structures extend the application of Pascal to solving a wide range of problems.

Array

An *array* is a structured data type consisting of a group of components, each component of the same type. For example, suppose we wish to find the largest of a group of numbers. If there are a few numbers, then we can solve this problem by using nested IF statements (see Chapter 5). Each IF statement would compare two numbers. However, suppose there are 1000 numbers to consider. A set of IF statements would be very impractical, as would having to declare the 1000 integer variables:

```
VAR
      num1, num2, num3, . . . num1000 : integer;
```

All 1000 variables names would have to be listed in this declaration!

12	number [1]	(* contains first number, say 12 *)
10	number [2]	(* contains second number, say 10 *)
7	number [3]	(* contains third number, say 7 *)
6	number [4]	(* contains fourth number, say 6 *)
.	.	
.	.	
.	.	
.	.	
.	.	
.	.	
18	number [1000]	(* contains last number, say 18 *)

Figure 9-1   Array of numbers.

What we would like to do is group these numbers under one name, say *number*, and access the individual components of the group as *number[1]*, *number[2]*, and so on, up to *number[1000]* (see Figure 9-1). This group of elements is an array of integers.

The number used to distinguish between components is called a ***subscript***, or ***index***. For example, the index of the component *number[10]* is 10, while the index of *number[3]* is 3. The index is used to access the individual components. The data type of the index does not have to be the same as the component type. In this example, the data type of the index is 1 . . 1000 and the data type of the components is integer.

Using Pascal we can define an array of elements consisting of 1000 components, each component being an integer, using a TYPE definition as follows:

TYPE matrix = ARRAY [1..1000] OF integer;

The reserved word TYPE is followed by an identifier *matrix* naming the structured data type. The type identifier is followed by an equal sign and then the reserved word ARRAY, which is followed by the range of the index type enclosed by brackets. The range of the index type is followed by the reserved word OF, which is followed by the data type of the components. The syntax diagram for the array type is shown in Figure 9-2. Packed arrays will be discussed in Chapter 10.

Figure 9-2   Syntax diagram for an array.

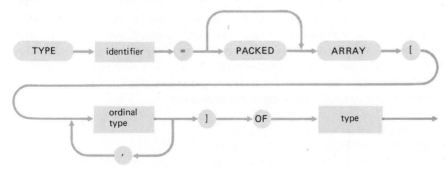

The following variable declaration will reserve the 1000 memory locations needed to store the numbers (note the data type *matrix* is defined above using the TYPE definition):

```
VAR number : matrix;
```

Actually, we may write the variable declaration without using the TYPE definition. Our previous declaration could be written as

```
VAR number : ARRAY [1..1000] OF integer;
```

However, as you learned in the previous chapter, this approach will not suffice when the array variable must be passed as a parameter. That is, the following procedure header is incorrect:

```
PROCEDURE example (VAR number : ARRAY [1..1000] OF integer);
```

The array structure must be defined previously using a TYPE definition. The following would be a valid procedure header, assuming the TYPE definition for matrix had been previously given:

```
PROCEDURE example (VAR number : matrix);
```

Let us look at some examples of array declarations.

Example 9.1

A class consists of 50 students. The array declaration to store a letter grade for each student would be

```
TYPE garray = ARRAY [1..50] OF char;
VAR lettergrade : garray;
```

or alternately

```
VAR lettergrade : ARRAY [1..50] OF char;
```

Notice the data type of the index in this case is a subrange of the integers, while the data type of each component is character. The variable *lettergrade* is an array variable (or a subscripted variable). Each component of the array can be used in the same way as variables with simple data types. This means they may appear in assignment statements, *read* and *write* statements, and as actual parameters to procedures and functions. For example, the assignment statements

```
lettergrade[1] := 'A';
lettergrade[2] := 'B';
```

will assign the character 'A' to the first component of the array and the character 'B' to the second component. In the next example we show that the index variable can be any ordinal type.

Example 9.2

A program to count the number of occurrences of each uppercase letter in a piece of text might use an array that has the uppercase letters as the index and an integer as the component type. This might be declared as

```
TYPE counts = ARRAY ['A'..'Z'] OF integer;
VAR lettercount : counts;
```

or alternately

```
VAR lettercount : ARRAY ['A'..'Z'] OF integer;
```

At this point you might be wondering when a noninteger index type should be used for an array. Consider this example: Suppose we would like to keep track of the number of people working at a particular company whose last name begins with the letter A, the letter B, and so on. We can use the array declaration from example 9.2 to store these counts. For example, the assignment statement

```
lettercount['W'] := lettercount['W'] + 1
```

would add one to the count of individuals whose names start with the letter W.

We can pictorially represent an array as a collection of boxes, one box for each component of the array. The contents of each box represent the contents of a component, and the subscript, or index, associated with a component is written next to

Figure 9-3   Array with char subscripts.

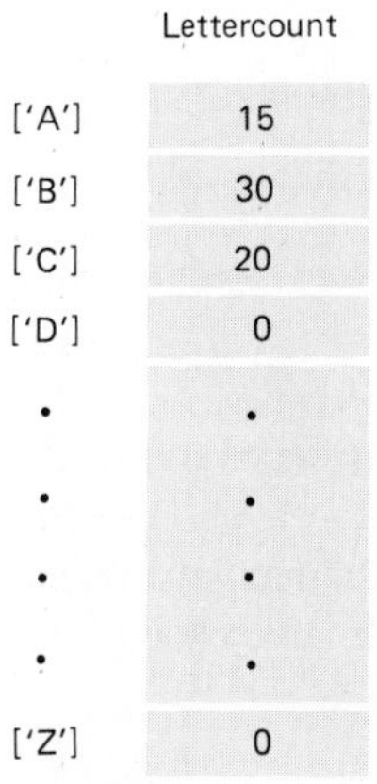

Lettercount

['A']	15
['B']	30
['C']	20
['D']	0
.	.
.	.
.	.
.	.
['Z']	0

the box. In Figure 9-3, for example, we see that the number of persons whose last name begins with *A* is 15, while the number whose last name begins with *B* is 30.

Example 9.3

This example contains a variety of array declarations:

```
TYPE
      grade = (A, B, C, D, F);
      trange = 0..4;
      score = ARRAY [1..100] OF trange;
      letter = ARRAY [0..10] OF grade;
      scale = ARRAY [A..D] OF real;
VAR
      final : score;
      mark : letter;
      value : scale;
```

The following table summarizes the characteristics of the arrays in example 9.3.

array name	index type	number of components	component data type
final	1..100	100	trange (0..4)
mark	0..10	11	grade (A,B,C,D,F)
value	A..D	4	real

In example 9.3 we can observe a variety of ordinal types used as index types. Any ordinal type, including subranges or entire type names, can be used as the index type. As a final example, consider the declarations

```
TYPE
      grade = (A, B, C, D, F);
      charcnt = ARRAY [char] OF integer;
      gradecnt = ARRAY [grade] OF 0..maxint;
VAR
      cfreq : charcnt;
      gcnts : gradecnt;
```

How many components will the array *cfreq* have as a result of this declaration? The answer depends on the particular computer system in use, but we can observe that there will be one component for every possible value of type char. On many machines, therefore, we will have 256 elements in *cfreq*. The array *gcnts* will have exactly five elements, since there are five possible values of type grade (A, B, C, D, F).

At this point you should have a good understanding of the difference between the type of data that can be stored in a component of an array and the type of data that is used to select (index, or subscript) an array to locate a particular component.

Array Processing

Now that we have seen how to declare an array, we are ready to look at some examples that manipulate the components of arrays. Assume the following declarations:

```
TYPE
      matrix = ARRAY [1..1000] OF integer;
      letter = ARRAY ['A'..'Z'] OF real;
VAR
      number : matrix;
      scale : letter;
      index : 1..1000;
      chrindex : 'A'..'Z';
```

Using the looping constructs, we can do some array processing one component at a time. The following FOR loop would read in 1000 numbers and store them in the array called *number*, one element at a time.

```
FOR index := 1 TO 1000 DO
      read (number[index]);
```

The following FOR loop will set all the components of the array *scale* to zero (initialize the array):

```
FOR chrindex := 'A' TO 'Z' DO
      scale[chrindex] := 0.0;
```

The following FOR loop will display twice the contents of each component of array *number*:

```
FOR index := 1 TO 1000 DO
      writeln ('Twice value is ', 2 * number[index]);
```

Finally, the following FOR loop will display the contents of the array *scale* in reverse order:

```
FOR chrindex := 'Z' DOWNTO 'A' DO
      writeln (scale[chrindex]);
```

Occasionally, we need to copy the contents of one array into a second array with the same component type. The next problem we consider is an example of this type.

Problem 9.1

Write a Pascal procedure that will copy the contents of the array scores, *storing the copy in the array* temp. *Assume that both arrays are of type char and the index type of each is the subrange type* $-10..10$.

To solve this problem we *must* globally define the type of the array, since the arrays will be used as actual arguments to the procedure:

```
TYPE list = ARRAY [-10..10] OF char;
```

The procedure itself can now be written as follows:

```
PROCEDURE copy (VAR : scores, temp : list);
(* Copy array scores into array temp *)
VAR index : -10..10;
BEGIN
      FOR index := -10 TO 10 DO
            temp[index] := scores[index]
END;
```

Notice the declaration of both *scores* and *temp* as formal VAR parameters, even though *scores* is used only as an input parameter. The reason for this is that if we declared *scores* as a value parameter, a copy of the entire array would be made to guarantee that the actual array parameter could not be modified. This copy (automatically created for every value parameter) would then be copied again (in the procedure) into the variable parameter *temp*. For an array of 21 elements this additional copying operation is not necessarily expensive. However, this copying of value parameters can become excessively time and memory consuming when large array parameters and frequently called procedures are used. In general, if a large (in terms of memory requirements) parameter will not be modified by the called procedure or if the modification performed by the procedure should be reflected in the actual parameter, then that parameter should be a VAR parameter.

An alternate solution to problem 9.1 involves assignment to the entire array. Since *temp* and *scores* have exactly the same type, we are permitted to write

```
temp := scores
```

which will cause each component of *temp* to contain the same value as the corresponding element of *scores*. Note, however, that we are not permitted to read or write an entire array in standard Pascal with a statement similar to

```
read (scores)
```

To read an entire array, we must use a loop that reads each individual component (with an index) of the array. For example, reading the *scores* array would typically be achieved by writing the following code. Assume *index* is an integer variable.

```
FOR index := - 10 TO 10 DO
     read (scores[index])
```

Parallel Arrays

Many problems require simultaneous processing of more than one array. For example, suppose an instructor has a class with 50 students and assigns letter grades to homework problems and numeric grades to examinations. The instructor wishes to write a Pascal program that will display, for each student, the letter grade obtained on the final homework problem and the numeric grade obtained on the final examination. The instructor has stored the letter grades and the numeric grades in separate arrays. The following TYPE definitions and VAR declarations are used for the arrays:

```
TYPE
     lgarray = ARRAY [1..50] OF 'A'..'F';
     ngarray = ARRAY [1..50] OF 0..100;
VAR
     lettergrade : lgarray;
     numericgrade : ngarray;
```

In this problem, *lettergrade* and *numericgrade* are called **parallel arrays**. This is because each element of *lettergrade* is paired with an element of *numericgrade*. We can display both grades for each student by using the same index for both arrays. The following Pascal segment could be used to solve the problem, assuming *index* has been declared as an integer variable:

```
writeln ('S t u d e n t          L e t t e r          N u m e r i c');
writeln ('N u m b e r            G r a d e                G r a d e');
writeln ('– – – – – – –          – – – – –            – – – – – – –');
FOR index := 1 TO 50 DO
writeln (index:4, ' ':10, lettergrade[index], ' ':12, numericgrade[index]);
```

The next example of parallel array processing also uses the arrays *lettergrade* and *numericgrade*. In this case, the instructor would like to know how many students are in each of the following categories:

1   Received a numeric grade less than 90 and a letter grade less than A.
2   Received a numeric grade less than 90 and a letter grade of A.
3   Received a numeric grade of 90 or better and a letter grade of A.
4   Received a numeric grade of 90 or better and a letter grade less than A.

An additional array called *catsize* will be used to store the number of students in each category. Its declaration is as follows:

```
VAR
    catsize : ARRAY [1..4] OF 0..50;
```

The solution to this problem is shown below. Note the use of the nested CASE statements to simplify the problem of categorizing the students' scores.

```
FOR index := 1 TO 4 DO
    catsize [index] := 0;
FOR index := 1 TO 50 DO
CASE numericgrade[index] < 90 OF
    false:  CASE lettergrade[index] = 'A' OF
                false:  catsize[4] := catsize[4] + 1;
                true:   catsize[3] := catsize[3] + 1
            END;
    true:   CASE lettergrade[index] = 'A' OF
                false:  catsize[1] := catsize[1] + 1;
                true:   catsize[2] := catsize[2] + 1
            END
END
END
```

Parallel array processing can be performed with more than two arrays. In our previous examples, the instructor could have included an array to store the results of each exam, not only the final. Again the same index or subscript can be used to access all the grades for each student.

A Summary of Array Processing

Summarizing, we find the following important points to remember about array definition and manipulation:

■ Array types should be defined using a TYPE definition. The usual form is similar to

```
TYPE name = ARRAY [index type] OF component type;
```

For example, the following definition would be used to introduce a new type representing a collection of real numbers indexed by the integers in the range -50 to 50:

```
TYPE list = ARRAY [-50..50] OF real;
```

■ Variables of an array type may be declared by referencing a previously defined array type or explicitly writing the array type in the variable declaration. For example, the variable value can be declared to have 101 real elements, indexed with the integers from -50 to 50 by writing either

```
VAR value : ARRAY [-50..50] OF real;
```

VAR value : list;

where *list* is the type previously defined.

■ The index type of an array can be any ordinal type.
■ The component data type of an array can be any type.
■ The number of possible values in the index data type determines the number of individual components in the array; there will be one component for each value in the index data type.
■ To access a particular component of an array, the form

array name [expression of index type]

is used. Note that an arbitrarily complicated expression may be used as the index, but it must yield a value of the same type as the index type specified when the array was declared.

■ In procedure or function headings, formal parameters corresponding to arrays must be declared with a type identical to that of the corresponding actual argument; the array type must therefore be given a name and defined globally to the actual parameter declaration and the procedure declaration. In many cases, it will be appropriate to use VAR parameters to avoid the copying of entire arrays necessary with value parameters.

EXERCISES FOR SECTION 9.1

1 Determine the number of components in each array listed in the following declaration.

```
TYPE
      letter = (A, B, C, D, F);
      range = -3..3;
      scale = ARRAY [0..99] OF letter;
      matrix = ARRAY [range] OF char;
      line = ARRAY [letter] OF letter;
VAR
      xarray : scale;
      yarray : matrix;
      zarray : line;
```

2 How many numbers are read into the array *number*?

```
TYPE
      list = ARRAY ['0'..'9'] OF integer;
```

```
VAR
      num : list;
      index : '0'..'9';
BEGIN
      index := '0';
      REPEAT
          read(num[index]);
          index := succ (index)
      UNTIL (index = '9')
END;
```

3 Which of the following assignments are valid given the following declaration?

```
TYPE
      list = ARRAY ['A'..'Z'] OF integer;
      data = ARRAY [-3..3] OF char;
VAR
      lista, listb : list;
      data1 : data;
```

(a) lista['A'] := listb['B'];
(b) lista['Z'] := listb['A'] + 1;
(c) lista['A'] := data[0];
(d) lista[data[0]] := 0;
(e) lista := listb;
(f) data1 := lista;
(g) data1 [lista['A']] := 'A';

4 Suppose $i = 3$ and $j = -2$. Find the value of the index of each expression for the array called *table*.
(a) table[i+j]
(b) table[7-i+j]
(c) table[2 * i + succ(j)]
(d) table[i * j + pred(7)]

5 Given the declarations

```
VAR
      tscores : ARRAY [1..500] OF integer;
      test, smallest, index : integer;
```

which program segment will locate the smallest value in this array, and save the array subscript where this value is located?
(a) FOR test := 1 TO 500 DO
     IF (tscores[test] < smallest)
     THEN smallest := tscores[smallest];

```
(b)  FOR test := 1 TO 500 DO
       IF (tscores[test] < smallest)
       THEN smallest := test;
(c)  smallest := tscores[1];
       FOR test := 2 TO 500 DO
       IF (tscores[test] < smallest)
       THEN smallest := tscores[test];
(d)  index := 1;
       FOR test := 2 TO 500 DO
       IF (tscores[test] < tscores[index])
       THEN index := test;
(e)  index := 1;
       FOR test := 2 TO 500 DO
       IF (tscores[test] < index)
       THEN index := test;
```

6 Consider the segment

```
TYPE
        a = ARRAY [1..4] OF integer;
VAR
        x, y : a;
        k, j : integer;
BEGIN
        FOR k := 1 TO 4 DO
        BEGIN
                read (x[k]);
                FOR j := k TO 4 DO
                        read (y[j])
        END
END
```

and the input data

1 2 3 4 5 6 7 8 9 10 11 12 13 14 15

After this code executes, what will be the contents of arrays x and y?

(a) x: 1 2 3 4
     y: 5 6 7 8

(b) x: 1 6 7 8
     y: 2 3 4 5

(c) x: 1 6 10 13
     y: 2 7 12 14

(d) x: 1 6 11 13
     y: 2 7 11 14

(e) Too much input, crash!

(f) Not enough input, crash!

7 Which of the following program segments will reverse an array of char named *str* that is 10 elements long?

(a) FOR switch := 1 TO 10 DO
     BEGIN
         temp := str[switch];
         str[11 − switch] := temp
     END

(b) FOR switch := 1 TO 10 DO
     BEGIN
         temp := str[switch];
         str[switch] := str[11 − switch];
         str[11 − switch] := temp
     END

(c) FOR switch := 1 TO 5 DO
     BEGIN
         temp := str[switch];
         str[switch] := str[11 − switch];
         str[11 − switch] := temp
     END

(d) FOR switch := 1 TO 5 DO
     BEGIN
         temp := str[switch];
         str[switch] := str[11 − switch];
         str[switch] := temp
     END

(e) FOR switch := 1 TO 5 DO
     BEGIN
         temp := str[switch];
         str[switch] := str[5 − switch];
         str[5 − switch] := temp
     END

8 Write a Pascal function called *alpha* that has as parameters a character array called *sentence* (maximum of 100 characters), an integer called *length* (number of characters in the sentence), and a char variable called *letter*. The function *alpha* returns the number of occurrences of the character *letter* in the array *sentence* (include all TYPE definitions outside the function).

SECTION 9.2 SEARCHING AND SORTING

Problems involving searching and sorting arrays are quite common in computer applications. *Searching* for an element in an array that satisfies a specified condition is the process of determining whether a particular element is or is not a component of the array. *Sorting* an array is the process of rearranging the components of the array so that a specified relation holds between adjacent elements in the array. For example, a typical sorting problem is to arrange the components so that the second component of every pair of adjacent components is equal to or greater than the first component. In this section we consider both topics.

The Linear Search

Assume an auto parts company has a computer program that uses an array to maintain the part numbers of items in the inventory. We might pictorially represent this array as shown in Figure 9-4. Further assume that each part number is a four-digit number with the first digit nonzero, that there are 100 part numbers in the array, and there is no relation that holds between each adjacent pair of part numbers in the array. That is, there is no apparent order to the arrangement of the part numbers in the array. There are 9000 possible part numbers (four-digit numbers in the range 1000 to 9999), but this particular store has only 100 different parts. How can we determine if a four-digit part number matches a part number stocked by this particular store?

The simplest solution to this problem is to compare the requested four-digit number with each part number stored in the array, sequentially, until either the requested part number is found or all the components (part numbers) in the array have been examined. This type of search is called a *linear* or *sequential search*.

For example, suppose our array has an index of 1..100, and the first six elements are as follows:

index	1	2	3	4	5	6
partnumber	8567	4612	7714	1362	1002	5117

We might ask if the part number 1002 is stocked by the store or if the number 1002 appears in the array. The linear search would first ask if *partnumber[1]* is equal to

Figure 9-4   Array of part numbers.

Partnumber

[1]	8567
[2]	4612
[3]	7714
[4]	1362
[5]	1002
[6]	5117
•	• • • •
•	• • • •
•	• • • •
[100]	6888

1002. Since this is not true and there are more components in the array, the linear search would continue by asking if *partnumber[2]* is equal to 1002. Again this is not true, and there are more components in the array, so the search continues in a similar manner until the component *partnumber[5]* is reached. Here *partnumber[5]* is equal to 1002, so the search would terminate successfully.

If we were searching for a part number that was not in the array, then we would need to examine all 100 components of the array before returning a negative answer. If a large array is searched in this way, the time required to obtain the answer to the question could be excessive, but for small arrays the linear search is quite appropriate.

The algorithm for the linear search appears below. Two Boolean variables are used to control the loop. The variable *found* is true if we have located the required component and false otherwise. The variable *done* is true when we have completed the search, either by finding the required component or by having examined each component and not found the desired component. The variable *done* is false as long as we have not located the desired component and there are more components to examine. An additional variable, *index,* has the same type as the index for the array being searched.

Linear Search Algorithm
Set done = false, found = false, and index = 1.
While not (done or found)   (more to search?)

If the item is found at element "index"   (yes; found?)
    Then set found = true   (yes, search ends)
    Else if index < array size   (no; tested all elements?)
        Then set index = index + 1
        Else set done = true

If the array to be searched has as its VAR declaration

```
partnumber : ARRAY [1..50] OF integer
```

then the variable *index* would have a variable declaration

```
index : 1..50
```

That is, the *index* variable is the same type as the index for the array. The code for the linear search to locate a four-digit integer *findme*, then, is

```
done := false;      (* we're not done yet *)
found := false;      (* and we haven't found "findme" yet *)
index := 1;      (* start with the first array component *)
WHILE NOT (done OR found) DO
    IF partnumber[index] = findme
    THEN found := true
```

```
ELSE IF index < 50
      THEN index := index + 1
      ELSE done := true
```

Returning to the auto part store, let us look at a complete function to locate a particular item (*partnumber*). Assume the following definitions are globally defined:

```
CONST
      size = 100;                    (* array size *)
TYPE
      number = 1000..9999;       (* a part number *)
      list = ARRAY [1..size] OF number;
```

The result of the function *search* (shown below) will be the index of the located item; zero is returned if the item is not found. The input parameters for this function are:

partnumber (array of part numbers (as a VAR parameter))

item (the part number to be located in *partnumber*)

size (the number of elements in the array.)

The result of the function will be the subscript of item in *partnumber* if it could be located, and zero otherwise.

```
FUNCTION search (size : integer;
                 item : number;
                 VAR partnumber : list) : integer;
(* linear search of array partnumber [1..size] for item *)
(* result is index of item in array, or zero if not found *)
VAR
      done, found : Boolean;
      index : integer;
BEGIN
      done := false;      (* we're not done yet *)
      found := false;   (* and we haven't found "item" yet *)
      index := 1;   (* start with the first array component *)
      WHILE NOT (done OR found) DO
          IF partnumber[index] = item
          THEN found := true
          ELSE IF index < size
                THEN index := index + 1
                ELSE done := true;
      IF found
      THEN search := index
      ELSE search := 0
END;
```

Suppose we would like to determine whether the *partnumber* 1002 is located in the array of part numbers. The following assignment statement in the main program will store the index of the located number in the variable *location*:

```
location := search (size, 1002, partnumber)
```

The following code could then be used to display an appropriate message:

```
IF location <> 0
THEN writeln ('The part number has been located.')
ELSE writeln ('The part is not in stock.')
```

What would happen if we tried to use a FOR loop instead of the WHILE loop? The following FOR loop will perform the task. However, the loop will continue to execute even after the item has been located! This will waste time, since if the item is in the array, only about half the elements need to be searched, on the average (see problem 3 at the end of the chapter).

```
found := false;
search := 0;
FOR index := 1 TO size DO
IF item = partnumber[index]
THEN BEGIN
            found := true;
            search := index
      END
```

Binary Search

Although the correctness of programs is our main concern, we should also consider the efficiency of our solutions. In our previous example we have assumed that the components of the array were unordered. That is, there was no way to predict the relationship that exists between two adjacent components in the array. If the array components are ordered, then a much more efficient search algorithm can be used to locate an item in the data, namely the **binary search**. The Binary Search algorithm operates similarly to the actions taken when you use the telephone directory to locate a telephone number for a particular person.

The telephone directory has names listed alphabetically. Suppose we wish to locate a person whose last name is Jones. We do not start by looking at those persons whose name begins with A, but rather start somewhere close to the middle of the directory. If we should then find ourselves looking at names beginning with L, we know that we must search further, but only in the first part of the directory, since J comes before L in the alphabet. Suppose we then look somewhere close to the middle of the first half of the directory, and find ourselves looking at the H's. Now we know that we have gone too far toward the beginning of the directory, and redirect our search to the part of the directory between the H's and the L's. With the telephone directory we continue this search until we reach the page where Jones should be located and then (using what amounts to a linear search) locate (or do not locate) Jones.

The Binary Search algorithm works on the same principle: Start in the middle of the array to locate the item. If the item is not in exactly the middle position, then we repeat the search, this time concentrating on either the first half or the second half, depending on whether the item we seek is smaller than or larger than the middle value.

Locating the middle item is easy if the components are numbered from 1 to N; it is just component N DIV 2. When we are searching, say, from component 40 to component 74, we must use a slightly different approach. We want to locate the item that is midway between 40 and 74. To do this, we take the average of 40 and 74, (40 + 74) DIV 2, or 57. Using this technique, let us apply the binary search to an example.

Suppose we have the following ordered set of characters stored in array *letter* of size 8:

index	1	2	3	4	5	6	7	8
letter	'A'	'C'	'D'	'E'	'G'	'H'	'K'	'W'

Let us search for the character 'H'. We first find the middle position in the entire array, (1 + 8) DIV 2, or 4. The letter in that position is 'E', which is smaller than the letter 'H' that we are seeking. Therefore, we redirect our search to that portion of the array containing letters greater than 'E', or those between components 5 and 8, inclusive. Again computing the middle position, we obtain (5 + 8) DIV 2, or 6. This time we find the letter in that position matches the letter we are seeking, so the search terminates successfully (see Figure 9-5).

Let us try the binary search once again, this time for the letter 'I' which is not present. The search for 'I' will begin exactly as the search for 'H'. When we examine the component 6, we find 'H', not 'I'. Since 'I' is greater than 'H', we confine our search to components 7 through 8. The "middle" of this range is component 7, the letter 'K', which is greater than 'I'. We have no components left to search. Therefore we conclude that 'I' does not appear in the array.

At the beginning of the search we have no way of knowing where the item we seek

Figure 9-5 Example of binary search.

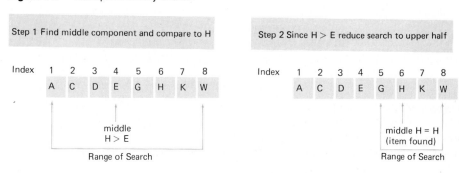

is located. After the first comparison we have narrowed our search "area" to about half the original array. After the second comparison we have only one-fourth of the original array left to search. This pattern continues to reduce the number of array components we need to search by 50 percent for each comparison we make.

Using a binary search, we can show that for an array of about 1000 entries we need to do only 10 comparisons to determine if a particular item is present, regardless of the position of the item in the array. For the linear search we need to do about 500 comparisons, on the average, to achieve the same goal. Thus, in this case, the binary search is about 50 times more efficient (in terms of comparisons) than the linear search. This efficiency gets even better as the arrays get larger. For smaller arrays, however, the advantage of the binary search over the linear search is not nearly as dramatic. Of course, the binary search does require that the components be ordered, and that requirement can cause significant problems in some applications. Later in this section we consider sorting arrays in detail. A discussion of analyzing the efficiency of algorithms can be found at the end of this chapter.

We now examine the pseudocode for the binary search. We assume that the array to be searched has index values between 1 and *LAST* and that the components are ordered such that the ith component has a value less than or equal to the i + first component, for i between 1 and *LAST* − 1. This sorted array will then be searched for *item*.

Four additional variables are used in the pseudocode. The variables *low* and *high* will contain the index values of the lower and upper ends of the portion of the array being examined, and *middle* will contain the index of the component in the middle of that portion. The variable *found* is a Boolean variable that will be true when we have located the desired item. Here, then, is the pseudocode:

Binary Search Algorithm

Set *low* = 1, *high* = *last*, and *found* = false.
While (*low* <= *high*) and not *found*   (more to search?)
    Set *middle* = (*low* + *high*) DIV 2.   (find midpoint)
    If *item* = *middle entry*,   (found the item?)
    Then set *found* = *true*,   (yes)
    Else if *item* < *middle entry*,   (in lower half?)
        Then set *high* = *middle* − 1,   (new upper bound)
        Else set *low* = *middle* + 1.   (new lower bound)
If *found* is true,
Then the *item* was located at *middle*,
Else the *item* was not located.

Now let us write a Pascal function with parameters like those used in the linear search to perform a binary search. We assume the *partnumber* array has been previously sorted.

```
FUNCTION binsearch (size : integer;
                    item : number;
                    VAR partnumber : list) : integer;
```

```
(* binary search of array partnumber [1..size] for item      *)
(* Array partnumber must already be sorted so that           *)
(* partnumber[i] <= partnumber[i+1], for i in the range 1    *)
(* to size-1. Result is index of item in array, or zero      *)
(* if the item is not found.                                  *)
VAR
        low, high, middle : integer;
        found : Boolean;
BEGIN
        low := 1;                                    (* initialize *)
        high := size;                                (* variables *)
        found := false;
        WHILE (low <= high) AND NOT found DO         (* more left? *)
        BEGIN                                        (* find middle *)
                middle := (low + high) DIV 2;            (* of range *)
                IF item = partnumber[middle]           (* test if found *)
                THEN found := true                   (* yes, we're done *)
                ELSE IF item < partnumber[middle]      (* which half? *)
                THEN high := middle - 1            (* new upper bound *)
                ELSE low := middle + 1             (* new lower bound *)
        END;
        IF NOT found
        THEN binsearch := 0                          (* item not found *)
        ELSE binsearch := middle                   (* item found at middle *)
END;
```

Sorting

The next problem we consider is how to sort an array. As we have just seen, one reason we need to know how to sort arrays is so we can prepare them for use in the binary search. The problem of producing sorted arrays is one of the most heavily researched problems in computer science. As a result, there are many different sorting algorithms with varying degrees of efficiency. Which algorithm should be used in a situation depends on whether there is any order to the existing data and the number of components to be placed in sequence. The analysis of sorting algorithms is a topic usually reserved for more advanced courses in computer science, but the topic is introduced in an optional section of this chapter.

In this section we consider the *Selection Sort* algorithm. This algorithm begins by locating the largest value in the array to be sorted and interchanging it with the component in the last position in the array. This step is then repeated, but on the portion of the array which does not include the last component. This will effectively move the second largest value in the original array just before the last component (which contains the largest value). We continue to repeat this process until each value has been moved to its proper component.

Note that we must perform the selection of the largest component in the array a total of $N - 1$ times, for an array that contains N components. The reason for this is that after $N - 1$ of the values have been reordered, the last value must necessarily be in the correct position.

Consider the following array of integers that require sorting:

index	1	2	3	4	5	6	7	8
array	48	23	56	92	63	90	46	80

In the first step, we must select the largest value in the array and interchange it with the component in the eighth position. The largest number is 92, so it is interchanged with the value 80 in the last position. The array now looks like this:

index	1	2	3	4	5	6	7	8
array	48	23	56	80	63	90	46	92

Now we repeat this basic operation but restrict our attention to the part of the array with index values between 1 and 7; the value in position 8 is already correct. After this step the array has the following appearance:

index	1	2	3	4	5	6	7	8
array	48	23	56	80	63	46	90	92

The process is then repeated five more times, after which the array is sorted:

index	1	2	3	4	5	6	7	8
array	23	46	48	56	63	80	90	92

The Selection Sort algorithm depends on the ability to locate the largest component in an array. Suppose the array to be sorted contains N components. We must find the largest number $N - 1$ times, each time for an array size of one less than the previous time. The reason is that once we have found the largest and placed it in the right position, we do not have to consider it anymore. Our algorithm for the selection sort, expressed in pseudocode, is shown below.

Selection Sort Algorithm

For $j = N$ downto 2 do

    Find the maximum value in positions 1 to j.

    Interchange the maximum value with that in position j.

To write the Pascal code implementing a selection sort, we first write a function called *findmax* whose result is the *index* of the largest component in the array (not the value of the largest component). We will assume that the array size is 500 elements and, for this example, that the element type is integer:

```
CONST
      size = 500;
TYPE
     list = ARRAY [1..size] OF integer;
```

The function must have the name of the array (here called *table*) and the index of the last position (*last*) as parameters.

```
FUNCTION findmax (last : integer;  VAR table : list) : integer;
(* find index of largest element in table[1..last] *)
VAR
      maxindex, index : 1..size;
BEGIN
      maxindex := 1;
      FOR index := 2 TO last DO
          IF table[index] > table[maxindex]
          THEN maxindex := index;
      findmax := maxindex
      END;
```

Now we write the procedure *sort*. Two parameters are required: the size of the array and the array itself. We will assume that function *findmax* has been defined prior to *sort*.

```
PROCEDURE sort (size : integer; VAR table : list);
(* selection sort of array elements table[1..size] *)
VAR
     temp, j, largest : integer;
BEGIN
      FOR j := size DOWNTO 2 DO
      BEGIN
            (* find the largest element in 1..j *)
            largest := findmax (j, table);
            (* interchange it with table[j] *)
            temp := table[largest];
            table[largest] := table[j];
```

```
                              table[j] := temp
                      END
END;
```

Now we put all these pieces together and write a complete Pascal program.

Problem 9.2

Write a complete Pascal program that reads an integer N (no larger than 500) and N additional integers. These N integers are to be sorted and then displayed.

The complete Pascal solution to this problem follows.

```
PROGRAM selection (input, output);
(* Read N, no larger than 500, and N integers. Sort *)
(* and display the N integers.                        *)
CONST
        size = 500;
TYPE
        list = ARRAY [1..size] OF integer;
VAR
        i, num : 1..size;
        table : list;
FUNCTION findmax (last : integer; VAR table : list) : integer;
(* find index of largest element in table[1..last] *)
VAR
        maxindex, index : 1..size;
BEGIN
        maxindex := 1;
        FOR index := 2 TO last DO
                IF table[index] > table[maxindex]
                THEN maxindex := index;
        findmax := maxindex
END;
PROCEDURE sort (size : integer; VAR table : list);
(* selection sort of array elements table[1..size] *)
VAR
        temp, j, largest : integer;
BEGIN
        FOR j := size DOWNTO 2 DO
        BEGIN
                (* find the largest element in 1..j *)
                largest := findmax (j, table);
                (* interchange it with table[j] *)
```

```
            temp := table[largest];
            table[largest] := table[j];
            table[j] := temp
        END
END;
(* Main Program *)
BEGIN
        writeln ('Selection sort of integers');
        (* obtain and validate the number of values to sort *)
        REPEAT
                write ('How many numbers (', size, ' or less)? ');
                readln (num)
        UNTIL ((num <= size) AND (num > 0));
        (* obtain the numbers to be sorted *)
    writeln ('Enter the numbers to be sorted.');
    FOR i := 1 TO num DO
        read (table[i]);
        (* invoke sort to reorder the array *)
    sort (num, table);
(* display the sorted numbers *)
    writeln ('The sorted numbers are: ');
    for i := 1 TO num DO
        writeln (table[i], ' ')
END.
```

Program Sort

```
Selection sort of integers
How many numbers (500 or less)? 8
Enter the numbers to be sorted.
48   23   56   92   63   90   46   80
The sorted numbers are:
23
46
48
56
63
80
90
92
```

Program Sort : Sample Execution

EXERCISES FOR SECTION 9.2

1 Consider the following list of numbers:

8 4 3 9 5 12 6

(a) How many comparisons are required to locate the value 12 when doing a linear search?
(b) Sort the numbers and determine the number of comparisons required to locate the value 12 using a binary search.

2 Suppose the selection sort is applied to an array that is already sorted, in ascending order, such as

1 2 3 4 5 6

and to an array that is sorted in descending order, such as

6 5 4 3 2 1

Compare the performance of the selection sort on these two arrays.

3 Write a Pascal program called *longmerge* whose input is two random arrays of integers of size m and n, respectively. The program should perform the following steps (you may use the selection sort in this chapter):
(1) Sort the first array of size m.
(2) Sort the second array of size n.
(3) Copy the first array into a long array of size $m + n$.
(4) Append the second array to the first array in the long array.
(5) Sort the long array.

4 Write a function similar to *findmax* in this chapter that will find the smallest value instead of the largest.

5 Write a selection sort procedure that sorts an array of integers in descending order by locating the smallest value in each iteration and switching it with the appropriate component.

SECTION 9.3 MULTIDIMENSIONAL ARRAYS

The arrays discussed so far are known as one-dimensional, or linear arrays, since each component can be located in the array by specifying a single index value. However, there are many problems where the data being manipulated would be better represented in a multidimensional format. For example, some parallel array processing problems can be considered to be multidimensional array problems. A table with two or more columns, for example, would be modeled as a two-dimensional array, while a collection of such multicolumn tables would be modeled as a three-dimensional array.

Consider the following table of mileages between selected cities in the United States.

from/to	New York	Los Angeles	Chicago	Houston	Miami
New York	0	2913	841	1675	1350
Los Angeles	2913	0	2175	1566	2817
Chicago	841	2175	0	1110	1388
Houston	1675	1566	1110	0	1300
Miami	1350	2817	1388	1300	0

The terms row and column are frequently used in discussing tables of this type. A *row* is a horizontal collection of data items; for example, the distances from New York to the various cities represents a row in the table above. A *column* is a vertical collection of data values; the distances to New York from the various cities is an example of a column. The entire table shown above contains five rows and five columns of mileages. We can locate the mileage from one city to another by using two index values: the name of the city we are coming from (row) and the name of the city we are going to (column). The first index selects a particular row of the table, and the second selects a particular column. The particular element selected is that located at the intersection of the particular row and column selected by the index values.

One way of looking at multidimensional arrays treats them as an array of arrays. This seemingly strange idea is really very logical. We can treat our table of mileages as five arrays, each of which has five elements. For example, the first array might contain the distances from New York to each of the five cities, while the second array might contain the distances from Los Angeles. Each of these arrays is just a component of the larger array. Let us consider the definition of these arrays.

First, the distance from any city to one of the five cities mentioned above is represented as five integers. We use the names of the cities as an enumerated type, and this type is used as the index type for the array type *row*:

```
TYPE
    city = (NewYork, LosAngeles, Chicago, Houston, Miami);
    row = ARRAY [city] OF integer;
```

Let us consider a variable that might represent a single row, say the distances from Houston to the various cities. This row, by itself, would be declared as a variable using the declaration

```
VAR
    fromHouston : row;
```

If the appropriate values were placed in the elements of this row, we could then determine the mileage from Houston to New York by referencing "fromHouston [NewYork]."

But to represent the table in a uniform fashion we really need a collection of such rows, one for each "from" city. To declare such a collection we would use a type that has one row for each city:

```
TYPE
      distance = ARRAY [city] OF row;
```

Of course, a variable of this type, representing the entire table, would be declared as usual:

```
VAR
      mileages : distance;
```

The type *distance* in this declaration could also be written explicitly:

```
VAR
      mileages : ARRAY [city] OF ARRAY [city] OF integer;
```

While you should continue to think of a two-dimensional array as an array of arrays, you can also write the type in an abbreviated form. Essentially we list, between the brackets, the two index types used. That is, we write the type of index used to select the row, a comma, and then the type of index used to select the column. Our mileages could then be declared as

```
VAR
      mileages : ARRAY [city, city] OF integer;
```

or, using the type declaration, as

```
TYPE
      distance : ARRAY [city, city] OF integer;
VAR
      mileages : distance;
```

The distance from New York to Houston would then be located in *mileages [New York, Houston]*.

Here is another example where two-dimensional arrays are useful. Suppose we want to store the following collection of names:

```
Cardiz
Johnson
Wileman
Tranh
Konvalina
Tennenbaum
```

This is essentially a table of characters, each row containing a complete name and each column containing the first, second, and so forth characters of all names. If we assume that there will never be more than 15 characters in a name (the number of

```
TYPE
      aname = ARRAY [1..15] OF char;
      names = ARRAY [1..6] OF aname;
```

or alternately

```
TYPE
      names = ARRAY [1..6, 1..15] OF char;
```

Let us declare a variable of type *names* and find out how to reference its elements.

```
VAR  folks : names;
```

would allocate space for 6 names, each having 15 characters. The first character of the sixth name would be referenced as *folks[6][1]*, or alternately as *folks[6,1]*. In the first form we explicitly used two subscripts (after all, there are two arrays being referenced). The first subscript selects the row containing the name, and the second subscript selects the particular character of the name in which we are interested. The second form is similar to the abbreviated declaration; we write the two subscript values separated by a comma in place of the two separate subscripts. Arrays of characters, with both one and two dimensions, are treated in greater detail in Chapter 10.

The number of elements in a multidimensional array is equal to the product of the number of index values in each dimension. Our mileage table has the same row and column index type (*city*), and as it has 5 values, there will be 25 integer mileages in the array *distance*, regardless of which of the various declarations we use. The *folks* array will require 90 characters, since the first index has 6 possible values and the second has 15. Note that in the case of the character array, characters not actually part of a name are still present in the array, and will usually be blanks.

Here are some additional type declarations representing two-dimensional arrays:

```
TYPE
      name  = ARRAY [1..20, 1..15] OF char;
      data  = ARRAY ['0'..'9', 1..10] OF integer;
      table = ARRAY [-10..10, 1..15] OF char;
```

Note that the index types need not be the same for the two dimensions of a two-dimensional array.

Consider the following declarations and code:

```
VAR num : ARRAY [1..3, 1..5] OF integer;
FOR i := 1 TO 3 DO        (* for each row *)
    FOR j := 1 TO 5 DO    (* for each column *)
        num[i,j] := i;
```

After execution of this loop the array would contain the following values:

	column				
	1	*2*	*3*	*4*	*5*
1	1	1	1	1	1
row 2	2	2	2	2	2
3	3	3	3	3	3

Observe that two indices are required to process two-dimensional arrays, one for the row and one for the column. The indices can be expressions as well as constants. For example, the Pascal segment

```
i := 1;
j := 2;
writeln (num[i + j, j − i])
```

would display the value in *num[3,1]*, or 3.

Two-Dimensional Array Processing

Assuming the following declaration

```
TYPE
    table = ARRAY [1..5, 1..10] OF integer;
VAR
    value : table;
```

the following Pascal segment would read into the array *value* row by row (*row* and *column* are declared as appropriate integer types):

```
FOR row := 1 TO 5 DO
    FOR column := 1 TO 10 DO
        read (value[row,column]);
```

To read the data in column by column, we would interchange the order in which the *row* and *column* variables are changed:

```
FOR column := 1 TO 10 DO
    FOR row := 1 TO 5 DO
        read (value[row,column]);
```

Suppose we change the declaration so that the number of rows equals the number of columns:

TYPE
        table = ARRAY [1..5, 1..5] OF integer;
VAR
        value : table;

We can directly write a Pascal segment to display the diagonal elements of the array. The components of the diagonal have the following positions: [1,1] [2,2] [3,3] [4,4] [5,5]. In this case only one index variable need be used, since the row position will equal the column position for each diagonal element. Here is the code, assuming *index* is an integer variable:

```
FOR index := 1 TO 5 DO
    writeln (value [index, index]);
```

Now suppose we want to display the other diagonal of the array. That is, suppose we want to write the elements in positions [5,1], [4,2], [3,3], [2,4], and [1,5]. To accomplish a task like this, we must find the relationship that holds between the row and column numbers. This relation should be invariant throughout the execution of the loop that displays the diagonal elements. A little thought will yield the correct relation in this case: the row number plus the column number is always exactly 6. Using this fact, we can write the code to display the diagonal:

```
FOR column := 1 TO 5 DO
    writeln (value[6 − column, column]);
```

Finding the relation between the row and column in problems like this is important, because the only other solution to the problem is to write statements that explicitly reference the desired elements in the order required. Thus to print the other diagonal, we would have to write

```
writeln (value[5,1]);
writeln (value[4,2]);
writeln (value[3,3]);
writeln (value[2,4]);
writeln (value[1,5]);
```

and it should be apparent that this solution is entirely unacceptable if there are many elements in the array.

Arrays with Three or More Dimensions

We may have arrays of more than two dimensions if they are appropriate for the problem we are solving. A three-dimensional array, for example, can be thought of as an array of arrays of arrays. In the declarations

TYPE
    box = ARRAY [1..5, 1..10, 1..5] OF integer;
VAR
    points : box;

a total of 5 times 10 times 5, or 250 integers, will be reserved. To access an element of the array *points,* we must use three indices, one for each dimension. For example, the following code will compute the sum of the entire collection of 250 integers in the array. Assume i, j, k, and *sum* are all declared as integer variables.

```
sum := 0;
FOR i := 1 TO 5 DO
    FOR j := 1 TO 10 DO
        FOR k:= 1 TO 5 DO
            sum := sum + points[i,j,k];
```

The method of declaring and accessing multidimensional arrays can be extended to any number of dimensions. However, three-dimensional arrays are usually the largest number of dimensions encountered in practical programs.

EXERCISES FOR SECTION 9.3

1 Examine the following array declarations. How many elements are present in this array?

TYPE
    rowindex = −5..5;
    colindex = 0..10;
    rowtype = ARRAY [rowindex] OF integer;
    matrixtype = ARRAY [colindex] OF rowtype;
VAR
    matrix : matrixtype;

2 Which of the following does *not* declare *mytable* with 100 rows and 200 columns?

  (a) TYPE
        slice = ARRAY [1..100] OF char;
        table = ARRAY [1..200] OF slice;
    VAR
        mytable : table;
  (b) TYPE
        slice = ARRAY [1..200] OF char;
        table = ARRAY [1..100] OF slice;
    VAR
        mytable : table;

(c) TYPE

        table = ARRAY [1..100] OF

        ARRAY [1..200] OF char;

   VAR

        mytable : table;

(d) TYPE

        table = ARRAY [1..100,1..200] OF char;

   VAR

        mytable : table;

(e) TYPE

        element = char;

        row = 1..100;

        col = 1..200;

        table = ARRAY [row, col] OF element;

   VAR

        mytable : table;

3 Determine what will be displayed when the following program is executed, assuming the declaration

```
VAR matrix : ARRAY [1..5,1..3] OF integer;

FOR i := 1 TO 5 DO
   FOR j:= 1 TO 3 DO
         matrix[i,j] := i + j;
j := 1;
FOR i := 1 TO 3 DO
      writeln (matrix[j+i,4-i]);
```

4 Consider the following declaration:

```
TYPE
      table = ARRAY ['0'..'9',1..9] OF Boolean;
VAR
      matrix : table;
```

(a) How many components does this table contain?

Which of the following are valid assignment statements?

(b) matrix[0,1] := true;

(c) matrix['9',9] := 0;

(d) matrix['0',1] := matrix['9',0] AND matrix['7',7];

(e) matrix['1',1] := '1' < 1;

5 Write a Pascal procedure called *change* that contains the parameters *rmatrix* (a two-dimensional integer array of 10 rows and 10 columns) and two integer variables

m and *n*. The procedure *change* interchanges rows *m* and *n* of *rmatrix*. Include any TYPE declarations.

6 Write a Pascal program called *swap* that performs the following:
    (a) Reads values for the integers *index1*, *index2*, and *index3* indicating the index values of a three-dimensional Boolean array called *logic* (of type "ARRAY [1..10, 1..20, 1..30] OF Boolean");
    (b) Reads the elements of the array *logic*; 0 in the input data represents false, while 1 represents true.
    (c) Invokes a procedure called *flipflop* that changes each true to false, and each false to true, for each component of the array *logic*.

SECTION 9.4 PROBLEM SOLVING USING ARRAYS

In this section we solve two problems using the material presented in this chapter. The first problem was stated in Chapter 1 and an algorithm was developed. Since we now can sort arrays, we can write the Pascal program.

Problem 9.3

The management of Apex Electronics Company would like to determine the median annual salary of its employees. Write a Pascal program that displays the number of employees and their median salary, given the number of employees and their salaries as input data.

Recall the algorithm we developed in Chapter 1:

1 Obtain the number of salaries *N* and the employees' salaries.
2 Sort the salaries.
3 Compute the median salary as follows. If *N* is odd, then the median is the middle salary. Otherwise, the median salary is the average of the two middle salaries.
4 Display *N* and the median salary.

    Let us assume a maximum of 500 employees for the company. The following Pascal program called *stats* will solve the problem. The program uses the function *findmax* and procedure *sort* from earlier in this chapter. The number of employees is stored in the variable *num*.

```
PROGRAM stats (input, output);
(* Compute median salary of 500 or fewer salaries, given *)
(* the number and value of the salaries as input data. *)
CONST
      size = 500;
```

```
TYPE
        list = ARRAY [1..size] OF integer;
VAR
        i, num : 1..size;
        salary : list;
        median : integer;
FUNCTION findmax (last : integer; VAR table : list) : integer;
(* find index of largest element in table[1..last] *)
VAR
        maxindex, index : 1..size;
BEGIN
        maxindex := 1;
        FOR index := 2 TO last DO
            IF table[index] > table[maxindex]
            THEN maxindex := index;
        findmax := maxindex
END;
PROCEDURE sort (size : integer; VAR table : list);
(* Selection sort of array elements table[1..size] *)
VAR
        temp, j, largest : integer;
BEGIN
        FOR j := size DOWNTO 2 DO
        BEGIN
                    (* find the largest element in 1..j *)
            largest := findmax (j, table);
                    (* interchange it with table[j] *)
            temp := table[largest];
            table[largest] := table[j];
            table[j] := temp
        END
END;
(* Main Program *)
BEGIN
    writeln ('Median Salary Calculator');
(* obtain and validate the number of employees *)
    REPEAT
        write ('How many employees (', size, ' or less)? ');
        readln (num)
    UNTIL ((num <= size) AND (num > 0));
(* obtain the employee salaries *)
    writeln ('Enter the salaries.');
    FOR i := 1 TO num DO
        read (salary[i]);
(* invoke sort to reorder the salaries *)
    sort (num, salary);
```

```
(* determine the median salary *)
    IF odd(num)
    THEN median := salary[(num + 1) DIV 2]
    ELSE median := (salary[num DIV 2]
        + salary[num DIV 2 + 1]) DIV 2;
(* display results *)
    writeln ('Number of salaries: ', num:1);
    writeln ('Median salary: ', median:1)
END.
```

Program Stats

```
How many employees (500 or less)? 5
Enter the salaries:
20000   30000   25000   60000   40000
Number of salaries: 5
Median salary: 30000
```

Program Stats: Sample Execution

In the next problem we use a two-dimensional array to solve a game problem.

Problem 9.4

Write a Pascal procedure called winner *that determines whether a completed tic-tac-toe game has a winner and, if so, identify the winner and type of win (row, column, or diagonal). That is, determine if a three-row, three-column array contains three X's or three O's in any row, column, or diagonal and, if so, which letter (X or O) appears three times and in which way.*

Examples of some completed tic-tac-toe games appear in Figure 9-6. There are three possible symbols that may appear in the game: *X*, *O*, and blank. The solution to this problem can be reduced to solving the following subproblems:

SUBPROBLEM 1: Check each row for three *X*'s or three *O*'s.
SUBPROBLEM 2: Check each column for three *X*'s or three *O*'s.
SUBPROBLEM 3: Check each diagonal for three *X*'s or three *O*'s.

Each subproblem can be solved using an appropriate IF statement to check for a winner. The details of the Pascal solution follow.

The TYPE definitions we will need include the various kinds of symbols that may

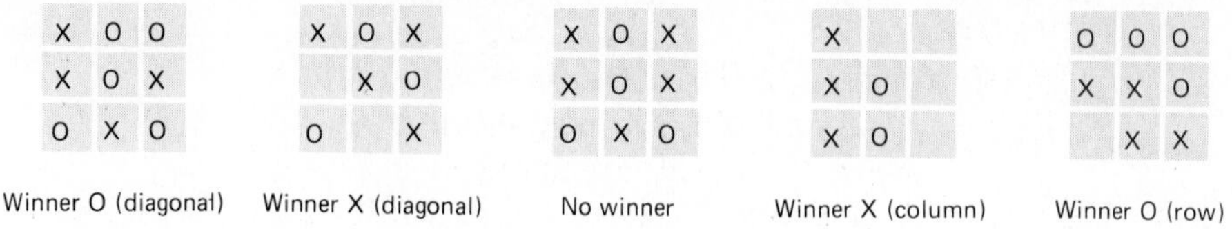

X O O	X O X	X O X	X	O O O
X O X	X O	X O X	X O	X X O
O X O	O X	O X O	X O	X X

Winner O (diagonal)   Winner X (diagonal)   No winner   Winner X (column)   Winner O (row)

Figure 9-6   Tic-tac-toe games.

appear (type *mark*), the various places where three symbols in a row may appear (type *place*), and the playing board itself (type *board*). Here is the Pascal TYPE definition for these:

```
TYPE
       mark = (X, O, BLANK);
       place = (row, column, diagonal);
       board = ARRAY [1..3, 1..3] OF mark;
```

We will write a procedure *winner* that determines who won and what type of win was made. It has an array parameter called *game* that is a two-dimensional array with a value of type *mark* in each component. The procedure will set the value of the parameter result to X if there are three X's in a row, to O if there are three O's in a row, or BLANK if there is no winner. If a win is indicated, then the parameter *wintype* is set to either row, column, or diagonal to indicate the type of win.

```
PROCEDURE winner (VAR game : board;
                  VAR result : mark;
                  VAR wintype : place);
(* Determine if, who, and what type of win was made *)
(* in a completed tic-tac-toe game.                  *)
VAR
       i : 1..4;                          (*index*)
BEGIN
       result := BLANK;          (* assume no winner *)
       i := 1;                    (* check rows for winner *)
       WHILE (i <= 3) AND (result = BLANK) DO
       BEGIN
          IF ((game[i, 1] = X) OR (game[i, 1] = O))
             AND (game[i, 1] = game[i, 2])
             AND (game[i, 1] = game[i, 3])
          THEN BEGIN
                       result := game[i, 1];
                       wintype := row
                END;
          i := i + 1
       END;
       i := 1;                         (* check columns *)
```

```
WHILE (i <= 3) AND (result = BLANK) DO
BEGIN
      IF ((game[1,i] = X) OR (game[1,i] = O))
          AND (game[1,i] = game[2,i])
          AND (game[1,i] = game[3,i])
      THEN BEGIN
                    result := game[1,i];
                    wintype := column
          END;
        i := i + 1
END;
IF (result = BLANK)          (* check diagonals *)
 AND ((game[2,2] = X) OR (game[2,2] = O))
 AND (((game[1,1] = game[2,2]) AND (game[3,3] = game[2,2]))
    OR ((game[3,1] = game[2,2]) AND (game[1,3] = game[2,2])))
 THEN BEGIN
                    result := game[2,2];
                    wintype := diagonal
          END
END; (* procedure win *)
```

SECTION 9.5 ANALYSIS OF ALGORITHM EFFICIENCY [OPTIONAL]

As you have probably discovered by now, there is often more than one correct algorithm that solves a given problem. However, some correct algorithms are better, or more *efficient*, than others. What does it mean for an algorithm to be efficient? In this chapter we said that, in general, the Binary Search algorithm was more efficient than the Linear Search algorithm. In this case efficiency refers to the amount of *time* it takes to locate an item in the array. We do not measure the efficiency of the algorithm for a specific case, since there are many cases where a linear search is faster than a binary search. For example, if the array size is small, a linear search is often very efficient. So when we compare the performance of two algorithms, it is reasonable to analyze the efficiency of each algorithm in a general setting. That is, compare the performance of each algorithm on arbitrary data, and determine which algorithm performs better on the average. This is not the only way to measure efficiency. For example, we can measure the amount of *storage* required by the algorithm.

In this section we discuss algorithm efficiency rather than computer program efficiency. Estimating the efficiency of the actual computer program can be a difficult task since it is heavily dependent on the actual computer system and programming language used. On the other hand, algorithms are machine-independent and can be analyzed to obtain estimates of their efficiency. In fact, significant gains in efficiency are usually made in the algorithm rather than the actual computer program.

In general, the time and space resources required by the execution of an algorithm depend on the size of the input to the algorithm. For example, in the Linear or Binary Search algorithms the amount of time required to locate an item and the amount of

each algorithm will depend on the size of the input. Suppose we let n represent the
size of the input. In order to analyze the efficiency of an algorithm, we must solve
the following problem: Given the algorithm and an input of size n, estimate the time
and amount of storage required by the execution of the algorithm.

How do we measure the time and storage requirements of an algorithm? The storage
requirements can be measured by the amount of memory used to store such objects
as variables, constants, and arrays. In the case of the Linear and Binary Search
algorithms, the measure of storage is not very useful, since both algorithms use
approximately the same amount of storage. To measure the time it takes the algorithm
to execute for a given input size n, we could count the number of instructions to be
executed. However, many instructions, such as initializations, require very little time
relative to the main activity of the algorithm. For example, in the Linear Search
algorithm most of the execution time is spent in comparing the item to be located with
the elements in the array. Since we are interested in the overall performance of the
algorithm, it is reasonable in the case of the Linear Search algorithm to measure its
efficiency by counting the number of comparisons.

Big O-Notation

Measuring the efficiency of a given algorithm exactly is often practically impossible.
Usually we settle for an estimate of the efficiency of the algorithm. Technically, this
estimate is called the ***order*** of the algorithm. The estimates of algorithm efficiency
are often written using the "big oh" notation, or ***O-notation***. Let's consider some
examples of the use of O-notation.

Suppose an algorithm requires $3n^2 + n - 1$ steps on the average to execute with
an input size of n. As the input size n gets very large, the number of steps $(3n^2 + n - 1)$ required in the execution of the algorithm is dominated by the first term, $3n^2$.
That is, when n is very large, $3n^2$ is much larger than the other term, $n - 1$. So we
can effectively neglect the term $n - 1$. This result is written as follows:

$$3n^2 + n - 1 = O(n^2)$$

The equation says, in effect, that the efficiency of the algorithm grows no faster than
a constant times n^2. In this example, the order of the algorithm is $O(n^2)$. Notice if the
input size n is doubled, the number of steps to execute the algorithm would increase
about four times.

It can be shown that the average number of comparisons required in a linear search
with an array of n elements is $n/2$. So the order of a linear search is $O(n)$, since $n/2$
grows no faster than a constant times n. Similarly, it can be shown that the Binary
Search algorithm is of order $O(\log_2 n)$ for a sorted array of n elements. As n gets
larger $\log_2 n$ becomes significantly smaller than n. This accounts for the binary search
being much faster in general than the linear search. These results are derived in
advanced computer science courses.

The following table lists some common orders of algorithms and their names. In
order for you to appreciate the significant differences between these orders, the table

includes a column showing the execution times of typical algorithms of each order for an input of size $n = 50$. The times assume the use of a computer that can execute one step each millisecond (10^{-6} seconds); that is, the computer can execute 1 million steps per second.

order	name	execution time
O (1)	Constant	10^{-6} seconds
O ($\log_2 n$)	Logarithmic	6×10^{-6} seconds
O (n)	Linear	5×10^{-5} seconds
O ($n \log_2 n$)	$n \log n$	3×10^{-4} seconds
O (n^2)	Quadratic	3×10^{-3} seconds
O (n^3)	Cubic	0.13 seconds
O (2^n)	Exponential	36 years
O ($n!$)	Factorial	10^{51} years

It is important to note, for example, if one algorithm has the order O(n^2) and another algorithm has order O(n^3), then the O(n^2) algorithm is more efficient than the O(n^3) algorithm for sufficiently large input sizes. Yet, it is possible for the O(n^3) algorithm to be more efficient than the O(n^2) algorithm for small input sizes.

We conclude this section with an example of analyzing the efficiency of an algorithm to find the largest element in an array called *list* with n elements. The largest value will be assigned to the variable *max*. The algorithm is outlined as follows:

STEP 1 Initialize *max* to *list[1]*.
STEP 2 For each integer value of i in the range 2 to n
    If *max* < *list[i]*
      then assign *list[i]* to *max*

Since most of the work of this algorithm is done inside the loop in step 2, we will measure the efficiency of this algorithm by computing the number of comparisons made inside the loop to find the largest element. Each time the body of the loop is executed a comparison is made. The loop is executed for $i = 2, 3, 4, \ldots, n$. That is, the loop body is executed $n - 1$ times. This implies the number of comparisons is $n - 1$. The order of the algorithm is O(n), since $n - 1$ grows no faster than a constant times n. So the algorithm is linear. In this case it means if the input size doubles, so will the number of comparisons required to find the largest element.

SECTION 9.6 TESTING AND DEBUGGING TECHNIQUES

One of the most common errors that can arise when using arrays is for the value of a subscript to fall outside the range of values allowed for the subscript. If the index or subscript is out of range, either the computation will not produce the correct result or, in some systems, an error will be indicated. Here is an example: Suppose we wish to search the array *list* for a number called *item* (assume *list* is declared as ARRAY [1..50] of integer). Consider the following Pascal program segment (*index* is a variable of type *1..50*):

```
index := 1;
WHILE list[index] <> item DO        (* search for value *)
    index := index + 1;
```

If *item* occurs in the array *list*, then *index* will contain the position of *item* in the array. But, if *item* is not in the array *list*, after the WHILE loop tests *list[50]*, the index will be incremented to 51 (outside the subrange specified in the declaration), and then the WHILE loop will reference an element that is not in the array (*list[51]*). Therefore it is necessary to verify that *index* is in the proper range before performing the test ("list[index] <> item").

Here is the modified solution to the previous problem:

```
index := 1;
WHILE (index <= 50) AND (list[index] <> item) DO
        index := index + 1;
```

Unfortunately, this "fix" does not solve the problem either. The reason is that the Boolean expression in the WHILE statement is evaluated completely, regardless of the value of "(index <= 50)." This means that when *index* finally becomes 51, evaluation of the Boolean expression will still reference *list[51]*, resulting in an error. One way to avoid the error is to check the last element of the array separately, as shown in the following code:

```
index := 1;
WHILE (index < 50) AND (list[index] <> item) DO
        index := index + 1;
IF (index = 50) AND (list[index] <> item)
THEN writeln ('Item not found.')
ELSE writeln ('Item found, index = ', index)
```

Here is another solution that uses a Boolean variable *found* to record whether the item has been located or not.

```
index := 0;
REPEAT
        index := index + 1;
        found := list[index] = item
UNTIL found OR (index = 50);
IF found
THEN writeln ('Item found, index = ', index)
ELSE writeln ('Item not found.')
```

Another source of subscript errors is declaring too few elements in the array. For example, suppose we have the following declarations:

```
TYPE
      list = ARRAY [1..100] OF integer;
VAR
      grade : list;
```

The array *grade* stores 100 integers. However, when input data is actually read into the array elements, there may be an unknown number of values terminated by an end of file. The following Pascal segment is typical of coding used to read the data (assume *index* is declared as a variable of type *0..100*):

```
index := 0;
WHILE NOT eof DO
BEGIN
      index := index + 1;
      read (grade[index])
END
```

If there are more than 100 values provided in the input data, the loop will cause *index* to become greater than 100 and then attempt to read a value into *grade[101]*.

When utilizing arrays in Pascal, you should make certain to declare at least as many elements as the maximum number of values you anticipate. In addition, if you are reading an unknown number of values, use a variable to record the number of values already obtained and verify that you are not attempting to read a value into an array element that does not exist.

Declaring arrays with too many elements usually does not cause serious problems, but unused elements do reduce the amount of storage available for other uses and can make your program run slowly. In addition, some systems with limited storage may not even be able to run your program. The declaration

```
VAR
      list : ARRAY [1..maxint] OF integer;
```

will almost certainly require too much storage to run reasonably on any computer system and usually will not run at all on microcomputer systems.

Here is a list of some important Pascal reminders to be noted when testing and debugging your programs.

PASCAL REMINDERS

- Array definitions cannot appear in a procedure or function header; use a global TYPE definition instead.
- The individual components of an array are referenced by using the array name followed by the index (or a list of indices) enclosed in brackets:

list[2]   table[2,3]

■ The index can be any valid expression that yields a value of the correct type:

list[2*index + 1]   table[trunc(sqrt(17.3))]

■ The index type can be any ordinal data type, while the component type can be any data type, including a structured data type:

TYPE
       table = ARRAY[1..5] OF ARRAY[1..10] OF char;

■ A linear search will sequentially search for an item in order from the first component of the array until either the search item is found or the last element of the array has been examined.
■ A binary search will search for an item in a sorted array by splitting the array in half each time.
■ A multidimensional array is an array of arrays, and can be declared in an abbreviated form:

TYPE
       names = ARRAY [1..50,1..15] OF char;

■ Subscript errors are the most common array processing problem.
■ Variables having identical array types can be assigned to each other.

SECTION 9.7 CHAPTER REVIEW

In this chapter we discussed defining and declaring arrays, both one-dimensional and multidimensional. We presented many Pascal segments in array processing. Also FOR loops and WHILE loops were used quite extensively in array processing. A multidimensional array can be thought of as an array of arrays.

Many problems using arrays require searching for an item in an array or sorting an array in some order. In this chapter we presented two search techniques: linear and binary. A sorting algorithm known as a selection sort was presented in detail. The sort algorithm was applied to the problem involving computation of the median salary of an array of employee salaries. A problem using multidimensional arrays was also solved. Algorithm efficiency and O-notation were discussed in an optional section of the chapter.

The following summary of the Pascal features presented in this chapter can be used for future reference.

PASCAL REFERENCE

1 Array: A named group of elements of the same type.

TYPE name = ARRAY [index type] OF component type;

Example:

```
TYPE list = ARRAY [ -10..10] OF char;
```

2 Multidimensional array: An array of arrays. Examples:

```
TYPE
     table = ARRAY [1..5] OF ARRAY [1..10] OF char;
```

or

```
table = ARRAY [1..5,1..10] OF char;
```

or

```
cols = ARRAY [1..10] OF char;
table = ARRAY [1..5] OF cols;
```

3 Accessing array components: Use array name followed by a list of subscript (index) expressions enclosed in brackets:

```
arrayname [ index expression ]
```

or

```
arrayname [ row index, column index ]
```

Examples:

```
table [3, 5] or table [3] [5]
list [2 * j]
```

Chapter 10 Preview

In the next chapter we will take a close look at nonnumeric data manipulation, including the manipulation of sequences of characters. Computers spend more time manipulating nonnumeric data than any other data type.

Keywords for Chapter 9

array
binary search
column
index
linear search
multidimensional array

O-notation
order
parallel arrays
row
selection sort
sequential search

CHAPTER 9 EXERCISES

⭐ ESSENTIAL EXERCISES

1   The dot product of 2 one-dimensional arrays of real numbers a and b defined as

```
VAR
      a, b : ARRAY [1..size] OF real;
```

is the sum of

```
a[1] * b[1] + a[2] * b[2] + . . . + a[size] * b[size]
```

where size is an integer constant. Write a function to perform this computation.

2   The transpose of a square two-dimensional array a is an array b with the same type and components with values satisfying the relation $b[i,j] = a[j,i]$ for all possible values of i and j. Write a procedure which will compute the transpose of a five-row, five-column array of real numbers.

⭐⭐ SIGNIFICANT EXERCISES

3   A symmetric matrix a is a square two-dimensional array with the property that $a[i,j] = a[j,i]$. Such a matrix can be stored in a compact form (in array ac), since duplicated elements need only be stored once. First, design a method for storing such arrays without repeating the duplicate elements. Then write a function *GETSYM (ac, i, j)* which yields the value of $a[i,j]$ and a procedure *PUTSYM (ac, i, j, val)* which stores *val* in the appropriate location of the compact array ac. (Hint: Only n elements from column n need be stored; consider a one-dimensional array containing the elements from column 1, then column 2, and so forth.)

4   Write a function *match* which has 2 one-dimensional arrays with the same component types and positive integer subscripts as parameters. The first of these has N elements and the second has M elements, where N and M are defined as constants. Also, *match* should determine if the elements of the second array appear, contiguously and in order, somewhere in the first array. If this is the case, then *match* returns the index of the leftmost component of the first array where the match occurred. Otherwise, *match* returns 0. For example, if the first array contains

```
9  7  12  7  85  2  5
```

and the second array contains

```
12  7  85  2
```

then *match* should return 3.

★★★ CHALLENGING EXERCISES

5 This exercise is basically the same as exercise 4, but now allow a match to "wrap around" the end of the first array. For example, if the first array contains

3 7 9 1 8

and the second array contains

1 8 3

then *match* should return 4.

CHAPTER 9 PROBLEMS FOR COMPUTER SOLUTION

★ ESSENTIAL PROBLEMS

1 Define the distance between two positive integers as the sum of the absolute value of the difference between the digits in corresponding positions, MOD 10. For example, the distance between 417 and 392 is

$$(\,|4-3| \, + \, |1-9| \, + \, |7-2| \,) \text{ MOD } 10$$

or 4. Write a program which will compute the distance between the pairs of integers that appear as input data. Note that it is necessary to assume leading zeroes if the numbers in a pair do not have the same number of digits.

Example input:

417 392   5 12

Example output:

Distance between 417 and 392 is 4.
Distance between 5 and 12 is 4.

2 Given as input an integer N and a set of N characters enclosed in apostrophes, determine how many comparison operations between elements of the data to be sorted are necessary for the selection sort to place these characters in ascending order.

Example input:

3   'D'   'G'   'B'

Example output:

To place the characters
D G B
into ascending order using the selection sort requires 3 comparisons.

3 It has been noted that on the average about $N/2$ elements of an N element array must be examined to determine if a particular value is in the array. The purpose of this exercise is to verify that this is the case. Write a procedure *linearsearch* which searches an array for a value known to be in the array, returning the number of array elements examined during the search operation. Then write a program which reads N, an integer, from the first input line and N unique characters from the second line. Each of these characters is to be placed in a separate array element. The program should then use *linearsearch* to find, in turn, the number of elements required to locate every element of the character array. The average of these numbers should then be reported, as well as the value of $N/2$, both as real numbers. If our original claim is correct, then the two values should be about the same. Explain why the results will not be identical.

Example input:

6
AFBECD

Example output:

The average number of comparisons required was 3.5
The value of N / 2 is 3.0

★★ SIGNIFICANT PROBLEMS

4 Given the same data as problem 2, perform a selection sort on the array, but manipulate only a second array containing the indices of the elements. If we assume the array d contains the data to be sorted, then a second array x will contain the indices of the components of array d. After the selection sort, $x[1]$ will contain the index in d of the smallest component and $x[n]$ will contain the index in d of the largest component. That is, after the sort $d[x[1]]$ is the smallest component's value and $d[x[n]]$ is the largest component's value. Display the array x.

Example input:

4 'G' 'A' 'I' 'C'

Example output:

The index array contains
2 4 1 3

5   The input data contains no more than 100 pairs of integers. Each pair of integers
    should be treated as one component and sorted such that the first integer in each
    pair is in ascending order. If the first components of several pairs have the same
    value, then those pairs should be further ordered so that the second components'
    values are ordered in descending sequence.

Example input:

```
12  41
9   304
12  63
8   12
9   512
```

Example output:

```
8   12
9   512
9   304
12  63
12  41
```

6   The *convolution* of an array of real components D with another array of real
    components F is defined as the sum of the dot products (see exercise 1) of F with
    every group of components of D that are adjacent. For example, if D contains

```
1    7    3    4    2
```

and F contains

```
0.2   0.6   0.2
```

then

$$\begin{aligned}
\text{Convolution} &= 1 * 0.2 + 7 * 0.6 + 3 * 0.2 \\
&\quad + 7 * 0.2 + 3 * 0.6 + 4 * 0.2 \\
&\quad + 3 * 0.2 + 4 * 0.6 + 2 * 0.2 \\
&= 5.0 + 4.0 + 3.4 \\
&= 12.4
\end{aligned}$$

Write a Pascal program which has as its input two integers M and N followed by
M real numbers comprising the D array and N real numbers comprising the F
array. Compute the convolution and display the result.

Example input:

```
5   3   1.0   7.0   3.0   4.0   2.0   0.2   0.6   0.2
```

Example output:

The convolution is 1.2400000e+01

★★★ CHALLENGING PROBLEMS

7 This problem is related to problem 6. We wish to compute the convolution again, but this time we define it to be the sum of all dot products that can be formed between D and F, including "wrap around" at the end of D. Using the same data as problem 6, we would additionally include

4 * 0.2 + 2 * 0.6 + 1 * 0.2
+ 2 * 0.2 + 1 * 0.6 + 7 * 0.2

making the value of the convolution 17.0. The forms used for the input and output are the same as in problem 6.

8 The input data contains positive integers M and N, no larger than 10, followed by the M rows of an M-row, N-column array of integers. This is followed by an integer P and P additional integers. Write a program which locates a match between the P integers read last and any sequence of contiguous integers in the M by N array in any row, column, or diagonal, forwards or backwards. If such a match cannot be found, then print an appropriate message. Otherwise, print the indices of the component of the M by N array where the match begins and the direction in which the match was found. (An even more challenging problem is to find all possible matches.)

Example input:

```
3  4
4  7  9  3
6  6  2  0
3  1  2  3
3
1  2  3
```

Example output:

Match begins at row 3, column 2 on upward diagonal, going right.

or

Match begins at row 3, column 2 on row going right.

(For the more challenging problem, both of these lines would be displayed.)

9 The input data contains pairs of lines. Each line contains a representation of an integer which (probably) exceeds *maxint*. Display each pair of integers and their sum. The number of digits in a single integer will not exceed 50.

Example input:

```
4000000000000000000000000001
7499999999999999999999999999
```

Example output:

```
 4000000000000000000000000001
 7499999999999999999999999999
11500000000000000000000000000
```

CHAPTER 10
CHARACTER STRING
PROCESSING

Strings
and Packed
Arrays

String
Processing
Routines

Problem
Solving

Conformant
Array
Parameters

CHARACTER
STRING
PROCESSING

OBJECTIVES

After completing this chapter, you should be able to:

- Recognize and apply packed arrays
- Recognize and apply string variables
- Recognize and apply the standard procedures *pack* and *unpack*
- Write string processing routines in standard Pascal
- Solve, test, and debug problems using strings
- Recognize and apply conformant array parameters to string operations [optional]

CHAPTER OVERVIEW

In the early years of computer programming (in the 1950s) computers were used principally for numeric data processing. However, in the past 20 years, nonnumeric data processing has emerged as a major source of computer applications. Text editors, language translators, user-friendly software, and large databases consisting of character data are just a few sources for nonnumeric data processing. In this chapter the emphasis is on character string processing. In particular, we show how character strings and string variables can be used most effectively when declared as *packed arrays* of characters. String variables can be written as one item with a single *write* statement, and not character by character as with an unpacked array of characters. Another advantage of string variables is that we can compare them using the relational operators. We will also discuss two standard procedures in Pascal that permit us to move between the packed and unpacked data formats: *pack* and *unpack*.

Unfortunately, standard Pascal does not include string-manipulating functions or procedures. In Section 10.2 we present techniques for writing string processing routines. We will apply some of the techniques to a problem involving a text editor in Section 10.3.

The chapter concludes with an optional section on conformant array parameters with applications to string operations.[1] Conformant array parameters permit the processing of variable length array parameters which can be quite effective and useful when writing string processing procedures.

SECTION 10.1 CHARACTER STRINGS AND PACKED ARRAYS

In the last chapter we showed how to declare an array of characters. For example, the declaration

```
TYPE
    word = ARRAY [1..6] OF char;
VAR
    firstname : word;
```

---

[1]Conformant array parameters are included in the ISO standard for the Pascal language, but not in the ANSI standard. Most standard Pascal systems will include conformant arrays.

declares an array of six characters. Using this declaration, six assignment statements and six memory locations would be required to store the name *BLAISE*, one location per character (see Figure 10-1).

Packed Arrays

For many computer systems this is a waste of memory, especially if the character array is very large. Therefore Pascal permits us to declare a ***packed array*** of characters. This suggests to the Pascal system that as many characters as possible should be packed into each memory location (or ***word***). The number of characters packed into a memory location varies with the particular computer system. Typical values on minicomputers are two characters packed per word, while on larger systems four characters may be stored in a single word. So if we use the declaration

```
TYPE
      word = PACKED ARRAY [1..6] OF char;
VAR
      firstname : word;
```

instead of the previous declaration, then the assignment statement would require only two words instead of six on a computer system that packs four characters per word. Figure 10-2 shows the word *BLAISE* packed into two words. Note that it is only necessary to include the reserved word PACKED prior to the reserved word ARRAY. A packed array of characters with a lower subscript of 1 is also known as a ***character string***. Variables declared as packed arrays of characters are called ***string variables***. So far we have already discussed character strings known as string constants. For example, the statement

```
writeln ('Beginning of execution')
```

includes a string constant 'Beginning of execution' which is stored as a packed array.

Figure 10-1   Storage of character array.

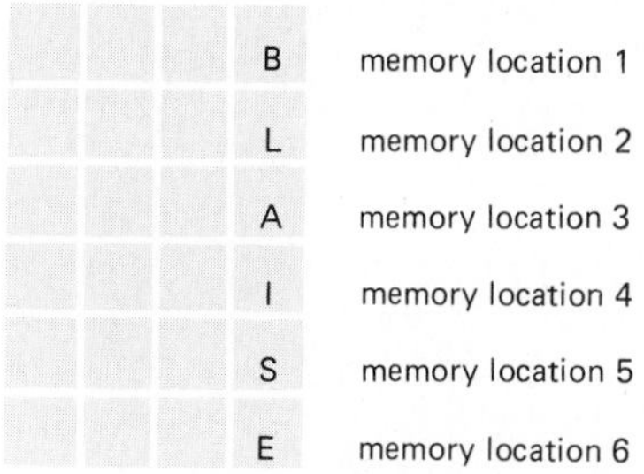

B	memory location 1
L	memory location 2
A	memory location 3
I	memory location 4
S	memory location 5
E	memory location 6

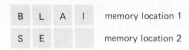

| B | L | A | I | | memory location 1 |
| S | E | | | | memory location 2 |

Figure 10-2 Packed array.

One virtue of using packed arrays is that a string constant or variable can be displayed directly, as the string constant above, instead of character by character. The following *write* statement will display the name contained in the string variable *firstname*, declared above as a packed array:

```
write (firstname)
```

Without the packed array definition we would have to write the contents of *firstname* character by character, as in the following code segment:

```
FOR i := 1 TO 6 DO
      write (firstname[i])
```

Packed array elements can be read just like unpacked arrays, one component at a time. For example, the following is acceptable in standard Pascal for the packed array *firstname:*

```
FOR i := 1 TO 6 DO
      read (firstname[i])
```

However, some nonstandard implementations do not permit a component of a packed array to appear as a parameter to *read* or *readln*. Instead, we must first read data into an unpacked variable and then assign the value obtained to the component of the packed array. For example, suppose we wish to read 15 characters from an input line (we assume there are at least that many) and then display them. The following is typical coding that must be used for input of packed arrays:

```
TYPE
      word = PACKED ARRAY [1..15] OF char;
VAR
      index : integer;                          (* array index *)
      first15 : word;               (* the packed array variable *)
      achar : char;                  (* an unpacked character *)
FOR   index := 1 TO 15 DO
BEGIN
      read (achar);
      first15[index] := achar
END;
writeln (first15)
```

Note that the *writeln* statement displays the contents of the packed array directly and without using any subscripts. Later in this section we show how the standard (built-in) procedure *pack* can be used to copy an unpacked array into a packed array without processing each character individually in a loop. When a value is assigned to an entire packed array in an assignment statement, the value must have *exactly* the same number of characters as the variable. For example, if a constant is involved, then the number of characters between the single quotes must be exactly the same as the number of characters in the packed array representing the string variable:

```
VAR
     string1 : PACKED ARRAY [1..6] OF char;
     string2 : PACKED ARRAY [1..8] OF char;
     string3 : PACKED ARRAY [1..6] OF char;
string1 := 'Pascal';
string2 := 'Standard';
```

It is typical to add extra blanks at the end of a string constant if it is to be assigned to a string variable with more characters:

```
string2 := 'Four_ _ _ _
```

String variables may be assigned to other string variables, but the same restriction applies. Thus, the assignment statement

```
string3 := string1
```

is correct, but the assignment statement

```
string2 := string1
```

is not. Note that string variables are not automatically padded with blanks when they are assigned the value of a packed array or string constant with a smaller number of elements. It is also important to recall that string variables *must* have a lower subscript of 1.

Another important advantage of using character strings as packed arrays is that they can be compared directly using the relational operators ($=$, $<$, $>$, $<=$, $>=$, and $<>$). The alternative is to compare the characters in the strings one by one, making for a tedious task, indeed.

The relations that hold between character strings is typified by the examples shown below.

'CAR'	$<$	'DOG'
'pig'	$>$	'cat'
'KENNEDY'	$>$	'JOHNSON'
'JOHNSEN'	$<$	'JOHNSON'

Blanks and upper- and lowercase letters can cause difficulty in understanding string comparisons. On most systems the blank character precedes all alphabetic characters in comparisons. Therefore, the following relation is true on such systems:

'JOHNSEN' > 'JOHN   '

Be careful, however, when mixing upper- and lowercase alphabetic characters in comparisons. If your system uses ASCII (see Appendix F), then the following relation will hold:

'Cat' < 'boy'

On the other hand, if your system uses EBCDIC, the opposite is true:

'boy' < 'Cat'

The ordering of strings is similar to the ordering of words in a dictionary. When comparing strings, the computer compares the ordinal values (the same that would be returned from the *ord* function) of characters from corresponding positions in each string from left to right, one by one, until the relation between the strings can be determined. As long as the character from one string is exactly the same as the corresponding character from the other string and there are more characters in each string, the comparison continues. If all the corresponding characters are identical, then the strings are equal. Otherwise, the relation that holds between the first pair of characters that are not identical defines the relation that holds between the strings.

Consider, for example, the comparison between 'KENNEDY' and 'JOHNSON'. The comparison proceeds as shown below. The relation that holds between each pair of characters is also shown.

```
K   E   N   N   E   D   Y
>   <   >   =   <   <   >
J   O   H   N   S   O   N
↑
```

This is the only comparison completed.

As soon as the computer determines that the first characters from the strings are not identical ('K' > 'J'), the relation between the strings is determined. Note that none of the relations between characters to the right of the first inequality can affect the relation between the strings. Therefore we see that 'AZZZZ' is less than 'ZAAAA', since 'A' is less than 'Z'. Strings that have different lengths cannot be compared directly. For example, it is improper to write

IF 'ABCD' < 'ABC'   (* incorrect *)

One way to compare strings that have different lengths is to append blanks to the end of the shorter string to make it the same length as the longer string. The preceding comparison could then be written

IF 'ABCD' < 'ABC '   (* correct, padded with blank *)

So far, we have found that string variables (declared as packed arrays of characters with a lower subscript of 1) have the following advantages over unpacked arrays:

1   Strings can be displayed as a single item in a *write* or *writeln* statement, instead of the character by character display necessary when unpacked arrays are used.
2   Strings can be compared directly, usually requiring less execution time than the comparison of unpacked arrays of characters.
3   In some systems, strings conserve storage space.

Unfortunately, there are some disadvantages when string variables are used:

1   While entire packed arrays may be used as parameters, components of packed arrays may not. However, a component of a packed array may be assigned to a component of an unpacked array or a simple variable, or vice versa. Thus the packed component can be copied to a simple variable, passed as a parameter, and then copied back to the packed component after the procedure invocation.
2   If the program requires frequent conversion between packed and unpacked arrays, execution time can be greater than if packed arrays were not used at all.

When you are deciding whether to use unpacked arrays or their packed counterparts, many factors must be considered. The volume of data to be manipulated, the available memory, execution time requirements, and the particular Pascal system being used all may influence the choice. Some implementations of Pascal may store packed and unpacked data in the same format, especially when the number of characters per word is one. In these cases, there appears to be no apparent advantage to using a packed array over the unpacked equivalent. But, in fact, there is! If a program is to be portable, it should be easy to move from one computer system to another. If the Pascal system originally used does not require packed data, the programmer is tempted to omit the word PACKED and ignore the restrictions imposed by packed arrays. If such is the case and the program is moved to a different computer that does have the packed array restrictions, much time will be spent modifying the program to conform with the requirements. This is due to the use of nonstandard Pascal features; try to avoid their use if possible.

Other Pascal arrays may be packed, too. For example,

TYPE
        survey = PACKED ARRAY [1..128] OF Boolean;

might result in a considerable savings of space. Strings, however, are the most frequently encountered packed structured data.

Standard Pascal Procedures: *Pack* and *Unpack*

Another way to move data into a packed array is to copy the contents of an unpacked array directly using the standard procedure *pack*. Suppose, for example, we want to read the first 15 characters of an input line (as in a previous example). If the declarations

```
TYPE
     word = PACKED ARRAY [1..15] OF char;
     unword = ARRAY [1..15] OF char;
VAR
     namepack : word;
     name : unword;
     index : integer;
```

are used, then the Pascal segment

```
FOR index := 1 TO 15 DO
     read (name[index]);
pack (name, 1, namepack)
```

will place the first 15 characters into the packed array variable *namepack*. The pack procedure effectively causes the same actions as

```
FOR index := 1 TO 15 DO
     namepack[index] := name[index]
```

but requires less explicit coding.

The standard procedure *pack* has the general form

```
pack (uarray, start, parray)
```

where *uarray* is the name of an unpacked array, *start* is an expression (of the same type as the index of *uarray*), and *parray* is a packed array (whose components are of the same type as those of *uarray*). Essentially the pack procedure causes the components of the unpacked array *uarray*, starting with the element specified by *start*, to be assigned, in order, to the components of the packed array *parray*. All components of the packed array are filled, so it is necessary that there be enough components in the unpacked array after and including the component indexed by *start* to fill the packed array. For example,

```
pack (name, 2, namepack)
```

will fail, since there are only 14 components between *name[2]* and *name[15]* and 15 are required to fill the packed array *namepack*.

The standard procedure *unpack* serves to perform the opposite function. In the invocation

unpack (parray, uarray, start)

the parameters *parray*, *uarray*, and *start* have the same interpretation as for the pack procedure, but the effect is for all components of the packed array *parray* to be copied, one by one, into the unpacked array *uarray* starting at index *start*. Again, there must be at least as many components from position *start* to the end of the unpacked array as there are in the packed array; otherwise, an error will occur. To reverse the packing operation

pack (uarray, 1, parray);

we would write

unpack (parray, uarray, 1);

EXERCISES FOR SECTION 10.1

1   Determine which of the assignments are valid given the declaration

```
TYPE
    word = PACKED ARRAY [1..15] OF char;
    sentence = PACKED ARRAY [1..80] OF char;
VAR
    worda, wordb : word;
    sent : sentence;
```

(a)   worda := wordb
(b)   worda := sent
(c)   worda[1] := 'A'
(d)   sent[1] := worda[15]
(e)   wordb := 'The word is OM!'

2   Which of the following is *not* an advantage of packed arrays?
(a)   The time required by the computer to access a particular element is shorter than with a normal array.
(b)   Packed arrays of the same type can be compared directly.
(c)   The array may take up less computer memory.
(d)   Packed arrays of char can be assigned a string of the same length.

(e) Packed arrays of char can be used as parameters to the *write* and *writeln* procedures.

3 Write a function called *compare* that returns a value of -1 if a packed array of 20 characters called *worda* precedes a similar array called *wordb*; returns a value of 0 if *worda* = *wordb*; and returns a value of 1 if *worda* follows *wordb*. Include the appropriate TYPE definitions.

4 Consider the following function:

```
TYPE
      word = PACKED ARRAY [1..80] OF char;
FUNCTION something (VAR aword : word) : integer;
CONST
      blank = ' ';
VAR
      temp : integer;
BEGIN
      temp := 81;
      REPEAT
          temp := temp - 1
      UNTIL (aword[temp] <> ' ') OR (temp = 1);
      IF (temp = 1) AND (aword[1] = blank)
      THEN something := 0
      ELSE something := temp
END;
```

Can you describe what the function is computing?

5 What is displayed by the following procedure if the actual parameter is *aword* = 'lacsap'?

```
TYPE word = PACKED ARRAY [1..6] OF char;
PROCEDURE what (VAR aword : word);
VAR
      ctemp : char;
      temp : ARRAY [1..6] OF char;
      index : integer;
BEGIN
      unpack (aword, temp, 1)
      FOR index := 1 TO 3 DO
      BEGIN
          ctemp := temp (index);
          temp (index):= temp (7 - index);
          temp (7 - index) := ctemp
      END;
```

```
        pack (temp, 1, aword);
        writeln ('The word is', aword)
END;
```

SECTION 10.2 STRING PROCESSING

In this section we examine a number of typical problems encountered when manipulating character string data. Standard Pascal does not include any string manipulation
functions or procedures, but some implementations may include nonstandard features
to accomplish these tasks. Currently, however, there are no standard facilities for
achieving such tasks.[2]

As our first problem, let's consider obtaining a person's full name from the input
data, placing it in a packed array.

Problem 10.1

Write a Pascal procedure readname *which will obtain a person's full name and
store it in a packed array. The maximum number of characters in the full name
will be no more than 50, and the end of the name in the input data is immediately
followed by an end of line. If the name is not exactly 50 characters long, then the
trailing characters in the packed array must be blank. For example, the input data
line*

```
Franklin D. Roosevelt<eoln>
```

would result in the packed array receiving the value

```
'Franklin D. Roosevelt
```

*which contains exactly 50 characters. If the name contains more than 50 characters,
the excess will be truncated, or left out of the name.*

The following procedure will correctly solve this problem, assuming the type

```
TYPE
      string = PACKED ARRAY [1..50] OF char;
```

has been globally defined.

---

[2]The standards for the Pascal programming language may be revised in the future to include a new data
type, operators, and standard procedures or functions to permit manipulation of character strings.

```
PROCEDURE readname (VAR fullname : string);
(* Read a full name terminated by <eoln> into fullname. *)
VAR
        j, index : integer;
        inchar : char;
BEGIN
        index := 0;
        WHILE NOT eoln AND (index < 50) DO
        BEGIN
                index := index + 1;
                read (inchar);
                fullname[index] := inchar
        END;
        (* Fill unused characters, if any, with blanks. *)
        FOR j := index + 1 TO 50 DO
            fullname[j] := ' ';
        readln
END;
```

Now suppose we wish to read a list of names, one per line, into an array of strings. We will assume that the list of names is terminated by an end of file and that no more than 100 names will be processed. The following procedure will accomplish this task, assuming the types

```
TYPE
        string = PACKED ARRAY [1..50] OF char;
        list = ARRAY [1..100] OF string;
```

have been globally defined. The parameter size will be set to the number of names actually read and stored in the array.

```
PROCEDURE readlist (VAR table : list; VAR size : integer);
(* Read a list of no more than 100 names terminated by *)
(* end of file, one name per line, no more than 50      *)
(* characters per name. The number of names read is     *)
(* returned in the variable size.                       *)
BEGIN
        size := 0;
        WHILE NOT eof AND (size < 100) DO
        BEGIN
            size := size + 1;
            readname (table[size])
        END
END;
```

Problem 10.2

Write a Pascal program that reads a list of names and then displays them in the order opposite to that in which they were read.

We assume the procedures *readname* and *readlist* from above. The program then could be written as follows.

```
PROGRAM reverser (input, output);
(* Read a list of no more than 100 names of 50 characters    *)
(* or less. Then display them in the order opposite to        *)
(* that in which they were read.                              *)
TYPE
      string = PACKED ARRAY [1..50] OF char;
      list = ARRAY [1..100] OF string;
VAR
      table : list;            (* the names in the order read *)
      nnames : integer;             (* the number of names *)
      namendx : integer;      (* index to name being printed *)
PROCEDURE readname . . .        (* as previously defined *)
PROCEDURE readlist . . .        (* as previously defined *)
(* Main Program *)
BEGIN
      readlist (table, nnames);          (* read the names *)
      FOR namendx := nnames DOWNTO 1 DO
            writeln (table[namendx])     (* display one name *)
END.
```

The operation of the program is quite straightforward, once the procedures *readname* and *readlist* are available. A sample of the input and output obtained when the program is executed appears below.

```
George Washington<eoln>         James Madison
John Adams<eoln>                Thomas Jefferson
Thomas Jefferson<eoln>          John Adams
James Madison<eoln>             George Washington
<eof>
```

The next problem will extract and display the first name of each full name in a list.

Problem 10.3

Write a Pascal procedure to display the first name of each full name appearing in the list of full names passed as a parameter.

The following procedure will perform the task. The procedure assumes the first blank character encountered separates the first and last names. Assume the declarations from the previous problems and that a first name has a maximum of 15 characters.

```
PROCEDURE extract (VAR table : list; size : integer);
(* Extract and display the first name from each full name *)
(* in table[1] to table[size], where the size of the list    *)
(* is passed as a value parameter.                           *)
CONST
      blanks = '                 ';    (* 15 blanks *)
TYPE
      word = PACKED ARRAY [1..15] OF char;
VAR
      firstname : word;              (* a first name *)
      achar : char;          (* one character of a name *)
      j,     (* subscript of the full name being processed *)
      index : integer;         (* subscript to first name *)
BEGIN
      FOR j := 1 TO size DO          (* for each name *)
      BEGIN
          firstname = blanks;     (* initialize with blanks *)
          index := 0;             (* no characters yet *)
          achar := table[j, 1];      (* get first letter *)
          WHILE (achar <> ' ') AND (index < 15) DO
          BEGIN
              index := index + 1; (* get another char *)
              firstname[index] := achar;      (* move it *)
              achar := table[j, index + 1]     (*get next
                                                    char*)
          END;
          writeln (firstname)    (* display the first name *)
      END
END;
```

If we invoke the procedure with the same input data as used in the previous example, the output would contain just what we expected:

```
George
John
Thomas
James
```

Concatenation

Concatenation is a very common string operation that joins two strings together, end to end, to form a single string. For example, suppose we have the following strings:

string1 = 'Today is'
string2 = ' the day before tomorrow.'

Then the concatenation of the two strings would be

'Today is the day before tomorrow.'

Here are some further examples of concatenation.

string1	string2	concatenation
'Tom '	'Jones'	'Tom Jones'
'I am '	'thirty'	'I am thirty'
'25'	'Main St.'	'25Main St.'
'ABC'	'DEF'	'ABCDEF'
'A'	'?'	'A?'

Our next problem is to write a procedure to concatenate two strings.

Problem 10.4

Write a procedure to concatenate two strings. The formal parameters should be the two strings and their lengths, together with the output string and its length. Assume all strings have a maximum length of 80 characters, and verify that the output string has no more than 80 characters.

The following procedure will solve this problem assuming we have the global TYPE definition

```
TYPE
      string = PACKED ARRAY [1..80] OF char;

PROCEDURE join (VAR string1, string2, result : string;
                length1, length2 : integer;
                VAR lengthr : integer);
(* Concatenate string1 and string2 (of length1 and length2 *)
(* characters respectively) to form result. Length1 plus    *)
(* length2 should be less than or equal to 80.               *)
VAR
      index : integer;
```

```
BEGIN
    IF length1 + length2 > 80
    THEN writeln ('ERROR in join: result > 80 characters.')
    ELSE BEGIN
                    result := string1;          (* copy string1 *)
                    (* append string2 to result *)
                    FOR index := 1 TO length2 DO
                        (* copy a char from string2 to result *)
                        result[length1+index] := string2[index];
                    lengthr := length1 + length2
            END
END;
```

The string-manipulating routines presented so far require the maximum string length to be a constant value. This is due to the requirement that a formal array parameter match exactly the type used for the actual array parameter. Later in this chapter we present general string-manipulating routines that permit the manipulation of strings whose maximum sizes differ using only standard Pascal.

EXERCISES FOR SECTION 10.2

1 Concatenate the following strings:
   (a) '2 + 2' and ' = 4'
   (b) 'The time' and 'is now'
   (c) '2500' and 'Rice Blvd.'
   (d) 'New York' and ', New York'
   (e) 'blank' and 'blank'

2 Write a function called *blankcount* that returns the number of blank characters in a packed array of 80 characters called *sentence*.

3 Which of the following methods will read in a packed array of char and fill in the remainder of the string with blanks. The end of the string is indicated by the end of an input line. Assume that the type of the array is as follows:

```
CONST
    max = 20;
    blank = ' ';
TYPE
    strtype = PACKED ARRAY [1..max] OF char;
VAR
    str : strtype;
    i : integer;
    total : real;
```

(a) read (str);

(b) i := 1;
     WHILE (i < max) AND (NOT eoln) DO
          read (str[i]);
     WHILE (i < max) DO
          str[i] := blank;

(c) FOR i := 1 TO max DO
          read (str[i]):

(d) i := 1;
     WHILE (i <= max) AND (NOT eoln) DO
     BEGIN
          read (str[i]);
            i := i + 1
     END;
     WHILE (i <= max) DO
     BEGIN
          str[i] := blank;
            i := i + 1
     END;

(e) FOR i := 1 TO max DO
     IF NOT eoln
     THEN read (str[i]);

4   What is displayed by the following procedure if the input parameter *aword* is
    'JOHN BROWN'?

```
TYPE word = PACKED ARRAY [1..10] OF char;
PROCEDURE who (VAR aword : word);
VAR
        count : integer;
BEGIN
        FOR count := 1 TO 5 DO
            aword[count] := ' ';
        writeln (aword);
        FOR count := 1 TO 5 DO
            aword[count] := aword[count + 5];
        writeln (aword);
        FOR count := 1 TO 5 DO
            aword[count + 5] := ' ';
        writeln (aword)
END;
```

5   Write a procedure similar to procedure *extract* that will extract the last name from
    each full name in a list. Assume each name is of the form used in problem 10.3:

Mamie Eisenhower

In this section we solve a problem that relies heavily on character strings. First, let us look at the problem definition:

Problem 10.5

The Portable Software Company specializes in the development of software that can be used on a variety of computer systems. The company would like to develop a simple text editor that is portable. Consequently, it has decided to write the program in standard Pascal. The text editor should be able to:

- Read a text file line by line, assuming a maximum of 72 characters per line and a maximum of 500 lines
- Delete any number of lines from the text
- Insert any number of lines into the text
- List or display any number of lines and their line numbers
- Substitute new lines for old lines
- Obtain help on available commands
- Terminate execution.

Write the standard Pascal program that will perform these tasks.

We can subdivide this problem into several subproblems:

SUBPROBLEM 1: Read the input text.
SUBPROBLEM 2: Read a command.
SUBPROBLEM 3: Process the command.

Subproblem 1 can be solved using techniques similar to those presented in the previous section for reading a list of full names from the input.

Subproblem 2 will read a legal command. We will abbreviate the commands to their first letter: D for delete, I for insert, L for list, S for substitute, H for help, and T for terminate.

Subproblem 3 will process the command using a CASE statement to select the actions. Each command will cause an appropriate procedure to be executed. The delete, insert, list, and substitute commands require line number references. They are followed by two integers, m and n, indicating the lines to be manipulated. The table below describes the actions of the editor in response to some sample commands.

command	editor action
D 2 3	Delete lines 2 through 3.
I 3 5	Insert 3 lines before line 5.
L 2 5	List lines 2 through 5.
S 5 10	The next six input lines replace lines 5 through 10.

The algorithm for the text editor is expressed by the following pseudocode.

Text Editor Algorithm

Read the input text.
Read a command.
While the command is not T (terminate):
    Read the integers *m* and *n*, if not H command
    Case command of:
        D: Delete lines *m* through *n*.
        I: Insert *m* lines before line *n*.
        L: List lines *m* through *n*.
        S: Substitute for lines *m* through *n*.
        H: Display brief command summary.
        Other: Display an appropriate error message.
    Read the next command.

The main program will contain the following TYPE definitions:

```
CONST
     maxfilesize = 500;
TYPE
     string = PACKED ARRAY [1..72] OF char;
     block = ARRAY [1..maxfilesize] OF string;
```

To read the text, we will read in one line at a time, searching either for an end-of-line character or a maximum of 72 characters. This is repeated until the end of the text is encountered or the maximum number of lines permitted in the file is read. We will assume the end of the text is indicated by any line that begins with two periods ('..'). This line is not a part of the text. It is a sentinel.

The procedure *readtext* will perform this task, thereby solving subproblem 1. The procedure *readtext* will call another procedure, *readline*, to read each line. This is similar to the organization used in processing the full names of a group of individuals.

```
PROCEDURE readline (VAR newline : string);
(* Read a line terminated by <eoln> into newline *)
VAR
     chrcount : integer;
     inchar : char;
BEGIN
     FOR chrcount := 1 TO 72 DO          (* Initialize line *)
          newline[chrcount] := ' ';      (* with blanks. *)
     chrcount := 0;
     WHILE NOT eoln AND (chrcount < 72) DO
     BEGIN
```

```
                        chrcount := chrcount + 1;
                        read (inchar);
                        newline[chrcount] := inchar
            END;
            readln
END;

PROCEDURE readtext (VAR textfile : block; VAR numlines : integer);
(* Read the existing text file (up to "..") and count lines. *)
VAR
        done : Boolean;
BEGIN
        numlines := 0;
        done := false;
        WHILE NOT done AND (numlines < maxfilesize) DO
        BEGIN
        numlines := numlines + 1;
        readline (textfile[numlines]);
        (* Check for the end of text sentinel, "..". *)
        IF (textfile[numlines,1] = '.') AND
          (textfile[numlines,2] = '.')
        THEN BEGIN
                done := true;
                numlines := numlines - 1 (* don't count .. *)
                END
        END
END;
```

We will first code the delete procedure. It can best be explained with an example. Suppose we have 10 lines of text. We want to delete lines 2 through 5. One way to perform the deletion is to shift lines 6 though 10 up (toward line 1) four lines, so that line 6 becomes line 2, line 7 becomes line 3, and so forth. The last line would now be line 6, since 4 lines were deleted from the original 10.

In general, deletion of lines m through n causes those lines following the deleted text to be shifted upward over the deleted text. The lines to be shifted are numbered $n + 1$ through *filesize*. Finally, *filesize* is reduced by $(n - m + 1)$, the number of deleted lines.

The parameters of the procedure include the array containing the lines of text, the line numbers to be deleted (m and n, where $m <= n$), and the number of lines currently in the file (*filesize*).

```
PROCEDURE delete (VAR textfile : block; VAR filesize : integer;
                        m, n : integer);
(* Delete lines m through n of the text, where *)
(*m <= n <= filesize.                          *)
```

```
VAR
        index, j : integer;
BEGIN
        (* Shift lines n + 1 to last line up n-m + 1 lines. *)
        FOR index := n + 1 TO filesize DO
        BEGIN
                j := index − (n + 1);
                textfile [m + j] := textfile[index]
        END;
        (* Recompute the file size. *)
        filesize := filesize - (n − m + 1)
END;
```

The insert procedure can also be explained with an example. The command I 2 5 is used to request the insertion of two lines before line 5. This requires that lines 5 through the last line (*filesize*) be shifted down two lines, so that line 5 becomes line 7, line 6 becomes line 8, and so forth. The new lines will become lines 5 and 6.

In general, to insert *m* lines before line *n*, we will shift lines *n* through *filesize* down *m* lines, then insert the *m* new lines of text, and finally recompute *filesize* by adding *m*. Note that shifting must begin with the last line and *not* the first line. Otherwise, the second line to be shifted would be destroyed (or overwritten) before it can be shifted.

```
PROCEDURE insert (VAR textfile : block; VAR filesize : integer;
                        m, n : integer);
(* Insert m lines prior to line n of the text, where   *)
(* m + filesize <= maxfilesize, and n <= filesize.    *)
VAR
        index : integer;
BEGIN
        (* Shift lines n to last line down m lines. *)
        FOR index := filesize DOWNTO n DO
            textfile [index + m] := textfile[index];
        (* Read m lines and insert into the textfile. *)
        FOR index := 1 TO m DO
            readline(textfile[n + index-1]);
        (* Recompute the file size. *)
        filesize := filesize + m
END;
```

The list procedure will display lines *m* through *n*, assuming *m* <= *n*. The lines will be prefixed by their line numbers.

```
PROCEDURE list (VAR textfile : block; m, n : integer);
(* List lines m through n, for m <= n <= filesize   *)
(* with prefixed line numbers.                       *)
```

```
VAR
     index : integer;
BEGIN
     FOR index := m TO n DO
          writeln (index:3, ': ', textfile[index])
END;
```

The substitute procedure will replace lines *m* through *n* with the same number of new lines.

```
PROCEDURE subst (VAR textfile : block; m, n : integer);
(* Substitute new lines for current lines m through n     *)
(* where m <= n <= filesize.                              *)
VAR
     index : integer;
BEGIN
     (* Call readline repeatedly to get replacement lines. *)
     FOR index := m TO n DO
     readline (textfile[index])
END;
```

Procedure *help* will have no parameters and just displays a brief message about each of the available commands.

```
PROCEDURE help;
(* Display a brief description of each available command. *)

BEGIN
     writeln ('Available commands:');
     writeln ('       D m n        Delete lines m through n');
     writeln ('       I m n        Insert m lines before line n');
     writeln ('       L m n        List lines m through n');
     writeln ('       S m n        Substitute for lines m through n');
     writeln ('       H            Display this help message');
     writeln ('       T            Terminate execution')
END;
```

The main program is relatively straightforward. We have but to read commands, validate the parameters, and call the appropriate procedures to effect the editing.

```
PROGRAM editor (input, output);
(*************************************************************)
(* A simple text editor with the following commands:     *)
(*   D m n     delete lines m through n                  *)
```

```
(*  I m n      insert m lines before line n            *)
(*  L m n      list lines m through n                  *)
(*  S m n      substitute for lines m through n        *)
(*  H          display a command summary               *)
(*  T          terminate execution                     *)
(*"m" and "n" are positive integers, and have some     *)
(* restrictions as noted in the code. The original     *)
(* file to be edited appears as input terminated by    *)
(* a line beginning with two periods.                  *)
(*****************************************************)
CONST
        maxfilesize = 500; (* maximum number of lines *)
(* text of the error messages *)
        message0 = 'Sorry, this is an unknown command.';
        message1 = 'No; first line # exceeds last line #.';
        message2 = 'No; maximum file size would be exceeded.';
        message3 = 'No; first line # exceeds file size.';
        message4 = 'No; last line # exceeds file size.';
        message5 = 'No; line numbers must be greater than 0.';
TYPE
        string = PACKED ARRAY [1..72] OF char;
        block = ARRAY [1..maxfilesize] OF string;
VAR
        textfile : block;
        filesize : integer;
        command : char;
        m, n : integer;
(* Each procedure mentioned below must be inserted here. *)
PROCEDURE readline . . .
PROCEDURE readtext . . .
PROCEDURE delete . . .
PROCEDURE insert . . .
PROCEDURE list . . .
PROCEDURE subst . . .
PROCEDURE help . . .
(* Main Program *)
BEGIN
        writeln ('Editor');
        writeln ('Type H for help');
        readtext (textfile, filesize);
        write ('Command: ');
        read (command);
        WHILE command <> 'T' DO       (* Terminate command? *)
        BEGIN
                (* No, so test for another valid command. *)
                IF command IN ['D', 'I', 'L', 'S', 'H']
```

```
            THEN CASE command OF
                (* the delete command *)
        'D': BEGIN
                readln (m, n);
                IF m > n
                THEN writeln (message1)
                ELSE IF n > filesize
                    THEN writeln (message4)
                    ELSE IF m < 1
                        THEN writeln (message5)
                        ELSE delete (textfile, filesize, m, n)
            END;


        (* the insert command *)
        'I': BEGIN
                readln (m, n);
                IF filesize + m > maxfilesize
                THEN writeln (message2)
                ELSE IF n > filesize
                    THEN writeln (message3)
                    ELSE IF n < 1
                        THEN writeln (message5)
                        ELSE insert (textfile, filesize, m, n)
            END;
        (* the list command *)
        'L': BEGIN
                readln (m, n);
                IF m > n
                THEN writeln (message1)
                ELSE IF n > filesize
                THEN writeln (message3)
                    ELSE IF m < 1
                        THEN writeln (message5)
                        ELSE list (textfile, m, n)
            END;


        (* the substitute command *)
        'S': BEGIN
                readln (m, n);
                IF m > n
                THEN writeln (message1)
                ELSE IF n > filesize
                    THEN writeln (message3)
                    ELSE IF m < 1
                        THEN writeln (message5)
                        ELSE subst (textfile, m, n)
            END;
```

```
                (* the help command *)
            'H': BEGIN
                    help;
                    readln      (* skip end of line *)
                END
            END (* case *)
       ELSE (* if not 'D', 'I', 'L', 'S', or 'H' *)
           BEGIN
                    writeln (message0);
                    readln (* skip parameters, if any, and eoln *)
           END;
          write ('Command: ');
          read (command)
     END
END.
```

SECTION 10.4 CONFORMANT ARRAY PARAMETERS AND STRINGS [OPTIONAL]

Standard Pascal is frequently criticized for its lack of built-in, or standard, procedures or functions to manipulate character strings. Therefore, many Pascal implementations have nonstandard extensions for character string processing. This is unfortunate for two reasons. The first is that there is little, if any, standardization of these facilities. A programmer using any of these nonstandard facilities will be unable to move his or her work from one machine to another without investing significant effort. The second reason that nonstandard extensions are unfortunate is that standard Pascal *does* include facilities that permit their processing!

The "secret" to character string processing in standard Pascal is the conformant array parameter. This facility allows us to write procedures that can have array parameters with variable index ranges. Later in this section we will examine a collection of procedures that can perform a variety of standard operations on variable length character strings with different maximum lengths.

Conformant Array Parameters

As you know, entire arrays can be passed as parameters to procedures and functions as long as the actual parameters have exactly the same type as the formal parameters. Thus the size of the array in the actual parameter must match the size of the formal parameter. For example, suppose a procedure called *readstring* reads a string of 80 characters. The following declarations and procedure header would be appropriate:

```
TYPE
     string = PACKED ARRAY [1..80] OF char;
```

```
VAR
     line : string;
PROCEDURE readstring (VAR aline : string);
```

A typical procedure invocation could then be written as

```
readstring (line);
```

Suppose we have the additional declarations

```
TYPE
     small = PACKED ARRAY [1..25] OF char;
VAR
     linepart : small;
```

We cannot use procedure *readstring* as it was originally formulated to read *linepart*, since *linepart* does not have exactly the same type as the formal parameter of *readstring*, *aline*. With the Pascal features we have seen this far, we would find it necessary to write several procedures to read strings, one for each string length we wished to read. This is clearly a poor solution, especially since standard Pascal provides a better one.

The solution provided by standard Pascal is to allow the index limits of formal array parameters to be variable. The effective array parameter then includes not only the array but the actual index limits. Let us look at an example for the procedure *readstring*. The new procedure header might be

```
PROCEDURE readstring
     (VAR aline : PACKED ARRAY [start..finish:integer] OF char);
```

Now we could invoke procedure *readstring* with both *readstring (line)* and *readstring (linepart)*. In the first of these invocations, *readstring* would have the bounds *start* and *finish* set to 1 and 80, respectively, while in the second invocation the bounds would be 1 and 25.

Only a few restrictions apply to the use of conformant array parameters. The first restriction is that only the last dimension in a multidimensional array may be packed. This, of course, presents no real difficulty. The second restriction is that the number of dimensions, the component type, and the base type of the array indices must be the same. Thus we may use any subscript bounds we wish for the actual parameter as long as the formal parameter subscript bounds have the same base type. Additional restrictions are similar to those we might expect for other parameter types. For example, we cannot use an unpacked array as an actual parameter when the corresponding formal parameter is packed, and vice versa.

The exact syntax of a conformant array parameter is given by the syntax diagram in Appendix A. In general, though, such a parameter is formed by writing the formal parameter name, a colon, and either ARRAY or PACKED ARRAY followed by the bracketed bounds. The bounds are represented by two identifiers separated by "..", followed by a colon and the base type of the bounds. To represent multidimensional array parameters, the bounds are repeated (inside the brackets) separated by semicolons. For example, any unpacked two-dimensional array of reals with integer subscripts would be acceptable as an actual parameter for the procedure *solver* whose procedure header is

```
PROCEDURE solver
    ( mat : ARRAY [low1..high1 : integer; low2..high2 : integer] OF real);
```

The formal parameter type does look complex, but it is really very simple. The first dimension's bounds are *low1* and *high1* (integers), and the second dimension's bounds are *low2* and *high2* (again integers). If we wanted to compute the sum of the real numbers in the array parameter we would write

```
sum := 0;
FOR index1 := low1 TO high1 DO
    FOR index2 := low2 TO high2 DO
        sum := sum + mat[index1,index2];
```

where *sum* is a real variable and *index1* and *index2* are integer variables.

String Operations

As an illustration of the use of conformant array parameters, we will write a series of string-manipulating procedures and functions that can be quite useful. In fact, few of the nonstandard Pascal compilers provide any more facilities than those presented here. In particular, we will examine procedures and functions to perform the following tasks:

- Copy a string constant or variable into another string (procedure *strcpy*).
- Create a zero-length string (procedure *strnul*).
- Determine the length of a string constant or variable (function *strlen*).
- Concatenate two strings (procedure *strcat*).
- Compare two strings (function *strcmp*).
- Extract a substring from a given string (procedure *substr*).
- Compute the position of the first occurrence of a given string in a second string (function *index*).
- Determine the first character in a string that is not also a character of a second string (function *verify*).
- Read a line into a string (function *rdline*).
- Display the contents of a string (procedure *putstr*).

There are two attributes of our strings that we would like to allow to vary. The first of these is the maximum number of characters in the string, and the second is the actual number of characters in the string. When we declare a string variable like

```
VAR
    astring : PACKED ARRAY [1..40] OF char;
```

we know that there will always be 40 characters in the string and the string can only be passed to procedures and functions with parameters of the same type. Using conformant array parameters will permit us to use different values for the maximum number of characters in the string and still use the same procedures and functions for each. But just because we have declared the array so it can store 40 characters does not mean that we will always have 40 valid characters. For example, suppose a string is used to store a person's last name. By specifying an upper limit of 40 characters for the variable, we are limiting names to 40 characters, but most names will require less than this. How do we indicate that the trailing characters are not really part of the name?

To do this, we must either implicitly or explicitly include a length specification in our character strings. To indicate the length implicitly, we would choose an otherwise unused character (for example, *chr(0)* on many machines) and arrange to have it appear immediately following the last "real" character in our data. If we stored the name 'Zarkov' in our 40-character array using implicit length specification, we would have the following arrangement of characters:

'Z'	'a'	'r'	'k'	'o'	'v'	chr(0)	?	?	. . .	?
1	2	3	4	5	6	7	8	9	. . .	40

Characters in positions 8 through 40 in this array are shown as question marks because we do not know, and do not care, what characters are stored there. Our special terminator, *chr(0)*, indicates that characters after that position are really not part of the string.

The explicit length specification requires that we allocate one (or more) of the characters in the string to store the length. For example, if we use the first character in the string to store the length, then 'Zarkov' would appear as follows:

chr(6)	Z	a	r	k	o	v	?	. . .	?
1	2	3	4	5	6	7	8	. . .	40

Note that the length is stored as a character whose ordinal value is the number of "real" characters in the string.

Both of these techniques require at least one additional character in the string to indicate the length. In addition, the implicit approach requires that we not use the special terminator character as a data character. The explicit approach limits the number of characters in the string to the largest ordinal value permitted for a character (typically 255) unless we consume two or more characters of the string to store its length. You should be aware, though, that these are the techniques, used in nonstandard Pascal implementations and other programming languages, for indicating the length of string variables, and therefore standard Pascal actually permits you to select which of the two techniques you wish to use.

In the procedures and functions that follow, we have chosen to use an implicit terminator character. The particular ordinal value used is specified by a global constant *terminator*. In the remainder of this section we will present a discussion of each of the procedures and functions, followed by a complete program that uses them to solve a real problem. The actual code for the procedures and functions appears in the program.

Procedure *Strcpy*

If we wish to copy a string variable or constant into a second string variable, we can use procedure *strcpy*. If the string being copied is longer than the number of characters permitted in the result string, the excess characters will be lost.

Procedure *Strnul*

In Pascal you may not write ''; that is, there is no string constant of zero length. You may ask why a zero-length string is useful. You will see an example of such a string in the problem at the end of this section, but in general, we can use a null, or zero-length, character string much like we use 0 in arithmetic addition. For example, if we concatenate the null string and a string S, the result is always the same as string S. The null string indicates that none of the characters in the string variable have significance. Procedure *strnul* allows a string variable to represent the null string by storing the terminator character in the first position of the packed array parameter.

Function *Strlen*

This function allows us to determine the number of characters actually used in a string variable. It does this task by counting the number of characters prior to the terminator, returning this count as its result.

Procedure *Strcat*

We have already examined the basic operation of string concatenation, and procedure *strcat* performs the same operation in the environment of our variable-length character strings. The algorithm used is very similar to that presented previously.

Function *Strcmp*

Function *strcmp* allows us to compare two character string variables even though they may not have the same current or maximum lengths. The code explicitly compares the characters of the two strings, one by one, until either all character pairs have been processed or an unequal pair of characters are encountered.

Procedure *Substr*

Procedure *substr* allows us to extract an arbitrary number of characters from any starting position in a string variable. This permits us, for example, to examine pieces of a character string, and, once located, to store a substring of interest in a separate character string variable for further processing. Alternately, it can be used to remove part of a string we no longer want by extracting (to a second string) the part we want to keep.

Function *Index*

Function *index* requires two character string variables as parameters. If we call them *search* and *find*, then the result is the position in *search* of the first occurrence of *find*. For example, suppose *search* contained 'MISSISSIPPI', and *find* contained 'SS'. Then "find (search, find)" would yield the integer value 3, since the string 'SS' occurs first starting at position 3 in 'MISSISSIPPI'. If the *find* string does not occur in *search*, then *index* returns zero. *Index* is frequently used to locate blanks in a string of words, so the individual words can be extracted using *substr*.

Function *Verify*

Function *verify* is frequently used to perform the inverse operation to that of *index*. It, too, requires two arguments, a string *search* to be searched and a string *nset* containing characters to be bypassed in *search*. Essentially, *verify* returns an integer indicating the position of the first character in *search* that is occupied by a character *not* in *nset*. If all characters in *search* also appear somewhere in *nset*, then *verify* will return zero. For example, suppose we want to locate the first nonblank character in a string. Then *nset* will contain the single character ' '. If all characters in the search string are blank, then *verify* returns zero. Otherwise, it returns the position of the first nonblank character.

Function *Rdline*

Function *rdline* will read an entire line of input data into a string variable supplied as a parameter (as a side effect). It will terminate after reading the end-of-line character and return the number of characters in the line. It will return -1 if the end of file was encountered.

Procedure *Putstr*

Procedure *putstr* will display the characters in its single parameter on the output file. No end of line is written, so multiple strings can be placed on a single output line.

A Complete Problem—Tabulating Word Usage

As an illustration of the use of these procedures and functions, let us write a complete Pascal program to produce an alphabetized list of the words used in a document supplied as input data. In addition, we will compute the number of occurrences of each word. For simplicity, we will define a word as any sequence of nonblank characters separated from other words by blanks, tabs, or end-of-line characters. A problem similar to this was presented in Chapter 6, but the actual words were not recorded or alphabetized.

```
PROGRAM sortword (input, output);
(* Read a varying length text and produce a sorted list of all *)
(* words (sequences of characters bracketed by blanks, tabs,   *)
(* and <eoln>s) and their frequency of occurrence.             *)
CONST
        terminator = 0;           (*suitable for computers using ASCII*)
        maxwords = 100;           (*maximum number of unique words*)
        maxwordlength = 20;       (*maximum word length + 1*)
        maxlinelength = 81;       (*maximum line length + 1*)
TYPE
        word = PACKED ARRAY [1..maxwordlength] OF char;
VAR
        words : ARRAY [1..maxwords] OF word;          (*the words*)
        counts : ARRAY [1..maxwords] OF integer;      (*the counts*)
        line : PACKED ARRAY [1..maxlinelength] OF char;(*the input line*)
        aword : word;                                 (*the current input word*)
        blank : PACKED ARRAY [1..2] OF char;          (*a single blank*)
        nwords : integer;                             (*number of unique words*)
(* Strcpy (b,a) will copy a string (a) into a string variable   *)
(* (b). If the length of a is such that it will not fit in b,   *)
(* it is truncated. Note that this procedure will work with     *)
(* either a string constant or a properly formed string        *)
(* variable.                                                    *)
PROCEDURE strcpy
        (VAR outstr : PACKED ARRAY [outlo..outhi:integer] OF char;
        instr : PACKED ARRAY [inlo..inhi:integer] OF char);
VAR
        i,j : integer;
        ch : char;
        more : Boolean;
BEGIN
        i := inlo;
        j := outlo;
        more := true;
```

```
(* Copy from instr[j] to outstr[i] as long as i is less    *)
(* than or equal to outstr's length, and j is less than    *)
(* or equal to instr's length, AND the terminator          *)
(* hasn't been copied.                                     *)
WHILE (more AND (i <= inhi) AND (j <= outhi)) DO
BEGIN
         outstr[j] := instr[i];
         IF ord(outstr[j]) <> terminator
         THEN BEGIN
                 i := i + 1;
                 j := j + 1
              END
         ELSE more := false         (* terminator copied okay *)
    END;
  IF more                            (* no terminator yet copied *)
  THEN IF j <= outhi
        THEN outstr[j] := chr(terminator)    (* no truncation *)
        ELSE outstr[outhi] := chr(terminator)    (* truncation *)
END; (*strcpys*)
(* Since it is impossible to represent a null string as a        *)
(* PASCAL constant, a special procedure is used to store null *)
(* in a string.                                              *)
PROCEDURE strnul
    (VAR outstr : PACKED ARRAY [outlo..outhi:integer] OF char);
BEGIN
    outstr[outlo] := chr(terminator)
END; (*strnul*)


(* This procedure will print a string character by character *)
(* on text file f.                                           *)
PROCEDURE putstr (VAR f : text;
              instr : PACKED ARRAY [inlo..inhi:integer] OF char);
VAR
     i : integer;
     more : Boolean;
BEGIN
     more := true;
     i := inlo;
     WHILE (more AND (i <= inhi)) DO
              IF instr[i] = chr(terminator)            (* terminator? *)
              THEN more := false           (* yes, no more to display *)
              ELSE BEGIN
                         write(f, instr[i]);        (* display 1 char *)
                         i := i + 1      (* increment the pointer *)
```

```
END; (* putstr *)

(* strlen will return the length of a string argument *)
FUNCTION strlen
    (instr : PACKED ARRAY [inlo..inhi:integer] OF char) : integer;
VAR
    i : integer;
    more : Boolean;
BEGIN
    more := true;
    i := inlo;
    WHILE (more AND (i <= inhi)) DO
        IF instr[i] = chr(terminator)        (* found terminator? *)
        THEN more := false                   (* yes, end of string *)
        ELSE i := i + 1;                     (* no, increment pointer *)
    strlen := i - inlo                       (* compute string length *)
END;

(* strcat (a,b) will concatenate the string b onto the end of *)
(* string a                                                   *)
PROCEDURE strcat (VAR a : PACKED ARRAY [alo..ahi:integer] OF char;
                b : PACKED ARRAY [blo..bhi:integer] OF char);
VAR
    i,j: integer;
    more : Boolean;
BEGIN
    i := strlen(a) + 1;          (* i is index of first unused char in a *)
    j := blo;                    (* j is index of first char in b *)
    more := true;
    (* Copy each character of b to end of a, while b isn't *)
    (* completely copied, and space remains in a.         *)
    WHILE (more AND (i <= ahi) AND (j <= bhi)) DO
    BEGIN
        a[i] := b[j];                        (* copy one character *)
        IF ord(a[i]) <> terminator           (* end of b? *)
        THEN BEGIN          (* no, update pointers to strings *)
                i := i + 1;
                j := j + 1
            END
        ELSE more := false    (* yes, terminator copied okay *)
    END;
    IF more                     (* no terminator yet copied *)
    THEN IF i <= ahi
```

```
              THEN a[i] := chr(terminator)          (* no truncation *)
              ELSE a[ahi] := chr(terminator)        (* truncation *)
END; (*strcat*)


(* Strcmp (a, b) returns − 1, 0, or + 1 depending on whether *)
(* a < b, a = b, or a > b. The longer of two strings of *)
(* unequal length is always larger. *)
FUNCTION strcmp (a : PACKED ARRAY [alo..ahi:integer] OF char;
                 b : PACKED ARRAY [blo..bhi:integer] OF char ) : integer;
VAR
      i, j, rslt : integer;
BEGIN
      i := alo;
      j := blo;
      rslt := 99;             (* rslt is 99 until an inequality is found *)
      WHILE (rslt = 99) DO          (* until an inequality isn't found *)
      BEGIN
            IF a[i] = b[j]                  (* are the characters equal? *)
            THEN IF (a[i] = chr(terminator))    (* yes, end of strings? *)
                    OR (i = ahi) AND (j = bhi)
                THEN rslt := 0              (* end of both strings *)
                ELSE IF i = ahi        (* not end of both strings *)
                    THEN rslt := −1     (* end a, not end b *)
                    ELSE IF j = bhi
                        THEN rslt := 1  (* end b, not end a *)
                        ELSE  BEGIN     (* not end of either
                                                   string *)
                              i := i + 1; (*both have more *)
                              j := j + 1
                              END
            ELSE IF a[i] < b[j]                  (* strings not equal *)
                THEN rslt := −1
                ELSE rslt := 1
      END;
      strcmp := rslt
END; (* strcmp *)


(* Substr (a, b, i, n) will assign to string "a" "n"          *)
(* characters from string "b" starting with the "i"th          *)
(* character of "b". If "n" characters cannot be stored in a,   *)
(* then the excess will be truncated. If "i" is outside the     *)
(* range 1 to strlen(b), or "n" is less than 1, then a null     *)
(* string will be stored in a. Finally, if "n" characters       *)
(* cannot be extracted from "b", the maximum number that can    *)
```

```
(* be extracted will be stored (unless truncated due to length     *)
(* of a).                                                          *)
PROCEDURE substr (VAR a : PACKED ARRAY [alo..ahi:integer] OF char;
                 b : PACKED ARRAY [blo..bhi:integer] OF char; i, n :
                 integer);
VAR
     j, lb : integer;
BEGIN
     lb := strlen(b);
                     (* validate i and n, and test for very small result string *)
     IF (i < 1) OR (i > lb)                (* i outside allowable range *)
         OR (n < 1)                                        (* n < 1*)
         OR (ahi = alo)                 (* a can only hold a terminator *)
     THEN strnul (a)                    (* set a to result for these cases *)
     ELSE BEGIN
                IF lb < i + n - 1     (* can't get n characters *)
                THEN n := lb - i + 1;      (* adjust downward *)
                IF n > ahi - alo            (* a can't hold it all *)
                THEN n := ahi - alo;
                j := alo;       (* j tells where to store next char *)
                WHILE n > 0 DO    (* while more chars in substr *)
                BEGIN
                   a[j] := b[i];           (* copy one character *)
                   i := i + 1;                (* increment pointers *)
                   j := j + 1;
                   n := n - 1 (* reduce number left to copy *)
                END;
                a[j] := chr(terminator)    (* put terminator in a *)
            END
END;
(* Index (a, b) will return an integer representing the       *)
(* leftmost position of string b in string a. If b does not   *)
(* occur as a substring in a, then the result of the function *)
(* is zero.                                                   *)
FUNCTION index (
            a : PACKED ARRAY[alo..ahi:integer] OF char;
            b : PACKED ARRAY[blo..bhi:integer] OF char) : integer;
VAR
     i,j,k,la,lb : integer;
     found : Boolean;
BEGIN
     la := strlen(a);
     lb := strlen(b);
     IF lb > la                          (* if b is longer than a *)
```

```
                THEN index := 0                    (* then it can't be found in a *)
                ELSE BEGIN
                        i := 1;              (* start with substr at first char of a *)
                        found := false;
                        (* continue until found, or no more matches are possible  *)
                        WHILE (NOT found AND (i <= la - lb + 1)) DO
                        BEGIN
                                j := alo + i - 1;
                                k := blo;
                                found := true;        (* assume we'll find it here *)
                        (* test each character of b with the substr of a at i *)
                                WHILE (found AND (k <= blo+lb-1)) DO
                                        IF a[j] <> b[k]   (* oops, we failed here *)
                                        THEN found := false
                                        ELSE BEGIN   (* got a match, move to
                                                                   next chars *)
                                                j := j + 1;
                                                k := k + 1
                                        END;
                                IF NOT found
                                THEN i := i + 1
                        END;                (* if we failed, move on to next substr *)
                        IF found            (* if we succeeded, then return the index *)
                        THEN index := i
                        ELSE index := 0                        (* else return zero *)
                END
END; (* index *)


(* verify (a,b) returns the index of the leftmost character in          *)
(* a that is not in b. If all characters in a also appear in            *)
(* b, then verify returns zero.                                         *)
FUNCTION verify (a: PACKED ARRAY [alo..ahi:integer] OF char;
                b: PACKED ARRAY [blo..bhi:integer] OF char) : integer;
VAR
        i, la : integer;
        c : PACKED ARRAY [1..2] OF char;
        more : Boolean;
BEGIN
        la := strlen(a);
        IF strlen(b) = 0                                (* special cases *)
        THEN IF la = 0
                THEN verify := 0          (* if b and a are null return 0 *)
                ELSE verify := 1             (* first char of a not in b *)
        ELSE BEGIN
                        c[2] := chr(terminator); (* c is a 1 char string *)
```

```
                    i := 1;
                    more := true;
                    WHILE ( (i <= la) AND more) DO
                    BEGIN
                            c[1] := a[alo+i-1]; (* get a character *)
                            IF index(b,c) > 0              (* is c in b? *)
                            THEN i := i + 1               (* looking *)
                            ELSE more := false (* no, we can quit *)
                    END;
                    IF more         (* if all chars in b were also in a *)
                    THEN verify := 0
                    ELSE verify := i    (* otherwise yes, keep return
                                               index of mismatch *)

            END
END; (* verify *)
(* Getline will read the next line from text file f into        *)
(* string a. If the entire line will not fit, then it is        *)
(* truncated. If an end of file is encountered before an end *)
(* of line, the function leaves the part of the line before     *)
(* the eof in a, and returns false. Otherwise it returns        *)
(* true.                                                        *)
FUNCTION getline (VAR f : text;
    VAR a : PACKED ARRAY [alo..ahi:integer] OF char) : Boolean;
VAR
        c : char;
        i : integer;
BEGIN
        i := alo;
        WHILE NOT (eof(f) OR eoln(f)) DO (* if not finished *)
        BEGIN
                read (f, c);
                IF i < ahi                      (* if space left in string *)
                THEN BEGIN
                        a[i] := c;       (* move in the new character *)
                        i := i + 1       (* update the string length *)
                    END
        END;
        a[i] := chr(terminator);               (* terminate the string *)
        IF eoln(f)
        THEN BEGIN
                readln(f);                       (* skip end of line *)
                getline := true                  (* and return true *)
            END
        ELSE getline := false                 (* otherwise return false *)
END; (*getline*)
```

```
(* nextword obtains the next word of the text and returns *)
(* true, or returns false at the end of file              *)
FUNCTION nextword ( VAR theword : word ) : Boolean;
VAR
        more : Boolean;
        i : integer;
        line2 : PACKED ARRAY [1..maxlinelength] OF char;
BEGIN
        more := true;
        WHILE more AND (verify (line, blank) = 0 DO
        BEGIN
                more := getline (input,line);          (* get the next line *)
                IF more                            (* if not yet end of file *)
                THEN BEGIN
                        (* replace each tab character by a blank *)
                        FOR i := 1 TO strlen(line) DO
                            IF line[i] = chr(9)
                            THEN line[i] := ' ';
                        strcat (line, blank)
                    END
        END;
        IF more
        THEN BEGIN
                i := verify (line, blank);       (* find first nonblank *)
                        (* store line w/o leading blanks into line2 *)
                substr (line2, line, i, strlen(line)-i + 1);
                i := index (line2, blank);          (* find first blank *)
                    (* store the word (all characters prior to blank) *)
                substr (theword, line2, 1, i-1);
                        (* store line2 w/o the leading word into line *)
                substr (line, line2, i, strlen(line2)-i + 1)
            END;
        next word := more
END; (* nextword *)


PROCEDURE initialize;
BEGIN
        strnul (line);                        (* no current input line is present *)
        nwords := 0;                              (* no words in the table yet *)
        blank[1] := ' ';                   (* blank is a string with only one blank *)
        blank[2] := chr(terminator);
END;
(* Update will locate the entry for a word in the table and    *)
(* update its count by 1. If the word is not yet in the table  *)
(* and space permits, the new word will be added at the end    *)
```

```
(* and its count will be set to 1. If no space exists, then a    *)
(* new word is "lost."                                           *)
PROCEDURE update( newword : word );
VAR
        found, more : Boolean;
        i : 0..maxwords;
BEGIN
        found := false;
        i := 1;
        more := i <= nwords;         (* more is false if table is empty *)
        WHILE NOT found AND more DO (*while more searching to do*)
        BEGIN
                IF strcmp(newword, words[i]) = 0    (* is this the word? *)
                THEN BEGIN
                        found := true;    (* yes, so we can quit *)
                        counts[i] := counts[i] + 1(* update count *)
                     END
                ELSE IF i < nwords               (* no match yet *)
                        THEN i := i + 1         (* but more to search *)
                        ELSE more := false       (* no more to search *)
        END;
        IF NOT found AND (nwords < maxwords)    (* if not found, and *)
        THEN BEGIN                              (* there's space for a new word *)
                nwords := nwords + 1;     (* increase word count *)
                strcpy (words[nwords], newword);    (* add the new
                                                        word *)
                counts[nwords] := 1         (* its been used once *)
             END
END; (* update *)


(* sort will perform an insertion sort of the words and counts *)
PROCEDURE sort;
VAR
        i, j, max : integer;
        temp : word;
BEGIN
        FOR i := nwords DOWNTO 2 DO
        BEGIN
                max := 1;
                FOR j := 2 TO i DO
                        IF strcmp(words[max],words[j]) = -1
                        THEN max := j;
                strcpy (temp, words[i]);
                strcpy (words[i], words[max]);
```

```pascal
            strcpy (words[max], temp);
            j := counts[i];
            counts[i] := counts[max];
            counts[max] := j
      END
END; (* sort *)


(* Ptbl will display the table of words and counts. The         *)
(* headings are automatically adjusted for different maximum *)
(* word lengths.                                                *)
PROCEDURE ptbl;
VAR
      i,j,n : integer;
BEGIN
      (*Display the headings for the table. *)
      (* Compute # of blanks to place on either side of "word" *)
      (* so it will be centered in "maxwordlength" columns. *)
      n := (maxwordlength − 4 (* strlen('Word') *) ) DIV 2;
      FOR i := 1 TO n DO write(' ');
      write('Word');
      FOR i := n+5 TO maxwordlength DO write(' ');
      writeln(' Count');
      FOR i := 1 TO maxwordlength DO write(' − ');
      writeln('     -----');
      FOR j := 1 TO nwords DO
      BEGIN
            putstr(output,words[j]);                  (* display a word *)
            FOR i := strlen(words[j]) + 1 TO maxwordlength + 5 DO
                  write(' ');                    (* space to correct column *)
            writeln(counts[j]:5)                  (* display the count *)
      END
END; (* ptbl *)


(* Main Program *)
BEGIN
      initialize;                                        (* setup for processing *)
      WHILE nextword(aword) DO update(aword);         (* count words *)
      sort;                          (* sort the words in ascending sequence *)
      ptbl                          (* display the words and occurrences *)
END.
```

One of the most common problems encountered in dealing with character strings in Pascal is failing to realize that character string constants really represent packed arrays of characters with a lower subscript bound of 1. This means that these constants cannot be assigned to unpacked arrays or packed arrays with lower subscript bounds other than 1. In addition, the upper subscript bound of the packed array variable used on the left side of an assignment statement must be exactly the same as the number of characters in the string constant or variable on the right side. For example, if we assume the declarations

```
VAR
     string10 : PACKED ARRAY [1..10] OF char;
     xstring10 : PACKED ARRAY [0..9] OF char;
```

then the assignment statements

```
string10 = '0123456789'
```

and

```
string10 = 'Nebraska    '
```

are valid, but

```
string10 = 'New Hampshire'
string10 = 'Iowa'
```

and

```
xstring10 = 'HoursLater'
```

are not. The same rules apply to string comparisons. While we can write

```
'Pascal' > 'Modula'
```

we cannot write

```
'Apples' <> 'Oranges'
```

since the strings do not have the same lengths. All these problems are eliminated when we perform the operations using the procedures and functions presented in the last section.

    The difference between upper- and lowercase characters can also cause confusion. Since these characters have different ordinal values, they are not equal. For example, if we compare the string constants 'UPPER' and 'upper', we will find they are not equal, and even worse, the comparison can yield different results on different machines! That is, many machines may report that 'UPPER' is smaller than 'upper', but on other machines 'UPPER' is greater than 'upper'. If you are writing code that you expect to be portable, you must pay particular attention to this problem area to ensure that code involving character comparisons will not yield unexpected results.

If fixed-length character strings are used to store data that is not necessarily as long as the fixed-length string, then the unused characters in the string should always be initialized to a constant value, usually blank. This can be accomplished in two ways. First, a string can be set in its entirety to blanks prior to storing actual data characters in it. This is the simplest of the two approaches but is more expensive since some characters in the string are referenced twice, once to store a blank and second to store the actual data. The second approach is to fill part of the string with the actual data and then store blanks in the unused portion. This is more efficient but is also more complicated since a loop must be used to store the blanks. Both these techniques have been illustrated in the programs shown in this chapter.

A final problem we mention has to do with the number of characters allowed in character variables. For example, suppose we are writing a program to deal with names of persons. We may anticipate that the longest last name an individual may have is 15 characters, but many persons may have longer last names. If we fail to check array bounds when storing characters into a string, a subscript error may occur. On the other hand, if we use procedures and functions similar to those presented in Section 10.4, we may lose data due to truncation of long names. Truncation is not always an error, but if it is a possibility, then our coding should include explicit tests for this condition and corrective actions to be invoked when truncation is detected.

Here is a list of important Pascal reminders regarding strings.

PASCAL REMINDERS

- Packed arrays are declared with the reserved words PACKED ARRAY.
- A component of a packed array cannot be passed as a variable parameter to a function or procedure.
- String variables are declared as

  PACKED ARRAY [1..maximum length] OF char;

  The lower subscript bound of string variables must be 1.
- The standard Pascal procedures *pack* and *unpack* can be used to convert between packed arrays and unpacked arrays.
- String variables and constants of the same size and type can be assigned directly and compared using the relational operators.
- Conformant array parameters can be used to pass variable-length array parameters.
- The component type of a conformant array parameter can be any element type, including another conformant array.

In this chapter we have discussed character strings and string variables declared as packed arrays of characters. Strings can be written or displayed entirely by a single *write* statement, without having to display the string character by character. However, strings must be entered as input character by character. Strings can be compared using the relational operators. We also discussed two standard Pascal procedures, *pack* and *unpack*, that can be used to convert entire arrays between packed and unpacked formats.

Application of strings to a variety of problems was also included in this chapter. Several string processing routines, including concatenation, were written and discussed. A simple text editor was written as an example of problem solving using strings. Conformant array parameters were discussed and applied to a variety of string manipulating routines. These routines were then used to solve a large string processing problem.

The following is a summary of the Pascal features discussed in this chapter, and can be used for future reference.

PASCAL REFERENCE

1 Packed array: An array whose components may be packed closer together than usual to save storage at the possible expense of processing speed.

Example declaration:

```
VAR
      string : PACKED ARRAY [1..10] OF char;
```

2 String variables: A packed array variable.

- Can be written using a single *write* or *writeln* statement:

  ```
  writeln (string);
  ```

- Can be compared with other strings or string constants using the usual relational operators:

  ```
  string > 'California'
  ```

- Can be assigned the value of a string constant or string variable with the same length:

  ```
  string := 'Washington'
  ```

3 Standard pascal procedures:

- "pack (uarray, start, parray)" copies enough characters starting with unpacked array element *uarray[start]* to fill the packed array *parray*.
- "unpack (parray, uarray, start)" copies all characters of the packed array *parray* to the unpacked array *uarray* starting at *uarray[start]*.

4 Conformant array parameters: Permit arrays with a variety of subscript bounds to be used as parameters to a single procedure or function by providing the function with the lower and upper subscript bounds of the array parameter. Example:

```
PROCEDURE strlen (VAR s :
    PACKED ARRAY [low..high : integer] OF char);
```

Chapter 11 Preview

In the next chapter we continue our discussion of structured data types by considering records. Unlike arrays, the components of a record may have differing data types. Arrays allow us to process similarly typed items as a group, but sometimes we want to process data items of different types as a group. As you will see, many problems, such as a student record system, can make effective use of the record data type.

Keywords for Chapter 10

character string
concatenation
conformant array parameter
pack
packed array
string
string variable
unpack
word

CHAPTER 10 EXERCISES

★ ESSENTIAL EXERCISES

1 Will the following segment be acceptable to standard Pascal? If so, what is the result of executing the segment? If not, why? Assume *c* is declared as a character variable and *n* as an integer.

```
n := 0;
FOR c := 'A' TO 'Z' DO n := n + 1
```

2 Determine whether the following expressions are valid or invalid. If an expression is valid, determine the type and value its result.

(a) ord('A') − ord('B')
(b) chr(−3) + 4
(c) 'Smith' = 'SMITH'
(d) 'A' = 'A'
(e) ord('Toll Free')
(f) 'MESSAGE'[4]
(g) ord(succ (chr (9)))

3   As you probably know, a string like 'STORAGE' actually has exactly the same data type as

```
PACKED ARRAY [1..7] OF char;
```

and therefore a variable of this type can be assigned such a constant. Therefore, the segment

```
VAR s7 : PACKED ARRAY [1..7] OF char;
s7 := 'STORAGE';
```

is completely legal.
Why, then, is the following code not permitted?

```
VAR s1 : PACKED ARRAY [1..1] OF char;
s1 := ' ';
```

4   Many computer systems store arrays of characters as tightly packed as possible without explicitly specifying the keyword PACKED. If you use a computer system where this is the case, why would you bother using PACKED ARRAYs at all?

5   Assuming the declarations

```
VAR
      string : PACKED ARRAY [1..10] OF char;
      c : char;
      i : integer;
```

what output is produced by the following program segment?

```
string := '0123456789';
FOR i := 1 TO 10 DO
BEGIN
      c := string[i];
      IF NOT odd (ord(c) − ord('0'))
      THEN string[i] := ' '
END;
writeln (string:10)
```

★★ SIGNIFICANT EXERCISES

6 In Pascal, single quotes may be used to enclose one or more characters, but not zero characters, as in ''. Some languages do permit this, and treat it correctly as a null character string. Why do you think standard Pascal does not permit this constant?

7 Assume a string contains four characters representing a 24-hour time (that is, between '0000' and '2359'). Write a Pascal segment that creates an eight-character string representing the corresponding 12-hour time, a colon separating the hours and minutes, a blank, and the appropriate letters *AM* or *PM*. For example, the string '1200' would result in '12:00 PM', and '0159' would result in '01:59 AM'.

★★★ CHALLENGING EXERCISES

8 Write a procedure *addcomma* which has two parameters. One parameter is an integer in the range 1 to 999999. The second parameter is to be set to the character representation of the integer, right justified, with a comma in the appropriate position if the value requires more than three digits. For example, if the integer is 999, then the character string returned should be '   999'. If the integer is 19999, then the string should be ' 19,999'.

9 Standard Pascal does not permit Boolean variables to appear as parameters in *read* or *readln* procedure invocations. Write a Boolean function *getBool* which skips leading blanks, tabs, and end-of-line characters and then returns true if the next character is 'T' or 't', and false otherwise.

CHAPTER 10 PROBLEMS FOR COMPUTER SOLUTION

★ ESSENTIAL PROBLEMS

1 Write a Pascal program that will convert an input text file containing tab characters by replacing the tab characters with the appropriate number of blanks. Each tab character is to be replaced by the number of blanks (at least one but no more than eight) that will make the total number of characters currently in the output line a multiple of eight.

Example input (tabs are represented by ^I:

This^Iis^Ia^Itest.<eoln>
^I^ISo is this!^I <eoln>

Example output:

This   is   a   test.<eoln>
        So is this!   <eoln>

2 The program does the inverse operation performed by the program requested in problem 1. Replace as many blanks as possible in the input data by tab characters.

Example input:

> Another   strange   personality.

Example output:

^I Another^I strange^I personality.

3   Write a program to center and underline a title read from the first line of the input. Centering the title can be done by first determining the number of characters in the title, subtracting that from the width of the output line, and then displaying half that number of blanks followed by the title. Underlining is accomplished by printing a minus sign under each nonblank character in the title.

Example input:

To Wake The Dead

Example output (assume an 80-character line):

```
To Wake The Dead
-- --  --- ----
```

4   Write a program to convert each occurrence of a decimal digit in the input data to its English equivalent, leaving unchanged all other characters.

Example input:

There were 4 values, specifically 7, 9,
3, and 0. The result had 10 digits.

Example output:

There were four values, specifically seven, nine, three, and zero. The result had onezero digits.

★★ SIGNIFICANT PROBLEMS

5   Each of the five lines in the input data contains a representation of a playing card as two strings separated by at least one blank and possibly preceded or followed by additional blanks. Determine what value the hand would have in a game of poker.

Example input:

```
9 SPADE   <eoln>
8    DIAMOND<eoln>
QUEEN CLUB<eoln>
   10  CLUB    <eoln>
JACK HEART
```

Example output:

STRAIGHT

6 Each line of an input file contains a name in the form last name, comma, and first name. There will be no blanks within the last or first name, but they may appear elsewhere. Write a Pascal program to read the names, sort them on last name and first name, and then display them, first name first.

Example input:

```
Charno, Fred
      Baker ,Huey
Favori , Sue
      Welch , Noah
Prono, Belle
```

Example output:

```
Huey Baker
Fred Charno
Sue Favori
Belle Prono
Noah Welch
```

★★★ CHALLENGING PROBLEMS

7 An instructor wants a program to score multiple-choice examinations. An input data file is provided which has the answer key and the responses of each student. Each line has student identification information in the first nine columns, followed by a variable number of responses. The student identification number in the first line is to be ignored, as the responses represent the correct answers to the questions. Responses are uppercase alphabetic characters or blank. Blank is used to indicate that a question is not to be scored. The remaining lines in the input represent student responses. Student responses to questions not indicated in the answer key should be ignored. Write the program that will score the exams, providing the student identification, number of correct responses, and percentage score for each student.

Example input:

```
      ADABECC DBE  ⟨eoln⟩
808732533ADABECCDDBEF⟨eoln⟩
808749266ABADEFBDABEC D⟨eoln⟩
813555121ADBCECCDDCAD⟨eoln⟩
```

Example output:

```
Student        Correct   Percentage
808732533        10         100
808749266         5          50
8113555121        6          60
```

8 Write a program to index all variable declarations in a Pascal program. Assume a limited form of variable declaration; the example input shows valid declaration forms. The output should include each variable name and the line number of the program where the declaration was encountered. Optionally sort the list by variable name, and include the type of each variable.

Example input:

```
VAR v1, v2 : integer;
VAR
    v5  ,  v6  :
        real;
VAR     v3,v4  ,v7:char;
```

Example output (with type extensions):

```
v1        integer      1
v2        integer      1
v3        char         5
v4        char         5
v5        real         3
v6        real         3
v7        char         5
```

CHAPTER 11

CHAPTER 11
RECORDS

Records

Hierarchical
Records
and Arrays
of Records

Problem
Solving

Variant
Records

RECORDS

OBJECTIVES

After completing this chapter, you should be able to:

- Recognize and apply the record structured data type
- Declare and apply hierarchical records (nested records)
- Declare and apply arrays of records
- Recognize and apply the WITH statement
- Sort an array of records
- Recognize and apply variant records [optional]
- Solve, test, and debug problems using records

CHAPTER OVERVIEW

Our discussion of structured data types will continue with the introduction of *records.*
Records are similar to arrays in the sense that they consist of components. But unlike
arrays, the components of a record can be of different data types. For example, a
record of a student's background may include name and address (packed array data
types), age (integer), grade point average (a real number), and class: freshman, sophomore, junior, or senior (an enumerated type).

In the Section 11.1 we show how records can be constructed using a TYPE definition
and a variable declaration. Methods used to access the different components of a
record are described. Records can contain arrays as components, as well as other
records. They can be nested, and a discussion of nested records is presented in Section
11.2. Recall that the component of an array can be any data type, including structured
types such as records. We will study arrays of records in detail. Accessing components
of complex structures, such as arrays of nested records, can lead to long and tedious
expressions. Pascal includes the WITH statement to simplify this process. We will
consider some examples in Section 11.2.

In the problem-solving section, we study the problem of sorting an array of records.
This problem differs from our previous sorting problem in two ways: the components
are records instead of integers and the items to be sorted are character strings located
inside each record. An optional section on variant records is also included. Variant
records are records containing a variant part of components that can change during
the execution of the program. The Testing and Debugging Techniques section includes
some common problems associated with records.

SECTION 11.1 RECORDS

An array consists of a number of components, each of the same type. However, there
are many applications where the components of a structured type should be of different
data types. To handle such cases, Pascal includes a structured data type known as a
record. For example, suppose a marketing company specializes in consumer surveys.
The information this company usually needs is the following:

Person's name (maximum of 35 characters)

Zip code (integer)

Age (integer)

Telephone number (12 characters)

Response (agree or disagree)

This information can be suitably placed in a Pascal record by using the following definition and declaration:

```
TYPE
    consumer = RECORD
                        name: PACKED ARRAY [1..35] OF char;
                        zipcode: 0..99999;
                        age: 21..99;
                        telephone: PACKED ARRAY [1..12] OF char;
                        response: (agree, disagree)
                END;
VAR
    person : consumer;
```

In the TYPE definition, the record type identifier *consumer* is followed by an equal sign and a semicolon-separated list of component descriptions called ***record sections*** enclosed by the reserved words RECORD and END. Each component of a record has a unique identifier known as the ***field identifier***. The variable section declares *person* as a record variable.

The following example shows sample data contained in the record variable *person*:

name	'FRANKLIN G. HOLLY '
zipcode	10021
age	39
telephone	212-551-0000
response	agree

The general form of a record TYPE definition is as follows:

```
TYPE
    identifier = RECORD
                        field identifier : type;
                        field identifier : type;
                        . . .
                        field identifier : type
                END;
```

The corresponding syntax diagram is shown in Figure 11-1.

Here is another example of a record definition and declaration. Can you find an application for this record?

```
TYPE
     info = RECORD
               name: PACKED ARRAY [1..35] OF char;
               class: (freshman, sophomore, junior, senior);
               gpa: real;
               credits, transfercredits: 0..maxint;
               sex: (male, female)
          END;
VAR
     student: info;
```

Field Designators

To access a component in an array, we used a subscript or an index. We must also be able to access the desired component of a record. Let us go back to our example of the record variable *person*. To access the name in the record, we use the record variable identifier (*person*) followed by a period, followed by the field identifier of the name field (*name*):

```
person.name
```

This expression is called a *field designator*. To access the other components, we use the following field designators:

```
person.zipcode        person.age
person.telephone      person.response
```

Field designators with simple (unstructured) types are treated just like ordinary variables with simple types. For example, they can be used in expressions and assignment statements. The following assignment statements will assign values to all the field designators of the record variable person:

```
person.name := 'Charles Dickens            ';
person.zipcode := 00001;
```

Figure 11-1   Syntax diagram of record.

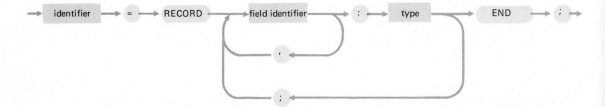

```
person.age := 55;
person.telephone := '213-861-4134';
person.response := disagree;
```

To read and write the values in a record variable, we use the field designators and the rules that apply to its associated data type. For example, the statement

```
writeln (person.name)
```

will display the name in the record since the type associated with *person.name* is packed array of character. If *person.name* was not packed, then it would be necessary to display each character separately, since entire arrays cannot be specified in the *writeln* statements parameter list. The field designator *person.response* has a value of an enumerated type. Therefore we cannot read or write the value directly. Instead we can use a CASE statement to indicate the value of this component:

```
CASE person.response OF
      agree: writeln ('Consumer agrees');
      disagree: writeln ('Consumer disagrees')
END;
```

Here is another example utilizing field designators with the record variable *person* to determine if the person is older than 65 years.

```
IF person.age > 65
THEN writeln ('Person older than 65 years.')
```

Some additional points to remember about records include the following:

- Records can be passed as parameters to functions and procedures.
- The result of a function cannot be a record.
- Records can be assigned to records with identical types. Suppose we have the definition and declarations

```
TYPE
background = RECORD
                name: PACKED ARRAY [1..35] OF char;
                age: 1..99;
                status: (citizen,resident,visitor);
                sex: (male, female)
                END;
VAR
      person1, person2 : background;
```

Since *person1* and *person2* have identical types, the assignment statement person2 := person1

is permitted and results in the assignment of the values from each field designator of *person1* to the corresponding field designator of *person2*.

■ The type associated with any field identifier of a record can be another record. This idea, nested or hierarchical records, will be discussed in the next section.

We conclude this section with an example of a procedure that will read an entire record from a text file.

Problem 11.1

Write a procedure to read a value for each field in a record defined as follows:

```
TYPE
      result = RECORD
                      lastname: PACKED ARRAY [1..20] OF char;
                      scores: ARRAY [1..5] OF integer;
                      idletter: 'A'..'Z';
                      grade: (excellent, good, fair, poor)
               END;
```

The line

```
Washington        90 80 95 92 91 Z A
```

represents some typical input data, where excellent is coded as A, good as B, fair as C, and poor as D.

The procedure that follows is one solution to this problem. Note that the entire structure is passed as a variable parameter.

```
PROCEDURE enterrecord (VAR data: result);
(* Read a record of type result from the input file. *)
VAR
      index : integer;
      inchar : char;
BEGIN
      FOR index := 1 TO 20 DO                    (* get the last name *)
      BEGIN
            read (inchar);
            data.lastname[index] := inchar
      END;
      FOR index := 1 TO 5 DO                     (* get the test scores *)
         read (data.scores[index]);
      read (inchar);                              (* skip blanks *)
```

```
          WHILE inchar = ' ' DO                   (* before idletter *)
                read (inchar);
          data.idletter := inchar;                 (* assign the idletter*)
          read (inchar); (* skip blanks *)
          WHILE inchar = ' ' DO                     (* before grade *)
                read (inchar);
          IF inchar IN ['A','B','C','D']            (* validate grade code *)
          THEN CASE inchar OF          (* convert to enumerated type *)
                    'A': data.grade := excellent;
                    'B': data.grade := good;
                    'C': data.grade := fair;
                    'D': data.grade := poor
               END
          ELSE writeln('Invalid letter grade.')     (* diagnose error *)
END;
```

EXERCISES FOR SECTION 11.1

1 Write a record definition for each of the following:
   (a) A bank record consisting of account name and address, social security number, current balance, and accumulated interest.
   (b) A listing in the telephone directory that includes name, address, and telephone number.
   (c) A criminal record with real name, alias name, age, height, weight, color of eyes, and number of prior arrests.

2 Decide which of the following are valid record definitions.
   (a) TYPE
       state = RECORD
                    name: PACKED ARRAY [1..30] OF char;
                    age: integer;
                    sex: (male, female)
   (b) TYPE
       example = RECORD
                    test: 0..100;
                    final: 'A'..'F';
                    rank: 1..100
                 END;
   (c) TYPE
       frankly = RECORD
                    test: 0..100;
                    exam: 0..10;
                    test: 0..100
                 END;
```
```

(d) TYPE
     scores = RECORD
          name,
          address: PACKED ARRAY [1..30] OF char;
          test,
          exam: 0..100;
          stype: (lazy, worker, sharp, late)
     END;

3 Consider the following definition and declaration:

```
TYPE
    date = RECORD
                month: 1..12;
                day: 1..31;
                year: 0..2001;
                leapyear: (yes,no)
            END;
VAR time : date;
```

Determine which of the following are valid:

(a) time.month := 12;
(b) time.date := 3-15-1900;
(c) time.date := month;
(d) time.year := 2002;
(e) time.leapyear := 1;
(f) time.day := time.month;
(g) time.time := time;

4 Consider the following definition and declaration:

```
TYPE
    info = RECORD
                name: PACKED ARRAY [1..30] OF char;
                age: 1..99;
                dateofbirth: PACKED ARRAY [1..10] OF char
            END;
VAR
    person : info;
```

Determine which of the following are valid statements:

(a) person.name := person.dateofbirth;
(b) person.name[30] := person.dateofbirth[10];
(c) person.age = person.age + 1;

(d) person.dateofbirth := '12-12-1912';
(e) person.dateofbirth[11] := '.';

5 Using the record declaration in problem 4, write a procedure to read such a record.

6 Using the record declaration in problem 4, write a procedure to display such a record with appropriate headings.

SECTION 11.2 HIERARCHICAL RECORDS AND ARRAYS OF RECORDS

In many applications a record may be just a component in a larger data structure. For example, in a student record system, each student record may be one component in an array of student records. Also within each student record may be a component that is also a record. In this section we show that a component of a record can be a record (nested records) and that the component type of an array can be a record (array of records).

Hierarchical Records

A record having a field identifier whose data type is also a record is called a *hierarchical record*, or a *nested record*. For example, a student record may contain a component recording the student's prior college experience:

```
TYPE
    prevcollege = RECORD
                    name: PACKED ARRAY [1..75] OF char;
                    address: PACKED ARRAY [1..50] OF char;
                    prevcredits: 0..maxint;
                    gpa: real
                  END;
```

Given the record definition of *prevcollege*, the actual student record would be defined as follows:

```
TYPE
    student = RECORD
                name: PACKED ARRAY [1..50] OF char;
                class: (freshman,sophomore,junior,senior);
                priored: prevcollege;
                gpa: real;
                credits: 0..maxint
              END;
VAR
    person : student;
```

In a record the field identifiers have limited scope. This permits the use of the same identifier in our main program or inside other records. Notice in our example the field identifiers *name* and *gpa* are used in both records. Within any given record, the field identifiers must be unique, but they may be used in other records.

An alternate way of writing the hierarchical record definition for *student* is as follows:

```
TYPE
     student = RECORD
                    name: PACKED ARRAY [1..50] OF char;
                    class: (freshman,sophomore,junior,senior);
                    priored: RECORD
                           name: PACKED ARRAY [1..50] OF char;
                           address: PACKED ARRAY [1..50] OF char;
                           prevcredits: 0..maxint;
                           gpa: real
                             END;
                    gpa: real;
                    credits: 0..maxint
                    END;
VAR
     person: student;
```

Suppose we wish to access the student's previous grade point average (*gpa*) and store the result in a real variable called *prevgrade*. The assignment statement

```
prevgrade := person.priored.gpa;
```

will do the task. Because the record is nested, we must use the period twice. The following statement displays the number of previous credits earned:

```
writeln ('Previous credits: ', person.priored.prevcredits:1)
```

and this statement assigns a value of zero to previous credits:

```
person.priored.prevcredits := 0
```

When dealing with hierarchical records, make sure you check the data type of the accessed component. Remember when doing assignments or evaluating expressions that Pascal will automatically perform type checking.

Arrays of Records

Let's return to arrays. Remember the component type of an array can be any data type, including structured data types such as arrays and records. For example, an employee may have an individual employee record. However, there may be 100 employees working at a company. Pascal permits us to define an array of 100 records as follows (notice the address is also a record):

```
TYPE
    info = RECORD
                name: PACKED ARRAY [1..35] OF char;
                address: RECORD
                                street: PACKED ARRAY [1..30] OF char;
                                town: PACKED ARRAY [1..30] OF char;
                                state: PACKED ARRAY [1..2] OF char;
                                zipcode: 0..99999
                            END;
                ssn: PACKED ARRAY [1..11] OF char;
                age: 16..99;
                exemptions: 0..maxint
                END;
    list = ARRAY [1..100] OF info;
VAR
    employee : list;
```

Figure 11-2 shows the array of records with sample data for the first employee (that is, *employee[1]*).

The variable *employee* is a 100-element array whose components are records of type *info*. The expression

```
employee[1].age
```

will access the first employee's age, while

```
employee[100].ssn
```

is the expression that will yield the last employee's social security number. To display the first three digits of this number, we might use the code

Figure 11-2   Array of records.

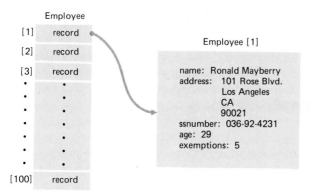

```
FOR index := 1 TO 3 DO
        write (employee[100].ssn[index])
```

where *index* is an integer variable.

Here are a few additional examples of assignment statements involving the *employee* array.

```
employee[1].name[1] := 'R';
employee[5].exemptions := 0;
employee[3].address.zipcode := 68114;
employee[100].address.state := 'NE';
employee[30].address.ssn := '516-08-5049';
```

The following table contains expressions and the associated data types. You should study this table carefully to help you determine the type of similar expressions.

expression	*data type*
employee[1].name	PACKED ARRAY [1..35] OF char
employee[1].name[1]	char
employee[1].address	RECORD . . .
employee[3].ssn	PACKED ARRAY [1..11] OF char
employee[3].address.zipcode	0..99999
employee[3].address.state	PACKED ARRAY [1..2] OF char
employee[4].address.state[1]	char
employee[5].age	16..99

WITH Statement

In our previous example, suppose we want to make the following changes to the first employee's record:

```
employee[1].age := employee[1].age + 1;
employee[1].exemptions := employee[1].exemptions - 1;
employee[1].address.street := '35 Maple Blvd.      ';
employee[1].address.state[1] := 'V';
```

We have repeated the record identifier in each assignment statement. Repeating the record identifier each time can be a time-consuming and error-prone process. Pascal permits us to abbreviate these assignments and other statements referencing similar components by using a WITH statement as follows:

```
WITH employee[1] DO
BEGIN
        age := age + 1;
        exemptions := exemptions - 1;
```

```
        address.street := '35 Maple Blvd.         ';
        address.state[1] := 'V';
END
```

The reserved word WITH is followed by the name of a record identifier (or a list of record identifiers separated by commas) which is followed by a statement or a group of statements enclosed by the reserved words BEGIN and END. The general form of the WITH statement is

```
WITH record identifier list DO statement
```

In the "statement" that appears in the WITH statement, references to a component of a record variable named can be abbreviated to just that part of the record designator appearing after the record variable. For example, consider the following variables:

```
VAR
    rec : RECORD
              f1 : integer;
              f2 : real;
              f3 : char
          END;
f3 : char;        (* not the same as rec.f3 *)
stuff : integer;
```

Then the statements

```
rec.f1 := stuff;
rec.f2 := 1.0 / rec.f2;
rec.f3 := 'X';
```

can be replaced by

```
WITH rec DO
BEGIN
        f1 := stuff;
        f2 := 1.0 / f2;
        f3 := 'X'
END
```

Note, however, that the statements

```
rec.f1 := stuff;
rec.f2 := 1.0 / rec.f2;
f3 := 'X';
```

cannot be replaced by

```
WITH rec DO
BEGIN
        f1 := stuff;
        f2 := 1.0 / f2;
        f3 := 'X'
END
```

because the statement f3 := 'X' would then be interpreted as meaning rec.f3 := 'X'. Note that the variable *stuff* can be referenced without problem in the statements enclosed by the WITH, since it does not appear as a field identifier in the record variable specified. If it did, then we would not be able to use the abbreviated form of reference permitted by the WITH statement, but rather be required to write the entire field designator. The syntax diagram for the WITH statement is shown below in Figure 11-3.

If we want to reference field designators repeatedly from nested, or hierarchical, records, we can use nested WITH statements. Consider the following program segment:

```
WITH employee[1] DO
    WITH address DO
        zipcode := 68182;
```

This is equivalent to the single statement

```
employee[1].address.zipcode := 68182
```

which is what you would normally write unless you have a group of statements with references to *employee[1].address*. Then the WITH statements are preferable, and the BEGIN-END would be used to bracket the group of statements containing the references. We can write the nested WITH statements shown above as

```
WITH employee[1].address DO
    zipcode := 68182
```

or alternately as

```
WITH employee[1], address DO
    zipcode := 68182
```

Figure 11-3 Syntax diagram of WITH statement.

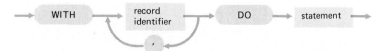

Note that the order in which *employee[1]* and *address* are written in the WITH statement is important. The following statement is wrong:

459

RECORDS

```
WITH address, employee[1] DO
    zipcode := 68182
```

In general, the notation

```
WITH rec1, rec2, rec3 DO
    statement;
```

means exactly the same as

```
WITH rec1 DO
    WITH rec2 DO
        WITH rec3 DO
            statement;
```

Suppose we have two field identifiers with the same name from different records referenced in the same WITH statement. Which of the nested WITH statements will supply the identity of the record variable? As you might expect, the innermost record variable will have precedence over the others. This is due, basically, to the same rule used when a local variable (in a procedure or function) has the same name as a global variable.

We will consider problems that can result from the use of WITH statements in the Testing and Debugging Techniques section.

EXERCISES FOR SECTION 11.2

1 Consider the following declarations:

```
TYPE
    datetype = RECORD
                    month : PACKED ARRAY [1..3] OF char;
                    day : 1..31;
                    year : 1900..2000;
                    hour : 0..2399
               END;
    nametype = RECORD
                    lastname : PACKED ARRAY [1..20] OF char;
                    firstname: PACKED ARRAY [1..10] OF char;
               END;
```

```
patient = RECORD
                name : nametype;
                sex : (male, female);
                maritalstatus : (single, married);
                doctor : nametype;
                appointment : datetype
          END;
VAR
     inpatient,
     outpatient : ARRAY [1..20] OF patient;
```

Determine which of the following are valid assignments:
(a) inpatient[5].name := 'John Jones';
(b) inpatient[1].sex := female;
(c) inpatient[6].appointment.month := 'Jun';
(d) outpatient[2].patient := inpatient[1].patient;
(e) outpatient[2].age := 0;
(f) outpatient := inpatient;
(g) inpatient[0].insurance := true;
(h) inpatient[1].doctor.firstname := 'Fredericks'

2 Read the following declarations:

```
TYPE
     word  =  ARRAY[1..25] OF char;
     structure  =  RECORD
                          value : integer;
                          legal : Boolean
                    END;
     list  =  RECORD
                   block : ARRAY [1..2000] OF word;
                   symbol : ARRAY [1..20] OF word
              END;
     coderec  =  RECORD
                        wordcode : word;
                        code : (A, B, C, D, E, L, M);
                        chart : list
                  END;
VAR
     codeblock : ARRAY [1..200] OF coderec;
     table : structure;
     complex : ARRAY [1..80] OF structure;
     acoderec : coderec;
     alist : list;
     i, count : integer;
     aword : word;
```

Determine which of the following are valid statements:

(a) codeblock[6].chart := alist;

(b) acoderec.wordcode[1] := alist.block[1];

(c) codeblock[100].chart.block[1,2] := aword[2];

(d) IF codeblock[20].code = L
    THEN codeblock[20].chart.block[1,1] := 'L'

(e) acoderec.value := i;

(f) IF legal
    THEN count := i;

(g) IF coderec.code = M
    THEN count := count + 1;

(h) codeblock[1].chart.block[2] := aword;

(i) complex[100].value := i;

(j) codeblock[20].block[1] := aword;

3 Consider the following declaration:

```
TYPE
    person = RECORD
                name: PACKED ARRAY [1..20] OF char;
                age: 1..99;
                status: (married, single, divorced);
                salary: real;
                exemptions: 0..maxint
            END;
VAR
    juanita: person;
    group: ARRAY [1..100] OF person;
```

Determine which of the following are valid:

(a) group[1] := juanita;

(b) group[1].name := 'juanita';

(c) read (group[1].status);

(d) WITH group DO
        writeln (name);

(e) WITH group[100] DO
    BEGIN
        writeln (name);
        read (age)
    END;

(f) WITH juanita DO
    BEGIN
        name := group[50].name;
        salary := group[1].salary
    END;

4 Using the declarations of problem 3, determine whether the following is a valid segment of code (assume *index* is an integer variable):

```
FOR index := 1 TO 100 DO
    writeln (group[101 − index].name);
FOR index := 1 TO 100 DO
    CASE status OF
            married : writeln (group[index].salary);
            single: writeln (group[index].name);
            divorced: writeln (group[index].exemptions)
    END;
```

5 Given the declarations in problem 3 and an integer variable *index*, assume the name in *group[1].name* is

'T. J. Booker   '

and the name in *group[2].name*, *group[3].name*, . . . *group[100].name* is

'Humpty Dumpty   '

Determine what is displayed by the following Pascal segment:

```
index := 1;
WITH group[index] DO
      WHILE index <= 100 DO
      BEGIN
            writeln (name);
            index := index + 1
      END;
```

6 Repeat problem 5 with the following Pascal segment:

```
index := 1;
WHILE index <= 100 DO
      WITH group[index] DO
      BEGIN
            writeln (name);
            index := index + 1
      END;
```

SECTION 11.3 PROBLEM SOLVING USING RECORDS

In this section we consider a common problem that involves the use of records. The problem concerns sorting an array of records.

Did you ever wonder why you are often asked to write your last name first when filling out a form? As you have learned in a previous chapter, when data is sorted, we can access items much faster (for example, by using a binary search) than if the data is unordered. The telephone directory you use is sorted in alphabetical order (technically, we say *lexicographical* order). Notice that in a telephone directory most entries have the last name appearing first, followed by the first name and then middle initial. Supplying last names first makes it easier to sort a list of names.

Problem 11.2

Write a program that will sort alphabetically by last name an array of records containing data on 100 computer science majors. To simplify the problem, assume that all last names are distinct. If this were not the case, we would have to sort on first names as well. Assume each record has the following structure:

Last name: maximum of 30 characters
First name: maximum of 30 characters
Middle initial: a single character
Class: freshman, sophomore, junior, or senior
gpa: a real number
Computer science credits: an integer

Our record definition and variable declarations will be as shown below. We have defined the student's name as a record too.

```
TYPE
     majnm  =  RECORD
                    lastname: PACKED ARRAY [1..30] OF char;
                    firstname: PACKED ARRAY [1..30] OF char;
                    middle : char
               END;
     major  =  RECORD
                    name: majnm;
                    class: (freshman, sophomore, junior, senior);
                    gpa: real;
                    cscredits: 0..maxint
               END;
     list   =  ARRAY [1..100] OF major;
VAR
     csstudent: list;
```

Now to sort the array of records, we must key in on the component containing the last name of a particular student (whose index is *i*):

csstudent[i].name.lastname

This component is a packed array of 30 characters. The component *lastname* is called the ***record key***. Previously, we wrote a procedure to sort integers in ascending order. In this case we must sort character strings. Since we have declared *lastname* as a packed array, we can use the relational operators to compare last names just like we do for integers. To introduce you to other sorting techniques, we will use a different sorting procedure called the ***bubble sort***.

Bubble Sort

Many sorting methods are based on interchanging pairs of items that are out of order until no such pairs exist. The bubble sort is a well known (but not particularly efficient) sort that uses this method. The idea of the algorithm is the following: scan adjacent pairs of names from left to right, repeatedly, interchanging any found to be out of order. Consider the following example of three-letter words to be sorted:

DOG CAT ZOO TOY GUY GAL

Starting from the left and working right, we compare the elements of pairs until we find a pair that is out of order. We immediately find that *DOG* and *CAT* are not in order, so they are interchanged:

CAT DOG ZOO TOY GUY GAL

Continuing, we see that *DOG* and *ZOO* are properly ordered, but *ZOO* and *TOY* are not, so we interchange them:

CAT DOG TOY ZOO GUY GAL

We then continue, interchanging *ZOO* and *GUY*, and then *ZOO* and *GAL*. After completing this first pass through the array, we have the order

CAT DOG TOY GUY GAL ZOO

Notice that the largest value has "bubbled" to the right end of the array. If we repeat this process (that is, do another pass), the next largest value will bubble to its proper position:

CAT DOG GUY GAL TOY ZOO

The next to the largest element, *TOY*, has bubbled to its proper position, just before *ZOO*. Since after the first pass the largest element was moved to its proper position, it was unnecessary to examine the last pair of values; we were certain that it was already in order. After the second pass, it is unnecessary to examine the last two pairs, since they must be in order. Similarly, we know that after the *I*th pass through the array, we need not examine the pairs involving the last I elements, since they are guaranteed to be in order.

We should also note that if there are N elements in the array to be sorted, we have only to make $N - 1$ passes of the data. Recall that after each pass another data item is moved to its correct position. Therefore after $N - 1$ passes, $N - 1$ of the data items will be in their correct positions in the array. Where does that leave the last data item? It must be in its proper location! The array in our example is completely sorted after five passes:

CAT DOG GAL GUY TOY ZOO

The algorithm for the bubble sort is shown below, where *name* is an array of N elements. Observe that an imbedded loop is needed. The inner loop (FOR) compares pairs of values. The outer loop (WHILE) repeats this process for the remaining values that are not yet in their correct positions until the array has been sorted.

Bubble Sort Algorithm

Set *control* equal to N (array size).
While *control* is not equal to zero do:
  Set *temp* equal to 0;
  For *index* = 1 to *control* − 1 do:
   If *name*[*index*] > *name*[*index* + 1]
      Exchange *name*[*index*] and *name*[*index* + 1];
      Set *temp* equal to *index*.
  Set *control* equal to *temp*.

An additional improvement has been incorporated into the algorithm as presented above. The variable *temp* is set to zero prior to each pass, and when an interchange is performed, *temp* is set to the index of the first element of the pair that was interchanged. On the next pass, we examine pairs only up to the position of the last interchange in the preceding pass, *because all pairs beyond that point must be in order!* If they were not, then *temp* would be set to the point at which the interchange was made. You should study this algorithm very carefully and test its correctness by applying it to the three-letter word example we used previously.

Problem Solution

Now let's return to solving our problem of sorting the student records in order by last name. The Bubble Sort algorithm will perform the task. It is important to note that instead of simply interchanging the last names, we must interchange the records in which the names appear. To do otherwise would "leave behind" the remaining data items associated with the students' records that were interchanged! The following program will perform the required tasks with the appropriate changes to the Bubble

Sort algorithm. Note that we must declare a temporary record to interchange two records in the array. The program includes invocation of two procedures, *readrecords* and *writerecords*, which are not included; they are the subject of exercise 4 at the end of the chapter.

```
PROGRAM sortrecords (input, output);
(* Read, sort on last name, and display the records for *)
(* up to 100 computer science majors.                   *)
CONST
        maxsize = 100;
TYPE
        majnm = RECORD
                        lastname: PACKED ARRAY [1..30] OF char;
                        firstname: PACKED ARRAY [1..30] OF char;
                        middle: char
                  END;
        major = RECORD
                        name: majnm;
                        class: (freshman, sophomore, junior, senior);
                        gpa: real;
                        cscredits: 0..maxint
                  END;
        list = ARRAY [1..maxsize] OF major;
        sizety = 0..maxsize;
VAR
        csstudent: list;
        size : sizety;      (* actual number of records *)
PROCEDURE readrecords;
(* read the records and set size *)
    (* see exercise 4 at the end of the chapter *)
PROCEDURE writerecords;
    (* see exercise 4 at the end of the chapter *)
PROCEDURE bubblesort (VAR recarray : list, size : sizety);
(* sort array of records by last name using bubble sort *)
VAR
        control, index, temp : 1..maxsize;
        temprec : major;        (* temporary record *)
BEGIN
        control := size;
        WHILE control <> 0 DO (* while array isn't sorted *)
        BEGIN
           temp := 0;
           FOR index := 1 TO control − 1 DO          (* for all pairs *)
              IF  recarray[index].name.lastname >      (* in order? *)
                  recarray[index + 1].name.lastname
                 THEN BEGIN               (* no, so swap the records *)
```

```
                    temprec := recarray[index];
                    recarray[index] := recarray[index + 1];
                    recarray[index + 1] := temprec;
                                    (* save index of last pair swapped *)
                    temp := index
            END
         control := temp              (* Now examine only that part *)
      END              (* of the array from 1 to the last pair swapped *)
END; (* bubblesort *)
(* Main Program *)
BEGIN
      readrecords;                    (* read the student records *)
      bubblesort (csstudent, size);            (* sort the records *)
      writerecords                 (* display the sorted records *)
END.
```

SECTION 11.4 VARIANT RECORDS [OPTIONAL]

In this section we present a brief introduction to variant records. Pascal permits records to contain components that can vary from record to record. A record that has two separate parts, a *fixed* part and a *variant* part, is called a ***variant record***. The fixed part of the record consists of those components (or ***fields***) common to all record variables of the given type. The variant part declares the possible fields that can exist depending on the value of a certain field (called the ***tag field***). For example, suppose we have a student record system that contains the field's name, address, gpa, total credits, and status. Depending on the student's status, more information may be desired. Suppose status is defined so as to indicate the need for additional information, as follows:

If freshman, need high school gpa.

If transfer student, need number of transfer credits.

If graduate student, need year of graduation.

Otherwise, no additional information needed.

The following is a TYPE definition of a variant record based on the above criteria:

```
TYPE
     status = (freshman,transfer,grad,other);
     student = RECORD
                    name: PACKED ARRAY [1..30] OF char;
                    address: PACKED ARRAY [1..50] OF char;
                    gpa: real;
                    credits: 0..maxint;
```

```
CASE current: status OF
    freshman: (hsgpa: real);
    transfer: (transcredit: 0..maxint);
    grad: (yeargrad: 1900..2000);
    other: ()
END
```

The fixed part of the record contains the field's name, address, gpa, and credits; it is always placed before the variant part of the record. The field *current* is called the *tag field*; in this example the *tag type* is *status*. The tag field is used to store a value that indicates which of the variant fields will be present in the variant record. Note that the variant part of the record is similar to a CASE statement, but *not* identical. The reserved word CASE is followed by the declaration of the tag component (*tag field: tag type*), then the reserved word OF and the variant fields. Each variant field contains a list of one or more constants, a colon, and the variant field definition enclosed in parentheses. Since the variant part of the record must appear at the end of the record, only one END is required to terminate its definition. The identifiers used in the variant fields must be different from those used in the fixed part of the record.

A variant record can have only one variant part. However, a variant part may contain a variant part of its own (that is, nested variants are permitted). Consider the following example:

```
TYPE
    string = PACKED ARRAY [1..25] OF char;
    computertype = (analog, digital);
    configuration = (standalone, hybrid);
    analogrec = RECORD
                    CASE config : configuration OF
                        standalone : ( );
                        hybrid : (digitalpart : string)
                END;
    digitalrec = RECORD
                    CASE config: configuration OF
                        standalone : ( );
                        hybrid : (analogpart : string)
                END;
    computer = RECORD
                    model : string;
                    manufacturer : string;
                    CASE ctype : computertype OF
                        analog : (arec: analogrec);
                        digital : (drec: digitalrec)
                END
```

Here each computer is expected to have a model name, a manufacturer's name, and a type (either *analog* or *digital*). A system of interconnected analog and digital computers is a hybrid computer, so if a computer is part of a hybrid system, the record includes the name of the other computer in the system.

The particular variant of a record that may be referenced is determined during the execution of the program. For example, assume the declaration

```
VAR
      person: student
```

has been given. We can reference the fixed components of the record variable *person* as usual: *person.name*, *person.gpa*, and so forth. To access a field in the variant part, the value of the tag field *(current)* must contain a value that selects the desired variant field. For example, the assignment statement

```
person.current := freshman
```

specifies that the variant of the person record that will be used is that containing the high school grade point average *(hsgpa)*. Now *person.hsgpa* can be accessed. For example, the statement

```
person.hsgpa := 3.10
```

is valid. This assignment would not have been permitted without a value in the tag field variable. For example, the assignment

```
person.yeargrad := 1985
```

is not valid unless the current value of the tag field is *grad*. We can set the tag field to *grad* by the assignment statement

```
person.current := grad
```

Suppose we declare two variables of the record type *student*:

```
VAR
      person1, person2 : student;
```

Notice below the variables *person1* and *person2* are of identical record type, but have different structures. The variant part is empty in *person2* and nonempty in *person1*. The following assignments for *person1* are valid:

```
person1.name := 'John Q. Rockyfella        ';
person1.gpa := 3.7;
person1.current := transfer;
person1.transcredit := 5
```

while the following assignments to *person2* are valid:

```
person2.name := 'Mary H. Lamb        ';
person2.gpa := 3.9;
person2.current := other
```

SECTION 11.5 TESTING AND DEBUGGING TECHNIQUES

In this section we look at some common errors arising from the misuse of records. Consider the following record definition and variable declaration:

```
TYPE
     wrong  =  RECORD
                    name: PACKED ARRAY [1..30] OF char;
                    sex: (male, female);
                    scores: ARRAY [1..5] OF integer
               END;
     list  =  ARRAY [1..50] OF wrong;
VAR
     student: list;
```

A common error in the record definition is the omission of the reserved word END to terminate the record definition. What would the compiler do in this situation? It would continue processing your source program, looking for field identifiers followed by the type identifier (recall the syntax diagram of a record type). This will usually result in a host of errors, depending on the syntax and the ability of the compiler to recover from errors; most compilers will try to continue the compilation after an error if at all possible.

Another very common record error is the use of the type identifier instead of the record variable. Referring to our example, here are some instances:

record error	corrected	reason
student[1].wrong	student[1].name	The record identifier is *wrong*.
student[1].list	student[1].name	The array type is *list*.
student.name	student[1].name	Subscript missing.

Errors arise when the type of the field identifier does not match the type of an assigned variable or constant. For example, the following assignment statement is invalid (assume *newscore* is an integer variable):

```
student[1].scores := newscore;
```

The field designator on the left is an array of integers, while the variable on the right is an integer. A correct assignment statement is:

student[1].scores[1] := newscore;

Record variables can be used as actual parameters corresponding to variable parameters of functions and procedures, but tag fields of variant records cannot. If we consider the *person* record variable of the previous section, then *person.name* could be passed as an actual parameter (to a formal packed array variable parameter), but *person.hsgpa* could not, as it is a component of the variant part of the record. A way around this problem is to copy the variant component to a second variable (not part of a packed array or structure) and use this second variable as the actual parameter. The value of the second variable after the procedure or function returns should then be reassigned to the variant component.

Next let us consider the errors that can arise from use of the WITH statement. Suppose we add the following variable declaration to our example:

```
VAR
     sex : char;
```

Sex also occurs as a variable of an enumerated type in our record definition. Therefore the statement

```
WITH student[1] DO
     sex := 'M'
```

is not valid, since the identifier *sex* in the WITH statement causes it to be equivalent to the statement

```
student[1].sex := 'M'
```

and 'M' is not a constant of the proper (enumerated) type. Statements referencing the character variable *sex* must not be in the scope of a WITH statement specifying an element of the array of records *student*. The statements

```
sex := 'M';
WITH student[1] DO
sex := male
```

are permitted.

In the previous examples we were required to use a subscript following the name of the array (*student*). This is because the WITH statement requires the specification of a record variable, and will not permit an array of records to be used (see the syntax diagram in Figure 11-3). Thus, the following WITH statement is incorrect:

```
WITH student DO
     [1].sex := male;
```

One final problem that can be encountered using the WITH statement involves the use of a variable to select a component of an array of records. Consider the following segment of code:

```
index := 1;
WITH student[index] DO
        FOR index := 1 TO 50 DO
            writeln ('Student ',index:1, ' name: ',name);
```

In this case the name in *student[1]* will be displayed 50 times! The first few lines of output will look something like this:

```
Student 1 name: John Smith
Student 2 name: John Smith
Student 3 name: John Smith
```

The value of index will change, as shown, but the name component does not. This is because the particular record that will be accessed in the WITH statement is fixed by the record variable specified, *at the time the WITH statement is executed.* Therefore whatever value *index* had prior to the WITH statement determines the name that will be displayed. The correct code to display each student name is

```
FOR index := 1 TO 50 DO
    WITH student[index] DO
            writeln ('Student ',index:1, ' name: ',name);
```

Here is a list of some useful Pascal reminders to aid in testing and debugging.

PASCAL REMINDERS

- The list of fields in a record definition is terminated with the reserved word END.
- The field identifiers in a record must all be unique. Different records may reuse the same identifiers.
- A field designator is used to access the components of a record. A period separates the record variable and the field identifier:

```
student[1].name
```

- The rules for reading and writing records are applied to each of the field designators based on the type of the field designator.
- Entire records can be assigned to other entire records with identical types.
- Records may be nested (hierarchical records).
- Field designators have types. These must satisfy the same requirements as the types of variables and constants when field designators are used in expressions or in assignment statements.

- The WITH statement must specify a record variable.
- The variant part of a record must appear only after the fixed part.
- A CASE clause is used to declare the variant part of a record. A tag field declaration immediately follows the CASE keyword. Each variant is supplied as a parenthesized field list preceded by a constant list and a colon.
- The value of the tag field is used to identify which of the variants are active.

SECTION 11.6 CHAPTER REVIEW

In this chapter we discussed the structured data type known as record. The characteristic property of records is that the components can be of different data types. Records are defined by listing field identifiers, followed by the corresponding type identifiers. We showed how complex data structures can be formed by combining records and arrays to form such structures as:

- Record of arrays (components of records can be arrays)
- Array of records (components of arrays can be records)
- Record of records (components of records can be records)

Accessing components of complex structures, such as an array of nested records, can be simplified by using the WITH statement.

The problem of sorting an array of records was also presented in this chapter. We showed how the Bubble Sort algorithm can be used to sort an array of student records such that the records are ordered by student last names. In an optional section on variant records we discussed the declaration of and accessing of components in variant records. The Testing and Debugging Techniques section provides a number of examples of common errors encountered when using records.

The following summary of the Pascal features discussed in this chapter should be used for future reference.

PASCAL REFERENCE

1 Record: A structured data type whose components may have different data types. General form:

```
TYPE
    identifier = RECORD
                    field identifier : type;
                    field identifier : type;

                    . . .

                    field identifier : type
                 END;
```

Example:

```
TYPE
    employee = RECORD
                    name: PACKED ARRAY [1..30] OF char;
                    salary: 0..maxint;
                    sex: (male, female)
               END;
```

2 Field designator: Used to access a component of a record.
   Example:

```
employee.name[1]
```

3 Hierarchical records: Nested record types.
   Example (using the employee record type from above):

```
TYPE
    department = RECORD
                      name: PACKED ARRAY [1..20] OF char;
                      boss: employee;
                      deptnum: integer
                 END;
```

4 Array of records: Array with component type of record.
   Example:

```
TYPE
    list = ARRAY [1..10] OF department;
VAR
    section : list;
```

5 WITH statement: Reference to field designator within WITH statement applies to
   record variable following keyword WITH.
   General form:

```
WITH record identifier DO
    statement;
```

   Example:

```
WITH section[1] DO
    deptnumber := 1
```

6   Variant Record: Contains fixed part and variant part. General form:

```
TYPE
     identifier = RECORD
                    (* fixed part *)
                    field identifier : type;
                    field identifier : type;
                    . . .
                    field identifier : type;
                    (* variant part *)
                    CASE tag : tag type OF
                        constant : (field list);
                        constant : (field list);
                        . . .
                        constant : (field list)
          END;
```

Chapter 12 Preview

Pascal has four structured data types: arrays, records, files, and sets (see Figure 11-4). In the next chapter we will consider file structures. Files are similar to arrays in that the components are all of the same type. However, files are normally stored external to the computer's primary storage on devices such as magnetic disks and tapes. The advantages of using files are that they do not have a predetermined maximum size and their contents have a lifetime distinct from the period of time during which the program is executing. Thus we can store large quantities of data without being restricted to the size of primary storage. The principal disadvantages of using files to store data are the relatively low speeds of the devices on which they are stored and the standard Pascal restriction that components be accessed only in strictly sequential order.

Figure 11-4   Structured data types.

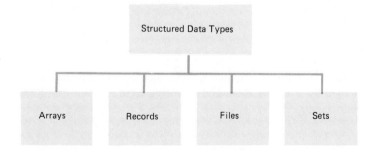

Keywords for Chapter 11

array of records
bubble sort
field
field designator
field identifier
fixed part
hierarchical records

lexicographical order
record
record key
tag field
variant part
variant record
WITH statement

CHAPTER 11 EXERCISES

★ ESSENTIAL EXERCISES

1   Describe the record that would be appropriate for each of the following types of data by giving an appropriate TYPE definition.
(a)   The books in a personal library.
(b)   The parts in a complex object. Be certain to allow for the description of parts which are composed of other parts.
(c)   A student's history of academic performance over several semesters of college.
(d)   A dictionary entry for an arbitrary word.

2   Suppose we have two record types, $T1$ and $T2$, defined as shown below. We can directly assign entire variables of type $T1$ to other variables of type $T1$ and similarly for type $T2$. We cannot assign an entire variable of type $T1$ to a variable of type $T2$, even though each field identifier of $T1$ also appears as a field identifier in $T2$. Write appropriate Pascal code to accomplish such a task. Find out whether your computer system has any languages that permit such an assignment operation to be specified.

```
TYPE
    T1 = RECORD
              f1 : integer;
              f2 : real
         END;
    T2 = RECORD
              f1 : integer;
              f2 : real;
              f3 : char
         END;
```

3   *Complex numbers* have two components, a *real* part and an *imaginary* part, each of which is represented by a real number. The following record type is useful for representing complex numbers:

```
TYPE
    complex = RECORD
```

END;

Write Pascal procedures with three parameters of type *complex* (two value and one variable) that perform addition and multiplication of complex numbers. If we let *re1* and *im1* represent the components of the first complex number and *re2* and *im2* the components of the second complex number, then

$$re3 = re1 + re2$$
$$im3 = im1 + im2$$

specifies the result of addition and

$$re3 = re1 * re2 - im1 * im2$$
$$im3 = im1 * re2 + im2 * re1$$

specifies the result of multiplication.

★★ SIGNIFICANT EXERCISES

4 Write the procedures *readrecords* and *writerecords* mentioned in the program of Section 11.3. Recall that the structure of the records to be processed is described by the definitions below:

```
TYPE
       majnm = RECORD
                      lastname: PACKED ARRAY [1..30] OF char;
                      firstname: PACKED ARRAY [1..30] OF char;
                      middle: char
               END;
       major = RECORD
                      name: majnm;
                      class: (freshman, sophomore, junior, senior);
                      gpa: real;
                      cscredits: 0..maxint
               END;
       list = ARRAY [1..100] OF major;
VAR
       csstudent: list;
```

Each record is represented externally as a sequence of variable-length fields separated from each other by at least one blank. For the class component of the record, a two-character code is used, as follows:

FR   freshman
SO   sophomore

JU junior
SE senior

Therefore, each of the following lines represents sample input to the program: (excessive blanks have been omitted)

```
Knickey Joe D SO 3.751 15
McGurgle William U FR 1.004 2
Evans Edith E SE 4.000 35
```

Procedure *readrecords* reads these records until an end of file is encountered or 100 records have been stored, whichever comes first. Flawed records are to be reported but are otherwise ignored. For each valid record, *readrecords* increments the integer size and sets the fields of *csstudent[size]*. Procedure *writerecords* reverses the process, producing a line acceptable to *readrecords* for every student in the *csstudent* array.

5 Consider the declarations shown below:

```
TYPE
     time =   RECORD
                  day : 1..366;     (* day of year *)
                  hour : 0..23;     (* hour of day *)
                  minute : 0..59   (* minute of hour *)
              END;
     evrec = RECORD
                  name: PACKED ARRAY [1..30] OF char;
                  starttime, endtime: time
              END
   VAR
       event :   ARRAY [1..100] OF evrec;
       window :  ARRAY [1..2] OF time;
```

Write a segment of Pascal coding which will display the name and duration in minutes of each event that will start and end during the "window" specified by the times *window[1]* and *window[2]*.

★★★ CHALLENGING EXERCISES

6 Suppose a genealogical society has an array of records indicating date of birth and subscript in the array of the fathers' and mothers' records for a number of persons. The array record and associated variables might be similar to the following:

```
CONST
     maxpersons = 1000;
TYPE
```

```
aname = PACKED ARRAY [1..50] OF char;
aperson = RECORD
              name: aname;
              dob: RECORD              (* date of birth *)
                       month: 1..12;
                       day: 1..31;
                       year: 0..maxint
                   END;
              motherindex,
              fatherindex : 0..maxpersons
          END;
VAR
    history: ARRAY [1..maxpersons] OF aperson;
    you: aname;
```

The fields *motherindex* and *fatherindex* contain the subscript in the history array of the mothers' and fathers' records. This value will be zero if the information (on the mother and/or father) is not available. Assume the variable *you* contains a person's name; then display the names and birthdates of that person's parents and both sets of grandparents.

CHAPTER 11 PROBLEMS FOR COMPUTER SOLUTION

⭐ ESSENTIAL PROBLEMS

1 Each line of the input data contains names that have two parts, a first name and a last name. Each part can be no longer than 20 characters. They may be preceded and followed by blanks, and are separated by one or more blanks. The example input gives illustrations of this form. Write a Pascal program that reads the input data and produces an alphabetized list of the names, ordered first by last name and then by first name.

Example Input:

```
John Smith
          Frank Smith
       Frank Martinez
Tseng-Ching Wang        Eugenia Smith
Caruthers Strockmorton
```

Example output:

```
Frank Martinez
Eugenia Smith
Frank Smith
```

John Smith
Caruthers Strockmorton
Tseng-Ching Wang

2 Each line of the input data for this problem contains a name, address, transaction type, and amount of transaction for a simple billing system. Name and address will be 20 characters each. The transaction type is either *C* (for credit) or *D* (for debit). The transaction amount is given in cents. If we assume each person's balance is initially zero, that a credit reduces the balance, and a debit increases the balance, write a Pascal program to produce a report, ordered on name, giving the final balance in dollars and cents in each account. If a balance is exactly zero, then that person's balance should not appear in the report.

Example input:

```
Fred Ehlers       213 Breakers Lane      D    4103
Sue Jones          9102 Tulane Circle     D     1000
Fred Ehlers       213 Breakers Lane      C  1
Baba Wawa          2000 E. 21st Street    D      45000
Sue Jones          9102 Tulane Circle        C   550
Jay Godchaux       9103 Hundred Oaks         C    2500
Fred Ehlers       213 Breakers Lane      C   4102
```

Example output:

Name	Address	Balance
Baba Wawa	2000 E. 21st Street	450.00
Jay Godchaux	9103 Hundred Oaks	−25.00
Sue Jones	9102 Tulane Circle	4.50

★★ SIGNIFICANT PROBLEMS

3 This problem is similar to problem 1 in that the input data has exactly the same format. The output, however, should contain the last names in alphabetical order, one per line, followed on the same line with the comma-separated, alphabetically ordered list of first names appropriate for that last name. If we use the same input data shown for problem 1, the output should be as shown below.

Example output:

```
Martinez       Frank
Smith          Eugenia, Frank, John
Strockmorton   Caruthers
Wang           Tseng-Ching
```

4 Write a program that has as its input another Pascal program. The purpose of this program is to produce a list of every procedure and function included in the

program, followed by a list of the line numbers where the procedures and functions were referenced. You may assume that there will be no more than 10 functions and procedures and that each is referenced no more than 10 times. Further assume that the names of procedures and functions are no longer than 15 characters. Assume that a function or procedure is always defined by the occurrence of FUNCTION identifier or PROCEDURE identifier. You may also assume the input is not "tricky." That is, there will not be lines like

```
(* PROCEDURE notreally; *)
```

Example input:

```
[Any Pascal program]
```

Example output (typical):

Name	Type	Invocations
GetInput	Function	75, 120, 215
WriteOutput	Procedure	90, 95, 96
SortData	Procedure	201
Initialize	Procedure	195

★★★ CHALLENGING PROBLEMS

5   A police department is developing a system to validate alibis provided by suspects in its investigations. One of the parts of the system is an array of records, each record having the following structure:

```
RECORD
        suspectname: aname;
        hasalibi: Boolean;
        alibiname: aname
END
```

where *aname* is a packed array of characters. If a suspect has no alibi, then *hasalibi* will be false. Otherwise *alibiname* will be the name of the person providing the alibi. Assume that each suspect's name appears in the first 25 columns of an input line and, if the suspect has an alibi, that the name of the person providing the alibi appears in the next 25 columns; otherwise the end of line appears after column 25. Write a Pascal program to read all the suspect and alibi data and produce two reports. The first report lists all those individuals with no alibi. The second report identifies groups of persons that supply the alibis for others in the same group (for example, A *alibis* B, B *alibis* C, and C *alibis* A). Assume there are no more than 50 suspects.

Example input:

Freddy Fingers   Sam Sharky
Sam Sharky   Big Eddie the Terminator
Mary Merciless   Freddy Fingers
Irma Innocence
Big Eddie the Terminator Sam Sharky

Example output:

Suspects With No Alibi
    1. Irma Innocence
Suspects With Circular Alibis
    1. Big Eddie the Terminator
    2. Sam Sharky

CHAPTER 12

CHAPTER 12
FILES

File Types
and
Variables

Text Files

Problem
Solving

FILES

OBJECTIVES

After completing this chapter, you should be able to:

- Define file types
- Recognize and declare file variables
- Recognize and apply the standard file manipulating routines: *reset, rewrite, get,* and *put*
- Write programs to perform text file processing
- Solve, test, and debug problems using files

CHAPTER OVERVIEW

In this chapter we consider another structured data type, the file. A *file* is an ordered sequence of components of the same type. Files differ from arrays in that the size of a file is not specified and can be arbitrarily long. As we shall see, files also differ from arrays in the way that they are accessed.

Files are usually stored on secondary storage devices, such as magnetic disks and tapes. The identification of a file can be passed as a parameter to the entire Pascal program by specification of parameters in the PROGRAM header. These files are called *external* files and, as such, have a lifetime independent of the programs that manipulate them. This makes them useful for permanent storage of data and programs. Files that do not appear as parameters in the PROGRAM header are *internal* files, and exist only during the period of time the program is executing; their contents are lost when the program terminates.

In the first section of this chapter we discuss the definition of files and declaration of file variables. Each file has an associated file buffer variable; this variable will be discussed in this chapter. File processing is also discussed in the chapter. Pascal has five standard file manipulating routines: *reset, rewrite, get, put,* and *eof.* We will apply these in the solution of the problem of copying a file.

In the Section 12.2 we examine the most commonly used file type, the text file. This file type is characterized by lines composed of characters, each of which is terminated by an end-of-line character. The additional procedures that manipulate text files are the familiar *read, readln, write,* and *writeln;* the *eoln* function is also used in text file processing. Applications involving text file processing are presented in this section.

The problem-solving section discusses the important file process known as *merging*, in which a single ordered file is produced by combining two or more ordered files. A detailed algorithm is discussed and then applied to a specific problem involving files. The Testing and Debugging Techniques section presents some common errors that can result when files are used improperly.

SECTION 12.1 FILE TYPES AND VARIABLES

Sometimes we want to store information permanently on secondary storage devices, such as disks and tapes. The reasons for this are varied, but frequently we want the data to be made available to other programs for processing, possibly on physically different computer systems, or we wish to store the data so we can perform further processing of the data at a later time. For example, suppose a large corporation has a file of 5000 employee records stored on magnetic tape. To access the information in this file, we must observe the following constraints:

1 Since the records are stored sequentially in the file, to access the Nth record of the file we must sequentially access the 1st, 2nd, . . . , $N - 1$st records of the file prior to accessing the Nth record. This is analogous to the way you might access a particular tune recorded on an audiocassette along with other tunes. You must skip past the tunes on the tape preceding the one in which you are currently interested.
2 If there are a large number of records in the file, we may not be able to read all records into the computer's primary memory at one time. Therefore we may be restricted to processing only a fraction of the records at a time, typically only one record.

To handle this type of information processing, Pascal includes a structured data type known as a *file*. A file can be described as a sequence of components, each of which has the same type. There is no predetermined limit on the number of components that may be stored in a file (but physical characteristics of the secondary storage of the computer system may, in fact, produce such limitations). Such files are also called *sequential files*, since accessing the components is done strictly sequentially. That is, when the processing of the file is initiated, the first component is the first one that must be processed. The very next component that can be accessed is the second component, and the pattern continues in this manner until all desired components have been processed.

Nonsequential processing of files is permitted by some languages and systems; nonstandard Pascal features may also permit you to access a particular component of a file without accessing all the preceding components. These are alternately called *random-access* or *direct-access* files. We will not consider such processing, though, since the nonstandard Pascal features required to do such processing vary from system to system. Just because these features are nonstandard, they can prove useful, and you should become familiar with them if they are available on your system. If you should choose to write programs using such features, be prepared to spend the necessary time to revise your program if you move it to a different computer system.

File Types

The definition of the file structured type resembles that of an array. However, when you are declaring an array, the size of the array must be (indirectly) specified by giving the index type. A file, on the other hand, has no predetermined size. Any number of components, zero or more, can be present in a file. In an array, any component can be accessed directly simply by supplying the array name and the appropriate index value. This is not the case with the components of a file. Only one file component (known as the *file window*) is available at any given time. Any other components, such as those preceding or following the file window, cannot be accessed immediately. The file window must be moved to the desired component.

The TYPE definition of a file has the following form:

```
TYPE
     identifier = FILE OF component type;
```

For example, the following are TYPE definitions of files:

```
TYPE
     numfile = FILE OF integer;
     book = FILE OF char;
     bingo = FILE OF ARRAY [1..5, 1..5] OF integer;
```

Note that the file identifier is followed by an equal sign and the reserved words FILE OF, which are followed by the component type specification. The component type can be any type, simple or structured, except file or any type that has a component type of file. Thus, a file that includes a file as a component, either directly or indirectly, is not permitted.

Pascal includes a predefined structured type called *text* that is used to declare text files. For example, throughout the book we have used the standard files *input* and *output*. These files are automatically declared type *text*. That is, the following declaration is automatically performed by the compiler:

```
VAR
     input, output : text;
```

Next to text files, the most common file types are files of records. For example, consider the example of a large company's file of employee records. Each record might be defined as follows:

```
TYPE
     employee = RECORD
                     name: PACKED ARRAY [1..30] OF char;
                     address: PACKED ARRAY [1..50] OF char;
                     ssn: PACKED ARRAY [1..11] OF char;
                     salary: real;
                     exemptions: 0..maxint
                 END;
```

Now we can declare a file variable for the employee records:

```
VAR personfile : FILE OF employee;
```

Alternately, we can define a file type and then use that type in the declaration of the file variable:

```
TYPE
      empfile = FILE OF employee;
VAR
      personfile : empfile;
```

File Parameters

The file variables *input* and *output* are predeclared, and have the type *text* (discussed in the next section); all other file variables must be explicitly declared. Any file variable, whether input, output, or one globally declared in the program, may be listed as a parameter in the PROGRAM header. Such files are called **external** files. They have a lifetime greater than the execution of the program that creates or uses them and have names that are used to reference them outside the Pascal program environment. They can be manipulated by the utility programs available on the computer system (for copying, deleting, editing, renaming, and so forth) and programs written in other programming languages. As far as the Pascal program is concerned, however, the only difference between external files and **internal** file variables is that external file variable names must appear in the PROGRAM header and internal file variable names must not. In most Pascal implementations, the only names that appear as **program parameters** are the names of file variables; the way in which these parameters are associated with values is not defined by Pascal. Usually the name of the file variable is explicitly associated with the name (external to Pascal) of the file. For example, consider the statement

```
PROGRAM update (input, output, database);
```

There will usually be some mechanism provided by the computer system to associate *input*, *output*, and *database* with file names. For example, your IBM system may use the commands

```
//OUTPUT DD SYSOUT=A
//DATABASE DD DSN=JAN85DATA
//INPUT DD *
     lines for the file variable input
/*
// EXEC UPDATE
```

or the DEC VMS commands

```
$ DEFINE DATABASE JAN85DATA
$ RUN UPDATE
```

or the CDC command

```
$ UPDATE(,,JAN85DATA)
```

or some other commands to request association of external files with the Pascal file variables and execution of the program. You should determine exactly how to associate the names of external file names with Pascal file variables by examining your system documentation.

File Buffers

When a file variable is declared, a file window is automatically created to permit us to look at the components of the file. This window is formally called the ***file buffer variable***. The name of this variable is the file variable's name with an arrow (↑) or circumflex (ˆ) appended to its right. (Most systems will not actually have an arrow, so the circumflex is used. For clarity, however, we use an arrow in the text.) For example, *input* ↑ , *output* ↑ , and *personfile* ↑ are all file buffer variable names. Each of these has the same type as the component type of the associated file. For *input* and *output*, the type of the file buffer variable is char, even though the type of these files is *text*. The type of *personfile* ↑ is *employee*. Figure 12-1 shows an example of the file buffer variable and its relationship to the file. Notice that a copy of the value currently in the file window (record 4) is in the file buffer variable (*personfile* ↑). The file buffer variable is the link between the program and the components of the file. Remember, a file buffer variable is created whenever a file variable is declared. So the declarations

```
TYPE
      numfile = FILE OF integer;
      gamefile = FILE OF ARRAY [1..3, 1..3] OF char;
VAR
      numbers : numfile;
      games : gamefile;
```

will result in the creation of two file buffer variables, an integer *numbers* ↑ and an array *games* ↑ .

Figure 12-1   File buffer variable.

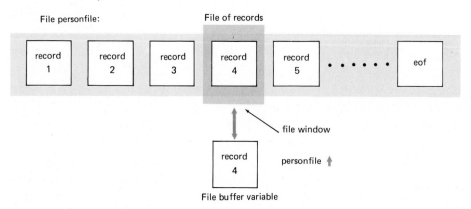

These file buffer variables are just like other variables, and can be manipulated in the same way. For example, each of the following is a valid statement involving a file buffer variable:

```
index := number ↑;      (* assign buffer variable to index      *)
number ↑ := 5;          (* assign 5 to the buffer variable       *)
writeln (personfile ↑ .name)     (* display name of an employee *)
```

Standard File-Manipulating Procedures and Functions

Pascal includes the standard procedures *reset*, *rewrite*, *get*, and *put* and the standard function *eof*. Collectively, these permit manipulation of file variables. We will examine each of these in detail.

First, we consider the steps necessary to retrieve information from an existing file. Prior to our accessing the file buffer variable, the file must be prepared for reading. This "opening" of the file is done by the procedure *reset*. If *infile* is the file variable associated with the file we wish to read, then

```
reset (infile)
```

will make the necessary connection between the file variable and the file. It also prepares the file for reading (or "inspection") and positions the file window so that the first component of the file is in the file buffer variable *infile* ↑ . Figure 12-2 illustrates the situation as it exists after the procedure *reset* has completed its task. The procedure *reset must* be invoked before reading can begin. It is only necessary to perform the reset once, however. The standard file *input* is automatically reset if its name appears in the PROGRAM header. If you wish to write a program that does not use the standard input file, it is unnecessary to include it in the PROGRAM header as a program parameter.

Similarly, if a file is to be written (or "generated"), the procedure *rewrite* must be invoked. For example, if *outfile* is a file variable, then

Figure 12-2 Reset.

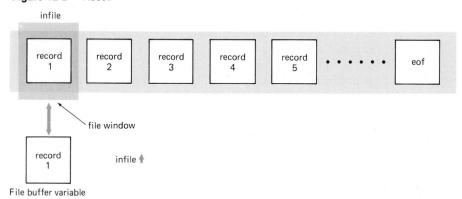

rewrite (outfile)

will prepare the associated file for writing. Like *reset*, *rewrite* establishes the connection between the file variable and the file. But *rewrite* "opens" a file for output, so any prior contents of the file are completely erased, and the window is at the beginning of the file, over a component whose value is undefined.

Once a file has been prepared for reading or writing, the first component of the file is available in the file buffer variable. For an input file, we may immediately use the first component as we wish. The statement

get (infile)

will move the file window to the next component of *infile* and make its contents available in the file buffer variable *infile* ↑ . If it is impossible to achieve this because we are at the end of the file and there are no remaining components, then an error occurs.

Writing to a file is similar, in that the file buffer variable provides the means by which values are communicated. The value to be written is assigned to the file buffer variable, and then the procedure *put* is invoked. For example, suppose *newdata* is a record variable of type *employee* as defined earlier. Then to write this value to the next component of *newfile*, a file of type *employee*, we would write

newfile ↑ := newdata;
put (newfile)

As with input files, we must invoke the procedure *rewrite* before the first attempt is made to invoke the procedure *put* for the file.

The function *eof* is used, as always, to determine if there are more components in an input file. It was used previously with the standard text file *input*, but can be used with files of any component type. For example, the expression

eof (infile)

will yield true if there are no more components in the file associated with file variable *infile*. This condition also means that the value of the file buffer variable *infile* ↑ becomes undefined, and should not be used. While it is normally of little value, *eof* will always be true if its file variable argument is being written (that is, in "generation" mode). Recall that *eof* without a parameter is treated as *eof(input)*.

Now let us look at a problem whose solution can make use of these facilities.

Problem 12.1

Write a procedure copyfile *that will make a duplicate of a file of records of type* student, *defined as follows:*

```
TYPE
     student = RECORD
                    name: PACKED ARRAY [1..30] OF char;
                    id: 0..maxint;
                    gpa: real;
                    class: (freshman,sophomore,junior,senior)
                END;
```

The solution to this problem requires a program with two file variables, one for input (*infile*) and one for output (*outfile*). The solution is shown below. Note the use of the file buffer variables.

```
PROGRAM copyfile (infile, outfile);
(* Copy a file of student records from infile to outfile. *)
TYPE
     student = RECORD
                    name: PACKED ARRAY [1..30] OF char;
                    id: 0..maxint;
                    gpa: real;
                    class: (freshman,sophomore,junior,senior)
                END;
VAR
     infile, outfile : FILE OF student;
BEGIN
     reset (infile);          (* open for input *)
     rewrite (outfile);         (* open for output *)
     WHILE NOT eof(infile) DO
     BEGIN
            outfile ↑ := infile ↑ ;(* copy record to output *)
            put (outfile);(* write component to output *)
            get (infile) (* advance to next input component *)
     END
END.
```

Notice that the statements in the program do not really depend on the type of file being copied. If we change the declaration of type *student*, we can then copy almost any kind of file. The single exception is the file type *text*. We will discuss the solution to the file-duplicating problem for text files in the next section.

File Variables

File variables, like *personfile* and *infile*, are similar to other variables in that they have values that can be modified. The values these variables possess are sequences of components, however, and may therefore be manipulated only by the predefined procedures and functions provided by Pascal. Specifically, the following points should be noted:

1 File variables may be used as actual parameters in procedure and function invocations, but the corresponding formal parameter must always be a VAR parameter. For example, a procedure that expects a file variable of type *filetype* would begin with the statement

PROCEDURE processfile (VAR f : filetype);

2 File variables may not be involved in assignment statements, even when the types of the variables involved are identical. Thus the two files *f1* and *f2*, each of type *filetype,* cannot appear in an assignment statement such as

f1 := f2;

Modification and access of the components of a file can only be performed component by component using the predeclared procedures provided by Pascal.

3 File variables cannot be simultaneously open for reading and writing. If a file is open for reading, the *write*, *writeln* and *put* procedures must not be invoked to manipulate that file. Similarly, if a file is open for writing, the *read*, *readln* and *get* procedures must not be invoked for that file. To do otherwise will result in an error.

EXERCISES FOR SECTION 12.1

1 Determine which of the following are valid TYPE definitions of files:
(a) TYPE mathfile = FILE OF real;
(b) TYPE file = FILE OF char;
(c) TYPE superfile = FILE OF file;
(d) TYPE myinput = text;
(e) TYPE bag = FILE OF ARRAY [1..10] OF integer;
(f) TYPE secret = FILE OF text;

2 Consider the following file declaration:

TYPE
    fileofnum = FILE OF integer;
    matrixfile = FILE OF ARRAY [1..100] OF real;
VAR
    numbers: fileofnum;
    scidata: matrixfile;

Determine which of the following are valid:

(a) numbers ↑ := 5;

(b) scidata[2] ↑ := 2;

(c) numbers ↑ := scidata ↑ [1];

(d) scidata ↑ := numbers ↑ ;

(e) scidata ↑ [100] := numbers ↑ * scidata ↑ [100];

3 Find two errors in the following program:

```
PROGRAM error (infile, outfile);
BEGIN
        rewrite (outfile);
        WHILE NOT eof(outfile) DO
        BEGIN
                outfile ↑ := infile ↑ ;
                put(outfile);
                get(outfile)
        END
END.
```

4 Write a procedure that duplicates all the positive numbers from a file of real numbers to another file of real numbers, and does not copy the nonpositive numbers.

5 Write a procedure that converts a file of reals to a file of integers by replacing each real number by the closest integer to it.

6 Explain the error in each of the following statements. Assume the following declaration:

```
TYPE
    name = FILE OF char;
    number = FILE OF integer;
VAR
    filename : name;
    numfile : number;
```

(a) PROCEDURE compfile (filename : name);

(b) filename := numfile;

(c) filename↑ := numfile↑ ;

(d) rewrite (filename);
     get (filename);

(e) reset (numfile);
     put (numfile);

SECTION 12.2 TEXT FILES

Recall that the standard files *input* and *output* are text files. A text file is unique in that it is comprised of a sequence of variable-sized lines, each containing a variable number of characters terminated by a special end-of-line character. The end-of-line characters cannot be written by a Pascal program (in a standard manner) except by the standard procedure *writeln*. In addition, the end-of-line character cannot be detected when a text file is read except by the standard function *eoln*. These differences mean that text files are *not* the same as files of type FILE OF char, which can be viewed as an arbitrarily long sequence of characters.

Text files are the most frequently used files because the characters are organized into lines. They correspond to the usual way we think of files of written material. As you read this book, you examine lines, each of which contains a variable number of characters. When you write a letter, you organize your words into lines.

The standard procedures *get* and *put* may be used to read and write text files. Since the lines in text files frequently contain representations of integer and real constants, the procedures *read*, *readln*, *write*, and *writeln* are also provided to make their input and output simpler. We have used each of these procedures (and called them statements) in previous chapters. Let us consider them in more detail now.

Consider the declarations:

```
VAR
      wordfile: text;
      achar: char;
```

The procedures *read* and *write* with *wordfile* and *achar* have equivalents in terms of *get* and *put*. The following table illustrates these equivalents.

read/write procedure call	*get/put equivalent*
write (wordfile, achar)	wordfile ↑ := achar; put (wordfile)
read (wordfile, achar)	achar := wordfile ↑ ; get (wordfile)

You should recall from previous use that the last action performed during an invocation of the procedure *writeln* is the writing of an end-of-line character. If the procedure *writeln* is invoked with no parameters, or just a file variable parameter, then it will write only an end-of-line character.

Recall also that the last action performed during an invocation of the procedure *readln* is skipping of the next end-of-line character and all preceding characters. If *readln* is invoked with no parameters, or just a file variable parameter, then it will just skip past the next end-of-line character.

The procedures *read*, *readln*, *write*, and *writeln* can have multiple parameters when they are used with text files. Such invocations are equivalent to a sequence of invocations, each of which includes just a single parameter and the same file variable (if one was used). For example, the statement

```
read (wordfile, chr1, chr2, chr3)
```

is equivalent to

```
read (wordfile, chr1);
read (wordfile, chr2);
read (wordfile, chr3)
```

but the statement

```
readln (wordfile, chr1, chr2, chr3)
```

is equivalent to

```
read (wordfile, chr1);
read (wordfile, chr2);
readln (wordfile, chr3)
```

since the skip past the end of line is performed only at the end of the procedure invocation. If we omit the file variable for a *read* or *readln* procedure, or *eof* or *eoln* function invocation, then the standard file *input* is used. Likewise, if the file variable is omitted from a *write* or *writeln* procedure invocation, then the standard file *output* is used.

In the last section we noted that the file buffer variable has the same type as the components of the file. Usually, the variables and expressions used with the *read*, *readln*, *write*, and *writeln* procedures must also be of the correct type. With text files this is not the case. Each parameter may be of type integer, real, or char; *write* and *writeln* invocations may also include parameters of type Boolean and packed arrays of character.

When an integer or real parameter is encountered in a *read* or *readln* procedure invocation, the text file being read is expected to have a sequence of characters representing an integer or real constant, possibly preceded by any number of blanks or end-of-line characters. The conversion between this sequence of characters and the internal form for an integer or real is performed automatically by the procedure. Likewise, when a parameter with a type other than char is encountered in a *write* or *writeln* procedure invocation, the sequence of characters that represent a constant of the same type is written to the text file, possibly adjusted by the formatting directions you include after the parameter. For example,

```
write (output, 17:4)
```

will cause two blank characters followed by the characters '1' and '7' to be written to the text file *output*.

The function *eoln(f)* returns true if the component currently in the file buffer variable for file f (that is, $f\uparrow$) is the end-of-line character. You might think, therefore, that you could copy the end-of-line character to a character variable by writing something like achar := f ↑

when *eoln(f)* is true. Such a statement can be written, but only the *eoln* function itself can detect that *f* ↑ contains an end of line; all other uses of *f* ↑ will yield a blank (' '). There is no single character constant that corresponds to the end-of-line character; therefore we cannot write one without using the standard procedure *writeln*.

Now we are ready to examine the problem of duplicating a text file. Our solution is organized in the same way text files are organized.

```
PROGRAM copytext (infile, outfile);
(* Duplicate a text file. *)
VAR
      achar: char;
      infile, outfile: text;
BEGIN
      reset (infile);
      rewrite (outfile);
      WHILE NOT eof (infile) DO
      BEGIN
            WHILE NOT eoln (infile) DO
            BEGIN
                  read (infile, achar);
                  write (outfile, achar)
            END;
            readln (infile);
            writeln (outfile)
      END
END.
```

Editing a Text File

As a further example of text file processing, let us assume that we wish to make changes in the content of a text file. For example, suppose we want to delete all misspelled words in a file. Since it is not possible to modify the input file, we can copy the input file to an internal file, making the modifications as we copy the text, then change to writing mode on the original file, and copy the internal file to it. This technique is somewhat dangerous, though, since a power failure or other problems with the computer hardware while we are rewriting the original file could result in disaster! Anyway, let's apply this technique to a real problem.

Problem 12.2

Write a program that will remove all debugging statements of the form

(*DEBUG*) write ... ;

from a Pascal source program. Assume that the characters "(*DEBUG*)" always appear at the beginning of such a line and they are followed, on the same line, by the debug statement to be removed.

The following program will solve this problem. Note that two procedures, *readline* and *writeline*, make the task of reading and writing lines from or to a text file very simple. Since the text file used is provided as a parameter, they can be used on both the input and output files. A function, *debug*, will determine if the current line begins with the debug flag.

```
PROGRAM deletedebugs (pascalprogin, pascalprogout);
(* Remove debugging lines from a Pascal source program. *)
CONST
      maxlinesize = 150;                          (* maximum line size *)
      flag = '(*DEBUG*)';                         (* flag for debug lines *)
      flagsize = 9;                               (* length of debug flag *)
TYPE
      line = PACKED ARRAY [1..maxlinesize] OF char;
      string = PACKED ARRAY [1..flagsize] OF char;
VAR
      pascalprogin,                               (* input program *)
      pascalprogout : text;             (* program without debugs *)
      currentline : line;
      currentlength : integer;

PROCEDURE readline (VAR infile : text; VAR inline : line;
                    VAR linelength : integer);
(* read one line from text file infile into inline, setting *)
(* linelength to the number of characters in the line       *)
(* eof(infile) must be false when readline is invoked.       *)
VAR
      c : char;
BEGIN
      linelength := 0;       (* initially no characters *)
      WHILE NOT eoln(infile) DO
      BEGIN
              read (infile, c);      (* get the next character *)
              IF linelength < maxlinesize
              THEN BEGIN       (* store it if space permits *)
                      linelength := linelength + 1;
                      inline[linelength] := c
                   END
      END;
```

```pascal
                          readln (infile)         (* skip the end of line *)
END; (* readline *)


PROCEDURE writeline (VAR outfile : text; outline : line;
                            linesize : integer);
(* write outline[1..linesize] to file outfile, and append *)
(* a new line character                                    *)
VAR
       i : integer;
BEGIN
       FOR i := 1 TO linesize DO      (* write each character *)
       write (outfile, outline[i]);
       writeln (outfile);       (* write the end-of-line character *)
END; (* writeline *)


FUNCTION debug (VAR aline : line; linesize : integer;
                            flag : string) : Boolean;
(* return true if aline begins with the debug flag, and *)
(* false otherwise *)
VAR
       temp : Boolean;
       i : 1..flagsize;
BEGIN
       IF linesize < flagsize        (* is line too short? *)
       THEN debug := false
       ELSE BEGIN
                temp := true;
                FOR i := 1 TO flagsize DO (* check for match *)
                temp := temp AND (aline[i] = flag[i]);
                debug := temp
           END
END;
(* Main Program *)
BEGIN
       reset (pascalprogin);
       rewrite (pascalprogout);
       WHILE NOT eof(pascalprogin) DO
       BEGIN
                readline (pascalprogin, currentline, currentlength);
                IF NOT debug (currentline, currentlength, flag)
                THEN  writeline (pascalprogout, currentline,
                                    currentlength)
       END
END.
```

Note that the input to this program is expected to be a Pascal program, but in fact could be any text file. The output will be an exact copy of the input with only the lines beginning with "(*DEBUG*)" removed. For example, consider the following input data.

```
    PROGRAM sample (output);
    VAR i : integer;
    BEGIN
            FOR i := 1 TO 10 DO
(*DEBUG*)  BEGIN
(*DEBUG*)          writeln ('Variable i = ', i:2);
                writeln ('Hello')
(*DEBUG*)  END
    END.
```

After execution, the output file would contain the following lines:

```
PROGRAM sample (output);
VAR i : integer;
BEGIN
        FOR i := 1 TO 10 DO
            writeln ('Hello')
END.
```

This program can be easily modified to perform a variety of transformations on the lines of text files while copying them from one file to another. For example, conversion of all lowercase characters to their uppercase equivalents could be accomplished with a simple modification. Such programs are called *filters*.

EXERCISES FOR SECTION 12.2

1 Suppose *sentences* is a text file containing the following data:

```
To be or not to be.<eoln>
This above all:<eoln>
To thine ownself be true<eoln>
The rest is silence.<eoln>
<eof>
```

Determine the output of the following Pascal segment (assume *sentences* is a text file, *unknown* is an integer, and *inchar* is a char variable):

```
reset (sentences);
unknown := 0;
```

```
        WHILE NOT eof (sentences) DO
        BEGIN
                WHILE NOT eoln (sentences) DO
                    read (sentences, inchar);
                unknown := unknown + 1;
                readln (sentences)
        END;
        writeln (unknown)
```

2   In problem 1 can you determine how the variable *unknown* is related to the text
    file contents? If so, determine the output if *sentences* is declared as

    FILE OF char;

3   Write a procedure that reads a text file where each line varies in length from 1 to
    72 characters and that creates another text file where each line is exactly 72
    characters long by padding (adding to the end of) each line with zero or more
    blanks.

4   Write a Pascal procedure that reads a text file as input and displays the number of
    nonblank characters in each line.

5   Write a Pascal procedure that reads a line of text from a text file and stores the
    line in a packed array. If the line is less than 72 characters long, pad the line with
    blanks. Assume the TYPE definition of the packed array is globally defined:

    TYPE
        string = PACKED ARRAY [1..72] OF char;

SECTION 12.3 PROBLEM SOLVING USING FILES

A common requirement that occurs in file processing is to produce a merged file. A
merged file is a single sorted file produced by combining two or more sorted files.
Consider the following problem.

Problem 12.3

*The hardware and software divisions of Apex Electronics are to be combined into
a single systems division. The employee records for each division are currently
stored on separate files in which the records are sorted in ascending order by social
security number. Write a program that will merge the two employee record files to
produce the employee file for the systems division. This new file must also be sorted
in ascending order by social security number.*

The main problem here is that of merging. Before we consider a detailed solution
of this problem, let us study a simpler example of merging using integers. This example
will provide us with the understanding needed to produce the solution to our problem.

Suppose we have two lists of integers sorted in ascending order and an empty merged list, as shown below. Note that the lists can be of different sizes.

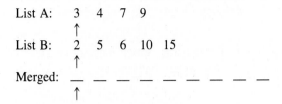

List A: 3   4   7   9
          ↑

List B: 2   5   6   10   15
          ↑

Merged: __ __ __ __ __ __ __ __ __
          ↑

Each list includes an indicator (↑) pointing to the smallest number in the list. To merge the two lists, we proceed as follows. Scan each list from smallest to largest, keeping track of the current positions (as noted by the indicators). The current positions are compared, and the smaller value is inserted into the current position of the merged list. The indicators pointing to the smaller value and the current position in the merged list are then moved one item to the right, while the third arrow (pointing to the value not inserted) is not moved. Repeat this process until one of the lists is empty; then add the remaining values from the nonempty list to the end of the merged list.

Returning to our example, after the first comparison and insertion our lists look as follows:

List A: 3   4   7   9
          ↑

List B: 2   5   6   10   15
              ↑

Merged: 2   __ __ __ __ __ __ __ __
              ↑

Notice the current position indicator has been advanced in list B, since the previous value was the smaller. The position indicator of the merged list is always advanced, since a value will always be inserted.

Repeating the process, we find the next iteration will result in the following changes:

List A: 3   4   7   9
              ↑

List B: 2   5   6   10   15
              ↑

Merged: 2   3   __ __ __ __ __ __ __
                  ↑

Now the position indicator in list A has been advanced, since 3 is less than 5 and the value 3 is inserted into the merged list. This process is repeated until list A (having no values larger than 9) is emptied. The result at this point is:

List A: 3   4   7   9

List B: 2   5   6   10   15

Merged: 2   3   4   5   6   7   9   __   __

The last step is to copy the remaining values of list B (which must all be greater than any value in list A) to the merged list. When we are finished, the indicators will be as shown below:

List A: 3   4   7   9

List B: 2   5   6   10   15

Merged: 2   3   4   5   6   7   9   10   15

Now we can outline our merge algorithm. Assume arrays *listA* and *listB* are to be merged, producing array *listC*. The position indicators are called *positionA*, *positionB*, and *positionC*.

Merge Algorithm

Initialize *positionA*, *positionB*, *positionC*.
While (not end of *listA*) and (not end of *listB*)
  If *listA[positionA]* < *listB[positionB]*,
  Then *listC[positionC]* = *listA[positionA]*.
    Increment *positionA*.
  Else *listC[positionC]* = *listB[positionB]*.
    Increment *positionB*.
  Increment *positionC*.
If end of *listA*,
Then copy rest of *listB* to *listC*.
Else copy rest of *listA* to *listC*.

Problem Solution

Now that we have outlined a solution to the merge problem, we can proceed with the solution of the original problem. Let us assume that the records of employees contained in the software and hardware divisions of Apex Electronics are described by the following record type:

```
TYPE
    employee = RECORD
```

```
                    ssn: PACKED ARRAY [1..11] OF char;
                    name: PACKED ARRAY [1..30] OF char;
                    salary: real;
                    exemptions: 0..maxint
            END;
      empfile = FILE OF employee;
```

The file variables can then be declared as

```
VAR
      software,
      hardware,
      systems : empfile;
```

We will use a procedure called *mergefiles* that will be based on our merge algorithm with appropriate modifications for the types of records being merged. For example, the position indicators in the algorithm are automatically implemented by the file type in Pascal, keeping a record of how many components have been processed in each file. We might want to maintain a count of the number of records processed, however, and in that case we would keep the position indicators. Our solution to the problem follows.

```
PROGRAM merge (software, hardware, systems);
(* Merge hardware and software division employee *)
(* files to produce the systems division employee *)
(* file.                                         *)
TYPE
      employee = RECORD
                    ssn: PACKED ARRAY [1..11] OF char;
                    name: PACKED ARRAY [1..30] OF char;
                    salary: real;
                    exemptions: 0..maxint
            END;
      empfile = FILE OF employee;
VAR
      software,
      hardware,
      systems : empfile;
PROCEDURE mergefiles (VAR in1, in2, out : empfile);
(* merge files in1 and in2 to produce file out in *)
(* ascending social security number order        *)
BEGIN
        WHILE NOT eof(in1) AND NOT eof(in2) DO
        BEGIN
```

```
                        IF in1 ↑ .ssn < in2 ↑ .ssn
                        THEN BEGIN
                                    out ↑ := in1 ↑ ;
                                    get (in1)
                              END
                        ELSE BEGIN
                                    out ↑ := in2 ↑ ;
                                    get (in2)
                              END;
                        put (out)
                  END;
                  (* copy remaining records to file out *)
                  WHILE NOT eof(in1) DO
                  BEGIN
                        out ↑ := in1 ↑ ;
                        put (out);
                        get (in1)
                  END;
                  WHILE NOT eof(in2) DO
                  BEGIN
                        out ↑ := in2 ↑ ;
                        put (out);
                        get (in2)
                  END
            END; (* merge *)
            (* Main Program *)
            BEGIN
                  reset (software);
                  reset (hardware);
                  rewrite (systems);
                  mergefiles (software, hardware, systems)
            END.
```

SECTION 12.4 TESTING AND DEBUGGING TECHNIQUES

In this section we consider some common errors associated with file processing. One frequent file handling error is confusing the *reset* and *rewrite* procedures. If you omit either the *reset* or *rewrite* procedure invocation in your program, you will not likely receive any compilation errors, but you can expect the program to fail when it is executed.

After the *reset* procedure has been applied to a file, the only operations that may be performed on that file are *read*, *get*, and *readln* if the file type is *text*. Similarly, after *rewrite* has been applied to a file, the only operations that should be used are *write*, *put*, and *writeln* if the file type is *text*. A file can be used for both input and output, as long as we use *reset* and *rewrite* properly, and do not try to read and write simultaneously. Remember, however, that as soon as the *rewrite* procedure is invoked, any previous file contents are lost.

Eof and *Eoln* Errors

Probably the most common errors in file handling occur with the *eoln* and *eof* functions. Suppose we have a text file called *infile* whose last components are as follows:

```
5 3_ 2 1 _ _ <eoln> <eof>
```

Consider the following code (assume *num* is declared integer):

```
WHILE NOT eof(infile) DO
BEGIN
        read (infile, num);
        write ('The number is ', num)
END
```

This loop will result in an error when it is executed due to an attempt to read past the end of file. The problem is that as soon as the integer 21 has been read, the next character is not the <eof>, but rather a blank. Even if the trailing blanks had been omitted, we would still have a problem, since the <eoln> would not "trigger" the *eof* function.

To prevent this error, you should precede end-of-file tests by a *readln* statement. Since the end of file can only occur after an end of line, this ensures that the test is made at the correct point.

Another similar problem can occur when reading more than one item in a single *read* or *readln* procedure invocation. Suppose the statement

```
read (infile, data1, data2, data3)
```

is used, but an end of file is encountered prior to satisfactory completion of a value for *data3*. The computer system will report an attempt to read past end of file in this case too. To avoid such problems, always perform a *readln* before testing for end of file, and if a variable number of data items are present (either intentionally or accidentally), read them one at a time, preferably reading only character data from text files.

The *eoln* function can be a source of many errors. Remember that *eoln* can be used only with text files, while *eof* can be used on any type of file. Recall that the end-of-line character is effectively a blank when it is read by your program and that the *eoln* function is the only way to detect its presence in an input file. Here is a segment of code that is designed to copy *infile* to *outfile* (both are of type text, and *inchar* is of type char):

```
reset (infile);
rewrite (outfile);
WHILE NOT eof(infile) DO
BEGIN
        read (infile, inchar);
        write (outfile, inchar);
        IF eoln (infile)
        THEN writeln (outfile)
        (* ERROR -- End of line has not been read!! *)
END;
```

In this example, we failed to read the end-of-line character (using *readln*, for example) when it was detected. As a result, an extra blank will be added to each output line except the first.

When a file is reset and happens to be empty, the *eof* condition is immediately true. So if the file *infile* is empty, the following code will cause an error:

```
reset (infile);
REPEAT
        read (infile, inchar);
        (* ERROR -- Failed to test for an empty file. *)
        write (outfile, inchar)
UNTIL eof(infile);
```

To avoid this problem, you should always check for the end of file before doing any processing of the file.

Here is a list of some important Pascal reminders regarding files.

PASCAL REMINDERS

- *Eoln*, *readln*, and *writeln* cannot be used with nontext files.
- When you are using *read* and *write* with nontext files, only one component may be read or written at a time.
- *Rewrite* opens a file for output; any previous file contents are lost.
- *Reset* opens a file for input; if the file is empty, *eof* is immediately true.
- The procedure *get* moves the file window and makes the next component of the file available in the file buffer variable.
- The procedure *put* appends the value of the file buffer variable to the end of the file.
- File variables cannot be assigned or assigned to.
- File variables can only be used as parameters to procedures and functions that expect VAR parameters.
- All file variables, other than *input* and *output*, must be explicitly declared.

In this chapter we discussed files and file processing. In Pascal, a file is a structured data type consisting of a sequence of components, each of which has the same type. Files are not limited in size (except by physical constraints). External files can be used to store data that has a lifetime independent of a program's execution. We discussed the definition and declaration of file types and file variables. The file buffer variable was also introduced. The procedures *reset*, *rewrite*, *get*, and *put* and the function *eof* were discussed and applied to a file duplication problem.

In Section 12.2 we discussed text files and the use of the *read*, *readln*, *write*, *writeln*, and *eof* Pascal procedures and functions. An application of file handling for file editing was presented.

Section 12.3 discussed merging two files. A merge algorithm was developed and modified to handle files.

The following summary of the Pascal features discussed in this chapter can be used for future reference.

PASCAL REFERENCE

1 A file is a sequence of components, each having the same type. General form for file TYPE definitions:

```
TYPE
        identifier = FILE OF component type;
```

Example:

```
TYPE
        chfile = FILE OF char;
```

2 File-handling routines.

2.1 *Reset* (*infile*) opens file *infile* for reading and makes the first component available in the file buffer variable (*infile*↑).

2.2 *Rewrite* (*outfile*) opens file *outfile* for output, erasing any prior contents it may have had.

2.3 *Get* (*infile*) makes the next component of *infile* available in the file buffer variable (*infile*↑).

2.4 *Put* (*outfile*) appends the current contents of the file buffer variable (*outfile*↑) to the file.

2.5 *Eof* (*infile*) is true if the file window is positioned beyond the last component of *infile*.

2.6 *Eoln* (*infile*) is permitted only if *infile* is a text file and the file buffer variable (*infile*↑) contains an end-of-line character.

3 Text files:
   3.1 Predefined file type.
   3.2 Organized as lines, each of which contains a variable number of characters followed by an end-of-line character.
   3.3 Most elementary components are characters.
   3.4 Integers and reals may be read from text files using *read* and *readln*.
   3.5 Integers, reals, and Booleans may be written to text files using *write* and *writeln*.
   3.6 *Eoln* may be used to test for the presence of an end-of-line character.
4 File declarations.
   4.1 External files appear as program parameters.

```
PROGRAM sample (infile, outfile);
VAR infile, outfile : FILE OF sometype;
```

   4.2 Internal files do not appear as program parameters.

Chapter 13 Preview

In the next chapter we will conclude our discussion of structured data types with the set type. We will also introduce the pointer data type with applications to other data structures, such as linked lists and trees.

Keywords for Chapter 12

direct-access file	merge
eof	*put*
eoln	random-access file
external file	*read*
file	*readln*
file buffer variable	*reset*
file parameter	*rewrite*
file window	sequential file
filters	text
get	*write*
internal file	*writeln*

CHAPTER 12 EXERCISES

★ ESSENTIAL EXERCISES

1 In many computer systems an end-of-line character is actually represented by a single character in text files. As a result, a file that can be read as a text file can also be read as a FILE OF char, with certain limitations. One of these is that the function *eoln* cannot be used on the file variable.

(a) What is another restriction placed on reading from a FILE OF char?

(b) Assume a global char variable *endofline* contains the character that represents the end-of-line in text files. Write a Boolean function *ceoln* with a file variable parameter of type FILE OF char that performs the same function as the *eoln* function.

2   Although it is grossly inefficient, a Pascal file can be accessed in a simulated direct-access manner. If a file f, for example, has been reset, then a second reset will just reposition the file so that the file buffer variable contains the first component of the file. The following procedure, for example, will "directly" access the ith component of file f (assumed to be of type *filetype*), leaving the selected record in the file buffer variable.

```
PROCEDURE directaccess (VAR f : filetype; i : integer);
BEGIN
        reset (f);
        WHILE (i > 1) AND NOT eof (f) DO
        BEGIN
                get (f);
                i := i - 1
        END
END;
```

Explain how this procedure works. In particular, explain what is in the file buffer variable when the input value of i is greater than the number of components in the buffer. What happens if i is 1 and the file is empty (that is, has no components)?

★★ SIGNIFICANT EXERCISES

3   Reconsider exercise 2, but assume we wish to extract n (an integer variable) records from the file, the record numbers of which have been stored in integer array components $loc[1]$ through $loc[n]$. Further assume the extracted records are to be stored in $rec[1]$ through $rec[n]$, where rec is an array whose components are the same type as those in the file. Write a Pascal procedure which will extract the desired records from the file, performing only one reset operation.

★★★ CHALLENGING EXERCISES

4   Directly accessing the records of a file for writing in standard Pascal is even more costly that direct access for reading, as shown below. One technique that can be used to simulate direct-access writing of record i of a file f of type FILE OF *componenttype* is summarized below:

(a) Rewrite an internal file *temp* with the same type as f.

(b) Copy records 1 through $i - 1$ from f to *temp*.

(c) Write the new data for record i to *temp*.

(d) Skip record i on f (that is, read it into a "junk" variable of type *componenttype*).

(e) Copy the remaining records from f to *temp*.

(f) Finally, copy *temp* back to f.

Write a Pascal procedure *directwrite* whose parameters are a file variable, an integer record position, and a record to be written in that position. Make certain to consider the exceptional condition of the specified record position being greater than the number of records currently in the file.

CHAPTER 12 PROBLEMS FOR COMPUTER SOLUTION

★ ESSENTIAL PROBLEMS

1 The standard procedure *page (f)* (see Appendix G) causes an action that is defined by the implementor of each Pascal system. Its purpose is to cause output to text file *f* to begin on a new "page." This may cause skipping to the top of the next form for output to printing devices or to clear the screen and begin displaying output at the upper-left corner on video terminals. Using the procedure *page*, write a program that lists a text file with line numbers, 50 lines per page. Assume the line numbers will occupy the first four positions on each output line, and follow the line number by two blanks and a line from the text file.

Example input:

```
This is line 1.
This is line 2.
...
This is line 50.
This is line 51.
...
```

Example output:

```
   1  This is line 1.
   2  This is line 2.
   ...
  50  This is line 50.
<at the top of the next page>
  51  This is line 51.
   ...
```

2 The standard input file contains a pair of integers *s* and *w*. A second text file containing no more than 500 lines, each having 80 characters or less, is to be sorted and written to a third text file. The file is to be sorted into ascending sequence on the characters in positions *s* to $s + w - 1$ of each line. If a particular line does not have at least $s + w - 1$ characters, then it should be padded with blanks *for purposes of determining its position in the output file*; any blanks used for padding should not appear in the output file.

3 A list of words, one per line, appears in a text file *f*. These words have variable lengths, the longest having no more than 19 characters. We desire to display these words in as many columns as possible, such that the total width of all columns is not greater than a specified (constant) number of characters and each column is separated from the others by at least one blank. Write a program which will accomplish this task. (Hint: Read file *f* through once to determine the maximum word length, then determine the maximum number of columns that may be displayed, and reread the text file, displaying the words in the columns.)

Example input;

Polish Notation
Powerset
Prime Numbers
Integer
Label
Letter
Merge
Chopped Liver
Infix
Empty

Example output (assuming a maximum width of 55 characters):

Polish Notation   Powerset   Prime Numbers
Integer   Label   Letter
Merge   Chopped Liver   Infix
Empty

4 A text file *p* contains a prototype advertising letter. This letter contains no more than 50 lines, each of which contains no more than 50 characters. At various places in *p* there appear, never split across the end of line, the characters @*n*@, where *n* is a decimal digit. A second text file *m* contains an arbitrary number of lines, each containing up to 10 fields of characters separated by commas. For each line in *m*, copy text file *p* to an output text file *j*, substituting the *n*th field of the line from *m* for every occurrence of @*n*@. If the character sequence @*n*@ appears in *p* so that *n* is greater than the number of fields in the current line from *m*, then just delete @*n*@ from the text written to *j*. Separate copies of the letter written to *j* by invoking *page(j)*.

Example file *p*:

Dear @0@ @1@,
    So you bought @2@ @3@ computer! Well, @0@, you certainly want
to get the most from your @3@, so you want to buy the Pleasurable

Pascal system. It's so full of extensions, you'll never be able to leave it! @0@, it's only $19.95 (forget that you'll spend many thousands rewriting the programs for other Pascal systems!)

Example file *m*:

```
Charlie,Computnik,a,Lemon
Bertha,Binary,an,Albatross
Mata,Hari,the,Crypto 100
```

Example of output on file *j*:

Dear Charlie Computnik,
   So you bought a Lemon computer! Well, Charlie, you certainly want to get the most from your Lemon, so you want to buy the Pleasurable Pascal system. It's so full of extensions, you'll never be able to leave it! Charlie, it's only $19.95 (forget that you'll spend many thousands rewriting the programs for other Pascal systems)!
<top of new page>
Dear Bertha Binary,
   So you bought an Albatross computer! Well, Bertha, you certainly want to get the most from your Albatross, so you want to buy the Pleasurable Pascal system. It's so full of extensions, you'll never be able to leave it! Bertha, it's only $19.95 (forget that you'll spend many thousands rewriting the programs for other Pascal systems!)
<top of new page>
Dear Mata Hari,
   So you bought the Crypto 100 computer! Well, Mata, you certainly want to get the most from your Crypto 100, so you want to buy the Pleasurable Pascal system. It's so full of extensions, you'll never be able to leave it! Mata, it's only $19.95 (forget that you'll spend many thousands rewriting the programs for other Pascal systems!)

★★★ CHALLENGING PROBLEMS

5 An archive file *ar* is a text file that has lines of the form

@modulename

followed by a variable number of lines of text comprising the contents of *module-name*. The end of the text comprising a module is indicated by the next line beginning with @, or the end of file. For example, a simple archive file might contain

```
@module1
Line 1 of module 1
Line 2 of module 1
```

@module2
Line 1 of module 2
@modulexy15
Line 1 of module xy15

Assume a second text file *progin* has a Pascal program with frequently used modules (whose text appears in the archive file) omitted. File *progin* contains two types of lines, those that begin with @ followed by a module name and those that do not begin with @. Write a Pascal program that will copy text file *progin* to a third text file *progout*, leaving the lines that do not begin with @ unchanged and replacing those that begin with @ by the lines of text file *ar* following the @*modulename* line. You may assume that module names contain no more than 20 characters and the lines in all text files involved will contain no more than 100 characters.

Example file *progin*:

```
PROGRAM sample (input, output);
@declarations
@reader
@writer
@sorter
BEGIN
        readstuff;
        sortstuff;
        writestuff
END
```

Example file *ar*:

```
@declarations
VAR
    numitems : integer;
    stuff : ARRAY [1..1000] OF things;
@reader
PROCEDURE readstuff;
    ...
@writer
PROCEDURE writestuff;
    ...
@sorter
PROCEDURE sortstuff;
    ...
```

Example output on file *progout*:

```
PROGRAM sample (input, output);
VAR
```

```
        numitems : integer;
        stuff : ARRAY [1..1000] OF things;
PROCEDURE readstuff;

    ...
PROCEDURE writestuff;

    ...
PROCEDURE sortstuff;

    ...
BEGIN
        readstuff;
        sortstuff;
        writestuff
END
```

CHAPTER 13

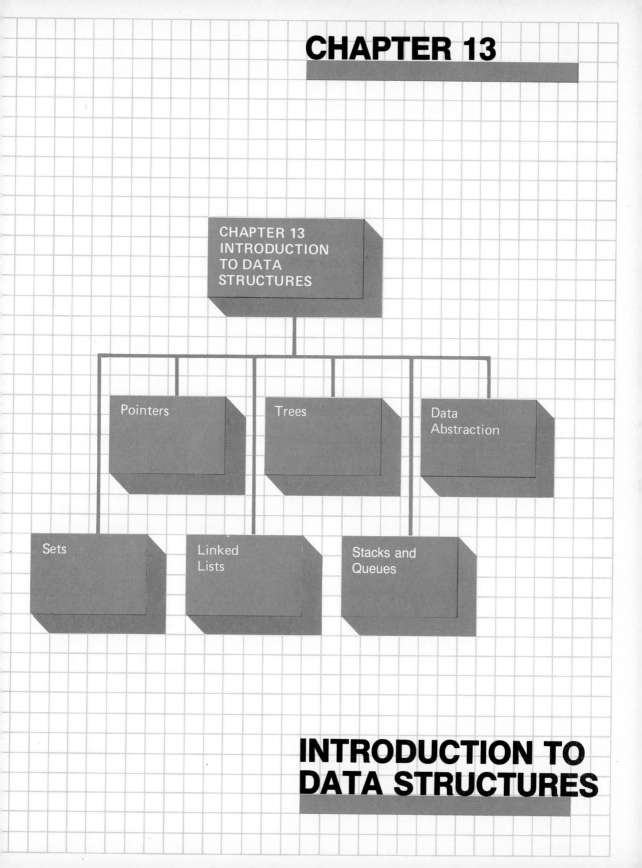

CHAPTER 13
INTRODUCTION
TO DATA
STRUCTURES

Pointers

Trees

Data
Abstraction

Sets

Linked
Lists

Stacks and
Queues

INTRODUCTION TO
DATA STRUCTURES

OBJECTIVES

After completing this chapter, you should be able to:

■ Recognize and apply the set data type and the set operations union, intersection, and difference
■ Define and declare pointers and pointer variables
■ Create dynamic variables
■ Create and apply dynamic data structures, such as linked lists, binary trees, stacks, and queues

CHAPTER OVERVIEW

In this chapter an introduction to data structures, especially dynamic data structures, is presented. Pascal includes the structured data types arrays, records, files, and sets. We have already discussed arrays, records, and files in previous chapters. In Section 13.1 we consider the set data type. Pascal is one of the few structured high-level languages that supports the set data type.

Pascal includes another predefined data type called a *pointer*. In Section 13.2 pointers are discussed. A pointer variable contains the address of a memory location. Using pointers, we are able to create *dynamic data structures*. These data structures can be expanded by adding new components or contracted by deleting components during the execution of the program. Dynamic data structures do not have the size restrictions that accompany data structures like arrays. Recall the size of an array must be specified before the program is executed. A data structure such as an array with a size that cannot be changed during execution of the program is called a *static data structure*.

The remainder of the chapter introduces dynamic data structures that can be constructed with the use of pointers. These data structures are discussed in more detail in advanced computer science courses. We discuss the following data structures: linked lists, binary trees, stacks, and queues. The application of such dynamic data structures often provides efficient and effective solutions to many complex data-handling problems. As you will see in a structured high-level language such as Pascal, these dynamic data structures can be readily implemented.

SECTION 13.1 SETS

Pascal includes a structured data type known as a set. An introduction to sets can be found in Chapter 8. A *set* is a collection of objects of the same type. For example, the set of positive even numbers less than 13 is represented as follows (note the square brackets are used when listing the set):

[2, 4, 6, 8, 10, 12]

Recall that this list is called a *set constructor*. The objects belonging to a set are called *elements*. So in this example, 2, 4, 6, 8, 10, and 12 are elements of the given set.

The elements must be distinct, and the order of the elements is not important. For example, the following set is equal to the set given above:

[12, 10, 8, 6, 4, 2]

To declare a set variable, we must first define the set type. For example, consider the following definition and declaration:

```
TYPE
      number = SET OF 1..50;
VAR
      numset : number;
```

The type statement defines the set of potential members. So a set of type number can include any collection of integers chosen from 1 to 50, including the *empty set,* [ ]. We can use an assignment statement to place elements in a set. For the above example, the following table shows several assignments to the set variable *numset*:

assignment	*elements in set*
numset := [1,2,9,10]	1, 2, 9, 10
numset := [1,3,5,7,9]	1, 3, 5, 7, 9
numset := [2,4,6,8,10,12]	2, 4, 6, 8, 10, 12
numset := [10,20,30,40,50]	10, 20, 30, 40, 50
numset := [1]	1
numset := [ ]	None (empty set)

A set type has the following form:

```
TYPE
      identifier = SET OF base type
```

The set type identifier is followed by the usual equal sign, then the reserved words SET and OF, and finally the base type which describes the type of members permitted in the set. The base type can be a simple or enumerated type, including the subrange types.

Most implementations of Pascal impose a restriction on the maximum number of elements that a set may contain. For example, one system requires that the base type specify no more than 64 values. In this case the set TYPE definition

```
TYPE
      number = SET OF 1..128;
```

would not be permitted, since there are 128 distinct values permitted by the type *1..128*. Likewise, the set TYPE definition

TYPE
    alfa = SET OF char;

might not be permitted if more than 64 unique characters existed. In addition, some systems also require that the smallest ordinal value of any set member be nonnegative. The set TYPE definition

TYPE
    number = SET OF −50.. −1

would not be permitted in such systems. You should determine if any such restrictions exist in your system.

The set consisting of all possible values of the base type is called the ***universal set***. The following statement will assign the universal set to the set variable *numset* previously declared:

numset := [1..50]

A set contained within another set is called a ***subset*** of that set. So every element of the first set is also an element of the second set. For example, given the set [*2,4,6,8,10,12*], the following are subsets of this set:

[2,4],   [6,8,10,12],   [12],   [2,8,12]

The following is another example of set declarations followed by valid and invalid assignments:

TYPE
    alphaset = SET OF 'A'..'Z';
    subject = (math, history, computer, english);
    courses = SET OF subject;
VAR
    vowels : alphaset;
    myclasses : courses;

Valid Assignments

    vowels := ['A','E','I','O','U']
    vowels := [ ]
    myclasses := [math,computer]
    myclasses := [math..english]

Invalid Assignments

    vowels := 'A'   (* type of 'A' is not set type *)
    myclasses := vowels (* set types are not identical *)

Set Operators

There are three set operators that may be used to combine two sets. Specifically, these operators are union (+), intersection (*), and difference (−). Suppose the variables *seta* and *setb* are both declared as sets of the same base type. Then the **union** of *seta* and *setb*

```
seta + setb
```

is a set whose elements appear in either *seta*, *setb*, or in both sets. The **intersection** of *seta* and *setb*

```
seta * setb
```

is a set whose elements appear in *both seta* and *setb*. Finally, the **difference** between *seta* and *setb*

```
seta − setb
```

is a set whose elements appear in *seta* but not in *setb*. The following examples should clarify the effect of these operators:

expression	*result*
[1,2,4,6] + [1,3,5,7]	[1,2,3,4,5,6,7]
[1,2,4,6] * [1,3,5,7]	[1]
[1,2,4,6] − [1,3,5,7]	[2,4,6]
[1,3,5,7] − [1,2,4,6]	[3,5,7]
[2,4,6] * [3,5,7]	[ ]
[1..20] + [16..50]	[1..50]
[1..20] * [16..50]	[16..20]
[1..20] − [16..50]	[1..15]

The order in which the set union, intersection, and difference operators are evaluated is the same as that of the corresponding arithmetic operators. That is, the set intersection operation is performed before the set union and set difference operations.

New elements can be added to a set using the union operator, and existing elements can be removed from a set using the difference operator. The statement

```
numset := numset + [10]
```

will add the element 10 to the set represented by variable *numset*. If *numset* already contained the element 10, then *numset* is not changed. Similarly, the statement

```
numset := numset − [10]
```

will remove the element 10 from *numset* if it existed; otherwise *numset* is not changed.

A set cannot be directly read from or written to a text file. The elements of a set, however, can be processed as usual. For example, we can read integer values from an input text file into the set *numset* as follows (assume *num* is an integer variable):

```
numset := [ ];                              (* initialize set *)
WHILE NOT eof DO
BEGIN
        WHILE NOT eoln DO
        BEGIN
                read (num);                 (* read the next number *)
                numset := numset + [num]    (* add it to the set *)
        END;
        readln
END
```

Reading is much simpler if we are processing an input file of a set type. If we assume the following declaration

```
TYPE
        number = SET OF 1..50;
VAR
        numset : number;
        f : FILE OF number
```

then to read the *entire* set, we need only write

```
reset (f);
read (f, numset)
```

Using the relational operator IN helps us display the contents of *numset* on a text file. Recall from Chapter 8 that we can test for the presence of an element in a set using the IN operator. For example

```
5 IN [1,2,4,5,6]
```

is true, but

```
3 IN [2,4,6,8]
```

is false. The following code will display the elements of *numset* (assume *index* is an integer variable):

```
FOR index := 1 TO 50 DO
        IF index IN numset
        THEN writeln (index)
```

Writing a set to a file of the appropriate type (consider the file *f* used previously) can be done as follows:

```
rewrite (f);
write (f, numset)
```

We may apply the relational operators $=$, $<>$, $<=$, and $>=$ to sets as well. The following table defines the result of applying each of the relational operators to a pair of sets, *seta* and *setb*. Note again that the result of the relational operators is Boolean.

expression	meaning	example yielding true
seta = setb	Sets are equal.	['A','E'] = ['E','A']
seta <> setb	Sets are unequal.	[2,4] <> [2,3]
seta <= setb	*seta* subset of *setb*.	[1,2,5] <= [1,2,4,5]
seta >= setb	*setb* subset of *seta*.	['A','C'] >= ['A']

In the next problem we will write a procedure to compute the symmetric difference of two sets *a* and *b*. The **symmetric difference** of two sets is defined as the set of elements in *a* and not in *b* together with the set of elements in *b* and not in *a*.

Problem 13.1

Write a procedure called symmetric *that forms the symmetric difference of two sets* a *and* b *having the following set type:*

```
TYPE
     alphabet = SET OF 'A' .. 'Z';
```

The following procedure will store the symmetric difference in *setc*:

```
PROCEDURE symmetric (VAR seta, setb, setc : alphabet);
(* compute symmetric difference of seta and setb *)
BEGIN
     setc := (seta − setb) + (setb − seta)
END;
```

In the next problem we consider an array of sets.

Problem 13.2

Write a Pascal program that will determine and display the set of divisors for each integer between 1 and 100 inclusively. The result should be stored in an array of sets called number.

The output from the execution of this program should begin as shown below:

Number	Divisor(s)
1	1
2	1 2
3	1 3
4	1 2 4
5	1 5
6	1 2 3 6

The algorithm used in the solution of this problem is presented below.

Divisor Algorithm

For each integer called *index* in the range 1 to 100:
    Initialize the set of divisors to include 1.
    For each number in the range 2 to *index*:
      If number evenly divides *index*,
      Then add number to the set of divisors.
For each integer called *index* in the range 1 to 100:
    For each integer called *divnum* in the range 1 to *index*:
      If *divnum* is in the set of divisors for *index*,
      Then display *divnum*.

The complete Pascal program is shown below. The program uses a "brute-force" approach to solve the problem. In the exercises a more efficient approach is suggested.

```
PROGRAM displaynum (input, output);
(* Determine and display the set of divisors for each *)
(* integer in the range 1 to 100.                     *)
TYPE
      divset = SET OF 1..100;
VAR
      number : ARRAY [1..100] OF divset;
      divisors : divset;
      divnum, index : 1..100;
BEGIN
      (* create the array of divisors *)
      FOR index := 1 TO 100 DO
      BEGIN
              (* initialize divisor set; 1 always included *)
              number[index] := [1];
              (* check for other divisors *)
              FOR divnum := 2 TO index DO
```

```
            IF index MOD divnum = 0
            THEN number[index] := number[index] + [divnum]
    END;
    (* display results *)
    writeln ('N u m b e r   D i v i s o r (s)');
    writeln ('– – – – – –   – – – – – – – – –');
    FOR index := 1 TO 100 DO
    BEGIN
            write (index:4, ' ':6);
            FOR divnum := 1 TO index DO
                IF divnum IN number[index]
                THEN write (divnum:1, ' ':1);
            writeln        (* skip to next line *)
    END
END.
```

EXERCISES FOR SECTION 13.1

1 Determine which of the following are valid set types:
   (a) TYPE digitset = SET OF 0..9;
        VAR num : digitset;
   (b) TYPE chrset = SET OF '0'..'9';
        VAR table : ARRAY [–10..10] OF chrset;
   (c) TYPE setarray = SET OF ARRAY [–10..10] OF char;
        VAR table : setarray;
   (d) TYPE
               mark = (comma,period,colon,semicolon,blank);
               special = SET OF mark;
        VAR symbol : special;
   (e) TYPE setchar = SET OF A..Z;
        VAR letter : setchar;

2 Given the set assignments

   seta := [1, 3, 5, 7, 9, 11]
   setb := [2, 4, 6, 8, 10, 12]
   setc := [1, 2, 3, 4, 5, 7]

   determine the sets resulting from the following expressions:
   (a) seta + setb
   (b) seta * setb
   (c) seta + setc
   (d) setb * setc

(e) seta − setb
(f) seta + setc * setb
(g) (seta − setb) * (setc − setb)
(h) seta * setc * setc
(i) setc − setc
(j) seta * (setc − setb) + setc
(k) seta * setc − setb

3 Determine the truth value of the following expressions:
(a) [1, 2, 3] = [3, 1, 2]
(b) [12, 14, 16] <= [12, 14, 16]
(c) [3, 6, 7] = [3, 6, 7] * [1, 3, 6, 7]
(d) [1..20] >= [1..30]
(e) 'B' IN ['C'..'T']

4 Given *seta* = [10], *setb* = [1, 3, 10], *setc* = [0, 1, 2, 3, 4], and *setd* = [3, 4, 5, 6], determine the result of each expression:
(a) seta * setb + setc − setd
(b) (setd − setb) − (setc * seta)
(c) (seta + setb) <= setc
(d) (setc * setd) <= setb
(e) 3 IN setb * setc * setd

5 Consider the declarations

```
TYPE
        name = (John,Paul,George,Ringo);
        group = SET OF name;
VAR combo : group;
```

List all possible sets that can be constructed from the base type *name* and stored in the set variable *combo*. (Hint: There are 16 possible sets, including the empty set.)

6 Write a Pascal program that reads two sentences in English and displays the set of letters appearing in either sentence but not both. Assume each sentence ends in a period. (Hint: Use procedure *symmetric* from Problem 13.1.)

7 Write a Pascal function that returns the number of members in a set of type

```
TYPE numset = SET OF 1..128
```

8 Modify program *displaynum* in Problem 13.2 so a more efficient solution is obtained. (Hint: Notice that divisors occur in pairs. For example, each divisor yields another divisor, namely the quotient. For example, the number 12 can be expressed as

$$12 = 1 * 12 = 2 * 6 = 3 * 4$$

We do not need to consider any divisors after 3, so the divisors are 1, 2, 3, 4, 6, and 12. The conclusion is that given a number, we need not consider any divisors beyond the integer part of the number's square root.)

SECTION 13.2 POINTERS

We have completed our discussion of the Pascal structured data types (arrays, records, files, and sets). Pascal includes yet another data type known as a ***pointer type***. Recall that the size of a Pascal array must be fixed and declared during compilation and before the program is executed. Because of these restrictions a Pascal array is called a ***static data structure***. Sometimes, however, we want to manipulate data that can change size during execution. A data structure that can be modified during the program's execution by expanding or contracting without specifying a fixed size is known as a ***dynamic data structure***. As you will see in the remainder of this chapter, complex dynamic data structures can be constructed by linking the components together using variables known as pointers.

In Pascal, a ***pointer*** is a variable that points to, or *references*, a memory location in which data is stored. Recall from Chapter 1 that each memory cell in the computer has an address that can be used to access that location. So a pointer variable points to a memory location. We can access and change the contents of this memory location via the pointer using the notation discussed below.

The following type definition defines a pointer type:

TYPE
        numpointer = ↑ integer;

In this example *numpointer* defines a pointer to a memory location that contains an integer value. The special symbol ↑, or the circumflex (^), must precede the type identifier to define a pointer type.

Now we can declare pointer variables:

VAR
        ptr1, ptr2 : numpointer;

The values stored in these pointer variables are initially undefined since no values have been assigned to them. Remember the value of a pointer variable will be a memory address. Such values are intrinsically dependent on the particular computer system being used. As a result, the ways in which we may manipulate pointer variables are restricted. We may not compare two pointer variables using the relational operators $>$, $>=$, $<$, and $<=$; we may only determine if two pointers are equal (that is, contain the same memory address) or not equal. Additionally, we may not read or write pointer variables from or to text files. That is, the pointer variables have no textual representation.

Since a pointer variable contains the address of a memory location, there are several ways in which such addresses can be assigned to a pointer variable. The first of these, the standard procedure *new*, obtains the address of an unused memory location of the appropriate type and assigns it to a pointer variable. For example, the statements

```
new (ptr1);
new (ptr2)
```

will obtain the addresses of two currently unused memory locations suitable for storing integers, then assign one of these to *ptr1* and the other to *ptr2*. The process of obtaining these memory locations is called **dynamic allocation**. The memory locations are also called **referenced variables**. We can only access these integer variables via the pointer variables as follows:

```
ptr1 ↑      (* integer variable pointed to by ptr1 *)
ptr2 ↑      (* integer variable pointed to by ptr2 *)
```

The following are valid assignments to the referenced variables:

```
ptr1 ↑ := 12;     (* store 12 in integer addressed by ptr1 *)
ptr1 ↑ := ptr1 ↑ + 4;     (* add 4 to integer addressed by ptr1 *)
```

Note, however, that the statements

```
ptr1 ↑ := 'A';
ptr1 := 12;
ptr1 := ptr1 + 4;
```

are invalid since the data types of the variables and constants involved are incompatible. That is, we cannot assign a character value to an integer or an integer value to a pointer variable because the types are not identical. Remember that the value of a pointer variable is an address that is dependent on the particular computer system being used. The assignment statement

```
ptr1 := ptr2
```

is allowed and causes *ptr1* to receive the same address as that stored in *ptr2*. After this assignment statement has been executed, the referenced variables *ptr1*↑ and *ptr2*↑ will be identically the same. That is, both *ptr1* and *ptr2* contain the address of the same memory location, and therefore *ptr1*↑ and *ptr2*↑ reference the same integer value.

Figure 13-1 illustrates three pointer variables *p*, *q*, and *r*, each pointing to a different referenced variable (memory location). Notice the referenced variable *p*↑ is of type integer, *q*↑ is of type real, and *r*↑ is a record type.

Pascal also provides a standard procedure *dispose* that will return a memory location to the "pool" of locations available for allocation by *new*. That is, *dispose* is the

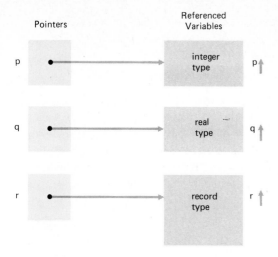

Figure 13-1   Pointers and referenced variables.

mechanism used to indicate that a memory location previously allocated with *new* is now no longer needed and to free that location for other use. For example,

```
dispose (ptr2)
```

will return the memory location pointed to by the pointer variable *ptr2*. Note that the pointer variable *ptr2* is still in existence. Its value, however, is undefined since it no longer references an available memory location.

Undefined pointer variables can often lead to unsuspected problems. Pascal includes a constant that can be assigned to any pointer variable to indicate that it does not point to any particular location. This constant is represented by the reserved word NIL. The statement

```
ptr1 := NIL
```

assigns this value to pointer variable *ptr1*. Note that a pointer variable with the NIL value is significantly different from one with an undefined value. We are permitted to compare a pointer containing a NIL value for equality or inequality with another pointer value, but a pointer variable containing an undefined address must never be used in a comparison; to do so would result in a run-time error or yield an undefined result. The following statement illustrates a valid comparison:

```
IF ptr1 = NIL
THEN writeln ('Ptr1 is nil.')
ELSE writeln ('Ptr1 points to ', ptr1↑)
```

We now have seen three different techniques for changing the address stored in a pointer variable:

1 Use the standard procedure *new* to assign the address of a newly allocated referenced variable.
2 Assign the address in a pointer variable of the same type.
3 Assign the value NIL.

Remember that pointer variables cannot be read from a text file or displayed. However, the referenced variables may be manipulated in any way permitted for variables of the same type. For example, *ptr1* is a pointer variable and therefore has several restrictions on how it may be manipulated. However, *ptr1*↑ is an integer referenced variable and may be manipulated just like any other integer variable. For example, the following are valid statements using the previously defined pointer variables *ptr1* and *ptr2*:

```
read (ptr1↑);
writeln (ptr2↑);
ptr2↑ := ptr1↑ * ptr2↑ + 3;
IF ptr2↑ < 0
THEN writeln ('Referenced variable is negative.')
```

The pointer variables presented so far contain the address of integer variables. However, pointer variables quite often point to structured data types, such as records. Study the following definitions and declarations very carefully:

```
TYPE
      recpointer = ↑recdata;
      recdata = RECORD
                     age : 21..99;      (* data fields *)
                     sex : (male, female);
                     salary : real;
                     recnext : recpointer      (* pointer *)
               END
VAR
      personrec : recpointer;
```

Notice the pointer TYPE definition *recpointer* includes the reference type *recdata* before the record is defined! In Pascal this is permissible for pointer TYPE definitions. After execution of the statement

```
new (personrec)
```

the contents of *personrec* will be the address of the allocated storage for the record. Notice that one of the fields of the record is also a pointer to a record. This is permissible, and as you will see in the next section, we can dynamically create a chain of records linked together by the pointer fields.

1 Determine which of the following are valid statements assuming the following definition and declaration:

```
TYPE
      lapointer = ↑integer;
      lepointer = ↑char;
VAR
      ptr1, ptr2 : lapointer;
      ptr3, ptr4 : lepointer;
```

(a) new (ptr1)
(b) new (ptr1↑)
(c) ptr1 := ptr3
(d) ptr2↑ := ptr2↑ + ptr1↑
(e) ptr1 := NIL
(f) ptr4↑ := NIL
(g) writeln (ptr2, ptr3)
(h) read (ptr1↑, ptr4↑)

2 Assume the declarations of the previous exercise. Determine the output of the following code:

```
new (ptr1);
new (ptr2);
new (ptr3);
ptr2 := ptr1;
ptr1↑ := 2;
ptr2↑ := 3;
ptr3↑ := 'A';
writeln (ptr1↑, prt2↑, ptr3↑)
```

3 Is there anything wrong with the following code? Assume that *ptr1* is a pointer variable referencing an integer variable.

```
new (ptr1);
read (ptr1↑);
writeln (ptr1↑);
dispose (ptr1);
writeln (ptr1↑)
```

4 Assume the declarations of exercise 1. Determine which of the following statements are valid:
(a) ptr1 := NIL
(b) ptr2 := new (ptr1)

(c) dispose (ptr3)

(d) ptr3↑ := NIL

(e) ptr3 := ptr4 AND (ptr3 = NIL)

5 Determine the output of the following code assuming the declarations of exercise 1:

```
new (ptr3);
new (ptr1);
ptr3↑ := 'Z';
ptr2 := NIL;
ptr4 := NIL;
IF (ptr3 <> NIL) AND (ptr2 = NIL)
THEN writeln ('Code A');
IF ptr3↑ = 'Z'
THEN writeln ('Code Z')
ELSE writeln ('Code X')
```

SECTION 13.3 LINKED LISTS

The most common pointer types are pointers to records. As we saw in the last section, each record can contain at least one field consisting of a pointer to another record. Given this situation, we can create dynamic variables that are records containing pointers to other records. These pointers can form a chain of records known as a ***linked list***.

Why bother with such a data structure when an array of records can be constructed without the need of a chain of pointers? Consider the problem of inserting or deleting a component in any array. For example, the text-editing program in Chapter 10 included procedures to insert and delete lines. The time required to add or delete lines in the array of lines can often be quite long, due to the necessary shifting of the components in the array. However, as you will see in this section, if the components form a linked list, insertion and deletion can often be done more rapidly by simply changing pointer values. The use of linked lists requires an increase in memory, due to the need to store pointers. In other words, there is a trade-off; using more memory in an effective manner can reduce the time required to perform the task.

Let us create a linked list of records. Suppose the following definitions and declarations are given (the actual record fields will not be specified except for the pointer field):

```
TYPE
     pointer =  ↑arecord;
     arecord = RECORD
                     field : type;     (* data field(s) *)
                     nextrec : pointer
                 END;
```

```
VAR
    startpointer : pointer;
    currentptr : pointer;
    index : integer;
```

Notice we have declared two pointer variables. *Startpointer* will contain the address of the start of the list, and *currentptr* will contain the address of the most recently created record. The following statements dynamically create the first record and initialize the pointers to the start of the list:

```
new (startpointer);
currentptr := startpointer
```

Now to create a linked list with, say, three more records and the pointer in the last record set to NIL, the following code will work:

```
FOR index := 1 TO 3 DO
BEGIN
        new (currentptr↑.nextrec);      (* get new record *)
        currentptr :=
            currentptr↑.nextrec   (* advance pointer *)
END;
currentptr↑.nextrec := NIL     (* terminate list *)
```

Figure 13-2 shows the construction of this linked list.
  The statement in the FOR loop

```
currentptr := currentptr↑.nextrec
```

Figure 13-2   Linked list.

will advance the pointer each time through the loop. The linked list is terminated with the value NIL. Note that the above loop merely creates the linked list by allocating the memory for each record and advancing the pointer to the next record. We could have included a *read* statement to enter the data into each record.

Searching a Linked List

Suppose in our previous example a linked list has been created where each record contains a character data value and a pointer to the next record. So our TYPE definition would be as follows:

```
TYPE
     pointer =  ↑arecord;
     arecord = RECORD
                     data : char;
                     nextrec : pointer
               END;
```

Further let us assume the pointer *startpointer* has been initialized to the beginning of the linked list and that the *nextrec* field in the last record in the linked list has the value NIL. Assume there are an unknown number of records and that the linked list is not empty; that is, there is at least one record. Refer to Figure 13-2 with each data field replaced by a character data value. Consider the following problem on searching the linked list.

Problem 13.3

Write a Pascal procedure called search *that displays a message indicating whether or not a character value called* code *occurs in one of the records in the linked list.*

The solution is shown in the following procedure that assumes the previous TYPE definition:

```
PROCEDURE search (code : char;
                     startpointer : pointer;
                     VAR currentptr : pointer);
(* Search for code in linked list, and display an *)
(* appropriate message.                           *)
BEGIN
     currentptr := startpointer; (* init. current pointer *)
     WHILE (currentptr ↑ .data <> code) AND (* code not found *)
         (currentptr ↑ .nextrec <> NIL) DO (* and not end of list? *)
         currentptr := currentptr ↑ .nextrec; (* advance *)
     IF currentptr ↑ .data = code(* code found? *)
     THEN writeln ('Code found in list.')(* yes, success! *)
     ELSE writeln ('Code not found in list.') (* no, failure *)
END;
```

Suppose a sorted array of integers is given and a new integer is to be inserted in its correct position in the array. As mentioned earlier, this process can often be quite time-consuming, especially when many elements must be shifted or copied. However, if the data structure is a linked list, then insertion can be performed by adjusting pointers. For example, consider the linked list shown in Figure 13-3a, where the integer values in the records are in increasing order as follows: 2, 6, 12, 15. The pointer from each record points to the next record, except, of course, for the last record which contains the NIL pointer.

Suppose a record containing the integer value 8 is to be inserted. As can be seen from Figure 13-3b, a new record containing the value 8 is created and the pointer from the record containing the value 6 now points to the new record, while the pointer of the new record points to the record containing the value 12. No components have to be shifted as is the case with arrays. A little reflection on this example should convince you of the efficiency of this method of inserting into a linked list as opposed to that of inserting into an array.

Figure 13-3 Linked list insertion.

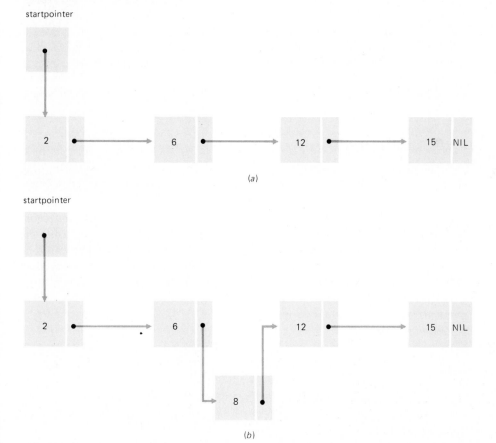

Now suppose we are given a linked list with the previous declarations where the values in the records are in increasing order. Suppose a record containing an integer value called *newnumber* is to be inserted in the correct position of the linked list so that the values in the records are still in order. Let's assume we have two pointers called *smaller* and *larger* that point to the records immediately preceding *newnumber* and immediately following *newnumber*. In the example, *smaller* would point to the record containing the value 6, while *larger* would point to the record containing 12. Now we can write the actual Pascal statements to perform the insertion.

The first step is to dynamically allocate storage to a new record and store the value *newnumber* into the record using the pointer variable *insertptr* (assume *insertptr* is declared pointer):

```
new (insertptr);
insertptr↑.data := newnumber
```

Now we can adjust the pointers using the pointer variables *smaller* and *larger*:

```
smaller↑.nextrec := insertptr;
insertptr↑.nextrec := larger
```

Note that in this example we have assumed that *newnumber* lies between two other values in the linked list. It may happen that *newnumber* is smaller than any value in the list or, perhaps, larger than any value in the list. These cases would have to be considered when writing a complete program to perform insertion in a linked list.

Linked List Deletion

Let's follow up on the same example and see how easy it is to delete an element from the list. Figure 13-4*a* shows the original linked list with values 2, 6, 12, and 15. Suppose the value 12 is to be deleted. Figure 13-4*b* shows the pointer adjustments.

The pointer from the record containing the value 6 is adjusted to point to the record containing the value 15, and the record containing the value 12 is freed using the procedure *dispose*. Assume the pointer variable *currentptr* points to the record to be deleted and *smaller* is a pointer variable pointing to the record immediately preceding the record to be deleted. Then the following statements will accomplish the deletion:

```
smaller↑.nextrec := currentptr↑.nextrec;
dispose (currentptr)
```

Again, this does not work if the record to be deleted is the first one, since there is no record immediately preceding the first one. That case must be handled separately in a complete program that performs deletion from a linked list (see exercise 5 in the section exercises that follow). Finally, if the last record is to be deleted, the pointer from the next to the last record must be set to the value NIL.

startpointer

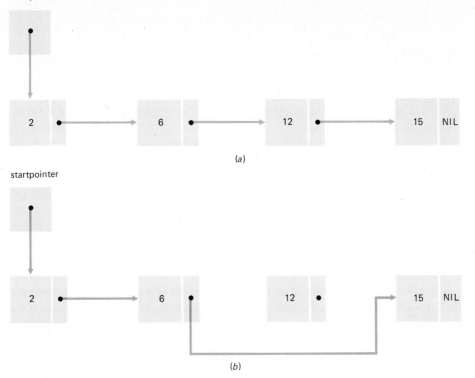

startpointer

(a)

(b)

Figure 13-4   Linked list deletion.

EXERCISES FOR SECTION 13.3

1   Why was the value NIL used to mark the end of the linked list?

2   Write a Pascal segment similar to the one presented at the beginning of the section on creating a linked list that includes a third pointer variable that points to the last record in the linked list.

3   Write a procedure similar to that shown for problem 13.3 that will display the contents of the data values in each record of the linked list.

4   Referring to the material on linked list insertion, write a Pascal segment to insert a new record at the beginning of the linked list.

5   Referring to the material on linked list deletion, write a Pascal segment to delete the first record in the linked list.

SECTION 13.4   TREES

If you examine the figures in this text containing top-down design diagrams, you will observe that they have a *tree structure*. That is, there is exactly one box at the top

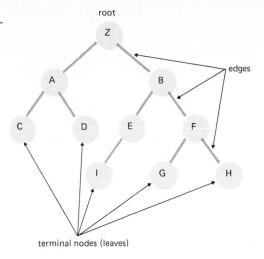

Figure 13-5   A binary tree.

level of the design called the *root* of the tree. The root of the tree design is connected to boxes at the next level below the root. Each of these boxes may, in turn, be connected to other boxes at the next lower level. Figure 13-5 shows an example of a general tree structure with the boxes replaced by labeled circles.

The labeled circles are called *nodes* and they are connected together by *edges*. The root in Figure 13-5 is labeled Z and has two offspring, a left offspring labeled A and a right offspring labeled B. The node labeled A also has two offspring, C and D. However, C and D do not have offspring and are called *terminal nodes*, or *leaves*.

If a tree has the property that each node has no more than two offspring, then it is called a *binary tree*. Figure 13-5 shows a binary tree since each node has either zero, one, or two offspring. Binary trees are important data structures in computer science that provide very efficient techniques for storing and retrieving data.

To construct a binary tree in Pascal we use records to represent nodes and pointers to represent the edges. In binary trees we need two pointers (left and right) to point to the offspring, if any. We set a pointer to NIL if there is no offspring in the corresponding direction. The definition of the node in a binary tree would be

```
TYPE
    pointer = ↑node;
    node = RECORD
              field : type;             (* data field(s) *)
              left : pointer;            (* ptr to left offspring *)
              right : pointer            (* ptr to right offspring *)
           END;
```

Notice the major difference between the linked list shown previously and the binary tree developed here is that the binary tree uses only two pointers.

Now let us see why binary trees are so useful. Suppose we have an array containing the following characters:

D F E B A C G

Recall from Chapter 9, "Arrays," that to determine whether a character is in the list, we can do a linear search (since the characters are not in alphabetical order). However, if the size of the array is large, a linear search is very inefficient, especially if the item is not in the list. To determine whether the item is not in the list would require searching the whole array. We can sort the array and use a binary search, which is very efficient. But suppose data items are being continually inserted and deleted. Then we have the same problem discussed in the previous section on inserting and deleting items in an array.

What is needed is a data structure where the items can be efficiently located, deleted, and inserted. One solution to this problem is a dynamic data structure known as a *binary search tree*. First we have to build the data structure. To construct a binary search tree we use the following algorithm:

STEP 1 The first data item is used to create the root of the binary search tree.

STEP 2 For each remaining data item, first compare with the root. If the item alphabetically precedes the root's value, then the item either becomes a left offspring or is compared to the existing left offspring and the process is repeated. If the item alphabetically follows the root, then the item either becomes a right offspring or is compared to the existing right offspring and the process is repeated.

Returning to our example and applying the algorithm, the character D is used as the data value for the root of the tree. The next item, F, follows D and becomes a right offspring of the root. Next, E is compared to the root. Since E follows D, it is compared to the right offspring F. As E precedes F, E is a left offspring of F. The process is repeated for each of the remaining data items. Figure 13-6 shows the resulting binary search tree.

We can now create a binary search tree from a collection of data items. Adding new data items to the tree is accomplished by executing step 2 of the algorithm used

Figure 13-6 Binary search tree.

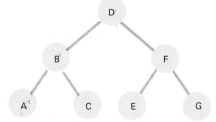

to build the tree initially. Algorithms for deleting items from a binary search tree will not be covered here.

It is important to note that the left offspring of the root and all its descendants (whether left or right offspring) have data items less than that of the root. The right offspring and all of its descendants have data items greater than that of the root.

To locate a data item called *key* in a binary search tree, the algorithm begins by comparing *key* to the root. If *key* equals the root, the search terminates successfully. If *key* precedes the root, the search continues with the left offspring. Otherwise, the search continues with the right offspring, since *key* follows the root. If there are no offspring remaining to compare, then *key* is not in the search tree. The following problem requires the use of this algorithm.

Problem 13.4

Write a Pascal function called bsearch *to determine if a character variable called* key *is located in a binary search tree. The value of search should be NIL if the item is not located or a pointer to the located node. Assume the following TYPE definition for the nodes in the tree:*

```
TYPE
     pointer = ↑node;
     node = RECORD
                  letter : char;
                  left : pointer;
                  right : pointer
               END;
```

The solution to this problem is presented below:

```
FUNCTION bsearch (bintree: pointer; key: char): pointer;
(* Search bintree for key, returning a pointer to its *)
(* record if found. Return NIL otherwise. *)
VAR done : boolean;
BEGIN
     done := false;
     REPEAT
            IF bintree = NIL
            THEN done := true
            ELSE IF key < bintree ↑ .letter
                    THEN bintree := bintree ↑ .left   (* key < value *)
                    ELSE IF key > bintree ↑ .letter   (* key > value *)
                            THEN bintree := bintree ↑ .right
                            ELSE done := true          (* key = value *)
     UNTIL done;
     bsearch := bintree
END;
```

In many problems it is important to *traverse* a binary tree. That is, we may need to examine each node in the tree, for example, to list the data values in the nodes or perform some other operation on each data value.

There are many ways in which the nodes in a binary tree may be visited. For example, there are six different orders in which the nodes in a binary tree with only three nodes may be traversed. Figure 13-7 shows a binary tree with three nodes labeled A, C, and E. The orders in which the nodes may be traversed are also included. For example, the order ACE means visit the root A, then visit C, followed by E.

Most frequently, though, only three orders of traversal are used, and these are easily implemented by visiting the root and traversing the **right subtree** and the **left subtree** (but not necessarily in that order). The left subtree of the root is the left offspring of the root and all its descendants. The right subtree of the root is similarly defined. This definition also applies at any node other than the root. Each subtree except the empty tree (NIL) also has a root.

The three most frequently used traversals of a binary tree always traverse left subtrees before right subtrees. These are called the *inorder*, *postorder*, and *preorder* traversals. These names reflect when the root is visited in the traversal: Inorder visits the root in the middle of the traversal, preorder visits the root first, and postorder visits the root last.

The inorder traversal has the following recursive algorithm:

STEP 1 Traverse the left subtree.
STEP 2 Visit the root.
STEP 3 Traverse the right subtree.

Applying this algorithm to the binary search tree in Figure 13-6, we would visit the nodes in the order

list root 1st time below

A   B   C   D   E   F   G

Note that this traversal algorithm will visit the nodes of a binary search tree in ascending order. This feature makes inorder traversal the most frequently used traversal type. The following recursive Pascal procedure implements this algorithm. The procedure *visit* is used to perform any desired operation on the node referenced by its parameter, and is not shown. Assume the same declarations as problem 13.4.

Figure 13-7 Tree traversals.

Six possible traversals: ACE,
AEC, CAE, CEA, EAC, ECA

```
PROCEDURE traversal (bintree : pointer);
(* Perform inorder traversal of binary tree. *)
BEGIN
    IF bintree <> NIL
    THEN BEGIN
        traversal (bintree↑.left);             (* left subtree *)
        visit (bintree);                       (* visit subtree root *)
        traversal (bintree↑.right)             (* right subtree *)
    END
END;
```

The postorder (or bottom-up) traversal has the following recursive algorithm:

list root when passed on the right

STEP 1 Traverse the left subtree.
STEP 2 Traverse the right subtree.
STEP 3 Visit the root.

When it is applied to the binary search tree of Figure 13-6, the nodes are visited in this order:

A   C   B   E   G   F   D

Finally, the preorder (or depth-first) traversal has the following recursive algorithm:

list root when passed on the left

STEP 1 Visit the root.
STEP 2 Traverse the left subtree.
STEP 3 Traverse the right subtree.

The preorder traversal applied to Figure 13-6 results in the nodes' being visited in the order

D   B   A   C   F   E   G

EXERCISES FOR SECTION 13.4

1 Construct a binary search tree for the following letters using the order given:

   H   J   A   C   B   Z   T

2 Construct a binary search tree for the following sequence of integers:

   7   3   6   2   1   4   8   5

3 Apply the three traversal algorithms to the binary search trees produced in problems 1 and 2.

4 Write a procedure to insert a new character called *newchar* in the binary search tree used in function *search*.

5 Write a recursive procedure similar to procedure *traversal* that visits the nodes of a binary tree in postorder traversal.

6 Write a recursive procedure similar to procedure *traversal* that visits the nodes of a binary tree in preorder traversal.

SECTION 13.5 STACKS AND QUEUES

In this section we present a brief discussion of two dynamic data structures, namely, stacks and queues, that are used in compilers, operating systems, and other applications. A **stack** is a dynamic data structure having a "top" with the property that the last element "pushed" onto the stack is the first element to "pop" off the stack. Access to each element is from one end called the **top** of the stack. Think of a stack of dishes in a cafeteria. The top plate is the only accessible dish, but as soon as it is removed, the dish immediately below it rises to the top.

A stack can be represented by a linked list with the starting pointer used as the top of the stack and the last pointer equal to NIL, as usual. Figure 13-8 shows a stack created with the insertion of the following characters in the order shown:

W   C   A   B

Notice the last element inserted is B, which is at the top of the stack. Assuming the TYPE definition

```
TYPE
    stackptr = ↑stackrec;
    stackrec = RECORD
                    symbol : char;
                    nextrec : stackptr
               END;
```

Figure 13-8   A stack.

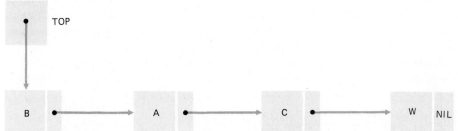

then the following procedure will push a new character called *newletter* onto the top of the stack.

```
PROCEDURE push (newletter : char; VAR top : stackptr);
(* Push newletter onto top of stack. *)
VAR
     temptr : stackptr;
BEGIN
     new (temptr);                    (* create new top of stack record *)
     temptr↑.symbol := newletter;              (* save newletter *)
     temptr↑.nextrec := top;          (* point to old stack top *)
     top := temptr                 (* update top of stack pointer *)
END;
```

The following procedure called *pop* will remove the element *outchar* at the top of the stack and adjust the top-of-stack pointer appropriately. Since you cannot remove an element from an empty stack, an error message is displayed if the stack is currently empty.

```
PROCEDURE pop (VAR outchar : char; VAR top : stackptr);
(* Pop top of stack element into outchar. *)
VAR
     temptr : stackptr;
BEGIN
     IF top = NIL
     THEN writeln ('Error in pop: stack is empty.')
     ELSE BEGIN
               outchar := top ↑ .symbol;        (* fetch top char *)
               temptr := top;             (* save pointer to top *)
               top := top ↑ .nextrec;       (* adjust top pointer *)
               dispose (temptr)         (* dispose of old record *)
          END
END;
```

Stacks have numerous applications in computer science. For example, when executing recursive procedures or functions, the computer uses a stack to keep track of the recursive invocations. Also, when the computer evaluates expressions, it translates them into an equivalent parenthesis-free form. Then using a stack for temporary storage, the computer can evaluate expressions efficiently.

A *queue* is a data structure where elements are entered in one end and removed at the other. The first element inserted is always the first element removed, unlike a stack in which the first element inserted is always the last element removed. This is analogous to the lines, or queues, formed at a grocery store checkout. The first person in line is (almost) always the first person out. Figure 13-9 shows a queue created with the insertion of the following characters in the order shown (note the necessity to use two pointers, front and rear).

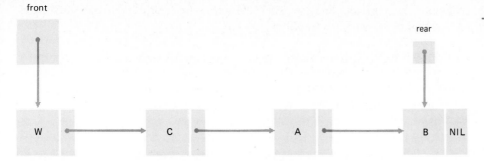

Figure 13-9 A queue.

W   C   A   B

Notice the element W which was inserted first is at the front of the queue and the element B was inserted last and is at the rear. To add an element to the rear of the queue, the procedure called *enqueue*, shown below, can be used. When the queue is empty (that is, *front* = NIL and *rear* = NIL), both pointers *front* and *rear* must be assigned the address of a newly allocated element. If the queue is not empty, a new element is added after *rear↑* and *rear* is adjusted to point to the newly added element. Assume we have declared two pointers, *front* and *rear*, of type *queptr* (defined as shown below).

```
TYPE
     queptr = ↑ querec;
     querec = RECORD
                    symbol : char;
                    nextrec : queptr
                END;
PROCEDURE enqueue(newletter : char; VAR front, rear : queptr);
(* Add new element to rear of queue. *)
VAR
     tempq : queptr;
     BEGIN
        new (tempq);                          (* allocate a new record *)
        tempq↑.symbol := newletter;           (* store the new letter *)
        IF rear <> NIL                        (* add to rear of *)
        THEN rear↑.nextrec := tempq;          (* existing queue *)
        tempq↑.nextrec := NIL;                (* terminate the queue *)
        rear := tempq;                        (* adjust rear pointer *)
        IF front = NIL                        (* if previously empty *)
        THEN front := rear                    (* adjust front pointer *)
END;
```

To remove an element from the front of the queue is similar to the procedure *pop* used to remove an element from a stack. In the procedure *dequeue*, shown below, however, we must consider the case of the queue becoming empty and also appropriately set the rear pointer to NIL.

```
PROCEDURE dequeue (VAR outchar : char; VAR front, rear : queptr);
(* Remove an element from the front of queue. *)
VAR
     tempq : queptr;
BEGIN
     IF front = NIL
     THEN writeln ('Error in dequeue: queue is empty.')
     ELSE BEGIN
               outchar :=  front↑.symbol;       (* save element *)
               tempq :=  front;                (* save front pointer *)
               front :=  front↑.nextrec;        (* adjust front *)
               dispose (tempq);           (* dispose of old record *)
               IF front := NIL          (* if queue is now empty *)
               THEN rear :=  NIL (* then reset rear pointer *)
          END
END;
```

EXERCISES FOR SECTION 13.5

1 Without using pointers, describe how a stack can be implemented using an array. How would you keep track of the top of the stack?

2 Write a Boolean-valued function that returns true if a stack is empty and false otherwise. Assume the same declarations as the procedures *push* and *pop*.

3 Is it necessary to test for a full stack? Explain your answer.

4 Write a procedure to display all the elements in a queue from front to rear. Assume the same declarations as the queue management procedures in this section.

5 Write a procedure that will initialize a queue to empty. If the queue is initially not empty, be certain to free all storage currently used.

SECTION 13.6 DATA ABSTRACTION

Throughout this textbook we have emphasized the top-down approach to algorithm design. In this approach many details of the problem solution are deferred until it becomes necessary to implement them during the stepwise refinement process. As you know, programs manipulate data used to model objects, and thus require the design of the data structures used in the model. In this chapter we have considered various types of data structures. The immediate question is how does one design and implement the appropriate data structure for a particular model? One answer to this question is characterized by a technique called ***data abstraction***.

The top-down approach can also be applied to the design of data structures. We refer to this as data abstraction. In this approach we begin with a general, or abstract, data structure and avoid specifying the implementation details. We need only specify the functions that the program will use to manipulate the data structure. In the next refinement we give the data structure in more detail, such as giving the pseudocode for the functions. In the final refinement we specify the implementation details for the functions and the storage organization of the data structure.

For example, consider the problem of alphabetically ordering a list of names. We have already described several sorting algorithms, any of which can be used in the solution of this problem. Let's consider the design of the data structure. At the highest level of data abstraction we have a list of names, each name except the last is followed by a single name, and each name except the first is preceded by a single name. The next level requires more detail to specify the data structure. We know that we must be able to compare individual names in the data structure (for ordering), and we must also be able to change the position of a name in the data structure, relative to its predecessor and successor in the list. These are the only functions necessary to completely order the list of names. Note that at this level we have left completely unspecified any details about how the names are actually stored. At more detailed levels of specification we must decide whether to use an array of records, with each record containing a name represented as an array of characters, or perhaps to use an array of arrays of character strings (that is, a two dimensional array of characters). Finally we must implement the functions and the storage for the list by writing Pascal code for each function we have identified, as well as the declarations for the data structure. These observations are summarized below.

level	data abstraction	example
Highest	Generalized data structure	A list of names
	Functions required to manipulate the data	Comparison of two names, Movement of a name.
Lowest	Pascal procedures, functions, and declarations	VAR name : ARRAY [1..100] OF PACKED ARRAY [1..25] OF char; FUNCTION comparenames (...) FUNCTION movename (...)

The specific data structure to be used depends on many factors, such as limitations of time and storage, program specifications and restrictions. The important point to remember is that data abstraction when applied effectively can simplify the problem solving process in a way similar to the top-down design of algorithms.

SECTION 13.7 TESTING AND DEBUGGING TECHNIQUES

Pointers are a potential source of many errors due to the rules regarding their use. For example, declaring a pointer variable is not sufficient to allow a memory location to be referenced. Either it must be assigned the value of a pointer that currently points to a memory location or it must appear as the argument of the new procedure. The pointer variable contains the address of a memory location. To access the referenced variable at that memory location we must suffix the special symbol ↑ to the pointer variable. If the pointer is undefined or NIL, attempting to access the referenced variable will cause a run-time error.

Using the procedure *dispose* on a pointer will leave the pointer logically undefined, and it should not be used to access a referenced variable. Unfortunately, some Pascal implementations will allow the pointer variable to be used to access the same referenced variable even after *dispose* has been applied, leading to the potential use of storage that has already been reallocated, perhaps to a dynamic variable of a different type!

Sometimes errors can result from the procedure *new* being invoked in an infinite loop, or just attempting to allocate more storage than is available on the computer system. Another potential reason for running out of storage is failing to use the procedure *dispose* to return unused storage. There is no way for the Pascal system to know when dynamic variables are no longer needed unless you explicitly indicate this using *dispose*.

Normally passing large data structures as value parameters is discouraged since it requires copying the entire data structure. With dynamic data structures this situation is improved since we need only pass the pointers to the data structure. A pointer requires only a small amount of storage, and copying pointers is a very efficient operation. You should be careful in passing dynamic data structures this way, though, since changes to the elements in the data structure affect the original, and not a copy of the structure.

Since dynamic structures such as linked lists and queues can be empty, it is important to include appropriate tests for this condition. Failure to do so can result in run-time errors or incorrect results.

If problems occur in programs using dynamic data structures, it is sometimes helpful to display the data stored in the structure and the relation between the elements. For example, if we are using a binary search tree, we can use any of the three traversal procedures to visit each node in the tree, and the procedure *visit* would contain only a *write* or *writeln* statement to display the data field (or fields) in the node.

The following are some important Pascal reminders to aid in testing and debugging.

PASCAL REMINDERS

■ Enclose set constructors with square brackets:

['A','E','I','O','U']

■ The individual elements of a set cannot be accessed directly; use the IN operator to test for membership.
■ Sets must be initialized prior to manipulation.
■ The set operators " + ", " − ", and "*", when applied to sets, are not the same as the corresponding arithmetic operators but do have the same precedence.

- Pointer variables contain addresses of memory locations.
- Pointer variables cannot be read from or written to text files.
- Pointer variables of the same type can be compared for equality or inequality or assigned to each other.
- To access the variable at the memory location specified by a pointer variable, use the name of the pointer variable followed by " ↑ ".
- When defining pointer data types, be certain to put the symbol " ↑ " before the type identifier:

```
TYPE pointer = ↑ integer;
```

- Pointer variables should not be left undefined; use the NIL value if necessary.
- *Dispose (ptr)* will leave *ptr* logically undefined; referencing *ptr* ↑ will cause either a logical or run-time error.

SECTION 13.8 CHAPTER REVIEW

In this chapter we discussed the structured data type known as the set. The set operations union, intersection, and difference were also discussed. The standard relational operators were shown to apply to sets.

Pascal includes a predefined data type known as a pointer. Using the standard procedure *new*, we can dynamically allocate a variable that can be referenced by the pointer variable name followed by the symbol " ↑ " . Using pointers, we showed how to build dynamic data structures such as linked lists, binary trees, stacks, and queues. Procedures were written to search for elements, insert and delete elements, and traverse binary trees.

The following is a summary of the Pascal features discussed in this chapter; it can be useful for future reference.

PASCAL REFERENCE

1   Set. A structured data type consisting of a collection of distinct elements chosen from the ordinal base type. Example:

```
TYPE numset = SET OF 1..128;
VAR numbers : numset;
```

1.1   Set operators yielding set results:
   +   Union
   −   Difference
   *   Intersection

1.2   Relational operators yielding Boolean results:
   =   Set equality
   <>   Set inequality

$<=, >=$ Subset or equal

IN   Membership

2 Pointer. Data type containing address of referenced variable. Example:

```
TYPE
    pointer = ↑ node;
    node = RECORD
                code : char;
                left : pointer;
                right : pointer
           END;
```

2.1 If *ptr* is the name of a pointer variable, then *ptr*↑ is the name of the referenced variable.

2.2 Standard procedures:

New (ptr). Dynamically allocates a memory location and assigns its address to *ptr.*

Dispose (ptr). Indicates storage pointed to by *ptr* is unused and makes *ptr* logically undefined.

3 Some dynamic data structures:

3.1 Linked lists

3.2 Binary trees

3.3 Stacks

3.4 Queues

Keywords for Chapter 13

base type	pointer variable
binary search tree	postorder
binary tree	preorder
data abstraction	queue
difference	referenced variable
dispose	root
dynamic allocation	set
dynamic data structure	stack
dynamic variable	static data structure
edge	subset
empty set	subtree
inorder	terminal node
intersection	traversal
linked list	tree
new	union
node	universal set
pointer	

⭐ ESSENTIAL EXERCISES

1 Which of the following set constructors are valid? For those that are valid, determine the number of members of the set constructed.
   (a) [1, 1+2, 1+3, 1+4]
   (b) [1..5, 2..6]
   (c) ['A', succ('A'), pred('A')]
   (d) [Monday..Friday] if the TYPE definition

   TYPE
           day = (Monday,Tuesday,Wednesday,Thursday,Friday);

   has previously appeared
   (e) [1.3, 2.7]
   (f) [sqr(2)..sqr(3)]
   (g) [abs(x)..x] if x is an integer variable containing 4
   (h) [abs(x)..x] if x is an integer variable containing −4

2 Describe an algorithm to compute the intersection of two sets using only set union and the membership test.

3 Describe an algorithm to determine the cardinality, or number of elements, in a set.

4 How is it possible to assign NIL to a pointer variable, regardless of the type of pointer? Doesn't this violate the strong typing rules of Pascal? What does this tell you about the probable representation of a NIL-valued pointer? Could Pascal "survive" without the NIL pointer? If so, what would you use to substitute for the null pointer?

⭐⭐ SIGNIFICANT EXERCISES

5 Why is it reasonable for Pascal to prohibit the use of the operators <, <=, >, and >= to compare two pointers? (Hint: Remember what pointers contain.)

6 It was mentioned in the text that there are six different orders in which the nodes of a binary search tree with three nodes could be traversed. Given the binary search tree created from the character values B, A, and C (in that order), list the order of these character values in all six traversals, noting those which correspond to preorder, inorder, and postorder traversal. How many different traversals are possible for a binary tree containing n nodes?

7 Describe an algorithm which will reverse the order of elements in a stack. That is, if a stack contains the elements A, B, C, X, Y, and Z, with A at the top of the stack, give an algorithm which leaves the stack with the elements Z, Y, X, C, B, and A, with Z at the top.

8 Define the height of a binary tree as the number of nodes in the longest path from the root node to a terminal node, including the root and the terminal node. Describe an algorithm to determine the height of an arbitrary binary tree.

9   Describe a nonrecursive algorithm to perform the inorder traversal of a binary tree.

★★★ CHALLENGING EXERCISES

10   Given the TYPE definitions

```
TYPE
      nodeptr = ↑node;
      node = RECORD
                   data : integer;
                   next : nodeptr
              END;
```

and a linked list whose nodes are of type *node*, describe algorithms to permit accessing the elements of the linked list as if the linked list was an array. Specifically, describe an algorithm to obtain the data field of the *i*th element of the linked list and another algorithm to store a new value in the data field of the *i*th element of the linked list, given the pointer to the first element of the linked list, the subscript of the requested element, and the new value as parameters. Be certain to address the question of storing a value into a new element of the array, perhaps one that is not contiguous to the existing elements.

11   Unfortunately, Pascal provides us with no mechanism to handle contingencies (like run-time errors) that may occur during execution. Many of these, like division by zero and attempted accesses to nonexistent array elements, can be avoided by performing appropriate tests prior to the operation that might yield the contingency. The standard procedure *new*, however, can fail when the available storage on the computer system is exhausted and there is no facility for anticipating or handling this failure in any portable way, since the storage available on different computer systems will vary in size. Describe at least one, and preferably more than one, technique to alleviate this situation. Estimate the impact of your technique on existing Pascal programs using the standard procedure *new*.

CHAPTER 13 PROBLEMS FOR COMPUTER SOLUTION

☆ ESSENTIAL PROBLEMS

1   The input data is a list of integers terminated by the end of file. Build two linked lists containing these integers, one with the integers in the same order as they appear in the input and another with the integers in ascending order. Then display those integers appearing in the same position in both lists.

Example input:

    4   3   7   5   9   6   1

Example output

3

5

2   In this problem you are to write a simulation for demonstrating the *push* and *pop* operations on a stack. Each line of the input will contain the word PUSH, POP, or SNAP in the first four positions (POP will always be followed by a blank). Lines containing PUSH will additionally include an integer value. For each line, read the word (and the integer for push operations), display the operation being performed, and then perform the actions indicated below.

PUSH   Push the integer value onto the stack.

POP   Pop an integer from the stack and display it. If the stack is empty, report that fact.

SNAP   Display the current contents of the stack, indicating the position of each element in the stack. Use only push and pop operations to perform this display.

Example input:

```
PUSH 4
PUSH 5
SNAP
POP
PUSH 2
POP
POP
POP
```

Example output:

```
PUSH 4
PUSH 5
Snap of Stack
     (top)    1  5
              2  4
POP
Popped 5 from stack
PUSH 2
POP
Popped 2 from stack
POP
Popped 4 from stack
POP
Cannot pop empty stack
```

3 Each line of the input data will contain between 1 and 20 integers in the range 1 to 63; the end of line will immediately follow the last integer on each line. Build a binary search tree that contains two data values in each node. The first data item contains the number of *unique* integers in a line of input data and is used to order the nodes of the tree. The second data item is the set containing the integers from that line of input data. In building the binary search tree, treat new nodes having the same number of integers as an existing node as larger than the existing node. That is, they are to be inserted to the right of the existing node. When the end of file is reached, perform an inorder traversal of the tree and display the integers in each node's set on a separate line. Separate the integers on each line with a comma and a blank.

Example input:

```
 4   7   1   9
 3
16   3   9   3
21   5   9   4   5
```

Example output:

```
3
3, 9, 16
1, 4, 7, 9
4, 5, 9, 21
```

★★ SIGNIFICANT PROBLEMS

4 The input data contains two columns of words (that is, each line in the input contains two words). Each word is delimited by single quotes and contains no more than 10 alphabetic characters (although both upper- and lowercase letters may appear). The words in each column are in alphabetic order. Build a linked list containing each column of words, then merge the two lists to form a third list containing all the words in alphabetic order. Display this resulting list.

Example input:

```
'Apples'      'Arrays'
'Bananas'     'BTrees'
'Coconuts'    'Files'
'Dates'       'HashTables'
```

Example output:

```
Apples
Arrays
BTrees
Bananas
```

Coconuts
Dates
Files
HashTables

5   The input data for this problem consists of a number of definitions, each arranged
    as a group of text lines. The first line of each definition begins in column 1 with
    the word being defined (of 10 characters or less), at least one blank, and the first
    few words of the definition. Additional lines of the definition always have a blank
    in column 1 followed by additional words of the definition. Build a binary tree of
    these definitions, and then display them in alphabetic order of the words being
    defined. Each node in the binary tree should contain a word being defined (used
    to order the nodes in the tree) and a pointer to a linked list of the words comprising
    the definition.

Example input:

    Node   A collection of data items used to represent the
                    data and edges in a tree.
    Binary   Having two parts, as in a tree.
    Link   That which joins separate parts, as in the link be-
                    tween nodes in a binary tree.

Example output:

    Binary   Having two parts, as in a tree.
    Link   That which joins separate parts, as in the link be-
                    tween nodes in a binary tree.
    Node   A collection of data items used to represent the
                    data and edges in a tree.

★★★ CHALLENGING PROBLEMS

6   The input data for this problem consists of a single integer, N. Generate N unique
    real random numbers between 0.0 and 1.0 using any random number generator
    you have available, and build a binary search tree with the resulting numbers.
    Display the smallest and largest random numbers generated. Then perform an
    inorder traversal of the tree, and compute the average difference between adjacent
    random numbers. In the example shown below, assume the random numbers that
    are generated are 0.4, 0.2, 0.7, 0.3, and 0.1. These numbers have been restricted
    to one digit to keep the illustration simple. The average difference computation is

    ((0.2 − 0.1) + (0.3 − 0.2) + (0.4 − 0.3) + (0.7 − 0.4)) / 4.

    (Note: If N is too large or the random number generator repeats after a small
    number of values, the program may loop. Devise a scheme to detect this problem.)

Example input:

5

Example output:

The smallest random number is 0.1
The largest random number is 0.7
The average difference between adjacent numbers is 0.15

APPENDIXES

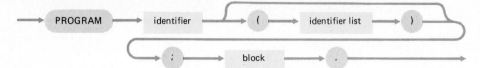

Figure A-1 Program.

Figure A-2 Identifier.

Figure A-3 Identifier list.

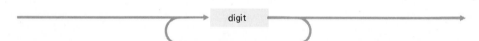

Figure A-4 Unsigned integer.

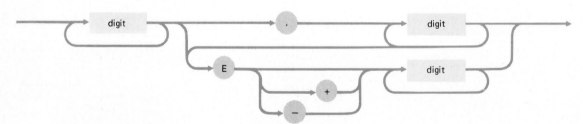

Figure A-5 Unsigned real.

Source: Programming with Pascal by B.S. Gottfried (Schaum's Outline Series, McGraw-Hill).

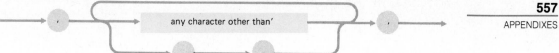

Figure A-6   String.

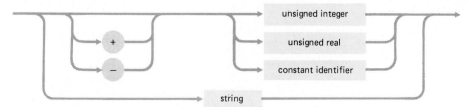

Figure A-7   Constant.

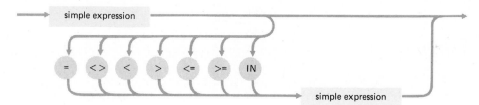

Figure A-8   Simple expression.

Figure A-9   Expression.

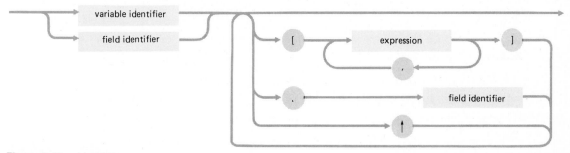

Figure A-10   Variable.

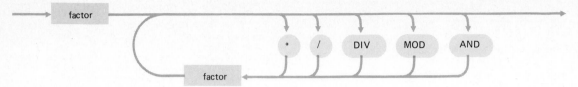

Figure A-11 Term.

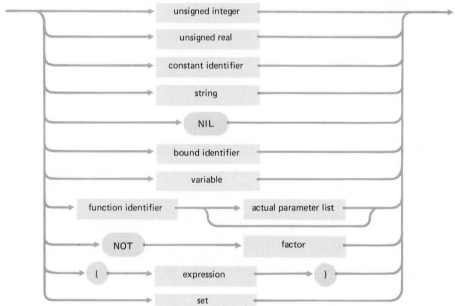

Figure A-12 Factor.

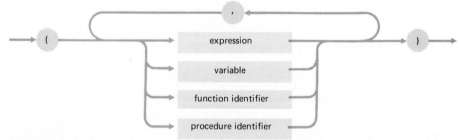

Figure A-13 Actual parameter list.

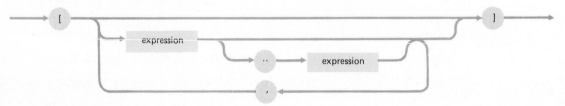

Figure A-14 Set.

558

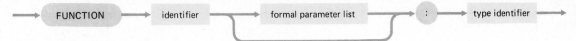

Figure A-15 Function heading.

Figure A-16 Procedure heading.

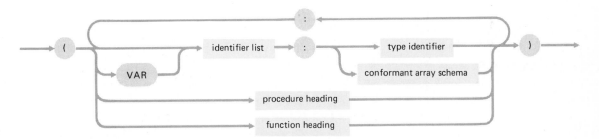

Figure A-17 Formal parameter list.

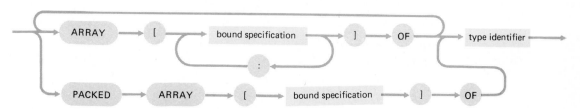

Figure A-18 Conformant array schema.

Figure A-19 Bound specification.

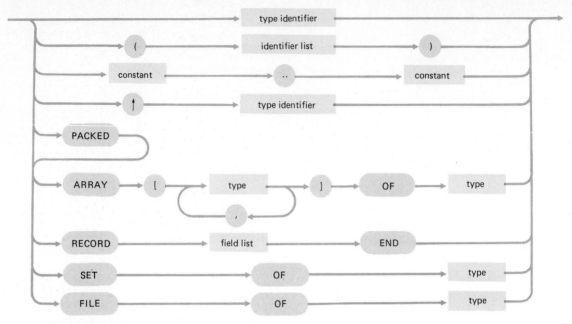

Figure A-20   Type.

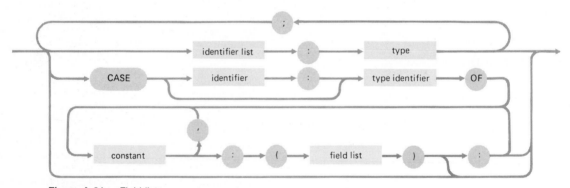

Figure A-21   Field list.

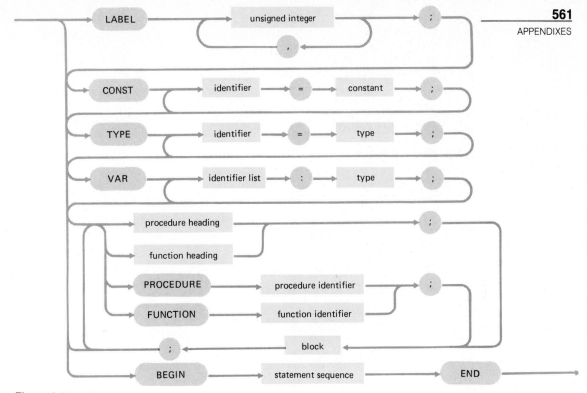

Figure A-22 Block.

Figure A-23 Statement sequence.

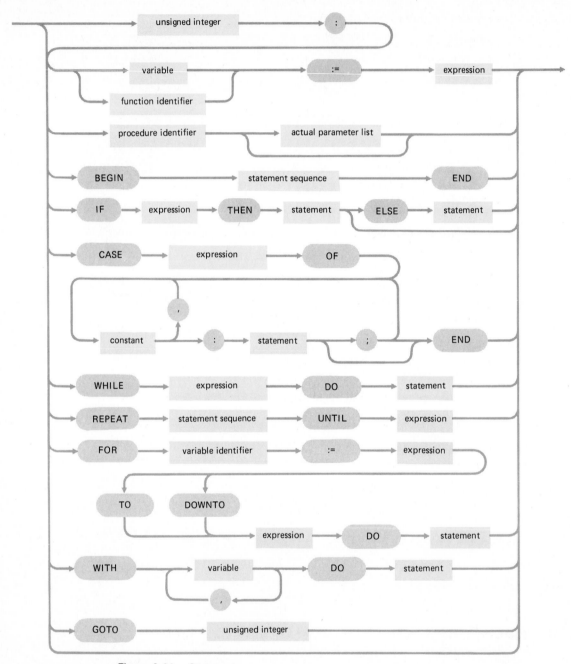

Figure A-24 Statement.

AND	END	NIL	SET
ARRAY	FILE	NOT	THEN
BEGIN	FOR	OF	TO
CASE	FUNCTION	OR	TYPE
CONST	GOTO	PACKED	UNTIL
DIV	IF	PROCEDURE	VAR
DO	IN	PROGRAM	WHILE
DOWNTO	LABEL	RECORD	WITH
ELSE	MOD	REPEAT	

APPENDIX C PREDECLARED IDENTIFIERS

STANDARD IDENTIFIERS

abs	false	pack	sin
arctan	get	page	sqr
boolean	input	pred	sqrt
char	integer	put	succ
chr	ln	read	text
cos	maxint	readln	true
dispose	new	real	trunc
eof	odd	reset	unpack
eoln	ord	rewrite	write
exp	output	round	writeln

STANDARD CONSTANTS

false	true	maxint

STANDARD TYPES

Boolean	integer	real	text
char			

STANDARD FILES

input	output

APPENDIX D STANDARD FUNCTIONS AND PROCEDURES

function	definition	type of parameter (x)	type of result
abs(x)	The absolute value of x	Integer or real	Same as x
arctan(x)	The arctangent of x	Integer or real	Real
chr(x)	The character represented by ordinal number x	Integer	Char
cos(x)	The cosine of x (x in radians)	Integer or real	Real
eof(x)	Test if an end of file has been detected	File	Boolean
eoln(x)	Test if an end of line has been detected	File	Boolean
exp(x)	e^x, where $e = 2.71828...$	Integer or real	Real
ln(x)	The natural logarithm of x	Integer or real	Real
odd(x)	Test if x is odd or even	Integer	Boolean
ord(x)	The ordinal number of x	Any ordinal	Integer
pred(x)	The predecessor of x	Any ordinal	Same as x
round(x)	Round the value of x to the nearest integer	Real	Integer
sin(x)	The sine of x (x in radians)	Integer or real	Real
sqr(x)	The square of x	Integer or real	Same as x
sqrt(x)	The square root of x ($x > 0$)	Integer or real	Real
succ(x)	The successor of x	Any ordinal	Same as x
trunc(x)	Truncate x	Real	Integer

STANDARD PROCEDURES

Procedure	Definition
dispose(p)	Indicates that the storage pointed to by p is available for reallocation; p becomes logically undefined.
get(f)	Advances file variable f so the next component of f is available for inspection in $f\uparrow$.
new(p)	Dynamically allocate storage for a variable of the type pointed to by p and assign p the address of this storage.

Procedure	Definition
pack(u,i,p)	Copy a[i], a[i + 1], . . . , to p starting with the first element of p.
page(f)	Append end of line to text file f if necessary, and arrange for next *put, write,* or *writeln* referencing f to place output on a new page.
put(f)	Append $f\uparrow$ as a new component of f; $f\uparrow$ becomes undefined.
read(f,list)	Read, and possibly perform conversions of textual data, from file variable f, assigning values to variables named in list.
readln(f,list)	Same as *read,* except advances past next end of line on text files as last operation.
reset(f)	Prepare for reading from file variable f; places f in input, or inspection, mode.
rewrite(f)	Prepare for writing or display on file variable f; places f in output mode.
unpack(p,u,i)	Copy elements of p starting with first element to *u[i]*, *u[i + 1]*, ...
write(f,list)	Write, possibly with conversion to textual form, the value of each expression in list to file f.
writeln(f,list)	Same as *write,* except appends end of line to text files as last operation.

APPENDIX E OPERATORS

The following table summarizes the various operators available in Pascal. The order of precedence is shown from highest to lowest precedence. Successive operators within the same precedence group are performed from left to right. Parenthesis may be used to force an alternate order of evaluation.

precedence	operator(s)
1 (highest)	NOT
2	* / DIV MOD AND
3	+ – OR
4 (lowest)	= <> < <= > >= IN

APPENDIX F

ASCII (AMERICAN STANDARD CODE FOR INFORMATION INTERCHANGE)

first digit(s) \ last digit	0	1	2	3	4	5	6	7	8	9
3				!	"	#	$	%	&	'
4	(	)	*	+	,	−	.	/	0	1
5	2	3	4	5	6	7	8	9	:	;
6	<	=	>	?	@	A	B	C	D	E
7	F	G	H	I	J	K	L	M	N	O
8	P	Q	R	S	T	U	V	W	X	Y
9	Z	[	\	]	^	_	`	a	b	c
10	d	e	f	g	h	i	j	k	l	m
11	n	o	p	q	r	s	t	u	v	w
12	x	y	z	{	|	}	~			

Codes 0 to 31 represent special control characters and are not printable. Code 32 represents a blank.

EBCDIC (EXTENDED BINARY-CODED DECIMAL INTERCHANGE CODE)

first digit(s) \ last digit	0	1	2	3	4	5	6	7	8	9
7					¢	.	<	(	+	|
8	&									
9	!	$	*	)	;	¬	‾	/		
10								,	%	_
11	>	?								
12		`	:	#	@	'	=	"		a
13	b	c	d	e	f	g	h	i		
14						j	k	l	m	n
15	o	p	q	r						
16		~	s	t	u	v	w	x	y	z
17							\		{	}
18	[	]								
19				A	B	C	D	E	F	G
20	H	I								J
21	K	L	M	N	O	P	Q	R		
22							S	T	U	V
23	W	X	Y	Z						
24	0	1	2	3	4	5	6	7	8	9

Codes 0 to 63 and 250 to 255 represent special control characters and are not printable. Code 64 represents a blank.

THE PAGE PROCEDURE

Pascal includes a standard procedure called *page* that will cause the next output item to be displayed at the top of a new page. Consider the following code segment:

```
writeln (2, 4);
page;
writeln (6, 8)
```

The integer values 2 and 4 are displayed on one line. Next, the output device is positioned so the next items displayed are on a new page. Finally, the values 6 and 8 are displayed on the new page.

The procedure *page* is implementation dependent. For example, on some interactive systems the page statement is ignored when the output is displayed on a terminal screen, while on other interactive systems the terminal's screen will be cleared. If the output device is a printer, the procedure *page* will likely cause the printer to output paper until it reaches the top of the next page. If you plan to use the procedure *page* be certain to read your system's documentation to verify the effect on the output device.

THE GOTO STATEMENT

Many programming languages such as FORTRAN and BASIC include a control structure that performs an unconditional branch; that is, control is transferred unconditionally from one statement to another statement that is labeled, usually by an integer.

In Pascal, such a control structure exists and is called the ***GOTO statement***. The statement is written by following the reserved word GOTO by an integer in the range 1 to 9999; this integer is called the ***label***. Control is unconditionally transferred to the statement in the same procedure, function, or main program that is prefixed with the specified label and a colon.

All labels used in a procedure, function, or main program must be declared prior to any other declarations. The following procedure illustrates the use of the GOTO statement and the label declaration; it reads 100 integers values and returns the total.

```
PROCEDURE sumdata (VAR total : integer);
(* Compute total of 100 input integer values. *)
LABEL
     10;
CONST
     max = 100;
VAR

     index, num, total : integer;
```

```
BEGIN
        total := 0;
        index := 1;
10:    read (num);
        total := total + num;
        index := index + 1;
        IF index < 101
        THEN GOTO 10
END;
```

Notice the reserved word LABEL is followed by one or more integers separated by commas declaring the labels. The labels are ignored during execution except when referenced by a GOTO statement. The same procedure can be written using any of the looping control structures discussed in this text (WHILE, REPEAT-UNTIL, or FOR). We have avoided the use of GOTO statements in our programs. Codes produced using only control structures, other than the GOTO statement have exactly one entry point and one exit point, whereas use of the GOTO provides several possible methods for entry to and exit from coding. Use of GOTO statements can therefore result in difficulty with reading, understanding, and debugging programs.

GOTO statements may not be used to branch to code that is part of other control structures unless, of course, the GOTO statement itself is part of the same code. There are also situations in which the GOTO statement can be used to terminate the execution of procedures and functions; these uses are fortunately rare.

You may be wondering if there are situations in which the use of the GOTO statement is appropriate. In those special situations where we want to terminate a procedure, function, or program immediately because of a significant error, it is usually acceptable to branch directly to the end of the executable statements. Even this use of GOTO is questionable, however, and you should attempt to avoid the GOTO whenever possible.

PROCEDURES AND FUNCTIONS AS PARAMETERS

If you examine the syntax diagrams (Appendix A) for actual parameter list and formal parameter list, you will discover that procedures and functions can appear as parameters. So, for example, an actual parameter of a procedure invocation can be a procedure or function. The following procedure header includes a function as a formal parameter:

```
PROCEDURE process (FUNCTION f (x : integer) : real;
                        left, right : integer);
```

Note that if the formal parameter is a function (or procedure), then it is written in the same form as the function (or procedure) header.

The actual function (or procedure) parameter passed to the procedure is the function name only. For example, the following are valid procedure invocations where *func1* and *func2* are real-valued functions, each having one formal value parameter of type integer.

```
process (func1, 0, 5)
process (func2, 1, 4)
```

There are restrictions on what procedures or functions can be passed as parameters. For example, the parameters of a passed function or procedure must be value parameters. Some Pascal implementations do not permit the standard procedures or functions to be used as parameters. Check the documentation on your system before attempting to use procedures or functions as parameters.

GLOSSARY

accuracy

A measure of the quality of correctness or precision.

actual parameter

The actual value passed by the invocation to a function or procedure.

algorithm

A step-by-step procedure to solve a given problem that terminates in a finite number of steps.

AND operator

Pascal logic operator that yields the value true if both operands are true, and false otherwise.

argument

The value given to a function in order to obtain the result.

arithmetic operator

An operator, such as +, -, *, /, DIV, and MOD, used in numerical calculations.

arithmetic/logic unit (ALU)

A component of the CPU that performs arithmetic and logic operations.

array

Structured data type with a fixed number of components of the same type. Each component is accessed by a subscript or index.

array of records

An array where each component is composed of a record.

assembler

A program that translates an assembly language program into machine language.

assembly language

A computer language closely related to machine language that uses mnemonics to represent machine language instructions.

assertion

A comment about the state of the program during execution at the point of the assertion.

assignment compatible

Refers to assigning values of one type to a variable having a compatible type.

assignment statement

A Pascal statement that includes the assignment operator : = and replaces the contents of the variable to the left of the operator with the value of the expression to the right of the operator.

base type

The type of the potential values that a set variable can assume.

batch processing

A mode of running programs that does not involve direct user interaction with the computer.

binary

Refers to two states, or base 2.

binary operator

An operator, such as addition or multiplication, that requires two operands.

binary search

A search technique for locating an item in an ordered list by repeatedly halving the search area until the desired item is located.

binary search tree

A dynamic data structure where data items can be efficiently located and inserted.

binary tree

A tree in which each node has zero, one or two descendants.

bit

A contraction for binary digit, which is either 0 or 1. Bits are the smallest unit of information used in a computer, and are used to represent data and instructions.

Boolean

A Pascal data type with only two possible values, true and false.

Boolean expression

An expression which, when evaluated, yields a Boolean value.

Boolean operator

In Pascal, one of the operators AND, OR, and NOT.

Boolean variable

A variable of type Boolean.

bottom-up testing

Testing of a program that is done by exercising the low-level procedures (those at the bottom of the design tree) before joining with others.

bubble sort

A well-known sort technique that interchanges adjacent elements until the desired value "bubbles" to the top.

bugs

Errors in a program such as syntax errors, run-time errors, or logic errors.

CASE statement

A Pascal statement that permits the selection of an action from many different courses of action.

central processing unit (CPU)

A major component of the computer that directs and controls the information processing done by the computer.

char

A Pascal data type consisting of characters such as those found on a keyboard or printer.

character string

A sequence of characters logically considered as a single unit.

chr function

A function that returns the character whose position (or code) in the collating sequence is the same as the integer argument to the function.

code

Statements or instructions referenced as a group.

collating sequence

The ordering of a particular character set (for example, ASCII or EBCDIC).

column

Normally refers to all elements in a two-dimensional array having the same second subscript value.

comment

A component of a computer program used for documentation and explanation of parts of the program, intended for human readers. Comments are usually ignored by the computer.

compatible types

Two types are compatible if either they are the same type, or one is a subrange of the other, or both are subranges of the same host type.

compile-time error

An error, such as a syntax error, detected during the compilation of a program.

compiler

A program that translates a program written in high-level language, like Pascal, into machine language for a specific computer.

computer program

A set of instructions to be performed (executed) by a computer.

concatenation

The operation of joining two or more data items, such as character strings, to form a single sequence.

conformant array parameter

A parameter which can be used in Pascal procedures and functions to allow separate invocations to have array arguments with different bounds.

constant

A value that does not change during the execution of a program.

control structure

A programming construct, such as selection or looping, that determines the order in which statements will be executed.

control unit

The component of the CPU that directs the execution of the computer instructions.

data abstraction

A data structure design process similar to top-down design wherein details of the actual data structure are deferred until needed.

data type

Representation of data, such as numbers and characters, as a well-defined type of object specified by syntax rules.

debugging

The process of removing bugs or errors from the program.

declaration

Pascal expression defining or declaring programming objects required by program, such as variables, constants, and procedures and functions.

definite control structure

A control structure, such as the FOR loop, where the number of passes through the loop is determined prior to execution.

delimiter

A symbol or character string, such as BEGIN and END, that delimits or marks a part of a program or an expression.

difference

In Pascal, a set operation to form the difference of two sets.

direct access file

A file where retrieving or storing a data item does not depend on the order of the components. For example, a random access device, such as a disk.

dispose

A Pascal procedure that frees the storage allocated to a dynamic variable.

divide and conquer

An approach to problem solving that involves the division of a problem into smaller, more manageable problems.

driver

A main program whose statements are primarily procedure invocations.

dynamic allocation

Allocating storage for dynamic variables during execution.

dynamic data structure

A data structure, such as a linked list, that can be expanded and contracted during execution.

dynamic variable

A variable accessed only through a pointer variable.

echo print

The displaying or printing of input data at the time of input, used principally for input validation.

edge

The connection between the nodes of a tree.

editor

An interactive program that permits the user to create and modify text files.

empty set

The set with no elements.

empty statement

A statement indicated by only a semicolon that implies no action.

enumerated type

A user-defined type consisting of an ordered set of new constants.

eof

The end of a file.

eof function

A Pascal function used to determine if any unread components exist in an input file.

eoln

The end-of-line marker used with a text file.

eoln function

A Pascal function used to determine if the next unread component of a text file is an end-of-line marker.

executable program

The actual machine language program executed by the computer.

executable statement

In a Pascal program, a statement which is translated to machine language instructions by the computer, as opposed to CONST, TYPE, and VAR declarations which produce no machine language instructions.

execute

To perform the steps in an algorithm or machine language program.

external file

A permanent file used or created by a Pascal program, referenced through a parameter in the PROGRAM statement.

field designator

In Pascal, an expression used to access the components of a record.

field identifier

In Pascal, the name of the component of a record.

file

A named sequence of components, usually stored on a magnetic disk or tape, and referenced in Pascal by read or write statements.

file buffer variable

A variable used to access the next sequential component of a file before it is actually processed by a read or write statement.

file name

The name used to permanently identify a file. This name is usually distinct from the name of the file variable used to access the file.

file parameter

A parameter, used in the PROGRAM statement, to connect a file variable to an external file.

file variable

A variable, of type FILE, used to access a file in reset, rewrite, read, or write statements.

file window

The portion of a file accessible through the file buffer variables.

filters

Programs that perform transformations on an input file to produce an output file.

fixed part

That part of a variant record common to all possible realizations of the record.

flag

A variable used to indicate the occurrence of an event or presence of a condition. In Pascal, a Boolean variable is frequently used as a flag.

floating point notation

Also called *scientific notation*. Used to represent real values.

FOR statement

A looping control structure or definite control structure where the loop control variable is automatically changed from an initial value to a final value.

formal parameter

An identifier appearing in the parameter list of a procedure or function header.

formatted

Refers to the organization, or representation, of the display of information on a text file.

forward

A Pascal procedure or function declaration appearing before its body.

FUNCTION

A Pascal reserved word used in the declaration of a function.

get

A Pascal procedure that advances the current position of the file window to the next component of a sequential file and assigns the value of the component to the file buffer variable.

global identifier

An identifier declared in a procedure or main program and therefore accessible in any procedure or function within the scope of the identifier.

global variable
A variable declared in a procedure or main program and therefore accessible in any procedure or function within the scope of the variable.

GOTO statement
A Pascal statement which unconditionally transfers control to a labeled statement.

hardware
The physical components of the computer, including the input/output devices, as opposed to the software.

hierarchical records
Records containing other records as components (nested records).

hierarchy
The order or precedence of evaluating an expression that includes more than one operator.

high-level language
A computer language, such as Pascal, in which the computer instructions are represented by statements written using English-like expressions.

host data type
The ordinal data type from which subrange data types can be derived.

identical types
Refers to programming objects having the same type name.

identifier
A word or sequence of characters that forms the name of a program object, such as a program name, a variable, a constant, a type, or a function or procedure.

IF-THEN statement
A Pascal statement used to conditionally execute a statement if a specified Boolean value is true.

IF-THEN-ELSE statement
A Pascal statement used to selectively execute one of two statements depending on a specified Boolean value.

IN operator
A Pascal operator used to test membership in a set.

indefinite control structure
A control structure, such as WHILE or RE-PEAT-UNTIL, where the number of iterations of the loop body may vary depending on the value of an arbitrary Boolean expression.

index
A subscript used to access the components of an array.

infinite loop
A loop that never meets its termination condition, and can only be terminated by means external to the program.

inorder
Refers to the tree traversal algorithm that traverses the left subtree first, then the root, followed by the right subtree.

input
In Pascal, a standard identifier representing the standard input file, used by default in read and readln statements.

input (value) parameter
A parameter associated with input to a procedure or function.

input device
A device, such as a keyboard, that permits the user to enter data and information into the computer.

integer
A Pascal data type consisting of positive and negative whole numbers including zero.

interactive system
A computer system where the user interacts directly with the operating system, usually through a video terminal.

internal file
A file whose corresponding Pascal file variable does not appear in the PROGRAM statement, and whose lifetime is the execution of a single program.

interpreter
A program that translates and executes the statements of a source program one statement at a time.

intersection
A set operation represented by * that forms the set of elements common to two or more sets.

invocation
The transfer of control from a procedure statement (or function) to the actual procedure (or function).

lexicographical order
The "actual" order of an ordinal data type. For example, alphabetic order.

library procedures

Commonly used software residing in a system library.

linear search

A search technique that locates a specified value by comparing it to every element in a list until the item is found or the list is exhausted.

link

A process where one or more object programs are linked with any library procedures used by the program.

linked list

A dynamic data structure consisting of a chained list of data items connected by pointers.

load

See "link."

local identifier

An identifier known only within its scope.

local variable

A variable declared in a procedure (or function) known only within that procedure (or function).

logic error

An error usually traced to the algorithm design.

loop control variable

A variable used to control the number of iterations of a loop.

loop invariant

An assertion that remains unchanged after each iteration of a loop.

loop variant

An assertion that changes with each iteration through the loop.

looping

A process that permits the repeated execution of a sequence of statements until a termination condition is met.

low-level language

A language expressing computer instruction in a symbolic form closely related to the particular computer system which is intended to execute the instructions.

machine language

A language expressing computer instructions in binary code.

main memory

The primary memory used by the computer system to store instructions and data to be directly accessed by the CPU. Also frequently known as "core."

main program

The executable statements of a Pascal program that appear after all constant, type, variable, procedure and function declarations. The main program is always that part of the entire program at which execution begins.

maxint

A predefined standard integer constant that represents the largest possible integer available on a particular computer system.

memory address

A unique number assigned to each memory cell of the memory unit, and used by the CPU to reference individual memory cells.

memory unit

A major component of the computer consisting of many memory cells used to store computer programs and data.

merge

The process of combining two or more ordered lists into a single ordered list.

mnemonics

Symbolic codes used to represent binary machine language expressions.

multidimensional array

An array which has arrays as components.

nested IF statements

IF statements contained within other IF statements.

new

A Pascal standard procedure that dynamically allocates storage for a variable.

node

The point or vertex of a tree, usually representing a data item.

NOT operator

A Boolean operator that yields the opposite truth value of the operand.

O-notation

Used to mathematically estimate the performance or efficiency of an algorithm.

object program

The machine language program resulting from the translation of the source program.

odd function

A standard Pascal function used to test if the integer parameter is even or odd.

operand

The value used when evaluating an operator such as addition (+) or multiplication (*).

operating system

A set of programs that manages a computer system and the system software.

OR operator

A Pascal logic operator that yields a value of true if either operand is true, and false otherwise.

ord function

A standard Pascal function used to determine the ordinal position of the input ordinal parameter.

order

An estimate of the efficiency of an algorithm.

ordinal data types

Data types, such as integer and char, that consist of an ordered set of distinct values having a first and last element.

output (variable) parameter

A parameter associated with the output of a procedure, occupying the same memory as the corresponding actual parameter.

output device

A device, such as a printer, that displays or outputs information from the computer to the user.

pack

A standard Pascal procedure that copies the elements of an unpacked array to a packed array.

packed array

An array that may conserve memory space by packing several components of an array into a single memory cell.

parallel arrays

Two or more arrays of the same bounds in which elements with the same subscripts are treated as a single composite element. Compare with *record*.

parameter

A value or variable appearing in the parameter list of a procedure or function header, or in the parameter list of a procedure or function invocation.

peripheral device

An I/O device usually external to the computer.

pointer

A Pascal data type containing the memory address of a variable of a specified type.

pointer variable

A variable of type pointer.

portability

The capability of transporting a program from one computer system to another with minimal change.

postcondition

An assertion that is true after a sequence of statements has been executed.

postorder

Refers to the tree traversal algorithm that visits the left subtree first, the right subtree, and finally the root.

precondition

An assertion that is true before a sequence of statements is executed.

pred function

A standard Pascal function that yields the predecessor of the ordinal input parameter.

preorder

Refers to the tree traversal algorithm that visits the root first, then the left subtree, followed by the right subtree.

primary memory

The main memory unit (as opposed to secondary storage).

PROCEDURE

A reserved word in Pascal used to declare procedures.

procedure

A subprogram with a name and optional parameters that can be called or invoked and executed.

program block

The Pascal program (excluding the program header) consisting of the declarations and executable statements.

program header

A single Pascal statement that begins with the reserved word PROGRAM and includes the program name and the names of file variables associated with external files.

program verification

A branch of computer science concerned with proving program correctness.

pseudo-random number

A number generated by a program in such a way as to appear random.

578

pseudocode

A mixture of English and computer instructions used to express an algorithm.

put

A standard Pascal procedure that appends the contents of the file buffer variable to the file.

queue

A dynamic data structure whose elements are entered at one end and removed from the other. Frequently called a first-in, first-out (FIFO) queue.

random access file

See *direct access file*.

random number

A number randomly generated.

read

A standard Pascal procedure that permits the input of data from a file.

readln

A standard Pascal procedure used only with text files that is similar to the read procedure, but advances the file window past the next end of line at its conclusion.

real

A data type in Pascal consisting of numbers with decimal points, decimal fractions, and exponents.

record

A structured Pascal data type with a fixed number of components that are accessed by name. The components may be of different types.

record key

A component of a record used as a key, or identifying value, when processing the records.

recursive function

A function that invokes itself, either directly or indirectly.

referenced variable

A variable accessed via a pointer variable.

relational operators

Pascal operators such as = and < that are used to compare data items of the same type. These operators return a Boolean value.

REPEAT-UNTIL statement

An indefinite control structure used in looping and similar to the WHILE statement.

reserved word

An identifier, such as PROGRAM, VAR, BEGIN, and END, reserved for special purposes in Pascal.

reset

A standard Pascal procedure that prepares a file for input or reading.

rewrite

A standard Pascal procedure that prepares a file for output or writing.

root

A distinguished node of a tree indicating the top of the tree.

row

Normally refers to the collection of all elements in a two-dimensional array having the same first subscript value

.run-time error

An error occurring during the execution of a computer program.

scientific notation

A shorthand mathematical notation using powers of ten to represent very large or very small numbers. Also called *floating point notation*.

scope

The portion of a program where an identifier is known.

secondary storage

Memory devices, such as disks and tape drives, that provide additional memory and storage capabilities.

seed

Initial value used in generating pseudo-random numbers.

selection

A fundamental control structure that selects one of many alternate choices of action depending on a condition.

selection sort

A commonly used sorting algorithm that finds the largest element in each pass through a list and places it in the proper position.

selector

In a CASE statement a variable used to select the course of action.

semantic error

An error related to the meaning of a statement.

sentinel

A special data item used to indicate the end of a data file.

sequential file

A file that requires the retrieval or storage of elements to be performed in sequential order.

sequential search

See linear search.

set

A Pascal structure data type consisting of a collection of different elements selected from the constants of the base type.

set constructor

An explicit list of members.

side effect

The result of modifying a variable declared outside a procedure or function without that variable being passed as a parameter.

simple data types

In Pascal, any user-defined ordinal type or the types integer, real, Boolean, and char.

software

The set of programs written for a computer.

sorted array

An array that has its elements ordered in a specified sequence.

source program

A program written in a computer language before translation to machine language.

stack

A dynamic data structure where the elements are added and deleted from one end (the top of the stack). Also referred to as first-in, last-out.

standard function

A Pascal built-in function, such as square root (sqrt).

standard identifier

A Pascal identifier, such as input or output, that is predeclared by the compiler and automatically associated with certain programming objects.

standard ordinal functions

The standard Pascal functions succ, pred, ord, and chr.

static data structure

A data structure, such as an array, whose size is fixed during compile-time.

stepwise refinement

The process of breaking down a problem in steps by continual refinement.

string

A sequence of characters considered as a single data item. A packed array of characters.

string variable

A variable declared as a packed array of characters.

strongly-typed language

A language, such as Pascal, where each identifier must be declared with an associated type. This permits the compiler to verify that objects are used only in the correct type context prior to execution.

structured data types

In Pascal, one of the types array, record, file, or set.

stub

A procedure used in testing and debugging that temporarily substitutes for the actual procedure.

subrange data type

A data type consisting of a given range of values from an ordinal data type.

subscript

A value or index used to access the components of an array.

subset

If every element in set A is an element of set B, then set A is a subset of set B.

subtree

A portion of a tree that is itself a tree.

succ function

A standard Pascal function that yields the successor of the ordinal input parameter.

syntax

The formal rules of constructing legal statements in a computer language.

syntax diagram

A visual aid used to express syntax rules.

tag field

Used in variant records to determine the current record structure.

terminal node

A node that has no descendants. Also called a leaf node.

text

A file containing characters and end-of-line markers, divided into lines, each of which is terminated by an end-of-line marker.

threshold

A value used in determining the termination of a loop.

top-down design

The process of dividing a problem into subproblems, and then dividing the subproblems further until they can be implemented for computer solution.

top-down testing

The testing of a program that is done by exercising the procedures at the top of the design tree first.

transfer function

A function, such as round, that converts from one data type to another.

traversal

Refers to visiting the nodes of a tree.

tree

A dynamic data structure containing a root node that has zero or more associated nodes known as descendants, each of which also has zero or more associated descendant nodes that can also have descendants, and so on.

truncate

The process of ignoring or dropping the fractional part of a real number.

TYPE definition

In Pascal, the definition of a data type.

unary operator

An operator, such as NOT, requiring only one operand.

unconditional transfer

The transfer of control unconditionally to a particular point in the program. In Pascal, this is effected with the GOTO statement.

union

A set operation on two or more sets that forms a set containing all the elements of each operand set.

universal set

In Pascal a set consisting of all the constants of the base type.

unpack

A standard Pascal procedure that converts a packed array of elements to an unpacked array.

user-defined function

A function defined and declared by the programmer.

user-defined type

See enumerated type.

value parameter

In Pascal a parameter representing input to a procedure or function.

variable

An object in a program that may change value during execution.

variable parameter

In Pascal a parameter representing output from a procedure. Also can represent input to a procedure or function.

variant part

The part of a variant record that can change depending on the particular record.

variant record

A record having two distinct parts: a *fixed* part and a *variant* part. The components of a variant record can vary from record to record.

WHILE statement

An indefinite control structure used with loops written in Pascal.

WITH statement

A Pascal statement permitting references to record components in an abbreviated form.

word

In computers, refers to a memory location or group of adjacent locations.

write

A standard Pascal procedure that permits the output of data to a file.

writeln

A standard Pascal procedure similar to write that also appends an end-of-line character to text files as the last operation.

ANSWERS TO SECTION EXERCISES

SECTION 2.2

1. (a) valid
   (b) valid
   (c) invalid
   (d) invalid
   (e) invalid
   (f) invalid
   (g) invalid
   (h) valid
   (i) invalid
   (j) invalid

2. (a) must begin with a letter
   (b) can't use *, as * is an arithmetic
      operator
   (c) reserved word
   (d) must begin with a letter
   (e) standard identifier
   (f) reserved word
   (g) standard function
   (h) must begin with a letter

3. (a) valid
   (b) invalid
   (c) valid
   (d) invalid

4. (a) CONST days = 7;
   (b) CONST weight = 185;
   (c) CONST salestax = 0.08;
   (d) CONST students = 50;

5. (a) valid
   (b) invalid
   (c) invalid
   (d) valid

6. (a) VAR ssn : integer;
   (b) VAR curryr : integer;
   (c) VAR irate : real;
   (d) VAR avegrade : real;

7. (a) PROGRAM
      BEGIN
      END
      VAR
      CONST
   (b) *integer*
      input
      output
      read
      writeln

SECTION 2.3

1. (a) valid
   (b) invalid
   (c) invalid
   (d) valid as long as
      -55555 is $>= -maxint$
   (e) invalid
   (f) invalid
   (g) valid
   (h) invalid
   (i) valid

2. (a) valid
   (b) invalid
   (c) valid
   (d) invalid
   (e) valid
   (f) invalid
   (g) valid
   (h) invalid
   (i) invalid

3. (a) invalid (quotes missing)
   (b) valid
   (c) valid (character string constant)
   (d) valid
   (e) valid
   (f) valid (character string constant)

4. (a) 6210 or 6.21e3
   (b) 0.0015 or 0.15e$-$2
   (c) 1660000.0 or 1.66e6
   (d) 0.000000224 or 22.4e$-$8.

5. (a) $2.6 \times 10^3 = 2600$
   (b) $-12 \times 10^{-2} = -0.12$
   (c) $4.56 \times 10^{10} = 45600000000.0$
   (d) $-66.5 \times 10 = -665.0.$

6. (a) needs a digit to the right of the
      decimal point
   (b) needs a digit to the left of the
      decimal point
   (c) exponent is not an integer
   (d) minus sign must be in front of
      number
   (e) no digit after decimal point
   (f) can't have . . . following a number

7. (a) valid, char
   (b) invalid
   (c) valid, Boolean
   (d) valid, integer
   (e) invalid
   (f) valid, integer
   (g) valid, real
   (h) valid, char
   (i) invalid

SECTION 2.4

1. (a) valid
   (b) invalid
   (c) valid
   (d) valid
   (e) invalid
   (f) valid
   (g) invalid

2. (a) 2
   (b) 3
   (c) 5
   (d) 8
   (e) 3
   (f) 1

3. (a) valid
   (b) invalid

   (c) valid
   (d) valid
   (e) invalid
   (f) invalid

4. (a) 4
   (b) 11
   (c) -4
   (d) 10
   (e) -13
   (f) 25
   (g) 12
   (h) -1

5. (a) 3.0
   (b) 2.5

6. (a) (x + y) / (y / z + 3)
   (b) (− b − sqrt (sqr (b) − 4 * a * c)) / (2 * a)
   (c) sqr (sqr (x) + sqr (y))
   (d) (x + y − z) / (2 * x + sqr (y) − x * y * z)

7. (a) $\dfrac{abc}{de}$

   (b) $x + \dfrac{y}{z}(a+b)$

   (c) $b^2 − 4ac$

   (d) $a − \dfrac{bc}{d} + ef$

8. (a) (2 * b) − a + ((b * d) / e)
   (b) f − ((e * d) / c) + (b * a)
   (c) (a * a) − ((b * c) / d) + sqrt (e + (2 * f))
   (d) (d * (a + b)) − trunc ((e * f) / g)
                                  + (b / (a − (b * c)))
   (e) ((6 DIV 2) * (5 MOD 3)) − (2 * 3)
   (f) ((2 * 3) MOD ((8 DIV 3) + 1)) + round (6.5)

9. (a) valid
   (b) invalid
   (c) invalid
   (d) valid
   (e) valid
   (f) invalid
   (g) valid
   (h) invalid
   (i) invalid

10. (a) 11
    (b) 6
    (c) 36
    (d) 2

SECTION 3.1

1. x = 8
   y = 7
   z = 2
   a = 1
   b = 1
   c = 4
   d = 3

2. (a) no errors
   (b) an error will occur when 2.3 is assigned to b

(c) an error will occur when 2.1 is assigned to c

(d) an error will occur because there will not be any input left to assign to z

3. Value1 is   3
   Value2 is   5
   Sum is   8

4.   86   39
   a =
     3.2500000000000e + 01
   a =   86b = 3.2500000000000e + 01

5. Values are   0   2   1 5.2000000000000e + 00

   ↑ line 1, column 1

   3.6000000000000e + 00 4.1000000000000e + 00
   ↑ line 1, column 62

   Sum is 1.2900000000000e + 01
   ↑ line 2, column 1

   Product is   0
   ↑ line 3, column 1

6. x -12

7. a = 2   b = 15
   c = 1
   d = 8

8. Value 4 -18

9. e

10. a

11. x = 12
    y = 7
    z = 11

12.   HELLO
    R = 6.10
    S = 7.2

SECTION 4.2

1. Speed is   50mph.
   Speed is   40mph.

2. 　2　　　4　　　2
　　　4　　　4　　　2

3. PROCEDURE trisum;
　 BEGIN
　　　　total := num1 + num2 + num3
　 END

4. PROCEDURE mean;
　 BEGIN
　　　　average := total DIV 3
　 END

5. PROGRAM compute (input, output);
　 VAR
　　　　num1, num2, num3 : integer;
　　　　total : integer;
　　　　average : integer;

　 PROCEDURE trisum;
　 BEGIN
　　　　total := num1 + num2 + num3
　 END;

　 PROCEDURE mean;
　 BEGIN
　　　　average := total DIV 3
　 END;

　 BEGIN (* main *)
　　　　writeln ('Please enter three integers');
　　　　readln (num1, num2, num3);
　　　　trisum;
　　　　mean;
　　　　writeln('The average value is', average)
　 END.

Execution:

　　　Please enter three integers
　　　34　67　159
　　　The average value is　　　　86

6. PROCEDURE circle;
　 BEGIN
　　　　area := pi * sqr(r)
　 END

7. Procedure worth determines how much money there is, depending on the number of nickels.

8. PROCEDURE money;
   BEGIN
           dollars := (0.05 * nickels) + (0.1 * dimes) + (0.25 * quarters)
   END

SECTION 4.3

1. x, y, and z are the input (value) parameters.
   a, b, and c are the output (variable) parameters.

2. Formal parameters are the parameters listed in the procedure header. They are used as placeholders for the actual values.

   Actual parameters are the actual values passed to the procedure when it is executed.

3. Formal parameters are time, space, day, and sign. Actual parameters are 3.5, 6.0, hour, and 'Z'.

   time = 3.5
   space = 6.0
   day = hour
   sign = 'Z'

4. When test is invoked it passes the value 2.0 to y. The problem is that 2.0 is a real constant and y is an integer parameter.

5. 4.0 cannot be passed to the variable parameter z. 4.0 must be replaced by a real variable's name.

6. The character constant Z must be enclosed in quotes ('Z').

7. tum, num, and temp.

8. clock

9. a, b, and c
   a and b are input parameters
   c is an output parameter

10. tum = 1, num = 2, temp

11. num = 1, tum = 0, temp

12. 1   2   4   3
4
1   0   2   1
2

Four lines of output were produced.

SECTION 4.4

1.   1   2   3
        3   5   4

2.
```
PROCEDURE cube (length : real; VAR volume : real);
BEGIN
        volume := length * length * length
END
```

3.
```
PROCEDURE magnitude (x1, x2 : real; VAR distance : real);
BEGIN
        magnitude := abs (x1 − x2)
END
```

4.
```
PROCEDURE digit (number : integer; VAR lowest : integer);
BEGIN
        lowest := number MOD 10
END
```

5.
```
PROCEDURE circle (radius : real; VAR area : real);
BEGIN
        area := 3.14 * sqr(radius)
END
```

6.
```
PROCEDURE rectangle (length, width : real; VAR area : real);
BEGIN
        area := length * width
END
```

7.
```
PROGRAM uncovered (input, output);
VAR
        floor, rug1, rug2 : real;
        uncover : real;

PROCEDURE circle (radius : real; VAR area : real);
BEGIN
        area := 3.14 * sqr(radius)
END;

PROCEDURE rectangle (length, width : real; VAR area : real);
```

```
                    BEGIN
                        area := length * width
                    END;
                    BEGIN (* main *)
                        circle (1.0, rug1);
                        circle (2.0, rug2);
                        rectangle (12.0, 15.0, floor);
                        uncover := floor − rug1 − rug2;
                        writeln ('The uncovered area is ', uncover)
                    END.
```

Execution:
      The uncovered area is $1.64300e + 02$

SECTION 5.1

1. (a) true
   (b) true
   (c) false
   (d) true
   (e) false
   (f) false

2. (a) true
   (b) true
   (c) true
   (d) false

3. (a) false
   (b) false
   (c) false
   (d) true
   (e) false

4. (a) true
   (b) true
   (c) false
   (d) true

5. (a) (NOT flag) OR (NOT switch)
   (b) flag OR (test AND (NOT switch))
   (c) NOT ((flag AND switch) OR test)
   (d) test OR (switch AND flag)

6. (a) NOT (1 < num)
   (b) (2 > num) OR (num < −2)
   (c) (NOT (0 < num)) OR (num > 10)
   (d) (1 > num) AND (num > 0)

SECTION 5.2

1. (a) Extreme
   (b) Extreme
   (c) Median

2. IF (a > b) AND (a > c)
   THEN write ('A is largest')

3. x = 7
   y = 9

4. (a) false
   (b) false
   (c) false
   (d) true

5. 'Never gets to here.' is displayed.

6. Nothing is printed.

7. B

SECTION 5.3

1. Value is 5.

2.
```
CASE k OF
        0 : r := r + 1;
        1 : s := s + 1;
    2,3,4 : t := t + 2
END
```

3. (b)

4.
```
CASE grade OF
    D, F : writeln ('Poor job.');
    C, B : writeln ('Good job.');
    A    : writeln ('Outstanding job.')
END
```

SECTION 6.1

1. -2

2. 9   15

3. 17

4. 30   2   0

5. 4   3

6. Sum = 18, value = 0

SECTION 6.2

1. One time

2. Primitive

3. -1

4. (c)

5. 1   3   2   5   3   7

6. 4   4
    3   4

SECTION 7.1

1. (c)

2. (d)

3. (b)

4. (a)

5. 4
   8

6.

4	4	2	4
1	0	4	
11	11	6	6
6	0	11	

7. (b)

8. (b)

9. (d)

10.

15	20	4	30
2	15	3	30
8	10	5	6
6	8	3	30

SECTION 7.2

1. (a) false
   (b) false
   (c) true
   (d) false
   (e) false

2. 2
   4

3. The count is 3

4. (c)

5. (d)

6. 2   3   4

7.
```
FUNCTION lastdig (x : integer) : integer;
BEGIN
        lastdig := x MOD 10
END
```

8.
```
PROGRAM grades (input, output);
VAR
i, grade, lowest : integer;
BEGIN
        i := 0;
        lowest := 101;
        WHILE NOT eof (input) DO
        BEGIN
```

```
        readln (grade);
        IF (grade >= 0) AND (grade <= 100)
        THEN BEGIN
                    i := i + 1;
                    IF grade < lowest
                    THEN lowest := grade
                END
        ELSE writeln ('Error, grade is too large.')
    END;
    writeln ('The total number of grades = ', i);
    writeln ('The minimum grade is ', lowest)
END.
```

SECTION 7.3

1. 15

2. 50

3. (a) 1! = 1
n! = n * (n − 1)! for n > 1

(b)
```
PROGRAM nfact (input, output);
VAR
        x, m : integer;
FUNCTION fact (n : integer) : integer;
BEGIN
        IF n <= 1
        THEN fact := 1
        ELSE fact := fact (n − 1) * n
END;
BEGIN
        readln (m);
        x := fact (m);
        writeln (m, '! = ', x)
END.
```

4. (a)
```
FUNCTION power (x : real; n : integer) : real;
(* Non-recursive function to compute Nth power of x *)
VAR
        i : integer;
        ans : real;
BEGIN
        ans := 1;
        FOR i := 1 TO n DO ans := ans * x;
        power := ans
END
```

(b) $x^1 = x$

$x^n = x * x^{n-1}$ for $n > 1$

(c) FUNCTION power (x : real; n : integer) : real;
(* recursive function to compute nth power of x *)
BEGIN
IF n = 1
THEN power : = x
ELSE power := x * power (x, n − 1)
END

5.   FUNCTION fib (n : integer) : integer;
(* compute nth Fibonacci number *)
BEGIN
IF (n = 1) OR (n = 2)
THEN fib := 1
ELSE fib := fib (n − 1) + fib (n − 2)
END

SECTION 8.1

1. (a) TYPE astate = (Alabama, Alaska, Arizona, Arkansas)
    (b) TYPE relative = (Cousin, Dad, Mom, Grandma, Grandpa)
    (c) TYPE softdrink = (MountainDew, Pepsi, DrPepper, Coke)
    (d) TYPE flavor = (Chocolate, Vanilla, Strawberry)

2. (a) invalid
    (b) invalid
    (c) invalid
    (d) valid
    (e) invalid
    (f) valid

3. (a) invalid
    (b) valid
    (c) invalid
    (d) valid
    (e) invalid
    (f) valid

4. (a) invalid
    (b) invalid
    (c) valid
    (d) invalid
    (e) valid

5. (c)

6. Travel to Chicago
Travel not recommended.

7. TYPE month = (Jan, Feb, Mar, Apr, May, Jun, Jul, Aug, Sep, Oct, Nov, Dec);

```
PROCEDURE display (name : month);
BEGIN
        CASE name OF
                Jan : writeln ('January');
                Feb : writeln ('February');
                Mar : writeln ('March');
                Apr : writeln ('April');
                May : writeln ('May');
                Jun : writeln ('June');
                Jul : writeln ('July');
                Aug : writeln ('August');
                Sep : writeln ('September');
                Oct : writeln ('October');
                Nov : writeln ('November');
                Dec : writeln ('December')
        END
END
```

SECTION 8.2

1. (a) nonneg : 0..maxint;
 (b) big : 101..maxint;
 (c) firsthalf : 'A'..'M';
 (d) sechalf : 'N'..'Z';

2. {99, 100, 101, ...999, 1000}

3. (a) yes
 (b) no

4. letter's range is 'A', 'B', 'C', 'D', ..., 'Z'
 negative's range is from −maxint to −1
 somedigits range is '0', '1', '2', '3'
 temp's range is from −32 to 32
 spring's range is Mar, Apr, May, Jun
 halfyear's range is Jan, Feb, Mar, Apr, May, Jun

5. (d)

6. (e)

7. PROGRAM palindrome (input, output);
 TYPE
         digits = '0'..'9';

```
VAR
        ch1, ch2, ch3, ch4, ch5 : digits;
BEGIN
        readln (ch1, ch2, ch3, ch4, ch5);
        IF (ch1 = ch5) AND (ch2 = ch4)
        THEN writeln('The sequence is a numeric palindrome')
        ELSE writeln('The sequence is not a numeric palindrome')
END.
```

SECTION 8.3

1. (a) 7
   (b) 2
   (c) −2
   (d) '7'
   (e) undefined
   (f) undefined

2. (a) −2
   (b) 100
   (c) '0'
   (d) '4'
   (e) 6
   (f) 'B'

3. (a) 0
   (b) 4
   (c) coodle
   (d) undefined
   (e) undefined
   (f) 5

4. (a) 7
   (b) 0
   (c) '3'
   (d) '0'

5. 2001
      37

6. It will execute with an error

7. It will execute without an error

8.
```
PROCEDURE convert (VAR num : integer);
VAR
        inchar : char;
```

```
  BEGIN
          num := 0;
          inchar := ' ';
          WHILE (inchar < '0') OR (inchar > '9') DO read (inchar);
          WHILE (inchar >= '0') AND (inchar <= '9') DO
          BEGIN
              num := num * 10 + ord(inchar) − ord('0');
              read (inchar)
          END
  END
END
```

SECTION 8.5

1. (a) 0, 1, 2, 3
   (b) 0, 1, 2, 3, 4, 5, 6, 7, 8, 9, 10, 13, 15
   (c) 'A', 'B', 'C', 'D', 'E', 'F', 'G', 'H', 'I', 'J', 'L', 'M', 'N', 'O', 'P', 'Q', 'R', 'S', 'T', 'U', 'V', 'W', 'X', 'Y', 'Z'
   (d) 'a', 'b', 'c', 'd', 'e', 'f', 'g', 'h', 'i', 'j', 'k', 'l', 'm', 'A', 'B', 'C', 'D', 'E', 'F', 'G', 'H', 'I', 'J', 'K', 'L', 'M'
   (e) '0', '1', '2', '3', '4', '5', '9'

2. (a) invalid
   (b) valid
   (c) invalid
   (d) valid
   (e) invalid

3. (a) false
   (b) true
   (c) true
   (d) false

4. (a) false
   (b) true
   (c) false
   (d) true

5. (a) false
   (b) false
   (c) true
   (d) true

6. 2
   2

7. ```
PROGRAM nondigit (input, output);
VAR
```
```

```
                    counter : integer;
                    i : integer;
                    ch : char;
              BEGIN
                    i := O;
                    counter := O;
                    WHILE (NOT eoln(input)) AND (i < 80) DO
                    BEGIN
                            read (ch);
                            i := i + 1;
                            IF NOT (ch IN ['O'..'9'])
                            THEN counter := counter + 1 (* it's a non-digit *)
                    END;
                    writeln ('The total number of non-digit characters is ', counter);
              END.
```

SECTION 9.1

1. xarray has 100
   yarray has 7
   zarray has 5

2. Nine numbers are read into array num.

3. (a) valid
   (b) valid
   (c) invalid
   (d) valid if data[0] is in ['A'..'Z']
   (e) valid
   (f) invalid
   (g) valid if lista['A'] is in [−3..3]

4. (a) 1
   (b) 2
   (c) 5
   (d) 0

5. (d)

6. (c) x: 1 6 10 13
       y: 2 7 11 14

7. (c)

8. TYPE sen = ARRAY[1..100] OF char;
   FUNCTION alpha (sentence : sen; length : integer; letter : char) : integer;
   (* Determine number of occurrences of letter in sentence *)
   VAR

```
          counter, i : integer;
BEGIN
          counter := 0;
          FOR i := 1 TO length DO                    (* go through the array *)
              IF sentence[i] = letter                      (* Found one? *)
              THEN counter := counter + 1;                      (* yes! *)
          alpha := counter                          (* report final result *)
END
```

SECTION 9.2

1. (a) It will take six comparisons to locate the value 12 using a linear search.

   (b) It will take three comparisons to locate the value 12 using a binary search after the values have been sorted.

2. The performance is the same.

3.
```
PROGRAM longmerge (input, output);
CONST
        size = 100;        (* maximum combined size *)
TYPE
        bigarr = ARRAY [1..size] OF integer;
VAR
        arr1, arr2 : bigarr;
        long : bigarr;
        i : integer;
        start : integer;
        m, n, tot : integer;

PROCEDURE sort (size : integer; VAR table : bigarr);
VAR
        temp, j, largest : integer;
        FUNCTION findmax (last : integer; VAR table : bigarr) : integer;
        VAR
                maxindex, index : 1..size;
        BEGIN
                maxindex := 1;
                FOR index := 2 TO last DO
                    IF table[index] > table[maxindex]
                    THEN maxindex := index;
                findmax := maxindex
        END;
BEGIN
        FOR j := size DOWNTO 2 DO
        BEGIN
```

```
                    largest := findmax (j, table);
                    temp := table[largest];
                    table[largest] := table[j];
                    table[j] := temp
              END
    END;

    PROCEDURE copy (start, stop : integer; table : bigarr; VAR longm : bigarr);
    (* this procedure appends arrays together *)
    VAR
          i, j : integer;
    BEGIN
          FOR i := 1 TO stop DO
          BEGIN
                longm[start] := table[i];
                start := start + 1
          END
    END;

    BEGIN
          (* main program *)
          writeln ('Please enter array sizes.');
          readln (m, n);
          tot := m + n;
          IF tot > size
          THEN writeln ('Arrays are too large.')
          ELSE BEGIN
                    writeln ('Enter first array elements.');
                    FOR i := 1 TO m DO read (arr1[i]);
                    writeln ('Enter second array elements.');
                    FOR i := 1 TO n DO read (arr2[i]);
                    readln;
                    sort (m, arr1);
                    sort (n, arr2);
                    start := 1;
                    copy (start, m, arr1, long);
                    copy (m + 1, n, arr2, long);
                    sort (m + n, long);
                    FOR i := 1 TO m + n DO writeln (long[i])
                END
    END.

4. FUNCTION findmin
        (last : integer; VAR table : list) : integer;
   (* find index of smallest element in table[1..last] *)
   VAR
          minindex, index : 1..size;
   BEGIN
          minindex := 1;
          FOR index := 2 TO last DO
          IF table[index] < table[minindex]
```

```
        THEN minindex := index;
        findmin := minindex
END
```

5.
```
PROCEDURE sort (size : integer; VAR table : list);
(* selection sort of array elements table[1..size] *)
VAR
        temp, j, smallest : integer;
BEGIN
        FOR j := size DOWNTO 2 DO
        BEGIN
                smallest := findmin (j, table);
                temp := table[smallest];
                table[smallest] := table[j];
                table[j] := temp
        END
END
```

SECTION 9.3

1. matrix contains 121 elements.

2. (a)

3. 5
   5
   5

4. (a) There are 90 components.
   (b) invalid
   (c) invalid
   (d) invalid − index out of range
   (e) invalid

5.
```
TYPE matrix = ARRAY [1..10,1..10] OF integer;
PROCEDURE change (m, n : integer; VAR rmatrix : matrix);
(* interchange rows m and n of rmatrix *)
VAR
        temp : matrix;
        i, j : integer;
BEGIN
        FOR i := 1 to 10 DO
        BEGIN
                temp[m,i] := rmatrix[m,i];
                rmatrix[m,i] := rmatrix[n,i];
                rmatrix[n,i] := temp[m,i]
        END
END
```

6. PROGRAM swap (input, output);
TYPE thrdim = ARRAY [1..10,1..20,1..30] of Boolean;
VAR

    index1, index2, index3 : integer;
    logic : thrdim;
    i, j, k : integer;
    total, data : integer;
    okay : Boolean;

PROCEDURE flipflop (logicarr : thrdim);
(* invert the logical sense of each element in logicarr *)
VAR

    i, j, k : integer;

BEGIN

    FOR i := 1 TO index1 DO
        FOR j := 1 TO index2 DO
            FOR k := 1 TO index3 DO
                logicarr[i,j,k] := NOT logicarr[i,j,k]

END;

BEGIN (* main *)

    writeln ('Please enter the array dimensions.');
    okay := true;
    readln (index1, index2, index3);
    IF (index1 > 10)
    THEN BEGIN
        writeln ('First array dimension too large.');
        okay := false
      END;
    IF (index2 > 20)
    THEN BEGIN
        writeln ('Second array dimension too large.');
        okay := false
      END;
    IF (index3 > 30)
    THEN BEGIN
        writeln ('Third array dimension too large.');
        okay := false
      END;
    IF okay
    THEN BEGIN
        writeln ('Enter data: 0 = false, nonzero = true.');
        FOR i := 1 TO index1 DO
            FOR j := 1 TO index2 DO
                FOR k := 1 TO index3 DO
                BEGIN
                    read (data);
                    logic [i,j,k] := data <> 0
                END;
        flipflop (logic)
      END

END.

1. (a) valid
   (b) invalid
   (c) valid
   (d) valid
   (e) valid

2. (a)

3.
```
TYPE word = PACKED ARRAY [1..20] OF char;
FUNCTION compare (VAR worda, wordb : word) : integer;
BEGIN
        IF worda < wordb
        THEN compare := -1
        ELSE IF worda = wordb
                THEN compare := 0
                ELSE compare := 1
END
```

4. The function searches for the first blank in the packed array starting from the end. It returns a zero if there were no blanks in the entire array, and returns the index of the blank if it found one.

5. pascal

SECTION 10.2

1. (a) $2+2=4$
   (b) The time is now
   (c) 2500 Rice Blvd.
   (d) New York, New York
   (e) blankblank

2.
```
TYPE sent = PACKED ARRAY [1..80] OF char;
FUNCTION blankcount (VAR sentence : sent) : integer;
VAR
        count, index : integer;
BEGIN
        count := 0;
        FOR index := 1 TO 80 DO
                IF sentence[index] = ' '
                THEN count := count + 1;
        blankcount := count
END
```

3. (d)

4. Output:

```
                    BROWN
               BROWNBROWN
               BROWN
```

5. PROCEDURE extlast (VAR table : list; size : integer);
```
(* Extract and display the last name from each *)
(* full name in table[1] to table[size], where   *)
(* the size of the list is a parameter.            *)
CONST
        blanks = '               ';        (* 15 blanks *)
TYPE
        word = PACKED ARRAY [1..15] OF char;
VAR
        lastname : word;                                    (* a last name *)
        achar : char;                              (* one character of a name *)
        j,                                 (* subscript of full name being processed *)
        index : integer;                    (* subscript to the first name *)
        ndx : integer;                          (* subscript to last name *)
BEGIN
        FOR j := 1 TO size DO                              (* for each name *)
        BEGIN
                lastname := blanks;
                index := 0;
                achar := table[j,1];
                WHILE (achar <> ' ') AND (index < 15) DO
                BEGIN
                    index := index + 1;
                    achar := table[j, index + 1]
                END;
                 ndx := 1;
                 WHILE (achar <> ' ') AND (ndx < 15) DO
                 BEGIN
                    index := index + 1;
                    lastname[ndx] := table[j, index + 1];
                    ndx := ndx + 1
                END;
                writeln (lastname)
        END
END
```

SECTION 11.1

1. (a) TYPE
```
        bank = RECORD
                        nameaddr : PACKED ARRAY [1..100] OF char;
                        ssn : PACKED ARRAY [1..11] OF char;
```

```
            currbal : real;
            accintr : real
         END
```

(b) TYPE
```
      phonedir = RECORD
                    name : PACKED ARRAY [1..40] OF char;
                    addr : PACKED ARRAY [1..50] OF char;
                    num : PACKED ARRAY [1..12] OF char
                 END
```

(c) TYPE
```
      crimrec = RECORD
                   realname : PACKED ARRAY [1..40] OF char;
                   aliasname : PACKED ARRAY [1..40] OF char;
                   age : integer;
                   height : integer;
                   weight : integer;
                   eyes : PACKED ARRAY [1..10] OF char;
                   priorarst : integer
                END
```

2. (a) invalid, no END statement
   (b) valid
   (c) invalid, test is duplicated
   (d) valid

3. (a) valid
   (b) invalid
   (c) invalid
   (d) invalid
   (e) invalid
   (f) valid
   (g) invalid

4. (a) invalid
   (b) valid
   (c) valid
   (d) valid
   (e) invalid

5. TYPE
```
      info = RECORD
                name : PACKED ARRAY [1..30] OF char;
                age : 1..99;
                dateofbirth : PACKED ARRAY [1..10] OF char
             END
   VAR
      person : info;
```

```
PROCEDURE reading (VAR human : info);
VAR
        n : PACKED ARRAY [1..30] OF char;
        d : PACKED ARRAY [1..10] OF char;
        i : integer;
BEGIN
        i := 1;
        WHILE (i <= 30) DO
        BEGIN
                read (n[i]);
                human.name[i] := n[i];
                i := i + 1
        END;
        read (human.age);
        i := 1;
        WHILE (i <= 10) DO
        BEGIN
                read (d[i]);
                human.dateofbirth[i] := d[i];
                i := i + 1
        END
END
```

6. ```
TYPE
        info = RECORD
                        name : PACKED ARRAY [1..30] OF char;
                        age : 1..99;
                        dateofbirth : PACKED ARRAY [1..10] OF char
                END;
VAR
        person : info;
PROCEDURE display (VAR human : info);
BEGIN
        writeln ('Name':35, 'Age':7, 'Date of Birth':15);
        writeln (human.name:35, human.age:7, human.dateofbirth:15)
END
```

## SECTION 11.2

1. (a) invalid
   (b) valid
   (c) valid
   (d) invalid
   (e) invalid
   (f) valid
   (g) invalid
   (h) valid
```

2. (a) valid
   (b) invalid
   (c) valid
   (d) valid
   (e) invalid
   (f) invalid
   (g) invalid
   (h) valid
   (i) invalid
   (j) invalid

3. (a) valid
   (b) invalid, not enough characters
   (c) invalid
   (d) invalid, group needs an index
   (e) valid
   (f) valid

4. It is not valid. CASE status OF should be
                                  CASE group[index].status OF

5. It will print 100 lines, each containing 'T. J. Booker   '.

6. The first line will contain 'T. J. Booker   '.
Lines 2 through 100 will contain 'Humpty Dumpty   '.

SECTION 12.1

1. (a) valid
   (b) invalid, file is a reserved word
   (c) invalid
   (d) valid
   (e) valid
   (f) invalid

2. (a) valid
   (b) invalid, ↑ should appear before index
   (c) invalid, reals cannot be assigned to integers
   (d) invalid, scidata should have a subscript
   (e) valid

3. 1. reset(infile) must be executed before read(infile,…)
   2. Eof(infile) and get(infile), not outfile
   3. declare infile, outfile

4. TYPE n = FILE OF real;
VAR
        num : n;
        posnum : n;

```
PROCEDURE duplicate (VAR number, positive = n);
BEGIN
        reset (number);
        rewrite (positive);
        WHILE NOT eof(number) DO
        BEGIN
                IF number ↑ > 0
                THEN BEGIN
                            positive↑: = number↑;
                            put (positive)
                     END;
                get (number);
        END
END
```

5.
```
TYPE
        r = FILE OF real;
        i = FILE OF integer;
VAR
        realnum : r;
        intnum : i;
PROCEDURE convert (VAR rn : r; VAR int : i);
BEGIN
        reset (rn);
        rewrite (int);
        WHILE NOT eof(rn) DO
        BEGIN
                int↑: = round (rn↑);
                get (rn);
                put (int)
        END
END
```

6. (a) filename must be a VAR parameter.
   (b) file variables cannot be assigned.
   (c) integers cannot be directly assigned to char variables.
   (d) Either
   ```
           reset (filename); get(filename)
   ```
   or
   ```
           rewrite (filename); put(filename)
   ```
   must be used.
   (e) Either
   ```
           reset (numfile); get(numfile)
   ```
   or
   ```
           rewrite (numfile); put(numfile)
   ```
   must be used.

1. 4

2. The variable unknown counts the number of end-of-line markers (or lines) in the text file. An error will result since the *eoln* function is used with text files only.

3. PROCEDURE readtext (VAR infile, outfile : text);
```
(* Readtext reads data from a text file which is then copied   *)
(* to a second text file. This second file will have lines     *)
(* of exactly 72 characters, padded if necessary with blanks. *)
VAR
        ch : ARRAY [1..72] OF char;
        i, count : integer;
BEGIN
        reset (infile);
        rewrite (outfile);
        WHILE NOT eof(infile) DO
        BEGIN
                count := 0;
                WHILE NOT eoln(infile) AND (count < 72) DO
                BEGIN
                        count := count + 1;
                        read (infile, ch[count])
                END;
                readln (infile);
                FOR i := 1 TO count DO write (outfile, ch[i]);
                FOR i := count + 1 TO 72 DO write (outfile, ' ');
                writeln (outfile)
        END
END
```

4. PROCEDURE nonblanks (VAR infile : text);
```
(* Read a textfile, and display the number of nonblank *)
(* characters on each line.                            *)
VAR
        count : integer;
        ch : char;
BEGIN
        reset (infile);
        WHILE NOT eof (infile) DO
        BEGIN
                count := 0;
                WHILE NOT eoln (infile) DO
                BEGIN
                        read (infile, ch);
                        IF ch <> ' ' THEN count := count + 1
                END;
```

```
                                    writeln (count);
                                    readln (infile)
                        END
            END


5.  PROCEDURE padblanks (VAR infile : text);
        (* Padblanks reads infile and stores it in a packed array. *)
        (* It then pads the rest of the array with blanks.         *)
        VAR
                    i : integer;
                    ch : PACKED ARRAY [1..72] OF char;
                    data : char;
        BEGIN
                    reset (infile);
                    WHILE NOT eof (infile) DO
                    BEGIN
                        i := 0;
                        WHILE NOT eoln (infile) DO
                        BEGIN
                            i := i + 1;
                                read (infile, data);
                                    ch[i] := data
                        END;
                            WHILE i < 72 DO
                            BEGIN
                                i := i + 1;
                                ch[i] := ' '
                        END;
                            readln (infile)
                    END
        END
```

SECTION 13.1

1. (a) valid
    (b) valid
    (c) invalid
    (d) valid
    (e) invalid

2. (a) [1, 2, 3, 4, 5, 6, 7, 8, 9, 10, 11, 12]
    (b) []
    (c) [1, 2, 3, 4, 5, 7, 9, 11]
    (d) [2, 4]
    (e) [1, 3, 5, 7, 9, 11]
    (f) [1, 2, 3, 4, 5, 7, 9, 11]
    (g) [1, 3, 5, 7]
    (h) [1, 3, 5, 7]

    (i) []

    (j) [1, 2, 3, 4, 5, 7]

    (k) [1, 3, 5, 7]

3. (a) true

    (b) true

    (c) true

    (d) false

    (e) false

4. (a) [0, 1, 2, 10]

    (b) [4, 5, 6]

    (c) false

    (d) false

    (e) true

5. [ ]

[John]

[Paul]

[George]

[Ringo]

[John,Paul]

[John,George]

[John,Ringo]

[Paul,George]

[Paul,Ringo]

[George,Ringo]

[John,Paul,George]

[John,Paul,Ringo]

[John,George,Ringo]

[Paul,George,Ringo]

[John,Paul,George,Ringo]

6.
```
PROGRAM english (input, output);

TYPE
        alphabet = SET OF 'A'..'Z';
        letters = 'A'..'Z';
VAR
        seta, setb, setc : alphabet;
        range : letters;
        ch : char;

PROCEDURE symmetric (VAR seta, setb, setc : alphabet);
(* compute symmetric difference of seta and setb *)
BEGIN
        setc := (seta − setb) + (setb − seta)
END;
```

```
BEGIN
        seta := [ ];
        setb := [ ];
        read (ch);
        WHILE ch <> '.' DO
        BEGIN
                seta := seta + [ch];
                read (ch)
        END;
        readln;
        read (ch);
        WHILE ch <> '.' DO
        BEGIN
                setb := setb + [ch];
                read (ch)
        END;
        readln;
        symmetric (seta, setb, setc);
        FOR range := 'A' TO 'Z' DO
                IF range IN setc
                THEN write (range)
END.
```

7.
```
TYPE
        numset = SET OF 1..128;

FUNCTION members (VAR num : numset) : integer;
VAR
        i, count : integer;
BEGIN
        count := 0;
        FOR i := 1 TO 128 DO
                IF i IN num
                THEN count := count + 1;
        members := count
END
```

8.
```
PROGRAM revise (input, output);
TYPE
        divset = SET OF 1..100;
VAR
        number : ARRAY [1..100] OF divset;
        divisors : divset;
        divnum, index : 1..100;
BEGIN
        (* create the array of divisors *)
        FOR index := 1 TO 100 DO
        BEGIN
```

```
             number[index] := [];
             FOR divnum := 1 TO trunc(sqrt(index)) DO
             IF (index MOD divnum) = 0
             THEN BEGIN
                          number[index] := number[index] + [divnum];
                          (* include the other half *)
                          number[index] := number[index]
                                                   + [index DIV divnum]
                   END
     END;
     (* display results *)
     writeln ('N u m b e r    D i v i s o r (s)');
     writeln ('– – – – – –    – – – – – – – ');
     FOR index := 1 TO 100 DO
     BEGIN
             write (index:4, ' ':6);
             FOR divnum := 1 TO index DO
                   IF divnum IN number[index]
                   THEN write (divnum:1, ' ':1);
             writeln
     END
END.
```

SECTION 13.2

1. (a) valid
   (b) invalid
   (c) invalid
   (d) valid
   (e) valid
   (f) invalid
   (g) invalid
   (h) valid

2. 33A

3. After dispose (ptr1↑), writeln(ptr1↑) is incorrect.

4. (a) valid
   (b) invalid
   (c) valid
   (d) invalid
   (e) invalid

5. Code A
   Code Z

SECTION 13.3

1. So that the last pointer is defined, thus permitting a search for the end of the list.

2. TYPE

```
        pointer = ↑arecord;
        arecord = RECORD
                        field : sometype;      (* data fields *)
                        nextrec : pointer
                END;
VAR
        startpointer : pointer;
        currentptr : pointer;
        endpointer : pointer;
        index : integer;
BEGIN
        new (startpointer);
        currentptr := startpointer;
        FOR index := 1 TO 3 DO
        BEGIN
                new (currentptr↑.nextrec);
                currentptr := currentptr↑.nextrec
        END;
        endpointer := currentptr;
        currentptr↑.nextrec := NIL
END.
```

3. PROCEDURE display (startpointer : pointer;
                                VAR currentptr : pointer);
(* display the contents of data values in the linked list *)

```
BEGIN
        currentptr := startpointer;
        WHILE currentptr ↑.nextrec <> NIL DO
        BEGIN
                write (currentptr ↑.data);
                currentptr := currentptr ↑.nextrec
        END
END
```

4. PROCEDURE insertbegin (startpointer : pointer;
                                recptr : pointer;
                                VAR currentptr : pointer);
(* insert item at the beginning of the linked list *)

```
BEGIN
        new (recptr);
        recptr ↑.nextrec := startpointer;
        startpointer := recptr
END
```

5. PROCEDURE delbegin (startpointer : pointer;
                        VAR currentptr : pointer);

(* delete an item at the beginning of a list *)
VAR
      temp : pointer;
BEGIN
      temp := startpointer;
      startpointer := startpointer ↑ .nextrec;
      dispose (temp)
END

SECTION 13.4

1.

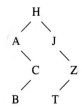

2.

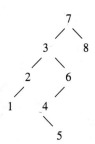

3. Inorder: A B C H J T Z
                 1 2 3 4 5 6 7

    Postorder: B C A T Z J H
                 1 2 5 4 6 3 8 7

    Preorder: H A C B J Z T
                 7 3 2 1 6 4 5 8

4. PROCEDURE insert (VAR bintree : pointer; key : char);
(* search bintree for right location to insert key *)
VAR
      done : Boolean;
      temp : pointer;
BEGIN
      done := false;
      temp := bintree;

```
            REPEAT
                    IF temp = NIL
                    THEN done := true
                    ELSE IF key < temp↑.letter
                            THEN temp := temp↑.left
                            ELSE temp := temp↑.right
            UNTIL done;
            new(temp);
            temp↑.letter := key;
            temp↑.left := NIL;
            temp↑.right := NIL
    END
```

5. ```
   PROCEDURE traversal (bintree : pointer);
   (* postorder traversal of binary tree *)
   BEGIN
           IF bintree <> NIL
           THEN BEGIN
                           traversal (bintree↑.left);
                           traversal (bintree↑.right);
                           visit (bintree)
                   END
   END
   ```

6. ```
   PROCEDURE traversal (bintree : pointer);
   (* preorder traversal of binary tree *)
   BEGIN
           IF bintree <> NIL
           THEN BEGIN
                           visit (bintree);
                           traversal (bintree↑.left);
                           traversal (bintree↑.right)
                   END
   END
   ```

SECTION 13.5

1. Use a subscript variable of the array to keep track of the top of the stack. Pushing and popping can be done by incrementing or decrementing the subscript.

2. ```
   FUNCTION empty (VAR top : stachptr) : Boolean;
   BEGIN
           empty := top = NIL
   END
   ```

3. Yes, it is necessary to check for a full stack if you are using an array instead of pointer. An array is a fixed size data structure, and you cannot add more elements to the array if it is full. Similarly, for dynamic allocations if the procedure new doesn't create a new variable there will not be any space to save the value on the stack.
   ```

4. PROCEDURE displayq (VAR front, rear : queueptr);
(* display all elements on a queue, front to rear *)
VAR
　　　　temp : queueptr;
BEGIN
　　　　temp := front;
　　　　WHILE temp <> NIL DO
　　　　BEGIN
　　　　　　　writeln (temp ↑ .symbol);
　　　　　　　temp := temp ↑ .nextrec
　　　　END
END

5. PROCEDURE emptyq (VAR front, rear : queueptr);
(* empty a queue *)
VAR
　　　　temp : queueptr;
BEGIN
　　　　WHILE front <> NIL DO
　　　　　　BEGIN
　　　　　　　　temp := front;
　　　　　　　　front := front ↑ .nextrec;
　　　　　　　　dispose (temp)
　　　　　　END;
　　　　rear := front
END

INDEX

INDEX

Sample Pascal Statements

Selection Statements

```
IF grade >= 90                          (* IF-THEN statement *)
THEN writeln ('Grade is A.')


IF grade >= 70                          (* IF-THEN-ELSE statement *)
THEN BEGIN
        writeln ('Passing grade.');
        writeln ('Your grade is ', grade)
     END
ELSE IF grade < 60                      (* nested IF *)
     THEN writeln ('Failing grade.')
     ELSE writeln ('Minimal passing grade.')


CASE vowel OF                           (* CASE statement *)
   'A': acount := acount + 1;
   'E': ecount := ecount + 1;
   'I': icount := icount + 1;
   'O', 'U': other := other + 1
END
```

Looping Statements

```
read (achar);
WHILE (achar = ' ') DO                  (* WHILE statement *)
BEGIN
     blankcount := blankcount + 1;
     read (achar)
END


REPEAT                                  (* REPEAT-UNTIL statement *)
     read (achar)
UNTIL (achar <> ' ')


FOR index := 1 TO 10 DO                 (*FOR statement *)
BEGIN
     read (number);
     total := total + number
END
```